HISTORY OF CIVILIZATION

Europe in the Twentieth Century

The angel of history has his face turned towards the past. Where a chain of events appears before us, he sees a single catastrophe which piles up a mountain of ruins before his feet. He would like to stay in place, resurrect the dead and reconstruct the wreckage; but his wings are forced back by a storm . . . which irresistibly propels him into the future to which his back is turned, while the pile of ruins mounts up before him heavenwards. This storm is what we call progress.

WALTER BENJAMIN
Theses on the Philosophy of History

Europe
in the
Twentieth
Century

GEORGE LICHTHEIM

PRAEGER PUBLISHERS
New York · Washington

BOOKS THAT MATTER

Published in the United States of America in 1972
by Praeger Publishers, Inc.
111 Fourth Avenue, New York, N.Y. 10003

© George Lichtheim 1972

Library of Congress Catalog Card Number: 70–187278

Printed in the United States of America

In Memory of My Parents

CONTENTS

CONTENTS

LIST OF ILLUSTRATIONS

Acknowledgement is due to the following for the plates used in this book: Camera Press Ltd., 1, 3, 4, 5b, 6, 10b, 11b, 12, 14a, b, 17a, 36, 37; Radio Times Hulton Picture Library, 2a, b, c, 8a, 17b, 33, 34, 42; Popperfoto, 5a, 7a, 9a, 13, 41; Keystone, 7b, 11a, 15, 16, 38, 39, 40; The Wiener Library, London, 8b; Fox Photos Ltd., 9b, 10a; The National Film Archives, 18, 19a, b, 20a, b; Ullstein Bilderdienst, 21, 23, 24, 25, 35; Fotomas, Barcelona, 22; H. Roger Viollet, 26; Museum of Modern Art, New York, 27, 29b, 32a; Kunstmuseum, Bern; 28a; Philadelphia Museum of Art: Louise and Walter Arensberg Collection, 28b; Rheinisches Bildarchiv 29a; Solomon R. Guggenheim Museum, 30; Service de Documentation Photographique, Paris, 31; The Tate Gallery, 32b.

LIST OF MAPS

PREFACE

The subject of this book is the transformation of European society since 1900, taking the term 'society' to stand for the entire structure of institutions and modes of life inherited from the past and constantly refashioned through the process of historical change. Both the date and the conceptual framework are arbitrary, and a different approach – an attempt, for example, to trace the crisis of the European nation state since the outbreak of war in 1914 – is equally legitimate. The nineteenth century is frequently said to have endured until 1914–18, in the sense that a particular civilization was disrupted by the First World War. Likewise there is no good reason why the account should be brought to a halt in 1970 merely to suit the convenience of the author or the reader. But historians have to terminate somewhere, and if their topic is the contemporary scene they are obliged to stop at a point in time dictated by the actual completion of their work. Similar considerations apply to a geographical frame which includes Russia and omits the United States. The fact that since 1945 the old Continent has been overshadowed by these two hegemonial powers does not by itself invalidate the traditional approach which counterposes Europe and America as two distinct entities. We shall return to the already ancient question how far Russia can be said to form part of Europe. For our present purpose it is enough that no rigid barrier separates the present-day USSR from its client states. It is open to anyone to adopt an 'Atlantic' perspective and then try to fit Western Europe into it, but for better or worse the present work adheres to the time-honoured practice of most historians. If the result is a certain geopolitical unbalance, the author can only plead that strategic considerations are not uppermost among his concerns.

The general standpoint adopted throughout is one of interpretation rather than narrative. Political and military affairs are briefly summarized, and the same applies to economic history. The aim has been to bring into view the totality of European civilization, the heaviest emphasis falling upon the transformation of inherited life styles under the impact of social and technological change. Such an approach inevitably imposes upon author and reader alike a willingness to embark upon generalization in fields normally reserved for specialists. Historians have become dependent upon the work done by sociologists and students of what might be described as the culture of an epoch. Being at the mercy of their own ignorance and their prejudices, they can claim some degree of authority only in so far as they are able to present an overall view of the entire field. This in turn presupposes the existence of certain definable trends shaping the totality of events during a given period. A writer who believes that European history is simply the aggregate of national histories will shy away from general statements bearing upon the peculiar character of society as a whole. If on the contrary one assumes the overriding importance of problems common to the entire culture, one will seek to lay bare the strains and stresses resulting from two world wars, a series of shattering revolutions, and the decline of the European nation state. The search for a central nexus mediating between the autonomous spheres of political, social and intellectual life has become fairly respectable in recent years, but there is no agreement as to the method proper to the enterprise. Quite probably there never will be. The approach adopted in this book must in any case justify itself in terms of the aim here set out.

Anyone who embarks upon this kind of enterprise is obliged to rely heavily on secondary literature. This circumstance is reflected in the composition of the text and the notes. The latter refer for the most part to sources which have actually been consulted and are not to be regarded as a reliable storehouse of information relating to the enormous mass of scholarly work performed in the various fields here briefly touched upon. The same applies to the bibliography, which in practice cannot be more than a guide to further study. The critical reader to whom this book is addressed will discover for himself where the author has done his own research, where he has relied upon others, and where ignorance has obliged him to omit what ought to have been presented. A study of history undertaken from a personal viewpoint cannot set itself aims proper to an encyclopaedia. Its purpose has been achieved if it sheds new light upon its chosen topic. The thematic unity running through these pages will, it is hoped, be apparent even to readers who reject the method here brought to bear, a method centring upon the category of totality. This concept, needless to say, is controversial, but then so is the empiricist approach still favoured by the majority of historians in the English-speaking world. For the rest, I am able to state that neither friends nor colleagues are responsible for the conclusions herewith presented to the public.

London, December 1971   G.L.

PART ONE

CHAPTER 1

THE AGE OF IMPERIALISM

The Europe of 1900 was articulated into a number of independent nation states bordering upon, or co-existing with, political structures antedating the rise of nationalism and democracy. The national principle was clearly expressed in France, Great Britain, Italy, Spain and various minor Western European states. Tsarist Russia, Austria-Hungary and the Ottoman Empire centring upon Turkey represented an earlier historical formation: that of empires not based upon nationality. Germany was somehow poised in the middle, being both a nation state (since the Bismarckian unification of 1871) and an 'empire' in the sense that its political organization dated back to the post-Napoleonic settlement of 1815. There had been a time when the three Eastern Empires – Prussia-Germany, Austria-Hungary and Russia – stood arrayed against the principles of the French Revolution: nationalism and democracy. The abortive revolution of 1848 had shaken all three, but they had survived into the modern age, and Germany at least had achieved something like national unification. From about 1878 onwards the three Eastern Empires no longer presented a common front, their dynastic rivalries giving rise to national antagonisms of which Pan-Germanism and Pan-Slavism were the ideological expression. Germany and Austria drew away from Russia, enlisting on their side the Ottoman Empire. In 1917–18 all four crashed to the ground, thereby validating the democratic perspective which since 1848 had treated the state and the nation as equivalents. Central and Eastern Europe around 1900 thus present a problem to the historian, in that the German Empire straddled a political landscape still encumbered by ancient formations antedating the rise of modern nationalism. To the West, Britain, France and Italy pursued their 'imperial' rivalries in Africa and elsewhere, but the domestic policies of their respective governments stood on a firm national-democratic foundation: the nation and the state were one. By contrast, the 'empires' of the Habsburgs, the Romanovs and the Ottoman Turks had remained dynastic creations increasingly riddled by the claims of nationalism and democracy. The German Empire represented an unstable compromise. Its policies were

3

already nationalist and imperialist in the modern sense of the term; its internal political structure resembled that of the ancient East European monarchies, and its ruling stratum was heavily weighted in favour of the landowning nobility which during the Bismarck era had come to terms with the industrial bourgeoisie. Germany was neither one thing nor another: no longer a purely dynastic creation, and possessed of a strong sense of national identity, it nonetheless lacked the democratic organization which in the West had placed the nation state on a popular basis. The resulting tensions translated themselves into attitudes which appeared irrational to the statesmen of the Western Powers and were in fact not suited to the role Germany's rulers intended her to play on the global scene. This peculiar configuration must be kept in mind if one is to grasp the complexity of the pre-1914 situation. There were two different kinds of imperialism on the scene: the modern bourgeois variety and that of the East European dynastic empires. Germany somehow managed to combine both. This circumstance resulted in the country's growing political isolation.[1]

The central paradox to be kept in mind is this: Europe alone had given birth to the nation state, but the nation and the state did not, over large areas of Europe, signify the same thing. National self-determination remained a revolutionary slogan in Eastern Europe long after it had been accepted in the West as the norm of political organiza-tion. The trend towards the establishment of states on a national foundation had been arrested in Central and Eastern Europe, although German nationalism paid lip service to the principle that the nation (or the folk) should constitute the basis of the State. For practical purposes, self-determination had since the French Revolution become a reality only in the Western half of the Continent, where nationalism and demo-cracy had entered an alliance. The movement launched in 1789 was blocked in Central Europe, had no serious impact on Tsarist Russia until 1905, and only began to reach the Ottoman Empire on the eve of 1914. In a sense the entire period from 1789 to 1914 may be described as an age in which democratic nationalism spread eastward, with conse-quences ruinous to the dynastic empires of the Habsburgs and the Romanovs. The German case was complicated by the fact that in the reign of William II (1888–1918) the ruling stratum made an attempt to refloat itself by coming to terms with middle-class nationalism. The practical outcome of this experiment was the Anglo-German naval race of 1900–14, and ultimately Germany's defeat in the First World War. This defeat stemmed in the last resort from the circumstance that Germany had embarked upon modern imperialism with a political armature dating back to an earlier age. The attempt to impose German hegemony upon the Slav nations of Eastern and Central Europe was undertaken in the teeth of those popular forces which the French

4

Revolution had unleashed and which continued to work beneath the surface of dynastic and aristocratic politics in the Europe of 1900.[2]

Nationalism and democracy, working separately or jointly, were by far the most powerful forces on the political scene, affecting bourgeois and peasant alike. Socialism added a new dimension, that of the class-conscious industrial proletariat. This new force was perceived as a rival by the older bourgeois-democratic movement with which nonetheless it frequently coalesced. It was seen as a mortal threat by the ruling classes of the Eastern Empires, and as a more or less serious challenge to the liberal-democratic consensus by the political elites of the Western nations. The self-awareness of the Socialist movement tended towards reformism, save where it came up against the autocratic political structures of Central and Eastern Europe. In these areas the movement could not help being revolutionary, even though its leaders might dislike the thought. Elsewhere, Social-Democrats and Syndicalists were at odds over the issue of political violence, the former in general opting for parliamentary democracy, the latter advocating the general strike as a means of mobilizing the working class for the decisive revolutionary struggle. Anarchism lingered on in Spain as a feature of that country's general backwardness. In Russia populist socialism, with its base in the intelligentsia and its hopes centred on the peasantry, slowly gave way to Marxism. Few people perceived the decisive nature of this development, occurring as it did in the Tsarist Empire which by general consent was not ripe for anything beyond an experiment in constitutional monarchy on the German pattern.

The foreground of the political scene in 1900 did not differ substantially from the spectacle presented by Europe's rulers in 1870–1 when Germany achieved her national unification. The only important political transaction of the preceding decade had been the formation of two rival military alliances pitting the Central Powers – Germany and Austria-Hungary – against France and Russia. The incongruous pact between the French Republic and the Romanov dynasty testified to the tacit acceptance of *raison d'état*, or *Realpolitik* as the Germans called it: internal political arrangements were not supposed to matter. Foreign affairs were conducted with a view to preserving or upsetting the precarious balance of power which modern Europe had inherited from the dynastic politics of an earlier age. Great Britain, still securely perched on the edge of the Continent, manipulated this unstable equilibrium so as to prevent the establishment of a Continental hegemony by some dominant power. From the British standpoint, European affairs were a nuisance, in as much as they absorbed energies which ought to flow into the world-wide system of British-controlled trade and financial investment. The European 'balance' became precarious as Germany grew stronger, but until the challenge inherent in the German naval building programme from 1900 onwards, British policy on the whole tended to favour the Central Powers. Russia and France were Britain's principal rivals in Asia and Africa. Germany had not yet made her bid for naval equality and for control of Ottoman Turkey and the Balkans. The Continental balance thus had its counterpart in Britain's 'splendid isolation', reluctantly abandoned from 1902 onwards, and definitely sacrificed in 1914 with Britain's entry into the First World War on the side of her former imperial rivals.

Imperialism is the key to European politics in the age that terminated in 1914, but the key fits the lock only if it is borne in mind that very disparate phenomena are covered by this term. The Eastern Empires – Habsburg, Romanov, Ottoman – were imperialist in a sense quite different from that intended by liberal and socialist critics of French, German, British or North American imperialism. These ancient dynastic empires had assembled territories and populations held together by military force, by religious belief, or by loyalty to the reigning dynasty. Their Western competitors had passed beyond this primitive stage, having assimilated the concepts of democracy and nationhood which in 1789 appeared revolutionary and by 1914 had become conservative so far as bourgeois society was concerned. There was a cleavage between the old dynastic empires and the modern Western Powers whose expansionism took the form of capital investment in Asia, Africa and Latin America. The French Republic and Tsarist Russia were allies against Wilhelminian Germany, but Germany's political system had affinities with the Romanov monarchy, while the Third Republic looked westward to the United States. In 1900 these differences lay concealed beneath the smooth surface of diplomatic palaver. In the crisis of 1914–18 the Western Powers – America, Britain, France – drew together in a common front against Imperial Germany, while Russia dropped out of the race altogether, and Austria-Hungary went to pieces, having failed to solve its long-standing nationalities problem. Ottoman Turkey was already moribund in 1900, when Germany's rulers conceived the notion that control of Turkey and the Balkans was the prerequisite of great power status in the 'imperial' age: the age that was about to leave the sovereign nation state behind, just as the Italian city state had been left behind in the sixteenth century, when the major European nations acquired their political shape.[3]

Bearing in mind the distinction between simple territorial aggrandizement on the part of the Eastern Empires and the new expansion born from the dynamic of capital investment, the period from 1880 to 1914 may be described as 'the age of imperialism', in the sense that all the major European Powers, plus Russia and the Unites States, were engaged in a race to partition the hinterland of the modern world. The intellectual rationale of this drive was supplied by Social Darwinism, that is, by the doctrine that the 'survival of the fittest' applied to nations no less than to individuals. This approach undercut the traditional liberal emphasis upon free trade as the economic foundation of cosmopolitanism. It represented a return to mercantilist doctrines which had gone out of fashion in the nineteenth century, but were now revived even in Britain as foreign competition became more menacing. The United States, too, appeared on the world scene as an expansionist power with the war against Spain in 1898, leading to the annexation of the Philippines and the establishment of an informal protectorate over much of the Caribbean. Statesmen and general staffs rationalized their new preferences with the help of 'geopolitics', a doctrine designed to show that the European nation state had become too small for the new age of empire-building. America made its contribution to the torrent of imperialist literature with A. T. Mahan's *The Influence of Sea Power upon History, 1660–1783*, a work of which it has been said that its publication in 1890 inaugurated something like a new era.

It was read eagerly and studied closely by every chancellory and admiralty; it shaped the imperial policies of Germany and Japan; it supported the position of Britain that its greatness lay in its far-flung empire; and it once more turned America toward those seas where it had been a power up to 1860, but which it had abandoned to seek its destiny in the conquest of its own continent. If the young Kaiser Wilhelm II 'devoured', as he himself said, Mahan's book, so did the young Theodore Roosevelt, and, in a later time, so did another Roosevelt.[4]

Taken in the global sense proper to the term, imperialism around 1900 signified the expansionist policies then pursued by the major European powers, by the United States and by Japan. It represented a carry-over into world politics of the competitive struggle familiar to every observer of the domestic scene in these countries. In practice it signified empire-building on the basis of colonial expansion, plus protectionist measures designed to shut out foreign competitors. The globe was being divided up among a handful of advanced industrial countries whose ruling classes found in the imperialist ethos an outlet for their own energies, as well as for latent tensions in the body politic. The trend affected Europe in two ways. In the first place it sharpened the antagonisms already dividing the principal European nations. Secondly, it set in motion forces which could not be effectively controlled within the framework of parliamentary government: not even in Britain which already possessed the world's largest empire and had managed to combine liberal democracy at home with colonial expansion abroad. The combination rested upon the fleeting triumph of *laissez-faire* economics in the mid-nineteenth century, a moment in time when Britain was briefly the world's only industrial power and thus able

7

to treat the rest of the globe as a market for her products. When this enviable monopoly crumbled under the impact of American, German and Japanese competition, reliance on free trade became difficult to defend. The renascence of the Tory Party went hand-in-hand with imperialism in the narrow sense, that is, reliance on the formal empire in India and Africa, as against the *de facto* empire of free trade secured by Britain's industrial monopoly in the middle of the nineteenth century. The German challenge, taking shape as it did around 1900 with the decision to build a major battle fleet in the teeth of British protests, thus impinged upon a situation which had already been destabilized by the loss of Britain's industrial and trade monopoly. The defensive reactions of the British governing class in the face of this threat in turn prompted the German government to accelerate its military and naval preparations for the expected showdown. The Anglo-German conflict thus superimposed itself upon Germany's and Austria's attempt to establish an unshakable hegemony in Central Europe and the Balkans, a line of policy which drove the Central Powers inexorably towards a military conflict with Russia and France. In this sense 1900 marked a watershed.

From the British standpoint it now became an urgent matter to ward off the German menace, either by agreement with Germany's rulers about a global share-out, or by building up an anti-German coalition. A move in the first direction was made by Joseph Chamberlain – not accidentally the chief exponent of protectionism and colonial expansion – when at the turn of the century he threw out some rather vague and grandiose proposals for a Triple Alliance between the British Empire, the United States and Germany, to make the world safe for the Nordic races. Like Chamberlain's plans for a centrally controlled British Empire secure behind tariff walls, this proposal fitted in with the clearly observable trend towards trans-national, or even trans-continental, political arrangements. "It would have been the translation into the sphere of power-politics of the classic methods of monopoly capitalism."[5] The trouble was that neither the Germans nor the Americans were ready to enter such a triumvirate, the former having staked too much on the High Seas Fleet and the coming showdown with Britain, the latter being as yet unwilling to emerge from behind their comfortable isolation. The Germans were in a hurry; the Americans felt they could wait and were suspicious of what looked like a scheme to perpetuate Britain's world empire. In retrospect it seems plain enough that Germany's rulers gambled with the fate of their nation when they rejected Chamberlain's proposals, but from the standpoint of a dynamic industrial country which already possessed Europe's best army, the decision to build a major battle fleet was logical enough. It would have given Germany the paramount position on the Continent necessary to break out of the Central European confinement and acquire the status of a genuine world power. But this was just the essential point no British government was ready to yield. In consequence there followed a British accommodation with France in 1904 and with Russia in 1907. Germany now had to face a coalition of potentially superior hostile forces. The knowledge that Russia was still far behind economically, Britain clearly past its peak, and France hampered by a stagnant population and stunted industrial growth, encouraged the German military and political leaders to seek a decision on the battlefield while time was on their side. The war of 1914–18 sprang from this peculiar constellation, within which Germany was the dynamic factor. There would in any case have been a showdown between the Central Powers and the Franco-Russian combination, for Germany's increasing control over Turkey represented a standing threat to Russia, while her senseless interference in North Africa antagonized even those French politicians who in principle favoured a Franco-German reconciliation. Such a war would in all likelihood have terminated with a rapid German victory. Precisely for this reason, the British government in 1914 intervened on the side of France and Russia.[6]

The tensions which exploded into war in 1914 were not different in principle from those that had given rise to earlier European conflagrations. What had changed was the character of society. That the major powers would one day come to blows was generally taken for granted, but all concerned thought in terms of a quick victory and a subsequent return to the state of affairs then regarded as normal: an unstable equilibrium politely dubbed 'balance of power', with Europe continuing to hold the centre of the world stage. It was just in this latter respect that the war of 1914–18 represented a turning-point: Europe's pre-eminence was no longer unchallenged. The European state system was disrupted by the collapse of the Central Powers and the Tsarist regime alike, while France was bled white and Britain had abandoned large areas of control to the United States. These unforeseen consequences of what in 1914 looked like a fairly traditional contest for European hegemony had their roots in socio-economic changes already visible in 1900. The industrialization of Europe had been driven to the point where millions of men could be mobilized for a struggle of unprecedented duration. The same process steadily undermined the social fabric of the Eastern Empires and to an extent also the foundations of the Wilhelminian regime in Germany. The series of revolutions in 1917–18 were not merely a response to the dreadful slaughter of the war years: they testified to the fact that the pre-1914 political arrangements no longer corresponded to social reality. Germany, Austria-Hungary and Russia underwent the revolution they had managed to stave off in 1848. In the case of Russia, the movement departed so far from its

bourgeois-democratic origins as to bring an entirely new social formation into being. There was no corresponding sequel in Western Europe,
notwithstanding the severity of the losses incurred during the war.
This circumstance points to a basic difference between Eastern and
Western Europe which was to become even more pronounced after the
1939–45 war had run its course. Eastern Europe lagged behind in its
socio-political development, and for this reason responded differently
to the challenge of war and revolution. To put the matter in a nutshell,
Western European society was predominantly bourgeois, in that the
propertied middle class had placed its imprint on politics and culture
alike. The Eastern half of the Continent, having never absorbed the
legacy of the French Revolution, or even the Protestant Reformation,
was pre-bourgeois and for this very reason ripe for a 'bourgeois revolution' which would create the preconditions for a subsequent development along industrial-capitalist lines. Germany stood in the middle,
not only geographically but socially and spiritually: the homeland of
the Reformation, yet not genuinely reconciled to the modern world of
industrialism and democracy. Its ruling stratum in 1900 had more in
common with the Tsarist bureaucracy than with the liberal bourgeoisie
of France, Britain and America: the nations which in 1914–18 were to
league together for the purpose of bringing the structure of Imperial
Germany to the ground.

The general concept of imperialism thus concealed an ambiguity. It
could be taken to refer to the Hohenzollern, Habsburg and Romanov
empires, and was so employed by liberals and socialists alike. It could
also relate to the growing protectionist and colonialist movements in
Britain, France and Italy, whose imperial claims were sustained at the
expense of backward non-European lands in Africa and Asia. German
imperialism combined both features in a mixture that appeared to its
critics peculiarly puzzling and repellent. It was modern all right, but
its ideology dispensed with liberal cosmopolitanism. In its place the
German theorists of imperialism placed *Realpolitik* – the doctrine that
power alone counted.

More generally it may be said that imperialism had different aspects
– political and ideological – and that there is a problem of relating one
to the other. An 'age of imperialism' is by definition one in which the
imperial urge has become articulate and self-conscious. In Britain this
phase dated from the 1870s, which is not to say that British imperialism
came to birth at this time: its roots were considerably older. French
colonial expansion after 1880 was in part a reaction to the military
defeat sustained in the Franco-German war of 1870–1. Russian expansion had vague but grandiose aims in Central Asia and at least one
clearly defined objective in the Near East: possession of Constantinople.
Austria-Hungary, already weakened by rebellious nationalities, was

nonetheless ready to acquire new subjects in the Balkans: nominally in the name of Christendom, actually by way of barring Russian expansion. Pan-Slavism and Pan-Germanism served to propagate political loyalties which might otherwise have taken a dangerously democratic turn. They also helped to cement the alliance between Germany and Austria-Hungary which triggered off the First World War in 1914. In all these respects it would have been difficult to say where political calculations ended and ideological self-deception took over. People have to believe in something, and the ruling classes of a decrepit East European empire were only too glad to hitch their wagon to the star of an ultra-modern movement which proclaimed the imminent demise of democracy and the nation state, in the name of geopolitics and the need for larger trans-national or trans-continental agglomerations. Seen in this light, the imperialist movement around 1900 had a dual aspect: it underwrote the existing pre-modern empires while at the same time pointing obscurely to concepts lying beyond the horizon of liberal democracy and national self-determination.

Global politics were the province of political leaders and military theorists. The topic held no attraction for the mass of the people whose loyalty went to the nation, the homeland, the fatherland – in short, to what was familiar and easily understood. Nations were supposed to have a mission, but this sort of talk did not excite the average man. What mattered to him was the linguistic group within whose confines he lived. The transition from nationalism to imperialism was effected by political elites no longer content with anything that fell short of a world role. The change was accelerated by the spread of an advanced technology transcending national frontiers, and by the backwash of inter-imperialist rivalries in the undeveloped lands colonized by Europeans. Friction between British, French and Russian governments involved in colonial pursuits had the effect of rendering more acute political tensions inherited from the past century. Inversely, the assertion of independent nationhood by Germany and Italy injected a fresh element of instability into the general European pattern. Liberalism and nationalism parted company. The Bismarckian construction had rested on an alliance between national sentiment and traditional conservatism. The Wilhelminian regime around 1900 became aggressively imperialist in the modern sense largely because 'world politics' cemented the alliance between the ruling caste and the great industrialists whose interests were served by this kind of globalism. It was commonly accepted that the future belonged to a handful of powers capable of empire-building on the British pattern: the remainder would be squeezed out or reduced to satellite status. This kind of reasoning was common to statesmen, financiers and academic theorists stemming from a middle class no longer content with the liberal nationalism of its ancestors. The change was not perceived by the mass of ordinary people whose naive patriotism guaranteed the reliability of the armed forces. Peasants traditionally attached to their plot of land, or recently urbanized workers who had barely begun to internalize the values of middle-class culture, could be relied upon to fight and die for the motherland when the call sounded. They did so in 1914–18, and it took years of slaughter in the trenches to alienate a substantial minority from governments already in pursuit of purely imperialist aims. Around 1900 this outcome was not foreseeable, which is why the major European powers played the imperialist game behind the back of electorates still wedded to nationalism and democracy. The 'pan' movements helped to bridge the gap, but their influence was restricted to the educated middle class. Pan-Germanism and Pan-Slavism made their principal impact upon school teachers, students and army officers. British imperialism became the special province of the Conservative Party, and by way of the press and popular literature reached sections of the electorate which could not conceivably hope to benefit directly from overseas expansion. French imperialism was not perceived as such: it sheltered behind patriotic emotions and France's 'civilizing mission' in North Africa and Indo-China. The economic interests directly involved in these enterprises were not very considerable, but they were strategically located at the core of the governing class, and for the rest it could plausibly be argued that the partition of the globe among the leading industrial powers – the United States and Japan included – was inevitable. To that extent, imperialism actually made sense: it implied a recognition that the European nation state was in danger of being left behind.

The common factor in all this theorizing was the pre-eminence of Europe. This was taken for granted down to 1918, which is why even the most rabid imperialists preserved a good conscience in advancing the respective claims of 'their' nation. Europeans and non-Europeans alike assumed that inter-continental relations would continue to follow the pattern they had assumed in the sixteenth century.[7] The German challenge to Britain's world position was seen as a move within a game whose rules were familiar. The Anglo-Japanese alliance of 1902 introduced a new factor, in that for the first time an Asian country was treated as an equal by the greatest of European empires, but there was no clear perception of the fact that the alliance heralded the termination of the European age. Russia was still intent on being recognized as a member of the European family, and the revolution of 1905, by introducing something like constitutional government, did in fact bring the Tsarist regime into line with its Central European rivals. There was not, on the eve of 1914, a marked dissimilarity in the political processes at work in Berlin, Vienna and St Petersburg. The reigning dynasties pursued their rival and incompatible aims in the name of what were supposed to be common values. Even the Ottoman regime modernized itself after 1908 to the extent of elevating Turkish national- ism, rather than religion, to the status of an overriding political prin- ciple. Further to the East, China underwent similar tremors in 1911. The ultimate source of all these adaptations to the Western model was the impact of European capital, education and military organization. Europe's cultural heritage was exported alongside the economic surplus which enabled rival British, German and French companies to under- take railway construction in the Near East or in Latin America. Britain had a long lead in this field, and competition grew intense as French banks financed Russian railway construction, while German capital began to pour into Turkey, with the clear intention of creating a Berlin–Baghdad connection linking Central Europe with the Near East by way of the Austro-Hungarian monarchy and the remaining Turkish possessions in the Balkans.[8] The whole enterprise was thoroughly traditional in terms of Europe's inherited national rivalries. These antagonisms cut across the common endeavour to draw the backward hinterland of European capitalism into the network of economic rela- tionships characteristic of the advanced countries. Down to 1914–18 it was tacitly assumed that both operations could go on side by side; that is to say, it was taken for granted that Europe would remain the centre of politico-economic decision-making, even if the rival European states came to blows. It took the First World War to shake this confidence, and the second to complete the awakening. It was then retrospectively perceived that national rivalries had destroyed the nexus of relations on which Europe's pre-eminence rested. On purely economic grounds, a consortium for the purpose of developing the non-European hinterland would have been preferable to war, but rational calculations were uppermost only in the minds of a handful of bankers. The bulk of what then counted as public opinion, and what was in effect middle-class opinion, was thoroughly committed to nationalism, and this circum- stance proved an insuperable obstacle to the pacifist schemes promoted by left-wing liberals in the hope of averting the threatening catastrophe. We are thus obliged to register the fact that the European nation state, after preparing the ground for the emergence of trans-continental im- perialism, promoted the destruction of Europe's historic pre-eminence. The 1914 war did not merely demolish the Eastern Empires: it delivered a knock-out blow to Britain's and Western Europe's hegemony as well. Imperialism had grown out of nationalism, and in the end had out- grown the fabric of the nation state. But the nation state was the only political instrument available for the attainment of supra-national aims. When Europe went to war in 1914, and again in 1939, means and ends came into conflict. What emerged from the wreckage was something no European patriot of 1900 was capable of foreseeing.

NOTES

1 For the political history of the period see A.J.P.Taylor, *The Struggle for Mastery in Europe 1848–1918* (Oxford: Clarendon Press; New York: Oxford University Press, 1954), esp. pp. 228 ff., 255 ff., 372 ff.; *The Habsburg Monarchy 1809–1918* (London: Hamish Hamilton, 1948), *passim*; H.Seton-Watson, *The Russian Empire* (Oxford: Clarendon Press; New York: Oxford University Press, 1967), pp. 430 ff., 567 ff., 677; Fritz Fischer, *Germany's Aims in the First World War* (London: Chatto & Windus; New York: W.W.Norton, 1967), first published in German under the title *Griff nach der Weltmacht* (Düsseldorf: Droste Verlag, 1961); also the same author's *Krieg der Illusionen: Die deutsche Politik von 1911 bis 1914* (Düsseldorf: Droste, 1970). For the general topic of imperialism in modern Europe see George W.F.Hallgarten, *Imperialismus vor 1914* (Munich: C.H.Beck, 1951), *passim*.

2 For the typology of nationalism see Alfred Cobban, *The Nation State and National Self-Determination* (London: Collins, 1969; New York: Crowell, 1970); Geoffrey Barraclough, *European Unity in Thought and Action* (Oxford: Blackwell; New York: Hillary, 1963) and the same author's *Factors in German History* (Oxford: Blackwell, 1946), pp. 104 ff.; F.L. Carsten, *The Origins of Prussia* (Oxford: Clarendon Press; New York: Oxford University Press, 1954). For the general European background on the eve of 1914 see vol. XII of *The New Cambridge Modern History* (1st ed., 1960, 2nd rev. ed., 1968). For the impact of the French Revolution on European thought in the liberal age, see Elie Kedourie, *Nationalism* (London: Hutchinson, 1960; New York: Praeger, 1961).

3 V.G.Kiernan, *The Lords of Human Kind: European Attitudes Towards the Outside World in the Imperial Age* (London: Weidenfeld & Nicolson; Boston: Little, Brown, 1969); E.J.Hobsbawm, *Industry and Empire* (London: Weidenfeld & Nicolson; Garden City, N.Y.: Doubleday, 1968); Bernard Semmel, *Imperialism and Social Reform: English Social-Imperial Thought 1895–1914* (London: Allen & Unwin, 1960); A.P.Thornton, *The Imperial Idea and its Enemies: A Study in British Power* (London: Macmillan; New York: St Martin's Press, 1959); L.C.B.Seaman, *Post-Victorian Britain 1902–1951* (London: Methuen; New York: Barnes & Noble, 1966); Heinz Gollwitzer, *Europe in the Age of Imperialism 1880–1914* (London: Thames and Hudson; New York: Harcourt Brace, 1969).

4 See the Introduction to the new edition of Mahan's work published in 1957 (New York: Sagamore Press). The standard indictment of colonial expansion from the traditional liberal standpoint is to be found in J.A. Hobson's *Imperialism*, first published in 1902 and several times reprinted. For a critical study of the imperialist movement from a Continental liberal standpoint see J.A.Schumpeter, *Imperialism and Social Classes* (Oxford: Blackwell, 1951; New York: World Publishing, 1955). Of the two papers in this volume, the more important is Schumpeter's essay "Zur Soziologie der Imperialismen", first published in the *Archiv für Sozialwissenschaft und Sozialpolitik* in 1919 (Vol. 46). The principal Marxist contribution to the pre-1914 debate was Rosa Luxemburg's *Die Akkumu-*

lation des Kapitals (1913), an English-language edition of which appeared in 1951 (London: Routledge; New York: Monthly Review Press, 1964), with an introduction by Joan Robinson. Lenin's well-known *Imperialism, the Highest Stage of Capitalism* was written in 1916 and represents a transposition of the earlier discussion among Socialists to the new situation brought about by the outbreak of war in 1914.

5 Seaman, *op. cit.*, p. 51.

6 *Ibid.*, pp. 52–9. The fact that war was declared in August 1914 by a Liberal government, while the decisive turn towards France in 1902–4 had been negotiated by the Conservatives, made no difference, save to a handful of left-wing Liberals who duly felt betrayed by Asquith, Grey, Haldane, Lloyd George and their colleagues. British foreign policy was shaped by the permanent officials of the Foreign Office who from 1904 onwards steadfastly held to their conviction that Germany's rulers meant to challenge Britain's world position – as indeed they did.

7 H.Stuart Hughes, *Contemporary Europe: A History* (Englewood Cliffs, N.J. Prentice-Hall, 1961), *passim*.

8 Fischer, *Germany's Aims in the First World War*, p. 19.

CHAPTER 2

SOCIAL FOUNDATIONS

The Europe on which the storm of the First World War burst in 1914 lay at the centre of a global network of trade relations policed by the British Navy and kept going by constant infusions of British capital, with France and Germany coming next in order of importance. These three, as well as some of the smaller West European countries, had absorbed the industrial revolution and built up a capital surplus which in turn underpinned the imperialist expansion described in the preceding chapter. Eastern Europe lagged behind, but Russian industrialization accelerated sharply in the 1890s, and by 1914 there had come into existence a class of industrial entrepreneurs whose performance seemed to duplicate the strides earlier made in Germany. The latter country had by then come to the forefront industrially and abandoned a predominantly rural economy in favour of an urban one. Germany's economy expanded at a faster rate than that of her competitors, while her population grew from about forty-five million in 1880 to fifty-six million in 1900 and close to seventy million in 1914. This demographic shift was accompanied by a rush to the towns, so that by 1910 the urban population accounted for sixty per cent of the total, as against thirty-six per cent in 1871, when the German Empire came into being. At the same time emigration to North America, which had been considerable, virtually came to a halt after 1900, a circumstance testifying to the absorptive capacity of a fast expanding industrial and commercial network. By contrast France's industrialization proceeded rather slowly, and her population remained almost stable at around forty million. The big jump in British population growth from twenty-six million in 1870 to forty-one million in 1910 helped to keep the country in the front rank of European powers, but technologically Britain had begun to lag by comparison with Germany. Italy by 1914 approached France in population, but was far behind industrially.

The demographic pattern had obvious military implications, especially when joined to an advanced industrial technology. During the period under review Germany was able to combine rapid population growth with an even faster expansion of industry, and this circumstance underlay the political schemes of a governing stratum which had begun to toy with the notion of effecting a rapid breakthrough from European to world status. Imperial Germany had outstripped France and embarked on a dual race with Britain – still predominant overseas – and the Tsarist Empire, whose population in 1910 was thought to be in the neighbourhood of 150 million. There was no precise correlation between manpower and military force, but Russia's rapid industrialization lent weight to the conflicting aspirations of Pan-Slav and Pan-German expansionists. It was, to say the least, plausible to suppose that Russia's huge reserves of manpower would make up for France's notorious weakness in this domain. The speculative projection of these factors into the future became an obsession with diplomats, general staffs and captains of industry alike. When the Central Powers went to war in 1914, they did so in part because their governments had been converted to the view that the Franco-Russian combine was becoming dangerously strong. In this sense industrialization promoted intra-European tensions which in the end wrecked Europe's predominance on the world scene.[1]

The topic can be approached in different ways, depending on the yardstick one applies. From the sociologist's viewpoint the whole of the Western world was undergoing a rapid transition from an agrarian to an industrial way of life. In this perspective, what stands out is the spread of the industrial revolution from its British birth-place to North America and Continental Western Europe, its phenomenal success in Germany, its gradual extension to Austria-Hungary and Russia, the marked contrast between Northern and Southern Europe, and the consequent weakening of French influence, along with a tendency to class France with Italy and Spain as members of a predominantly Latin-Catholic culture which adapted rather slowly to the modern age. This approach cuts across the political and military factors discussed earlier. In a perspective of this kind, North America's population growth from about forty-five million in 1875 to 100 million in 1914 takes precedence over other considerations, notably in the light of the fact that between 1870 and 1914 some twenty-two million European immigrants were added to the American population. We are then concerned with the internal structure of what at a later date would come to be known as the Atlantic community. But in 1900 the dismal result of Europe's internal wars was not foreseeable. Russia counted as a backward country trying to Europeanize itself, not as a global super-power overshadowing the Eastern half of the Continent. Germany was plainly about to make a bid for European hegemony, and this tendency was fed by an uncommonly successful process of technological modernization along familiar capitalist lines. Britain was beginning to lose ground to foreign competitors, but remained pre-eminent in foreign investment, with perhaps £4,000 million invested abroad, as against less than £5,500 owned by the USA, Germany, France, Belgium and Holland put together.[2] Outside the Western world, Japan had made a successful start with industrial modernization, although her political institutions remained archaic. The general picture was heartening from the liberal viewpoint, although the menace of war remained constantly on the horizon. There was no clear perception of the fact that European civilization as such stood in peril, or that the nation state was about to be overtaken by the fate of the German and Italian city state in an earlier age. Equally, the prevailing consensus rested on an uncritical acceptance of bourgeois society as the final goal of the historical process. Its institutions – parliamentary government included – were expected to spread outward in the wake of European capital investment. The possibility that large tracts of the world might choose to modernize along entirely different lines had not yet been seriously considered even by socialist critics of the liberal consensus.

On the assumptions generally prevalent down to 1914, it did not seem particularly odd to suppose that Russian industrialization would follow the German example, and that the country's political institutions would be remodelled in such a way as to produce a semblance of parliamentary government. Such an outcome was in fact regarded as likely even by Russian Marxists, not to mention the Conservatives who admired Prussia, and the Liberals who were determined to follow the Western model.[3] Russia was still relatively backward compared with Germany, but apparently launched upon a course that could only result in a duplication of the German pattern. The principal obstacle in the way of such a solution was the inability of the peasantry to defray the costs of industrialization.[4]

The Russian government not only put the peasantry under heavy fiscal pressure: it left the village economy to its own devices, at a time when population was growing rapidly, so that by 1900 Russian agriculture produced less breadgrain per head than had been the case in 1870. At the same time, governmental intervention in industry concentrated on strategic railway building on the one hand, iron and steel on the other. The result was a lopsided development, advanced technology and large modern plants being grafted upon a primitive agriculture. The process was self-contradictory, in that industrialization at the expense of the village caused political tensions which exploded in 1905, and more violently in 1917. "A central principle of governmental policy was to impound a larger share of the peasants' output rather than to take active steps to raise that output."[5] In this respect the Tsarist government under Witte and Stolypin carried on a tradition which after the Revolution became part of the Bolshevik inheritance. Although not driven to Stalinist extremes, this deliberate exploitation of the peasantry, under conditions of political instability and in the absence of a strong entrepreneurial middle class, created the pre-conditions for revolution. By 1914 Russian industry and banking had come to resemble the admired German model, but politically the country was drifting towards an explosion on the pattern of the French Revolution. This was an extreme case. Austria-Hungary was socially closer to Germany, but here too the governmental fabric was archaic and unable to withstand the strain of a major war. The series of revolutions in 1917–18 significantly occurred on the territory of the three Eastern Empires, and the German upheaval of 1918 was the least radical of the three. Radicalism was a function of backwardness, which is merely another way of saying that these structures collapsed because they were pre-bourgeois. Where the industrial revolution had been successfully carried through under bourgeois leadership in the nineteenth century, the labour movement tended to be reformist and the intelligentsia was well integrated within the socially dominant class.

Sociologically speaking, capitalism represents the bourgeois form of industrialization. It cannot get under way successfully in the absence of a social class which embodies the values of the private entrepreneur. Even where such a stratum exists it may be hampered by the prevailing social attitudes, a circumstance attested to by the relatively slow growth of modern industry in France, Italy and Spain, by comparison with Germany, Britain and the United States. It is important to bear in mind, however, that the spectacular German development around 1900 was largely a matter of the country's top structure being transformed, while underneath there remained a mass of conservative attitudes centring on the family firm. It has been estimated that in Germany and France before the First World War 94·59 and 97·98 per cent, respectively, of all enterprises in industry and mining occupied no more than ten persons.[6] Socially speaking, this state of affairs signified that the prevailing values were those of the small entrepreneur, rather than the modern banker or 'captain of industry'. It was precisely the lack of such a broadly based stratum of entrepreneurship which in Russia – and to a lesser degree in Austria-Hungary – drove the state into the sphere of capital investment. In this sense the real dividing line ran between Central and Eastern Europe, rather than between Germany and France, notwithstanding the superior German performance after 1870, when the cession of Alsace-Lorraine handicapped France's iron and steel industries.[7] Down to the 1870s the French development was if anything more spectacular than the German.[8]

Coming closer to the facts of industrial strength, we may note that in 1871, the year the Bismarckian Empire was put together, Germany's mines produced twenty-nine million tons of coal and 8·5 million tons of lignite, as against 118 million metric tons for Britain and 13·3 million for France. By 1913 Britain's output had risen to 292 million tons, but Germany was hard on her heels with 191·5 million tons of coal and 87·5 million tons of lignite, while France had dropped far behind with less than forty-one million tons, closely followed by Belgium with about twenty-three million. "Disunited Germany had been helped by her railways and her far superior resources to get ahead of France and Belgium. United Germany was almost ready at the last to challenge England on England's chosen ground." [9] The figures for iron and steel are instructive too:

TABLE I OUTPUT IN METRIC TONS

		1890	1910
United Kingdom	Pig iron	8,031,000	10,172,000
	Steel	5,301,000	7,613,000
Germany			
(with Luxemburg)	Pig iron	4,658,500	14,794,000
	Steel	3,164,000	13,149,000
France	Pig iron	1,962,000	4,038,000
	Steel	1,407,000	2,850,000

Germany had moved far ahead during the period 1890–1910 and came to rank second behind the United States as an iron and steel producer. In the modern chemical and electrical industries, Germany's lead over her European competitors was even more pronounced. This spectacular leap forward occurred against a background of tariff protection and cartelization which cut the ground from under the liberal doctrines inherited from an earlier era. Imperial Germany was governed by an irremovable *bloc* of industrialists and landowners whose conversion to protectionism since the 1880s rendered illusory all hopes of internal liberalization. The Reich government was committed to the perpetuation of archaic social patterns ultimately rooted in the circumstance that Prussia had historically been ruled by a class of noblemen, the Junkers.[10] The protectionist bloc of East German landowners and West German industrialists was obliged, as a matter of self-preservation, to oppose the democratization of the country's political institutions, since democracy at home would have involved a conversion to free trade abroad. Rather than risk this experiment the ruling stratum embarked upon *Weltpolitik* in the imperialist spirit referred to in the preceding chapter. The Russian situation was similar, in that a comparable alignment of forces became evident after the semi-successful revolution of 1905–6. In both cases the authoritarian political structure centring upon the reigning dynasty won the loyalty of a bourgeoisie which had skipped the liberal stage and moved straight from mercantilism to imperialism in the modern sense of the term. If there was a difference it lay in the fact that in Russia a land-hungry peasantry constituted a potentially revolutionary force, whereas the German peasants followed the lead of the great landowners who taught them to regard all city-dwellers as enemies of the country folk. The vastly superior performance of the German Army in 1914–18, as compared with its Russian opponents, is not unconnected with this ambience.

Because of its peculiar combination of technological modernity with social archaism, Germany became the dynamic factor in European politics during the three decades terminating with the collapse of 1918. The strength of the country's technological base is well illustrated by the fact that the eastern province of Silesia alone in 1913 produced 43 million tons of coal, more than all of France, while its reserves were said to exceed those of the United Kingdom.[11] Demographically, militarily and industrially, Germany's advance between 1890 and 1914 was so fast that the country's rulers in the end felt able to gamble on rapid victory in a two-front war against France and Russia. Even though they misjudged the British reaction, believing to the last that an accommodation with the British Empire in Africa would keep London neutral in the event of a Continental European war, their behaviour cannot be said to have been wholly irrational. It was sustained by the conviction that a rapid military victory was possible, and this belief in turn was grounded in the indisputable fact that in the industrial field Germany had outdistanced her European rivals. No other country could show a comparable record, save for the United States, whose exports developed at an even more rapid pace than Germany's.[12] Russia was seen as a potential menace in the distant future rather than an immediate threat. The decision to go to war in 1914 thus had the aspect of a preventive move. It was designed to forestall the time when Russia's resources would be fully developed. It also took account of the fact that the Dual Monarchy of Austria-Hungary was not likely to stay in existence much longer, and that the construction of a unified Central Europe could only be undertaken with Austrian help. *Mitteleuropa*, as it came to be known, was visualized as a customs union embracing not only Austria, but Italy, Switzerland and the Netherlands as well. The aim had the support of leading industrialists with access to the Emperor and the Chancellor.[13] Given the mounting disparity between Germany and her neighbours, it was not illogical. It could, however, be attained only by first delivering a military knock-out blow to France, or alternatively by inducing France to enter a German-led combination directed against Britain and the United States.

At every stage, the economics of cartelization intermingled closely with purely strategic schemes. Thus in 1912, after the failure of the last British attempt to arrive at a naval settlement (the Haldane mission), William II expounded to the great industrialist Walter Rathenau his ideas for "an economic unification of the Continent as a defensive measure against the American reprisals policy of high tariffs. 'His plan' was for a 'United States of Europe against America.' He thought that this would not be disagreeable to the British, and that they would come in...."[14] This sort of theorizing had been rendered respectable by economists and geopoliticians since the 1890s. It was essentially an extension into the political sphere of the rationality that underlay the cartelization of industry under the patronage of the banks. A German-dominated Central Europe fitted into this kind of oligopolistic thinking, a not so distant forerunner of Hitler's rather similar plans in 1939, with the difference that in 1912–14 European civilization had not yet spawned the phenomenon of the totalitarian one-party state. The British Empire, on this assumption, would have become an associate of Germany in the inevitable economic showdown with a protectionist America. If one subtracts William's personal fantasies, which were inevitably of the Pan-German variety and included gloomy visions of a racial struggle between Slavs and Teutons, the scheme had all the familiar characteristics of politico-economic manipulation in the age of trustified capitalism. This is just what made it attractive to bankers and industrialists who in other respects had little use for the Hohenzollern dynasty.

Imperialist thinking in Britain after 1900 ran along broadly similar lines, with the important difference that the country was committed to free trade, a doctrine described by *The Economist* in 1848 as "a good, like virtue, holiness and righteousness, to be loved, admired, honoured and steadfastly adopted, for its own sake, though all the rest of the world should love restrictions and prohibitions, which are of themselves evils, like vice and crime, to be hated and abhorred under all circumstances and at all times". More than half a century later, after the first flush of enthusiasm over free trade had long departed, imperialism was still described by J.A.Hobson as a "depraved choice of national life". This was emphatically not the opinion of men like Joseph Chamberlain, Alfred Milner or Cecil Rhodes, who around the time of the Boer War (1899–1902) set out to make the British conscious of their imperial responsibilities. But although they gradually converted most of the Conservative Party to their views, the section of opinion they represented was decidedly in the minority down to 1914–18. On the opposing side were arrayed not only the Liberal Party and its allies among the City bankers, but the intellectual weight of a tradition going back to John Stuart Mill, Cobden, Bright, Gladstone, Herbert Spencer and T.H.Green. The premises of their thinking were pacifist and cosmopolitan, and the nascent labour movement inherited this orientation, even though a substantial number of Fabian Socialists were in tacit agreement with the new imperialist school.[15] The 'tariff reform' campaign launched by Chamberlain in 1903 split the Conservatives and was a major factor in promoting the Liberal comeback in 1906. The imperial federation favoured by the tariff reformers was the counterpart of German *Mitteleuropa* schemes. It failed because the electorate preferred the Liberal solution of free trade and cheap imports from overseas, and because the self-governing white-settler colonies were lukewarm: they were already thinking in terms of independent nationhood, an impossibility within an integrated empire based on a customs union. Liberal imperialism, the line pursued by the ruling Liberal Party between 1906 and 1914, rested on an illogical compromise, but in the short run it was popular both with the electorate and with the City, which still regarded the entire world as its oyster and had no desire to be dragged into an imperial customs union on bad terms with America and the rest of the world. The logic of imperialism, in the Chamberlainite sense of the term, pointed straight towards global war. It is arguable that war was inevitable, and that Britain would have been in better shape to wage it had it adopted the social-imperialist legislation urged by theorists like Karl Pearson and leading Fabians such as the Webbs and Bernard Shaw.[16] But this is to overlook the fact that the Liberal government was able to bring Britain into the war in 1914 only because its principal figures were ostensibly wedded to pacifism and hostile to everything Chamberlain stood for. A Conservative government committed to massive armaments, high tariffs and military alliances against the German menace would have split the nation. Paradoxically, the Liberals were able to make imperialism work in practice just because in principle they were *not* committed to it, or to the aristocratic outlook which its proponents – in this respect heirs of Carlyle and Matthew Arnold – were trying to put across. As for the trade unions, they had imbibed the doctrine that free trade meant cheap food for the working man, but their leaders also supported it because it fitted in with their inclination towards peace and internationalism. Protection could be sold to the British working class only after the Liberal Party had surrendered the ghost. On the left, the Fabians were alone in denouncing liberal economics as a do-nothing programme. They did not speak for the main body of the British labour movement, which obstinately supported the radical wing of liberalism.

The Liberal–Labour coalition, which had come into being around 1900, was committed to the extension of democracy. The Tories were not, and this was a crucial factor in causing the unions to cast their weight on the Liberal side. As late as 1911 only fifty-nine per cent of Britain's adult male population (some eight million out of a total nearing forty-one million) had the vote, and there were seven different types of franchise, of which the two major ones related to ownership or occupation of land, or of any house defined as a separate dwelling. Half a million voters belonging to the wealthier stratum had two or more votes.[17] Women were disfranchised until 1918, when the radical clamour for an extension of the vote to millions of second-class citizens, who had done their duty during the war, could no longer be resisted. Democracy thus remained an important issue on which Liberals and Labourites could coalesce. In contrast to Germany, where the all-important Prussian franchise effectively excluded the working class from public life, it was possible in Britain to envisage a non-violent passage from oligarchic to democratic forms of rule, and this was among the major reasons why the union movement retained a pre-dominantly liberal–radical outlook down to 1918, when the Labour Party committed itself to Fabian Socialism. Violence entered British public life by way of Ireland, where by 1914 conflicting national and religious passions held the threat of civil war. It is true that from 1910 onwards a fall in real wages helped to stimulate a wave of strikes and the spread of syndicalist doctrines imported from France and America. But only in Ireland, where Protestant Ulstermen and Catholic National-ists had begun to prepare for an armed confrontation, was the authority of the British government seriously challenged.

France's domestic problems differed sharply from Britain's, a circum-stance obscured by the informal Anglo-French alliance against Ger-many which became a factor in European politics from 1904 onwards. Alone among the major Western nations, pre-1914 France had remained predominantly a rural country, although from about 1875 onward the population officially classed as rural began to decline in absolute terms, the total French population growing slowly from less than thirty-seven million at that date to just under forty million in 1911. During the same period the proportion of Frenchmen living in predominantly rural communes of less than 2,000 inhabitants went down from about seventy to fifty-six per cent.[18] Official statistics before 1914 assumed that by 1920 half the country's population would be urban. By contrast, the urban percentage for Germany in 1910 was already three-fifths out of a total population of sixty-five million. Britain was even more highly urbanized, its 580,000 farmers in 1911 employing only a fraction of the 15·6 million wage-earners, to whom must be added 1·2 million salaried men and women usually reckoned as belonging to the lower middle class. By the 1930s agriculture provided work for only five per cent of the occupied population, and this outcome was already visible three decades earlier, notwithstanding the social eminence of the landowning class which down to 1914 retained its stranglehold upon both Houses of Parliament. Britain's socio-political structure thus resembled that of Germany rather than France: the latter a bourgeois Republic based on a numerous landowning peasantry. French politics in consequence shared common features with those of Italy and Spain, all three pre-dominantly Roman Catholic cultures with traditional values quite different from those of the Protestant North on the one hand, and Eastern Europe with its Slav populations on the other. Foreign policy cut across these alignments: it did not reflect them, being a matter of political calculation and military strategy. In terms of social composition and inherited outlook, it would have seemed natural for France to become the leader of a Mediterranean group of countries, rather than an ally of Russia and Britain. The major moves on the political chessboard before 1914 were quite unrelated to such considerations, which was just what *Realpolitik* signified: alliances were formed in response to balance-of-power considerations. What in a later age was called 'ideology' hardly entered into the matter, else Tsarist Russia and the French Republic could not have become allies. This circumstance was to cause a good deal of trouble after 1914, when the belligerents had to rationalize their respective positions in terms that made sense to the mass of ordinary people. It was, however, axiomatic that unconditional loyalty was owed to the nation state. As long as this principle went unchallenged, the military and diplomatic professionals had a free hand. In the case of France, they could also rely on popular sentiments stemming from the war of 1870-1 and the loss of Alsace-Lorraine. Any alliance that promised the recovery of the lost provinces could count on a large measure of public support.

Nationalism was overwhelmingly the most important factor in European affairs, if one abstracts from the geopolitical chess moves referred to earlier. Even these were rooted in national sentiment, for imperialism was too esoteric a doctrine to become genuinely popular. The Franco-Russian alliance was kept going by French hatred of Germany, the German–Austrian combination by the conviction that one day Germans and Slavs would come to blows. Imperial Germany's most sensitive domestic problem – the incomplete Germanization of formerly Polish lands incorporated within the Bismarckian Empire – likewise stemmed from the clash of rival nationalisms. A systematic attempt to Germanize these lands was set going in the 1880s. It proved unsuccessful, and its failure was largely responsible for the resurrection in 1919 of an independent Poland which promptly laid claim to Prussian territory in Silesia. The Dual Monarchy of Austria-Hungary was torn apart by irreconcilable national hatreds which in the end drove the ruling German and Magyar minorities to the point of seeking a solution of their problem in a military showdown with Serbia and its Russian backers. Italy in 1915 sided with the Anglo-French Entente against the Central Powers on account of irredentist claims to Austrian territory dating back to the nineteenth century. Even Britain had by 1914 been driven to the point of constitutional breakdown and armed violence by the Irish problem. By comparison with these stresses, the class antagonisms unleashed by the industrial revolution took second place. They came to the forefront only in 1919, by which time the map of Europe had been redrawn in accordance with national principles and the ancient multinational empires had disappeared.

This is not to say that class conflict was absent, but it assumed violent forms not at the core of the system, but rather along its outer rim. Russia was shaken by revolution in 1905, whereas Germany stayed quiet. France possessed a Syndicalist movement with revolutionary aims, but it was in retrograde Spain that Anarcho-Syndicalism assumed the character of a deliberate secession from society.[19] Italy witnessed a decline of faith in parliamentary institutions even before the 1914–18 war gave Fascism its chance.[20]

It was a foretaste of the future when, in 1908, the landowners of Emilia collected a defense fund and formed a motorized volunteer force equipped with arms. This force assisted the troops in street-fighting at Parma and marched through a barrage of missiles and boiling water to surround and occupy the working-class quarter of the city. Similar scenes were to occur more frequently in the not so distant future.[21]

Some of the Syndicalist leaders on the extreme left of the Italian labour movement reacted to this experience by throwing in their lot with the Nationalists on the right, in the hope of bringing the parliamentary system down. In so doing they set a precedent for a youthful Socialist named Mussolini who at the time still stood on the radical wing of his party. They also confirmed eminent thinkers such as Gaetano Mosca and Benedetto Croce in their gloomy conviction that liberalism and democracy could not be successfully combined.[22]

Overall, the European system which collapsed into war in 1914 was highly unstable, a circumstance not immediately obvious to the middle class which during the preceding century had been borne along by the industrial revolution and in the process had amassed both material fortunes and a reasonably good conscience. It was this class which had given birth to nationalism and liberalism alike. When national passions were translated into imperialist politics, liberal-democratic institutions proved unable to keep the peace. For that matter, neither the Catholic Church nor the Socialist International did any better. The torrent of hatred unleashed in 1914 bore witness to the fact that European civilization had nurtured destructive forces which found their outlet in war and revolution.

NOTES

1 Solomon F. Bloom, *Europe and America* (London: Longmans; New York: Harcourt Brace, 1961), pp. 392 ff., 402 ff.; J. H. Clapham, *The Economic Development of France and Germany 1815–1914* (Cambridge: University Press, 1921; New York: Cambridge University Press, 4th ed., 1935), pp. 232 ff., 278 ff.

2 E.J.Hobsbawm, *Industry and Empire* (London: Weidenfeld & Nicolson; Garden City, N.Y.: Doubleday, 1968), p. 125.

3 H.Seton-Watson, *The Russian Empire 1801–1917* (Oxford: Clarendon Press, 1967), pp. 531 ff.

4 Alexander Gerschenkron, *Economic Backwardness in Historical Perspective* (London: Oxford University Press, 1963; Cambridge, Massachusetts: Harvard University Press, 1962), pp. 124 ff.

5 *Ibid.*, p. 126

6 *Ibid.*, p. 64 n.

7 Clapham, *op. cit.*, p. 237.

8 Gerschenkron, *op. cit.*, p. 65.

9 Clapham, *op. cit.*, p. 281.

10 Gerschenkron, *Bread and Democracy in Germany* (Berkeley, Calif.: University of California Press, 1943), p. 67 and *passim*.

11 Clapham, *op. cit.*, p. 282.

12 Fritz Fischer, *Germany's Aims in the First World War*, (London: Chatto & Windus; New York: W.W.Norton, 1967), p. 12.

13 *Ibid.*, pp. 28–9.

14 *Ibid.*, p. 28.

15 A.M.McBriar, *Fabian Socialism and English Politics 1884–1918* (Cambridge University Press, 1966; New York: Cambridge University Press, 1962), pp. 119 ff.

16 Bernard Semmel, *Imperialism and Social Reform* (London: Allen & Unwin, 1960), pp. 128 ff.

17 Arthur Marwick, *Britain in the Century of Total War* (London: The Bodley Head; Boston: Atlantic Monthly Press, Little, Brown, 1968), p. 26.

18 Clapham, *op. cit.*, p. 159.

19 Raymond Carr, *Spain 1808–1939* (Oxford: Clarendon Press; New York: Oxford University Press, 1966), pp. 430 ff.

20 Denis Mack Smith, *Italy: A Modern History* (Ann Arbor: University of Michigan Press, rev. ed. 1969), pp. 254 ff.

21 *Ibid.*, p. 256

22 *Ibid.*, p. 259.

CHAPTER 3

LIBERALISM AND NATIONALISM

With the concluding remarks of the preceding chapter we have over-stepped the somewhat artificial barrier between the politics and the culture of pre-1914 Europe. The area where both may be said to have had their vital centre was liberalism, taking the term to denote the self-interpretation of the social order resulting from the impact of capitalism and democracy. The society born from the dual revolution had taken shape around 1830 and attained its peak in the closing decades of the nineteenth century. By the start of the twentieth it gave signs of strain already pointing forward to its subsequent dissolution. In this perspective, what has been called 'the revolt against positivism' in the 1890s was a harbinger of increasingly profound disturbances.[1] The more pessimistic liberals located the era of transition at an earlier point, in the 1870s, when faith in unrestricted individualism and *laissez-faire* began to flag, socialism was seen as a challenge to the bourgeois order, and Bismarckian Germany effected a divorce of nationalism from liberalism. As one historian has noted, "Benedetto Croce (1866–1952) saw in the years after 1870 a change in the public spirit of Europe which ended the nineteenth century and began the twentieth."[2] Yet another writer has observed, "The story of the German youth movement begins about 1896. According to some historians it ended in 1914, according to others in 1933. . . ."[3]

These considerations cut across the more familiar concerns of the economic historian, for whom the 1890s and 1900s are chiefly remarkable for revolutionary technological developments linked to the invention of the internal combustion engine, the appearance of the motor car, the aeroplane, the telephone, the use of oil and electricity as sources of power, and the production by the growing chemical industry of synthetic fibres and plastics. Perhaps a link may be effected by noting that these aspects of what has sometimes been called the second industrial revolution made possible the subsequent mechanized slaughter of human cannon-fodder in 1914–18. Industrialization and urbanization had social consequences which translated themselves into political unrest. By 1910 London and New York had populations of over five million, Paris about three million, Vienna two million, Greater Berlin some four million. These masses of wage- and salary-earners were not likely to stay content with an individualist outlook proper to the European bourgeoisie in its creative phase. They responded to novel slogans – nationalism on the one hand, socialism on the other. The crisis of liberalism as a political creed, which dates from this period, had its source in the cleavage between faith in the independent individual and the actual life-style of the urbanized masses whom the industrial revolution had called into being. At its lowest level, the new culture was given shape by the popular press, for the most part in the hands of entrepreneurs who combined vague liberal reminiscences with the tenets of imperialism and Social Darwinism: life was a struggle in which the weak went to the wall, and specifically an unending global contest in which loyalty to one's nation served the greater cause of spreading European civilization all over the world. This was what 'progress' had come to signify around 1900, and this militant doctrine increasingly took the place of an older liberalism not yet effectively severed from the pacifism and cosmopolitanism of the Enlightenment. The world having been for the most part shared out among the European countries and North America, it appeared plain to the growing number of Social Darwinists that this fortunate arrangement was due to the racial superiority of their fellow countrymen, itself presumably brought about by some process of natural selection. In this sense, racism was an essential ingredient of the imperialist ideology. Its principal competitor, socialist internationalism, addressed itself to the industrial proletariat. Liberalism was caught between these new mass movements, which is why the more old-fashioned kind of individualist began to feel uncomfortable well before the 1914–18 catastrophe terminated the golden age of the European bourgeoisie.[4]

Politically speaking, European liberalism reached its peak in the 1870s. After this date there gradually occurred what the more consistent liberals regarded as a regression to the age of mercantilism, that is to say, protectionism and state intervention. The latter was urged by socialists on behalf of the growing labour movement, by nationalists in support of their competing claims, and by the great industrial and financial combines which had come to see the government as their chosen instrument. All three concurred in pressing state intervention beyond the point regarded as permissible in classical liberal doctrine, which allotted to the public authorities a regulative function only in respect of activities demonstrably beyond the capacity of private individuals. Protectionism in the economic sphere and colonial expansion abroad, plus the silent concentration of capital in larger units no longer subject to effective competition, sapped the foundations of the liberal creed.

After 1900 the Anglo-German arms race added another dimension to this process of disillusionment.

War had always been the weak point in the liberal construction. Classical economics itself conceded that defence came before opulence, which was only another way of saying that society stood in need of the state in its war-making capacity, just as it required official protection from dangerous mass movements. For obvious reasons it was easier to stress this heritage of pre-liberal thinking in Continental Europe than in Britain, but the end result was the same. Imperialism provided the rationale for a steady drift away from the attitudes prevalent within the entrepreneurial middle class in the century from 1775 to 1875. There had been a time when protective tariffs conferred their benefits mainly upon landowners. The alignment of interests altered when cartelized industries were induced to shelter behind customs barriers which enabled them to enforce monopolistic price policies at home, while dumping their surpluses abroad. The resulting change in the political climate underlay the mounting clamour for possession of colonies and spheres of interest adequately protected against foreign competition. From an overall European viewpoint these quarrels were irrational, but Europe was articulated into states divided not merely by tariff barriers, but by long-standing national animosities. Nationalism and liberalism thus came into conflict, and nationalism won out, in the process transforming itself into imperialism.

What has been called "the civilization of capitalism"[5] rested upon social arrangements of which classical liberalism briefly served as the political expression. By 1900 this outlook had become outmoded in its British homeland and was passing out of fashion in the Western world generally, with a time-lag in the United States, where as late as 1917 the decision to participate in the struggle against Germany could be rationalized as "a war to end war and make the world safe for democracy". Woodrow Wilson took up where Gladstone had left off. Inevitably his rhetoric sounded quaint to Europeans, although for decency's sake this circumstance was not publicly emphasized by America's British and French allies. We know from the memoirs of a distinguished British participant in the 1919 Versailles conference how deep was the gulf between the American President and his European colleagues, even though all were committed to the same principles. What was then said of Georges Clemenceau might have been said of virtually every statesman in Europe: "He felt about France what Pericles felt of Athens – unique value in her, nothing else mattering: but his theory of politics was Bismarck's."[6] This is simply to say that Clemenceau had no use for make-believe. There was nothing extraordinary about his outlook. He embodied a code of conduct which was traditional, had survived the brief liberal interlude, and underwent a substantial change only after Europe's pre-eminence itself had been destroyed in two world wars:

Nations are real things, of whom you love one and feel for the rest indifference – or hatred. The glory of the nation you love is a desirable end – but generally to be obtained at your neighbour's expense. The politics of power are inevitable, and there is nothing very new to learn about this war or the end it was fought for; England had destroyed, as in each preceding century, a trade rival; a mighty chapter had been closed in the secular struggle between the glories of Germany and of France. Prudence required some measure of lip service to the 'ideals' of foolish Americans and hypocritical Englishmen; but it would be stupid to believe that there is much room in the world, as it really is, for such affairs as the League of Nations. . . .[7]

This was written in 1919 by a disillusioned critic of the Versailles settlement, but the attitudes described by J.M.Keynes in his celebrated work had long been dominant and were not confined to France or Germany. In so far as European society possessed something like a common outlook, this community of mind and feeling took the paradoxical form of national exclusiveness. That is to say, what was common to all Europeans was their mutual detestation and their readiness to go to war against one another. The imperialist creed did not create this state of mind; it merely helped to aggravate its consequences. The logic of economic development called for larger trans-national agglomerations. Given the existing European state system, it was unlikely that this aim would be attained peacefully. Liberal pacifism and socialist internationalism alike were ineffective when matched against the intransigent claims of the sovereign state. The nation state might be obsolete, but it remained the focus of popular loyalties, and it was governed by political elites who had made the transition from the age of absolute monarchy to the imperialist era without altering their basic outlook:

The steel frame of that structure still consisted of the human material of feudal society and this material still behaved according to precapitalist patterns. It filled the offices of state, officered the army, devised policies – it functioned as a *classe dirigente* and, though taking account of bourgeois interests, it took care to distance itself from the bourgeoisie. . . . All this was more than atavism. It was an active symbiosis of two social strata, one of which no doubt supported the other economically but was in turn supported by the other politically.[8]

The description fits the major European states in the age that terminated in 1914. Even the bourgeois French Republic relied for its safety upon an army largely officered by the landed gentry, and for the rest French patriotism was in tune with the Jacobin tradition inaugurated in 1793: a tradition which did not rule out war, provided it was waged in the service of the nation. As for Britain and Germany, there was never any doubt that the call to arms would evoke a popular response in an age when war was glorified as the noblest and most heroic of human pursuits. Russia and Austria-Hungary could rely on their peasant masses, though in the end the strain of war proved too much for them. All told, there was no reason why liberal democracy, where it existed, should have been regarded as an effective barrier to national chauvinism, and where it did not exist, the traditional ruling classes moved within a mental orbit in which war still figured as a perfectly natural pastime. Granted that such sentiments were pre-bourgeois, it is nonetheless the case that the European bourgeoisie had come to terms with them. Liberal individualism was never more than the creed of an intellectual elite. For practical purposes, democracy implied nationalism – for the sound reason that the state was supposed to embody the general will. The more democratic a society, the more likely was it to make a total claim upon the loyalty of the citizens composing it. In this sense, liberalism and democracy could even be said to be at odds. But these philosophical puzzles did not burden the common man in the age which ended in 1914. His unquestioning loyalty went to political formations – the competing states and nations of Europe – whose traditional behaviour rendered it certain that sooner or later the accumulated tensions would find their outlet in a major war.[9]

In Western Europe, liberalism had by 1900 gone on the defensive. In Central and Eastern Europe it could not even be said to have enjoyed a brief hour of glory. The conservative reaction of the 1880s, which gained mass support in the new century, occurred against a background of rampant nationalism allied to retrograde social forces which had never been effectively challenged. The German Enlightenment had on the whole been a failure, and the miscarriage of the liberal-democratic experiment in 1848 laid the ground for the subsequent fusion of German nationalism with a conservatism rooted in archaic values and modes of life which were threatened by modernity. Historians have given insufficient weight to the existence of a form of anti-capitalism allied to the political Right. Its intellectual roots went back to the Romantic movement, while its popular base lay in the peasantry and the small towns. In Central Europe at least this form of conservatism was far more deeply embedded than the liberal movement, with its enthusiastic glorification of progress and rationality. Germany was to become a disaster area in the twentieth century for reasons having to do with the conservative rejection of the modern world. The implantation of industrial capitalism had occurred with unprecedented rapidity, and the brilliant economic achievements registered by the statisticians concealed an underlying malaise. Traditional ways of life were disrupted, with consequences only dimly perceived at the time.

The patent miseries of late eighteenth-century industrialization did not appear in Germany. The real cost, the psychic cost, has been ignored. Yet the history of Germany from 1871 to 1945 records not only the most extreme economic antagonisms of an industrial society, but the violent resentment against the new industrialism, which in different guises erupted time and again in German life. To a people sentimental about nature and their ancient towns, the sudden rise of monstrously big and ugly cities was distressing. Nor did Germany do things by halves; by 1910, it had almost as many large cities as the entire rest of the Continent.[10]

It is understandable that the country folk should have reacted with hostility to this development. What lent a dangerous edge to the conservative reaction was the readiness of the urban middle class to espouse political sentiments incompatible with the proper functioning of a liberal system. Parliamentary life was largely a sham anyway, the Bismarckian regime had aggravated class tensions, and there was widespread yearning for a return to the past, or alternatively for an authority that would somehow transcend the tiresome game of party politics. "These feelings found expression in the great exaltation of August 1914, when at last the cultural boredom of the nation was lifted, when politics were suspended, when the nation in danger would soon become the nation triumphant."[11] The sense of elation was not confined to one class: it briefly engulfed almost the entire country. But it was strongest among the educated, with school teachers and students in the lead. War had unified the nation under the leadership of its traditional ruling class, while at the same time offering an outlet to vague idealistic yearnings hitherto confined to the youth movement: itself the offspring of a predominantly Protestant middle-class culture threatened with disintegration by the spread of Western liberalism and individualism. The Germans, it might be said, were paying for their earlier failure to create a democratic political system which would have permitted a certain amount of steam to escape from the political cauldron. As matters stood, the patriotic orgy of 1914 appeared to conservative intellectuals as Germany's response to the French Revolution. The so-called 'ideas of 1914' – in reality formulated in the 1880s and 1890s – translated into political terms the heritage of German Romanticism. A people estranged from its own past by the shattering impact of capitalist industrialization for a brief moment felt united – in war against its neighbours.

The conservative counter-movement had its roots in the past, specifically in the 'war of liberation' against Napoleon in 1813, when German nationalism first began to take shape. In its modern form the movement represented a reaction to the dissolution of all organic ties incompatible with the urban civilization which had come into being in the wake of the industrial revolution. This kind of conservatism was a general European phenomenon, and Germany was not the only area

33

where nationalism acquired an anti-liberal flavour: France and Italy displayed similar tendencies. But only in Central Europe did the movement capture the bulk of the middle class. That class saw itself as the guardian of values and sentiments threatened by the inroads of Western rationalism, liberalism, secularism and materialism. It was only natural that the churches should lend their support to such a defensive reaction. The novelty lay in the fact that much of the resentment against the inroads of modernity was expressed by writers alienated from traditional religious faith. What they were after was a return to the folk community of the pre-modern age. Folk is a more comprehensive term than people: it signifies a kind of spiritual cosmos ultimately traceable to man's link with his ancestors, and through them with the natural environment in which the original folk community acquired its characteristic essence. From such vague sentiments it was only a short step to the notion that the various folk characteristics were not merely unique but incommunicable and eternally closed off from each other. This belief served as a rationale for the widespread anti-Semitism of the period, stronger for historical reasons in Russia, Germany and Austria than in Western Europe. It likewise became the foundation of political myths which were tested on the battlefield in 1914.[12]

With the wisdom of hindsight we can now perceive that the generation of reactionary ideologists who came to the forefront between 1880 and 1910 effected a transition from the older religious conservatism to the modern racialist faith. So far as the Jews were concerned, this change signified that anti-Semitic orators replaced the conventional charge of deicide by appeals to blood and soil. By definition the Jews were not members of the folk community, and since the State was supposed to be an emanation of the folk, it followed that they had no claim to equal citizenship. Similar conclusions were drawn by French nationalists during and after the Dreyfus affair (1894–1902), but they sounded eccentric to Frenchmen brought up to believe that the unity of the nation, as conceived in 1789, transcended racial heritage and religious belief alike. In contrast, the Germans suffered from the after-effects of a belated and incomplete national unification imposed by Prussia, which left twelve million Germans outside the borders of the *Reich*. Such as it was, the German Empire saw itself encircled by the Franco-Russian alliance. In Austria-Hungary the dominant German nationality felt even more insecure, constituting as it did only one-third of the population of the Habsburg Monarchy's western half. Nationalism, a unifying force in Germany, was a centrifugal one in Austria-Hungary, where the other nationalities far outnumbered the Germans. In the circumstances, an obsession with tribal politics gradually brought about a wholly irrational state of mind which fastened on the obvious connection between political liberalism, the Jewish community and the inroads of modern capitalism. In so far as they pioneered capitalism and liberalism alike (and later socialism as well), the Jews laid themselves open to the charge of undermining the tribal cohesion of the folk. Since by 1910 in Vienna they numbered 175,000 out of a total population of two million – and in Budapest nearly one-quarter of a population half the size of Vienna's – it was impossible to affirm that what was at stake was simply their individual assimilation into the surrounding culture. In the end, the problem was perceived as a national one by all concerned from the 1890s onward when Zionism came into being in Vienna, after an earlier hesitant start in Russia following the pogroms of 1881. That is to say, it was seen that in Eastern Europe the Jews constituted a nationality, not simply an assemblage of individuals who happened to stem from a dissolving religious community. The resounding failure of Austrian liberalism merely aggravated a problem which was anyhow bound to cause a good deal of trouble. As the nationalities drew farther apart, German nationalism was gradually divorced from constitutional liberalism; in its place there arose a populist current which combined Pan-German racism and anti-Semitism with vague anti-capitalist slogans: the forerunner of the National-Socialist movement.[13] Alongside it there ran the major stream of Church-supported Christian-Social conservatism with its own built-in antagonism to Jews, liberals and socialists. Symbolically, Christian-Social anti-Semitism captured Vienna in the general election of 1897, while the first Zionist Congress assembled under the chairmanship of the Viennese intellectual Theodor Herzl at Basle later in the same year. A certain degree of anti-Semitism was endemic in Hungary and in the Slav lands as well. Thus during the Dreyfus affair Thomas Masaryk, later to become the founder of the Czecho-Slovak Republic, complained that nearly all Czech papers were anti-Dreyfus. But only among German Austrians was anti-Semitism elevated to the dignity of a political principle.[14]

Speaking more generally, both German and Slav nationalism were retrograde by Western standards in that they substituted the folk community for the rational and democratic concept of citizenship. In practice this meant that national minorities could not be effectively integrated, since it was assumed that the nation was co-extensive with the 'natural' community held together by ties of kinship. Pan-Germanism and Pan-Slavism generalized these notions into aggressive political doctrines which by 1914 had come to shape the policies of the Russian, Austro-Hungarian and German governments. In all three cases, pre-liberal traditions assumed a post-liberal cast, the connecting link being the antecedent failure to create a self-governing community whose members freely determined the public life of their respective polity. Democracy and the nation state signified one and the same thing in Western Europe and North America, in that popular control of the already existing national states did not raise insurmountable problems; whereas in Central and Eastern Europe the establishment of nation states on the Western pattern presupposed the dissolution of older dynastic ties cutting across linguistic and national frontiers. For the Tsarist Empire and the Habsburg Monarchy this is obvious. The German case was less clear-cut, in that the non-German minorities were important only in some of the Prussian provinces and in Alsace-Lorraine. Given a larger degree of internal democratization, Germany might have been reconstructed along classical nation-state lines even before the military defeat of 1918. What actually happened was that the German Empire embarked upon national expansion with an ideology which rendered peace impossible, in that the modern variety of imperialism was superimposed upon a more ancient foundation reaching back to the days when the Germans constituted the *Herrenvolk*, or master race, in Central Europe. Racism thus became an important ingredient of the German political outlook. The Pan-German ideology combined an archaic cast of mind antedating the liberal era with militant expansionism in the name of the *Volk*. This illogical mixture did not arise spontaneously; it was the conscious creation of theorists responding to practical needs. The same applies to anti-Semitism with which Pan-Germanism (and Pan-Slavism) became intertwined. In Eastern Europe it was the economic function of the Jewish trader or financier, in Central Europe the pro-Western ideological commitment of the Jewish community as a whole, that laid them open to nationalist attacks. Pan-German anti-Semites were conscious of the fact that, as one of them put it, "the German Jewish community signified a kind of prolongation of the Western world, born of the French Revolution, towards the East".[15] Their Pan-Slav antagonists held similar views, and for good measure were able to exploit the resentments of a peasantry and lower middle class who generally encountered the Jew in the role of primitive capitalist entrepreneur. In this sense, the rise of a broadly based anti-Semitic movement in Central and Eastern Europe from the 1880s onwards has nothing surprising about it. The more lunatic expressions of this faith, in the writings of 'Aryan' fanatics nurtured on racist literature, were both the vehicle and the literary by-product of a deep-seated cultural malaise, ultimately traceable to the fact that these societies had not really come to terms with the modern world. There were analogous phenomena in Western Europe, but they encountered a more principled resistance even in areas where liberalism had by 1900 passed its peak. There capitalism had not been suddenly imposed upon cultures untouched by the bourgeois revolution; democracy was taken seriously; citizenship was not confused with membership of a mythical folk community; and the role of the Jews in the economic sphere was comparatively trivial. For the same reason, Jewish nationalism – when it arose as a response to the anti-Semitic movement – remained for the most part confined to Eastern and Central Europe.

The organizational links forged during these years were destined to endure. In 1904 there was founded in Trautenau (Bohemia) the "German Workers' Party" (*Deutsche Arbeiterpartei*), with a programme which combined anti-Semitism, nationalism, anti-clericalism and defence of the artisan against the inroads of big business and high finance. Years before this organization in 1918 adopted the title "Deutsche National-sozialistische Arbeiterpartei" (DNSAP), its adherents were generally known as "National Socialists".[16] Their theoretical inspiration was in large part derived from Eugen Dühring, the butt of Engels' well-known exposition of Marxism. Dühring, a fanatical anti-Semite, had in the 1870s begun to preach what Engels described as "specifically Prussian socialism", and what later generations would come to regard as a link between the more ancient conservative mentality and the German variant of Fascism. With Paul de Lagarde, Julius Langbehn and Houston Stewart Chamberlain, Dühring may be counted among the precursors of the Third Reich. All the authors in question shared the central tenet of the new Right: modern civilization – indifferently condemned as Western or Jewish – was fatal to Germany's ancient traditions. This doctrine made an appeal not only to the lower middle class, but to intellectuals disoriented by the decline of religious faith, the spiritual emptiness of urban civilization and the dissolution of the ancient organic community of the *Volk*. From the 1890s onward the Youth Movement helped to spread such notions among a middle class which had lost its faith in liberalism, was repelled by Marxism and yearned for a return to a simpler society founded on independent peasants and artisans. Matters were not eased by the fact that liberals and Marxists alike spoke the language of modernity in a country where the Enlightenment had failed to strike root. What they termed 'progress' could readily be dismissed as crass materialism. The widespread identification of capitalism with Jewish high finance did the rest.[17]

The French and Italian counterparts of this movement took shape at roughly the same time. Edouard Drumont's *La France juive* (1886) revived an already ancient battle-cry: France's ancient civilization was being corrupted by the Jewish spirit in general, and Jewish financiers in particular. In 1898 the nationalist *Action française* came into being as a right-wing response to democratic campaigns on behalf of Captain Dreyfus, wrongly accused of having sold military secrets to Germany. From this promising start the movement gradually broadened out into an attack on liberalism and parliamentary government in general. Its principal theorist, Charles Maurras, was a monarchist and never managed to understand the modern world, a circumstance which effectively prevented the *Action française* from turning into a genuinely

37

Fascist movement. Its defence of French Catholic civilization against the inroads of Anglo-German Protestant modernity lent an archaic flavour to its literature, as did its attempts to undo the effects of the French Revolution. For all that, the movement spread to the universities and had some influence among students in the years immediately preceding the 1914 war, when national passions were aroused by the spectre of the German menace. The working class remained indifferent, notwithstanding nationalist flirtations on the part of a few Syndicalist leaders inspired by the doctrines of Georges Sorel (1847–1922).[18] Nor was the Italian Nationalist Party founded at Florence in 1910 under the leadership of Enrico Corradini markedly successful in propagating the doctrine that Italy was a 'proletarian nation' locked in combat to win its freedom from stronger plutocratic powers. The fusion of this nationalist rant with elements of the Syndicalist tradition had to await the 1914–18 war and the conversion to nationalism of former Socialists led by Benito Mussolini.[19]

The cult of violence in general, and of war in particular, was common to all these movements. For the rest, they made do with the rags and tatters of Social Darwinism, dreams of a new aristocracy, and badly digested fragments of Nietzsche – a writer who managed to combine Europeanism with worship of power, and who in general was too elitist to suit the tastes of his countrymen. There was a marked difference between the Italian and the German school in their respective attitudes to cultural modernism. The German neo-Romantics, as befitted people who lamented the rise of monstrous slag-heaps on the ruins of ancient picturesque towns, would have nothing to do with modern art and literature. The Italian Nationalists, over-burdened with tradition and yearning to see their country become powerful and prosperous, favoured modernism as a radical break with a past they despised. F.T.Marinetti's *Futurist Manifesto* of 1909 somehow managed to glorify both military conquest and modern technology. "We proclaim that the world is the richer for a new beauty of speed, and our praise is for the man at the wheel. There is no beauty now save in struggle, no masterpiece can be anything but aggressive, and hence we glorify war, militarism and patriotism."[20] Marinetti and his friends longed to rid Italy "of the innumerable museums which cover it with innumerable cemeteries". Gabriele d'Annunzio proclaimed himself at once a follower of Nietzsche and an admirer of the aeroplane. This kind of technological Romanticism sounded more revolutionary in France and Italy than in Germany, which already possessed modern technology and had recently witnessed a current of revolt against it: the Youth Movement. The Futurists, a group of displaced Italian intellectuals who had acquired their ideas in Paris, were all for progress, as long as it was accompanied by plenty of violence. The 1909 manifesto was explicit on this topic:

We are on the extreme promontory of the centuries! What is the use of looking behind. ... We are already living in the absolute, since we have already created eternal, omnipresent speed.

We want to glorify war – the only cure for the world – militarism, patriotism, the destructive gesture of the anarchists ... and contempt for woman.

We want to demolish museums, libraries, fight morality, feminism and all opportunism and utilitarian cowardice. We will sing of great crowds agitated by work, pleasure and revolt; the multicoloured and polyphonic surf of revolution in modern capitals; the nocturnal vibration of the arsenals and the workshops beneath their violent electric moons; the gluttonous railway stations devouring smoking serpents; factories suspended from the clouds by the thread of their smoke; ... and the gliding flight of the aeroplane whose propeller sounds like the flapping of a flag and the applause of enthusiastic crowds.[21]

This nihilism already contained in germ some elements of the future Fascist creed, just as it reflected the influence of Sorel's *Reflections on Violence* (1906–8), a work much admired by Mussolini and Marinetti alike.[22] Futurism made better sense in Italy than in Germany, where proto-Fascist longings took the form of a back-to-the-land movement. If one believed the peasantry to constitute 'the life-spring of the Nordic race', one could not well advocate in the same breath a radical break with the past. The gap was never completely bridged, the less so since the Italian Nationalists in 1915 dragged their country into war against the Central Powers. Moreover, anti-Semitism was not an issue in Italy, there being no Jewish influence to worry about. Paradoxically, the Italian branch of the movement was more deeply influenced by Nietzsche than were the German nationalist intellectuals of the period; where they all concurred was in their glorification of war and violence.

That public opinion – or what passed for such in pre-1914 Italy – was getting ripe for the practical application of nationalist doctrines became obvious in 1911, when the Liberal government of Giovanni Giolitti (1842–1928) declared war on Turkey for the purpose of annexing the North African territory of Libya. While the Socialists opposed the move, some of Sorel's Syndicalist pupils approved of it, on the grounds that war was a school of courage and a defiance of bourgeois international law. Mussolini's conversion to this doctrine in 1914 was to have farreaching consequences after 1918, when Fascism came into being as an organized movement. For the purpose of a colonial war against Ottoman Turkey a Liberal government was adequate, and hysterical poetasters such as d'Annunzio and Marinetti could join Corradini and the Nationalists in proclaiming that Italian labour would make the African desert bloom like a rose. What is perhaps more remarkable is the support given to the 1911 war by old-fashioned Liberals like Croce and Mosca, who affirmed that patriotic sentiments were beneficial for national morale.[23] The establishment of a French protectorate over most of Morocco in this and the following year likewise produced a remarkable outburst of patriotism, heralding the so-called *réveil national* associated with war preparations against Germany and the tightening of the Franco-Russian alliance in 1913–14. The European powder-keg was nearing the point of explosion. Britain had already been drawn in by way of the Anglo-German naval race, which continued under the Liberal government of Asquith and Lloyd George, much as it had done under the Tories. Liberalism had ceased to be a guarantee of peace – if indeed it ever was. The changing intellectual climate reflected a general· drift towards violence, Germany setting the pace and the others adapting themselves as best they could. Even Spain, long dormant in decay, was affected by the general fever: during the decade before 1914 its government tried to establish a protectorate over northern Morocco which would keep the coast line facing Spain out of French control.[24] The reason given was the familiar one: if Spain had no share of North African territory, she would cease to count in the councils of Europe.

This manner of reasoning had become so much part of the common consciousness of Europe that it scarcely occurred to anyone, save for a handful of pacifists and socialists, to question it. Liberal governments devoted to peaceful expansion via commercial treaties, and conservative army officers interested in war and promotion, could count on solid public backing for any move they made to keep abreast of rivals. The pattern remained substantially unchanged even in those countries where parliamentary rule had replaced authoritarian forms of government. Moreover, pacifism was on the decline; the intellectuals were increasingly drawn towards violence, and their rhetoric helped to create the public mood which greeted the outbreak of war in 1914 as a relief from the boredom of existence. Liberalism and nationalism could and did enter into conflict, but never to the extent of questioning an underlying commitment to aims and values held in common by the European middle class, the class which had laboriously constructed the proud edifice of European civilization. That a major war might be fatal to this structure was not then perceived by more than a handful of thinkers, and their warnings fell on deaf ears. It took the 1914–18 bloodbath to make pacifism respectable, and the greater wreckage of 1939–45 to terminate the age of European wars.

NOTES

1 Stuart Hughes, *Consciousness and Society: The Reorientation of European Social Thought 1890–1930* (New York and London: Knopf, 1958), pp. 33 ff.
2 George L. Mosse, *The Culture of Western Europe* (London: Murray, 1963; Chicago: Rand McNally, 1961), p. 213.

3 Walter Z.Laqueur, *Young Germany, A History of the German Youth Movement* (London: Routledge & Kegan Paul; New York: Basic Books, 1962), p. xi.

4 Jürgen Habermas, *Strukturwandel der Öffentlichkeit* (Neuwied: Luchterhand, 1962), pp. 158 ff.

5 Joseph A.Schumpeter, *Capitalism, Socialism and Democracy* (London: Allen & Unwin; New York: Harper & Row, 3rd ed., 1950), pp. 121 ff.

6 John Maynard Keynes, *The Economic Consequences of the Peace* (London: Oxford University Press; New York: Harcourt, Brace & Howe, 1920), pp. 32 ff.

7 *Ibid.*, p. 33.

8 Schumpeter, *op. cit.*, p. 136.

9 Guido de Ruggiero, *The History of European Liberalism*, tr. by R.G.Collingwood (Boston: Beacon Press, 1959), pp. 370 ff.; Elie Kedourie, *Nationalism* (London: Hutchinson, 1960; New York: Praeger, 1961), *passim*.

10 Fritz Stern, *The Politics of Cultural Despair* (Garden City, N.Y.: Doubleday, 1965), pp. 19–20.

11 *Ibid.*, p. 21. Karl Dietrich Bracher, *Die deutsche Diktatur* (Cologne: Kiepenheuer & Witsch, 1969), trans. *The German Dictatorship*, tr. by Jean Steinberg (London: Weidenfeld & Nicolson, 1971; New York: Praeger, 1970), *passim*.

12 George L.Mosse, *The Crisis of German Ideology. Intellectual Origins of the Third Reich* (London: Weidenfeld & Nicolson, 1966; New York: Grosset & Dunlap, 1964), Introduction and *passim*; Peter G.J.Pulzer, *The Rise of Political Anti-Semitism in Germany and Austria* (New York and London: John Wiley & Sons, 1964), pp. 76 ff., 128 ff., 171 ff.; *Propheten des Nationalismus*, ed. Karl Schwedhelm (Munich: List Verlag, 1969), *passim*; Paul W.Massing, *Vorgeschichte des politischen Antisemitismus* (Frankfurt: Europäische Verlagsanstalt, 1959); trans. from the American original, *Rehearsal for Destruction* (New York and London: Harper, 1949); Eleonore Sterling, *Judenhass: Die Anfänge des politischen Antisemitismus in Deutschland (1815–1850)* (Frankfurt: Europäische Verlagsanstalt, 1969).

13 Pulzer, *op. cit.*, pp. 148 ff., 199 ff. The founders of the Austrian anti-Semitic movement, notably Georg von Schönerer, were dissident ex-liberals who deplored the impact of 'Jewish capitalism' on the economy in general and the peasantry in particular. From the 1880s onward the party became frankly anti-Jewish as well as pan-German, thus differentiating itself from the more traditional anti-Semitism of those Catholic conservatives who had no desire to join Bismarck's Empire.

14 Pulzer, *op. cit.*, p. 224, notes that by 1913 the Austrian section of the *Wandervogel* youth movement had succeeded in excluding 'Slavs, Jews and Latins', at a time when the racialist wing of the movement in Germany had not yet gained complete control. In general, extreme racialism was more pronounced in Bavaria and Austria than in the Protestant North, which down to 1918 was fairly content with the Prussian tradition of 'German Christendom'. The elaboration of 'Aryan' symbols such as the swastika occurred in the Munich of the 1890s; see Pulzer, p. 244.

15 Pulzer, *op. cit.*, p. 298. Cf. also the same author's remark "Lagarde and

Langbehn were the leading anti-Semites of that school and the Youth Movement the main offspring of their neo-Romanticism", p. 302.

16 Andrew G.Whiteside, "Nationaler Sozialismus in Österreich vor 1918", *Vierteljahreshefte für Zeitgeschichte*, 1961, no. 4. Bracher, *op. cit.*, pp. 53 ff.

17 F.L.Carsten, *The Rise of Fascism* (London: Batsford, 1967; Berkeley, Calif.: University of California Press, 1969), pp. 22 ff., 32 ff.

18 *Ibid.*, pp. 12 ff.; Ernst Nolte, *Three Faces of Fascism* (London: Weidenfeld & Nicolson; New York: Holt, Rinehart & Winston, 1966), pp. 48 ff.; trans. from the German original, *Der Faschismus in seiner Epoche* (Munich: Piper, 1963).

19 Carsten, *op. cit.*, p. 19; Nolte, *op. cit.*, pp. 145 ff.; Denis Mack Smith, *Italy: A Modern History* (Ann Arbor: University of Michigan Press, 1959), pp. 268 ff.

20 *Ibid.*, p. 270. For an analysis of the Futurist movement and its links with Fascism, see James Joll, *Intellectuals in Politics* (London: Weidenfeld & Nicolson, 1960; New York: Pantheon, 1961), pp. 133 ff.

21 *Ibid.*, pp. 139–40.

22 Georges Sorel, *Réflexions sur la violence* (1908); originally published in 1906 in the Syndicalist journal *Mouvement socialiste*. For a discussion of the topic see Stuart Hughes, *op. cit.*, pp. 90 ff.; I.L.Horowitz, *Radicalism and the Revolt against Reason* (London: Routledge & Kegan Paul, 1961; Carbondale, Ill.: Southern Illinois University Press, 1968), *passim*. Cf. *Reflections on Violence* (Glencoe: The Free Press, 1950), with an introduction by Edward A.Shils. For the extreme Right in France see Eugen Weber, *Action française: Royalism and Reaction in Twentieth Century France* (Stanford, California: University Press, 1962).

23 Smith, *op. cit.*, p. 279.

24 Raymond Carr, *Spain* (Oxford: Clarendon Press, 1966; New York: Oxford University Press, 1966), pp. 517 ff.

CHAPTER 4

POSITIVISM AND ITS CRITICS

The civilization which went over the brink in 1914 centred upon the original heartland of Europe: France, Britain, Germany-Austria and Italy. Scandinavia and the Iberian Peninsula stood a little apart and were not directly involved in the catastrophe of 1914–18. Russia was half in and half out: not altogether European, yet the possessor of a magnificent literature and promising ventures in the arts. Its complete Europeanization appeared to be only a matter of time. The others shared a common heritage and an outlook which could broadly be described as a fusion of aristocratic and bourgeois values. They also shared a sense of foreboding which contrasted with the complacent optimism of the Victorians and their contemporaries on the Continent. The overhanging menace of a great European war does not wholly account for this change in the intellectual climate. Much of the pervasive unrest was due to the contrast between traditional life-styles and the second industrial revolution: that which from 1900 onwards brought the motor car and the aeroplane into general view. The great estates of the landed nobility remained in being, all the way from Russia to Spain, but the aristocracy had entered into a symbiosis with the upper middle class, thus creating a civilization of which wealth was the only common denominator. At the opposite pole, the socialist movement had effected something like a secession from bourgeois society on the part of organized labour, but the labour movement did not as yet represent a serious challenge to the social order. Political conflict assumed revolutionary dimensions only where that order had not been firmly implanted: in Russia, and to some degree in Spain and Italy. Where capitalism reigned supreme, the working class appeared content with reformist legislation which took the basic elements of the status quo for granted. Unionized workers participated to some extent in the benefits derived from technological progress while the lower strata who thronged the slums of the great cities in search of badly paid work were not organized and constituted no serious threat to the established system.

The strains increasingly felt in Western Europe before 1914 arose for the most part from the impact of modern technology upon antiquated modes of life, some of them pre-bourgeois, others inherited from the Victorian era. Suffragettes agitating for the vote looked and sounded spectacular, but were only pressing for the application of liberal-radical principles inherited from the democratic revolutions of the nineteenth century. The association of feminism with socialism is a case in point. The same applies to reform movements in child education, which were taken up by socialists because liberalism had run out of steam. Sexual morality was another area in which the modernist movement collided headlong with social conventions derived from Christian conservatism. These conventions took for granted a set of institutions built up around the cellular family of bourgeois society. To the extent that industrialization undermined the foundations of middle-class conservatism, it could plausibly be argued that bourgeois civilization was no longer able to accommodate the forces let loose by its own technology. But socialists were not alone in making this point. It was possible to diverge from the existing consensus in different directions: by way of aesthetic detachment from a repulsive environment, or by urging the formation of a new aristocracy which would create an elitist culture open to a minority of free spirits. If Henrik Ibsen (1828–1906) and his followers throughout Europe stood for feminine emancipation and the consistent extension of democracy, the delayed impact of Nietzsche – paradoxically beginning in the year of his collapse into madness (1889) – portended a very different outcome.

The modernist movement in literature and the arts possessed no single theme, save for a general dissatisfaction with what was vaguely known as the bourgeois way of life. Its representatives frequently managed to combine socialist sympathies with Nietzschean longings for a new order run by supermen. Marinetti informing the staid readers of *Le Figaro* in 1909 that, as he put it, "a roaring motor-car which seems to run on machine-gun fire is more beautiful than the Nike of Samothrace", clearly regarded himself as a revolutionary of sorts. In retrospect it seems plain that his "manifesto of ruinous and incendiary violence", as he proudly called it, gave expression to something that was going on among the offspring of an overfed middle class: young men tired of liberalism and in need of bloodshed to keep them from getting bored. Hence those frantic invocations to the future to provide wars and other excitements. The future obliged, and Marinetti (who lived until 1944) had the satisfaction of witnessing the disappearance of some of those historic monuments which he and his friends so disliked because they cluttered up a landscape not yet given over to the worship of the internal combustion machine.

The British took things more calmly, as befitted people who had originally pioneered the industrial revolution. The prevalent mood in British intellectual circles around 1900 was one of restrained optimism, faith in applied science being linked to belief in social progress: to be brought about not by revolution, but by the application of scientific rationalism to statecraft. Herbert George Wells (1866–1946), who did much to create this mental climate, was not accidentally a prominent member of the Fabian Society, which was originally brought together in the 1880s by Sidney Webb (1859–1947) and others with the object of promoting a gradualist version of socialism. Its principal literary exponent, George Bernard Shaw (1856–1950), lived to see the practical application of Fabian principles by Britain's post-1945 Labour government. Shaw's plays and Wells's novels popularized a doctrine which made liberalism sound old-fashioned; but what they put in its place was basically the positivist faith in limitless scientific progress administered by a self-chosen elite of technocrats. The founding of the London School of Economics and Political Science (1895) buttressed a tentacular enterprise which looked to the peaceful take-over of the State by social scientists and enlightened civil servants. Shaw and Wells did much to make the public aware of the fact that science and technology were about to create a global environment indifferent to national frontiers. Wells in particular, through the new medium of science fiction, gave artistic expression to a creed which affirmed the unity of mankind. His exuberant optimism was considerably dimmed by the First World War, and wholly shattered by the second. It is arguable that he was never quite free from doubt as to the beneficial consequences of applied technology. In that remarkable piece of science fiction, *The First Men in the Moon* (1901), the Grand Lunar is not a wholly reassuring figure. *A Modern Utopia* (1905) presented the Wellsian creed in a manner closely linked to the author's political fancies, which then centred upon the idea of an order of self-appointed 'samurai' dedicated to the welfare of mankind.[1]

Shaw had similar elitist longings, and for the rest tried to make socialism palatable to a generation of readers and playgoers who had been profoundly affected by the worship of bigness, speed and benevolent autocracy on the imperial model. Among the first to bring Marx, Ibsen and Wagner to the attention of the British public, he also indulged in the cult of the Superman. Anglo-Irish by extraction, he stood a little apart from the late Victorian and Edwardian consensus, playing the role of an intellectual rebel in the tradition of other notable Irish expatriates. Starting as a music critic in the 1880s, he turned himself into the most celebrated playwright of the age, and for good measure took up a host of causes from socialism to anti-Darwinism. During the period of his active dramatic composition (1893–1939) he wrote forty-seven plays, an average of one a year. They established his reputation as the country's foremost wit, a latter-day Voltaire whose lengthy prefaces, as much as the plays themselves, mocked the certitudes of the wealthy public which crowded the theatre stalls. His misfortune was that after 1914 he no longer had much to say, while his faith in enlightened absolutism degenerated into eulogy of dictators. His later plays, from *Heartbreak House* onward, are the record of a progressive disenchantment with the scientific rationalism of his earlier years. In so far as he still possessed a faith, it was distilled out of Henri Bergson (1859–1941), whose *L'Évolution créatrice* (1907) had greatly impressed him. Bergson's philosophy is expounded in a comparatively late play, *Back to Methuselah* (1921), which opens up a prospect of redemption from the flesh through the progressive unfolding of the Life Force – a cosmic agent destined to carry mankind to new heights. This was a reasonable faith for an artist who made no claim to being a systematic thinker, but on the whole Shaw was more effective as a social critic, and a champion of the Ibsenite new woman, than in the role of prophet. *Saint Joan* (1923), exhibiting the Maid as a Protestant hero before her time, is a marvellous play, but it is also quite false to reality, and the religious mysticism is unconvincing. The author was too much of a rationalist to believe in his own creation. If one identifies God with the Life Force, one cannot seriously engage the topic of supernaturalism. Shaw had the misfortune to outlive the era to which his thinking was appropriate. Persisting in creativity into advanced old age, he applied commonsensible standards to a generation which witnessed the rise of Mussolini, Hitler and Stalin. Inevitably he began to sound rather dated, but his *Sixteen Self-Sketches*, published in 1949 when he was ninety-three, offer a splendid self-portrait. The licensed court jester of the Edwardian bourgeoisie was also a writer of genius. If there was a void at the centre, it was filled with talk whose brilliance has rarely been matched. The high point of the Irish genius, it has been said, is pure destructiveness for its own sake. Though an offspring of the Protestant ascendancy, Shaw was enough of an Irishman to become the embodiment of this particular gift of the gods. After 1914 the world caught up with him, and his message began to stale. In a civilization bent upon destroying itself, the self-appointed successor of Swift no longer sounded particularly outrageous.

Shaw had remote intellectual cousins in other European countries, but the only major writer of his time who subscribed to similar standards was François Anatole Thibault (1844–1924), better know as Anatole France. For about forty years he carried on the Voltairean tradition in a manner that made him the dominant figure in French literature. An intellectual sceptic of the *haute bourgeoisie*, he gradually evolved from a kind of learned dilettantism to the seriousness of *Les Dieux ont soif* (1912) and *La Révolte des anges* (1914): the former an account of the French Revolution, the latter an attempt to grapple with religion. The mood of pessimistic irony that runs through his mature work is epitomized in the figure of his hero and mouthpiece, Professor Bergeret, who addresses his learned observations to his dog. The author had been driven out of his ivory tower by the Dreyfus affair, which convulsed the country around 1900, and his subsequent political attitudes reflected the rather vague radicalism of a Left traditionally opposed to Church and State, sceptical of socialism, and on the whole fairly content with the institutions of the Third Republic. To the extent that this bourgeois radicalism possessed a philosophy, it was adequately expressed by the modest *lycée* professor and essayist Émile-Auguste Chartier, better known by his pen-name, Alain. What he stood for – provincial earnestness, distrust of Paris and of governmental corruption in general – was also what the Radical Party professed to stand for, which is why both he and it went into eclipse after 1930. The new age was still wedded to capitalism, but no longer bourgeois in the traditional meaning of the term. The family firm began to crumble, and so did the family, even in a country like France which appeared retrograde by comparison with Britain and Germany. The 'ideas of 1789' were not wholly devalued in 1914–18, but their defence became an enterprise best suited to stoics. In Germany these ideas had never won a secure foothold, save among Social Democrats or members of the Jewish community, and few important writers could be trusted to defend liberalism, let alone republican democracy. In France, the official creed represented a middle way between the Romantic royalism of the *Action française* and Syndicalist stirrings which went beyond the parliamentary politics of the Socialist Party. At the intellectual level, the crisis of liberalism took the form of an assault on the positivist faith associated with the Third Republic. We shall return to the topic of positivism in a different context. What matters for our immediate purpose is the intellectual current associated with the names of Henri Bergson and Georges Sorel. Both writers won public recognition in the 1890s, a decade conventionally associated with the aestheticism of J.K.Huysmans (1848–1907), Stéphane Mallarmé (1842–98), Oscar Wilde (1856–1900) and the early W.B.Yeats (1865–1939). Aestheticism could be described as a defensive reaction on the part of literary intellectuals against a culture in which science had begun to set the tone. But Sorel was an engineer by training, Bergson a professional philosopher and the holder of a chair at the prestigious Collège de France. His lectures were major events, and *Creative Evolution* (1907) was a success with the general public, as were Sorel's *Reflections on Violence* (1906–8). This kind of notoriety was not a minor matter. It pointed to a change in the intellectual climate.[2]

"Creative evolution" was the name given by Bergson to a doctrine which had originally started out as an attempt to salvage introspection, and intuition generally, from the determinism of the physical sciences. In counterposing felt 'duration' to the abstractions of physics and mathematics, Bergson inaugurated a method of speculation which gradually grew into a system. By the time he published his major work in 1907, he was ready to give an account of how the universe worked. Its operation turned out to be in tune with the general doctrine of evolution, but Bergson departed from other evolutionists by introducing a dualism between life, ever climbing upwards, and inert matter which descends in a downward direction. The actual evolutionary development of plant, animal and human life in turn gives rise to a new bifurcation, this time between instinct and the intellect. The latter recognizes only material bodies and the logic pertaining to them, notably mathematics. It is unable to grasp the cosmic force of life, a vital impulse that struggles to make its way against the inert resistance of matter. Life proceeds in conformity with a motion of time which is not mathematical, but relates to felt duration. The latter is perceived by intuition, not by the intellect which relates only to the spatial movement of material bodies. Life is a kind of cavalry charge.

All organized beings, from the humblest to the highest, from the first origins of life to the time in which we are, and in all places as in all times, do but evidence a single impulsion, the inverse of the movement of matter and in itself indivisible. All the living hold together and all yield to the same tremendous push. The animal takes its stand on the plant, man bestrides animality, and the whole of humanity, in space and in time, is one immense army galloping beside and before and behind each of us, in an overwhelming charge able to beat down every resistance and to clear many obstacles, perhaps even death.[3]

This doctrine was a great comfort to French students tired of positivism, and to the more philosophically minded army officers, some of whom in 1914 tried to apply it in practice, with unfortunate results. It was only in 1916, during the battle of Verdun, that Captain (as he then was) Charles de Gaulle discovered the modern age in the act of standing up to the German artillery barrage at Fort Douaumont.

Bergson, although Jewish by origin, was very much an Establishment figure. When in 1918 he was elected to the Academy, it seemed that no further honours could be bestowed upon him, but in 1927 he obtained the Nobel Prize for literature. Towards the end of his life his intellectual development brought him into the vicinity of Catholicism, a circumstance noticeable from a late publication of his, *Two Sources of Morality and Religion* (1932). On his death in 1941 his will disclosed that only a sense of solidarity with the persecuted Jewish community prevented him from formally adhering to the Catholic Church. That eminent convert to Catholicism, Charles Péguy (1873–1914), had argued many years earlier in favour of letting students in Catholic seminaries read Bergson. His intellectual progeny may be said to have included another gifted Jewish writer with Catholic sympathies, Simone

religion and idealist metaphysics. The Darwinian theory of evolution by way of natural selection reinforced this bias, as did the positivist interpretation of Marxism put forward, from about 1875 onwards, by Friedrich Engels (1820–95) and his successors. Nature and history alike appeared to be governed by 'iron laws' unalterable at will and indifferent to the fate of individuals. The eternal order of nature had its prolongation in the life process of the human species. Social evolution was comparable to biological change. The disappearance of inferior races, or their displacement by stronger and better equipped rivals, was part of the order of things, as was the dominance of superior classes over their inferiors: this last a Social Darwinist doctrine disputed by the Marxists, though the arguments they employed did not differ radically from those advanced by bourgeois positivists. Progress was inevitable; it would result in the conscious application of science and technology to the social life of man. Science was bound to advance towards the elucidation of hitherto unexplained phenomena, and in so doing would dispel the remnants of the theological world picture. Society too would evolve further in the direction it had taken since the industrial revolution: on this point at least there was no quarrel between liberals and socialists, although they differed over the social setting proper to a successful prolongation of present trends.

The older positivism associated with Auguste Comte (1798–1857) had largely faded out by 1900, leaving behind a residue of notions associated with his celebrated Law of the Three Stages. The Law states that human thought inevitably progresses from a theological through a metaphysical to a 'positive' or scientific stage. The human mind does not, however, arrive at a scientific viewpoint in all domains at once. Some areas lag behind, the science of society having matured a long time after the study of nature. There is a hierarchy of sciences, of which sociology forms the apex, being the latest arrival and hence the crowning glory of mind's evolution. This was rather too much for Comte's successors, who were put off by his implied claim to have personally disposed of all earlier forms of thought. It was also too much for the academic philosophers, Comte having excluded philosophy from his hierarchy of sciences. A mathematician by training, he shared the anti-metaphysical bias of most natural scientists, but his attempt to found what he described as a Religion of Humanity discredited his enterprise in the eyes of more rigorous empiricists. Herbert Spencer (1820–1903), enormously influential in his own day, propagated views similar to those of Comte in the English-speaking world. A thorough-going determinist, he aimed at a "natural history of society" subject to causal laws which it was the sociologist's task to discover. An evolutionist, he was also a functionalist, holding that "there can be no true conception of a structure without a true conception of its function". These intellectual enterprises ran parallel to Marxism and intermingled with it, a circumstance that caused some of the anti-positivist animus after 1900 to be discharged in the general direction of Marx's successors. At the political level, Comte's and Spencer's endorsement of individualism and *laissez-faire* led in the direction of Social Darwinism, but socialists as well as liberals were affected by the prevailing positivist climate of thought. In the social sciences, Émile Durkheim (1858–1917) based the French branch of modern sociology upon an intellectual foundation in part derived from Comte and Spencer alike. Durkheim's view of society as a functioning system susceptible to scientific study owed something to Spencer, but in the main he stood within a specifically French tradition of scientific rationalism. His major works, starting with *De la division du travail social* (1893), and his numerous monographs, established a framework within which the new discipline of sociology gradually took shape. Originally a descendant of Comte, he gradually emancipated himself from what he termed "positivist metaphysics", though never to the extent of repudiating his allegiance to the founder. From 1902 onwards a professorship at the Sorbonne enabled him to gather around him a group of disciples with whose help he edited the journal *L'année sociologique*.

The impact of Durkheim's work, culminating in a study of religion (1912), owed something to his ability to incorporate intellectual currents emanating from England and Germany. At the same time his descent from Saint-Simon and Comte induced him to work out the concept of organic solidarity, meaning the ability of a social system to integrate all its diverse elements into a stable whole. Solidarity in turn was related to its underlying ground, described by Durkheim as *conscience collective*: a term translatable as collective conscience or collective consciousness. This "system of beliefs and sentiments" held in common by the members of a society establishes a common bond transcending interest conflicts. When the bond is loosened, pathological symptoms make their appearance. Durkheim had been struck by the fact that industrialization was everywhere accompanied by a rise in suicide rates, a topic to which he devoted a separate study (1897). This led to the problem of investigating the individual's relationship to the normative principles of the social system of which he forms part, whence the concept of *anomie* to denote a dangerous slackening of the common bond. Comparative suicide rates among Catholics and Protestants led to the conclusion that the Protestant stress upon individual responsibility had introduced a new type of human personality – a theme developed some years later by Max Weber in his celebrated study of the link between capitalism and Protestantism (1904–5). Empirical investigation into topics such as suicide thus laid the ground for the notion that every type of society requires the functional equivalent of a religious system, even though traditional beliefs may die out.

Durkheim's approach, for all his awareness of British and German thinking, remained within the tradition founded by Comte. The Central European development ran along different lines, German thought being hospitable to the study of history, which Comte and Spencer had neglected. Historiography, the special pride of Germany, was heavily indebted to Hegel and for the rest in tune with the Romantic tradition which looked for spiritual entities intuited by the mind of the historian. The resulting disjunction between *Naturwissenschaft* and *Geisteswissenschaft*, science of nature and science of mind or spirit, did not encourage the application of sociological methods to history. It was the Marxists rather than the followers of Comte who introduced the sociological approach, but Marxism had no foothold in the universities, where Kant and Hegel reigned supreme. When Wilhelm Dilthey (1833–1911) became sceptical of philosophical idealism, he turned to psychology for an understanding of history. Among natural scientists the eminent chemist Wilhelm Ostwald (1853–1932) could be counted an admirer of Comte, but he found few imitators. The empiricists among the philosophers were not particularly interested in Comte either: their starting-point was the neo-Kantian rejection of metaphysics which dated back to the 1870s. Neither Ernst Mach (1838–1916) nor Richard Avenarius (1843–96) found Comte to their liking, even though they shared his general bias. The 'Vienna Circle' of logical positivists arose in the new century on foundations in part laid by Mach, a physicist by training and a rigid empiricist whose general standpoint in philosophy went back to Hume and Kant. The same applies to the Cambridge school associated with the names of G.E.Moore and Bertrand Russell. Logical positivism reached the British Isles by way of Vienna, and by then the older positivism associated with Comte was no longer a serious issue. Sociology proper made even slower progress in Britain than in Germany. L.T.Hobhouse, the first professor of sociology in England (at the London School of Economics), may be claimed among the spiritual descendants of Comte, with the qualification that in philosophy he tended towards idealism. His successor and biographer, Morris Ginsberg, was friendly to Comte's general purpose, but rejected the implied claim that sociology could provide a comprehensive philosophy.

Taken as a whole, sociology represented something like an academic response to the challenge of Marxism which by 1900 had become a serious matter: at any rate on the Continent, less so in Britain, where traditional modes of thought predominated for another generation. Marx himself had been so far ahead of his time that his own followers failed to make proper use of his methodology. What they extracted from it was, however, quite enough to alarm the academic community in Germany, France and Italy, where Marxist socialism had become a force to be reckoned with. The work of Weber, Durkheim and Vilfredo

Pareto (1848–1923) must be seen in this context. All three made it their business to refute Marx, while at the same time taking over an entire stock of ideas from historical materialism: notably the concept of a social science capable of integrating political philosophy with the study of economic structures not reducible to individual transactions in the market place. Marx had presented both a theory of the bourgeois revolution and an analysis of capitalism as a system bound in the long run to disintegrate and make room for a higher stage of societal evolution. His major work was sub-titled *Kritik der Politischen Ökonomie*, and his criticism of classical political economy amounted to a demonstration that theoretical economics reflected the social relations peculiar to capitalism. At the same time he developed the thoroughly classical notion that the economy was in the last resort preponderant within the totality of bourgeois society. From this it followed that the insoluble contradictions of capitalism as a system of production were bound, sooner or later, to disrupt the social relations characteristic of bourgeois civilization. This was what 'scientific socialism' signified, even though Marx had been prevented by illness from carrying out the vast project of a study of society within which the critique of political economy would have occupied the central place. By 1900 enough had been published by his followers to make it clear that Marxism could not be ignored by the academic establishment, notably in Germany and Austria where Social Democracy then had its stronghold. If Marx was to be refuted, it could only be done by constructing an alternative model which submerged the 'materialist conception of history' within a more general perspective of social evolution. This was substantially what Weber, Durkheim and Pareto undertook to do. In this context it is irrelevant that Weber was a German nationalist, Durkheim a French positivist and Pareto an Italian aristocrat whose critique of liberal democracy anticipated some aspects of Fascism. What matters is that all three set out to formulate an alternative to Marx's totalizing synthesis of philosophy, history and economics. The new discipline of sociology, which arose from this enterprise, resembled Marxism in that it integrated separate levels of social reality within a unified science of society. It differed from the Marxian synthesis in that it eliminated the notion of dialectical contradiction. Instead, the social system was conceived as a totality within which all the elements determined each other in such a way as to prevent a radical rupture between the 'material base' and the 'superstructure' of institutions and beliefs. The socialist perspective was replaced by the descriptive analysis of a self-regulating system, or alternatively by the vision of a cyclical movement proceeding via temporary crises and disorders to a different sort of stable and self-perpetuating order.[5]

Pareto's *Trattato di sociologia generale* (1916) crowned a body of work which had originated in mathematics and physics. By training an engineer – a circumstance he shared with Sorel – Pareto had come first to economics, and later to sociology, by way of the physical sciences. When in 1893, at the age of forty-five, he took up the Chair of Political Economy at Lausanne, he made it his task to give precise formulation to what he himself described as "an outline of economic science considered as a natural science based exclusively on facts". His subsequent development led, by way of a critical study of socialist thought (*Les Systèmes socialistes*, 1902–3), to his *Trattato* of 1916 which established him as a major figure in contemporary sociology. He approached the subject from the positivist standpoint he shared with Durkheim, but with a pessimistic bias not to be found in his French contemporary. The basic assumption he makes throughout his major work is that economic, social and political gradations correspond to differences in natural ability. From this it follows that democratic egalitarianism is utopian, and so is socialism which had sprung from the earlier democratic faith. Every society is ruled by an elite, a point already made by Gaetano Mosca (1858–1941) two decades earlier. Political domination of the masses by an elite of rulers is a quasi-biological circumstance which cannot be eliminated by any kind of social rearrangement. This notion leads to the question why elites are sometimes unable to prevent a revolution from occurring, but Pareto meets this difficulty by arguing that they are simply replaced by other elites. Aristocracies do not last. For one reason or another, they tend to degenerate, and their place is then taken by a new caste of rulers. This "circulation of elites" is the reality masked by liberal-democratic talk about equality. Class conflict is real (on this point Pareto accepted Marx's critique of liberalism), but it does not lead to the classless society: it simply produces a different sort of class rule. Robert Michels (1876–1936) – half French, half German and an Italian citizen by choice – developed a similar thesis in his study of political parties.[6]

One advantage of the new approach was that its central thesis could not be falsified, since in every society – indeed in any organized grouping – there will always be individuals of outstanding ability who may be said to constitute an elite. But while this is undoubtedly true, it tells one nothing about the mechanism whereby one ruling class is replaced by another. The ideal case postulated by Pareto, Mosca and Michels is one in which a state of free competition enables the most gifted individuals to circulate without hindrance, so that the elite is always composed of the ablest people who happen to be available. In bourgeois society this free circulation is blocked by the institution of private ownership of the means of production. On Pareto's assumption the abolition of private property does not lead to free self-government on the part of the producers, but to the establishment of a different kind of social hierarchy manipulated by an elite of those best able to manage the system. But even if this is conceded, it still makes a difference whether the political institutions are of the democratic type, or whether the ruling stratum is irremovable and able to exercise unhampered control. If it does, one must assume that the elite represents a powerful vested interest, in which case we are not far from the Marxian theory of class conflict. What Pareto might have said, but did not, was that the Marxian schema is only applicable to bourgeois society, and specifically to the bourgeois revolution, that is to say, the process whereby the middle class acquires political power. This argument was subsequently outlined by J.A.Schumpeter (1883–1950). It does not form part of the Paretian system, or of Weber's theory of politics, to which we now turn.[7]

Max Weber (1864–1920) stands at the confluence of economics, history and sociology, which is why it has been possible to describe him as a 'bourgeois Marx'. The characterization is apt, provided one bears in mind that Weber grew up in a Germany unified by Bismarck, and thereafter had to endure the spectacle of Bismarck's *Reich* being ruined by the government of William II. The circumstance is of some importance for the understanding of his theorizing. Bismarck was the only statesman of genius Germany ever produced, but the landed gentry whom he represented, and whose traditions he embodied, was quite incapable of adapting to the modern world. The problem Weber confronted as a German patriot was the political incapacity of the German middle class, its subordination to the aristocracy, and the consequent injection of social strains which the Western democracies had avoided. A fair proportion of Weber's thinking revolved around the failure of the German middle class to throw up a political elite capable of governing the State. As matters stood, the great landowners who controlled Prussia were driving the German peasants on their estates into emigration, their place being taken by Polish seasonal workers whose presence conflicted with the official policy of Germanization. Weber recommended that the government abandon the landowners and seal the frontier against the Polish invasion. His advice was not taken, and Prussia-Germany continued to be ruled by a class whose political leadership had become incompatible with the national interest. This state of affairs was Weber's starting-point in the 1890s, not only politically but theoretically: he had discovered that class conflict was a reality, not a Marxist invention. At the same time he had no faith in the middle class or in the labour movement. Nor did he have much confidence in the quasi-parliamentary institutions with which Germany had been endowed between 1848 and 1871: he perceived that they were a sham, and that the real political power lay with an uncontrolled bureaucracy centred on the Emperor and the General Staff. The question then was how Germany could be modernized short of revolution. When the structure collapsed in 1918–19, Weber was instrumental in bringing about those constitutional changes which endowed the Weimar Republic with a President exercising quasi-monarchical powers. It was his legacy to the nation. A few months later, in June 1920, he died.[8]

Weber is best understood as the outstanding political theorist of post-Bismarckian Germany, a country trying to become a world power. The National–Liberal Party, of which his father had been a prominent member, had been used and then destroyed by Bismarck after 1871. Being personally acquainted with its leaders, as well as with historians like Mommsen and Treitschke and philosophers such as Dilthey, Weber lived and moved in an atmosphere heavily charged with memories of political and intellectual combat. National Liberalism was the militant offspring of the earlier cosmopolitan and pacifist liberalism whose day had passed. It was liberalism adapted to *Realpolitik*, the politics of power pure and simple as practised by Bismarck. Weber never renounced this heritage, not even after the German Empire had crashed in 1918. The other lesson Bismarck taught him was the importance of *charisma*: a gift of grace bestowed by providence upon political leaders able to cast a spell upon parties or entire peoples. The *Reich* founded by Bismarck had been ruined by the ineptitude of his successors, but all was not lost, for the nation had displayed its strength during four years of warfare. One had to pass through a troubled interval. "And then history, which has given to us, and only to us, a second springtime, will give us a third. Of that I have no doubt."[9] He did not live to see a charismatic leader driving the nation over the brink, this time for good. Nor could he have imagined the monstrosities of the Third Reich. Yet there is a strain of pessimism in Weber, ultimately traceable to his Lutheran heritage. Politics and ethics could never be made to run in harness. "The ancient Christians too knew very well that the world is ruled by daemons, and that involvement in politics means allying oneself with power and violence ... and sealing a pact with diabolic forces."[10]

Then why engage in politics at all? Because it was one's duty, and because a nation could not evade its destiny, which in Germany's case was to struggle for recognition as a world power. His Freiburg inaugural lecture of 1894 set the theme for the remainder of his life: "It is not peace and human happiness that we have to pass on to our descendants, but the *eternal struggle* for the maintenance and upbreeding of our national kind." More than two decades later, at the peak of the 1914–18 war, the tone had not changed:

Future generations, and above all our descendants, will not hold the Danes, the Swiss, the Dutch and the Norwegians responsible if the mastery of the

57

world – and in the last resort this means the disposal over the civilization of
the future – is divided up between the regulations of Russian officials and the
conventions of Anglo-Saxon society, perhaps with an infusion of Latin
raison. They will hold *us* responsible, and rightly so, for we are a Power
(*ein Machtstaat*) and unlike the smaller nations we are able to cast our weight
in the scale. . . .[11]

This kind of reasoning subsequently helped to persuade a generation
of high-minded academics and civil servants to follow the Leader, until
it dawned upon the more perspicacious among them that he was leading
Germany to perdition. National Liberalism paved the way for National
Socialism – among the elite of the nation above all. Yet Weber's
generation was profoundly committed to a civilization and a moral
code inherited from the nineteenth century, an age in which politics
had not yet been divorced from ethics. He never resolved the conflict,
having posed it in terms which rendered a solution impossible: there was
a plurality of values, each claiming absolute validity. One had to choose,
and the patriot would choose the good of his country. The older liberalism had placed politics in the service of humanity. Weber stoutly
denied that this kind of equation made sense. Cosmopolitanism was a
chimera; religion was other-worldly; socialism was utopian. Politics
and morals could not be squared. Weber's ethical pessimism was rooted
in the duality of factual statement and value-judgement which troubled
other thinkers of his generation; he was unique in turning this dualism
into the very centre of his *Weltanschauung*.

In sociology one did not encounter these problems, for as a science
it was solely concerned with the way in which the social system actually
worked. Weber's influential studies on the relationship of religious
faith to economic activity were meant to demonstrate that historical
materialism could be stood on its head: so far from being an ideological
expression of bourgeois reality, as the Marxists maintained, Protestantism appeared in Weber's writings as a precondition for the effective
functioning of capitalism. *The Protestant Ethic and the Spirit of Capitalism*,
the first part of which was published in 1904 in the *Archiv für Sozialwissenschaft*[12] has been endlessly debated. One's understanding of it is considerably helped by recognition of the fact that Weber was operating
with what he termed "ideal types", that is to say concepts which are not
meant to portray slices of empirical reality; rather their function is to
delineate what human actions of a certain kind would be like if they
were strictly purposive – that is, rationally oriented and undisturbed
by error or sentiment.[13] Even with this qualification the thesis has not
worn well. It seems to cast more light on what the Puritans, or some of
them, said about the world than on the manner in which society was
actually being transformed in Catholic and Protestant areas alike.
Weber's recognition of a link between religious belief and socio-economic

patterns of behaviour was a fruitful starting-point for the new discipline of sociology which had grown out of the dispute between German economists and historians around the turn of the century; he was inquiring into the historical origins of capitalism, something neither the academic historians nor the economists of the classical school – with the obvious exception of Marx – had yet done. But his approach was flawed by a principle he had inherited from Hegel: the belief that every historical epoch has its own peculiar "spirit" (*Geist*) which imparts a characteristic mode of behaviour to all human transactions. The "spirit" of capitalism having been reduced to a certain type of rational activity, the conclusion presented itself that the absence of this spiritual predisposition accounted for the failure of non-European civilizations to give birth to capitalism. Along this road Weber encountered a fellow-traveller, the economic historian Werner Sombart who was likewise intensely preoccupied with the "spirit" of capitalism. Unlike Weber he held the Jews rather than the Calvinists responsible for the flowering of a mentality no longer tied to the asceticism of the Catholic monastery. Other variations on this theme could be played by historians of culture familiar with the Renaissance. They threw much needed light on the history of Europe, but then Marx had already stressed the link between the bourgeoisie and Protestantism in *Capital* and elsewhere. It did not induce him to alter his basic approach, nor has the obvious connection between bourgeois civilization and religious individualism induced economic historians to adopt Weber's approach. In the modified form represented by R. H. Tawney's *Religion and the Rise of Capitalism* (1926), the thesis that Calvinist ethics made room for the early entrepreneur is not seriously disputed, but Tawney's discussion of the subject owed more to Marx than to Weber. He saw Calvinism as the ideology of the rising middle class, Lutheranism as a socially conservative doctrine still tied to medieval values. On this assumption it could be argued that the more radical variant of the Protestant Reformation was effective in creating an environment favourable to the adoption of a middle-class work ethic, but it did not follow that Calvinism was the parent of capitalism; at most it could be said to have expressed the spirit of the new order with fewer inhibitions than the Lutheran faith.[14]

Unlike some of his more uncritical followers, Weber did not go so far as to derive the rise of European and American capitalism from an antecedent change in the religious climate. He was after all aware that European capitalism antedated Protestantism. His aim was rather to show that a really radical break with the medieval cast of mind occurred only in those areas where Calvinism had taken hold for reasons quite unconnected with economic change. If cause and effect were interrelated in this manner, then the historical process appeared as a circular movement, spirit determining matter and vice versa, whereas Marxism insisted on the crucial role of one particular element within the social structure, the economic. On Marx's assumption, capitalism was readily accepted by Protestants not because they were Protestants, but because they were bourgeois. In this perspective the essential precondition of the bourgeois revolution was the existence of self-governing cities which made it possible for the burgher class to evolve a distinctive culture. The Protestant Reformation appeared as a link in the chain of historical causation whereby modern society had come into being. Weber's emphasis upon the unique significance of Calvinism within this process is compatible with a dialectical view of history. One may say if one likes that Calvinism did for the bourgeoisie what Marxism at a later date did for the industrial working class. A statement of this kind is actually closer to the spirit of Marx's own approach than the mechanical derivation of religious or irreligious beliefs from changes in the social structure. What Weber's emphasis upon the psychology of the early entrepreneur fails to account for is the peculiar mechanism whereby the capitalist mode of production, once it has come into being, creates a social environment adapted to its functioning. Once the process has been set in motion, it matters little what the individual agents imagine themselves to be doing, and what sets it in motion is the emergence of a new mode of production.

Weber did not on this point seek to refute Marx: he merely explained in detail what had happened in a particular area: the self-governing city of Northern Europe. Originally a commune of former serfs who had escaped from their masters and were held together by an oath (*coniuratio*), the Northern European city was bourgeois from the start – quite unlike the city of classical antiquity or of the Orient. The burgher culture of the free city was central to Weber's sociology. *Wirtschaft und Gesellschaft*, a massive treatise published posthumously, centres on the occidental city as the birth-place of modern society. The strain of pessimism that runs through Weber's later writings was induced by the belief that the civilization originally created by free and independent citizens would fall victim to all-round bureaucratization, state control and the consequent loss of personal freedom. It was a vision he shared with Pareto – a cultivated patrician who had ceased to believe in the liberal perspective. They resemble each other also in that their work lacks a single central theorem around which a school or a party could have gathered. Ultimately what they convey is a sense of the dilemma induced by the spectacle of an increasingly rationalized society which somehow fails to exhibit the traits peculiar to liberal civilization in the age of its greatest creativity. This is perhaps no more than to say that they arrived on the scene at a time when the culture they had inherited was beginning to disintegrate. The war of 1914–18, which speeded this process, also marked the effective termination of their work.

This brief survey does not exhaust the subject of comparing Marx's and Weber's respective methods, as distinct from the results at which they arrived. Here the key issue is Marx's commitment to a particular philosophy and a political practice appropriate to it, as against Weber's belief that – granted the influence which value-judgements necessarily have in the social sciences – it is nonetheless possible to construct a value-free political sociology which will be genuinely scientific. Weber conceded at the outset that basic standpoints are arbitrary, and then went on to outline a sociology which nonetheless tried to attain the maximum of scientific objectivity possible under human conditions.[15] Unlike the extreme positivists he held that the social sciences differ from the natural in that they cannot eliminate the subjective element altogether. At the same time he was quite clearly convinced that his own freely chosen standpoint enabled him to give an objective account of social reality. It is difficult to see how objectivity can follow from the admission that all standpoints are arbitrary. Moreover, Weber's own basic approach, so far from being value-free, quite clearly embodied a particular view of man which comes to the surface in his use of the term 'disenchantment'. It requires no great effort to show that the concept of 'rationalization' occupies as central a position in Weber's analysis of modern society as does that of 'alienation' in Marx's writings. It is true that where Marx offers a cure, Weber contents himself with a diagnosis; but his view of history as a relentless process of secularization, schematization and bureaucratization is evaluative as well as descriptive. Perhaps the most that can be claimed for Weber is that he raised the problem of value-relevance for the social sciences; he cannot be said to have solved it. And if his political philosophy was implicit, where Marx's was explicit, it was distinctive enough to give life and shape to the body of his work.

NOTES

1 H.G.Wells, *Experiment in Autobiography* (London: Jonathan Cape, 1934, 1969).
2 For the general background see Stuart Hughes, *Consciousness and Society*, (New York and London: Knopf, 1958), pp. 33 ff. and *passim*. For the *fin de siècle* poets see Graham Hough, *The Last Romantics* (London: Methuen; New York: Barnes & Noble, 1961); Richard Ellmann, *Yeats: The Man and the Mask* (London: Faber, 1961; New York: Dutton, 1958).
3 *L'Évolution créatrice*, tr. as *Creative Evolution* (New York: Modern Library, 1944), pp. 293, 295. For a critical dissection of Bergson's philosophy see Bertrand Russell, *A History of Western Philosophy* (London: Allen & Unwin, 1945; New York: Simon & Schuster, 1945), pp. 791 ff.
4 Georges Sorel, *La décomposition du marxisme* (Paris: Marcel Rivière, 1908); *Réflexions sur la violence* (11th ed., Paris: Marcel Rivière, 1950); *De*

l'utilité du pragmatisme (Paris: Marcel Rivière, 1921). Gaëtan Pirou, *Georges Sorel: 1847–1922* (Paris: Marcel Rivière, 1927). Pierre Andreu, *Notre maître, M.Sorel* (Paris: Grasset, 1953). For Sorel's lack of influence on the Syndicalist labour movement see Édouard Dolléans, *Histoire du mouvement ouvrier*, vol. II, 1871–1936 (Paris: Armand Colin, 1946), pp. 126–7.

5 For this topic see Talcott Parsons, *The Structure of Social Action* (New York: The Free Press, 1968), *passim*; Walter M.Simon, *European Positivism in the Nineteenth Century* (Ithaca, N.Y.: Cornell University Press, 1963); Carlo Antoni, *From History to Sociology: The Transition in German Historical Thinking* (London: Merlin Press, 1962; Detroit, Mich.: Wayne State University Press, 1959); Emile Durkheim, *Socialism and Saint-Simon*, ed. Alvin W.Gouldner (London: Routledge & Kegan Paul, 1959; Yellow Springs, Ohio: Antioch Press, 1958), tr. from the French *Le Socialisme* (1928); W.G.Runciman, *Social Science and Political Theory* (Cambridge and New York: Cambridge University Press, 1963); Franz Borkenau, *Pareto* (London: Chapman & Hall, 1936); Vilfredo Pareto, *Sociological Writings*, ed. S.E.Finer (London: Pall Mall Press; New York: Praeger, 1966); Gaetano Mosca, *The Ruling Class*, ed. Arthur Livingston (New York and London: McGraw-Hill, 1939); James H.Meisel, *The Myth of the Ruling Class: Gaetano Mosca and the Elite* (Ann Arbor: University of Michigan Press, 1958, 1962); Robert Michels, *Political Parties* (New York: Dover, 1959); T.B.Bottomore and M.Rubel eds., *Karl Marx: Selected Writings in Sociology and Social Philosophy* (New York and London: McGraw-Hill, 1964); Reinhard Bendix, *Max Weber: An Intellectual Portrait* (London: Heinemann; Garden City, N.Y.: Doubleday, 1960); H.H.Gerth and C. Wright Mills eds., *From Max Weber: Essays in Sociology* (London: Kegan Paul, 1947; New York: Grosset & Dunlap, 1946); Raymond Aron, *German Sociology*, tr. by M. and T.Bottomore (Glencoe: The Free Press, 1957).

6 Borkenau, *op. cit.*, pp. 106 ff.; T.Bottomore, *Elites and Society* (London: C.A.Watts, 1964; New York: Basic Books, 1965).

7 Joseph A.Schumpeter, *Capitalism, Socialism and Democracy* (London: Allen & Unwin; New York: Harper & Row, 1950), *passim*; Stanislaw Ossowski, *Class Structure in the Social Consciousness* (London: Routledge & Kegan Paul; New York: Free Press, Macmillan, 1963), pp. 69 ff.

8 For biographical data see J.P.Mayer, *Max Weber and German Politics* (London: Faber & Faber, 1944; New York: Hillary, 2nd ed., 1956), *passim*.

9 Carlo Antoni, *op. cit.*, p. 135.

10 "Politik als Beruf", in *Gesammelte Politische Schriften* (Tübingen: J.C.B. Mohr, 1958), p. 542.

11 "Zwischen zwei Gesetzen" (1916); in *Gesammelte Politische Schriften*, p. 140. For the Freiburg lecture see p. 14.

12 Reprinted in vol. I of the collected works, *Gesammelte Aufsätze zur Religionssoziologie* (Tübingen: J.C.B.Mohr, 1947).

13 Werner J.Cahnman, "Max Weber and the Methodological Controversy in the Social Sciences", in Cahnman, W.J. and Boskoff, A., eds., *Sociology and History* (London: Macmillan; Glencoe: The Free Press, 1964), pp. 103 ff.

14 For a critical dissection of Weber's views see Gabriel Kolko, "Max Weber on America: Theory and Evidence", in George H. Nadel ed., *Studies in the Philosophy of History* (London: Macmillan; New York: Harper & Row, 1965), pp. 180 ff. For an analysis of Weber's general procedure in working out a logic of the social sciences see W. G. Runciman, *Social Science and Political Theory* (London and New York: Cambridge University Press, 1963), esp. pp. 57–63.

15 *Ibid.*, pp. 54 ff.; Karl Löwith, "Max Weber und Karl Marx", in Löwith, *Gesammelte Abhandlungen* (Stuttgart: Kohlhammer, 1960), pp. 1–67.

CHAPTER 5

A NEW VIEW OF THE WORLD

From the sociologist's viewpoint the twentieth century began in 1914, just as the nineteenth started in earnest around 1830, when the middle class placed its stamp on public affairs in Western Europe. What happened in 1914–18 shattered a way of life that looked solid but had been undermined by the processes described in the earlier chapters of this study. This circumstance creates a difficulty for the historian who takes as his starting-point the apogee of bourgeois civilisation around 1900. The dominant outlook in philosophy, science and art down to the 1920s was founded on nineteenth-century models. At the same time, the forces which created a new kind of culture were already at work around 1900, whether one thinks of physical science, applied technology, depth psychology or modern music and painting. The motor car, the aeroplane, the tractor, the telephone and the cinema all made their appearance well before 1914. So did the new theoretical model in physics, which indeed may be said to date from the discovery of X-rays and radioactivity in 1895–6.[1] Sigmund Freud (1856–1939) worked out the technique of free association around 1895, and published *The Interpretation of Dreams* at the close of 1899, although the publisher chose to put the date 1900 on the title page. Six hundred copies of the book were printed, and it took eight years to sell them.[2] The same sort of lag afflicted his countryman Adolf Loos, one of the founders of modern architecture, whose buildings in Vienna around 1910 looked forward to the international style of the 1930s. The post-impressionist painters assembled in Paris – Matisse, Rouault, Utrillo, Picasso, Derain, Braque, Léger and others – were more fortunate, in that their work created an immediate sensation, whereas their German and Russian colleagues did not reach a wider audience until the 1920s. Lastly, the new style of writing associated with James Joyce dated back to 1906, but impinged on the consciousness of the reading public only two decades later.

If for convenience we start with science, we may note that the breakthrough in physics occurred between 1895 and 1905 against the background of a technology based on nineteenth-century models. Electric light and power, wireless telegraphy and the internal combustion machine represented the application to industry of discoveries made by men like Michael Faraday (1791–1867) and Clerk Maxwell (1831–79) at a time when physics was still committed to the Newtonian picture of a universe composed of fixed particles created by God and destined to last for eternity. These particles – atoms and molecules – were limited in number and unchangeable. The discovery of radioactivity by J.J. Thomson, Becquerel, Röntgen and others cast doubt on the permanence of the atom and at the same time suggested that the break-up of atomic particles released energy. Max Planck (1858–1947), following Ernest Rutherford (1871–1937), showed in 1900 that atoms gave off energy in discrete quantities or constants, a discovery which confirmed the theory of the atom subsequently put forward in 1913 by Niels Bohr (1885–1962). Albert Einstein (1879–1955) demonstrated in 1905 that space and time were interchangeable, depending on the motion of an observer. This was a radical departure from Newtonian cosmology, although Planck and others came to regard relativity as the completion of classical physics.[3] Einstein's general theory of relativity (1915) centred on the equivalence of mass and energy, and the limiting character of light's velocity. His formula provided the theoretical expression for an understanding of the energies locked in the atom. The practical application of this model belongs to a later period, starting with Rutherford's discovery in 1919 that the nucleus of the atom could be broken up by bombarding it with suitable physical particles, and going on to the release of atomic energy through nuclear fission during the 1939–45 war, with all the familiar consequences that have flowed from this revolutionary device.[4]

The Rutherford–Bohr atom was no longer the simple uncuttable particle of ancient philosophy. It could be broken up, even though it still had a centre, the nucleus. The atom was now pictured as a solar system, with electrons orbiting around the nucleus and giving off a negative charge equal to the positive charge of the nucleus. It thus became possible to predict the properties of atoms from the number of electrons they contained.

Complex spectra could be interpreted and the *energy levels* of the electrons in the different atoms could be found. The very concept of an energy level is a quantum one. It implied that every atomic or molecular structure could exist in a great number of states with different vibration characters like the overtones of a musical instrument and that the *differences* of energy between the states could be found by measuring the *frequencies* of the light emitted or absorbed.[5]

The new model helped to bridge the gap between physics and chemistry. It also explained why certain atoms formed metals, while others did not. These discoveries represented an application of Planck's quantum theory to the study of the atom, Planck having suggested as early as 1900 that the energy of atoms comes off in discontinuous pieces. An element of indeterminacy entered into the picture. A certain state of affairs persists in an atom and then is suddenly replaced by a different one. Continuity of motion, hitherto taken for granted, appeared to have been discredited. While this reorientation was going on, Einstein quite independently suggested that events should replace particles as the basic constituents of the universe. Commonsense thinks of the world as made of discrete things, a notion elevated to philosophic dignity by the concept of material substances, each consisting of particles subsisting through all time. Einstein held that events rather than particles were the stuff of physics, from which it followed that 'matter' was merely a convenient shorthand formula for describing sub-atomic events having physical properties. He also substituted space-time for the traditional distinction between time and space. According to his theory, Euclidean geometry applied only to empty space: near heavy bodies space is curved. These concepts could not easily be translated into non-scientific language and relativity thus set up a barrier between the world-view of science and the outlook of the ordinary man.

The world of visual experience no longer bore any relation to that of the physicist, chemist or astronomer. Einstein's thought reflected the influence of the Austrian physicist and philosopher Ernst Mach (1838–1916) whose *Die Mechanik in ihrer Entwicklung* (1883, tr. into English as *The Science of Mechanics* in 1902) dispensed with time, space and causality as useless metaphysical concepts. Nature simply 'goes on', and the task of science is to work out a set of functional relationships which compress the workings of nature into formulae which can be tested in experience. Absolute time and space are metaphysical entities of no interest to science. A body's spatial or temporal position can only be defined in relation to that of another body. In 1895 Mach became professor of physics at the University of Vienna, and from this date may be reckoned the gradual rise of the 'Vienna Circle' whose intellectual leader, Moritz Schlick, succeeded Mach after having already made his reputation as an interpreter of Einstein. Mach's hostility to traditional metaphysics was inherited by the logical positivists who came to the fore in the 1920s, as was his belief that scientific hypotheses are justified if they stand up to empirical verification. His empiricism was a link between the neo-Kantian school, prominent in Germany since the 1880s, and the subsequent rise of logical positivism. Freud no less than Einstein inherited from Mach a bent towards empiricism and a consistent indifference to metaphysics of the traditional kind. In this sense, logical positivism, psychoanalysis and the new physics associated with Einstein, belong to the same spiritual family. This also applies to the theory of science worked out by the French physicist Pierre Duhem (1861–1916), who made a point of stressing the independence of physics from metaphysics, as did his countryman Henri Poincaré (1854–1912), for whom physical laws were conventions constructed by scientists to account for the motion of particles.

Speaking generally, the new outlook in theoretical physics since the beginning of the century demolished the classical picture of a static universe made up of particles whose motions conform to the laws of mechanics. The physical world of modern science is still composed of particles, but all may be transformed into others and none are eternal in the Newtonian sense:

Given an appropriate and fixed system of equations, one can hope to explain physical processes from the sub-atomic up to the molecular and macroscopic, and even the astronomical, scale; and this can be done without exempting any physical objects whatever from the flux of time – which means accepting that there are no permanent material 'atoms' in the original sense.[6]

Whether there were laws of nature at all became a matter for dispute among scientists, some of whom doubted whether stellar evolution could be reduced to constants not subject to change over suitable dimensions of time. The topic had no practical significance, save for theologians still tied to a geocentric picture of the universe, or mechanical materialists wedded to the 'ineffaceable characters' of atoms and molecules. The same applies to modern cosmology. A universe which may (or may not) have come into existence through a cataclysmic explosion some 10,000 million years ago still presents some logical problems – after all, it is legitimate to ask what was there before this event occurred – but it is no longer related to the familiar environment inhabited by human beings. Astronomers who favour the notion of an absolute beginning in time, because it fits in with religious doctrines about the Creation, plainly give vent to their personal preferences. Philosophers who prefer the Stoic picture of a recurring cycle of creation and destruction are in the same position.[7]

Setting metaphysics aside, the new model impinged upon the philosophy of science in that it lent some substance to the revolt against determinism associated with Bergson and with the American pragmatist school founded by William James (1842–1910) on the basis of C.S.Peirce's earlier work. The older empiricist tradition had been determinist, in accordance with Newtonian physics. When applied to psychology it led to the unsatisfactory conclusion that men's actions are wholly explicable in terms of causal determinants. Kantian idealism postulated a distinction between causally conditioned phenomena and moral actions stemming from a real or 'noumenal' self to which causation does not apply. The problem for philosophers unwilling to follow Kant was how to reconcile determinism with free will. Bergson, as we have seen, disposed of the matter by affirming that the intellect creates a conceptualized universe which must not be confused with reality. Pragmatism suggested that natural laws are merely statistical regularities. No situation is ever completely describable in terms of causal laws. Novel features develop out of previous situations which do not contain them. This doctrine, which James and Bergson had worked out independently of each other, was a great comfort to the anti-rationalist school of thought already prominent as a reaction to the rigid determination of the previous generation. Once the revolution in physics, notably the quantum theory, had introduced an element of indeterminacy within the order of nature, philosophers could draw some support from science for the contention that free will is not an illusion. It is, however, noteworthy that Planck's own standpoint did not permit the inference that the chain of causality contains a missing link. He contented himself with the argument that the causal motives determining an action can only be understood after the event; one cannot predict one's own future behaviour, for every observation introduces a new factor, in that it supplies a new motive for the will.[8]

Pragmatism implied a departure from what one of its later exponents, John Dewey, called "the spectator theory of knowledge" – the view, that is, that philosophic knowledge consists in the passive contemplation of an eternal and immutable reality.[9] In Germany, Nietzsche had already paved the way for a different kind of philosophizing with his attacks on intellectualism, while Bergson somewhat later pursued a similar line of thought. Now pragmatism, with its stress on practical usefulness as the criterion of truth, gained a following in France, where Georges Sorel, already influenced by Bergson, welcomed James as an ally in the struggle against scientism. In Italy, Mussolini at a later stage was to number James among his teachers.[10] Since the American pragmatists were ardent democrats, this embarrassing circumstance cannot be employed for polemical purposes, the less so since the official philosopher of Italian Fascism, Giovanni Gentile, was a Hegelian. But the pragmatist emphasis upon experience and living reality as the test of truth did help to create a mental climate in which irrationalism could flourish. The more radical pragmatists, notably F.C.S.Schiller in Britain, explicitly denied that there is an objective reality given independently of the thinking subject. Schiller's polemics were largely directed against F.H.Bradley (1846–1924), who had introduced into British philosophy an anti-empiricist line of thought nourished on German idealism in general and Hegel in particular.[11] The Anglo-Hegelian synthesis promoted by Bradley, Bernard Bosanquet and J.E.McTaggart in turn became the special target of British thinkers in the empiricist tradition, notably George Edward Moore and Bertrand Russell, neither of whom had much use for pragmatism, whereas some of the leading pragmatists displayed more than a touch of sympathy for Hegel.[12]

Hegelian thinking traditionally centred upon the understanding of history, whereas empiricism had at least one foot solidly planted in natural science, itself largely dependent upon mathematics. For this reason, new developments in mathematics became crucial for the restatement of the empiricist standpoint undertaken around the turn of the century by Bertrand Russell (1872–1970) and A.N.Whitehead (1861–1947). "There was an odd exchange of international roles at this point; the Boole–De Morgan logic originated in England, but was given its classical formulation by Schröder in Germany; the logic of mathematics was a Continental creation which yet achieved its classical form in Russell and Whitehead's *Principia Mathematica*."[13] As published in 1910–13, this work carried further a new conception of mathematics already outlined in Russell's earlier *Principles of Mathematics* (1903). In the autobiographical fragment which introduces the volume of essays titled *The Philosophy of Bertrand Russell* (1944), the process leading to his mature standpoint is briefly described as follows:

The most important year in my intellectual life was the year 1900, and the most important event in this year was my visit to the International Congress of Philosophy in Paris. Ever since I had begun Euclid at the age of eleven, I had been troubled about the foundations of mathematics; when, later, I came to read philosophy, I found Kant and the empiricists equally unsatisfactory. I did not like the synthetic *a priori*, but yet arithmetic did not seem to consist of empirical generalizations. In Paris in 1900, I was impressed by the fact that, in all discussions, Peano and his pupils had a precision which was not possessed by others. I therefore asked him to give me his works, which he did. As soon as I had mastered his notation, I saw that it extended the region of mathematical precision backwards towards regions which had been given over to philosophical vagueness. Basing myself on him, I invented a notation for relations. Whitehead, fortunately, agreed as to the importance of the method, and in a very short time we worked out together such matters as the definitions of series, cardinals, and ordinals, and the reduction of arithmetic to logic.[14]

The new mathematics was a 'science of order' which had cut its connection with empirical reality. It was no longer a demonstration of timeless truths, but an analysis of logical implications. As outlined in the writings of the German mathematician Gottlob Frege between 1893 and 1903, and by a group of Italian logicians headed by Giuseppe Peano between 1895 and 1908, arithmetic and algebra were founded on a few elementary logical ideas and propositions. The logical symbolism invented by Peano was in turn adopted by Russell and Whitehead.[15] Russell's principal achievement, it has been said, is to have freed logical analysis from the domination of grammar. In the works he composed jointly with Whitehead, and in subsequent writings, he put forward a theory of descriptions which replaced spurious entities by logical constructions. Building on his Continental predecessors, he maintained that mathematics and formal logic are one, and that the whole of pure mathematics can be deduced from a small number of logical axioms. The method was carried further in such later works as *The Analysis of Mind* (1921) and *An Inquiry into Meaning and Truth* (1940). In Russell's own words:

All definitions are theoretically superfluous, and therefore the whole of any science can be expressed by means of a minimum vocabulary for that science. Peano reduced the special vocabulary of arithmetic to three terms; Frege and *Principia Mathematica* maintained that even these are unnecessary, and that a minimum vocabulary for mathematics is the same as for logic. This problem is a purely technical one, and is capable of a precise solution.[16]

Russell's and Whitehead's paths diverged from about 1919 onwards, when Whitehead departed from the tradition of British empiricism. The best-known works of his later period, notably *The Concept of Nature* (1920), *Science and the Modern World* (1925), *Process and Reality* (1929) and *Adventures of Ideas* (1933), represent the gradual unfolding of a metaphysical system in some respects similar to that outlined by Samuel Alexander in *Space, Time and Deity* (1920). After his appointment in 1924, at the age of sixty-three, to the Chair of Philosophy at Harvard, Whitehead became a force to be reckoned with in American philosophy as well. The metaphysical doctrine he developed in his later works has been variously described as Platonist and neo-Hegelian. It represented a complete break with the Russellian picture of the world. On the traditional view, ultimately derived from Plato, mathematics stated certain truths about the world; on the new assumption, it merely spelled out what followed from given postulates. Hence various different systems of geometry could be set up alongside each other, deriving from different postulates, and there was no answer to the question which was truer than the others. This discovery facilitated the acceptance of Einstein's theory with its relativization of Euclidean geometry. It also induced philosophical laymen to dispense with the criterion of truth altogether, a consequence which did not follow from the new theory of science, but was read into it by the growing number of irrationalists who pullulated in Europe after the 1914–18 war.

So far as the British Isles are concerned, the principal issue in philosophy between 1900 and 1914 was the tension between the native tradition of empiricism and the Anglo-Hegelianism of Bradley and

Bosanquet – "Hegelianism modified by Anglo-Saxon caution", in the words of a later writer, H.J.Paton.[17] Technically known as Absolute Idealism, this philosophy was a derivation of German metaphysics in that it centred on the concept of totality or 'the whole'. When Moore and Russell turned against it after 1900 they were symbolically joining hands "with at least two centuries of British philosophy, across a gap of a few years occupied with new and strange things".[18] Moore adopted a commonsense viewpoint which undercut the idealist position, in that he questioned the need for elaborate metaphysical solutions of perfectly ordinary problems. On his supposition the commonsense view of the world was likely to be the true one, and any departure from it required justifications which the idealists were notoriously unwilling to provide. Russell's position was different, inasmuch as he always aimed at a total system of truth about the world, where Moore was content with the analysis of important but neglected truisms. Deeply influenced by recent developments in logic and mathematics, Russell expounded what came to be known as logical atomism; that is to say, he tried to arrive at a notation whereby complex propositions were broken up into their simplest elements, atomic propositions relating to atomic facts. Although metaphysical, in that it tried to comprehend the nature of language and of the world, this procedure was in tune with the general spirit of British philosophy before the recent incursion of German idealism. Russell, the godson of John Stuart Mill, "so far as is possible in a non-religious sense",[19] did not require a great deal of persuasion to make him return to the native tradition founded by Locke, Berkeley and Hume. The Continental situation was quite different. While French thinkers had never taken much notice of Hegel, the Italians were about to absorb him in the diluted form presented by Benedetto Croce (1866–1952), while in Germany something like a Hegel renaissance made itself felt from about 1906 onwards. For the rest, the principal newcomer on the Central European scene after 1900 was the phenomenological school of Edmund Husserl, whose roots went back to Kant and ultimately to Cartesian rationalism.[20]

What Husserl (1859–1938) put forward in his *Logical Investigations* (1900–1) and in subsequent writings was a theory of experience which departed radically from Mill's attempt to derive logical concepts from psychology. Logical and mathematical conclusions could not, he argued, be grounded in empirical premises, nor could the psychological study of the thinking process cast light on the validity of theoretical concepts which by their nature are independent of contingent empirical data. What Husserl termed phenomenology is indeed descriptive, but what it describes are pure essences, not particular existences. These essences are not metaphysical entities, but neither are they generalizations derived from an inductive study of experience. In describing phenomena one necessarily describes their essential properties, that is to say, those general structures which are disclosed by an act of insight not reducible to empirical experience. The latter is uncertain and changeable, whereas phenomenological intuition of essences brings out those characters which constitute their meaning – e.g., the redness of red objects. Essences are independent of existence. It is possible to know what something is without having to decide the question whether it actually exists. Knowledge of reality is knowledge of the signification of things, and this meaning is lodged in our consciousness. Or one may say that the essence of something is that which is what it is, irrespective of whether or not it exists. The whole train of thought goes back to Kant, and ultimately to Descartes, whose example Husserl followed in his later writings from 1913 onwards by screening out, or 'bracketing', the actual world of experience; not doubting its existence, but suspending judgement about it, in order to arrive at a consciousness completely separated from the world of fact. This purification of consciousness enables the mind to grasp the validity of propositions which – like the axioms of mathematics – are eternally true, whether or not anyone has ever thought of them. At the same time, all objects of consciousness are considered only as they appear to the mind. Phenomenology restricts itself to what is given. It describes the structures of appearances, without in any way affirming or denying an objective existence of things independent of the thinking mind.[21]

Husserl's later development disclosed a growing concern with the status of science within the general context of European philosophy. He remained true to his early programmatic faith that only phenomenology can be truly scientific, and that only a scientific philosophy can be true. But he increasingly came to believe that European science had reached a critical stage which was related to a more general crisis of culture. The theme is spelled out at great length in his final work, which occupied him between 1934 and 1937, *Die Krisis der europäischen Wissenschaften und die transzendentale Phänomenologie.*[22] Down to 1914 he disclosed no doubt as to the possibility of establishing philosophy on a scientific basis, although independent of the methods employed in the natural sciences. In this respect his development parallels that of his contemporary Sigmund Freud, who may be said to have introduced a phenomenological approach into psychology, in that – in his early work at least – he confined himself to a pure description of the behaviour he encountered.

Both men emerged from an Austro-Jewish culture which was wiped out after they had left the scene. In other ways they did not have a great deal in common, even though Freud was influenced by Mach. To the extent that he was affected by metaphysics, Freud displayed something of the pessimism of Schopenhauer, a circumstance irrelevant to his scientific work. The Husserlian ideal of a strictly scientific and presuppositionless approach to the study of phenomena was also his own, but as a scientist he was inevitably concerned with the truth of particular statements about empirical reality, rather than with the analysis of the process whereby thinkers arrive at general concepts. Whether they do so by generalizing from experience, as the empiricists maintained, or through the intuition of general properties (essences) in the Husserlian sense, was not a question that troubled him in his professional capacity. In so far as Freud reflected on his own work, he plainly adhered to the customary notion that psychological statements are generalizations subject to correction in the light of experience; but this did not make him a subjectivist in the sense of holding that reality is in some sense a product of the mind. Scientific statements are either true or false, and if true they correspond to a reality independent of the notions which men at different times entertain about them. One may say that, although by profession a psychologist, Freud did not adhere to 'psychologism', if by this term is meant the doctrine that logic itself can be dissolved into psychology. He appears to have held with the philosopher Franz Brentano (an important precursor of Husserl) that the psychologist has a direct apprehension of the realities which constitute his subject matter. We know from his biographer that he attended Brentano's lectures as a student in Vienna in the 1870s.[23] Since it was of the essence of Brentano's doctrine that mental acts are known with greater certainty than anything in the outside world, Freud had no need to trouble himself as to the nature of cognition. He could be an agnostic in the neo-Kantian fashion, and still retain his solidly grounded conviction that in psychology we perceive our own mental acts, whereas in the other sciences we observe external phenomena whose ultimate nature must remain a matter for conjecture. Knowledge of one's mental life is peculiarly certain as compared to knowledge of anything else. This was Freud's philosophical starting-point, and for the rest he held the conventional view that there is no mind without a brain, and no psychical process apart from a physiological one. As for the ultimate nature of mind and matter, it was unknown and probably unknowable.[24]

Freud's investigations into the psychology of the unconscious have been so influential that there is a natural temptation to inquire how far they were promoted by his philosophical beliefs. In the sense that he was an irreligious Jew born of German-speaking parents in Moravia and then brought up in Vienna, he may be said to have epitomized a particular culture and a way of life which was destroyed after 1933. Beyond this obvious circumstance it is difficult to see wherein his general philosophy differed from that of his teachers and colleagues. He clearly shared the positivist belief in the universality of causally definable laws of nature. He was an agnostic rather than a materialist, in that he did not believe the essential nature of mind or matter was known, or that mental processes could be described in physical terms and vice versa. He was a determinist who nonetheless held that hidden processes at work in the unconscious could be influenced by being brought to the level of consciousness. All choices were determined, but they might be 'over-determined' by a plurality of psychic forces, so that it was not possible to establish a one-to-one relationship between cause and effect. The unconscious mind (a term he did not invent) drew its energy from instinctual drives which might be pictured in mechanistic terms, but once brought to light these motivations yielded to treatment and underwent a change. Perhaps all this is merely to say that Freud made use of whatever scientific terminology lay ready to hand. His positivist outlook was not really adequate to his dialectical view of the relationship between the conscious mind and the dreamlike processes constantly at work in the unconscious regions, but he never abandoned the vocabulary he had acquired as a student.

The imposing structure later to be known as psychoanalysis arose from modest beginnings. As a physician who specialized in neurology, Freud gradually came to the conclusion that many of his patients were suffering from psychological disorders, began to study hypnosis, spent some time in Paris, and in 1895, together with Josef Breuer (1842–1925), published *Studien über Hysterie*, a description of clinical cases treated with the aid of what he then described as "the cathartic method", whereby the patient was encouraged to remember and relate forgotten experiences. The term 'psychoanalysis' was first employed in 1896, and by 1898 Freud had developed the technique of free association which then became the foundation of his psychotherapy. The appreciation of sexual factors in the genesis of neuroses developed gradually out of the treatment of hysterical patients who were encouraged to let their minds roam freely and not to conceal anything from the therapist who assumed the neutral role of a listener. The interpretation of dreams followed from the new conception of the unconscious as a dynamic force drawing its energy from instinctual drives, some of them disturbing to the ego and thus kept below the level of consciousness. This form of repression was seen as an unconscious process, the true nature of the drive disclosing itself only in the form of dreams or free associations, some of them very shocking to the patient. Neurotic symptoms on this assumption were compromise attempts at instinctual gratification inhibited by the conscious personality and the cultural environment dominant in the patient's existence as a member of society. Subsequent disputes within the psychoanalytic school turned on the role of sexual gratification, the crucial significance of which was disputed by Alfred Adler, Carl Gustav Jung and other psychologists who accepted the general notion of the unconscious, but took a different view of its peculiar dynamic. Jung in particular adopted Bergson's philosophy and defined the Freudian notion of 'libido' as an overflow of psychic energy not specifically related to sexuality. The central importance of the latter became the hallmark of orthodox Freudianism.[25]

The decisive step was the introduction of the free association method. If causality was taken seriously, then no mental association, however obscure or aberrant, could be wholly meaningless: it must relate to some unknown agency directing the flow of memory. Repression and resistance were directly observable in clinical treatment. But why did they occur? Here Freud committed himself to the doctrine, not acceptable to all his followers, that repressed sexual drives going back to early childhood – and to the childhood of the human race – were at the bottom of the instinctive resistance which the unconscious opposes to the therapist. As he put it in *The Interpretation of Dreams*: "It is the fate of all of us, perhaps, to direct our first sexual impulses towards our mother and our first murderous wish against our father." This notion was elaborated in his later anthropological studies, of which *Totem and Taboo* (1913) is the best known.[26] The publication of this work precipitated the conflict with Jung and his followers, a circumstance foreseen by Freud who told his pupil Karl Abraham that the book "would serve to make a sharp division between us and all Aryan religiosity".[27] By nailing his colours to the mast of what came to be known as the Oedipus complex, Freud introduced a principle which could be employed to bridge the gap separating individual psychology from the study of society; but he also made it impossible for therapists who did not accept the central importance of infantile sexuality to describe themselves as psychoanalysts. The debate ran its course, various amendments being proposed by Freud's own followers, e.g., a biological interpretation which linked attachment to the mother and the pre-natal state with a desire to return to the womb; the Oedipus complex on this assumption is rooted in anxiety derived from the birth trauma. More serious dissension arose from Freud's speculative reconstruction of primitive human society as a horde of brothers who rebel against their father and kill him; totemism and the incest taboo common to most religions figured in this hypothesis as historically acquired consequences of the primeval crime of murdering the despotic father of the clan. The construction was disputed by anthropologists such as Malinowski, Kroeber and Westermarck, and it has never been wholeheartedly accepted by all of Freud's followers. Freud's reading of the anthropological evidence available to him was inevitably selective. Even if one accepted the plausibility of his hypothesis in relation to monogamous patriarchal society, there was still no way of proving that totemism and the incest taboo had actually come into existence in the manner postulated by his theory. As Malinowski pointed out, it was very difficult to envisage primitive parricide as a shattering event whose consequences spread by a process of cultural diffusion, or alternatively as an epidemic of minor parricides occurring among all primitive hordes. Among later writers, Claude Lévi-Strauss, in his *Les Structures élémentaires de la parenté*, rejected the hypothesis of a parricidal act transmitted by some obscure process to all human beings. Psychoanalysts have remained divided on the topic. Only the most rigid Freudians still adhere to the notion that the Oedipus complex is central to the rise of civilization, as well as accounting for the origins of religion and morality.

Setting aside the therapeutic treatment of neurotic disturbances, psychoanalysis made its greatest impact in the region of sex education. On the conventional view, backed by the Churches and predominant in the European middle class of Freud's own age, sex was that part of man's animal inheritance which had to be brought under control, or even sacrificed, in order to keep the soul pure. Freud did not challenge the notion that instinctual repression is a precondition of civilized existence, but he shifted the balance in the direction of making sexual activity respectable. On his assumption, the sexual instinct was defined as a special kind of psychic energy seeking release. It existed in a certain quantity and sought appropriate discharge in actions which restored the internal equilibrium. It differed from other forms of psychic energy in that it could be diverted from its biological aim and sublimated into cultural activities, but in one form or another it must be satisfied, on pain of causing grave mental disturbances. This view of the matter was quite novel, as was the related discovery that sexual activity occurs long before puberty. The gradual acceptance of these notions has revolutionized the mental climate of the modern world and born fruit in a less authoritarian pattern of parental behaviour towards their offspring. It has also induced the Churches to question or amend the traditional equation of sin with sensuality. Certain taboos ingrained in the bourgeois family structure of Freud's own culture have been quietly abandoned – paradoxically under the influence of a thinker whose own personality and conduct were rigidly puritanical. Irrespective of the value one attributes to the therapeutic effects of psychoanalysis in the treatment of neuroses, Freud ranks with Darwin as one of the liberators of the modern mind. Once his message had sunk in, it was no longer possible to overlook the instinctual derivation of psychic phenomena which had previously been classified solely with reference to the prevailing standards of moral behaviour. At the same time the ancient view of human instincts as automatic animal responses to given stimuli was replaced by the concept of a relatively undifferentiated energy capable of variation through learning and education.[28]

One of the less fortunate effects of the new method was a tendency to indulge in a facile kind of paradox. Freud had postulated that conscious behaviour may spring from unconscious tendencies opposite in character; thus a pacifist may be compensating for unconscious aggressive urges. By playing upon these possibilities some of Freud's disciples achieved startling literary effects of no value to science. They also helped to discredit useful concepts such as over-compensation and reaction-formation which actually do relate to observable patterns of behaviour. Statements which can neither be verified nor falsified are of no use to science, and too many of Freud's followers went in for intellectual games of this kind. At a different level it has been urged that behavioural therapy often yields better results than psychoanalysis, even though it is only concerned with symptoms, not with the total personality. On the Freudian hypothesis this is quite probable and does not invalidate the theoretical framework of analysis. At most it suggests that for the majority of patients there are forms of therapy available which are less time-consuming than analysis.

The pre-1914 period was fertile in new advances in the psychological field. What became known as *Gestalt* psychology developed alongside psychoanalysis, and quite independently from it, against a similar German-Austrian background. Its origins go back to 1912, when one of its founders, Max Wertheimer (1886–1943), investigated the apparent movement brought about if two points of light, each static, occur in rapid succession – the fundamental principle of the film camera which had begun to develop during these years. In this case the sense of movement is not to be found in the elements that contribute to it, and is quite different from the succession of sensations that occur if the interval between them is a little longer. Wolfgang Köhler (1887–1967) and Kurt Koffka (1886–1941), who took part in Wertheimer's experiment, joined him in a sustained onslaught on the conventional atomistic, or associationist, theory of sense impression. During the 1914–18 war, Köhler (then interned on the island of Tenerife) undertook studies of problem-solving on the part of animals, later reported in *The Mentality of Apes*. In 1921 he was appointed Director of the Institute of Psychology at Berlin University, and this became a centre of *Gestalt* psychology until the founders of the school were obliged in the 1930s to emigrate to the United States, where a number of psychoanalysts had preceded them. *Gestalt* psychology took issue with the orthodox view that a scientific account of behaviour must be analysed or atomized into its constituent parts. As against this time-honoured notion the new school emphasized that in perception (possibly also in learning and memory) a whole 'figure' is an immediate experience and not analysable into an assembly of its parts. It cannot even be described as an assembly of parts related to each other, for the component parts may be altered by the whole to which they contribute. This approach had implications for general psychology, as well as for psychotherapy, since in the assessment of personality it led away from the consideration of separate traits. *Gestalt* psychology affected the Austrian educational system in the 1920s and is thought to have had an important influence on the philosophy of Ludwig Wittgenstein and Karl Popper. It is probably no coincidence that the Swiss linguist Ferdinand de Saussure (1857–1913) had in the meantime begun to pioneer studies of language in which the emphasis lay on systems of relations rather than linguistic 'atoms'. There is also a resemblance between *Gestalt* psychology and the phenomenology of Husserl, with its slogan *Zurück zur Sache* (freely rendered as "back to the matter"). This might be read as meaning "back to perception" and was so understood by some later thinkers, notably the French philosopher Maurice Merleau-Ponty. Phenomenology, on this interpretation, meant going back beyond science to the world actually encountered in perception by the living subject. From there a road pointed to the existentialism which became fashionable in Germany after the first European war, and in France after the second.[29]

This topic leads back to our earlier considerations about the interaction between science and philosophy. The general trend during the period under review led away from metaphysical idealism. For Brentano, Husserl and the logical positivists who assembled in Vienna after 1919, philosophy was scientific or it was nothing. The same might be said of their British contemporaries, among whom Russell was personally acquainted with Wittgenstein during the latter's residence in Cambridge between 1912 and 1913. The trouble is that at this point the chronology becomes confusing, for Wittgenstein's *Tractatus Logico-Philosophicus* appeared in 1921, and in an English translation the following year. Since the present chapter is meant to provide a sketch of the philosophical scene on the eve of the 1914–18 earthquake, we are obliged at this point to abandon the topic of science and turn our attention to other matters. The purpose of these introductory remarks will have been served if it has become clear that the general revolution in science and philosophy, which attracted public attention during the 1919–39 inter-war period, had already begun before 1914. In the words of an eminent literary critic:

1914 has obvious qualifications; but if you wanted to defend the neater, more mythical date, you could do very well. In 1900 Nietzsche died; Freud published *The Interpretation of Dreams*; 1900 was the date of Husserl's *Logic*, and of Russell's *Critical Exposition of the Philosophy of Leibniz*. With an exquisite sense of timing Planck published his quantum hypothesis in the very last days of the century, December 1900. Thus, within a few months, were published works which transformed or transvalued spirituality, the relation of language to knowing, and the very locus of human uncertainty, henceforth to be thought of not as an imperfection of the human apparatus but part of the nature of things. . . . 1900, like 1400 and 1600 and 1000, has the look of a year that ends a *saeculum*.[30]

NOTES

1 J.D.Bernal, *Science in History*, vol. III (London: C.A.Watts and Pelican Books, 1969; New York: Hawthorn Books, 1965), pp. 726–7.

2 Ernest Jones, *Sigmund Freud: Life and Work*, vol. I (London: The Hogarth Press; New York: Basic Books, 1953), p. 395.

3 Max Planck, *The Universe in the Light of Modern Physics* (London: Allen and Unwin, 1937; New York: Norton, 1931), p. 18.

4 Bernal, *op. cit.*, pp. 733–58.

5 *Ibid.*, p. 740.

6 Stephen Toulmin and June Goodfield, *The Discovery of Time* (London: Pelican Books, 1967; New York: Harper & Row, 1965), pp. 305–6.

7 Albert Einstein, *Relativity: A Popular Exposition*, tr. Robert W.Lawson (London: Methuen, 1960; New York: Crown Publishers, 1961). Werner Heisenberg, *The Physicist's Conception of Nature*, tr. from the German original, *Das Naturbild der heutigen Physik* (London: Hutchinson; Westport, Conn.: Greenwood Press, 1958). Stephen Toulmin, *The Philosophy of Science* (London: Hutchinson; New York: Hutchinson and Humanities Press, 1953).

8 Max Planck, *Vom Wesen der Willensfreiheit* (Leipzig: Barth Verlag, 1936).

9 John Passmore, *A Hundred Years of Philosophy* (London: Penguin Books, 1968; New York: Basic Books, 3rd ed., 1966), p. 117.

10 *Ibid.*, pp. 118–19. Sorel seems to have come across James during the 1914–18 period. His *De l'utilité du pragmatisme* appeared in 1921.

11 Richard Wollheim, *F.H.Bradley* (London and Baltimore: Penguin Books, 1959, 1969).

12 For G.E.Moore see his *Principia Ethica*, first published in 1903 (Cambridge and New York: Cambridge University Press, 1959), and P.A.Schilpp ed., *The Philosophy of G.E.Moore*, published as vol. IV in *The Library of Living Philosophers* (Evanston and Chicago: Northwestern University Press, 1942).

13 Passmore, *op. cit.*, p. 145. For Russell and Whitehead see *inter alia* vols. III and V in Schilpp ed., *The Library of Living Philosophers*; also Whitehead, *Adventures of Ideas* (Cambridge: University Press, 1933, 1961, 1964); *Science and Philosophy* (London: Cambridge University Press, 1948; New York: Philosophical Library, 1948); and Lucien Price, *Dialogues of Alfred North Whitehead* (Boston and London: Little, Brown & Co., 1954). For Russell, in addition to his numerous publications, see his three-volume

autobiography (London: Allen & Unwin, 1967, 1968, 1969). A useful introduction to his thinking before 1914 is contained in *The Problems of Philosophy*, first published in 1912 (London–New York–Toronto: Oxford University Press, 1967)

14 *Op. cit.*, in vol. V of Schilpp ed., *The Philosophy of Bertrand Russell*, vol. V of *The Library of Living Philosophers*, pp. 12–13. See also D.F.Pears, *Bertrand Russell and the British Tradition in Philosophy* (London: Collins-Fontana, 1967).

15 Passmore, *op. cit.*, p. 147.

16 "My mental development", in Schilpp ed., *The Philosophy of Bertrand Russell*, pp. 14–15.

17 G.J.Warnock, *English Philosophy since 1900*, 2nd ed. (Oxford and New York: Oxford University Press, 1969), p. 4.

18 *Ibid.*, p. 8.

19 Schilpp ed., *The Philosophy of Bertrand Russell*, p. 3.

20 Edmund Husserl, *Cartesian Meditations: An Introduction to Phenomenology*, tr. Dorion Cairns (The Hague: Martinus Nijhoff, 1960); see also Quentin Lauer, *Phenomenology: Its Genesis and Prospects* (New York: Harper & Row, 1965).

21 Husserl, *Logische Untersuchungen* (Halle: Niemayer, 2nd ed. 1913), *passim*; see also Husserl, *Ideen zu einer reinen Phänomenologie* (1913) trans. *Ideas: A General Introduction to Pure Phenomenology* (New York: Collier Books, 1962), reprinted in vol. III of the *Gesammelte Werke*. An English translation of the *Logische Untersuchungen* by J.N.Findlay appeared in 1970 (London: Routledge), under the title *Logical Investigations*.

22 Published in 1954 and 1962 (The Hague: Martinus Nijhoff) as vol. VI of the *Husserliana* edited by the Husserl Archives at Louvain. Parts I and II of this work had appeared in the Belgrade review *Philosophia* in 1936. See also Quentin Lauer ed., *Phenomenology and the Crisis of Philosophy* (New York and London: Harper & Row, 1965), which contains the translation of a lecture delivered by Husserl in Vienna in May 1935 on the relation between European history and philosophy.

23 Ernest Jones, *Sigmund Freud: Life and Work*, vol. I (London: Hogarth Press; New York: Basic Books, 1953), pp. 41–2, 61–2.

24 Passmore, *op. cit.*, pp. 176–8; Jones, *op. cit.*, pp. 402–5. See also the discussion of the topic in Stuart Hughes, *Consciousness and Society* (New York and London: Knopf, 1958), pp. 125 ff.

25 Jones, *op. cit.*, pp. 243 ff.; Hughes, *op. cit.*, pp. 153 ff.; J.A.C.Brown, *Freud and the post-Freudians* (London and Baltimore: Penguin Books, 1961).

26 Jones, *op. cit.*, vol. II, pp. 103, 395 ff.

27 *Ibid.*, p. 396. For Freud's account of these and other dissensions see his essay *Zur Geschichte der psychoanalytischen Bewegung* (1914), reprinted in vol. X of the *Gesammelte Werke*.

28 Brown, *op. cit.*, p. 10. For a critical assessment of the Freudian heritage see Ian D.Suttie, *The Origins of Love and Hate* (London: Kegan Paul, 1935; Penguin Books, 1960, 1963); Charles Rycroft ed., *Psychoanalysis Observed* (London: Constable, 1966; New York: Coward-McCann, 1967).

For a brief outline of Jungian psychology see C.G.Jung, *Analytical Psychology: Its Theory and Practice* (London: Routledge & Kegan Paul; New York: Pantheon, 1968). This volume makes available the text of five lectures which Jung delivered, in English, at the Institute of Medical Psychology (The Tavistock Clinic) in London, in 1935. For the subsequent development of anthropology see Edmund Leach, *Genesis as Myth and other Essays* (London: Jonathan Cape, 1969) and the same author's *Lévi-Strauss* (London: Collins-Fontana; New York: Viking Press, 1970).

29 Wolfgang Köhler, *The Task of Gestalt Psychology*, with an introduction by Carroll C. Pratt (Princeton, N.J.: Princeton University Press, 1969); Passmore, *op. cit.*, pp. 499–500, 511. Merleau-Ponty's account of the matter is to be found in his *Phénoménologie de la perception* (Paris: Gallimard, 1945).

30 Frank Kermode, *The Sense of an Ending* (London and New York: Oxford University Press, 1966, 1967), pp. 97–8.

CHAPTER 6

A NEW STYLE IN THE ARTS

Earlier parts of this study contained casual references to new currents in literature and art on the eve of 1914. The present chapter is intended as a brief guide to modernism, taking the term to signify the more or less conscious break with tradition that occurred during the first two or three decades of the twentieth century. This arrangement necessarily imposes a departure from chronology, inasmuch as the 1914–18 war appears as an external disturbance, instead of being treated as the decisive rupture with the nineteenth century. In what follows we thus anticipate a good deal of what from a different viewpoint belongs to the post-war era. This cannot be helped, for the new movements which rose to prominence in the 1920s had already made themselves felt before 1914. In some degree this also applies to technology and politics, but the technological speed-up in 1914–18, and the crash of the three Eastern Empires in 1917–18, had no precise artistic correlative; inversely, the emergence of a new artistic style around 1910 occurred at a time when the socio-political order in Europe was relatively stable. In the arts, as in science and philosophy, one cannot speak of a sharp cleavage between pre-war and post-war. Pre-1914 architecture, to take an example, had already made a radical break with the past, and there were similar stirrings in music and painting. We shall therefore ignore the war, leaving until later a consideration of what happened to European society in 1914–18 and the years following.

The autonomy of art is of course only relative. What occurred in architecture, music and painting – and to a lesser degree in literature – around 1910 was a response to challenges occasioned by new life-styles, themselves shaped by the second industrial revolution, the general acceptance of the machine age, and the loss of emotional certitudes rooted in a stabler order of society. Bourgeois art passed out of fashion because the middle class was no longer in secure possession of the world view it had brought into existence between 1830 and 1890. At the same time, the relative autonomy of the aesthetic realm enabled a vanguard of artists from the 1890s onward to evolve new styles appropriate to the social reality of the 1920s. The effective conditioning of modernism by the forces shaping it was concealed from the participants by the nature of the aesthetic experience. Art, it has been said, cares nothing for the difference between the true and the false: it simply ignores the distinction. "There is no such thing as the so-called artistic illusion, for illusion means believing in the reality of that which is unreal, and art does not believe in the reality of anything at all."[1] The context within which artistic production takes place nonetheless imposes its own standards upon the participants, even if they are in rebellion against the prevalent public taste. What turns them into forerunners of a new life-style is their sensitivity to changes in the environment. The aesthetic experience may be indifferent to factual statements; it is never indifferent to formal considerations, and the forms it evolves bear a relation – positive or negative – to the artist's surroundings. The Romantic reaction against industrialism during the first half of the nineteenth century was intimately related to contemporary life. The early twentieth century witnessed the emergence of new aesthetic patterns which would have been inconceivable half a century earlier.[2]

This interrelation of form and content is not just a matter of social conditioning. It extends to the core of the creative process, to the symbols employed by the artist, to the way in which artistic form responds to felt need:

The novel develops its formal principle from the idea of the corrosive effects of time, just as tragedy derives the basis of its form from the idea of the timeless fate which destroys man with one fell blow. And as fate possesses a superhuman greatness and a metaphysical power in tragedy, so time attains an inordinate, almost mythical dimension in the novel.[3]

Marcel Proust's work mirrored the Bergsonian concept of time, not because Bergson and Proust were contemporaries, but because *À la recherche du temps perdu* is the title of a work which has Bergson's *durée* for its real theme.[4] This is not to say that Proust set out to affirm the truth of Bergson's philosophical propositions: merely that both were struggling with the same sort of problem. In Proust's case the intellectual structure is wholly embedded in the work, incapable of being abstracted from its material and set over against it as a thesis distinguishable from the novelistic account of Parisian high society on the eve of 1914. But this is merely to say that Proust was an artist, not a philosopher. His work spells out in elaborate and concrete detail a concept of time which invests memory with meaning far beyond anything present in the naturalistic novel of the nineteenth century. There is for Proust no happiness but that of remembrance. Time that is past is not worthless. On the contrary, it gives meaning to our lives by enabling us to recall the lost paradise of childhood. Time is the medium in which we become aware of our spiritual existence, itself the antithesis of dead matter. This particular significance of time as *durée* is explicit in Bergson, implicit in Proust, for whom memory has become the only way in which we can possess our lives. It is a contemplative attitude and at the same time a highly individualistic one, closely allied to the Symbolist belief that the world exists for the sake of art. This kind of writing descended from the aestheticism of the 1890s, whereas the modern breakthrough in painting and sculpture was prompted by quite different motivations. A good deal of it stemmed from a vague sense of unease with modern civilization and a consequent readiness to seek refuge in simpler modes of thought associated with archaic cultures. African Negro art became fashionable in Paris around 1906, at the very time when nascent Cubism and Futurism toyed with the symbols of the machine age. Masks discovered in junk shops started a craze which, thanks to Matisse and his juniors Vlaminck, Derain and Picasso, spread to influential art collectors. The seeming paradox dissolves if it is borne in mind that all concerned were doing their best to get away from the art of the nineteenth century. If the traditional sources of feeling had been exhausted, then one could uncover new and unspoilt layers by turning inward, by escaping to the primitives, or by extolling the possibilities of the new technology. The poet Guillaume Apollinaire (1880–1918) and his friends idolized a 'naive' painter, Henri (Douanier) Rousseau, for reasons not unconnected with Proust's obsession with his own childhood. World-weariness and primitivism were two sides of the same coin. Simultaneously a group of innovators, the Cubists, decided to abandon portraiture and invent a new world of appearances determined only by the exigencies of composition. In due course Cubism was succeeded by Purism. Abstract art made its way from the painter's studio to the architect's office. Design once more conformed to a model, but now it was no longer nature that supplied the criterion of realism, but the highly artificial universe of modern technology. The circle was closed.

When one speaks of 'modern art' one thinks in the first place of the kind of architecture that had assimilated the new technology within its formal principle of construction. Not accidentally this approach was pioneered in America, where engineering was directly translated into an architecture literally resting on iron and steel. "The incongruity of building skyscrapers in Chicago and covering them with decorations from European pattern books was apparent."[5] It was plainly obvious to Louis Sullivan (1856–1924) who dispensed with ornamentation in putting up his office buildings, and to Frank Lloyd Wright (1867–1959) who applied similar principles to domestic architecture. From the United States, the new style invented by the Chicago School spread to Vienna, where Adolf Loos (1870–1933) introduced it from 1896 onwards, and to Paris, where Auguste Perret (1874–1954) and Tony Garnier (1869–1948) worked along similar lines with reinforced concrete. At first these innovators had to contend with the craze for ornamentation associated with the then fashionable Art Nouveau style typified by the work of the Catalan architect Antoni Gaudí (1852–1926); but by the time Loos published his essay *Ornament and Crime* in 1908, the battle had been won and Art Nouveau had petered out. The rationalist Purism of the Chicago School was translated into a Central European idiom by the German architect Peter Behrens (1868–1940) who in 1906 became chief adviser to the Allgemeine Elektrizitätsgesellschaft, and ultimately into the *Bauhaus* style pioneered by Behrens' pupils Walter Gropius (1883–1969) and Mies van der Rohe (b. 1886). The *Bauhaus* in its creative phase took shape in 1919, but its principles were anticipated by Behrens and others well before 1914. All concerned were agreed in holding that good design, whether applied to office building or to private dwellings, demanded a radical break with the kind of ornamentation associated with Art Nouveau.[6]

The general principle underlying the new approach was simple enough: art and engineering, which in the nineteenth century had been kept in separate compartments, were to be brought together again. What came to be known as 'functionalism' could be summed up in the thesis that anything designed to serve its purpose would turn out to be aesthetically pleasing as well. This rather sweeping claim made no allowance for individual success or failure in designing structures that were both functionally correct and in tune with the persistent human craving for harmony. The masterpieces of the new style were the work of distinguished artists who had somehow managed to retain beauty while dispensing with useless decoration. The extreme statement of the new doctrine, Otto Wagner's (1841–1918) affirmation that "nothing that is not useful can be beautiful", begged too many questions. But functionalism cleared the ground for what was later to become the specifically modern type of industrial design. By the time Gropius, Le Corbusier and others had acclimatized the new style in the 1920s, its general principles had won wide acceptance. To complicate matters further, Charles Édouard Jeanneret, better known as Le Corbusier (b. 1887), was Swiss by birth, a Frenchman by adoption and a painter-sculptor as well as the creator of revolutionary new designs in architecture. That is to say, he belongs to the history of modern art, and specifically to the Cubist school from which he drew his original inspiration, before championing an even more abstract style which he and his friends termed Purism. This event took place in November 1918, a few hours before the official termination of the First World War. The new model in architecture was intended to make the most of the technological environment as it then stood.

The earlier emergence of Cubism in painting was likewise no accident. Its pioneers, Pablo Picasso (b. 1881) and Georges Braque (1882–1963), took up around 1906 where Cézanne and other Impressionists had left off. In their later development the picture became what a member of the school, Juan Gris (1887–1927), called "coloured surface architecture". The 1900s were a time of remarkable vitality in painting, mostly centred on Paris. Besides Cézanne, who left the scene in 1906, there were Braque, Picasso, Matisse, Rouault, Utrillo, Derain, Vlaminck, Léger and others, all hard at work along lines that were then quite novel. These were also the years when the Dutchman Piet Mondrian (1872–1944) created a style of his own; when two important groups of German expressionist painters formed the schools respectively known as *Die Brücke* (Dresden) and the *Blaue Reiter* (Munich); when the Rumanian sculptor Constantin Brancusi (1876–1957) made the obligatory visit to Paris in 1904 and shortly thereafter effected a notable departure from the neo-classicism of his teachers; and when the Russians appeared on the scene in the persons of Kasimir Malevich (1878–1935), Vassily Kandinsky (1866-1944) and others. The formation in 1911 of the *Blaue Reiter* group by Kandinsky and Franz Marc (1880–1916) established a link between the German and the Russian modernists, the latter being joined on the eve of 1914 by Vladimir Tatlin (b. 1885) and Alexander Rodchenko (b. 1891) who after the October Revolution tried with some success to implant what they called Constructivism. The Russians were among the pioneers of the modern movement. As early as 1913 Malevich painted pictures which consisted of a black square or circle on a white ground and in 1918 he painted 'white on white' in a fashion not seen again until the 1950s. In addition there were the Italian Futurists already mentioned, the Norwegian Edvard Munch (1863–1944), and the Belgian James Ensor (1860–1949). The Van Gogh memorial exhibition held in Paris in 1901 may in retrospect be said to have inaugurated the new wave, but Munch had already been to Paris in 1889 and his work had created a scandal in Berlin as early as 1892. Around 1905, when the *Brücke* group came together in Dresden, on the heels of yet another Van Gogh exhibition, Expressionism may be said to have arrived on the scene, thereafter to draw its inspiration from the violence of an age that relegated academic painting to the attic. The *Bauhaus* – originally a pre-war arts-and-crafts school drastically reorganized by Walter Gropius in Weimar in 1919, and subsequently located in Dessau – drew all these threads together. Mies van der Rohe worked there, and so did Kandinsky, Paul Klee, Feininger, Moholy-Nagy and others. The architects and designers set the pace, but painters and sculptors formed part of the ensemble. The *Bauhaus* manifesto of 1919 explicitly rejected the distinction between arts and crafts. "The artist is the craftsman intensified. . . . Together we will conceive and create the new building of the future in which all will be fused in a single image: architecture and sculpture and painting. . . . "[7]

It is arguable that the break with the past was less radical than it appeared at the time both to the innovators and the public. The principal trends in the art of the new century had their predecessors in the earlier period: Cubism in Cézanne (1839–1906), Expressionism in Van Gogh (1853–1890), Surrealism in Rimbaud (1854–91) and Lautréamont (1846–70).[8] The Swiss painter and innovator Paul Klee (1879–1940) and the American painter Lyonel Feininger (1871–1956) were born early enough to span the generational gap between the first modernists and the *Bauhaus* style. Both had been to Paris in 1912, where they found the world of art "agog with Cubism".[9] It has been suggested that Picasso and his friends took as their guide-line the advice Cézanne had given to a young painter, namely to look at nature in terms of spheres, cones and cylinders. Whether Cézanne meant to be taken quite literally is another matter. His authority was invoked by a new group of artists who no longer aimed at representation in the Impressionist manner. Instead of merely copying they were going to construct, relying on the mind's eye rather than on actual sight. Of Picasso's celebrated still life of a violin (1912) it has been said that it represents a return to the pre-classical, Egyptian, principle of drawing the object from an angle which displays its characteristic form most clearly.[10] The artist constructs the picture out of parts that are present to his reflective mind, which is more or less what the first artists did before such a thing as perspective had been invented. What matters is no longer the imitation of nature, but the manifestation of thought and feeling, a principle common to Expressionism and Cubism alike. A sculptor such as Ernst Barlach (1870–1938) alienated conservative opinion by representing an aged beggar woman with a cloak drawn over her face in such a manner that nothing but her misery was allowed to capture the eye of the beholder. Not surprisingly, his works were banned by the National Socialist dictatorship. Representations of human misery and ugliness were not wanted by a regime whose leaders had been brought up on Nietzsche's philosophy. For it is a mistake to suppose that only bourgeois philistines were shocked by the Expressionist emphasis on the ugly side of existence. The neo-pagan worship of life, an essential element of the Fascist creed, was likewise incompatible with everything the Expressionists stood for.

But this is to anticipate. The pre-1914 breakthrough into modernity did not at first arouse violent emotions on the part of a public whose basic certainties had not yet been shattered by political earthquakes. A certain amount of head-shaking was only to be expected when the Expressionist painters burst on the scene, and the same applies to the radical experiments in music then undertaken by Stravinsky (1882–1971), Ravel (1875–1937) and Debussy (1862–1918) in Paris; by Schönberg (1874–1951) and his pupils Anton Webern (1883–1945) and

Alban Berg (1885–1935) in Vienna; and by Bela Bartók (1881–1945) in Budapest. Stravinsky's *Fire Bird* (1910), *Petrushka* (1912) and *The Rite of Spring* (1913) encountered the sort of resistance to be expected by a composer who had broken with classical models, but his orgiastic music also drew applause from a public inclined to make some allowance for Russian primitivism. It has been remarked that the distinctive feature of Russian history is the lack of anything corresponding to the Renaissance, and the consequent indifference of Russian artists to the preoccupation with personal feeling characteristic of most European art from the sixteenth century to the twentieth. The obverse of this coin is the treatment of art as primitive ritual, and in Stravinsky's case this natural bent was allied to a sophisticated understanding of what a modern audience might crave for.[11] Schönberg, Bartók, Hindemith (1895–1963) and Debussy arrived at similar results by a more complex route, against the background of a tired romanticism which had ceased to convey hope to a sick civilization, and was duly replaced by a pessimism foreshadowing catastrophes yet to come. The formal expression of the new mood was the dissociation of harmony and melody from rhythm. "Both the pandemonium of Stravinsky's *Rite of Spring* and the whisper of Debussy's *Voiles* deprive music of the sense of motion from one point to another."[12]

Any consideration of the modern movement in art leads inescapably to questions of value which are of concern to philosophy. For whatever the practitioners may imagine themselves to be doing, their work is intimately related to the social order which has nurtured them. To say that the meaning of pre-1914 modernism disclosed itself in 1914–18 is to make a statement of fact which is at the same time a judgement on European culture. An assessment of this kind inevitably sounds far-fetched to artists who in their daily work are concerned with technical problems of writing, drawing or composition, but it is not on this account to be dismissed as irrelevant. The difficulty consists in establishing a precise link between formal analysis and wider considerations which are ultimately philosophical. "Analysis of an aesthetic experience may lead down through proportion and harmony to patches of pigment, which may in turn be dissolved into their chemical constituents. To a purely analytic thinker it must remain a sheer mystery that these products of analysis should have anything to do with intrinsic value."[13] The mystery is not removed by an unmediated employment of socio-political concepts, for what needs to be explained is just how and why a given trend in the arts comes to be associated with one particular social, political or religious current rather than another. It is easy to see why autocratic rulers will favour a monumental style. It is more difficult to trace the link between Malevich's new manner in painting and Mies van der Rohe's sketch for an all-glass office building twenty storeys high in 1919. But such connections do exist, and their analysis is the business of the art historian.[14] Similarly, there is no arbitrariness involved in treating Austrian musical composition, before and after 1914, against the background of a collapsing culture. Of Arnold Schönberg it has been said with truth that he "was a Jew and in that sense an isolated spirit".[15] It has also been observed by the same historian that Schönberg's invention of the twelve-tone or serial technique was "at once a technical and a spiritual necessity".[16] The technical need arose from a feeling that the traditional tonal basis of European music appeared to be exhausted; the spiritual content relates to the fact that Schönberg's music is fundamentally religious, a circumstance evident enough from his unfinished opera *Moses und Aron*, in which the composer identifies himself with Moses: as Freud had done in his own manner when he undertook the laborious task of creating the new depth psychology. Bartók for his part was very much a Hungarian patriot. With Debussy and Ravel we are in an altogether different world: that of the French musical tradition which around 1900 drew some inspiration from Impressionist painting and Symbolist poetry, but whose roots went back all the way to the eighteenth century and even to the Renaissance. It has been possible to say of Delius (1862–1934) and Elgar (1857–1934) that they composed in the German Romantic manner because England had forgotten her own musical tradition. This kind of interplay was then less common than it became in a later age, when something like a European consciousness had begun to replace the unquestioning adherence to a specific national inheritance. Part of the difficulty with our theme is due to the circumstance that tendencies common to the whole of Europe had to be translated into the local idiom, and indeed were experienced by artists and public alike as issues peculiar to the national tradition. Again, the turning away from humanism and romanticism occurred simultaneously in poetry, painting and music, but it took some time before all concerned became aware of the fact that they were engaged in the momentous enterprise of creating a new European style in the arts.

The pattern is similar in literature. Major innovators such as Thomas Mann (1875–1955), Hermann Hesse (1877–1962), André Gide (1869–1951), Paul Valéry (1871–1945), Marcel Proust (1871–1922) and Joseph Conrad (1857–1924) made their debut before 1914, and indeed transmitted to the post-war generation something of the nineteenth-century culture which at its peak had produced Ibsen (1826–1906), Strindberg (1849–1912) and Chekhov (1860–1904). W.B. Yeats (1865–1939) belongs both to the nineteenth century and to its successor. The same may be said of Paul Claudel (1868–1955). Thomas Mann's novel *Buddenbrooks* was published in 1901, his novella *Tonio Kröger* in 1903, *Death in Venice* in 1913. The Hungarian literary critic Georg Lukács (1885–1971), later to become an influential figure in the European

Communist movement, began his career as an admirer of Mann's work which may fairly be described as the consummation of German bourgeois Romanticism. Rainer Maria Rilke (1875–1926) and Franz Kafka (1883–1924) altered the style of Central European poetry and prose in a manner recognizably inherited from the later Romantics. Gide pointed the way for Proust who between 1905 and 1911 drafted his great work, the first volume of which appeared in 1913. D.H.Lawrence published *Sons and Lovers* in 1913, *The Rainbow* in 1915. James Joyce's story collection *Dubliners* made its appearance in 1914, and work on *Ulysses* (1922) was begun in the same year. In short, the modern movement was already well under way when the 1914–18 war disrupted the culture whose internal strains had given birth to what was specifically new and startling in the work of these writers. They became major figures in the 1920s because their sensibility was attuned to the crisis of European civilization, but their roots were in the society whose decomposition they portrayed.

The principal change in literature during this period is the decline of the novel as social portraiture, and the rise of a type of fiction whose hero, or anti-hero, broods on the human predicament. Thomas Mann's *Buddenbrooks* was still cast in the ancient mould: at once a solid bourgeois family chronicle and a comedy of social manners. By the time James Joyce (1882–1941) and Virginia Woolf (1882–1941) had won public recognition, the avant-garde had abandoned the novel of manners to the lending-library public. Proust's work falls somewhere between Mann's chronicle and the internal dialogue of *Ulysses* with its by now familiar stream-of-consciousness technique. *À la recherche du temps perdu* is the work of a recluse who from the sanctum of his cork-lined bedroom describes the decay of the aristocracy.[17] The subject-matter is traditional; the style represents an innovation, being derived from Proust's theory of memory as a bottomless well, from which there may be dredged up chance associations more real than the original experience later evoked by casual reminiscences. The story is narrated in the first person by the central character, who is quite simply Proust himself. His memory enables him to take possession of his past life, which happens to be intertwined with the complex existence of Parisian high society: a decomposing culture much given to introspection. He is still writing about man in a social context, not just about the individual locked up within himself, and to that extent he descends from Stendhal and Flaubert. But what really matters to the narrator is his own subjectivity, the unfolding of his memory and the retrospective possession of experiences no longer forgotten. Stylistically, there occurs an imposition upon one another of different impressions: the trick is to see them all simultaneously. To that extent Proust is a predecessor of Joyce in whom the subjective element has become even more pronounced. *Ulysses* is the story of a single day, 16 June 1904, in the lives of a group of people in

Dublin, but it is also the account of a spiritual journey. Virginia Woolf's *The Waves* (1931) belongs to the same category.[18]

Can one point to a common feature inherent in all this experimentation? If everything that occurred after 1900 is indiscriminately lumped together as being constitutive of something called 'the modern world', the intellectual revolution in physics traced in an earlier chapter falls under the same heading as the emergence of what has been described as 'the film age'.[19] Once embarked on this route one may try to establish a link between Cubism and Einstein's non-Euclidean four-dimensional space–time continuum. On the whole it seems advisable to avoid such extravagances. The case of psychoanalysis is different, if only because the writers of the Surrealist school – André Breton being the best known – were influenced by Freud. What fascinated them in the first place was the new prominence allotted to dreams and other manifestations of the unconscious; but the more philosophically minded among them appear also to have perceived the significance of Freud's attempt to investigate the level of psychic activity which lies halfway between the physiological and the moral. The notion of mental integration forms a bridge between the pursuit of health and the attainment of morality. It was possible to sense this without taking over the entire apparatus of Freudian depth psychology. It was likewise advantageous to adopt Marxian insights into the role of ideology as a phenomenon independent of individual volition. Once this had been done, criticism disposed of an arsenal of concepts which spanned the distance separating traditional aesthetics from modern sociology.[20]

Marx and Freud made their major impact on literature after 1918, a topic to which we shall have to return in another context. The *Surrealist Manifesto* was issued by Breton and others in 1924, by which time the Russian Revolution had popularized Marxism, while simultaneously a number of transplanted Central Europeans had begun to acquaint the artistic and literary vanguard in Paris – then the unquestioned centre of the arts – with Freudian insights into the operation of the unconscious. So far as modernism around 1910 is concerned, we have to look for indigenous sources. It has often been observed that a historian of the modern movement in French poetry would have to go back at least as far as Charles Baudelaire (1821–67), not to mention Arthur Rimbaud (1854–91) and Jules Laforgue (1860–87). There was no corresponding development in England, where the *poète maudit*, living in his garret and damning the bourgeoisie, was a rare phenomenon, at any rate until the 1920s. French Symbolism reached the British Isles by way of W.B. Yeats and the expatriate American T.S.Eliot who in 1911 wrote a poem so novel in tone that he could not get it published until 1915: 'The Love-Song of J. Alfred Prufrock.' Thus around 1910 something new crystallized in the poetry of the youthful Eliot and the mature Yeats, and that something was clearly neither Victorian nor Romantic. The proximate source of this stylistic innovation was Symbolism, an importation from France where a mood of alienation from the official culture had set in a generation earlier. Between 1910 and 1920 the *poète maudit* gave place to an outwardly more reassuring, but actually quite subversive figure: the writer whose spiritual exile had become so much part of his existence that he was able to perform a routine job while composing a kind of poetry that could be appreciated only by his fellow-artists. Mallarmé's disciple Valéry, working in a newspaper agency for many years; Eliot gracing a publisher's office; or Wallace Stevens, to his death the respectable vice-president of a New England insurance company, represent a kind of internal emigration. Inwardly withdrawn from their daily surroundings, they go through the motions of respectable citizenship, while their poetry is selfconsciously addressed to an invisible elite of kindred spirits. What matters is not life but the poem, and the more remote its style from what passes for reality, the better.[21] This kind of withdrawal stands in marked contrast to the attitude of the representative essayists, poets, novelists and dramatists before and after 1914: Thomas Hardy, G.B.Shaw, Rudyard Kipling, E.M.Forster, Hilaire Belloc and G.K.Chesterton in Britain; Anatole France, Maurice Barrès, Romain Rolland, Jules Romains, Georges Duhamel and Roger Martin du Gard in France; Thomas and Heinrich Mann in Germany; Maxim Gorky in Russia. It prefigures the even more radical alienation of the artistic vanguard after 1945.

So far as style can be distinguished from content, the major change during the period under review is the turning away from the notion of art as something that is faithful to nature. The post-Impressionist artist abandons the portraiture of reality and expresses his basic intuition by the deliberate deformation of natural objects. The outcome is an 'ugly' art which discards pictorial values in painting, agreeable images in poetry and melody in music.[22] The aim is to shock and startle, to renounce the sentimental mood of the later nineteenth century, and to create new structures purified from the emotions. Whether this tendency should be described as 'formalism' depends on the view one takes of the reciprocity between form and content. In Croce's *Estetica* (1902) their identity is stressed, to the point of asserting that "the aesthetic fact is form and nothing but form". For Croce, form is "expression-intuition", which amounts to saying that it is simply another term for the work of art. If this is accepted, then what is called form may equally well be termed content.[23] Valéry, with his "there is nothing but form", appears to be saying the same thing, but is actually in opposition to Croce, since for him "content" disappears altogether, or is dismissed as "impure form". Eliot seldom refers to the topic and appears to take it for granted that, in the perfect work of art, form and content are identical. His

The Waste Land and Joyce's *Ulysses*, both published in 1922, mark the definite emergence of modernism in literature; they are the counterpart of Schönberg's twelve-tone system and of post-Impressionism in painting and sculpture. The conventional means of expression having broken down, Expressionism and Surrealism invade writing, as Symbolism had done before 1914. Kafka's work adheres to the same general pattern. His subject is the absurdity of existence, not the psychology of the representative individual character. The decay of the psychological novel corresponds to the dissolution of reality in the visual arts. At a later stage it will be shown that these tendencies – implicit before 1914 and explicit thereafter – reflect a crisis of civilization which entered the general consciousness during and after the Second World War.

At the same time it is well to bear in mind that the writers whose work was acclaimed by a small avant-garde in the 1920s, and by the general public after 1945, belonged to a generation whose outlook had been formed before 1914. Of Joyce it has been said with truth that "in his tacit political assumptions he belonged to an age that had never experienced totalitarianism or total war".[24] Much of his work, notably his collection of short stories, *Dubliners*, had been either published or at least drafted before 1914. *A Portrait of the Artist as a Young Man* was serialized in a small British magazine, the *Egoist*, in 1914–15, and around the same time Joyce began to map out *Ulysses*, the action of which is laid in the Dublin of 1904 – a sleepy provincial town on which the modern world had barely begun to impinge. The book is shot through with borrowings from popular culture and its central characters belong to the lower middle class from which Joyce had himself emerged before becoming an internationally known writer. The self-consciously modernist element is much stronger in his last work, *Finnegans Wake*, which most readers found incomprehensible and which discerning critics have come to view as a grandiose aberration. "In *Ulysses* language is already beginning to work loose from its hinges; in *Finnegans Wake* it breaks free completely, and words take on a capricious life of their own."[25] The significance of Joyce's early work lies in the fact that it evokes the kind of stable provincial life which was the principal casualty of the age of mass production and mass communication. By contrast, *Ulysses* introduced a new technique, the interior monologue, which was to revolutionize fiction from the 1920s onward. It also contributed to the modern awareness that the world we live in is dependent on linguistic conventions tacitly accepted by everyone. This curious medley of archaism and modernism is just what constitutes the originality of Joyce. He was capable of effecting a stylistic revolution because he was still rooted in the old world that came to a violent end in 1914. It is arguable that he never again wrote anything as good as *Dubliners*, but the stylistic innovation came later.

I have permitted myself the liberty of describing *Finnegans Wake* as an aberration on account of its incomprehensibility so far as the ordinary reader is concerned. But in dealing with a writer of genius one must be careful to specify the peculiarity of his work, even if one is unable to derive satisfaction from some parts of it. As Richard Ellmann has pointed out in his biography of Joyce, there is a close connection between his earliest and his latest writings. In the story *The Dead*, which was written in 1907 and published in the collection titled *Dubliners*, the relationship of the living to the dead is the central theme. It recurs in *Ulysses*, but it is in *Finnegans Wake* that the topic which had haunted Joyce all his life finds its ultimate consecration in the closing section of the work. Here Anna Livia Plurabelle, the river of life, flows towards the sea, which is death: the fresh water passing into the salt, a bitter ending, to quote Ellmann. The movement, moreover, is circular, linking the end with the beginning. Joyce is the central figure in the avant-garde literature of his time – in the English-speaking world anyway – because he worked out an artistic form appropriate to the post-religious consciousness of an age which was about to discover the ultimate pointlessness of existence. It is significant that he was influenced by Vico, whom he discovered during the years he spent in Italy. The circular movement of life, the return to the origins, was an aspect of Irish nationalism, a movement for which Joyce had some sympathy, and whose political triumph he was destined to witness. But it also symbolized an occurrence in the general European consciousness of his age which was genuinely an end, not the start of something new. Joyce had begun his literary career as an admiring follower of Ibsen, but his work testifies to a growing sense of disillusionment with mankind. In this he was not alone, but it was the peculiar quality of his genius to endow this feeling of alienation and exile with a power that transcends its accidental personal origins.

NOTES

1 R.G.Collingwood, *Speculum Mentis* (Oxford: Clarendon Press, 1924, 1946; New York: Oxford University Press, 1924), p. 60.
2 Arnold Hauser, *The Social History of Art* (London: Routledge & Kegan Paul, 1962; New York: Knopf, 1951), vol. IV, *passim*.
3 *Ibid.*, p. 78.
4 Cf. *Remembrance of Things Past*, tr. by C.K.Scott Moncrieff (London: Chatto & Windus; New York: Random House, 1927–32), *passim*; George D.Painter, *Marcel Proust: A Biography* (London: Chatto & Windus; Boston: Atlantic Monthly Press, Little, Brown, 1965), *passim*.
5 E.H.Gombrich, *The Story of Art* (London and New York: Phaidon Press, 1950 and 1967), p. 424.
6 *The Styles of European Art*, introduced by Herbert Read (London: Thames and Hudson, 1965; New York: Harry N.Abrams, 1967), pp. 416 ff.

7 *Ibid.*, p. 438. For architecture see especially Peter Blake, *Mies van der Rohe* (London and Baltimore: Penguin Books, 1964, 1966), *passim.*
8 Hauser, *op. cit.*, p. 214.
9 Gombrich, *op. cit.*, p. 440.
10 *Ibid.*, p. 436.
11 Wilfrid Mellers, *Man and his Music.* vol. IV (London: Barrie & Rockliff, 1962, 1969; New York: Oxford University Press, 1958), pp. 198–9.
12 *Ibid.*, p. 200.
13 G.R.G.Mure, *Retreat from Truth* (Oxford: Blackwell; New York: Fernhill House, 1958), pp. 173–4.
14 Blake, *op. cit.*, p. 28.
15 Mellers, *op. cit.*, p. 181.
16 *Ibid.*, p. 186.
17 Paul West, *The Modern Novel* (London: Hutchinson, 1963 and 1967; New York: Humanities Press, 2nd ed., 1969), vol. I, pp. 18 ff.
18 *Ibid.*, p. 30. For a detailed analysis of Proust's work see Harry Levin, *The Gates of Horn* (New York: Oxford University Press, 1963), pp. 372 ff. For Joyce see Richard Ellmann's magisterial study *James Joyce* (London and New York: Oxford University Press, 1966), *passim.* See also the same author's *Yeats: The Man and the Masks* (London: Faber & Faber, 1961; New York: Dutton, 1958) for another aspect of Anglo-Irish literature.
19 Hauser, *op. cit.*, pp. 214 ff.
20 Ernst Fischer, *Art Against Ideology* (London: Allen Lane, 1969; New York: George Braziller, 1970); *The Necessity of Art: A Marxist Approach* (London and New York: Penguin Books, 1963, 1964). On the relevance of the new psychology for the understanding of human personality, see "Freud and Psychoanalysis", in George Mosse, *The Culture of Western Europe* (London: Murray, 1963; Chicago: Rand McNally, 1961), pp. 263 ff.
21 G.S.Fraser, *The Modern Writer and his World* (London: Penguin Books, 1964; New York: Praeger Publishers, 1965), pp. 34 ff., 96 ff.
22 Hauser, *op. cit.*, pp. 217 ff.
23 René Wellek, *Concepts of Criticism* (New Haven, Conn. and London: Yale University Press, 1964), pp. 56–9. Richard Wollheim, *Art and its Objects* (New York: Harper & Row, 1968; London; Penguin Books, 1970), pp. 52 ff. and *passim.*
24 John Gross, *James Joyce* (New York: The Viking Press, 1970), p. 4.
25 *Ibid.*, p. 75.

PART TWO

CHAPTER 7

WAR AND REVOLUTION 1914–19

In an earlier chapter it was remarked that the conventional periodiza-
tion of history takes no account of technological change, or of those
subtler processes which signal the advent of a major social mutation.
A related inconvenience stems from the national approach common
until lately to most European historians. On any reckoning, the wars
of 1914–18 and 1939–45 were overwhelmingly the most important
events in European history during the first half of the twentieth century.
These wars, and the social upheavals they brought in their train, revolutionized society and simultaneously terminated the age of Europe's
global predominance. Their unintended consequences included the
Russian Revolution, the liquidation of the British Empire, the partition
of Germany and the emergence of supra-national organizations from
the wreckage brought about by the conflicting aims of sovereign nation
states. Yet their history tends to be written from the national standpoint,
even though the author in question may be aware of the parochialism
inseparable from such an approach. Similarly, the twenty-years' armistice from 1919 to 1939 is rarely described in terms appropriate to the
subject. In what follows an attempt will be made to transcend the
national framework and to see Europe as a whole. We shall likewise be
concerned with the political upheavals occasioned by the two great
European wars, as much as with the military operations preceding
them. Finally, some space will be devoted to those technological changes
which the wars helped to accelerate.

The last-mentioned topic is in some ways the easiest to deal with,
for the simple reason that technical progress can be measured and
quantified. It can also be related to distinct events occurring on definite
calendar dates. The Wright brothers, two American inventors originally
associated in the bicycle repair business, built a power-driven heavier-
than-air machine which was piloted by Orville Wright, and serviced
by his brother Wilbur, on its first successful flight at Kitty Hawk, on
17 December 1903. On 12 September 1908 an aeroplane established a
new record by remaining in the air for an hour and a quarter. The
French aviator Louis Blériot crossed the Channel in one of these new

machines in 1909. By 1920, after years of rapid development during the 1914–18 war, an aircraft flew for the first time at a speed of 100 miles an hour. In 1945 a jet plane passed the sound barrier at about 700 miles per hour, and by 1970 a spacecraft moved at 25,000 miles per hour. This is the sort of progress everyone can understand. Likewise there is no disputing the fact that in 1914–18 the most lethal weapon at the disposal of the belligerents was a bomb that might kill a few hundred people if aimed at a suitable target, whereas in 1945 the first and still rather primitive atom bomb wiped out something like a hundred thousand victims at Hiroshima, and in 1970 some eight million people could be killed, and millions of others injured by radiation, if a single hydrogen bomb landed on New York, Moscow, Tokyo, London or Paris. In 1920 wireless communication was in its infancy, and as late as 1945 there were only 60,000 television sets in the British Isles. By the summer of 1969, a thousand million people all over the world saw and heard an American astronaut set foot on the surface of the moon. These circumstances provide the frame of reference for our understanding of what technology has done to traditional ways of life during the twentieth century.

In turning to the political landscape it becomes rather more difficult to quantify one's generalizations; yet certain basic facts do stand out. In 1900 the British government controlled the destinies of about one-quarter of the human race. Britain had no allies, because she needed none; the Royal Navy policed the oceans; Germany was not as yet a real menace; France had long ceased to be one; Russia for all its huge size was too backward to be taken seriously and in 1904–5 underwent a military humiliation at the hands of Japan. The United States, a recent newcomer to the imperial game, was still for the most part busy with internal problems. Yet the peak of British power had already been passed, for America and Germany had gained a lead in the newer industries, notably chemicals and electricity. Britain's short-lived world hegemony in the later nineteenth century was a function of her own industrial leadership, French defeat, German disunity and American inexperience.[1] From the 1880s onward, and more rapidly after 1900, these factors ceased to operate, and on the eve of 1914 the German challenge had become sufficiently grave for Britain to be drawn into an informal alliance with France and Russia. The 1914–18 war produced a hollow victory; that of 1939–45 brought America and Russia to the forefront as hegemonial powers with whom Britain could no longer compete. On the Continent of Europe, Germany, France and Italy emerged from the two holocausts so weakened as to be, for the first time in their respective histories, willing to cooperate and even to shed some part of their sovereignty, Germany having also lost one-third of her territory and the whole of her recently (1871) gained national unity. These cataclysmic changes resulted from the collapse of the British-controlled world system which in 1900 still looked remarkably solid. Its dissolution was both cause and consequence of the two wars which permanently wrecked Europe's global pre-eminence.[2]

The 1914–18 war came when it did owing to an accident – the assassination on 28 June 1914, of the Archduke Francis Ferdinand, and the consequent Austrian ultimatum to Serbia: an ultimatum formulated in terms which made war inevitable. But the storm clouds had been gathering for years, and in Berlin at least there was a growing disposition to believe that time was working against Germany, if only because her only reliable ally, Austria-Hungary, was visibly falling to pieces under the stress of national antagonisms. There was on the German side a fatalistic acceptance of the need for a showdown with Russia, a firm conviction that France could be knocked out in a matter of weeks, and some hope of keeping Britain neutral, notwithstanding the growing antagonism fed by Germany's naval building programme. The German Chief of Staff, Helmuth von Moltke, merely translated these feelings into words when in 1913 he told his Austrian colleague that a European war was bound to come sooner or later, and that ultimately the struggle would be one between Teuton and Slav.[3] On the opposing side, Britain and Russia were only very loosely allied, by way of their respective commitments to France, and the tensions between them went so deep that in the absence of the German menace they would have gone their separate ways:

No Power of the Triple Entente wanted a European upheaval; all three would have liked to turn their backs on Europe and to pursue their imperial expansion in Asia and Africa. Germany, on the other hand, had come to feel that she could expand her overseas empire only after she had destroyed the European Balance of Power; and Austria-Hungary wanted a Balkan war in order to survive at all.[4]

There is no proof that the German General Staff deliberately timed war for August 1914, but there is every evidence that its coming was welcomed by the Emperor and his advisers as the only way out of an increasingly intolerable situation. Germany and Austria-Hungary must strike before the threatening expansion of Russian manpower got under way: that was the sum and substance of their collective wisdom. If a preventive war involved France and Belgium, and if in consequence Britain abandoned the posture of neutrality, that was too bad, but the risk had to be taken. It was in this spirit that the European governments drew nearer to the abyss. The Austrian ultimatum to Serbia on 23 July 1914, merely served as detonator.

Underlying this configuration there were conflicting aims which could not be resolved by diplomacy: Germany's bid for world power,

Britain's determination to maintain her naval supremacy, the incompatibility of German-Austrian and Russian ambitions in the Balkans and in Turkey. In so far as the German government after 1900 possessed something like a considered policy, it rested on the hope of keeping Britain neutral in the Continental war which everyone saw coming. From the British standpoint this would have amounted to letting Germany become the hegemonial power in Europe and in the Near East as well. There were those who regarded this prospect as preferable to letting Russia become paramount in Eastern Europe and the Balkans, but when the crunch came the Liberal Cabinet of Asquith, Grey, Haldane, Lloyd George and Churchill acted on the advice of its permanent officials: Germany must not be allowed to crush France and Russia, for it would then become impossible to restrain her imperialist appetites and her determination to challenge Britain's maritime supremacy. For similar reasons, Franco-German reconciliation – an improbability in any case – must not be encouraged, lest it lead to the formation of a Continental bloc impervious to British influence. From 1908 onwards the acceleration of Germany's naval building programme served to prepare public opinion in both countries for the crash that came in 1914. Yet the British choice between Germany and Russia hinged on considerations which made more sense to the Foreign Office than to the average backbencher, let alone the proverbial man in the street: Russia must be sustained because her defeat, coupled with that of France, would make Germany all-powerful in Europe. This kind of logic swayed Sir Edward Grey and his colleagues; it could not be publicly avowed, and for this reason there could be no formal alliance with France and Russia. Both were repeatedly warned not to count on British support, just as the Germans were warned not to gamble on British neutrality. In point of fact Germany's rulers were committed to a military strategy which entailed an invasion of France through Belgium, and consequently the near-certainty of British intervention. They would have liked Britain to stay neutral, but in the final analysis they were resigned to her entry into the great European war they had come to regard as inevitable.

Once war had broken out, it developed a momentum of its own, and so did the process of formulating political aims. These were necessarily framed in ideological language and thus concealed the fact that Germany had gone to war for the purpose of becoming the dominant power in Europe, and that the Allies were fighting to deny her this goal. What the Germans really wanted was an impregnable *Mitteleuropa*: a German-controlled bloc in the centre of Europe, plus a subservient Turkey and vast annexations in Africa.[5] Austria-Hungary fought for self-preservation and a share of influence in the Balkans and Turkey. Russia was officially trying to protect Serbia, and actually concerned to obtain control of Constantinople and the Dardanelles. The Western Powers were fighting to deny Germany the means to redraw the map of Europe, and France was also intent on recovering Alsace-Lorraine. Italy, having belatedly entered the war in May 1915, saw Austria-Hungary as her principal opponent, and annexations in Istria, Dalmatia and the Tyrol as the goal to be pursued. There was no way of reducing all these aims to a common denominator, although the British and French tried hard to make an issue of German militarism, while the Germans insisted that they were waging a defensive war against a coalition of hostile powers plotting the downfall of everything German. The United States only came in during the opening months of 1917, and then on the issue of the 'freedom of the seas', which had been challenged by Germany's proclamation of unrestricted submarine warfare. The Germans in fact, with their customary obtuseness, drove America into war when it would have been in their interest to cultivate Woodrow Wilson's hankering for the role of peace-maker, to which he owed his re-election as President in November 1916. Even so, the United States government, having declared war on Imperial Germany on 2 April 1917, did not formally ally itself with the Anglo-French Entente; it preferred to come in as an 'Associated Power' with a number of mental reservations on the subject of a future European settlement. Meanwhile, Russia underwent two revolutions in 1917: one in March when the Romanov dynasty fell, the second in November when the Bolsheviks took over, on a platform of immediate peace without annexations. By then Britain and France – now personified by Lloyd George and Clemenceau – were committed to ending the war by delivering a knock-out blow to Germany.

The Germans for their part were encouraged by their military victories to hold out for terms which could only be imposed by force: not merely a German-controlled *Mitteleuropa* centred on an Austro-German customs union, but military control of Belgium, the annexation of France's remaining iron-ore fields, a Polish satellite state, the detachment of the Ukraine from Russia and the cession of Russian territory in the Baltic as far as Riga. Some of these aims had already been formulated before the war by leading industrialists and financiers who counted as moderates by comparison with the Pan-Germans; others were incorporated in an informal programme drawn up by the Imperial Chancellor, Bethmann Hollweg, in September 1914, when for a moment it looked as though Germany had won the war; still others were sponsored by the German High Command, whose nominee, a faceless bureaucrat called Michaelis, succeeded Bethmann Hollweg in July 1917. Some of the more lunatic Pan-German notions, such as the cession of French territory and the expulsion of its inhabitants in favour of German settlers, had the personal support of the Emperor.

The official German line was more moderate: it merely called for the vassalization of France and Belgium, the break-up of Russia and a German colonial empire in Central Africa.[6] These aims had the active backing not only of Krupp, Stinnes, Thyssen and other representatives of heavy industry: they were sponsored by men such as Gustav Stresemann, Walter Rathenau and Matthias Erzberger, who subsequently played a leading role during the short-lived Weimar Republic. Nor were they effectively resisted by the Social Democrats, who had voted for war credits on 4 August 1914, and thereafter contented themselves with urging moderation in dealing with France and Belgium. The liberation of non-Russian people from the Muscovite yoke had their support, and indeed the German government had been able to plunge into war in 1914 only because it knew that in a conflict with Russia the Social Democrats could be relied upon to take the patriotic line. As the war lengthened and the pacifists set up a party of their own, the Social Democratic leaders gave their tacit consent to annexationist aims, even though in principle they rejected Pan-Germanism. As for the Conservative and Liberal parties, their support for *Mitteleuropa* never wavered. What this would have portended in practice was not clearly spelled out, if only because the Austrians had reservations about it. In practice it signified the creation of a politico-economic unit strong enough to compete in the world market with Britain, Russia and the United States. As conceived by the German Foreign Office, the General Staff, the magnates of banking and industry and their academic advisers, *Mitteleuropa* would have included not only Austria-Hungary, but Turkey and Bulgaria as well. Thus a German-controlled bloc would have stretched from Antwerp via Hamburg, Vienna and Constantinople to Baghdad; if it also proved possible to detach Finland from Russia, this German Empire would extend from the North Cape to the Persian Gulf.[7]

On the Allied side, the collapse of Tsarism, Russia's withdrawal from the war in 1917–18 and America's simultaneous entry into it, had the effect of producing a clear-cut political and ideological alignment which had been lacking in 1914: the Western democracies, at grips with German militarism, were no longer embarrassed by the awkward alliance with Tsarist Russia. America, Britain and France now presented a common front and a common strategy. Lloyd George and Clemenceau were at one with Wilson in preaching the need to bring Imperial Germany to the ground. Given this aim and the concurrent mobilization of popular sentiment on both sides of the Atlantic, there could no longer be any talk of a compromise peace. If William II and his advisers sought to stimulate an Islamic revolt against Britain throughout the Middle East, Persia and India, the Western democracies for their part enrolled their peoples in what was described as a crusade against militarism. Once Russia had left the war and America had come in, this could be done with some plausibility, even though the British and French were at times embarrassed by the enthusiasm with which the Americans projected anti-imperialism as a war aim. So far as Europe was concerned, agreement was possible. Wilson's Fourteen Points, published on 8 January 1918, outlined a peace settlement whose precondition was total victory in the field. Not only must Germany evacuate Belgium and return Alsace-Lorraine to France: there must be a surrender of all conquered Russian territory, an independent Poland, self-determination for the peoples of Austria-Hungary and the Balkans, an end to secret diplomacy and a League of Nations to supervise the settlement. This statement of aims was of some importance to Russia's new rulers who were obliged to sign a peace treaty at Brest Litovsk on 3 March 1918, whereby the Germans got what they wanted: control of the Baltic States and the Ukraine. Militarily, Germany had won the war in the East, before losing it in the West. Politically, a compromise had become impossible once the Allied war aims had been formulated in the language of liberal democracy, for national self-determination spelled the doom of Austria-Hungary and therewith of German hopes for *Mitteleuropa*. In his own fashion Wilson was no less doctrinaire than Lenin. The Fourteen Points were, among others, a rejoinder to the Bolshevik peace proclamations of November 1917. America and Russia had been launched upon the competitive enterprise of stating the principles on which the post-war order was to rest.

But before the Allies could impose their terms they had to defeat the German Army in the field, an aim which eluded them for years and was only attained in October–November 1918, when a war-weary Germany faced with a mounting flood of American manpower felt obliged to sign an armistice. The four years' butchery preceding this event was chiefly remarkable for the failure of generalship on both sides to keep in step with technical innovations. The machine-gun existed already when war broke out in 1914, but the tank was a later invention, and air power had yet to come into its own. The outcome was deadlock, symbolized by endless lines of trenches defended by barbed-wire entanglements. Artillery failed to destroy these defences, and the hapless infantry was driven into the slaughterhouse in numbers unprecedented in history. The result was eloquently described after the event by Winston Churchill, himself deeply involved in military strategy, although lacking the political authority he was to gain a quarter century later:

The Great War differed from all ancient wars in the immense power of the combatants and their fearful agencies of destruction, and from all modern wars in the utter ruthlessness with which it was fought. All the horrors of all the ages were brought together, and not only armies but whole populations were thrust into the midst of them. The mighty educated States involved conceived with reason that their very existence was at stake. Germany having let Hell loose kept well in the van of terror; but she was followed step by step by the desperate and ultimately avenging nations she had assailed. Every outrage against humanity or international law was repaid by reprisals often on a greater scale and of longer duration. No truce or parley mitigated the strife of the armies. The wounded died between the lines: the dead mouldered into the soil. Merchant ships and neutral ships and hospital ships were sunk on the seas and all on board left to their fate, or killed as they swam. Every effort was made to starve whole nations into submission without regard to age or sex. Cities and monuments were smashed by artillery. Bombs from the air were cast down indiscriminately. Poison gas in many forms stifled or seared the soldiers. Liquid fire was projected upon their bodies. Men fell from the air in flames, or were smothered, often slowly, in the dark recesses of the sea. The fighting strength of armies was limited only by the manhood of their countries. Europe and large parts of Asia and Africa became one vast battlefield on which after years of struggle not armies but nations broke and ran. When all was over, Torture and Cannibalism were the only two expedients that the civilized, scientific, Christian States had been able to deny themselves: and these were of doubtful utility.[8]

The author of these lines was destined to preside over the even greater and more frightful torment of 1939–45, when mass murder of prisoners and civilians was added to the horrors he had catalogued, and when air power was employed for the purpose of levelling entire cities to the ground. The interval of so-called peace in 1919–39 had been spent in preparing for mechanized warfare, and when it came, the massive employment of armour brought some relief to the foot soldier, no longer obliged to spend years in the trenches as he had done on the earlier occasion. In all other respects the Second World War proved even more destructive of human lives and civilized habits than its predecessor. Yet it was the 1914–18 war that left the deeper mark on the consciousness of the belligerents. In retrospect it appears as the true dividing line between the nineteenth century and the twentieth. By 1939 people were already habituated to the notion that war placed the very structure of civilization at risk, whereas in 1914 all concerned still thought in terms of a brief shock involving only the soldiers, not the civilians. Total war – the mobilization of all human and material resources for military purposes – was an innovation forced upon the belligerents by the generals' failure to win quick victories in the field. The Germans had gambled upon a lightning war in the West, followed by a few months' campaigning against Russia. The French and British from 1914 to 1917 put their faith in the Russian steamroller, which obstinately refused to roll. The resulting stalemate on the Western front, the introduction of trench warfare, the discovery that cavalry had become obsolete, the reliance on fire-power, and the first clumsy attempts to employ armour in the field, marked a deep division between traditional and modern strategy. Unrestricted submarine war against merchant shipping was another novelty added to the general picture. Air power was as yet undeveloped – its efflorescence belongs to the post-war period and the war of 1939–45. Yet by 1919 it was already evident that the next round of combat among the Great Powers would largely centre upon the employment of the aeroplane.[9]

The actual conduct of operations was determined by the failure of the Schlieffen Plan on which the Germans had based their hope for a quick victory. As it stood in 1914, after various alterations during the preceding decade, the plan committed Germany to an offensive strategy in the West, as against the military doctrine of the Bismarck era which assumed a defensive posture towards France, and by implication British neutrality in a war waged by Germany against Russia and her French ally. After 1892, and more especially after 1906, the basic assumption was that France must be knocked out within six weeks, whereafter the bulk of Germany's forces would be shifted eastward. To this end Schlieffen and his successor, the younger Moltke, laid it down that the German offensive should wheel through Belgium and around Paris, thus pinning the whole French army against the Moselle fortresses, the Jura and Switzerland. This was a colossal gamble which presupposed a degree of coordination and initial success very difficult to attain in practice, and in fact the plan went wrong in September 1914, when the German advance was brought to a halt on the Marne. The French for their part were committed to a great offensive in Lorraine, which was duly delivered and very nearly wrecked their Army at the very outset. In the East, Austria-Hungary was to stand on the defensive until Germany could come to her aid, and this part of the general programme was actually adhered to, even though Italy's entry in May 1915 on the side of the Anglo-French Entente introduced an unforeseen complication, as did Rumania's brief and unsuccessful attempt in August 1916 to emulate Italy's example. Britain's contribution was at first limited to the dispatch of a relatively small expeditionary force which did not play a major part in 1914; but by the summer of 1916 the British army in France had been built up to a strength of fifty-seven divisions, as against ninety-five French and 117 German divisions in the West. Organized by Lord Kitchener (1850–1916) and commanded by Sir Douglas Haig (1861–1928) this enormous volunteer force was flung into the battle of the Somme in July 1916. It met with wholesale disaster, even though artillery was employed on an unprecedented scale to make a break-through possible. The battlefields of the Somme were the grave of Kitchener's army, much as the French and Germans had been bled white at Verdun some months earlier. After these massacres there occurred a distinct shift in popular sentiment in all the belligerent countries, foreshadowing the weariness of 1917, by which time Russia was out of the war altogether and only the entry of the United States kept the Entente going. The Germans had suffered proportionately less heavily than the French, but by 1918 they too were close to breaking-point, and the failure of their gigantic offensive in France that year led to a politico-military collapse which shattered the structure of Imperial Germany and its Austro-Hungarian ally. Defeat in the field, plus strikes and naval mutinies at home, brought the colossus to the ground. It was the logical outcome of a gamble on which the Central Powers had in 1914 staked their existence. Total victory having been aimed at, defeat when it came was total too.

From the historian's viewpoint what stands out is the fact that much of the pre-war planning proved delusive. France was not knocked out in the first round; the Russian 'steamroller' was ineffective against Germany, although dangerous to Austria; trench warfare on the Western front was wholly unforeseen; the major battles waged around Verdun, the Somme and in Flanders (1917) exhausted the armies and undermined their morale without yielding the expected results; cavalry proved wholly useless in the West, where 700,000 horses were kept in idleness behind the Allied lines throughout the war; the British Grand Fleet and the German High Seas Fleet spent most of their time in harbour, and when on 31 May 1916 they briefly came to grips at Jutland the outcome was inconclusive, although British losses were heavier than German; submarines proved more effective than battleships: they almost won the war for Germany in 1917 by sinking British and neutral ships, albeit at the cost of driving America into the fight. Such major innovations as steel helmets worn by the infantry, and the use of armour in place of cavalry, were clumsily improvised from 1915 onwards, in an attempt to adapt warfare to the conditions created by all-round mechanization and the mounting effectiveness of fire-power. Generalship on the whole was mediocre, though better on the German side, where it partly made up for the imbecility of the political leadership. Nothing came of German efforts to promote an Islamic revolt against the British Empire in India and the Middle East. German financial aid to the anti-war forces in Russia boomeranged upon the Central Powers when the Bolsheviks seized power in November 1917, thereby starting a political landslide which a year later swept away the Hohenzollern and Habsburg monarchies, though not the Western democracies whose power of resistance to revolutionary slogans was consistently underrated in Moscow.

None of the participants achieved their pre-war aims. France obtained Alsace-Lorraine at the Versailles peace settlement in 1919, but got no real security against her German neighbour; Britain received a few German colonies and precious little besides, even though the British Admiralty had the satisfaction of watching the scuttling of Germany's High Seas Fleet; Austria-Hungary and Turkey went to pieces; Russia fell into revolution; the United States blundered away its chances at Versailles and thereafter withdrew into isolation. All told, statesmen and diplomatists proved as helpless as the generals. Down to 1914 they had been able to control the march of events because they were operating in accordance with a complicated set of rules for the most part worked out in the preceding century. The outbreak of war did not take the governments by surprise: it had long been expected, and when it came the various armies and navies were ready for it. What upset everyone's calculations was the stalemate on the Western front and the uselessness of frontal assaults against positions defended by machine-guns. Joffre, Pétain, Nivelle and Foch among the French commanders, Falkenhayn and Ludendorff among the Germans, Kitchener, Haig and Robertson on the British side, were all committed to the belief that a rapid victory was attainable, and so were the governments they served. Even Austria and Russia produced field commanders who were able to win occasional battles against inferior forces. What no one could do was to work out an operational strategy that took account of the new technical realities. In the end the Allies won because their reserves of manpower were larger and because Germany's war-making capacity had been undermined by the British blockade. When Ludendorff suddenly insisted upon an immediate armistice in September 1918, no major Allied breakthrough had materialized, notwithstanding the successful employment of tanks. But Austria's resistance was crumbling and the constant arrival of American reinforcements made certain Germany's defeat in 1919. The decision to seek an armistice on the basis of Wilson's Fourteen Points was a political gamble which miscarried when German morale cracked in October–November, the Fleet mutinied and the Kaiser was driven to flight and abdication. Germany had not suffered an overwhelming defeat in the field, but she had clearly lost the war, and the High Command opted for an armistice. What the German plenipotentiaries actually had to sign on 11 November 1918 was an unconditional surrender, for by then the home front had collapsed and the new republican authorities had neither the will nor the power to continue the struggle. In this sense the German revolution in November 1918 hastened the inevitable.

As the consequences of the war gradually disclosed themselves, it became evident that Eastern and Central Europe were destined to follow separate and divergent ways. On the Eastern front the war had been one of movement rather than attrition. The Germans and their Austrian allies had penetrated deeply into Russian territory, and the

Russian Army had by 1917 lost both the will and the capacity to carry out major offensive operations. The last of these, in July 1917, by its failure undermined the authority of the Provisional government established in March after the fall of the Tsarist autocracy, thereby opening the road for Lenin's seizure of power four months later. Russia had in fact suffered military defeat, and the German Army in the East had by 1918 emerged as victor, even though its Austro-Hungarian allies were barely able to maintain themselves. This circumstance was to have major political consequences. Victory in the East, paralleled by defeat in the West, left the German officers' corps and its political allies in a state of mind quite different from that of the democratic parties who in 1919 made themselves responsible for carrying out the onerous terms of the armistice. These provided not only for the surrender of all German conquests in the West and the handing over of the Fleet; they included the nullification of the Brest Litovsk settlement imposed upon the Bolshevik authorities in March 1918, when for all practical purposes Germany had attained its aims in Eastern Europe. German nationalists were thus left with the feeling that victory had been snatched from them at the eleventh hour by American intervention, aided by sedition on the home front, for which they held the extreme Left responsible. In point of fact neither the pacifist Independent Socialist Party formed in 1917, nor the more radical Spartakus group headed by the future leaders of the German Communist Party, had made much of an impact on the morale of Germany's armed forces, until a sailors' revolt exploded at Kiel on 3 November 1918, when the mutinous crews seized control of their vessels and of Kiel itself. The ninth of November witnessed the Emperor's abdication and the proclamation of a Republic, followed two days later by the signing of the armistice. The revolution – such as it was – thus appeared as cause and consequence of a military defeat which the German Right refused to acknowledge, save in so far as it was conceded that the Western Allies had won thanks to superior resources and manpower. In due course German nationalism recovered an aggressive colour, its central illusion being the myth that the German Army had not been defeated in the field, but rather stabbed in the back by Jews, pacifists and Social Democrats. These obsessive beliefs were strengthened by the terms of the Versailles settlement imposed upon the new German Republic by a Treaty signed on 28 June 1919, in the Hall of Mirrors where forty-eight years earlier the German Empire had been proclaimed by Bismarck. The Treaty not only returned Alsace-Lorraine to France and northern Schleswig to Denmark: it gave the newly reconstituted Polish Republic access to the sea through the so-called Polish Corridor which cut off East Prussia from the rest of Germany. The notion that Germany would ever put up with such a state of affairs could only have been entertained by people unfamiliar with her history. By comparison, the scaling down of her armed forces to 100,000 men, and the imposition of mountainous reparations, weighed less heavily in the balance, as did the 'war guilt' clause which fastened exclusive responsibility for the whole disaster of 1914 upon the Imperial Government. The basic weakness of the Treaty lay in the fact that it left the German people in a frame of mind not conducive to a lasting peace. Germany, as the nationalists saw it, had been starved into surrender, and then stabbed in the back, after having won the war on land. The conclusion they drew was that on the next occasion they must be better prepared. As for accepting the Versailles settlement as it stood, the thought never entered their minds.[10]

Taking the peace settlement as a whole, one can see in retrospect that its endurance depended upon a united front being presented by America, Britain and France for at least a generation. In actual fact the United States failed to ratify the Treaty of Versailles, while the British and French soon began to quarrel over its enforcement. Germany had been disarmed and stripped of some territory, but remained a powerful state in the centre of Europe and before long began to challenge the terms imposed upon her in 1919. Their enforcement rested theoretically with the League of Nations, a toothless body wholly dependent for action upon British and French readiness to go to war. The League Council first met in January 1920, the Assembly in November. The United States was not represented, the Senate having abandoned Wilson's brain-child. Russia of course was not a member and neither was Germany. The League therefore became the instrument of its two strongest components, Britain and France, who were soon at cross-purposes. The heart of the problem was Germany's unwillingness to accept her new status in Europe, coupled with the inability of the Western Powers to formulate a coherent policy. This was most notable in the persistent Anglo-French quarrel, but the rise of Fascism in Italy also made a contribution by rendering illusory the claim that the League existed for the purpose of safeguarding liberal democracy. Meanwhile the failure of Allied intervention in Russia on the side of the 'White' armies meant that the Bolshevik regime, having weathered the storm, would be resolutely hostile to the West and inclined to encourage German revisionism. The revival of Poland was no compensation for this state of affairs, the less so since the Poles, with French encouragement, invaded Russian territory in 1920, thereby prolonging a war which at one moment threatened their newly won independence.

Next to the replacement of Imperial Germany by a Republic ostensibly committed to peace abroad and liberal democracy at home, the principal change in Central Europe resulted from the break-up of the Austro-Hungarian Monarchy and the establishment of successor states, among which Czechoslovakia was unique in that it was a genuine democracy. The same could not be said of Hungary, where a 'White' counter-revolution triumphed in August 1919 after a brief Communist experiment; or of Poland, which was reconstituted on what had formerly been German, Austrian or Russian territory. The peace settlements with Austria and Turkey followed the general pattern established at Versailles. They confirmed the principle of national self-determination and to that extent represented a belated triumph of democratic liberalism, even though the doctrine was difficult to apply in practice: notably in the Balkans and as between Italy and the newly created state of Yugoslavia. In the event, Italian nationalism was left with a grievance which became an important factor in the rise to power in 1922 of the Fascist movement. The Austrian settlement deprived Hungary of almost three-quarters of its ancient territory, and two-thirds of its inhabitants, for the benefit of Czechoslovakia, Rumania and Yugoslavia – France's client states during the inter-war period that ended in 1939. Turkey, after having been expelled from Europe, was now also relieved of its Arab dominions, but a Greek attempt to carve out territory in Asia Minor ended in disaster in 1922. All told, the Allies imposed the sort of settlement to be expected from former radicals such as Lloyd George and Clemenceau who took national self-determination seriously, but restricted its application to Europeans. The Peace of Paris conformed to their principles, even though the vindictive treatment of Germany contained the seeds of another war. Meanwhile the Treaty of Riga in March 1921 left Russia dissatisfied, turned Poland into a French client state and encouraged dangerous delusions of grandeur on the part of her rulers.

The human costs of the settlement are difficult to compute. They were less devastating than those incurred during the 1939–45 war, but gigantic by nineteenth-century standards. Germany had lost two million dead, Russia as much or more, France a million and a half, the British Empire just under a million, Italy half a million, the United States a mere 100,000. Large areas of France and Belgium had been devastated seemingly beyond hope of recovery. Eastern Europe suffered famine, typhus and cholera which carried off millions; Germany and Austria had been relentlessly blockaded, and by 1919 the populations of Berlin and Vienna were close to the point of actual starvation. Russia underwent a civil war which raged for three years, from 1917 until 1920, when the Bolshevik regime at last triumphed over the 'White' armies, only to be confronted by a major famine that devastated large areas of the country in 1921–2. The Russian upheaval followed the pattern of the French Revolution in the eighteenth century, including wholesale terrorism. By comparison the German and Austrian revolutions in 1918–19 were harmless affairs; even so the restoration of 'order' in Berlin and Munich claimed hundreds of victims, while the

Hungarian counter-revolution was bloodier still. A generation of revolutionary leaders – Karl Liebknecht and Rosa Luxemburg are the most celebrated – went to their deaths, and the resulting Socialist–Communist split was envenomed to the point of insurmountable hatred. These events had no parallel in Western Europe, where no serious attempt was made by the handful of Communists to overstep the boundaries of democratic legality. The Russian Revolution left its mark upon the labour movements of all European countries, but actual bloodletting was confined to territories formerly incorporated in the Hohenzollern and Habsburg Empires. This circumstance pointed a lesson which the emerging Communist International was slow to grasp. Its leaders thought in terms of proletarian revolution in all the industrially advanced countries, but in point of fact the Communist message made its major impact in the less developed areas of the continent.

The Russian Revolution provides the historian with an inexhaustible array of topics. All that needs to be said here is that it did for Eastern Europe what the French Revolution in an earlier age had done for the Western half of the Continent: it created a new political model radically different from anything previously in existence. At the same time it involved the Russian Communist Party in the solution of problems which had already baffled the Tsarist regime: not least among them the need to drag the country's peasant masses into the industrial age. The Revolution likewise brought to the fore the ancient cleavage between the ruling Great Russian people and the other nationalities inhabiting the Empire. Like the Jacobins before them, the Bolsheviks approached these tasks in an apocalyptic mood which gradually gave way to greater realism, and in the end became a cover for traditional *Realpolitik*. The seizure of power in November 1917 under the leadership of Lenin (1870–1924), Trotsky (1879–1940) and their colleagues was originally intended to spark off a proletarian revolution in Germany and regions further west. When the German and Austrian revolutions of 1918–19 failed to overstep the borderline separating bourgeois democracy from Soviet Communism, the new Russian regime – conventionally known since 1922 as the Union of Soviet Socialist Republics (USSR) – was faced with the task of preserving itself within a hostile world environment, while at the same time catching up economically with the more advanced countries. In 1919 this outcome was not foreseen, principally because the almost simultaneous collapse of the Romanov, Hohenzollern and Habsburg dynasties in 1917–18 concealed from view the fact that the Russians were alone in confronting a genuinely revolutionary situation. The Russian peasant-soldier made the Bolshevik seizure of power possible by backing the urban revolt, whereas in Central Europe the conservatism of the peasantry supplied the majority faction of the Social Democratic movement with an adequate reason for not attempting a revolution on the Russian model. Moreover, such revolutionary sentiment as existed in Berlin and Vienna in 1918–19 was principally due to war-weariness. The termination of the war led to the isolation of the radical vanguard which was thereupon decapitated by the forces of 'order'.[11]

The principal issue which in 1919 came to divide Communists from Social Democrats had to do with the Bolshevik seizure of power in the teeth of democratic legality and majority opinion, as expressed in the elections to the Constituent Assembly a few weeks after Lenin and Trotsky had taken over in Petrograd in the name of an altogether new and different authority: that of the Soviets (councils) of workers and peasants, supposedly the supreme governing body. It now became a matter of principle for Communists to affirm, and for their Social Democratic opponents to deny, that a socialist revolution could achieve its aims only if it dispensed with bourgeois legality and parliamentary institutions, not to mention freedom of the press and the existence of rival political parties. Since all these assertions were methodically demolished by Rosa Luxemburg in a tract composed in 1918, shortly before she became the co-founder of the German Communist Party (KPD), it has never been easy for Leninists to claim the authority of Marx for what Lenin and Trotsky did in 1917–18, when they dissolved the recently elected Constituent Assembly, in which the Bolsheviks could not hope to gain a majority. The electorate had cast its vote in favour of the Social Revolutionaries, a party which broadly speaking represented the interests of the peasantry.[12] In a predominantly agrarian country this outcome was scarcely surprising. Lenin dealt with the issue by claiming that the Social Revolutionaries no longer existed as a party, their extreme left wing having made common cause with the Bolsheviks. Ever since those dramatic days the Communist movement has been saddled with the difficult task of explaining why socialist democracy must necessarily take the form of one-party dictatorship, or at least go through a lengthy period of single-party rule. To the German and Austrian Social Democrats in 1918–19 it appeared that workers' councils were not an adequate substitute for democratically elected national assemblies, and the resulting cleavage made it impossible for Communists and democratic Socialists to speak the same political language.

At the same time the helplessness of reformist Social Democrats when installed in office, their reliance on the old State apparatus, and their readiness – at least in Germany – to employ the armed forces against workers' councils established in imitation of the Russian model, deepened the split and drove all genuinely radical elements into the camp of the Third International. For practical purposes an informal alliance was struck in November 1918 between Ebert, the leader of the Majority

European politics and society

1900–1914

1 Nine reigning monarchs attended the funeral of Edward VII in London, May 1910: seated, Alphonse XIII of Spain, George V of Great Britain, Frederick VIII of Denmark; standing, Haakon VII of Norway, Ferdinand I of Bulgaria, Manuel II of Portugal, Wilhelm II of Germany, George I of Greece and Albert I of Belgium.

2 (Top) The interior of the Krupp works at Essen, a leading German industrial producer; (centre) C. S. Rolls driving the future George v in an early Panhard car; (bottom) an early view of the interior of the Berlin telephone central.

3 The German war leadership: Ludendorff, the Kaiser and Hindenburg.

4 The use of propaganda to rouse national passions: a French poster of the last year of the war, with the slogan '*On ne passe pas*': They shall not pass.

5 The 1914–18 war saw several new forms of fighting: (above) trench warfare: British troops go over the top under a German barrage in Flanders; (below) victims of poison gas, first introduced by the Germans in the second battle of Ypres, 1915.

6 Heads of state of the victorious powers at the 1919 Versailles peace conference:
Vittorio Orlando, David Lloyd George, Georges Clemenceau, Woodrow Wilson.

7 The Russian Revolution:
Lenin addressing a meeting
in Moscow, with Trotsky on
his left (in later years this
photograph was circulated
with Trotsky cut out);
street fighting in Petrograd,
July 1917.

8 The troubled thirties: men
queuing up at the Wigan labour
exchange; German soldiers march
through the streets of Nuremberg
during the 1938 Nazi rally; the
emblem of the international
brigade in the Spanish civil war.

9 Mussolini and Hitler, 1938; below, Chamberlain waves the famous piece of paper that promised 'peace in our time' on returning from Munich, September 1938.

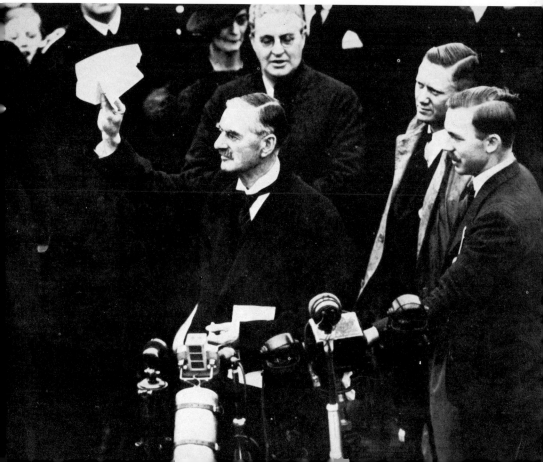

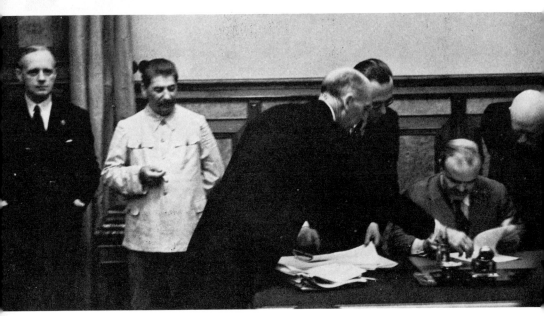

10 Signing the Nazi–Soviet non-aggression pact, 23 August 1939: German Foreign Minister Ribbentrop at left next to Stalin; Molotov, the Russian Foreign Minister, is seated affixing his signature. (below) Hitler declares war on Poland, 1 September 1939, to the cheers of the Reichstag; Goering, President of the Reichstag, is seated behind him.

11 Winston Churchill. (below) Charles de Gaulle, as leader of the Free French.

12 The eastern front: Red Army trench mortar gunners supporting the infantry in an advance against the Germans, during the Russian winter offensive of 1942–3.

13 The concentration camp Sachsenhausen, a photograph taken in February 1941. The thinly-clad inmates were forced to stand in the cold for hours while the district was searched for one prisoner who had escaped.

14 The war in the air: (right) on the
eastern front, German planes over
Russia; (below) allied paratroopers
over southern France, August 1944.

15 Dresden after the fire bombing of February 1945.

16 Allied conference at Potsdam, July 1945: left-centre, top, Stalin with Molotov;
extreme right, Truman; bottom-left, Attlee, who replaced Churchill during the
conference.

17 The division of Europe: (top) the Russian delegation signing the Warsaw Pact, May 1955; (below) Western European leaders with American ally: Eden, Adenauer, Acheson, Schumann.

Socialists, and Groener, representing Hindenburg and the other Army leaders after the Emperor's abdication. The alliance, it was hoped, would commend the German Republic to the Western Powers as a shield against Bolshevism. The bloody suppression of the Spartakist revolt in January 1919 by the forces of the Ebert government did in fact establish the government's credibility in the eyes of the Allied Powers. They tacitly permitted Germany to keep her troops in the East until they could be relieved by Allied forces. This form of cooperation between the Allies and the new German authorities persuaded many Germans that a compromise peace might yet be concluded in the West. All the greater was the shock when the Treaty of Versailles had to be signed by the German delegates. The Weimar Republic – so called because the National Assembly had taken refuge in Weimar from the political storms in Berlin – never recovered from the blow.

At a different level the events of 1918-19 produced a spirit of fratricidal hatred on the part of the German Communists whose leaders had been murdered by armed forces nominally controlled by the Ebert government. This state of affairs was peculiar to Germany. Elsewhere the great schism dividing Socialists from Communists was not sealed in blood, and the subsequent rivalries between them lacked the element of mutual hatred peculiar to the mental climate of the Weimar Republic. The separation was, however, accomplished all over Europe. Even where massive strikes and factory occupations had Socialist support, as was the case in Italy in 1920, a formal secession occurred nonetheless because the Socialists clung to parliamentary democracy and political pluralism, whereas the Communists interpreted 'proletarian dictatorship' to mean one-party rule on the Russian model. The debate ran its way, both sides citing Marx and Engels in support of their theses, and neither making much of an impact on the other. In the end the Second International, originally founded in 1889, was reconstituted, with the German SPD and the British Labour Party playing the major role. Communist parties everywhere represented a minority, save for France where the split left them in control of the party's machinery; and even in France the Socialists subsequently managed to outnumber their Communist rivals throughout the 1920s. Nor was the German KPD successful in its attempt to win over a majority of the working class, let alone the electorate. It remained a political sect, albeit one that could count on a few million supporters at election time. The great schism did not as yet translate itself into national terms, as was the case in 1945-8, when the Communists, with Russian support, seized power all over Eastern Europe. It remained an internal affair of the European labour movement.

The founding of the Third International in 1919 is nonetheless a decisive date in world history: it placed the resources and the prestige of the Russian Communist Party at the service of a world-revolutionary cause which attracted numerous supporters all over Europe. The Fascist response to this challenge validated the central truth of Hegelian dialectics, though all concerned were slow to grasp the point. The inter-war period from 1919 to 1939, to which we now turn, was to furnish ample proof that history does indeed proceed by way of internal contradictions seeking a synthesis at a higher level. Had the Communists taken their own philosophy more seriously the rise of Fascism would not have come as a surprise to them.[13]

NOTES

1 Arthur Marwick, *Britain in the Century of Total War* (London: The Bodley Head, 1968; Boston: Atlantic Monthly Press, Little, Brown, 1968), p. 22.

2 A.J.P.Taylor, *The Struggle for Mastery in Europe 1848–1918* (Oxford: Clarendon Press, 1954; New York: Oxford University Press, 1954), pp. 457 ff., 483 ff., 511 ff.

3 *Ibid.*, p. 496.

4 *Ibid.*, p. 518. See also the same author's *The Habsburg Monarchy 1809–1918* (London: Hamish Hamilton, 1948), pp. 214 ff., for Austria-Hungary's domestic problems which eventually resulted in the decision to go to war in 1914.

5 Fritz Fischer, *Germany's Aims in the First World War* (London: Chatto & Windus; New York: Norton, 1967); Hans W.Gatzke, *Germany's Drive to the West* (London: Oxford University Press; Baltimore: Johns Hopkins Press, 1966), *passim*.

6 For the German programme of annexations see Fischer, *op. cit.*, pp. 98 ff., pp. 162 ff. For the pre-history of German imperialism see George W.F. Hallgarten, *Imperialismus vor 1914* (Munich: C.H.Beck, 1951), vol. I, pp. 255 ff., vol. II, pp. 159 ff. For the role of the Social Democrats in Imperial Germany see Carl E.Schorske, *German Social Democracy 1905–1917* (London: Oxford University Press; Cambridge, Mass.: Harvard University Press, 1955), *passim*.

7 Fischer, *op. cit.*, pp. 441–3.

8 Winston Churchill, *The World Crisis 1911–1918*, abridged and revised edition (London: Thornton Butterworth, 1931; New York: Macmillan, 1942), pp. 19–20. Lloyd George's *War Memoirs* (London: Odhams, 1938) and Lord Beaverbrook's *Politicians and the War 1914–1916* (London: Oldbourne; Hamden, Conn.: Shoe String Press, 1960) are important sources of information for anyone curious to understand Britain's management of the 1914–1918 war. See also A.J.P.Taylor, *Politics in Wartime and Other Essays* (London: Hamish Hamilton, 1964; New York: Atheneum, 1965). The German political scene has been adequately documented and analysed by Professor Fischer. Official sources made available after 1918 by the belligerents are listed in the bibliographical annex of Mr Taylor's *Struggle for Mastery in Europe 1848–1918*. They include such multi-volume collections of documents as the German *Die grosse Politik*

der europäischen Kabinette (1922–6) and the official French publication titled *Documents diplomatiques français 1871–1914* (1929 *et seq.*). *British Documents on the Origins of the War*, ed. Gooch and Temperley (1927 *et seq.*), covers the period from 1898 to 1914. Russian material was published spasmodically by the Soviet authorities in the magazine *Krasny Arkhiv* for about twenty years.

9 B.H.Liddell Hart, *A History of the World War 1914–1918* (London: Faber, 1930–8; New York: Modern Library, 1939), *passim*. See also the relevant chapters in A.J.P.Taylor, *English History 1914–1945* (New York and Oxford: Oxford University Press), *passim*.

10 H.Stuart Hughes, *Contemporary Europe: A History* (Englewood Cliffs, N.J. Prentice-Hall, 1961), pp. 102 ff.

11 L.Schapiro, *The Origin of the Communist Autocracy* (London: Bell and Sons; Cambridge, Mass.: Harvard University Press, 1955), *passim*; E.H.Carr, *The Bolshevik Revolution 1917–1923* (London: Macmillan, 1950, 1953). For a popular introduction see J.P.Nettl, *The Soviet Achievement* (London: Thames and Hudson, 1967; New York: Harcourt Brace, 1968), *passim*.

12 O.H.Radkey, *The Election to the Russian Constituent Assembly of 1917* (London: Oxford University Press; Cambridge, Mass.: Harvard University Press, 1950), *passim*.

13 F.Borkenau, *The Communist International* (London: Faber & Faber, 1938; New York: Norton, 1939), *passim*; *The Communist International 1919–1943*: Documents Selected and Edited by Jane Degras (London–New York–Toronto: Oxford University Press, 1956 *et seq.*). See also the companion series likewise issued under the auspices of the Royal Institute of International Affairs: *Soviet Documents on Foreign Policy*, ed. Jane Degras, vol. I (1917–24), vol. II (1925–32), vol. III (1933–41); all published by the Oxford University Press in 1951–3. F.L.Carsten, *Revolution in Central Europe 1918–1919* (London: Temple Smith, 1972).

CHAPTER 8

EUROPE BETWEEN THE WARS 1919–39

A   FROM VERSAILLES TO MUNICH

I believe that . . . men are beginning to see, not perhaps the golden age, but an age which at any rate is brightening from decade to decade, and will lead us some time to an elevation from which we can see the things for which the heart of mankind is longing.[1]

When Woodrow Wilson delivered himself of these edifying sentiments in December 1918, on the occasion of a visit to Manchester, he spoke a language familiar to British audiences who were simultaneously being treated to the same kind of rhetoric by Lloyd George during the brief election campaign of November–December 1918. There was, however, a substantial difference in their respective attitudes to the peace treaty. The Americans had come late into the war and suffered little. Britain had suffered a great deal, and her rulers were determined to make the Germans pay, literally and not just metaphorically. Lloyd George's pledge to the electors of a "country fit for heroes to live in" was necessarily balanced by his statement, on 11 December at Bristol: "We propose to demand the whole cost of the war" from Germany. The French went further: they were hoping to detach substantial portions of territory from the *Reich*, over and above the return of Alsace-Lorraine. These aims were not fully achieved, but under the terms of the Versailles settlement most of Posen and West Prussia, which had been seized by Prussia in the eighteenth-century partitions of Poland, went to the newly constituted Polish Republic; moreover, so as to give Poland access to the sea, the Treaty, as noted before, cut a 'corridor' separating East Prussia from the rest of Germany and leading to Danzig which became a free port. Altogether Germany lost thirteen per cent of her territory and nearly seven million people, two-thirds of her iron deposits (which lay in Lorraine) and much of her other subsoil resources.[2] She surrendered nine-tenths of her merchant marine, to make up for submarine sinkings, and virtually the whole of her Navy, although the officers scuttled the ships rather than hand them over to the victors. Germany furthermore lost the whole of her colonial empire: over a million square miles of territory with twelve million inhabitants, for the most part in Africa. The holdings and investments of German citizens overseas, representing one-tenth of Germany's capital, were forfeited. Under the 'war guilt' clause of the Treaty, Germany assumed responsibility for all the loss and damage done to the Allies, though in point of fact the Germans were only asked to pay for "damage done to the civilian population" and for the entire loss suffered by Belgium. The precise amount of reparations was a matter for controversy among the Allies, and the United States asked no payment to herself, but acquiesced half-heartedly in fairly fantastic claims computed by the British and French. As a first instalment the Weimar Republic was to make a payment equivalent to five billion dollars by 1 May 1921. These terms were less harsh than those imposed by the Germans upon the Bolsheviks at Brest Litovsk in 1918, but they caused a degree of resentment which was of itself sufficient to demolish the standing of any German politician willing to accept the Versailles settlement. This was in part at least a consequence of Germany's own war-time measures. The Imperial government had financed the war less by taxes than by loans: the victims of Germany's triumph were to repay the sums which the German government had borrowed from its own citizens. But Germany did not win and was now saddled with huge reparations claims in addition to her internal debts. In March 1921 Germany declared that she had paid the interim bill, but the Allies proclaimed her in default. The zone of occupation was enlarged – a foretaste of the French occupation of the Ruhr in 1923 – and taxes were levied on German exports to Allied countries. The reparations total was then fixed at 132 billion gold marks, payment to be made by annuities of two billion marks plus twenty-six per cent of the value of exports. These terms were subsequently modified and by 1932 the whole issue had been virtually shelved, but in the meantime the Weimar Republic had exhausted its domestic stock of goodwill. By resorting to the printing press instead of taxing the wealthier classes, the German government destroyed its own currency, so that in 1923 an American dollar was worth millions of paper marks. Money became meaningless and the middle class lost its savings. Mortgages, government bonds, savings accounts and insurance policies were all wiped out. The subsequent economic recovery from 1924 onward did not erase these memories, which played a part in bringing Hitler to power a decade later.[3]

In some respects the French did not get all they wanted. Clemenceau's demand for the Rhineland to be set up as an independent buffer state was successfully resisted by Wilson and Lloyd George, and in the end he agreed to a provision whereby the Rhineland was demilitarized and Allied troops would occupy the most important bridgeheads for fifteen years. The German army was limited to a professional force of 100,000 men, conscription was abolished, and the General Staff disbanded (on paper). For good measure, Lloyd George and Wilson promised France a guarantee of aid in the event of German aggression. The House of Commons unanimously approved the guarantee, which thus became an integral part of the Versailles settlement signed on 28 June 1919. The United States Senate by contrast failed to endorse Wilson's signature by the required majority, while Wilson himself in September 1919 suffered a nervous breakdown. Neither the Versailles Treaty nor the League of Nations obtained official American sanction, so that when the League was duly convened in January 1920, the United States was not a member. The resplendent League buildings which eventually arose at Geneva, in neutral Switzerland, housed an Assembly in which Asia, Africa and Latin America were represented alongside Europe, but Germany and Russia were not invited to join, and the USA was conspicuous by her absence. As for the Anglo-American guarantee to France, which was really the keystone of the whole Versailles settlement, Britain withdrew her promise after the United States Senate had failed to ratify the Treaty. The French therefore felt cheated, and the history of the succeeding twenty years is largely the story of unavailing efforts on the part of France to find a substitute for the Anglo-American guarantee: first with the help of Poland and the so-called Little Entente (Czechoslovakia, Rumania and Yugoslavia) formed in 1921; between 1934 and 1939 with the assistance of Soviet Russia. Except for a brief interval between 1926 and 1929, when the Weimar Republic appeared to have struck roots, and its permanent Foreign Secretary, Gustav Stresemann (1878–1929), had taken Germany into the League of Nations, the French never felt reasonably secure, and their nervousness translated itself into an unavailing search for allies against the resurgent German *Reich*, whose steel production by 1925 equalled the pre-war level. Despite her losses Germany had in fact emerged from the war as the most powerful nation on the European continent, and her neighbours were aware of it. Once the 'succession states' carved out of the Austro-Hungarian Monarchy had effected the shift from a pro-French to a pro-German orientation, the rearmed Germany of the later 1930s was strong enough to make another bid for European domination.

The area in which the renewed German challenge made itself felt straddled Central and South-Eastern Europe, plus Italy where Fascism had taken control in 1922, thus removing one more prop of the Versailles settlement. The national problems of the succession states were an inheritance from the Austro-Hungarian past, as was the agrarian problem which affected them all with the exception of Czechoslovakia. The new boundary lines did not help. The Habsburg

Empire had possessed two free-trade areas: Austria and Hungary. The two became six as the result of the Empire's break-up.[4] The Danube now flowed through half a dozen countries separated by tariff and currency walls. Czechoslovakia's industries found outlets in Western Europe, but lost their former Austrian markets. Hungary was badly placed to export its foodstuffs. Austria's six and a half million people were saddled with Vienna, a metropolis which had lost its function and whose Social Democratic administrators were detested by the peasants of the provinces. Yugoslavia was torn by nationality conflicts so violent that by 1929 parliamentary government had collapsed. Poland was governed dictatorially by Piłsudski (1867–1935) and his army officers who permitted only a semblance of political life. Rumania, like Yugoslavia a constitutional monarchy, suffered the rule of a 'liberal' party which stayed in power by making sure that at election time the votes were properly counted. Of all these countries only Czechoslovakia produced a functioning liberal-democratic system, thanks in part to the leadership provided by Thomas Masaryk (1850–1937) and Eduard Beneš (1884–1948). The country had a reasonable balance of modern industry and efficient farming, an energetic middle class and a liberal-minded intelligentsia. Its German minority was fairly treated and had no substantial grievances, a circumstance which did not prevent most of it from rallying to Hitler's cause in 1938. All told, Eastern Europe might just conceivably have solved its problems if the Weimar Republic had remained in being. Its collapse and the advent of Hitler destroyed the French-controlled system, and with it the only barrier to another German bid for hegemony.

'Revision' of the Versailles settlement was the unifying theme which linked all the losers of 1914–18, plus Italy which counted officially as a victor, but had not obtained territorial gains commensurate with the military losses sustained during the war. Mussolini (1883–1945) rode to power on a wave of nationalism he had helped to foment after his break with the Socialist Party in 1914. In October 1922 the 'march on Rome' of some 40,000 uniformed Fascists resulted in an unopposed political takeover in which the Monarchy, the Church and the ruling Liberals all collaborated, largely from fear of an imaginary Communist danger. Once installed, the Italian dictator became the leader of the revisionist campaign. He had no trouble finding allies, though eventually the task became too much for him and he ended up as Hitler's subordinate. The settlements with Germany's war-time allies had followed the pattern of Versailles. The Treaty of Saint-Germain with Austria created an artificial state, whose people would have liked to join the German Reich but were specifically forbidden to do so. The Treaty of Trianon with Hungary deprived that country of nearly three-quarters of its territory and two-thirds of its inhabitants, for the benefit of Czechoslovakia, Rumania and Yugoslavia. The logic of the settlement was soundly national-democratic, for in the ancient kingdom of Hungary the Magyars were the rulers of national minorities which together constituted a majority of the population. The question was whether the Western Powers could and would impose liberal democracy on Central and Eastern Europe, and the answer is that they tried but failed. The defection of Italy did not help, but the real trouble was that France could not sustain the burden unaided and was given insufficient support by Britain. While the Weimar Republic lasted this did not matter too much. When National Socialism rose to power in Germany, Italian Fascism ceased to look like an oddity. It became apparent that the Western democracies would have to defend both constitutional government and the Versailles settlement against the 'revisionist' territorial claims of Fascist Italy and National Socialist Germany. This was not at all what the victors had expected to happen in 1919 when the map of Europe was redrawn on national-democratic lines. It was, however, a necessary consequence of Germany's refusal to play the game according to the rules. As long as the Weimar Republic lasted, Italian and Hungarian revisionism could be tolerated as a minor nuisance. When Germany joined the revisionist camp and at the same time dispensed with liberal democracy, it became evident that the League of Nations had failed. The only question now was whether the Western powers, including the United States, were willing to fight for the principles proclaimed in 1919. In the end they did so, but not before Germany had overturned the European order and made a shambles of constitutional government at home and abroad.[5]

It is important to grasp that Fascism and revisionism were related phenomena. The Fascist powers and their camp-followers aimed at the overthrow of the 1919 settlement, both in its territorial aspect and inasmuch as it institutionalized the rule of liberal democracy in Europe. From a different viewpoint the Russia of Lenin (1870–1924) and Stalin (1879–1953) likewise stood for the repudiation of Versailles: at any rate until 1934, when the USSR briefly adhered to the League of Nations as a reinsurance against the anti-Russian aspect of German revisionism. The complex entanglements resulting from this situation were not foreseen in the middle 1920s when for a brief while it looked as though the League settlement might endure. Under the terms of this arrangement Germany was expected to pay reparations and otherwise conform to the Versailles Treaty, while refraining from rearmament and from pressing territorial claims against Poland. The Soviet Union for its part would remain outside Europe, even though geographically linked to it by way of the Baltic States which had obtained their independence after 1919. The whole construction was bound to come unstuck as soon as Russia and Germany had recovered from their war losses. Meanwhile their tacit rapprochement in the military sphere, while the Weimar Republic was still intact and a member of the League, threw an additional strain on Poland, and indirectly on the entire French-controlled system of political relations. The system endured only because the Weimar Republic was too weak to challenge it. This circumstance was not lost upon some outside observers who took a realistic view of the situation. Thus when in 1925 the chief historical adviser to the British Foreign Office, Sir James Headlam-Morley, in what has been described as "a remarkable and prophetic memorandum", warned the Foreign Secretary, Sir Austen Chamberlain, of coming conflicts between Germany and her neighbours, he observed that the chief danger point in Europe lay not on the Rhine but on the Vistula:

Has anyone attempted to realise what would happen if there were to be a new partition of Poland, or if the Czechoslovak State were to be so curtailed and dismembered that in fact it disappeared from the map of Europe? The whole of Europe would at once be in chaos. There would no longer be any principle, meaning or sense in the territorial arrangements of the Continent.[6]

This was an accurate forecast of what in fact occurred in 1938–9, when another partition of Poland between Germany and Russia followed upon the dismemberment of Czechoslovakia. One cannot therefore say that the perils were being ignored. At most it might be said that the British government indulged for too long in the national habit of hoping for the best.

There was some excuse for cautious hope in 1926, when a seemingly flourishing Weimar Republic became a member of the League, and Gustav Stresemann joined Aristide Briand and Austen Chamberlain as arbiters of Europe's destiny. In France, the Radical Party of Herriot, with the assistance of unorthodox Socialists like Briand, had successfully reversed the chauvinism associated with the policies of Raymond Poincaré and begun negotiations for the evacuation of the Rhineland. Most Germans seemed to have accepted the Republic, and in the Reichstag elections of 1928 only twelve of Hitler's followers obtained a parliamentary mandate. The economic boom was at its height. Its collapse, following the Wall Street crash of October 1929, was not predictable. Even so it required a good deal of optimism to believe that the Germans would permanently put up with the frontiers of 1919, notably in the East. While Stresemann did his best to improve relations with France, the German General Staff was informally continued under another name, and new arms were being tested in Russia with the active cooperation of the Bolshevik authorities. The ground was being prepared for the rapid rearmament of Germany which became the principal feature of Hitler's dictatorial regime from 1933 onward. Since rearmament helped to relieve unemployment – swollen to monstrous proportions by 1932, when the depression reached its nadir – the National Socialist regime could count on the passive cooperation of a working class bereft of leadership by the brutal destruction of the Social Democratic and Communist parties. In all these respects German Fascism followed the precedent set by Mussolini in the 1920s, with a violence proportionate to the deeper tensions of German society: an industrial country rendered desperate by the world economic depression of the early 1930s. The link between the pre-war order and its Fascist successor was provided by the senile Field Marshal von Hindenburg, elected President of the Republic in 1925 and again in 1932, with whose help Hitler was legally installed as Chancellor in 1933. The Weimar Republic crumbled without offering serious resistance. Democracy was not merely unfamiliar: it had manifestly failed. Above all, it had failed to provide work. The totalitarian regime which arose from the ruins turned rearmament into a means of getting the unemployed back into the factories. The recipe was so successful that by 1939 Germany had both achieved full employment and become the strongest military power in Europe.

In view of what has been noted in an earlier chapter about the social roots of Austro-German National Socialism, the speed with which this successor of the Pan-German movement expanded into all strata of society in the 1930s need occasion no surprise. Something must be said, however, about the differences between Italian Fascism and the Central European variety. Both movements arose from an older nationalist tradition which in the Italian case intermingled with stray elements of Syndicalism, as expressed in Sorel's writings. Both centred upon the glorification of war in general and imperialist war in particular. Both were anti-liberal, contemptuous of democracy and hostile to the internationalism preached by the Socialists. Here the resemblance ends. Italian Fascism represented a corruption of syndicalist teachings which in Mussolini's case degenerated into violence for violence's sake. His principal theme, that of the "proletarian nation", was an inheritance from the nationalism of Corradini. In a poverty-stricken country economic issues were dominant, and the Milanese origins of Fascism in 1919 helped to give a socialist colouration to its early out-pourings: there was a good deal of talk about taxing war profiteers and helping the workers to a share in industrial management. Hitler (1889–1945) was from the start much more clearly identified with racialism of the Pan-German variety, his Austrian predecessors having identified Jews and Slavs as the principal enemies of the German *Volkstum* in Bohemia-Moravia, where Czech and German workers were in contact, but also in conflict, with one another. Austria in the early twentieth century had been something of a melting-pot, but there was no genuine fusion of the various nationalities: rather a stalemate which encouraged extremism of every variety. The *Deutsche Arbeiterpartei* of 1904 and its post-war successors operated in an atmosphere in which the defence of Germanism against the Slav hordes and their Jewish allies took precedence over all other issues. The youthful Hitler of 1914, who welcomed war as a blessed relief, shared the general obsession with the creation of a German-controlled *Mitteleuropa* which would drive the Slavs back and colonize the empire of the Romanovs. These notions were not peculiar to Hitler: they evoked an echo from German nationalists of every variety.

This is not to say that the National Socialist triumph in 1933 was inevitable. What was inevitable, once the parliamentary regime had shown itself unable to cope with mass unemployment, was the collapse of the Weimar system; but this might have led to a military dictatorship of the classic Right for which all the preconditions existed by the end of 1932: a presidential regime centred upon Hindenburg, an authoritarian government led by General von Schleicher, and a general mood of disillusionment with democracy. What turned this state of affairs into something resembling a political earthquake was the personality of Hitler, his ability to out-manoeuvre the traditional Conservatives after forming an alliance with them, and the weakness of the labour movement which offered no serious resistance to the Fascist take-over. It is no exaggeration to say that without Hitler the National Socialists would not have come to power, and certainly would not have been able to dispense with their Conservative allies within six months of Hitler's installation as Chancellor on 30 January 1933. In Italy it had taken Mussolini six years to achieve a similar result after his seizure of power in 1922, and even then the 'totalitarian' party had in fact to share power with the Monarchy and the Church. The German dictatorship was not only vastly more brutal: it was also far more effective in eliminating all other political forces, starting with the Communists and ending with dissenters in its own ranks. By August 1934, Hindenburg's death had turned Hitler into the official head of state and master of the country's armed forces, who took a solemn oath of loyalty to the Leader. No such phenomenon had been witnessed in a European country for over a century, which is why the more pessimistic Conservatives began to experience some qualms even before Hitler had led the country into war in 1939.

In fact the German Counter-Revolution parodied the French Revolution by giving a populist colouration to what was a profoundly reactionary movement. And it could do so because the aborted revolution of 1918 had not done its work. The Social Democrats had not altered the highly stratified class composition of German society and done nothing to resolve the tensions resulting from war and defeat. National Socialism presented itself as a 'revolutionary' movement. It was in fact a plebeian one, deeply rooted in the traditional illusions and aspirations of the peasantry and the lower middle class who for a century had seen their way of life disintegrate under the impact of industrialization. National Socialism promised them stability, at the same time that it held out to the workers the hope of full employment, and to the ruling stratum the certainty that Communists and Social Democrats would be smashed. For good measure, Hitler appealed to nationalism and promised to undo the Versailles settlement. National Socialism thus made an effective appeal to all classes of a society profoundly disoriented by the war of 1914–18, the raging post-war inflation which by 1923 had wiped out the savings of the middle class, and the mass unemployment consequent upon the great economic depression of the early 1930s and the deflationary policies pursued by the Brüning government with Social Democratic acquiescence in 1930–2. The movement spread like an epidemic, students and school-teachers being among its most effective propagandists. Even so it required Hitler's uncommon political talents to head off the classical Right with its faith in military dictatorship. The one-party State, legitimized by populist appeals to the masses, was an innovation, and the more intelligent Conservatives soon realized its latent dangers. But having entered into a partnership with their plebeian allies for the purpose of overthrowing the Weimar Republic, they became the prisoners of the daemonic forces they had helped to let loose. Once the armed forces had sworn an oath of loyalty to the Leader, and the Churches – Catholic and Protestant alike – had joined the anti-Communist crusade, the regime could no longer be dislodged by anything short of war. The anti-Jewish measures decreed from 1933 onward encountered no clerical resistance, nor did the academic community take a stand against them. In a certain sense it could be said that the entire phenomenon was in tune with German middle-class opinion, always excepting a handful of superannuated liberals who for many years had been fighting a rearguard action against this type of nationalism. As for the labour movement, the Social Democrats retired into passivity, while the Communists at first positively welcomed the new regime in the mistaken belief that it would be wrecked within months by its inability to cope with mass unemployment.

This illusion, like many others, was destined to be shattered in the course of the next twelve years. Hitler and his principal economic adviser, Dr Hjalmar Schacht – a fairly typical representative of the *haute bourgeoisie* who had once been a liberal – proved able to institute full employment without drawing upon the wisdom of Keynes. They simply refused to be guided by orthodox economics. That they chose to seek a way out by massive rearmament, instead of devoting the country's productive resources to peaceful purposes, is another matter. What counted was that they had broken away from economic liberalism, and in so doing discovered undreamed-of sources of energy which lay latent beneath the surface of society. State regulation proved superior to the uncontrolled market economy – this was the great discovery German Fascism made in the 1930s and which duly impressed foreign countries struggling with similar problems. If parliamentary democracy had to be sacrificed, that was too bad, but then the Germans had never really taken to it in the first place. Nor, for that matter, had the East Europeans who were Germany's neighbours and chief customers. The prestige of German National Socialism in the 1930s was rooted in a fairly widespread conviction that there must be a 'third way' distinct from capitalism and Communism, and that the Germans had found it. Since capitalism was identified with the West and Communism with Russia, this line of thought led to the already familiar notion that *Mitteleuropa* was destined to evolve a way of life peculiar to its Germanic heritage. In this fashion, Hitler's 'Third Reich' (the term went back to the literature of Romanticism) became identified with the 'third way': allegedly a rejection of capitalist values, in reality the imposition of State capitalist planning in the name of populist socialism.[7]

For all that the new regime had to be imposed by wholesale terrorism, the murder or imprisonment of thousands of opponents and the establishment of a secret police dictatorship unparalleled outside Stalinist Russia. The concurrent regimentation of cultural life benefited from the active cooperation of numerous writers and artists, academics and clergymen. Opposition was silenced or identified with the Jewish community, the greater part of which emigrated between 1933 and 1939. The civil service on the whole cooperated wholeheartedly with the new regime, in marked contrast to the coolness it had shown the Weimar Republic. This was particularly true of the judiciary. The crucial factor, of course, was the willingness of the Army leaders to back a government which embarked upon massive rearmament. Even the murder of General von Schleicher on 30 June 1934 – when Hitler caused a large number of potential opponents to be assassinated – did not shake the loyalty of the officers' corps: Schleicher's funeral was attended by the former Commander of the Army, General von Hammerstein, and one junior officer. It was only much later that something like a resistance movement began to form among officers, and even then it comprised only a small minority. The ecclesiastical leaders caused even less trouble. For the Catholic Church, the conclusion of a concordat with the Holy See in 1933 proved the decisive factor which ensured its loyalty to the Third Reich during the twelve stormy years that followed. The Protestant clergy, with few exceptions, cooperated even more enthusiastically, many of them joining the so-called 'German Christians' for whom anti-Semitism had become a bridge to something not far removed from neo-paganism. In sum, middle-class resistance was virtually non-existent, while the working class was either won over or reduced to silence by the SA and SS gangs and the Gestapo (political police). The regime could rely on the support of the lower middle class and peasantry, while its terrorist measures were ruthlessly enforced by the heirs of the *Freikorps* of 1919–20: military shock troops who had already shown their worth during the brief civil war of 1919, when among others they bludgeoned Karl Liebknecht and Rosa Luxemburg to death in the streets of Berlin. As later events were to show, there was no limit to which these hard-core terrorists were not prepared to go in the war to exterminate Slav or Jewish 'sub-humans'. Meanwhile they amused themselves by torturing political prisoners at Dachau and other concentration camps.

Inherited attitudes do not wholly explain the speed with which this collapse into barbarism occurred in what after all was the most highly industrialized country of Continental Europe. The fact is that Germany had been thoroughly brutalized by the 1914–18 war, the civil war of 1919, the inflationary dispossession of the old middle class, mass unemployment after 1930 and the impact of modern technology upon millions of uprooted people who crowded the big cities. Once the rule of law had broken down, the veneer of civilization proved to be much thinner than had been supposed by complacent liberals and Social Democrats. Fascism also profited from the anti-Communist hysteria which gripped the middle class from 1919 onwards. That the tide of revolution should have been checked in 1919 along the historic frontier between Russia and Germany was crucial for the subsequent failure of the German Communists to evolve into a genuine mass movement. Historically, the Germans were disposed to think of the Russians as barbarians. When this prejudice obtained additional nourishment from what was in fact a barbarous civil war in Russia, the German middle class reacted with a mixture of fright and fury that goes far to explain the behaviour of Hitler's followers and the tolerance with which they were viewed by the ruling stratum, the civil service and the clergy. Bolshevism became a scarecrow in a country whose indigenous Communists were far too few and incompetent to seize power. To some extent this was also the case in other European countries, but only in Germany was the disposition to exterminate Slavs and Jews linked to actual fears stemming from the collapse of 1918–19. Germany's ambiguous position between Eastern and Western Europe rendered the country liable to fits of crusading hysteria rooted in a centuries-old conviction that Teutons and Slavs were destined to be enemies. Russia stood for backwardness and barbarism. After 1917 its regime also figured as a standing menace to bourgeois values, a circumstance underlined by the bloodcurdling language with which the German Communists consoled themselves for their actual impotence. From this fateful conjunction of circumstances there arose in due course the monstrous programme of National Socialism: nothing less than a determination to enslave or exterminate Germany's Slav neighbours. This was a notable departure from the standard Conservative attitude which combined anti-Bolshevism with a disposition to revive the historic alliance between Russia and Prussia. To Hitler, an Austrian, this line of reasoning made no appeal. He thought in terms of crushing the Slav peoples and if necessary exterminating them wholesale. Russia was the principal target by virtue of its association with Communism, but Poland was not exempt, even though at times he toyed with the notion of using the Poles as allies and compensating them with Ukrainian territory for what they would have to give up to their German overlords. As for Czechoslovakia it would of course have to become part of the Greater *Reich*. There was a certain insane logic about all this: if the Pan-German aims of 1914 were to be revived under cover of an anti-Bolshevist crusade, it made sense to fuse racialism and imperialism at the expense of Germany's eastern neighbours. At the same time the anti-Communist aspect of the whole campaign offered a chance of keeping the Western democracies neutral, thus saving Germany the need to fight a war on two fronts. After all, why should America, Britain and France object to a German onslaught on Communist Russia? In point of fact this kind of reasoning proved highly effective between 1933 and 1939 in winning the Third Reich political sympathies both in the West and among the more frantic anti-Communists in Eastern Europe, the Poles included. Hungarian revisionism could be roped in as a matter of course. As for anti-Semitism, its popularity was of long standing, and the more or less fanciful association of Communism with the Jews did the rest.

The Jews in fact were destined to suffer a catastrophe of unparalleled dimensions, for no better reason than that out of a world total of fourteen million about half this number inhabited the thirteen countries grouped in and around Central Europe. A minority everywhere and a majority nowhere, they were distinguished from the surrounding populations by their religion, their traditions and their occupations. In an age of mounting rural distress they were an urban people; in an era of inflamed nationalism they adhered for the most part to some form of liberal or socialist cosmopolitanism, although in the end sheer despair drove masses of them into the Zionist movement. The bulk – about four and a half million – lived in Poland and Rumania, where they experienced both popular hatred and governmental disfavour.

Emigration to America, the traditional outlet for harried East European minorities, was increasingly barred from 1921 onwards, when quotas were assigned to the various European countries on the basis of America's own national composition in 1920, as revealed by census figures. Schools and universities throughout Eastern Europe imposed limitations upon the number of Jewish students, who for good measure were frequently beaten up with the connivance of the police. With the exception of Czechoslovakia all the governments of the area encouraged a pogrom mentality. The priesthood fed the masses with horrendous tales of Jewish crimes, and the *Protocols of the Elders of Zion*, a Tsarist police fabrication dating back to 1903, was widely accepted as a true account of Jewish designs to rule the world. It only needed the association of the Jews with Communism – rendered plausible during the early years of the Russian Revolution by the prominence of Trotsky and other leading figures of Jewish origin – for the ground to be prepared for the great massacre of 1939–45. Even so the actual extermination of some five or six million Jews during these years required a considerable organizational effort on the part of the Germans, plus widespread cooperation among their East European allies. During the inter-war years this outcome was not foreseeable, but the pressures were already sufficient to stimulate a considerable emigration to Palestine, then a British-mandated territory. In the circumstances it is not surprising that the Jewish intelligentsia was increasingly divided between Zionist and pro-Communist currents, the Soviet regime in those years being relatively tolerant where its own Jewish minority was concerned. Hitler did not create these conditions: he merely applied his own 'solution' to them.

By comparison with the forces let loose in Central Europe by war, defeat, inflation, depression, mass unemployment and the collapse of liberalism, Italian Fascism was a relatively minor affair. In some respects it wore a comic-opera aspect, as did Italian nationalism generally. Its significance lay in the fact that an important Western European nation had been prized away from the liberal-democratic camp. As noted before, this development had its roots in the pre-1914 era, when Nationalists, Syndicalists and Futurists began to converge towards a viewpoint subsequently identified with the Fascist movement. The transition was effected during the war years and the troubled post-war era, when the Nationalists won active support from hordes of ex-servicemen, especially the blackshirted *Arditi* of the Commando units, who were unwilling to return to civilian life.[8] Italian revisionism, antedating the rise of Fascism, was largely directed against Yugoslavia and centred on territorial claims in the Adriatic which the 1919 Peace Conference had failed to award to the Liberal government of Orlando and Sonnino. The Nationalists and their Fascists allies could therefore claim that whereas Italy had helped to win the war, Liberalism had lost the peace. D'Annunzio's theatrical 'occupation' of Fiume (a formerly Hungarian port coveted by Yugoslavia) in September 1919 was a harbinger of bigger things to come. The fact that the Socialists and the Catholic *Popolari* were much the largest parties in the parliament elected in November 1919 recoiled upon them when they proved unable to cooperate. A major strike in September 1920 frightened the middle class, and the newly founded Communist party, which had split away from the Socialists at Livorno in January 1921, added its share to the general confusion by calling for proletarian revolution. The upshot was the Fascist seizure of power already referred to. The Army, the Church and big business were all heavily implicated, while Western public opinion got used to the notion that Communism and Fascism were rival contenders for power, at any rate in unstable countries such as Italy. The Fascist dictatorship in consequence paved the way for Hitler's triumph, and in general set the tone for a style of government no longer compatible with the liberal tradition. It also made possible the subsequent formation of what became known as the Rome–Berlin Axis.

Unlike National Socialism, Italian Fascism remained something of a compromise since, despite the original Fascist programme of 1919, the Monarchy and the Senate survived. The Church likewise retained more influence than it could exercise in the Germany of Hitler. On the other hand, the one-party state – a novelty borrowed from Russia – became the model of all future Fascist regimes. What was known as the Corporative State theoretically replaced parliamentary democracy and free bargaining in the labour market. As constituted in December 1929, when the National Council of Corporations was formally established, each corporation, in addition to employers and employed, contained three members of the Fascist Party "to represent the public". The whole organization was subject to the Ministry of Corporations, which was another name for the Fascist bureaucracy. Mussolini was extremely proud of this invention, which was supposed to have overcome the class conflict, and Western observers fell into the habit of comparing Italian Fascism favourably with Russian Communism. In fact the regime represented a terroristic one-party dictatorship which operated in the interest of the employers and did its level best to speed industrialization along State-capitalist lines. In 1925 it was officially described by its leaders as 'totalitarian', a label destined to endure long after its inventors had been speeded to the grave. From the 1930s onwards it became openly aggressive in the military sphere, starting with an unprovoked assault on Abyssinia in 1935 which showed up the League of Nations for the hollow sham it was. The alliance with Germany was at first blocked by differences over the future of Austria, but became a reality in 1938. From then on it was evident that, if Britain and France wanted to uphold what was left of the 1919 settlement, they would have to go to war against Germany and Italy. For obvious reasons this unattractive prospect disposed the British and French governments of the period to opt for a different solution: a Four Power agreement which would ensure peace in the West while giving Germany a free hand in the East. This was the essence of what came to be known as the policy of appeasement.

The Austrian episode furnishes a good example of how politics were conducted in the 1930s. Hemmed in by Germany and Italy, with revisionist Hungary as an additional source of trouble, only a very solidly based democratic regime could have maintained the country's independence. Instead, Dollfuss and Schuschnigg in 1934, at the bidding of Mussolini, destroyed the Social Democrats and parliamentary government, only to be deserted by Mussolini in their hour of need. A further turning point came in July 1936 when an agreement between Germany and Austria proclaimed the latter "a German State" and obliged its leaders to follow in the wake of German policy. Schuschnigg's last gesture of defiance in 1938, a referendum on Austrian independence, was promptly revoked on orders from Berlin, whereupon the Germans marched in, to loud cheers from at least one-third of the populace. No resistance was offered, and Austria became part of the Greater *Reich*. Six months later it was the turn of Czechoslovakia.

Eastern Europe in the 1930s presented a picture very different from the confident optimism of the 1920s.[9] The great depression undid what economic progress there had been during the previous decade and undermined the foundations of whatever there was in the way of constitutional government. Political movements modelled on Italian and German Fascism filled the vacuum created by the decline of their rivals. By 1938 Czechoslovakia had become a lonely outpost of democracy; Austria had been forcibly amalgamated with Germany after going through a brief period of home-brewed authoritarianism; and the agrarian countries of East-Central Europe were in the process of shifting from a pro-French to a pro-German orientation. This was the case even in Poland, notwithstanding that country's territorial conflict with Germany over Danzig and the 'Polish Corridor' to East Prussia. The primacy of Germany was now such that only a coalition of the Western democracies and the USSR could have blocked Hitler's progress. This was perceived in Paris and London, but the alternative policy of giving Germany a free hand in the East possessed so many influential advocates that in the end the Czechoslovak bastion was sacrificed at the Munich conference in September 1938. Britain and France, by allowing Germany to annex the German-speaking parts of Czechoslovakia, in fact destroyed what was left of the Versailles settlement. The formal incorporation of Bohemia and Moravia in the *Reich* six months later, in March 1939, merely spelled out the consequence of the Munich surrender. At the same time, however, the event proved a turning-point, for Hitler had now unmasked himself and clearly launched out along a road mapped out in advance by the ideologists of Pan-Germanism. For this reason the complex of issues involved in the Munich settlement deserves some consideration, quite apart from the significance which this particular episode later assumed for public opinion in Britain and France.[10]

France was officially bound to come to Czechoslovakia's assistance if attacked, and the French government's failure in 1938 to live up to this solemn pledge showed how deep the rot had gone. Individual politicians in the tradition of Clemenceau, such as M. Paul Reynaud (with Colonel de Gaulle at his elbow), had for some years preached rearmament, mechanization and firmness in the face of German and Italian threats. The Right on the whole was more concerned with the Red Peril, while Léon Blum's Socialists inclined towards pacifism. The reigning Radical party of Édouard Daladier and Georges Bonnet, like the Baldwin–Chamberlain regime in Britain, dreaded war and proceeded very slowly with defensive armaments. The Maginot Line, which had become the centre-piece of French stategy, left a defensive gap of 350 kilometres along the French frontier. From 1934–5 onwards de Gaulle and Reynaud drew attention to the need for building up a mechanized professional army, but in the face of Radical inertia and Socialist hostility they made no progress. As for French diplomacy, the Quai d'Orsay was paralysed by the doctrine that nothing could be done without British cooperation. Reynaud, like Churchill, was denounced as a warmonger. Daladier's expert on foreign affairs, Bonnet, sided with Mussolini over Ethiopia, dreaded involvement in Spain, had no faith in an alliance with Russia and after the Austrian *Anschluss* in March 1938 gave up Czechoslovakia for lost, as did Paul-Boncour who happened to be Foreign Minister at that moment. The French, in short, were no longer in a mood to defend the Versailles settlement, although Bonnet in his memoirs claims to have warned the Chamberlain Government in April 1938 that the destruction of Czechoslovakia must not be allowed. By September of that year he had become the arch-appeaser in the French Cabinet, to the point of doing everything he could to promote a Czech capitulation to Hitler's demand for the cession of the German-speaking Sudetenland. The Prime Minister, Daladier, rather more reluctantly took the same line and after Munich he carried the great majority of the Chamber of Deputies with him.

On the British side, the threat posed by Hitler's claims had by 1938 induced Neville Chamberlain to toy with the notion of letting Germany have a large chunk of Africa: an amateurish scheme which was opposed by some of his own colleagues and by the Foreign Office. Chamberlain had not grasped that what Hitler wanted was control of Central Europe, preparatory to an onslaught on Russia and the annexation of the Ukraine. His proposal for diverting the Germans in the direction of Africa (presumably at the expense of Belgium and Portugal) did not obtain Cabinet backing. When it came to Austria and Czechoslovakia there was the argument that Hitler was only asking for revision of the Versailles settlement affecting German-speaking areas. For the rest, the Chamberlain government was convinced of its own helplessness. The decisive argument was quite simply that Britain was not ready. A 'scenario' submitted by the Chiefs of Staff on 14 September 1938 envisaged Britain having to fight Germany, Italy and Japan, with the United States and Russia neutral, the Middle East in rebellion, the British Isles subject to massive air raids and a submarine campaign, and the French probably not to be relied upon beyond a purely defensive stand along their frontier. It was also predicted that Czechoslovakia would crumble in a week. All this was disputable, but the Cabinet took the view that a 'breathing space' was necessary before Britain and France could think of confronting Germany. Unfortunately no such breathing space was granted by Hitler, who was determined to make the most of his temporary advantage. Having swallowed Austria, he promptly unleashed a campaign for the dismemberment of Czechoslovakia. When Daladier informed Chamberlain on 13 September that a German invasion must be avoided "because in that case France would be faced with her obligations", the British Cabinet was won over to the cause of capitulation. In the circumstances, Hitler could proceed with his threats of military action, confident that the decadent democracies would not fight. Some of his military advisers were less certain, but his gambler's instinct did not let him down on this occasion.

The Munich conference of 29–30 September 1938 involved only four Powers: Germany, Britain, France and Italy, respectively represented by Hitler, Chamberlain, Daladier and Mussolini. Mussolini played the impartial mediator, although in fact the plan he produced was that supplied to him in advance by the Germans. It differed from Hitler's original demands only in that the occupation of the German-speaking Sudetenland was to be spread over ten days instead of taking place at once. After the agreement had been signed, Chamberlain and Daladier saw the Czech representatives, who had been left waiting in an anteroom, and told them that their country had been partitioned by the Big Four. On the following day Chamberlain and Hitler signed a statement which read in part: "We regard the agreement signed last night and the Anglo-German Naval Agreement [of 1935] as symbolic of the desire of our two peoples never to go to war with one another again." This was the high-water mark of appeasement. Chamberlain was cheered when he returned to London and waved the statement at the airport. It meant, he said, "peace in our time", a sentiment echoed by many Conservatives and most of the business community, but not by the section of the Tory Party led by Winston Churchill and Anthony Eden; or by the Labour Party, which at this point renounced its rather sterile pacifism and decided that Hitler's further progress would have to be resisted. Munich in fact undermined Chamberlain's position, for Hitler now felt encouraged to embark on the military conquest of Eastern Europe. This was not at all what the British government had in mind when it decided to sacrifice the Czech bastion. Its leading figures seem to have supposed that Hitler would content himself with a revision of the Versailles settlement along national lines. When Munich turned out to be a surrender which had made Germany more rather than less aggressive, the traditional Tory forces began to mobilize behind Churchill. It was after all not safe to let Germany dominate the European Continent, and British rearmament was speeded up. From there the road led, by some surprising turns and twists, to the Anglo-French declaration of war on Germany in September 1939. Appeasement had failed, and its failure was due to the fact that after Munich the Germans were in no mind to let the British government dictate the shape of European politics.

The road to Munich had been a lengthy one. In a sense it may be said to have begun at Versailles. In the words of a leading British historian:

After 1918 France concluded alliances with Poland and the Little Entente against Germany, Russia, Italy, Hungary and Bulgaria; Britain refused to endorse a policy which she deemed short-sighted and, in the long run, exceedingly dangerous. In time its insufficiency became patent; France veered towards Britain and gradually accepted her lead even in Continental affairs. And then, after Czechoslovakia had been lost and Yugoslavia estranged, Chamberlain made the Polish-Rumanian rump of the French system – two countries allied against Russia – into the base of his defensive system against Germany, without ascertaining whether, or how, their interests and policies could be squared with those of Russia.[11]

This is the best available summary of what occured during those years, but in the nature of the case it leaves a great deal unsaid. In particular it ignores the exceedingly complex web of diplomacy spun by the professionals in charge. In view of the failure which crowned their efforts this is perhaps no great loss, but it obliges the historian to deal in desperate brevity with events which consumed a great deal of time and patience. Munich was the end of a long road. It was also a signal triumph for the Axis Powers over the Western democracies; and it made war certain, unless Britain and France were prepared to sacrifice Poland as well, in which case they might stand aside and let Germany and Russia fight it out. That the latter solution was in the end not adopted is the more remarkable since the logic of 'appeasement' unmistakably pointed in this direction. Instead, Germany and Russia agreed upon another partition of Poland in August 1939, whereupon the Western Powers reluctantly went to war in order to defend Poland from the Germans.

The turning-point was a British guarantee to Poland on 31 March 1939, a fortnight after Hitler had swallowed up what remained of Czechoslovakia. The Polish alliance was a major miscalculation, which in the end precipitated war under conditions unfavourable to the Western Powers. Britain had no means of guaranteeing Poland against a German onslaught, and France lacked the will. In point of fact Chamberlain and his associates did not think in terms of war. They thought a paper guarantee would suffice to moderate German ambitions, and for the rest the German claim to Danzig was negotiable. They reckoned without Hitler, who now determined on the destruction of Poland, and to this end postponed his long-planned crusade against Soviet Russia. On 23 August 1939 the German Foreign Minister, Ribbentrop, and his Soviet colleague, Molotov, signed a pact whereby Russia promised to stay neutral if Germany were involved in war; there were also secret clauses determining Russian and German shares in the partition of Poland. The German–Soviet pact was meant to neutralize Western influence in Eastern Europe. Neither the Germans nor the Russians seem to have thought that Britain and France would embark on the hopeless enterprise of saving Poland without Russian assistance. In this they were mistaken, for the spectacle of Communism and Fascism in alliance against the West destroyed the basis of appeasement: Hitler could no longer be portrayed as the West's defender against Russia. The British Conservatives now reverted to their traditional line of resistance to German hegemony in Europe. On 25 August an Anglo-Polish treaty of mutual assistance was signed, and by 3 September Britain and a reluctant France were at war with Germany. The Versailles settlement was to be defended by force of arms after all. The decision came too late. Germany had grown too strong to be checked by the Western Powers, and Soviet neutrality ensured the rapid destruction of Poland. Nonetheless the Anglo-French declaration of war on 3 September closed an epoch. Twenty years earlier the Western democracies had dictated peace terms to the heirs of Imperial Germany. They were now called upon to draw the sword in defence of what was left of the 1919 settlement.[12]

B REVOLUTION AND REACTION

The inter-war period was distinguished by a polarization of attitudes due to the impact of the Russian Revolution on Central and Western Europe. The resulting competition between the Communist and Fascist movements, to which reference has already been made, had its roots in the pre-1914 situation, but it assumed political dimensions only after 1918. The Bolshevik seizure of power in November 1917, and the founding of the Communist International in March 1919, created an entirely new political climate. In Lenin's conception the Russian up-heaval was only one element of the coming world revolution. The theme recurs in the letters he addressed to the Bolshevik Central Committee in the autumn of 1917. In a motion he pushed through the Central Committee on 10 October (23 new style) he placed first among his considerations "the international position of the Russian revolution (the revolt in the German navy, which is an extreme manifestation of the growth throughout Europe of the world socialist revolution)". He de-veloped this line of reasoning in other statements, public and private. "The ripening and inevitability of the world socialist revolution cannot be doubted." "We stand on the threshold of a world proletarian revolu-tion." "We shall be genuine traitors to the International if at such a moment, under such propitious conditions, we answer such a summons from the German revolutionaries only by verbal resolutions." "The international situation gives us a number of objective data showing that if we act now we shall have on our side the whole of proletarian Europe."[13] This was Lenin's considered opinion on the eve of the Bolshevik uprising. He regarded it as a signal for a European cataclysm, and the latter in turn as a guarantee for the revolution's triumph in Russia. That a proletarian regime in Russia could maintain itself only if the European working class followed suit was axiomatic. From 1917 until the spring of 1921, when the German movement had been de-feated, a kind of messianic mood predominated in Moscow. Thereafter it became a matter of holding out until the European proletariat had re-assembled its forces, and ultimately the Bolsheviks were obliged to acknowledge that their seizure of power was doomed to remain a strictly Russian experience.

The Bolshevik illusions of 1917-19 had their counterpart in the West. At Versailles the Allied statesmen reckoned with the possibility that Germany might follow the Russian example, and the German delegates did what they could to exploit such fears by representing their country as a bulwark of 'order', but a bulwark which was in danger of being carried away by the revolutionary flood. In actual fact the German revolution of 1918-19 never transgressed the boundaries of bourgeois society; it did not even make a clean sweep of the monarchist heritage. The same applies to Austria-Hungary. As for the Western democracies there was never a single moment when their governments were in serious danger. The Leninist world picture was illusory. Events such as the strike movements in Germany and Austria-Hungary in January 1918 sprang from war-weariness; if the strikers desired anything it was peace and democracy, not the overthrow of capitalist class rule. The subsequent military collapse of the Central Powers did sweep away the Hohenzollern and Habsburg monarchies, and disappointment with Social Democratic rule eventually gave rise to the formation of Communist parties; but they remained mere sects without impact upon the great mass of the workers. As for the notion that a revolutionary situation might arise in France or Britain, it was not shared even by the majority of Communists in these countries.

During the opening months of 1919 it was still possible to believe that the Russian Revolution would spread westward. Soviet republics were proclaimed in Budapest on 21 March and in Munich on 7 April. In February, a few weeks after the sanguinary suppression of the Spartakus rising in Berlin, and the murder by monarchist officers of Karl Liebknecht (1871–1919) and Rosa Luxemburg (1871–1919), there were bloody clashes between armed workers and government troops in Central Germany, and in March a second round of fighting in Berlin cost the lives of 1,200 people. Mass strikes swept the Ruhr industrial area. In April the French Fleet in the Black Sea mutinied, and in Paris on 1 May tens of thousands of demonstrators clashed with the police. In June 200,000 engineering workers came out on strike in Paris, and in April 1920 there was something approaching a general strike in France, followed a few months later by similar movements in Italy.[14] Lenin and his colleagues could also draw encouragement from the fact that in 1919–20 the Socialist parties of Italy, Norway and Bulgaria decided to affiliate to the Communist International, while the German USPD, the French Socialist Party and the British ILP entered into negotiations with Moscow. But when the Second Congress of the Communist International met in July 1920, the overwhelming majority of the workers in Britain, Germany, Austria, Belgium, Holland and Sweden were still under reformist leadership, and the subsequent splits in Western Europe left the Communists in a minority everywhere save in France. In the circumstances Lenin felt obliged to note that "the international working class is still under the yoke of the labour aristocracy and the opportunists", and the Congress manifesto recognized that when "the moment comes for direct action to achieve the Communist revolution", it would be essential to snatch control of the masses from the Social Democrats. The struggle against Social Democracy in fact became the principal business of the newly founded Communist parties, strengthened in their faith by writings such as Lenin's *Left-Wing Communism – an*

Infantile Disorder (1920), which spelled out the correct line to be followed. Somehow the right moment never came, until the Soviet Army was employed after 1939 for the purpose of imposing Communist parties on occupied countries. The open avowal of civil war, dictatorship and terrorism simply proved too much for the majority of workers in Central and Western Europe.

Instead of spreading westward, the Communist movement began to make headway in the East. At the Second Congress of the International, Armenia, Azerbaijan, Bokhara, China, Korea, Persia, India, Turkey and the Dutch Indies were represented, albeit with a total of only seventeen delegates out of 217. In later years it became increasingly evident that the great revolutionary reservoir lay in the backward countries, but during the 1920s the conviction prevailed that the decisive battle would be fought in Germany. In a sense this proved true, inasmuch as the collapse of the German labour movement in 1933 showed up the illusory character of the original Leninist perspective. The Bolshevik model was not applicable to the European workers' movement. At the same time the Communist example was copied and caricatured by the Fascists, who took over the notion of dictatorship and the one-party State. In this fashion the European civil war of the 1930s and 1940s obtained its ideological preparation.

Both Socialists and Communists invoked Marx, and they could do so with a perfectly good conscience. Communists had only to cite the 1848 *Manifesto* and Marx's 1871 defence of the Paris Commune, *The Civil War in France*. Socialists could point to the fact that the First International (1864–76) had been a democratic organization, that Marx had in 1872 got rid of Bakunin and his followers, and that on the same occasion he publicly expressed the view that countries with a democratic tradition – he particularly mentioned North America, Britain and Holland – might effect a peaceful transition to socialism.[15] In his preface to the first English edition of *Capital* in 1887 Engels underlined the point with special reference to Britain, and in 1891 he gave it as his opinion that:

the old order could grow peacefully into the new in countries where all power lies with Parliament and where one can have one's own way quite constitutionally so long as the majority of the people is behind one – i.e., in democratic republics like France and America or in monarchies like Britain, where the throne is powerless to act against the popular will.

He was simply elaborating on Marx's observation in 1879 that:

one need not be a Socialist to foresee sanguinary revolutions coming in Russia, Germany, Austria and possibly in Italy if the Italians carry on in the same manner as hitherto. In these countries the events of the French Revolution might once more occur. . . . Yet these revolutions will be performed by the majority. Revolutions are made not by a party but by the whole nation.[16]

The Central European upheavals of 1918–19 fitted into this perspective. Lenin's expectation that the Bolshevik seizure of power would be duplicated in the West did not. He had meanwhile shifted the emphasis from class to party, so that it no longer mattered to him what the majority actually wanted: it was enough if there was a Communist vanguard to take the lead in revolutionary uprisings. These notions ignored the actual state of mind of the working class in all advanced industrial countries and thus condemned the Communist parties to the hopeless task of preaching revolution to a labour movement which was militant and yet thoroughly reformist, even where it employed Marxist language. In the end this recognition spread to the West European Communists themselves, while those in Eastern Europe continued with some success to proclaim themselves the heirs of the Russian Revolution.

For the time being a succession of reverses had to be endured: the defeat of the Red Army at the gates of Warsaw in August 1920; the collapse of the Italian factory occupations in September 1920 and the subsequent rise of Fascism; the ignominious failure of a German rising in March 1921; and in Russia itself the naval mutiny at Kronstadt in the same month. This revolt shook the regime to its foundations and obliged Lenin to introduce the New Economic Policy which made extensive concessions to capitalism. By 1924, when Lenin had left the scene, the 'German Revolution' had been shown up as a mirage, and the International had become a mere extension of the Soviet Communist Party. Russia now became the spiritual fatherland of Communists the world over, and the activities of the International were guided by the assumption that the defence of the Soviet Union was the prime duty of all Communists. The parties of the International were thus turned into auxiliaries of the Soviet regime, to the point of abandoning their anti-militarism whenever the Soviet government felt obliged to sign a military alliance with a foreign power. This development was speeded up when Stalin and his associates monopolized the leadership of the Soviet party from about 1928 onwards. The simultaneous abandonment of the New Economic Policy, and the decision to industrialize at breakneck speed, while collectivizing agriculture against the stubborn resistance of the peasantry, made it all the more necessary that the USSR should obtain the resolute backing of Communist parties the world over. The International was transformed into a mere instrument of Russian policy, and the Old Guard of Bolshevik leaders who resisted this trend were ruthlessly slaughtered in the Great Purge of 1936–8.[17]

By accident this massacre – in effect the destruction of Lenin's party – coincided with the Spanish civil war of 1936–9, which for the last time turned 'proletarian revolution' into a genuine political issue in a major European country. Soviet assistance to the Spanish Republic was predicated on the avoidance of anything that might stir up the passions of 1917-21, but in the event it proved impossible to manipulate mass emotions in Spain to suit the convenience of Russian foreign policy. While the Republic on the whole avoided anything in the nature of wholesale socialization, Anarchist and Trotskyist participation in its defence against the Army and its Falangist allies resulted in something like a re-enactment of the Russian civil war. This was not to Stalin's taste, and his political police did its best to keep the movement within safe limits, to the point of murdering the Anarchist and Trotskyist leaders. But the international line-up – Germany and Italy versus Russia, with the Western democracies on the side-lines – provided a foretaste of the Second World War. From the Soviet standpoint it now became highly probable that the Western Powers would give Germany a free hand in the East, as indeed very nearly happened in 1939. Stalin drew his own conclusion by entering into an alliance with Hitler in August 1939, thereby obliging the Western Powers to fight. In the meantime Communist and Fascist intervention in what was essentially another round in the perennial conflict between Left and Right in Spain had transformed a civil war into the curtain-raiser for the Second World War. Spain inflamed political passions, not least among Roman Catholics, large numbers of whom rallied to the defence of the Church against its assailants. To that extent the Catholic peasantry of Europe was conditioned to support Hitler's subsequent crusade against Soviet Russia in 1941 when he went back on the 1939 Ribbentrop–Molotov agreement. Stalin's reputed query in 1945, "How many divisions has the Pope?" might have been answered by his British and American interlocutors by pointing out that Hitler's unsuccessful drive to Moscow was in part sustained by the peasant masses who had been taught to regard Communism as a mortal threat to their faith and their way of life.[18]

The Spanish civil war did not merely destroy the parliamentary Republic proclaimed in 1931: it divided European opinion along lines which proved durable. It also helped to wreck the Popular Front government established in France in 1936 under Socialist direction, with Léon Blum presiding over a coalition of Socialists and bourgeois Radicals which rested on Communist support. The French government having failed to sustain the Spanish Republic, it was an easy guess that France would succumb to an all-out onslaught by the Fascist Powers, which was duly delivered in 1940. How far the rot had gone became visible only in May–June 1940, when the French Army collapsed and the veteran Marshal Pétain presided over a military capitulation which before long spawned a reactionary dictatorship at the expense of France's democratic institutions. The 1930s had witnessed what can only be described as a European counter-revolution, as well as the destruction of the Versailles settlement. French foreign policy was geared to Britain's, and from this circumstance stemmed Blum's non-intervention in Spain, as well as Daladier's capitulation at Munich in 1938. It took the German challenge to Britain in the summer of 1940 to reverse this process, and by then Continental Europe was lost and had to be reconquered – principally by the military forces of Russia and America.

Throughout this confused period every move made by the European governments was conditioned by the prevailing estimate of the Russian Revolution and the Communist movement which was its offspring.[19] It was the peculiarity of Soviet Russia that it was far behind the Western countries in economic development, and at the same time ruled by men determined to pass beyond the West by skipping the capitalist phase. Bourgeois society had no real roots in Russia, and once the Tsarist regime had fallen the choice lay between Bolshevism and a military dictatorship of the Right. Lenin and his followers at first rationalized their actions by proclaiming that the Russian Revolution had to incorporate the heritage of its French predecessor, and then to pass beyond it by industrializing the country along socialist lines. The national emphasis became more pronounced with the passing of Lenin (1924), the expulsion of Trotsky (1929) and the arrival on the scene of a second generation of Bolshevik leaders who had few contacts with the West and viewed their own revolution in patriotic terms. The drive to turn Russia into a first-class industrial power, begun in earnest in 1929, soon absorbed all available energies and at the same time made necessary a degree of political centralization wholly incompatible with Lenin's quasi-anarchist pronouncements in 1917. The transition from Marxism to Leninism, and then from Leninism to Stalinism, was effected by a self-constituted bureaucratic elite which had become independent of the working class in whose name it ruled. This reconstitution of the familiar Russian tradition of autocracy and state control was made possible by the institution of a single-party monopoly supposedly designed to safeguard the 'dictatorship of the proletariat'. Without quite knowing what they were doing, the Soviet leaders stood Marx on his head. Socialism, so far from being a stage beyond capitalism, became an alternative way of pushing the industrial revolution through. With the termination of the mixed-economy experiment hesitantly begun in 1921 and abrogated in 1928–9, there were no capitalists to do the job, the profit motive was ruled out, and the State had to develop its own administrative organs for supervising the industrialization of a vast and backward country. Its prime instrument was the Party, officially the guardian of 'proletarian dictatorship', in fact a terrorist organization which imposed the decrees of a self-elected political autocracy.

The system had certain built-in advantages from the standpoint of the planners, in that there was no need to make concessions to the consumer.

Historically, capitalism in the West had begun from the market, under-selling the independent artisans who were gradually driven out of business. Only thereafter did it tackle the job of developing large-scale industries. The Stalinist regime reversed this order: it built up the basic industries first, without bothering about cost, or about the cost in lives. In this it pursued a strategy already inherent in the tentative experiments of the pre-revolutionary regime, but with the advantage of not having to worry about trade unions or public opinion. Nor was there any political party to defend the interests of the peasants, who were ruthlessly driven into collectives or drafted into the new industrial centres. The operation, achieved at the cost of millions of lives, was then baptized socialism, in contrast to the traditional Marxist analysis, which derived the necessity of socialism from the over-ripeness of capitalism. The drive to modernize the country came from the higher echelons of the Party, inheritors of a tradition which had deep roots within the pre-revolutionary intelligentsia. The whole process had only the remotest connection with the traditional aims of the labour movement, and the Bolshevik claim to speak on behalf of the workers and peasants sounded more and more incongruous as one Five Year Plan followed another, each imposing heavier burdens on the masses for the purpose of capital accumulation. The conquest of power in a backward country whose peasants clung to private ownership had its own logic: if the Party was to retain power, the peasantry must be brought under control, and this was done by herding it into collectives. Lenin had hoped that the peasants would accept a gradual process of modernization. When this expectation faded, Stalin embarked upon forced collectivization as the only means of preserving the Party's monopoly of power. At the same time he wrenched the Party loose from its moorings, destroyed or imprisoned millions of its members, and turned the others into willing instruments of his autocratic leadership. On balance the production drive was successful at the expense of the Revolution's egalitarian aims. The Soviet Union became a major industrial power, and the fact that in the process 'proletarian dictatorship' had been replaced by bureaucratic omnipotence was veiled by the retention of the Leninist vocabulary. The great terror of the later thirties, which turned the Party into an obedient instrument of the State leadership, set the seal on that 'revolution from above' which Stalin and his colleagues had been practising since 1929. The State had become all-powerful, peasant ownership had disappeared, and the working class was subjected to a degree of discipline unheard of in Europe since the early years of the industrial revolution. If this was socialism, it was certainly not the sort Marx and Engels had looked forward to.

Throughout these stormy years the identification of Marxism with Leninism prevented the Bolshevik leaders and the Comintern functionaries from working out conceptual tools that took account of the world situation. Neither Trotsky nor Bukharin – the theorist of the moderates who opposed Stalin's policies after 1928 – possessed an adequate understanding of the European labour movement. Western Communist leaders who tried to inject some sense into the Comintern's strategy were purged or ignored. The only successful adaptation of Leninism to local conditions occurred in Italy and was largely the work of the Communist Party's co-founder Antonio Gramsci (1891–1937), a theoretician of uncommon ability whose prison writings later became the foundation of Italian Communism during the post-Fascist period. His subtle distinction between political hegemony and Party dictatorship represented a return to the authentic Marxist tradition. Gramsci accepted the Leninist concept of Party dictatorship, but restricted it to the political sphere of *dominio* or State power. The basic change would have to occur in the realm of civil society, where socialism would introduce a new cultural consensus superior to the old. In this perspective, socialism transcended the intellectual and moral universe of Roman Catholicism and bourgeois liberalism alike. No other European Communist movement produced a thinker of equal distinction, although the German philosopher Karl Korsch came close to it, and the Hungarian theorist Georg Lukács made a promising start, until he was mired in the Stalinist bog.

It is remarkable that in these circumstances a substantial fraction of the European working class should have conserved its faith in the existence of something called 'Soviet power', which was visualized as the direct rule of workers and peasants. It is perhaps less surprising that the European governments should have reacted with unreasoning fear to the spread of Communist influence. Even a comparatively harmless and peaceful affair such as the British General Strike of 1926 gave rise to emotions ludicrously disproportionate to the actual situation. The true impact of the Bolshevik Revolution occurred in the West's pre-industrial hinterland, notably in the British, French and Dutch colonial possessions. Lenin's identification of Western capitalism with colonial imperialism struck a chord even among nationalists who otherwise had no use for Communism. It was the peculiarity of the Russian Revolution that it could be represented as a challenge to the industrial West and the backward East alike. If Stalin had been less ready to squander the moral capital he inherited, it is just conceivable that Lenin's dream of an alliance between the Asian peasant and the European or American city-worker might have come off. Even as it was, Communism made significant inroads among the intelligentsia of backward countries and it conserved its hold upon a minority of the European working class. But whereas Marxism reached Asia, Africa and Latin America in its Leninist incarnation, in Europe the Third International had to compete with the traditional Socialist movement which retained the loyalty of most industrial workers. Communism likewise helped to trigger off the Fascist reaction which sprang from the fears and hatreds of a ruined middle class. By the later 1930s the Fascist one-party State had come to confront its Communist rival in what looked like a battle for the inheritance of European civilization. The Bolsheviks had banked upon a German revolution. What in the end confronted them was the Third Reich of 'National Socialism'.

C THE CRISIS OF LIBERAL DEMOCRACY

The 1919 settlement rested upon the preponderance of America, Britain and France. Their failure to present a united front encouraged the revisionist onslaught which by 1939 had effectively destroyed the order enshrined in the Versailles Treaty and its various annexes. From a different viewpoint what was at stake during these years was the liberal-democratic system of government, itself the political counterpart of market economics. When in the 1930s the market economy failed to prevent the growth of mass unemployment in the industrial countries, and the ruin of peasant proprietors in the West's industrial hinterland, liberalism came under fire from Right and Left alike. By a curious coincidence the 1919–39 period was neatly bisected by the great Wall Street crash of October 1929 which ushered in a decade of economic depression and political crisis. From 1919 to 1929 the Versailles settlement had looked stable. Thereafter it went to pieces, and this disintegration expressed itself in every sphere of society, from politics to the arts. It was of course in the political realm that the crisis manifested itself most dramatically, and it was in Central Europe that the biggest eruption occurred. The fall of the Weimar Republic in 1933 was directly due to the great economic depression, and this political catastrophe in turn led inexorably to war in 1939. When liberal democracy failed in Germany, the most powerful and dynamic country in Europe was launched upon a path of dictatorial government and massive rearmament to which there could be only one outcome. In this sense the American crash of 1929 may be said to have triggered off the train of events leading to the Second World War.

The 1930s furnished proof that Central Europe was the weak link within the world system economically controlled by New York and London. Taken by itself the American stock market crash was more dramatic than its European counterparts; but whereas American democracy could ride out a prolonged depression, with unemployment mounting to twelve million, the Weimar Republic was destroyed by the consequences of the great slump. Britain and France suffered less, and in any case possessed stabler institutions, as well as greater financial reserves. For Britain the depression simply meant an aggravation of troubles that had become endemic since 1919. France was not yet fully industrialized and was to some extent sheltered by her backwardness. The depression bore heaviest on Germany where unemployment by 1932 had mounted to seven million. In these circumstances the country became ungovernable. In the presidential election of March 1932 Hindenburg was re-elected for a second term by nineteen million votes, but thirteen million ballots were cast for Hitler. Thereafter it only needed a political pact between the Conservatives and the National Socialists to install the latter in power, quite legally and with the blessing of the Army, the Churches and big business.

The British situation differed from the German in that Britain had emerged in 1919 as a victor power and by 1925 had reverted to the gold standard, thus lending a spurious appearance of solidity to the country's world economic status. In actual fact Britain had been in a state of economic depression since the end of the war. The country was heavily dependent on foreign trade, and the advantages once reaped in the pioneering age of the industrial revolution were over. A world turning to oil for power had less need for coal.[20] There was no catastrophic smash, merely prolonged stagnation. In 1925, a tolerably good year, industrial production was ten per cent above the 1913 level. Yet there were more than a million unemployed, three-quarters of them in the old staple industries – coal, iron and steel, textiles, shipbuilding – which traditionally supplied the bulk of British exports. Imports in 1925 were ten per cent higher than in 1913, whereas exports had shrunk by twenty-five per cent.[21] The decline of the older industries should have been offset by the growth of new ones, and to a limited extent it was; but this could not save the old staple industries and their work-people who became used to continuous unemployment. The Conservative viewpoint was adequately expressed by the Prime Minister, Stanley Baldwin, who on 30 July 1925 informed the public: "All the workers of this country have got to take reductions in wages to help put industry on its feet." The sequel included a prolonged conflict between the miners and the mine-owners, and at its peak a General Strike in May 1926, which was called off by the unions in the face of governmental intransigence. Thereafter the miners were driven back to work by starvation after holding out for another six months. The Labour Party and the unions got their revenge in May 1929, when the Conservatives were driven from office in the last general election in which the Liberals figured as major contenders for power. They were led by Lloyd George who, with the help of Keynes and others, had worked out a programme for countering unemployment by public works. Nothing was done about it by the Labour government headed by Ramsay MacDonald, and in October 1931 the Labour Party was heavily defeated in a panic election in which some of its own leaders made common cause with the Conservatives and Liberals to set up a 'National government'.

Even before the financial crisis of September 1931, which drove sterling off the gold standard, certain things had become clear about Britain's world position. In 1929, a good year, the volume of imports was twenty per cent above pre-war, while the volume of exports was twenty per cent lower, and this at a time when world trade was expanding. The conventional reaction consisted in demanding that export prices should be brought down by cuts in wages. In reality the export industries were producing goods for which world demand was not rising. For most people the blow was softened by the fall in the price of primary products which Britain was importing. But this was no unmixed blessing, for the resulting impoverishment of the producer countries made them poor markets for British exports. For the rest, the trading account was balanced by 'invisible' income from banking, shipping, insurance and profits derived from overseas investment. Britain was thus cushioned from the worst effects of the great depression, and once the panic of 1931 was over, the country adapted itself to the Conservative remedy of tariff protection. There was some degree of economic recovery, coupled with political apathy. Fascism never became a serious menace, and the Communist Party had trouble holding its membership above 10,000. The country was living on its reserves, which included faith in representative institutions. It also benefited from a stroke of luck in the form of lower import prices. Throughout the thirties, the terms of international trade moved steadily in Britain's favour; the fall in world commodity prices, which was greater than the drop in export prices, meant that Britain could import the former volume of goods at two-thirds of the former cost, a saving of about £400 millions annually.[22] This accounts for the paradoxical fact that average living standards improved slightly despite heavy unemployment which reached a peak of three million in January 1933 and thereafter fell to about half that figure. Except for those who were out of work, life became somewhat more tolerable, a circumstance reflected in the housing boom and the continuing growth of consumer industries. The recovery occurred at the expense of the foreign producer and the unemployed, particularly those in the depressed areas which were heavily dependent on export trades. Devaluation helped, and so did the formation of a sterling bloc consisting of Britain, the Dominions and the Scandinavian countries. The age of free trade was over for good.

The intellectual counterpart of this transformation was the spread of a new economic orthodoxy. As formulated by J.M.Keynes in *The General Theory of Employment, Interest and Money* (1936), the new academic doctrine – which, however, was not officially accepted before 1945 –

provided a theoretical basis for expansion by government action whenever the economy showed signs of running down. The emphasis shifted from saving to investment, and governments were urged to incur budgetary deficits in the interest of providing the unemployed with work. Similar proposals had already been put forward by Lloyd George in 1929, and were applied on a fairly large scale by President Roosevelt in the United States from 1933 onwards. In Britain they had an advocate in the trade union leader Ernest Bevin, who unfortunately failed to convince the leaders of the 1929–31 Labour government that balancing the budget was less important than getting men back to work. The events of 1929–31 in fact showed that the Labour Party had neither the will nor the capacity to govern.

Taken as a whole, the Baldwin–MacDonald era of 1922–37 was uncongenial to what was left of liberal optimism after the searing experience of 1914–18. The war had already shattered a good many illusions. In the words of E.L.Woodward, the historian:

> The novels and poems of D.H.Lawrence, the early novels of Aldous Huxley, Lytton Strachey's *Eminent Victorians*, Mr Keynes's *Economic Consequences of the Peace*, bear evidence of minds 'scorched' by war and reacting against a nervous strain which was almost unbearable. The strain was caused not by any doubt about the issue of the war, but by the very fact of a European war and the breakdown of accepted standards.[23]

It is arguable that a serious attack on Victorian beliefs and standards had already begun before 1914 under the leadership of Bernard Shaw, H.G.Wells and the members of the Bloomsbury set; but these writers were rationalists, whereas the intellectual fashion of the 1920s and 1930s was a revolt against reason.[24] The reaction never went as far as it did in Germany, but it was drastic enough to make novelists such as John Galsworthy and E.M.Forster seem rather dated. Popularized versions of Marxism and Freudian psychology fed a general unease which alienated a significant number of intellectuals from previously accepted standards. It became fashionable to maintain that the intellectualism of the eighteenth-century Enlightenment had crippled the individual. The theme was worked with great effect in the novels of D.H.Lawrence and Aldous Huxley, in the poetry of T.S.Eliot, and in the writings of their various associates and imitators. Lawrence flirted with blood and soil mysticism; Eliot opted for Anglo-Catholicism and a genteel version of anti-Semitism; Evelyn Waugh and Graham Greene became converts to Roman Catholicism; some of the more embattled poets of the 1930s, notably W.H.Auden, toyed with Communism. About the only thing they all had in common was the rejection of humanism in its liberal-individualist form. The process went on steadily throughout the inter-war period, paralleling the slow decay of the

Liberal Party and a growing cynicism on the part of the electorate where parliamentary politics were concerned. It was briefly halted in 1940, when Britain made a lonely stand against the Axis Powers, to be resumed after the war and the contemplation of what was left of European civilization when Hitler and Stalin had done their work.

The discovery that the individual no longer counted underlay the growing mood of pessimism. The more realistic war-time poets of 1914-18 had already made a dent in the conventional belief that wars are decided by individual bravery. What mattered quite obviously were technology and organizational ability, but it was difficult to derive heroic poetry from such insights. The Fascists tried, but Italian Fascist literature did not rise to great heights, if only because the Italian Army had notoriously never won a battle. In the 1930s Soviet collectivism produced a spate of poetry devoted to the theme of industrialization; but since the writers were not free to comment upon the fact that ten per cent of the country's population was being worked to death in what were euphemistically known as labour camps, their literary endeavours never rose markedly beyond the glorification of technology – a hackneyed theme by Western standards. Artistic modernism had a brief fling during the Weimar Republic, only to be stamped out when Hitler took over. All told, it was not an era which the historian of culture can view with enthusiasm. Its most significant achievement – the spread of the cinema-going habit to the masses – did little to raise cultural standards. Most of what the cinema offered was rubbish and the resulting mass culture – originally an American importation – trivialized the traditional subjects of the novel, itself a declining art form too closely bound up with its bourgeois origins to dominate the new audio-visual age. The commercialization of art in its turn gave rise to a conservative counter-attack which attributed the degradation of modern culture not to capitalism but to democracy. The spokesmen of this movement held the 'revolt of the masses' responsible for the decline of civilized values. Most of the better-known writers of the period were self-consciously reactionary. Bergson, Barrès, Maurras, Ortega y Gasset, Chesterton, Yeats, Eliot, Valéry, Spengler, Toynbee, Keyserling and the rest took issue with liberal democracy and humanism in the name of tradition, aristocracy and the proto-Fascist longings of an elite unconsciously in search of a hierarchical order which was simply the old Romantic fairyland of the European counter-revolution.[25]

The attack was the more effective because the "Decline of the West" was not simply the invention of Oswald Spengler (1880-1936), whose two-volume diatribe against modern civilization (1918-22) revived most of the old battle-cries of German Romanticism. It corresponded to a dissociation of the European mind which Nietzsche had begun to sense in the later nineteenth century. Spengler has been called the poor man's Nietzsche, and there is no doubt that he popularized a line of reasoning which sought refuge in the hope that a new barbarism might rejuvenate the civilization of old Europe. During the 1914–18 war even Thomas Mann had expressed himself in rather ambiguous terms: his conversion to liberal democracy came later and was a painfully slow affair. The Enlightenment had never really taken hold in Germany, whence the explosion of popular fervour when National Socialism declared war on the 'soulless' scientific world-view of positivism. For practical purposes Hitler and his followers contented themselves with shadow-boxing: capitalism was left untouched, but the ideological label was changed. Artists and novelists could not be expected to perceive this. Fascism gained ground among them to the extent that it promised an escape from the world created by the industrial revolution. The more consistent pessimists rejected even this refuge: the West could not be saved at all, and its decline had to be accepted.[26]

The question has occasionally been asked why the major literary figures of the age did not put up a stouter defence of humanist values. Given the fact that liberalism had landed Europe in the catastrophe of 1914, a certain amount of disillusionment was to be expected, but why was there such a flight from reason as such? Perhaps one has to allow for the fact that the Romantic credo comes naturally to artists. Here is D.H.Lawrence on the rejection of the intellect:

My great religion is a belief in the blood, the flesh. We can go wrong in our minds. But what our blood feels . . . is always true. The intellect is only a bit and a bridle. What do I care about knowledge? All I want is to answer to my blood, direct, without the fribbling intervention of mind, or moral, or what not.

It was perhaps fortunate for Lawrence's reputation that he died in 1930 before Hitler's rise to power provided him with an occasion to display his political innocence. The visionary neo-primitivism, the regression to an archaic mode of perception which dissolves the distinction between nature and culture – it is all there, waiting for a suitable outlet. In fairness it has to be noted that with Lawrence the cult of 'blood-consciousness' had no racial overtones. It was merely a confused way of trying to appropriate what Freudians called the Unconscious. For the rest, Lawrence would have nothing to do with machine-civilization, whereas the true Fascists positively gloried in it: it was after all the chosen instrument for imposing their rule on the 'lower races'. Lawrence's exaltation of life at all costs had no political implications. There was to be a return to the origins. The origins of what? He did not know, but then he was no theorist and it is pointless to search his writings for a message applicable to modern society. At the same time it would be wrong to overlook the Nietzschean strain in Lawrence's frantic vitalism.

God was dead all right, and something had to be put in his place. Nietzsche had set the tone:

The great majority of men have no right to exist, but are a misfortune to higher men. I do not . . . grant the failures the right. There are also peoples that are failures. . . . Unfortunately, man is no longer evil enough; Rousseau's opponents who say 'man is a beast of prey' are unfortunately wrong. Not the corruption of man, but the extent to which he has become tender and moralized is his curse.

This was heady stuff. It took time for Nietzsche's "transvaluation of values" to grip the minds of some Germans sufficiently to make Auschwitz possible. Meantime a watered-down version of the faith reached the British public by way of his disciples.

Nietzscheanism is a difficult topic, for despite the vast body of literature to which it has given rise, there is still a good deal of uncertainty as to Nietzsche's standing as a man of letters – that he was not a philosopher in the ordinary sense goes without saying. Moreover, the exegetical labours of his editors are not free from apologetic motivations.[27] The fact that his most influential work, *The Will to Power*, was edited and published by his sister, Elisabeth Förster-Nietzsche, after his death, has been represented as a reason why its employment by National Socialist 'philosophers' such as Alfred Bäumler (and its effect on Hitler himself) ought not to be blamed on the author. But whatever Nietzsche may have *intended* it is quite clear what his work *portended*: namely the spread of attitudes which were wholly incompatible with the Judaeo-Christian inheritance, including its humanist off-shoots. Nietzsche's obsessional hatred of democracy, his exaltation of violence and his readiness to let the weak go to the wall, all became part of the Fascist creed. As early as 1884 he had jotted down these thoughts:

A doctrine is needed powerful enough to work as a breeding agent: strengthening the strong, paralyzing and destructive for the world-weary. The annihilation of the decaying races. Decay of Europe – The annihilation of slavish evaluations – Dominion over the earth as a means of producing a higher type – The annihilation of the tartuffery called 'morality' (Christianity as a hysterical kind of honesty in this: Augustine, Bunyan) – The annihilation of *suffrage universel*; i.e., the system through which the lowest natures prescribe themselves as laws for the higher.[28]

The impact this kind of stuff had on the minds of educated Germans became apparent only in 1933, when Nietzsche was popularized by his disciples (Bäumler himself was made a professor of philosophy in Berlin after Hitler had come to power). The consequences were dramatic, for Nietzsche had provided a section of the intellectual elite with a *Weltanschauung* wholly consistent with Hitler's long-term aims. This statement holds true for every aspect of National Socialism, including its murderous onslaught on the Jews. Much has been made by Nietzsche's apologists of the fact that he was contemptuous of the anti-Semites of the 1880s and on occasion even expressed a kind of admiration for the Jews. What he preached was anti-Christianity, not Jew-hatred. But this is to overlook the fact that what he detested about Christianity was precisely its Jewish origins. His contempt for the vulgar anti-Semites of his day stemmed from the fact that they were not radical enough: they did not grasp that they were themselves carriers of that Jewish infection, Christianity. The Jews, he wrote in one of his last pamphlets, *The Anti-Christ*, "have made mankind so thoroughly false that even today the Christian can feel anti-Jewish without realising that he is himself *the ultimate Jewish consequence*". As has rightly been observed, Nietzsche was the most radical anti-Semite who ever lived, as well as the most radically anti-Christian writer known to history.[29] His atheism had nothing whatever in common with that of pre-Marxians such as Feuerbach, for whom humanism had replaced theism. At the same time he did away with the old naive and self-contradictory Christian anti-Semitism by indicting the Jews collectively as the original inspirers of that poisonous infection known as belief in Christ. No more deadly doctrine could have been preached to the Germans after 1900 and especially after 1933. It is not too much to say that but for Nietzsche the SS – Hitler's shock troops and the core of the whole movement – would have lacked the inspiration which enabled them to carry out their programme of mass murder in Eastern Europe.

There is good reason for including this topic under the general heading of 'liberalism at bay', for by the 1930s Nietzsche had become a European influence. The German National Socialists were merely the most fanatical among his admirers. Not a single Fascist – from Mussolini to Oswald Mosley – escaped his pervasive influence. It is quite irrelevant that he was also admired as a poet by people to whom Fascism was abhorrent: what counted was the doctrine spelled out at great length in *The Will to Power* and in the final half-mad pamphlets he composed before his collapse into insanity in 1889. That it should have taken half a century for his message to captivate that section of the German political elite which seized power in 1933 and then went to war in 1939 is not particularly surprising: the Enlightenment of the eighteenth century too was a gradual affair before it culminated in the French Revolution. Ideas need time to take root, especially if they challenge a whole stock of inherited beliefs. Nietzsche had long been an underground influence. In 1933 his German disciples seized power, and suddenly it turned out that all over Europe there were intellectuals who preached elitism to their fanaticized followers.

It is arguable that so far as Western Europe was concerned the impact of Nietzsche had by then already been absorbed. After all, it was possible for left-wingers like Malraux to take a tolerant view of him. The same may have been true of his literary admirers in Britain. In the German context the attack on liberalism and democracy had an overtly political character. Thomas Mann's original acceptance of a clash between (Germanic) culture and (Western) civilization was in the conservative tradition. His subsequent conversion to democratic liberalism remained a half-hearted affair, as may be seen from his major novelistic achievement, *The Magic Mountain* (1924), in which the issue is neatly side-stepped. The Weimar Republic stood for nothing in particular, unless it was freedom to experiment with artistic forms. These ranged from the nationalist Romanticism of Ernst Jünger on the Right to Bertolt Brecht's denunciation of bourgeois convention on the Left, a subject complicated by the fact that Brecht moved from his original Anarchist position to the acceptance of a Communist standpoint.[30] At a lower level, Expressionism, Dadaism and Surrealism assailed the false values of a philistine middle class which in actual fact had begun to lose faith in itself. It was comparatively easy to make the German public believe that liberal democracy was a hollow fraud. In France, where the Republic was solidly implanted – not least among the school teachers – the reactionary movement stagnated in the 1920s and only gathered force in the 1930s under the impact of the Spanish civil war, which drove large numbers of Catholics to the Right.[31] Even so, an instinctive Romantic like André Malraux turned to the extreme Left before becoming a Gaullist. It was not easy to make the French renounce their revolutionary heritage. In Italy, memories of the liberal *Risorgimento* imposed some limits upon Fascist brutality. No such obstacles blocked Hitler's path in Germany, traditionally the stronghold of conservative Romanticism, though even here the counter-revolution was obliged to dress up in revolutionary clothing. 'National Socialism' had to sound plebeian and anti-capitalist to get a hearing. The trick was done by identifying capitalist exploitation with the Jews, who in point of fact played a minor role in banking and none whatever in heavy industry. An unemployed white-collar class did not inquire too closely into the facts. It yearned for a charismatic leader, and in the end it got what it wanted.

For the full political consequences to make themselves felt by 1939, the Spanish civil war had to be fought and won by the Right, with Britain's benevolent assistance; and the French Popular Front experiment of 1936–7 had to fail. Once matters had reached this point it only needed the Munich settlement of 1938 to give the Third Reich control of Central Europe. Paradoxically, it was at this point that a counter-movement set in among British and French conservatives who had begun to realize what was at stake. As noted before, their enlightenment was helped along by the Hitler–Stalin pact of August 1939 which made nonsense, at least temporarily, of Hitler's pose as the defender of Europe against Bolshevist Russia. By then the Western Powers had been thrown on the defensive, the Rome–Berlin Axis threatened France with destruction, and the British government had to weigh the probability of having to fight Germany, Italy and Japan simultaneously. On Johnson's principle that it clears a man's mind if he knows he is to be hanged, the awakening which dates from the summer of 1940 is thoroughly comprehensible. The Western leaders who now came forward – Churchill and de Gaulle above all – were aristocrats who stemmed from the conservative Right. This gave them a realistic insight into the mentality of their Fascist opponents, but it handicapped them as spokesmen of the democratic cause. Perhaps the democrats deserved no better. After all, they had wasted twenty years in futile squabbles and for good measure failed to re-arm in time. Now the twenty years' armistice was over, and what was left of the 1919 settlement had to be defended in the only area where an effective stand was possible: on the field of battle.

D OLD ELITES AND NEW IDEOLOGIES

The society on which the war of 1914 broke was in some respects a stable and civilized one. It was also a society in which those in control were able, broadly speaking, to make effective use of the instruments at their disposal. Public opinion was virtually identical with middle-class opinion, and the middle class, with the help of elected parliaments and the press, saw to it that governments did not stray too far from their duties. Russia was the great exception, and even Russia after 1905 acquired a semblance of constitutional rule and the hope of better things to come. By tacit consent the aristocracy throughout most of Europe exercised political power in the interest of the bourgeoisie which kept a close watch over its nominal rulers. The trade unions, on the whole, knew their place. Revolutionary socialism was a fringe phenomenon, for the most part confined to countries like Russia and Spain which did not enjoy the blessings of liberal democracy. Belief in progress was not seriously shaken by conservative complaints and Syndicalist mutterings. America was something like a provincial hinterland of Europe. Asia and Africa were quiescent. Except for a few eccentrics no one questioned the hegemony of Europe, which even socialists for the most part equated with the spread of civilized values. Living standards were rising and world trade was expanding. In the sphere of culture there had gradually occurred a fusion of aristocratic and bourgeois values which satisfied both the elite and the middle class. Religion, outside the Roman Church, had come to terms with science and abandoned the hopeless struggle against Darwinism. There seemed to be no reason why this happy state of affairs should not go on forever.

The war of 1914–18 shattered these arrangements and inaugurated a series of political convulsions which led to the even greater catastrophe of 1939–45. Except for a brief lull in the mid-twenties there was a constant sense of danger arising from the Versailles settlement, the reactivation of German nationalism, the unpredictable behaviour of Soviet Russia and the danger of Japan encroaching upon Western preserves in Asia. Liberal democracy was under fire. Communism and Fascism attracted the discontented, whose numbers were swelled by mass unemployment in the 1930s. The ancient dynastic empires had collapsed and the aristocratic-bourgeois cultural symbiosis was no longer effective. The war itself had spawned a revolutionary new technology which the military authorities (other than the Germans) did their best to ignore. Air power and armoured warfare made non-sense of the old textbooks, but the military staffs were slow in catching up. The outstanding British theorist of modern warfare, Basil Liddell Hart (1896–1970) found apt pupils among the Germans who employed his doctrines with devastating effect in 1940. In Britain he had reason to complain about the opposition of the Army (notably the Cavalry) to the tank, and their desire to get back to what they considered 'real warfare'. As he wrote in 1933, the Army's expenditure on horsed cavalry could not be justified unless it had a scheme for breeding bullet-proof horses. Charles de Gaulle had no better luck in France.[32] It took the catastrophe of 1940 to overcome conservative resistance to the new modes of warfare which the Germans had meanwhile adopted. As in economic management, Fascism seemed better adapted to the needs arising from the new technology than its democratic opponents.

Setting aside the incalculable factor of ordinary stupidity it was easier for the vanquished to make a new start. The disparity between Germany's technological equipment and the military means at her disposal in the 1920s and the early 1930s was such that only the boldest kind of experimentation could hope to close the gap. The integration of science and technology was anyhow farther advanced in Germany than elsewhere. Mechanized warfare came easily to a nation which had for decades pioneered in the new mass-production industries. Moreover, the relationship of theory to practice was changing. "From the beginning of the century, in some industries such as the chemical and electrical, it could fairly be claimed that science had now more to contribute to industry than to learn from it."[33] Significantly, these were the industries in which Germany had gained a lead over her competitors.

The inter-war period was remarkable for the transformation it wrought in ordinary civilian life through the application of the internal combustion machine and its offspring, the internal combustion turbine which had made aviation possible. Motor-cars and aeroplanes had already existed in 1914, but their massive employment was reserved for the Second World War. Here too the Germans raced ahead of their competitors, until they were overtaken by the Americans. The process began during the Weimar Republic and was stepped up after its collapse. Putting an army on wheels was a notion that appealed to the futurist side of the Fascist mentality, even though the modernism associated with the *Bauhaus* did not. The artistic *Kitsch* of which Hitler and his followers were so fond represented the petty-bourgeois side of the movement, its dislike of modernity. But such considerations were not allowed to interfere with military needs, which is why modern-minded technocrats like Albert Speer had no trouble adjusting themselves to the Hitler regime.[34]

This circumstance leads to a more general consideration regarding the Third Reich and its origins. Its relationship to the traditional conservatism of the middle class was dialectical, embodying some of its values while sacrificing others on the altar of industrial modernity. The very term 'middle class' is misleading; there is no adequate equivalent for the German *Mittelstand*, which literally signifies 'middle estate', implying possession of a fixed status in a hierarchical social order, as distinct from 'class' which relates to a market economy. Given the way it had developed in the nineteenth and early twentieth century, the term *Mittelstand* had come to designate shopkeepers, civil servants, artisans, peasants – in short everyone who was threatened by the new industrial-capitalist nexus. As seen by the conservative theorists who worked it out, the term stood for social status independent of wealth. Since the medieval guilds could not be revived, hope centred on the establishment of what the sociologist Ferdinand Toennies in 1887 had termed *"Gemeinschaft"* as distinct from *"Gesellschaft"*.[35] "Family", "clan", "village", "friendship" may serve as approximate examples of *"Gemeinschaft"*, while "city", "state", "industry", "public opinion", may serve as types of *"Gesellschaft"*.[36] According to Toennies, human societies were fated to develop from *"Gemeinschaft"* (communal village organization), through "individualism", to *"Gesellschaft"*, which would in all likelihood be planned, bureaucratic and socialistic. Max Weber held much the same view when he interpreted economic history as the triumph of "rationalism". Toennies considered the trend towards *"Gesellschaft"* as a process of "ageing", while Weber treated the heyday of capitalism as "the dawn of an iron age". From there it was no great jump to Spengler with his pessimistic forecast of wars and tyrannies yet to come. The more educated strata of the *Mittelstand* imbibed all this as a psychological refuge from liberalism and socialism alike. The Weimar Republic had ruined them through inflation, and then completed their destruction by mass unemployment which hit the new middle class of salaried employees particularly hard. The wonder is not that they turned to Hitler, but that it took them over a decade to make the transition from traditional conservatism to National Socialism. The ideology of the movement promised them what they most wanted; security, social status independent of income and the warmth of *"Gemeinschaft"* in the shape of the German *"Volksgemeinschaft"*, from which Jews and Slavs were of course excluded. Economists such as Werner Sombart (1863–1941) had for years been preaching that state planning should be directed towards curbing the power of big business and big labour alike. In this way the old middle class would be regenerated, and so would the nation of which it formed the backbone. The key to it all lay in the rejection of an economic theory fashioned on the model of the natural sciences. Instead, economics should become the servant of social and moral aims. A ruined middle class thus embraced a caricature of socialism and then became the prisoner of a dictatorship which was nothing if not modern and technocratic. This is not to say that Hitler and his associates did not at some stage share the Romantic dream of a world made up of peasants and artisans, but once in power they contented themselves with a few gestures designed to provide the middle class with psychological satisfactions. The communitarian impulse was deflected into militarism, nationalism and rhetorical exaltation of the peasantry. A new Germany was to be created which would embody the virtues of a mythical past. Racism replaced the social emphasis on class: all true Germans were part of the *Volk*, while the Jews became the symbol of everything that was wrong with the world, liberalism and Marxism above all. The intoxication lasted just long enough to permit Hitler to carry out his rearmament programme. Thereafter Europe was at his feet, and the *Volk* had cause to feel some satisfaction at its newly won status.

So far as the schools and universities were concerned no radical break with the past was necessary. Emphasis on race and folk, and the view of history as a murderous struggle between superior and inferior races, had been embedded in German historical writing and thinking since the later nineteenth century. In this respect Germany was not unique, but the counter-forces were uncommonly weak. Anglo-American imperialism and Social Darwinism encountered obstacles lacking in Germany, where the democratic tradition had virtually died out during the Bismarck era, in so far as it was not kept alive by the Social Democrats, who had no influence within the educational establishment. By 1918, when the old order finally broke down, German liberalism had dwindled into a mere sect, largely sustained by the Jewish community. There was no institutional resistance when Hitler took over. The universities acquiesced, and so did the Catholic and Protestant Churches, setting aside a few hundred courageous dissidents who joined the Protestant 'Confessional Church' inaugurated in 1934 by a handful of theologians who could not stomach 'German Christendom'. Worship of a romanticized past and anti-liberalism had become part of the mental make-up of the declining *Mittelstand*. Conservatives who on social or religious grounds refused to associate with the plebeian National Socialist movement nonetheless for the most part expressed views almost indistinguishable from those of the genuine folk enthusiasts. They included former Rhodes scholars who favoured Anglo-German understanding and looked forward to an age when a community of 'Teutonic nations' would rule the world. This notion even found its way into Hitler's *Mein Kampf*, a circumstance which did not escape the attention of his numerous and influential British admirers. The fact is that the Third Reich could build on foundations laid by its conservative predecessors. Most of the *völkisch* doctrines had already flourished in Imperial Germany, notably among the youth movement and the student community. The collapse of 1918 did not discredit them. Instead, it engendered a sense of desperation which came to the surface in the 1920s. "True Socialism is the community of the *Volk*", as one of its numberless ideologists put it in 1928.[37] Thus was born the 'conservative revolution' which triumphed in 1933.

The Italian development differed from the German in that the Liberals had actually been in power for decades and it was their disintegration that promoted the Fascist takeover:

> The liberal heirs of Cavour were at last proving unable to absorb the new forces in Italian politics, and perhaps they acted on the false assumption that the fascists would prove more easily digestible than either the Catholics or the socialists, both of whom were by definition enemies of liberal government. Croce and Mosca had been elaborating their theories about the antithesis between liberalism and democracy, and some of Giolitti's liberals were so confused that they allied against democracy with men who ostentatiously despised the liberal state.[38]

Croce, a member of Giolitti's Cabinet in 1920–1, held that Fascism was harmless because it had no programme. He certainly did nothing to stop the armed violence whereby the Fascists won control of hundreds of localities. In the two years before the takeover of October 1922 some 300 Fascists and 3,000 of their opponents were killed in riots instigated by Mussolini's Blackshirts. Considering that there were 240,000 men in the armed services, plus 65,000 *carabinieri* and 40,000 *guardie regie*, the only possible conclusion is that the government, including the magistrates and the police, were in active collusion with the Fascists even before they had seized power. The Liberals simply refused to govern, Socialists and Catholics would not cooperate and the Blackshirts had a free hand in terrorizing their opponents. By 1923 Freemasonry was banned and the Church had been won over. The murder of the Socialist deputy Matteotti in 1924 produced a brief flurry which terminated with the ceremonial secession of the remaining opposition deputies to the Aventine hill, where they accomplished exactly nothing. Croce, who in 1924 had publicly sanctioned the use of violence as the only means of obtaining a Fascist majority, repented of his error when in January 1925 the Liberal Party, which had helped Mussolini into the saddle, was outlawed together with all others. The fact is that Italian Liberalism committed suicide. The Italian case is the more noteworthy in that it involved the entire Liberal elite and its most distinguished philosophers. Croce later tried to exculpate himself for his support of Mussolini in the critical years 1922–4 by describing Fascism as a disease which had come to Italy from abroad.[39] This was not what he had said in January 1924 when he affirmed that "the heart of fascism is love of Italy. . . . Fascism is overcoming the traditional indifference of Italians to politics . . . and I value so highly the cure which Italy is undergoing from it that I rather hope the patient will not get up too soon from his bed and risk some grave relapse."[40] The patient in fact took twenty years to get out of bed, and then only with the help of the Allied armies who invaded Italy in 1943–4, by which time Croce's reputation as a defender of liberty had somehow been restored. Mussolini for his part tried to fill the ideological vacuum by concocting a strange brew for the most part taken over from Nietzsche, Sorel, Pareto and the French followers of Charles Maurras:

We represent a new principle in the world, the clear, final and categoric antithesis of democracy, plutocracy, Freemasonry, and the immortal principles of 1789.
The ideals of democracy are exploded, beginning with that of 'progress'. Ours is an aristocratic century; the state of all will end by becoming the state of a few.
Fascism is the purest kind of democracy, so long as people are counted qualitatively and not quantitatively.
The fascist conception of the state is all-embracing, and outside of the state no human or spiritual values can exist, let alone be desirable.
Perpetual peace would be impossible and useless. War alone brings human energies to their highest state of tension, and stamps with the seal of nobility the nations which dare to face it.[41]

These sentiments were given their classic form in the article on Fascism in the *Enciclopedia Italiana*, an article written in 1931 and signed by Mussolini, but in fact composed by a number of authors, including his tame philosopher Giovanni Gentile (1875–1944), a former associate of Croce and a purveyor of a debased form of pseudo-Hegelianism. Here it was laid down that Fascism had its own political doctrine, that of the State which allowed no allegiance to anything other than the Nation in Arms. For his services in rounding up a number of compliant intellectuals, Gentile became Minister of Education, president of the

Istituto Fascista di Cultura and general editor of the *Enciclopedia*. Unlike Croce, who had for years preached the need for a strong State, only to draw back when the full consequences of Fascism unfolded themselves, Gentile stuck to his principles. These included a belief that Catholic doctrines were suitable only for the pupils of primary schools, whence his fall from grace when the Concordat of 1929 handed the entire educational system over to the Church. Italian Fascism was less thorough-going than German National Socialism, but then Italy was a country where the Monarchy and the Church had retained strong roots. The French Fascist leagues, which never came to power, fell somewhere between the Italian and the German pattern. They suffered from the handicap that in *Mein Kampf* Hitler had singled France out for special abuse:

France is and remains the most terrible enemy. This nation, which is increasingly subject to negroization, is tied to the aims of Jewish world domination and thus presents a lurking danger to the existence of the white race in Europe. . . . For Germany, however, the French danger means the obligation . . . to stretch out the hand to those who, equally threatened as we are, do not want to suffer and to countenance France's lust for domination. In Europe there will for the foreseeable future only be two allies for Germany: England and Italy. . . .[42]

With the best will, no one on the political Right in France could overlook this awkward evidence of Hitler's ultimate intentions.

The various West European Fascist movements of the 1930s, from the Spanish Falangists to the Belgian Rexists and Sir Oswald Mosley's British Union of Fascists, took Italy rather than Germany for their model. In Central and Eastern Europe German influence predominated, especially after the German cloaca had spilled over into Hitler's native Austria in 1938. The movement as a whole drew sustenance from the evident failure of liberal democracy to live up to the promises of 1919. Beyond this lay the fact that the social and psychic costs of industrialization had somehow to be paid for. Big business profited from what liberals were pleased to term progress; big labour, in the form of the trade union movement, was able to shield itself from the worst fluctuations of the market economy, although it proved unable to do anything about unemployment. The peasantry and the lower middle class were badly organized and unprotected. Unless the State came to their assistance, they stood in danger of being squeezed out. Hence the popularity of slogans which equated nationalism with socialism: if everyone, or almost everyone, counted as a member of the sacred *Volksgemeinschaft*, there was some chance of escaping from the remorseless logic of capitalism. The Social Democrats never grasped the point, and neither did the Communists, for whom Fascism was by definition 'petty bourgeois', hence not really dangerous. It took the Second World War to cure them of this illusion. Meanwhile the alliance between the old en. and the new technologies produced a mental climate which somehow made Fascism look up-to-date when compared to parliamentary democracy. By 1940 a movement drawn from the sweepings of the gutter had come close to conquering Europe. A century and a half after the French Revolution, the principles of 1789 were being challenged in their own homeland; the chief threat came from Germany, a country which for long had been the bulwark of the European counter-revolution. If Fascism did nothing else, it brought politics back to first principles. It also revived what had once been conservative battle-cries, and thus secured for itself the benevolent neutrality of the aristocracy and the Churches – above all the Catholic Church. It is a matter of more than historical interest that the nominal Catholic Adolf Hitler was never excommunicated, nor were his writings ever placed on the Index. The notorious silence of Pius XII during the years when the 'final solution' was being enacted in Eastern Europe had its ultimate root in a thousand years of Christian identification of the Jew with the Devil, but it also testified to the solidity of the political compact between the Fascist regimes and the Vatican.

NOTES

1 Cited by Charles Loch Mowat, *Britain Between the Wars 1918-1949* (London: Methuen; Chicago: University of Chicago Press, 1955), p. 1.

2 Solomon F. Bloom, *Europe and America* (London: Longmans; New York: Harcourt, Brace, 1961), p. 534.

3 For the controversy over reparations see J.M.Keynes, *The Economic Consequences of the Peace* (London: Oxford University Press; New York: Harcourt, Brace, 1920), *passim*. The reparations muddle was aggravated by the problem of inter-Allied indebtedness, which Keynes reckoned to be in the neighbourhood of twenty billion dollars. The United States was a lender only, whereas Britain had lent about twice as much as she borrowed, and France borrowed about three times as much as she lent. Hence the determination of French politicians to extract the highest possible reparations from Germany. Keynes, *op. cit.*, p. 271.

4 Bloom, *op. cit.*, p. 594.

5 H.Stuart Hughes, *Contemporary Europe* (Englewood Cliffs, N.J., and London: Prentice-Hall, 1961), pp. 102 ff; Denis Mack Smith, *Italy: A Modern History* (Ann Arbor: University of Michigan Press, 1959), pp. 321 ff; Elizabeth Wiskemann, *The Rome–Berlin Axis* (London–New York–Toronto: Oxford University Press, 1949), *passim*; F.L.Carsten, *The Rise of Fascism* (London: Batsford, 1967; Berkeley, Calif.: University of California Press, 1969), *passim*.

6 Hajo Holborn, *The Political Collapse of Europe* (New York and London: Knopf, 1951), pp. 128-9.

7 *Propheten des Nationalismus*, ed. Karl Schwedhelm (Munich: List Verlag, 1969); Karl Dietrich Bracher, *Die deutsche Diktatur* (Cologne: Kiepenheuer & Witsch, 1969), trans. *The German Dictatorship*, tr. by Jean Steinberg (London: Weidenfeld & Nicolson, 1971; New York: Praeger, 1970); Gotthard Jaspers ed., *Von Weimar zu Hitler 1930–1933* (Cologne: Kiepenheuer & Witsch, 1968); F.L.Carsten, *Reichswehr und Politik 1918–1933* (Cologne: Kiepenheuer & Witsch, 1964) trans. *The Reichswehr and Politics* (London: Oxford University Press, 1966); Ernst Nolte, *Der Faschismus in seiner Epoche* (Munich: Piper Verlag, 1963); Guenther Lewy, *The Catholic Church and Nazi Germany* (London: Weidenfeld & Nicolson, 1964; New York: McGraw-Hill, 1965); Heinrich Brüning, *Memoiren 1918–1934* (Stuttgart: Deutsche Verlagsanstalt, 1970).

8 Elizabeth Wiskemann, *Fascism in Italy: its Development and Influence* (London; Macmillan; New York: St Martin's Press, 1969), p. 5.

9 C.A.Macartney and A.W.Palmer, *Independent Eastern Europe* (London: Macmillan; New York: St Martin's Press, 1966), pp. 272 ff.

10 Martin Gilbert and Richard Gott, *The Appeasers* (London: Weidenfeld & Nicolson, 1967; Boston: Houghton Mifflin, 1963); Paul Reynaud, *Mémoires: Venu de ma montagne* (Paris: Flammarion, 1962); Georges Bonnet, *Le Quai d'Orsay sous Trois Républiques, 1870–1961* (Paris: Librairie Arthème Fayard, 1962), trans. *Quai d'Orsay*, (London: Anthony Gibbs, 1966; New York: International Publications).

11 L.B.Namier, *Europe in Decay: A Study in Disintegration 1936–1940* (London: Macmillan, 1950; Gloucester, Mass.: Peter Smith, 1963), p. 241. See also the same author's *Diplomatic Prelude 1938–1939* (London: Macmillan, 1948) and *In the Nazi Era* (London: Macmillan, 1952). For the related themes of Zionism, Jewish emigration to Palestine, and the Arab reaction thereto, see Leonard Stein, *The Balfour Declaration* (London: Vallentine-Mitchell; New York: Simon and Schuster, 1961) and Elie Kedourie, *The Chatham House Version and other Middle-Eastern Studies* (London: Weidenfeld & Nicolson; New York: Praeger Publishers, 1970).

12 *Documents concerning German-Polish Relations and the outbreak of hostilities between Great Britain and Germany on September 3, 1939* (London: H.M. Stationery Office, 1939).

13 Quoted in I.Deutscher, *The Prophet Armed: Trotsky 1879–1921* (London–New York–Toronto: Oxford University Press, 1954), pp. 292–3. For the original texts see Lenin, *Collected Works* (Moscow: Progress Publishers, 1964), vol. 26, pp. 74 ff., 182 ff., p. 190. The date '10 October' corresponds to the pre-revolutionary calendar. For Western purposes it has to be updated to '23 October'.

14 Julius Braunthal, *History of the International*, vol. 2 (London: Thomas Nelson; New York: Praeger Publishers, 1967), p. 168.

15 *Ibid.*, p. 180.

16 *Ibid.*, p. 181.

17 Robert Conquest, *The Great Terror* (London and New York: Macmillan, 1968).

18 Hugh Thomas, *The Spanish Civil War* (London: Eyre & Spottiswoode; New York: Harper & Row, 1961); Raymond Carr, *Spain 1808–1939*

(Oxford: Clarendon Press; New York: Oxford University Press, 1966); Gerald Brenan, *The Spanish Labyrinth* (Cambridge and New York: Cambridge University Press, 1967); Franz Borkenau, *The Spanish Cockpit* (London: Faber & Faber, 1937; Ann Arbor: University of Michigan Press, 1963); Gabriel Jackson, *The Spanish Republic and the Civil War 1931–1939* (Princeton, N.J.: University Press, 1965); Stanley G.Paine, *Falange: A History of Spanish Fascism* (Stanford, Calif.: Stanford University Press, 1961).

19 Leonard Schapiro, *The Origin of the Communist Autocracy* (London: Bell & Sons; Cambridge, Mass.: Harvard University Press, 1955); J.P.Nettl, *The Soviet Achievement* (London: Thames and Hudson, 1967; New York: Harcourt Brace, 1968); Alec Nove, *An Economic History of the USSR* (London: Allen Lane, 1969); Franz Borkenau, *The Communist International* (London: Faber & Faber, 1938; New York: Norton, 1939); Antonio Gramsci, *The Modern Prince and Other Writings* (London: Lawrence and Wishart, 1957, 1967; New York: International Publishing Co., 1959); Karl Korsch, *Marxism and Philosophy* (London: New Left Books, 1970); Günther Hillmann, *Selbstkritik des Kommunismus* (Hamburg: Rowohlt, 1967).

20 Charles Loch Mowat, *Britain Between the Wars 1918–1940* (London: Methuen; Chicago: University of Chicago Press, 1955), p. 259.

21 A.J.P.Taylor, *English History 1914–1945* (New York and Oxford: Oxford University Press, 1965), p. 238.

22 Mowat, *op. cit.*, p. 435.

23 Cited by Arthur Marwick, *Britain in the Century of Total War* (London: The Bodley Head; Boston: Atlantic Monthly Press, Little, Brown, 1968), pp. 113–14.

24 L.C.B.Seaman, *Post-Victorian Britain 1902–1951* (London: Methuen; New York: Barnes & Noble, 1966), p. 155.

25 Arnold Hauser, *The Social History of Art*, vol. 4 (London: Routledge & Kegan Paul, 1962), p. 216.

26 George Mosse, *The Culture of Western Europe* (London: Murray, 1963; Chicago: Rand McNally, 1961), pp. 293 ff.

27 See for example Professor Walter Kaufmann's new edition of *The Will to Power* (London: Weidenfeld & Nicolson, 1969; New York: Random House, 1967).

28 *Op cit.*, pp. 458–9.

29 Conor Cruise O'Brien, in *The New York Review of Books*, 5 November 1970.

30 Martin Esslin, *Brecht: A Choice of Evils* (London: Mercury Books, 1965).

31 H.Stuart Hughes, *The Obstructed Path* (London: MacGibbon & Kee, 1968; New York: Harper & Row, 1968), pp. 102 ff.

32 Charles de Gaulle, *Le Fil de l'épée* (Paris: Berger-Levrault, 1932); *Vers l'armée de métier* (Paris: Berger-Levrault, 1934); for a biographical study see Paul-Marie de la Gorce, *De Gaulle entre deux mondes* (Paris: Fayard, 1964).

33 J.D.Bernal, *Science in History*, vol. 3 (London: C.A.Watts and Pelican Books, 1965, 1969; New York: Hawthorn Books, 1965), p. 805.

34 George L.Mosse, *Nazi Culture: Intellectual, Cultural and Social Life in the*

Third Reich (London: W.H.Allen, 1967; New York: Grosset & Dunlap, 1966); Peter Gay, *Weimar Culture: The Outsider as Insider* (London: Secker & Warburg, 1969; New York: Harper & Row, 1968); Herman Lebovics, *Social Conservatism and the Middle Classes in Germany, 1914–1933* (Princeton, N.J.: Princeton University Press, 1969).

35 Ferdinand Toennies, *Community and Society* (East Lansing: Michigan University Press, 1957); cf. Toennies, "Mein Verhaeltnis zur Soziologie", in Richard Thurnwald, *Soziologie von Heute* (Leipzig: Hirschfeld, 1932).

36 Werner J.Cahnman, "Max Weber and the Methodological Controversy in the Social Sciences", in Cahnman,W.J. and Boskoff,A., eds., *Sociology and History* (London: Macmillan, 1964; Glencoe: The Free Press, Macmillan, 1964), pp. 103 ff.

37 Paul Krannhals, *Das Organische Weltbild* (1928); cited in G.L.Mosse, *The Corporate State and the Conservative Revolution in Weimar Germany* (Brussels: Éditions de la Librairie Encyclopédique, 1965). Walter Z.Laqueur, *Young Germany: A History of the German Youth Movement* (London: Routledge & Kegan Paul, 1962).

38 Denis Mack Smith, *Italy* (Ann Arbor: University of Michigan Press, 1959), p. 341.

39 *Ibid.*, p. 399.

40 *Ibid.*, p. 383.

41 *Ibid.*, pp. 411–12.

42 *Mein Kampf* (Munich: Eher Verlag, 1939), pp. 704–5; see also F.L.Carsten, *The Rise of Fascism* (London: Batsford; Berkeley, Calif.: University of California Press, 1969), p. 119.

CHAPTER 9

NATURAL AND SOCIAL SCIENCE

A   PHYSICS AND CHEMISTRY

It was remarked at the beginning of this study that there is a certain arbitrariness about letting the twentieth century commence in 1900 rather than in 1914. The statement obviously applies to the economic basis of European society rather than to the politico-military super-structure which was radically reshaped in 1914–18, and then once more in 1939–45. On occasion, though, the distinction becomes a trifle artificial. Consider, for example, the application of science to industry in those cases where the result had a direct bearing on a country's war-making capacity.[1] In 1898, at the Bristol meeting of the British Associ-ation for the Advancement of Science, Sir William Crookes in his presidential address declared that "England and all civilized nations stand in deadly peril of not having enough to eat ... land is a limited quantity ... it is the chemist who must come to the rescue of threatened communities". He calculated that if all the wheat-growing countries added the utmost to their area of cultivation, the increased yield could keep pace with the growth of population for only about thirty years; the solution was increased yield per acre. To this end the supply of nitrogen fertilizer had to be increased, and since the world's chief natural source, Chilean nitrates, would probably be depleted in thirty years, chemistry must step into the breach.

Crookes's warning applied especially to Germany, then the world's largest importer of Chilean nitrates. The challenge was promptly taken up by the country's leading scientists. The atmosphere contained enough free nitrogen to supply man's needs, for every square yard of the earth's surface has about seven tons of nitrogen gas pressing down on it. The problem was to fix this nitrogen in a usable form, and it was duly solved before 1914 by the Haber–Bosch process which combined nitrogen with hydrogen to produce synthetic ammonia. Fritz Haber (1868–1934) and the engineer Carl Bosch (1874–1940) in turn drew upon the advances made in chemical thermodynamics by Walter Nernst (1861–1941) and others. By 1909 Haber proved on a laboratory scale the feasibility of fixation, and by 1913 a small Haber–Bosch plant was in production at Oppau near Ludwigshafen. Had there been no world war, the plant's output would probably have increased very gradually, but the 1914–18 war, by cutting off Germany's normal supply of Chilean nitrate, speeded a technological upheaval. Nitrogen was needed not only for fertilizer, but for the production of explosives. The original plant was expanded from an annual capacity of 7,000 tons in 1913 to 100,000 tons early in the war, a mammoth new plant was constructed at Leuna near Merseburg, and by the end of the war Germany had the industrial capacity to produce about 550,000 tons of nitrogen annually, about half of it by the Haber–Bosch method. In due course the company expanded into an industrial empire, the celebrated *I.G.Farbenindustrie* of which Carl Bosch became the foremost director. Oppau and Leuna increased production from 122,000 tons in 1920 to 635,000 tons in 1928–9. The next step was to produce synthetic gasoline from coal by hydrogenation, thereby getting around the country's oil shortage which hampered its motor-car industry. Between 1924 and 1933 Germany produced about twenty per cent of the world total of coal and seventy-five per cent of the world total of lignite (brown coal). If lignite could be converted into gasoline to feed the internal combustion engine, Germany might regain her former status among the world's powers.

After 1933 synthetic gasoline made rearmament possible, but even at the peak of the Weimar period the Foreign Minister, Stresemann, developed the habit of saying that without coal and I.G.Farben he had no foreign policy. By 1932 the firm was deeply involved in politics, to the point of confidential meetings of its directors with Hitler, then still in opposition, but clearly on the threshold of power. Thereafter there was no stopping them, especially since Hitler's commitment to motor roads and the *Volkswagen*, not to mention rearmament, all depended upon the synthetic gasoline project. The history of hydrogenation in Germany between 1913 and 1933 thus discloses a growing momentum fed by war and the expectation of war. The process was exciting to the scientists because Germany could overcome a natural handicap with a synthetic product of technology. By coincidence this was also what Hitler needed in the interests of economic autarchy. Karl Haushofer and other geopoliticians had long argued that Germany could not attain her aims unless all the vital economic resources were within the national *Lebensraum*. Economic self-sufficiency was part of the National Socialist programme. Leuna happened to fill the bill. The most revealing aspect of the whole story is that as late as February 1933 Carl Bosch was confidentially described as "a south-west German liberal known for being an opponent of the Nazis". Personal likes and dislikes had ceased to matter. Bosch may have preferred the Brüning government (which fell in 1932), but once the existence of a gigantic industrial empire was at stake, he and his colleagues had to make the best of it. This, by the way, shows how absurd it is to characterize Hitler as a tool of big business. By 1933 the boot was on the other foot: the State was getting stronger than society, and even the biggest industrialists had to reckon with the fact that they were at the mercy of government policies. The systematic use of political power to sponsor technology was just what distinguished the new regime from its predecessor. When in December 1933 I.G.Farben contracted to provide the Hitler government with synthetic gasoline, a political pact was concluded between two autonomous powers. Fourteen years later, at the Nuremberg Tribunal, the prosecution argued that the contract was evidence of a conspiratorial alliance to prepare for war. It would have been more sensible to suggest that the technological momentum which had created I.G.Farben was part of a more general process whereby industry and the government had become interlinked.

Rocketry provides another example. The first scientific writing on the subject was published in 1903 by a Russian schoolmaster, K.E. Ziolovsky, who worked out mathematically some of the requirements of space travel.[2] R.H.Goddard, an American physicist, experimented on a small scale with rocketry between the two wars. Ignorant of the work of both, Hermann Oberth published *The Rocket in Interplanetary Space* in 1923, while he was still a student, and thereby set numbers of young men in Germany thinking about the subject. Amateur rocket societies were formed in various countries during the 1920s, but most of the practical work was done in Germany. Owing to an oversight on the part of the Versailles Treaty makers, rocketry was not mentioned among the restrictions imposed on Germany, and from 1929 onward the German government decided to undertake rocket research for military purposes. The decision ultimately resulted during the Second World War in the establishment at Peenemünde of a gigantic establishment which employed 12,000 people and enlisted the support of numerous research institutes. Dornberger, the head of the enterprise, employed Oberth among many others, and after the successful launching of the V2 rocket paid tribute to his pioneering work. Hitler, for some reason, was at first unenthusiastic about rockets and in the spring of 1940 rocket development was struck off the priority list. Eventually he changed his mind, and from then on the highest priority was given to the project. By the closing months of the war all technical handicaps had been overcome and launchings were completely successful. In brief, an invention sponsored by a mathematics student in 1923 had within two decades become a colossal development into which the German Army poured countless funds. Private enterprise could never have done the job – State backing was essential and it was provided by the military while the Weimar Republic was still in being. On a larger scale, the same applies to jet-propelled aircraft and indeed to the aeronautical industry in general.[3] The technicians took the lead, and the governments eventually provided the funds.

The most celebrated case of all, that of nuclear physics, also belongs to the inter-war period. Planck's original quantum theory, as interpreted by Niels Bohr of Copenhagen in 1913, had become questionable by 1925, when de Broglie in France, Schrödinger and Heisenberg in Germany, and Dirac in England, proposed various amendments.[4] The 1930s witnessed a burst of physical discovery, with radioactivity giving rise to a series of experiments that culminated in the actual control of nuclear processes. Between 1932 and 1938 a number of crucial discoveries were made by Joliot (1900–58), Fermi (1901–54) and others which had the effect of showing that most of the energy in the universe was derived from nuclear processes. By 1938 it had become possible to split the uranium atom, and since the discovery of nuclear fission occurred on the eve of war, the Western physicists were able to interest the British and American governments in what they were doing: largely on the grounds that if they did not act, the enemy would be first with a nuclear bomb. In fact the Germans lagged behind, while European refugee scientists who had made the controlled release of atomic energy possible were put to work in the United States. The actual splitting of the atom was achieved by Hahn and Strassmann in 1938, but fortunately for the Allies the Germans proved slow in trying to produce a bomb. The rest of the story is too well known to need recapitulation. The moral, so far as there is one, is that much of the drive to produce practical results came from the military. In quiet times the economics of nuclear fission, when measured against those of conventional power, might have taken decades to result in anything on the scale of the new production processes. As it was, the identification of the neutron by Chadwick in 1932 set off a train of events which within little more than a decade carried mankind over the threshold of the atomic age.

In retrospect it is evident that the first half of the twentieth century proved to be a period of advance in physics surpassing that of all preceding ages. In these fifty years the harvest of four centuries of modern science was reaped.[5] In 1897–9 J.J.Thomson had identified the first component to be known in the structure of the atom, now familiar as the electron. Shortly afterwards another particle, carrying a charge of positive electricity equal in amount to the negative charge of the electron was detected: the proton. In 1911 Rutherford showed that the alpha rays, as they were called, which were emitted in radioactive disintegration, were in fact not rays but positively charged helium atoms. They were known to pass through matter easily and at a high velocity, but with occasional large deflections. Rutherford concluded that the inside of the atom was mostly empty. Thus the ancient solid atom was revealed as a structure consisting of a minute but massive central nucleus with a positive electric charge, surrounded at a distance by a peripheral shell of negatively charged electrons – a kind of solar system in miniature. Next came the discovery that protons and electrons might form slightly different structures with different atomic weights, termed 'isotopes' by Soddy in 1913. The discovery that atoms differed chemically, because of the different number of protons and electrons of which they were composed, brought science back to the ancient but discredited notion that matter was transmutable, and by 1919 the first such transmutation was achieved by Rutherford when he succeeded in obtaining hydrogen by bombarding certain light elements with alpha particles. From there the road led straight to the cyclotron and later to the atomic pile; it also led to the production of new elements, the identification of the neutron by Chadwick in 1932 and the practical consequences already described.

Biology and chemistry, being of less practical import, made less sensational progress. In biology the key event was the rediscovery in 1900 of the Bohemian monk Gregor Mendel (1822–84) who in the 1860s had worked out the mechanism of inheritance. Mendel, experimenting with peas in his monastery garden, had come across indivisible and unalterable units called *genes* whose infinitely varied combination resulted in the process of heredity. This led to the conclusion that acquired characteristics were not inherited and it also limited the import of Darwin's theory of natural selection. In 1901 de Vries discovered abrupt changes which were termed mutations and for which chance variations appeared to be responsible. Mendel's law obtained further reinforcement when T.H.Morgan in America established a link between the unit genetic characters and the chromosomes which had been observed in the nuclei of dividing cells. Subject to mutation, it was thus established that to each inherited character in the adult organism there corresponded a material particle, the gene, in one of the chromosomes of its parents. Each cell of an organism contains a set pair of chromosomes, one derived from each parent, and should therefore possess a pair of genes for every character. The process of breeding thus reduced itself to different ways of dealing out the genes of the offspring. Discussion turned on the question how far the genes were subject to chance variation resulting in new mutations. This became an intensely topical issue when it was found that radiation from atomic and hydrogen bombs could lead to mutations in plants, animals and human beings. It also proved necessary to modify the Darwinian theory of natural selection in terms of the Mendelian theory of genes. Gene mutation obviously occurs for reasons having nothing to do with the adaptive value of the resultant character in the adult organism. On this view natural selection is still operative, but it works not on the characters but on the gene combinations, thereby changing in a mathematically determinable way the gene composition of the population.[6] In its latest development the study of ecology has grouped together the older evolutionary and genetic theories in such a way as to make possible the understanding of how the total environment – the balance of nature – is affected by man's interference with other organisms, with the soil and even with earth's climate. Soil conservation is now a major issue, and the ancient concept of conquering nature for man's benefit is beginning to give way to a more sensible concern for preserving a natural balance in danger of being undermined by unrestrained technology, the waste of natural resources, air pollution and unrestricted population growth in areas which can barely keep their present inhabitants alive. Most of these problems date from the post-1945 period. During the inter-war years they had barely begun to impinge upon the public consciousness.

The application of science to medicine meanwhile produced startling results, from the discovery in 1900 that malaria and yellow fever were transmitted by mosquitos to the effective control of these diseases. Artificial immunization was greatly developed, and typhoid, hitherto the scourge of armies, had only a negligible incidence in both world wars. Blood transfusion became a normal hospital routine from 1940 onwards. Antibiotics transformed medicine by reducing the danger of infectious diseases. The discovery between 1928 and 1938 of penicillin by Alexander Fleming (1881–1955) and Howard Florey (1898–1968) was a particularly notable victory in the struggle against bacteria. Biochemistry made it possible to use what came to be known as vitamins for curative purposes. Along with the unravelling of the genetic code this has probably been the most important advance made in recent decades in building up what may be called a science of life.

The philosophical implications of these discoveries are a matter for dispute.[7] The reformulation of Darwinism in the language of Mendelian genetics is only one instance. It has not proved possible to obtain agreement among scientists and philosophers on the ancient question whether reality is to be understood as a hierarchical system, the higher levels of which lend themselves to interpretation in teleological terms. In the 1920s much was heard of 'emergent evolution', its most distinguished exponent being A.N.Whitehead.[8] Since then the pendulum has swung in the other direction, but the notion that the higher levels of existence have emerged from the lower level of matter by the impact of natural selection on chance variations (mutations) remains unsatisfactory to many thinking people, not all of them metaphysicians. In all probability the issue will continue to be debated as long as there are philosophers who continue to believe that even at the lowest level of organic evolution something like a germ of freedom can be discerned.

B PSYCHOLOGY AND ANTHROPOLOGY

The brief discussion of psychology in the first part of this study (see Chapter 5) dealt in the main with Freud's work down to 1914, and secondly with the founders of the *Gestalt* school who came together around 1912. An attempt must now be made to sketch the development which took place between 1919 and 1939, and at the same time the field must be widened so as to make room for the newcomer known as Behaviourism. This procedure is eased by the fact that although the founder of Behaviourism, J.B.Watson, had already defined his main principles by 1914, his *Psychology from the Standpoint of a Behaviorist* appeared in 1919.[9] After 1920 Watson abandoned the academic world and worked in the advertising business, a fruitful partnership which gave rise to many interesting experiments in guiding the public taste. Watson's basic ideas, as outlined in his *Behavior: An Introduction to Comparative Psychology* (1914) and in his later writings, were rooted in his study of animal psychology, begun at Chicago in 1903 and continued at Johns Hopkins University after 1908. It was his contention that psychology, in order to become an exact science, must discard introspection and cease to take the field of consciousness as its chief datum. Instead, attention should be fixed upon overt behaviour. Most psychological functions could be described in terms of responses to stimuli, since they involved the task of adaptation to the environment. Even if there was an 'inner aspect', this could be ignored without great loss. In short, the study of mental events should be replaced by the study of actual behaviour. In his later writings Watson argued that the mechanism controlling the association between stimulus and response was the conditioned reflex and its refinements in the nervous system. The proper field of investigation was constituted by limb movements, gland secretions, verbal utterances, tensing of muscles – together with the environmental stimuli which may evoke such responses. Hence 'mental' science must change into 'physical' science.

Watson's writings made a decisive impact upon American psychology in the 1920s and from the United States they spread to Europe, where their influence coalesced with the interest taken in the work of the Russian psychologist Ivan Petrovich Pavlov (1849–1936) who had received the Nobel Prize in 1904. Pavlov's studies of conditioned reflexes in animals antedated Watson's work and probably influenced him by way of the American psychologist R.M.Yerkes (1876–1956) who in 1909 brought Pavlov to the attention of the English-speaking world and in 1910 collaborated with Watson in the study of animal behaviour.[10] Pavlov, using dogs as experimental subjects, had noticed that salivation, which is a purely reflex action occurring when food is felt in the mouth, often appeared before the dog was actually fed. Various stimuli associated with feeding – not only the sight of the food container, but even the sound of a buzzer – were sufficient to set off salivation. In the end the dog salivated in response to the buzzer alone, even if no food was produced. This experiment suggested to Pavlov that certain simple forms of 'learning' or 'habit formation' could be induced by conditioning the nervous system without any mental associations being formed. Whether or not fully conversant with Pavlov's work through his collaboration with Yerkes, Watson adopted the notion of conditioning and made it central to his system of human psychology. In this respect he followed a line of thought already suggested by the pragmatist philosopher William James in his article "Does Consciousness Exist?" (*Journal of Philosophy*, 1904).

When Watson moved out of academic psychology, his work was continued by others, among whom E.R.Guthrie and B.F.Skinner became the best known. In the 1930s Skinner worked with rats and established that a hungry rat in a box may 'learn' to press a lever which produces food pellets. Generalizing from this discovery he gradually built up a theory of behaviour which he applied to problems of learning and adaptation in human beings. As an example he gave the work-behaviour of employees who respond to high wages and good conditions with efficient work and the absence of strikes. These effects, in his opinion, were controlled responses to stimuli provided by the management.[11] This kind of thinking left its mark on American industrial sociology and its European offshoots. With the emergence of industrial psychology in the 1920s and 1930s, theories of learning and adaptation acquired a practical importance they had not possessed before, and Behaviourism made a contribution to the methods increasingly employed to rationalize industrial management. For the most part these innovations grew out of empirical studies on the factory floor, in which respect F.W.Taylor's *Principles of Scientific Management* (1911) was path-breaking in promoting what came to be known as 'time-and-motion' study. In this manner academic research and industrial psychology became more closely linked, but Skinner's version of Behaviourism, which derived from Watson and Pavlov, was only one factor, and perhaps a minor one, in promoting this fusion.

In the later 1930s the extremes of Behaviouristic thinking were modified by the influence of the *Gestalt* school, whose founders, being mostly German and Austrian Jews, were driven to the USA, where their work was absorbed into American psychology. While the *Gestalt* theorists agreed with the Behaviourists in attacking introspection and introducing methods of work which could be applied in the laboratory, their insistence on the importance of 'wholes' which are more than the sum of their parts had implications unfavourable to Behaviourism. In itself the view that 'wholes' have emergent properties not derived from their parts was not new: it possessed an anchorage in the psychology of William James and Lloyd Morgan. But the *Gestalt* school laid special emphasis on the notion that the basic data of consciousness are grasped in organized, structured and dynamic 'wholes'. Thus melodies are perceived as formally constituted units, not as a sequence of separate tones. Perceptual fields are organized in terms of specific *Gestalten*, or forms, whose parts are connected in relation to the dominant form. These and other conclusions had been worked out jointly by Wertheimer, Koffka and Köhler, whose periodical, *Psychologische Forschung*, appeared in Berlin from 1921 until 1938, when it was suppressed by the Hitler regime – a fate that also overtook the German and Austrian branches of the psychoanalytic movement.

The contrast between the intellectual climate of the 1920s and that of the 1930s is striking. In the earlier decade *Gestalt* psychology attained academic respectability in Weimar Germany, where Wolfgang Köhler was appointed to a professorship in Berlin in 1922. At the same time the influence of the Freudian school spread throughout Central Europe, while in Soviet Russia it briefly enjoyed Lenin's tolerance and Trotsky's active encouragement. In the 1930s everything went to pieces: the Stalinists turned against psychoanalysis as part of their struggle against 'Jewish cosmopolitanism'; and their example, in this as in other fields, was aped by Hitler's followers after their accession to power in 1933. At the same time the psychoanalytic movement was riven by doctrinal quarrels between orthodox Freudians and heretics such as Wilhelm Reich (1897–1957), an active Communist who for a time tried to synthesize Marxian insights with his own highly personal interpretation of Freud. While the latter was tolerant of left-wing disciples such as Otto Fenichel and Siegfried Bernfeld, whose Marxist leanings were well known, he could not abide Reich, who in consequence was expelled from the International Psychoanalytical Association in 1934 (and not long before from the Communist movement).[12]

At a distance of some four decades it is not altogether easy to take seriously Freud's suggestion (in the *Internationale Zeitschrift für Psychoanalyse*, vol. 18, 1932) that Reich's controversial theory of sadism was somehow linked to his membership of 'the Bolshevist party'. Reich's sociological interpretation of some of Freud's more metaphysical concepts was notorious, but Freud probably overshot the mark when on the same occasion he affirmed that Reich had described the "death instinct" (*Todestrieb*) postulated by Freud as "a product of the capitalist system". Reich's subsequent career in the United States as the inventor, among other novelties, of an 'orgone box' for the storage of biological energy efficacious in the treatment of cancer, laid him open not merely to legal proceedings, but to charges of mental imbalance. Mrs Reich's biography of her late husband, which appeared in 1969, makes it clear that he identified himself with Christ, whom he believed to have been in direct communication with the 'cosmic orgone forces', and that he considered *The Murder of Christ* to be his most important book. Yet while his private manias, as well as his notions about orgones and cosmic energy, have generally been rejected as fanciful, it has been argued that in the 1920s he made a contribution to psychoanalysis in various papers on character-analysis which were then accepted as orthodox by the Viennese analysts. As for the compatibility of Marxian sociology and Freudian psychology, Reich was by no means the only analyst to interest himself in the topic. An attempt to revise psychoanalysis in the light of Marxian humanism was subsequently made with some success by Erich Fromm, while in the 1950s the discussion was renewed by Herbert Marcuse.[13]

In some respects the controversy stirred up by Freud's Marxist colleagues and critics was a sequel to the earlier dispute between Freud and his distinguished Viennese contemporary Alfred Adler (1870–1937), from whom he had felt obliged to part before 1914.[14] It was Adler's prime contention that human beings are more influenced by conscious fears, ambitions, hopes and strivings than by unconscious drives or the residues of past experience. In particular he stressed man's aggressiveness, his search for conquest and security. At the same time he emphasized the central importance of overcoming the sense of inferiority induced by the fact that during infancy and childhood all human beings feel weak and insecure. These sentiments, Adler held, could be sublimated by education and socialization which lead the individual to understand that he must cultivate 'social interest' in the place of more egoistic striving. The neurotic, who fails to make this transition, remains an outsider. Among those whom Adler influenced, Erich Fromm (born in Frankfurt, 1900) and Karen Horney (born in Hamburg 1885, died in New York 1952) became the leading figures in what from the orthodox Freudian viewpoint was a 'revisionist' school which underplayed the role of the unconscious and overstressed the need to overcome the anxiety human beings inherit from their childhood. Freud himself, in a series of writings published in the 1920s and 1930s, deepened his original approach and at the same time gave a more pessimistic emphasis to his analysis of the human condition. His most important publications during this period were *Jenseits des Lustprinzips* (*Beyond the Pleasure Principle*) (1920); *Die Zukunft einer Illusion* (*The Future of an Illusion*) (1927); *Das Unbehagen in der Kultur* (*Civilization and its Discontents*) (1930); and his study of the origins of Judaism, *Der Mann Moses und die Monotheistische Religion* (*Moses and Monotheism*), published in 1939, by which time Freud had been driven from his native Vienna and obliged to seek refuge in London.

It has been suggested that during these years Freud shifted from his original explanation of behaviour in terms of mechanical causes towards a more descriptive psychology showing what functions are served by neurotic symptoms.[15] At the same time, however, he introduced the meta-scientific concepts of Eros and Thanatos which were not accepted by all his followers. Eros (the life instinct) represents the libidinal energy plus the urge for self-preservation. Thanatos (the death wish) is an impulse towards aggression and destruction which may be turned inwards against the self and lead to suicide. This dualism – ultimately perhaps an echo of Schopenhauer's philosophy which had helped to shape the outlook of the youthful Freud – was inherently incapable of scientific proof. On the sound empiricist principle that all theoretical constructions are merely hypotheses rather than conclusions arrived at by induction, this circumstance in itself perhaps did no great harm; but the introduction of these dualist concepts did have the effect of turning Freudian psychoanalysis into something akin to a *Weltanschauung*, which was certainly not what Freud had aimed at in his earlier days. His highly speculative reconstruction of Jewish religious history in *Moses and Monotheism* falls into the same category. Moreover, in suggesting that men possess an archaic heritage which includes not only dispositions, but memory traces of the experiences of former generations, Freud appeared in 1939 to have taken a step towards the theory of archetypes hitherto associated with the rival system of Jung.

Carl Gustav Jung (1875–1962) had worked in Zürich as a psychiatrist and between 1907 and 1913 became an associate of Freud. He then struck out on his own, formulating a different view of psychology and at the same time collecting anthropological data and developing an interest in comparative religion, folklore and primitive mythology. A writer of enormous erudition, he acquired a wide following among laymen, while within academic psychology and psychoanalysis alike he came to be regarded as something of an eccentric, with interests ranging from alchemy to mysticism. His theory of archetypes in particular depended on the notion of a collective unconscious, a concept not acceptable to Freudians, or indeed to academic psychiatrists. By comparison with Jung's system, even Freud's later writings have a severely empirical bent.

Jung had been able for some years to cooperate with Freud because he agreed with him in postulating the existence of an unconscious, for which evidence could be found in hypnosis, dream-analysis and free association. But his picture of the unconscious eventually came to differ from that of Freud in important respects. First, the unconscious mind of the individual is said by him to contain not only repressed infantile impulses, but also unapprehended personal experiences and ideas which have been forgotten because they lost "a certain energetic value". Secondly and more important, the personal unconscious is only a fraction of the total mass of unconscious material. Below it there lies an inheritance which contains the collective myths and beliefs of the human race, and at a yet deeper level the heritage of man's animal past. Evolution has predetermined the human mind to react in ways derived from this remote past. The tendency to do so Jung describes as 'archetypal'. Archetypes manifest themselves in dreams and symbols common to human beings belonging to widely different cultures. They emerge from the deepest levels of the collective unconscious and are not directly accessible. Dream symbols may be individual, but they may also relate to archetypes and have affinities with the folklore of all human cultures and races, rooted as they are in the primitive experience of birth and death, food and drink, or the cycle of the seasons. Hence the study of myths and religious symbolisms gives access to the working of the collective unconscious. This conclusion was disputed (by among others the orthodox Freudian analyst and anthropologist Géza Roheim), on the grounds that members of all cultures necessarily share common experiences: all individuals have parents, are born and die, have sexual desires, are dependent on the sun and earth, and so on. It is therefore not surprising that they should all tend to create myths of the Great Father, the Great Mother, sun-gods and the like. No collective unconscious need be postulated to account for the similarity of primitive myths, for their analysis will lay bare the shared experiences of all mankind, whereas the study of the individual ego will disclose the specific features of different cultures. For Jung, however, the archetype is not a metaphorical concept which simply translates the fact of universally-shared experience. It is is a real entity underlying the conscious mind as well as the personal unconscious. At a deeper level, groups of individuals are joined together in the racial unconscious, e.g. of the Aryans or the Semites, while at the most primitive level of all the collective unconscious contains the heritage of humanity as a whole, including its animal past. As for the motive force of human existence, the 'libido', it is non-sexual and represents a sort of life-force: a concept for which Jung was indebted to the philosophy of Henri Bergson.

The reception of these rival schools outside their Central European homeland was marked by wide differences. France proved resistant to psychoanalysis in all its forms until the 1940s, when the shock of military defeat paradoxically led to a wholesale adoption of German, or German–Jewish, importations: from the philosophy of Husserl and Heidegger to psychoanalysis and neo-Marxism of the Frankfurt variety. In Great Britain during the 1920s and 1930s Freudian concepts were pioneered by Dr Ernest Jones, the only native of Britain among Freud's early followers and ultimately his biographer. At the same time an eclectic combination of Freudian and traditional concepts was put to use at the Tavistock Clinic in London, founded by Dr Crichton Miller and associated with such names as Dr Emanuel Miller, Dr J.A.Hadfield and Dr Ian Suttie. With the gradual break-up of the German and

Austro-Hungarian psychoanalytic movements under the stress of political persecution, prominent members of the school settled in Britain, including Freud himself, his daughter Anna Freud and Melanie Klein.[16] Adherents of Adler and Jung likewise made their appearance, the Jungians in some cases being helped by the relatively favourable echo which their doctrines encountered in some Roman Catholic circles. In general, however, the empiricist bent of British academic psychology provided a less hospitable climate than that encountered by *émigre* psychoanalysts in the United States. Freud and his more or less orthodox followers were read in both countries, but whereas in America they exercised a direct influence upon practising psychiatrists, in Britain they tended to be read by intelligent laymen rather than by practitioners. This situation altered in some degree after 1945, but for the period under review it may be said that psychoanalysis, in its various manifestations, remained the affair of a limited circle of intellectuals. It was only in the 1960s that an original work such as Suttie's *Origins of Love and Hate* (originally published in 1935, shortly after the author's death) appeared in paperback format. To some extent the resolve of Freud's principal British followers, notably Edward Glover and Ernest Jones, to maintain a high intellectual standard may have been responsible for this state of affairs.[17] It remains a noteworthy fact that while the English *Standard Edition* of Freud's work in twenty-four volumes is generally regarded as the best in the world, there has until recently been no British counterpart of the massive distribution of his writings in popular format which occurred in the United States during the 1950s and in Continental Western Europe thereafter. It may or may not be coincidental that in respect of Marxism a similar situation prevailed in Britain during the inter-war period and beyond, when the identification of Marx's thought with the simplified Leninist version propagated by the Communist Party came to an end at long last.

Anthropology – to which Jung made a somewhat eccentric contribution with his theory of archetypes and his investigations into primitive myths – was already strongly entrenched in Britain when Bronislaw Malinowski (1884–1942), a displaced Polish intellectual, transferred himself from Germany to England in 1910. His principal field-work, interrupted by visits to Australia, was carried out between 1914 and 1918 in New Guinea, an area opened to research by A.C.Haddon, W.H.R.Rivers, C.G.Seligman and others who shaped his thinking while he was working as a post-graduate student at the London School of Economics between 1910 and 1913. He was also influenced by Westermarck (1862–1939) and to some extent by Freud, although he remained critical of the anthropological concepts employed by the Freudian school.[18] After a few years of strenuous field-work and the publication of his *Argonauts of the Western Pacific* (1922), Malinowski was appointed to a readership in anthropology and in 1927 to the first chair in anthropology at the University of London. Between 1923 and 1938 he poured out a stream of publications on such diverse subjects as *Crime and Custom in Savage Society* (1926), *Myth in Primitive Psychology* (1926), *The Sexual Life of Savages in Northwestern Melanesia* (1929) and *The Foundations of Faith and Morals* (1936). His death in 1942 occurred while he was teaching at Yale University in the United States. Science, magic and religion provided the main topics of his theoretical work which was guided by the concept of a dual reality: the natural world studied in observation, and a supernatural sphere grounded in emotional needs which give rise to faith. While differentiating between magic and religion, Malinowski treated the former as an essentially pragmatic response to fear, the latter as a self-fulfilling ritual linked to myth. His analysis of the Trobriand Islanders' social customs, which first brought him to public attention, may be described as a fusion of sociological and anthropological concepts. In all these respects his work aroused controversy, but it also stimulated the further development of the British school, of which A.R.Radcliffe-Brown, W.H.R.Rivers, E.E.Evans-Pritchard, Raymond Firth and Edmund Leach came to be regarded as the most distinguished representatives.[19]

Thus in the 1920s and 1930s there occurred a confluence of psychology and anthropology which led to a greatly increased interest in the study of primitive societies. The new scientific fashion was not confined to Britain, although the British school took the lead – if only because Britain's possession of a world-wide empire afforded an important advantage to fieldworkers in touch with colonial administrators. As it happened, these were also the years when Freudian psychology reached the British Isles, so that a certain degree of mutual interpenetration took place. Malinowski himself operated with Freudian concepts, although his study of the Trobriand Islanders led him to the conclusion that the Oedipus complex could not be operative in a culture in which not the father but the maternal brother was the child's custodian. Among the older generation of British anthropologists, W.H.R.Rivers, who during the 1914–18 war was engaged in treating cases of battle-neurosis, also accepted Freud's findings, though with reservations.[20] More generally, the leading figures of the school, especially Radcliffe-Brown and Malinowski, worked out a functionalist theory of primitive society which in turn stimulated the work of British and American sociologists. Functionalism implied that the various aspects of social life, from kinship to religion, formed a whole which was kept in being by an intricate balance of all the interconnecting parts. The implications for sociology were obvious, and were duly worked out by the American school founded by Talcott Parsons and its various British and Continental counterparts.

At the same time a wholly different approach, more in tune with the tradition of James Frazer (1854–1941), author of *The Golden Bough*, was inaugurated by the French anthropologist Claude Lévi-Strauss who between 1934 and 1937 taught at São Paulo University in Brazil and made some trips into the interior, supplemented by further field-work in 1938–9 when he had resigned his teaching post.[21] Lévi-Strauss, who had been influenced by Marxism as well as psychoanalysis, elaborated what in later years came to be known as a 'structuralist' approach; this has some resemblance with Marxism in that it aims at a grasp of totality, but unlike the Marxists Lévi-Strauss draws a rigid line between primitive societies, which are supposed to be timeless and static, and advanced cultures which elude anthropological analysis because they are "in history". Then there is the difficulty that Lévi-Strauss – like Edward Tylor, James Frazer, and other nineteenth-century evolutionists – tries to establish conclusions about the workings of the human mind, but his time-sense is very different from theirs, being geological rather than historical. He has said: "Unlike the history of the historians, history as the geologist and the psychoanalyst sees it, is intended to body forth in time . . . certain fundamental properties of the physical and psychical universe."[22] This makes it difficult to classify him as a Marxist, while his tendency to see primitive peoples as models of what is basic in all mankind suggests a certain affinity with Rousseau. It has been remarked that he takes his cue from Rousseau in arguing that it is language which constitutes the essence of humanity as distinct from animality, a transition that accompanies the shift from nature to culture. This leads on to the notion that verbal categories provide the means whereby universal characteristics of the human brain are transformed into patterns of behaviour, and this is where structuralism makes contact with the historical, or geological, part of the argument. For if such universals exist, they must in the course of human evolution have become elements of the human psyche, along with the development of those parts of the brain that are directly linked with speech formation.

The theory owed something to the Prague school of structural linguistics developed by Roman Jakobson, who was associated with Lévi-Strauss during the latter's stay in the United States in 1941–7. It differs from Malinowski's functionalism, which was much closer to empirical evidence, and must be regarded as a self-contained body of thought peculiar to Lévi-Strauss and his French disciples.[23] This is not to say that structuralism and functionalism are necessarily incompatible. The term 'social structure' draws attention to the interdependence within a social system of all the different classes of relations found within a given society. So defined, structuralism makes no claim to the possession of special insights denied to anthropologists or sociologists working with empirical material. The rather abstract model favoured by Lévi-Strauss is not for this reason radically divorced from the sort of explanation by origin or function favoured by historians and sociologists. Where it differs from the historical approach is in its attempt to decipher a code instead of tracing a pedigree. The basic assumption of structuralism resembles Noam Chomsky's theory of language, according to which all human languages derive from a finite set of universals common to all men and anterior to cultural variants. Similarly, Lévi-Strauss believes that the structures of kinship, social organization and economic exchange in primitive society are the manifest expressions of structural laws embedded in the unconscious. To take the best known example, the binary organization which men give to their perceptions – the universal habit of classifying experiences in pairs of opposites such as hot and cold, high and low, heaven and earth – is said to be grounded in the neurology of the human brain. Human beings are able to communicate because all languages and all codes of behaviour are rooted in cerebral universals. Like Chomsky's "generative grammar", Lévi-Strauss' "structural anthropology" wears a Cartesian look, but it can also be described as materialist in that it postulates a physico-chemical foundation underlying the patterned structure of social behaviour. In this it resembles the Freudian model, a circumstance familiar to students of Freud's early work, which presupposed a physiological basis of mental behaviour, even though Freud emphasized that this layer of the mind was not accessible to the science of his day. It is arguable that psychoanalysis, generative linguistics and structural anthropology in the form given to it by Lévi-Strauss share a common belief in the existence of an as yet unexamined biological foundation, similar to the genetic code whose decipherment ranks among the major intellectual advances of the present age. In this sense, Lévi-Strauss, like Freud, is a materialist, the chief difference being that Freud was concerned with the interpretation of dreams, Lévi-Strauss with the analysis of the collective dreams known as mythologies.

NOTES

1 For the following see Thomas Parke Hughes, "Technological Momentum in History: Hydrogenation in Germany 1898–1933", *Past and Present*, No. 44, August 1969, pp. 106–32.
2 John Jewkes, David Sawers and Richard Stillerman, *The Sources of Invention* (London: Macmillan; New York: St Martin's Press, 1958), pp. 355 ff.
3 *Ibid.*, pp. 314 ff.
4 J.D.Bernal, *Science in History*, vol. 3 (London: C.A.Watts and Pelican Books, 1969; New York: Hawthorn Books, 1965), pp. 748 ff.
5 Douglas McKie, "Science and Technology", in *The New Cambridge Modern History*, vol. XII (second edition), pp. 87 ff.

6 Bernal, *op. cit.*, p. 958.

7 See P.B.Medawar, *The Art of the Soluble* (London: Methuen; New York: Barnes & Noble, 1967), *passim*; also the same author's BBC Reith lectures of 1959 published under the title *The Future of Man* (London: Methuen, 1960).

8 Hans Jonas, *The Phenomenon of Life* (New York: Harper & Row, 1966); Marjorie Grene, *The Knower and the Known* (London: Faber; New York: Basic Books, 1966); Erwin Schrödinger, *What is Life? and Other Scientific Essays* (New York and London: Doubleday, 1956).

9 See Robert Thomson, *The Pelican History of Psychology* (London and Baltimore: Penguin Books, 1968), pp. 163 ff., 226 ff.

10 *Ibid.*, pp. 160–1.

11 *Ibid.*, p. 232. For a critique of Behaviourism see Gordon Rattray Taylor, "A New View of the Brain", *Encounter*, February 1971.

12 Reimut Reiche, *Sexuality and Class Struggle*, tr. by Susan Bennett (London: New Left Books, 1970; New York: Praeger Publishers, 1971); Herbert Marcuse, *Five Lectures*, tr. by Jeremy J.Shapiro and Shierry M. Weber (London: Allen Lane; Boston: Beacon Press, 1970); Hans Peter Gente ed., *Marxismus, Psychoanalyse, Sexpol*, vol. I (Frankfurt: Fischer Bücherei, 1970); Paul A.Robinson, *The Freudian Left* (New York: Harper & Row, 1969), published in Britain under the title *The Sexual Radicals* (London: Temple Smith, 1970). See also Wilhelm Reich's *Selected Writings*, ed. Mary Boyd Higgins (New York: Farrar, Straus, 1969); Charles Rycroft, *Reich* (London: Collins–Fontana; New York: The Viking Press, 1971).

13 Herbert Marcuse, *Eros and Civilisation* (London: Routledge & Kegan Paul, 1956; Boston: Beacon Press, 1955), tr. from the American original into German as *Eros und Kultur* (Stuttgart: Ernst Klett Verlag, 1957); see also the controversy between Fromm and Marcuse in *Voices of Dissent* (New York: Grove Press, 1958).

14 Thomson, *op. cit.*, pp. 264 ff. See also J.A.C.Brown, *Freud and the Post-Freudians* (London and Baltimore: Penguin Books, 1961); Charles Rycroft ed., *Psychoanalysis Observed* (London: Constable, 1966); Ian D. Suttie, *The Origins of Love and Hate* (London: Penguin Books, 1960, 1963); David Stafford-Clark, *What Freud Really Said* (London: Macdonald, 1965; New York: Schocken, 1966); C.G.Jung, *Analytical Psychology: Its Theory and Practice* (London: Routledge & Kegan Paul; New York: Pantheon, 1968).

15 Thomson, *op. cit.*, p. 254.

16 J.A.C.Brown, *op. cit.*, pp. 56–7.

17 See Edward Glover, *Freud or Jung* (London: Allen & Unwin, 1950; New York: Meridian Books, World Publishing, 1956); Ernest Jones, *Free Associations: Memories of a Psychoanalyst* (London: The Hogarth Press; New York: Basic Books, 1959).

18 See his *Sex and Repression in Savage Society*, first published in 1927 and reissued as a paperback in 1960 (London: Routledge & Kegan Paul; New York: World Publishing, 1955), where he observes that the Oedipus complex is not traceable in a matrilinear society. The work that first

brought him to public attention, *Argonauts of the Western Pacific*, appeared in 1922 and was re-issued in 1960 (London: Routledge; New York: Dutton).

19 For a relatively late specimen see Edmund Leach, *Genesis as Myth and other Essays* (London: Jonathan Cape; New York: Grossman Publishers, 1969). For a general introduction to the subject see M.F.Ashley-Montagu ed., *Culture: Man's Adaptive Dimension* (London–Oxford–New York: Oxford University Press, 1968) and the same author's *The Biosocial Nature of Man* (London: John Calder; New York: Grove Press, 1956). For an earlier American contribution to the topic see Ruth Benedict, *Patterns of Culture* (London: Routledge & Kegan Paul, 1935, 1961; Boston: Houghton Mifflin, 1959).

20 Brown, *op. cit.*, pp. 62–3, 115.

21 For an introduction to the subject see Edmund Leach, *Lévi-Strauss* (London: Collins–Fontana; New York: The Viking Press, 1970). This brief work also contains a useful bibliography.

22 Leach, *op. cit.*, p. 18.

23 *Ibid.*, pp. 27 ff. Lévi-Strauss, *The Elementary Structures of Kinship* (London: Eyre & Spottiswoode, 1969).

CHAPTER 10

ART AND LITERATURE BETWEEN THE WARS

Something has already been said about the crisis of liberalism and its reflection in the literary sphere during the inter-war period. A rather more coherent attempt must now be made to deal with the manifestations of a new sensibility. In the nature of the case, art as such was less directly affected by the 1914–18 war than science, which received a major stimulus from military technology. By 1914 the central themes of the modern age had for the most part been stated. Cubism, Futurism and Expressionism had been launched upon their respective careers. The only significant war-time newcomer was Dadaism, founded in Zürich in 1916 by Tristan Tzara and others who hit upon the production of absurdities as a means of ridding themselves of conventional forms. Dadaism was not designed to make sense – that was the whole point about it. The Surrealists who built upon it were less playful and more solemn. André Breton's *Surrealist Manifesto* of 1924 centred upon the newly discovered notion of unconscious creativity. Improvisation was given its due and fantasy was allowed to roam freely, as were dreams and nightmares. Art and life were to be merged, a principle already at work in the Cubist *collage* with its introduction of real objects into the ideal picture plane. One may say that Dadaists and Surrealists attempted to take over a territory previously inhabited by fantasy, allegory and satire. The movement tried *inter alia* to dissociate painting from the conventions of the easel canvas, and sculpture from the human figure. Behind these experiments lay the Dadaist yearning for a return to chaos and the Surrealist belief that automatic writing, by drawing upon the resources of the unconscious, would dredge up new truths from the hidden depths of nature. Dreams and the uncontrolled regions of the mind were invited to yield up their secrets, the censorship of reason was to be by-passed, and inspiration restored to its true role as the begetter of art.[1]

At this point the movement overstepped its origins and broadened out from representational art into literature. In the formal sense neither Proust nor Joyce nor Kafka can be termed Surrealists, since they did not subscribe to the doctrines of the school. Yet there is a sense in which they belong to the same general current. Proust still describes the social scene, but he locates reality in the mind of the observer, and Joyce replaces the current of events by the stream of consciousness. The basic experience of the specifically modern artist or writer is the discovery of what has been termed a 'second reality', fused with ordinary experience, but nonetheless significantly different from it. The dream becomes the stylistic ideal of the artist because it makes possible that peculiar intertwining of reality and unreality which corresponds to the feeling that we live simultaneously on different levels of existence. Such effects are more easily achieved in painting than in literature, whence the prominence of the Paris School in the 1920s, with Picasso, Matisse, Braque, Dufy, Chagall and Soutine in the lead. The sewing machine and the umbrella on the dissecting table, the donkey's corpse on the piano, the naked woman's body which opens like a chest of drawers, are symbols of an unreality which has invaded everyone's existence. The Surrealist writer attains the same end by turning his nightmares into sober accounts of alleged occurrences in the everyday world of the ordinary citizen. In the classical nineteenth-century novel the hero or heroine confronts an external world. In the modern novel the content of the mind is all that matters. There is no longer a self at odds with circumstances, merely a flux of inner experience. We do not inquire how the hero is going to solve his problems. There is no hero, and the only problem is to keep up with the author's relentless flow of association.

The problem for the historian lies in relating these experiments to the simultaneous spread of new attitudes in painting and architecture which ran counter to the subjectivist trend. The triumph of the 'international style' in building during the 1920s seems at first sight to have no connection at all with the exploitation of inwardness. Gropius in Germany and Le Corbusier in France continued a tradition which, as we have seen, had its origins in the functionalism of 1900, when the pioneers of the new model came to the conclusion that the modern world of vast industrial cities demanded a wholly impersonal style of building. What the artists assembled at the *Bauhaus* after 1919 (first in Weimar and later at Dessau) had in mind was essentially an attempt to bridge the gap between art and industry. This necessarily involved an underlying shift towards an abstract and non-representational art which in painting had already found its expression in Cubism and was now spilling over into architecture. The principle can be stretched to accommodate Arnold Schönberg's invention of the twelve-tone scale which consists in using all the notes of the scale.[2] But it is not at all clear in what way Schönberg and his pupils, Anton Webern and Alban Berg, were attuned to the new literary pattern, even though Berg's opera *Wozzeck* (1922) has for its theme a macabre story reminiscent of Kafka.[3] The analogy works better if one takes the film as an example, since in it the boundaries of space and time are fluid, which corresponds to what the Surrealists were after. An early German post-war filmic masterpiece such as *The Cabinet of Doctor Caligari* (1919–20) might reasonably have been called 'Kafkaesque'. Its makers were consciously trying to apply Expressionist and Cubist principles,[4] and for good measure the audience was expected to share the distorted notions of the madman in the asylum to which both the lunatic and the spectators were confined for the length of the performance.

This corresponded well enough with what Franz Kafka (1883–1924) was trying to do in his novels and stories. The hero of *The Trial* finds himself condemned for a crime he is not aware of having committed and whose very nature remains obscure. *The Castle* has for its central figure a man who has been appointed to act as agent for authorities he never manages to contact, and who cannot discover what duties he is supposed to perform. These writings were strangely prophetic of what was to happen to countless people in Kafka's native Prague after 1938, but in addition they made an appeal to a very generalized sense of anxiety and bewilderment in a culture which had lost its ancient bearings. Kafka wrote out of a personal dilemma quite unconnected with politics, but he happened to strike a chord which reverberated long after his death, for reasons he could not possibly have foreseen. His modernity was not willed: it came about because his temperament happened to fit the circumstances of an age in which millions of people were shuffled about like mice in a laboratory. For all the difference in age, Kafka had affinities with the celebrated Viennese critic Karl Kraus who for almost forty years, from 1899 onward, in his periodical *Die Fackel* belaboured the collapsing culture of Austria-Hungary in general, and the German–Jewish liberal bourgeoisie in particular. His 750-page monster drama *Die letzten Tage der Menschheit* ('The Last Days of Mankind') deals with the First World War, and specifically with that peculiarly unreal aspect of the Austrian situation which was invariably "hopeless but not serious". Kraus knew that the situation was in fact desperate, and Kafka in his intuitive manner likewise had a premonition of disasters yet to come. Being Jews both men were born outsiders – a considerable help at a time when things were radically out of joint. Kraus lived to witness Hitler's rise to power in Germany, an event which failed to surprise him, since he had long concluded that Central European society was rotten to the core.

Perhaps it is best to think of the inter-war period as a transitional age in which the pre-1914 innovators – André Gide, Marcel Proust, Paul Valéry, Thomas Mann, Hermann Hesse, J.A.Strindberg, Frank Wedekind, E.M.Forster, G.B.Shaw, W.B.Yeats, in literature; Picasso, Braque, Léger, Mondrian and others in painting – overlapped with a new generation which made its mark in the 1920s, even though some of them (Pirandello, D.H.Lawrence, T.S.Eliot, James Joyce) had already been active before 1914. The post-war disillusionment made it possible for the avant-garde to obtain a hearing, a circumstance which accounts for the sudden popularity of what before 1914 would have been judged scandalous – the uninhibited treatment of erotic themes above all. Radical innovations in technique are quite another matter. There are none to be found in 'daring' novelists such as D.H.Lawrence and Aldous Huxley, who made full use of the new freedom. Across the Channel the break with tradition was even less sharp. Gide, Valéry, Jules Romains, Roger Martin du Gard and François Mauriac continued as though nothing had happened, and even newcomers such as Georges Bernanos, André Malraux and Antoine de Saint-Exupéry effected no real innovations in style. The first thoroughly 'modern' piece of writing to come out of France before 1939 was Jean-Paul Sartre's *La Nausée* (1938), but then Sartre had the advantage of being a philosopher. The essential point about *La Nausée* is that the action – what there is of it – takes place almost entirely in the head of the author (ostensibly a diarist in search of historical material) and what bothers him is the sheer absurdity of existence as such. Not a very promising theme, one might think, but *La Nausée* is vastly more readable and entertaining than most conventional novels. It has been related that at the age of thirty Sartre was troubled by hallucinations of lobsters pursuing him. In *La Nausée* they are still after him, and his attempt to shake them off is nothing short of a masterpiece.

Sartre was a portent. For the most part the years between the wars witnessed the *roman-fleuve* in full spate. Romain Rolland (1866–1944) had earlier set the tone in his ten-volume panorama *Jean-Christophe* between 1904 and 1912, and after the war Jules Romains (b. 1885) explored the human scene in the twenty-seven volumes of *Les Hommes de bonne volonté* (1932–47). Over a hundred characters are introduced in the early part, and it takes a dozen volumes to get from 1908 to 1915.[5] In the Preface Romains explains that there is no central character because society itself is his theme. Roger Martin du Gard's *Les Thibault* (1922–40) is constructed on the same pattern, except that he makes it clearer that his real theme is the bourgeoisie, a principle also applicable to Georges Duhamel's *La Chronique des Pasquier* (1933–45) which runs from the 1890s to the 1920s. The nearest English equivalent is Galsworthy's *Forsyte Saga*. The difficulty with categorizing Proust stems from the fact that while he too depicts society at considerable length, he writes in the first person from the standpoint of the central character who is quite simply the author–narrator himself. At the end the reader is informed how and why Marcel came to be writing the book we have been reading. All the same Proust is a social realist of the first order when it comes to describing the decay of aristocratic society between the 1880s and the 1920s. To that extent he is still in the succession of Balzac, while simultaneously his subjectivism makes him 'modern' and places him among the avant-garde. He is both inside and outside the bourgeois tradition, a tradition which underlies the structural scheme of the classical novel – the sense of time unfolding within a stable universe in which certain values are tacitly taken for granted. Once self-consciousness has been driven to the extreme to which Proust takes it, the novel has been transformed into something else. The author no longer bothers to hide behind his central character, and to that extent the aesthetic illusion has vanished. This is the sense in which it may be said that after Proust and Joyce the novel in the traditional sense had ceased to exist.

The newcomers of the 1920s and 1930s were not troubled by Proust's nostalgia for an age that had vanished and could only be reconstituted in memory. Whether they were conservative Catholics like Georges Bernanos (1888–1948), romantic knight-errants like Antoine de Saint-Exupéry (1900–1944), or ex-Communists turned Gaullist like André Malraux (b. 1901), they took it for granted that the stable bourgeois universe had been shattered by the 1914–18 war. Bernanos had seen death all around him during the war, to the point of becoming obsessed with the topic. Saint-Exupéry escaped from the tedium of ordinary existence into the profession of commercial aviator at a time when there was nothing routine about flying; became a combatant during the Second World War; joined the Gaullists in 1943, and disappeared with his plane to the north of Corsica in July 1944, in a manner befitting his Romantic temperament and his elitist conviction that a new kind of chivalry had become possible in the age of technology. His writings correspond to the cult of heroism made popular in Britain after 1919 by T.E.Lawrence, another adventurer who did not greatly care which side he was on, or what he was doing, as long as it was sufficiently dangerous and remote from everyday life. Malraux, the archetypal artist-adventurer, boxed the political compass, starting as a Communist fellow-traveller in the 1920s and ending as de Gaulle's Minister of Culture after the General's return to power in 1958. *La Condition humaine* (1933), a study of the Chinese Revolution in which at one time he was actively involved, is his finest work. It is also a testimony to the fact that it was then possible for a French intellectual to cast his lot with the Communists while preserving a Nietzschean sense of man's loneliness in a world from which God had disappeared. His later writings derived from his experience as a combatant in the Spanish civil war and in the French Resistance movement after 1940. His break with the Communists occurred when the Hitler–Stalin pact of 1939 shattered his political illusions. It did not affect his fundamental commitment to what was coming to be known as 'engagement'. Gaullism after all was simply another form of death-defying commitment to what looked like a hopeless cause. This is the sense in which Sartre and Malraux may be said to have exemplified the same kind of break with tradition.

Some of these topics were given a brief airing in an earlier section (see Chapter 6). The need to go over them again arises from a shift in perspective. One can think of early modernism in the arts and literature as a harbinger of what was to come in the 1940s, or alternatively as the dominating trend in the post-1918 age. In the latter case one has to treat the 1919–39 period as a unity. This works better for the film than for the novel or the drama, for the simple reason that the cinema became important only after 1918. The decline of the traditional novel, and the lessening relevance of the theatre, prepared the way for the growing prominence of the film. The novel and the drama were the representative literary forms of the nineteenth century because they excelled in the difficult task of interpreting character in psychological terms. Moreover, they did so from the standpoint of the autonomous individual who had arisen in the lengthy process of bourgeois evolution. This is true even of the Russian novel, notwithstanding the social weakness of the Russian middle class and the fact that the masterpieces of Russian literature were for the most part composed by dissident representatives of the landed gentry. The problem of the Russian, German, French, English or Scandinavian novel before 1914, like the problem of Ibsen, Hauptmann or Shaw, centres on the role of the autonomous personality which finds itself at odds with society, while at the same time embodying its central faith: the belief that each individual is the maker of his or her own fate. To understand oneself is to understand the part one has to play. Psychological complexity thus becomes the principal theme of the novel and the drama. Literature is valued in the measure in which it contributes to the analysis of human character. The unspoken assumption of the German *Bildungsroman* and its various equivalents is the belief that the conflict between subject and object, the self and the world, is in principle capable of a solution. The hero comes to terms with life, or alternatively he is destroyed by a flaw in his character.

These assumptions vanished when the individual's existence was felt to be contingent, unrelated to his personality, and in the last analysis unpredictable and meaningless. The true subject of representation then is no longer the psychology of the central character, but the absurdity of life. In literature the process begins with Proust, who still has one foot in each camp, and is carried further by Kafka, with Joyce and Virginia Woolf occupying a kind of intermediate position. The film, by mixing up spatial and temporal dimensions, makes it easier to portray the new sensibility which can no longer be adequately rendered by the novel or the drama.[6] At the same time it necessarily sacrifices the psychological profundity of these forms. Everything happens at once and at the expense of continuity. Moreover, the film addresses itself to a shapeless mass public, whereas the novel and the drama were quite consciously created by and for the educated elite of the middle class. It is true that within the mass audience of modern society a new kind of differentiation occurs in the measure in which films and television plays are produced by and for intellectuals. But in the inter-war period this change had not yet taken place. The cinema addressed itself to the masses and only in rare instances did it aim at artistic complexity. The first decade after the Russian Revolution was a for-tunate period in this respect, with film directors such as Eisenstein and Pudovkin being given a free hand in portraying the tremendous events of the period at an artistic level rivalling that of the drama. It was not the only sphere in which the youthful Soviet Republic had important artistic achievements to its credit, but with the coming of Stalinism and 'Socialist Realism' in the 1930s, mediocrity set in in this as in all other dimensions of Soviet existence.

Russia presents special difficulties on account of the radical dis-continuities introduced by the Revolution. By 1917 the literary and artistic avant-garde had turned to Symbolism, Futurism and other Western importations, while their elders continued the realistic tradi-tion established in the second half of the nineteenth century. Maxim Gorky (Alexey Peshkov, 1868–1936) derived from Tolstoy, but was also influenced by Chekhov (1860–1904). Having left Russia after the civil war, he eventually (in 1928) decided to quit Italy and risk his lungs by returning to his native country, where he made his peace with the Soviet regime. He was, in part at least, responsible for the trans-formation of what became known as 'Socialist Realism' into an official orthodoxy to which even anti-Stalinists paid tribute in their writings. Ivan Bunin (1870–1953), who emigrated to France in 1919 and in 1933 received the Nobel Prize, also belonged to the Tolstoyan school. The pre-revolutionary *fin de siècle* style had been represented by Leonid Andreyev (1871–1919), whose morbidity had something in common with Dostoyevsky's brooding sense of evil; the same may be said of Alexander Blok (1880–1921) and Andrei Bely (1880–1934). Among the other members of this group, Leo Shestov (1866–1938) is perhaps better described as a philosophical essayist and critic who helped to develop a mental climate favourable to Symbolism on the one hand, religious revivalism on the other. Soviet literature after 1917 at first became associated with the rhetorical poetry of Mayakovsky and Yesenin, both by temperament inclined towards anarchism, while Expressionists and Constructivists flourished in painting and sculpture. During the 1920s those whom Trotsky called "fellow-travellers" were briefly allowed to write in their own manner, while yet accepting the Revolution. Boris Pilnyak – later 'purged' like so many others – belonged to this group, and so did Mikhail Bulgakov whose novel *The White Guard* (1924) became better known in its author's own dramatized version of it, *Days of the Turbins*: for many years a standing feature of the Moscow Art Theatre repertoire. The Turbins are an upper-class counter-revolutionary family, engulfed in their native Kiev during the confused civil war winter of 1918–19. They are treated with a good deal of sympathy and there is a certain ambiguity about Bulgakov's attitude towards them, which perhaps explains why in later years he fell out of favour and did not live to see the publication of his most original piece of work, the novel *The Master and Margarita*, an English translation of which appeared in 1967. Novels dealing with the civil war generally tended to be heavily propagandist. *The White Guard* was an exception: it infused an element of tragedy into the story by presenting the doomed Turbins and their friends in agreeable colours. The Red armoured train, "The Proletarian", whose arrival puts an end to their world, has a symbolic quality, as is proper in a Soviet novel; but the symbolism is reminiscent of the figure of Christ leading the Red Guardsmen at the close of Blok's celebrated poem "The Twelve" which drew qualified praise from Trotsky in his brilliant pamphlet *Literature and Revolution* (1923).

As long as Trotsky held the scene, and for a few years after his political star had declined, 'fellow-travellers' such as Blok, Pilnyak and Bulgakov were allowed free rein, on the tacit understanding that they would not challenge the basic principles of the Revolution. All this changed with the triumph of Stalin and his stony-faced henchmen at the end of the 1920s. From then on the political authorities laid down the law and did not tolerate the smallest deviation. Among the official celebrities of the 1930s and 1940s, F.V.Gladkov was the most tedious, Mikhail Sholokhov the most successful in winning Stalin's favour. His *Tikhy Don* ("The Quiet Don", 1928–40) runs to 1,300 pages and deals mainly with the civil war of 1918–21, while *Podnyataya tselina* ("Virgin Soil Upturned", 1932–3) celebrates the enforced collectivization of the villages after 1929. At one time every supervisor of a collective farm was required, by government order, to read it. Among satirists with counter-revolutionary leanings, Y.I.Zamyatin (1884–1937) made such a nuisance of himself that in 1931 he was accorded the unusual favour of being allowed to leave the country and settle in Paris. His utopian story *My* ("We", 1922) has been likened to Aldous Huxley's *Brave New World* and Orwell's *1984*, but since Soviet readers were not allowed to read either of these works, the subject aroused no debate in Russia. The story of Dudintsev's *Not by Bread Alone*, Pasternak's *Zhivago* (unpublished in the USSR), and the writings of Alexander Solzhenitsyn, belong to the post-Stalin era. At the latter's peak, during the great purge of 1936–9, some of the most committed Communists were shot or otherwise liquidated, while cynical turncoats such as Alexey Tolstoy and Ilya Ehrenburg were left alone. The ravages of the purge, and the continued existence of a bureaucratic censorship, make it difficult to guess what Soviet literature might have become if the relative tolerance of the 1920s had been perpetuated, but the aestheticism predominant among the literary vanguard on the eve of 1917 would in any case have had to give way to a more committed form of writing. This was among the reasons why Boris Pasternak (1890–1960) struck even some of his foreign admirers as old-fashioned when *Zhivago* finally saw the light in 1958. Of Solzhenitsyn, whose *Ivan Denisovich* appeared legally in 1962, while his later works had to be published abroad, it may perhaps be said that more than any other Russian writer since 1917 he revived the tradition of Tolstoy. Experiments in the arts were discouraged from the 1930s onwards, but Dimitri Shostakovich somehow managed to win official recognition for his music despite its modernist character, and the sculptor Neizvestny was able in the 1950s and 1960s to continue, in the teeth of official disfavour, the tradition created by Malevich, Lissitsky, Kandinsky, Tatlin, Pevsner, Rodchenko and other modernists, some of whom were briefly prominent in the early 1920s, having come to terms with the Revolution.

For different reasons the 1920s proved fruitful in Germany, to be followed by the National Socialist retreat into folk *Kitsch* and Teutonic pseudo-heroics.[7] Germany, unlike Russia, had not undergone a social revolution, but it had experienced a political collapse which incidentally discredited the dismal artistic standards of the Wilhelminian regime. The drive towards genuine self-expression, which had begun around 1900 with Frank Wedekind (1864–1918), now engulfed the whole of modern art, literature, the drama and the film. Expressionism did for the Germans in the 1920s what Surrealism accomplished for the French: it turned the outsiders into insiders. From about 1916 onwards the movement made contact with the anti-war radicalism of the political Left, and after 1918 it sprouted a crop of utopianism, typically represented in literature by Georg Kaiser, George Heym, Ernst Toller, Walter Hasenclever, Else Lasker-Schüler and the philosophical essayist Ernst Bloch; by Oskar Kokoschka and others in painting; and by the artists assembled around the *Bauhaus*, who were joined by Kandinsky when he had to take his syllabus out of Russia. By 1925 the movement had run out of steam, to be followed by the functionalism which the Germans termed *Neue Sachlichkeit*. The personal fortunes of the leading Expressionists reflected the circumstances of the age. The Jews among them emigrated after 1933; Gottfried Benn, a latter-day Nietzschean, briefly invested his faith in Hitler; and Johannes Becher ended his days as the poet laureate of the Ulbricht regime in East Germany. Whether the early Brecht should be included among the Expressionists appears to be a question on which no two critics are in agreement, but at least it can be said without fear of contradiction that his subsequent conversion to Leninism was preceded by a phase in the later 1920s when he paid tribute to the matter-of-factness typical of the then fashionable *Neue Sachlichkeit*. The celebrated *Threepenny Opera*, first performed in 1928, belongs to this period, which is why Communist critics have never been comfortable with it. In so far as it had a message, it was of the anarchist variety, and for the rest its genial cynicism was not to the taste of Party puritans.[8]

Bertolt Brecht (1898–1956) has by now become the subject of books and academic theses from every quarter of the globe. The body of his work is extremely varied, covering as it does not only poetry and drama, but politico-philosophical writings as well. Measured by the crudest yardstick, the collected works include over 1,000 pages of poetry, as against 3,000 pages for the plays and 1,300 for theoretical writings on the theatre. The prose, including a large number of short stories, runs to 1,500 pages and miscellaneous writings on literature and politics account for another 1,000.[9] In the circumstances it is not perhaps surprising that a Brecht industry has come into being, and not only in Germany. For our purpose it must be sufficient to say that Brecht's progress from a kind of youthful nihilism via *Neue Sachlichkeit* to Communism, and then within the Communist orbit from conformist Party orthodoxy to an undercurrent of submerged criticism of the Stalinist establishment, has made it possible to claim him for Expressionism and the modern movement generally, while enabling the less hide-bound Communists to treat him as a representative of Socialist Realism. It is questionable whether Brecht ever made up his mind about the possibility – as distinct from the desirability – of reforming the Stalinist bureaucracy, such as he encountered it in East Berlin, where he settled in 1949 after having characteristically arranged a line of retreat by acquiring an Austrian passport and a West German publisher. Brecht combined a good deal of native Bavarian peasant shrewdness with his commitment to Communism: originally an outgrowth of his passionate opposition to German nationalism and the mass slaughter of 1914–18. He had few illusions and even fewer inhibitions about fooling the authorities. What mattered to him was to get his message across. If this required a certain amount of double-talk and double-dealing, he was ready for it.

The message changed a good deal from the anarchic cynicism of the youthful post-1918 poems and plays, via the *Threepenny Opera* and the straitlaced Communism of *Die Massnahme* (1931) – a pretty accurate forecast of the Stalinist purge trials – to the eloquent humanism of the great plays written between 1937 and 1947: *Mother Courage, Puntila, Galileo, The Good Soul of Szechuan* and *The Caucasian Chalk Circle*. These established Brecht as a major dramatist – possibly the foremost in the German language since the tragically short-lived Georg Büchner (1813–37) whom he rightly placed above Schiller. It has been observed that in rejecting the classicism of the German Enlightenment Brecht reverted to an older tradition, that of the Austrian and Bavarian folk theatre.[10] The exuberance of the Baroque was close to his heart, as was the vigorous prose of Luther's translation of the Bible. Other 'sources' ranged from Villon to Rimbaud, from Swift and Gay to Kipling, and from the Japanese *No* play to Arthur Waley's translations from the Chinese. Many of his plays are adaptations of earlier originals, from Marlowe's *Edward II* and Gay's *Beggar's Opera* to Jaroslav Hasek's *Schweik*. He was never very particular about borrowing from earlier writers, and charges of plagiarism pursued him for years. He was also quite willing to adapt his work to local circumstances, including his status as a tolerated genius in post-war East Berlin who frequently came into conflict with the authorities. After the operatic version of his *Trial of Lucullus* had been banned by the cultural commissars of the regime, he told a Swiss journalist with his habitual cynicism that after all the authorities had paid for the production and were therefore entitled to demand alterations. "When princes commissioned works of art, they too interfered a great deal with the artist." In general he managed to get his own way, and the compromises enforced by his equivocal relationship with the East German government he treated as minor nuisances due to the stupidity of the officials. For the rest he found relief in private jokes, such as the poem he composed after the 1953 workers' rising against the Ulbricht regime:

> After the rising of the 17th June
> The Secretary of the Writers' Union
> Had leaflets distributed in the Stalinallee
> In which you could read that the People
> Had lost the Government's confidence
> Which it could only regain
> By redoubled efforts. Would it in this case
> Not be simpler if the Government
> Dissolved the People
> and elected another?

Brecht seems to have resolved his private doubts by telling himself that the Eastern camp was the Camp of Peace. Theoretical reasoning was never his *forte*; having once and for all decided around 1930 to become a Leninist, he stayed one until the end. The regime for its part put up with his equivocal attitude because his *Berliner Ensemble* was the only genuine artistic achievement it could show off to Westerners. The recipient of the 1954 Stalin Prize deposited most of the money in his Swiss bank account. The Party officials said nothing because the success of the *Berliner Ensemble* at the Paris Festival of 1954 had become a propaganda asset. So it went on until his death which – fortunately for all concerned – came a few weeks before the Hungarian rising of 1956.

Brecht's status as a theorist is generally held to be a function of his 'non-Aristotelian' approach, technically known as his use of the *Verfremdungseffekt* – an untranslatable term suggesting that the theatre should try to make the audience *think*, instead of inviting it to wallow in sentiments derived from emotional identification with the characters on stage. In the place of the theatre of illusion, which pretends that the happenings on stage actually occur, there is to be an 'epic' theatre which invites the spectators to reflect on the meaning of events enacted long ago in the historical past. Instead of emotional catharsis there is to be an enlargement of the understanding. The study of human nature is replaced by that of human relations. "Everything depends on the *story*; it is the centre-piece of the performance."[11] What Marx and Engels, with their enthusiasm for Shakespeare, would have made of all this it is difficult to say, but at least it can be urged in Brecht's support that Marx had no use for Schiller. Unfortunately for Brecht, the Party authorities had made up their minds that the only proper form of acting was the Stanislavsky method of the Moscow Art Theatre which depended on making the audience identify itself with the characters on stage. This ran directly counter to Brecht's conviction that the spectators ought to see the world in a detached and critical spirit. In due course the post-Stalin thaw put an end to the virtual ban on Brecht throughout the Soviet-controlled bloc, but his private brand of Communism never failed to alarm the orthodox. After all, *Mother Courage* is an anti-war play, and pacifism does not exactly fit the prevailing atmosphere in the USSR. Brecht's 'formalism' was another source of trouble. However formalism may be defined, it is incompatible with the kind of writing in which a political message is relentlessly hammered into the audience's head by treating all the characters as Communist heroes or Imperialist villains. The truth is that Brecht belonged to the age of the Weimar Republic, when there was a public which enjoyed parody, irony and complexity. His early plays adhered to the spiritual world of Joyce and Kafka – the universe of the *condition humaine*. In his later works he made an heroic attempt to infuse hope into the description of life, but his underlying pessimism seldom failed to show through. "I see the world in a mellow light: it is God's excrement", he had written in *Baal*, when he was still in his youthful anarchist phase. For all his subsequent efforts, he never quite shook off that early intuition.

The brief and brilliant interlude of the Weimar Republic witnessed an explosion of creative and critical writing, much of it due to the sudden prominence of Jewish intellectuals who trod the path of exile after 1933. The then fashionable association of radicalism with the Jewish intelligentsia does not, however, hold for Karl Korsch (1886–1961) whose philosophical writings did much to dissociate authentic Marxism from its Leninist version. There is some evidence that Korsch had a certain amount of influence on Brecht, who in turn did his best to convert the great critic Walter Benjamin (1892–1940) to his own private version of Marxism: not, it must be said, to the advantage of literary criticism as practised by Benjamin, a born metaphysician whose later writings testify to the trouble he had in harnessing his instinctive intuitionism to Brecht's rather simple-minded historical materialism.[12]

If these topics are given a brief airing here, instead of being reserved for the discussion of philosophy in the following chapter, the excuse must be that in some cases it is more profitable to deal with the intellectual scene of a given period as a whole. There was something unique about the spiritual climate of the Weimar Republic, not to mention its aftermath. In what other country, and at what other moment in European history, could a professional philosopher such as Martin Heidegger have addressed his students at Freiburg, in the critical month of May 1933, in the following remarkable terms:

> Out of the resolve of German students to hold their ground towards German destiny in its extreme trial, there comes a will towards the being (*Wesen*) of the university. This will is a true will inasmuch as the German students, by virtue of the new university statutes, are voluntarily placing themselves under the law of its being (*Wesen*) and so defining that being for the very first time. To give oneself laws is the supreme freedom. The much-lauded 'academic freedom' will be expelled from the German university; for this freedom was false because only negative. . . . The concept of freedom of the German student will now be brought back to its truth. From it in future will grow the commitment and service of the German students. The *first* commitment is that to the unity of our people. . . .[13]

Heidegger was by no means the only German philosopher who jumped down the sewers in 1933, but the enthusiasm he evinced at the sight of the Hitler cloaca had few parallels. He placed *Geist* (spirit), *Schicksal* (destiny) and *Wesen* (being) at the service of a movement which in a few short years undid what centuries of civilization had accomplished. But then we have it on Heidegger's authority that "thinking begins only at the point where we have discovered that thought has no more stubborn adversary than reason, that reason which has been glorified for centuries". Perhaps the matter can be summed up by saying that Heidegger stood in approximately the same relation to his Romantic and irrationalist forerunners around 1810 in which Hitler stood to Napoleon. The German counter-revolution had to have its philosopher, and Heidegger was available. For the rest there was Oswald Spengler with his *Decline of the West* and his readiness to help the decline along by eliminating whatever traces the Enlightenment had left in Germany. Once more there seems no reason to reserve this topic for the discussion of philosophy. Spengler was neither a philosopher nor a historian, but a learned autodidact with a gift for dramatic metaphor which struck his readers as profound for the same reason that their elders had mistaken Nietzsche for a major thinker, when all he could reasonably claim to be was a brilliant essayist. Spengler, like Nietzsche before him, had an intuitive sense that European civilization was on the brink of a major breakdown. Some of his predictions have actually come true, notably his belief that the modern megalopolis would make liberal democracy unworkable. This is the reason for taking him seriously. It does not make his "morphology of history" a genuinely scientific study of culture. His subsequent appeal (in *Preussentum und Sozialismus*, 1919) for a heroic master race was in the tradition of German nationalism. The National Socialists first used and then discarded him. He was not sufficiently plebeian for their taste and his pessimism was not to their liking. For all that, he had done his share in paving the way for their short-lived triumph.

With Thomas Mann (1875–1955) one runs into another kind of problem: that of differentiating between the poet and the thinker. His *Reflections of an Unpolitical Man* (1918) were in the spirit of conservative and anti-democratic aestheticism fashionable in the German middle class before the war. Like the poet Stefan George, whose *Star of the Covenant* (1914) celebrated the cult of the elite, Mann was then decidedly anti-Western: German *Kultur* was different from, and superior to, Western *civilization*. This was the heritage of Romanticism and the credo of the German patriciate of which Mann was a distinguished representative. By 1924, in his celebrated novel *The Magic Mountain*, he had worked around to a rather ambiguous neutrality on the issue. His subsequent development carried him so far into the democratic camp that his bitter dispute with his pro-Western brother Heinrich (1871–1950) in 1918 could be treated as a family joke, the more so since in the 1940s both had come to share the same Californian exile. Mann's pictures of the German middle class in *Buddenbrooks* (1901), of pre-1914 Germany as seen in retrospect in *The Magic Mountain* (1924) and finally of the Hitler catastrophe in *Doctor Faustus* (1947), though separated by less than half a century, are so remote from each other that no single formula is applicable to them. The tetralogy *Joseph and his Brothers*, set on the borderland between Biblical history and myth, was composed in the 1930s, when the German–Jewish symbiosis (what there was of it) had gone to pieces and Mann himself had turned his back on his native country: one of the relatively few 'Aryan' authors to have done so. It has been observed that while Goethe's Faust wins eternal salvation in the hour of death, Mann's hero, the musician Adrian Leverkühn, goes to the Devil. It is perhaps more relevant that his creator assumed the role of *praeceptor Germaniae* in full awareness that his work would be measured by Goethean standards. There is a certain self-consciousness about Mann's relationship to Goethe: he is in the line of descent and never allows one to forget it. "Where I am, there is Germany", he is reputed to have said in 1949, when invited by the East German authorities to deliver a lecture in Weimar on the occasion of Goethe's bicentenary. It is difficult to imagine any of his contemporaries, with the possible exception of Yeats, making that kind of remark.

Across the Channel the break with the pre-war era was less sharp, for the simple reason that Britain had undergone neither defeat nor revolution. Even before 1914 the modernists tended to be naturalized foreigners: Shaw, Yeats and Joyce were Irish, Conrad of Polish extraction, Eliot (like Henry James) a transplanted American. Among the native-born, E.M.Forster and Virginia Woolf reflected the values of the Bloomsbury set, which were liberal rather than radical, and the same applies to Aldous Huxley. D.H.Lawrence (1885–1930) is the exception. An intruder of working-class origin, married to a German and something of an irrationalist in his personal philosophy, he comes close to the Continental type of the artist who is also a revolutionary. As noted before, he had no coherent view of society, but he was sufficiently out of humour with bourgeois civilization, scientific rationalism and a banalized Christianity to have concocted a Nietzschean brew which appealed to lesser minds for the same reason that his German contemporary Ernst Jünger converted thousands of impressionable youngsters to a primitivism born in his case from the experience of war.[14] The dominance of primeval instincts and the quest for adventure is very marked in both cases. Jünger exalted war and called for a new elite: "A completely new race, cunning, strong and packed with purpose . . . battle proven, merciless both to itself and others." There is no saying how Lawrence would have reacted if this message had come to his attention. All we know is that as early as 1913, when *Sons and Lovers* was published, he had already declared war on the Galsworthys, the Shaws and "the rule and measure mathematical folk".[15] *The Rainbow* followed in 1915, *Women in Love* in 1921, *Kangaroo* in 1923, *St Mawr* in 1925, *The Plumed Serpent* in 1926 and *Lady Chatterley's Lover* in 1928. They were stages in the growth of a mythology filled, in the words of a critic already cited, with "Trances, raptures, ecstatic catalepsy, ecstatic bouts of frenzy, swoonings over flower-beds, dances in the presence of cattle, daisies planted in pubic hair, a continual litany of fruits, crops, horses, figurines, symbolic rods, sterile barons of industry, fertile peasants, milkmen and redskins, horserubbers and scarabs, resurrections and dragons. . . . There is far too much Frazer, Tylor, Frobenius and Jane Harrison, too much Blavatsky and Wagner in his novels."[16] But these are matters of taste. It is undeniable that Lawrence's earth-ecstasies had a liberating effect upon an entire generation of readers. His general notions we are not obliged to take seriously. As might be expected, they exhibit the cocksureness of the autodidact: Freud had exaggerated the importance of incest, Jung was wrong about the unconscious, Dostoyevsky was too cerebral, Proust and Gide were arid, Joyce was 'putrid', Keynes and his Cambridge friends reminded him of beetles, etc. The matter can safely be left to the growing army of literary critics. What counts is that after Lawrence the genteel upper middle class no longer had things quite its own way. It still produced major writers in Aldous Huxley, Evelyn Waugh and Graham Greene, but it no longer had the stage entirely to itself.

The 1920s were taken up with the inevitable reaction against the 1914–18 war and the Edwardian age that preceded it. On the poetical side the mood of the conservative intelligentsia was captured by T.S.Eliot's *The Waste Land* (1922) with its sense of hopeless drift, sterility and general dereliction. He followed it up in 1928 with a collection of essays, *For Lancelot Andrewes*, which defined a type of conservatism of a rather outlandish kind. In the preface Eliot wrote: "The general point of view may be described as classicist in literature, royalist in politics, and Anglo-Catholic in religion." It has been shown by later critics that this tripartite self-definition derived from a Maurrassian formula. In 1913 an editorial note in the *Nouvelle Revue Française*, to which Eliot was a subscriber, had described the "three traditions" of Charles Maurras as "classique, catholique, monarchique". Eliot first encountered the writings of Maurras on a visit to Paris in 1910, and the influence of Maurras remained crucial in his later intellectual development. As a publicist and leader of the monarchist *Action française*, Maurras was deeply involved in public affairs; as a supporter of the Catholic Church he extolled the Roman virtues of order and authority, while rejecting the 'Jewish' or mystical elements in Christianity. None of this was an issue in England, but Eliot stuck to his admiration for Maurras even after the Vatican had condemned him for his atheist and anti-Christian tendencies. The formulation "classicist, royalist, Anglo-Catholic" represented an adaptation of the Maurrassian faith to the English environment, with the accent on late-sixteenth and early-seventeenth-century tradition as a 'classical moment' unfortunately abandoned by subsequent generations of Englishmen. In later years Eliot dropped the controversial preface and made his peace with the Anglican *via media*.[17]

He also abandoned the pro-Fascist inclination which in 1928 had induced him to indulge in fulsome adulation of the British Union of Fascists, only regretting "that a nationalist organization should have to go abroad for its name and symbol". The publication he edited since 1922, *The Criterion*, had much to say about the problem of reconciling the "aristocracy of culture" with the "demagogy of science", a topic which had already troubled Eliot's spiritual predecessor W.B.Yeats. Similarly, "the governors of the people" must be encouraged to sustain "the conviction of their right to govern". Who "the governors" were was never clearly spelled out, but they appear to have been envisioned as an hereditary caste. On the subject of Marxism, *The Criterion*'s readers were informed that since Marx was a Jew, and since Jews had become "more and more openly the exploiters of the Western world today", Marx's revolutionary doctrine merely represented "the desire of the inferior to revenge himself on the superior (as Nietzsche points out, characteristic of the Judaic psychology)". Against this background it is hardly surprising that throughout the 1930s *The Criterion* maintained a policy of complete silence about Hitler and what was going on in Germany. Sympathetic references to Fascism occurred in 1937 and 1938, but comment on these matters was left to contributors, the editor himself preferring to maintain a discreet silence. By 1939 the game was up and the magazine ceased publication. "In the present state of public affairs," Eliot wrote in a valedictory note, "I no longer feel the enthusiasm necessary to make a literary review what it should be."

In retrospect the evolution of this group of writers appears as a more or less conscious cultivation of a distinctly elitist point of view which had grown out of a reaction against the democratization of society and culture. Inasmuch as Fascism was a demagogic mass movement, the expression of pro-Fascist sympathies on the part of writers committed to 'classicism' and the rule of aristocracy represents a striking example of political naïveté, but it is a fact that political authoritarianism was seen by them as the only cure for the real or imagined evils of democracy. These issues fascinated a portion of the intellectual elite in the 1920s. The 1930s introduced the theme of class struggle which around the time of the Spanish civil war (1936–9) induced a group of poets led by W.H.Auden to mistake themselves briefly for Communists.[18] Among prose writers this was the time when George Orwell (Eric Blair, 1903–50) took the first steps on an arduous journey whose full significance only became apparent in the 1940s with the publication of *Animal Farm* and *1984*. Orwell, a socialist and a realist (unlike the fraudulent 'Socialist Realists' who concocted romantic fiction for the benefit of the Soviet bureaucracy), had fought in Spain on the revolutionary side and seen through the pretensions of the Stalinist clique, a circumstance which naturally rendered him unpopular with the literary fellow-travellers then swarming around a number of British journals and publishing houses. His hour was to come in 1940, when the country awoke from its trance and confronted the German menace unaided.

Even a cursory account of European literature during this period must at least mention Luigi Pirandello (1867–1936) and Italo Svevo (Ettore Schmitz, 1861–1928). Italy contributed less than France, but Pirandello's plays and novels achieved genuine distinction and won him the 1934 Nobel Prize. Svevo, an acquaintance of James Joyce who may have influenced him, produced a minor masterpiece in *La coscienza di Zeno* in 1923, but gained public recognition only some years later, when he was sixty-three. 'Ignazio Silone' (Secondo Tranquilli, 1900–) broke with the Communist Party in 1930 and thereafter led the uncomfortable life of a solitary exile in Switzerland until his return to Italy in 1944. A 'political' writer and a sombre realist, he was not appreciated at his true worth in Italy, where his literary shortcomings counted for more with the critics than his harsh description of Abruzzese peasant life in *Fontamara* (1933) and *Pane e vino* (1937). Spain produced a major poet, Federico Garcia Lorca (1898–1936), who was murdered by Franco's followers during the opening stages of the Spanish civil war; and a minor essayist, José Ortega y Gasset (1883–1955), whose inflated reputation among European conservatives was chiefly sustained by a rambling piece of writing best known under its English title, *The Revolt of the Masses* (1930). Miguel de Unamuno (1864–1936) belonged to an older generation, while Ramón José Sender (1902–) and Arturo Barea (1897–1957) became expatriates as a result of the civil war.

NOTES

1 Arnold Hauser, *The Social History of Art*, vol. 4 (London: Routledge & Kegan Paul, 1962; New York: Knopf, 1951), pp. 222–3.
2 H.Stuart Hughes, *Contemporary Europe* (Englewood Cliffs, N.J. and London: Prentice-Hall, 1961), p. 189.
3 *Ibid.*
4 Paul Rotha, *The Film Till Now* (London: Vision Press, 1951; New York: Twayne Publishers, 3rd ed., 1960), p. 98.
5 Paul West, *The Modern Novel* (London: Hutchinson, 1963; New York: Humanities Press, 2nd ed., 1969), vol. 1, pp. 159–60.
6 Hauser, *op. cit.*, pp. 227 ff. Camilla Gray, *The Russian Experiment in Art 1863–1922* (London: Thames and Hudson, 1971).
7 Peter Gay, *Weimar Culture* (London: Secker & Warburg, 1969; New York: Harper & Row, 1968), *passim*; Wolfgang Rothe ed., *Expressionismus als Literatur* (Bern: Francke Verlag, 1970); Karl Ludwig Schneider, *Zerbrochene Formen* (Hamburg: Hoffman und Campe, 1970); John Willett *Expressionism* (London: Weidenfeld & Nicolson, 1971).

8 Martin Esslin, *Brecht: A Choice of Evils* (London: Mercury Books, 1965); Frederick Ewen, *Bertolt Brecht* (London: Calder and Boyars, 1970; New York: Citadel Press, 1969); Bertolt Brecht, *Manual of Piety: Die Hauspostille:* a bilingual edition with English text by Eric Bentley and notes by Hugo Schmidt (New York: Grove Press, 1968); see also Bertolt Brecht, *Gesammelte Werke*, general editor Elisabeth Hauptmann, vols. 1–8; *Werkausgabe*: vols. 1–20 (Frankfurt: Suhrkamp Verlag, 1967). The original scholarly edition planned by his Frankfurt publishers was gradually expanded to a total of forty volumes, including a good deal of material that had never been printed before. On the occasion of the poet's seventieth birthday in 1968 a completely new and revised edition was issued, or rather two: an India-paper edition in eight large volumes, and a web-offset semi-paperback edition in twenty volumes. The standard East German edition is incomplete and, as one might expect, does not include the poems written in East Germany itself.

9 See *The Times Literary Supplement*, London, 8 August 1968.

10 Esslin, *op. cit.*, p. 94.

11 *Ibid.*, p. 118.

12 Karl Korsch, *Marxism and Philosophy* (London: NLB, 1970); cf. *Marxismus und Philosophie* (Leipzig: Hirschfeld, 1923; 2nd rev. ed. 1930; reprinted by Europäische Verlagsanstalt, 1966). See also his *Karl Marx* (London: Chapman & Hall, 1938; reprinted by Russell & Russell, New York, 1963). For Benjamin see Hannah Arendt, *Men in Dark Times* (London: Jonathan Cape; New York: Harcourt Brace, 1970), pp. 153 ff.; Gershom Scholem, *Judaica II* (Frankfurt: Suhrkamp Verlag, 1970), pp. 193 ff.

13 Reprinted in *Nation im Widerspruch* (Hamburg, 1963); see Michael Hamburger, *From Prophecy to Exorcism* (London: Longmans, Green & Co., 1965; New York: Barnes & Noble, 1968), p. 22.

14 George L. Mosse, *The Culture of Western Europe* (London: Murray, 1963; Chicago: Rand McNally, 1961), pp. 297 ff.

15 Paul West, *The Modern Novel* (London: Hutchinson, 1963; New York: Humanities Press, 2nd ed., 1969), vol. 1, p. 74.

16 *Ibid.*

17 T. S. Eliot, *For Lancelot Andrewes* (London: Faber & Faber, 1928; Garden City, N.Y.: Doubleday, 1929). For Eliot's political views, as expressed in *The Criterion*, see the collection of essays and reviews from *The Times Literary Supplement* in 1968, published under the title *TLS* (London and New York: Oxford University Press, 1969), pp. 45 ff. The article originally appeared in the *TLS* of 25 April 1968.

18 G. S. Fraser, *The Modern Writer and his World* (London: Penguin Books, 1964; New York: Praeger Publishers, rev. ed., 1965), pp. 294 ff.

CHAPTER 11

PHILOSOPHY AND THEOLOGY BETWEEN THE WARS

The discussion of pre-1914 positivism in Chapter 4 drew no distinction between philosophical, sociological and literary attitudes character-istic of the prevailing culture. In what follows a different approach will be adopted. We shall deal first with the philosophical school generally known under the title of logical positivism; thereafter, Marxism, Existentialism, idealist metaphysics and theology will be examined separately. The advantage of this procedure is so obvious that the question may arise why it was not adopted from the start. The answer is that in the pre-1914 period one encounters a style of thought char-acteristic of the majority of representative thinkers, whereas after 1919 it becomes much more difficult to establish a common denominator. Newcomers like Existentialism and dialectical theology clearly demand separate treatment. This circumstance is itself an index to the dis-integration of the common culture which Europe possessed before 1914, a culture for which liberalism is still the best available label. There is a sense in which Bergson, Durkheim, Weber and Freud can all be styled liberals, and the same applies to representative Protestant theologians such as Albert Schweitzer and Ernst Troeltsch, to historians of culture like Wilhelm Dilthey, and to philosophers such as Edmund Husserl or Bertrand Russell. For the period between 1919 and 1939 it would be difficult to define a shared attitude, unless it be a sense of crisis. We are therefore obliged at this point to renounce the previous arrangement and to draw sharper dividing lines between the conflicting schools. So far as Communism and Fascism are concerned, it has already been shown that their simultaneous emergence signified something like a civil-war situation. In philosophy and theology the divisions were less rigid, but sharp enough to warrant separate treatment.

Logical positivism, the doctrine associated with the so-called Vienna Circle, and with Ludwig Wittgenstein (1889–1951), is itself a subject of sufficient complexity to warrant book-length treatment. Since this is not practicable, we simply note some of the relevant facts. The crucial date is 1922, when Moritz Schlick succeeded Ernst Mach as professor in the philosophy of the inductive sciences at Vienna, an appointment which coincided with the English translation of Wittgenstein's *Tractatus Logico-Philosophicus*.[1] Around Schlick, Rudolf Carnap (1891–1970) and others the Circle took shape in the later 1920s, the term *Wiener Kreis* (Vienna Circle) being first employed in 1928. The best known members, apart from Schlick and Carnap, were Friedrich Waismann, Otto Neurath, Herbert Feigl, Hans Hahn, Karl Menger and Kurt Gödel; its main medium of publicity was the journal *Erkenntnis* (1930), renamed for 1939–40 (by which time the majority of the members had emigrated) *The Journal of Unified Science*. The Circle worked in close association with the "Society of Empirical Philosophy" in Berlin, which included Hans Reichenbach – joint editor with Carnap of *Erkenntnis* – and others. Wittgenstein was not in any formal sense a member of the Circle, and neither was Karl Popper, whose *Logik der Forschung* was published in Vienna in the autumn of 1934 (with the imprint 1935) and subsequently caused a stir in Anglo-American academic quarters under the title *The Logic of Scientific Discovery* (1959). Carnap, who had been introduced to Schlick by Reichenbach, became a lecturer at the University of Vienna between 1926 and 1931, later went to Prague and in 1935 emigrated to the United States, as did Feigl and Reichenbach. It is a point of some importance that Schlick, Carnap and Neurath had already worked out some of the basic doctrines of logical positivism before they and the other members of the Circle read the *Tractatus* and encountered Wittgenstein. In the English-speaking world, Viennese logical positivism – as distinct from Wittgenstein's highly personal doctrine – was for the first time popularized in 1936 by A.J.Ayer in his brief and brilliant study *Language, Truth and Logic*. The subsequent development of linguistic philosophy – a heritage of the later Wittgenstein – belongs to the 1950s and represents a divergence from the original creed of logical positivism.[2]

To complete the picture it has to be added that Wittgenstein originally obtained his early philosophical training at Cambridge in 1912–13, where he studied under Russell whose *Principles of Mathematics* (1903) had already affected his philosophical outlook. Again, Russell's and Whitehead's *Principia Mathematica* were known to the members of the Vienna Circle, who found a common theme in discussing the work. Thus there is a certain circularity about the movement of ideas connecting Vienna and Cambridge. Wittgenstein's earliest philosophical discussions dealt with problems with which Frege and Russell were then occupied. Hence it is not surprising that Russell should after 1919 have taken an active interest in having the *Tractatus* translated into English. The book itself was composed during the 1914–18 war, while Wittgenstein was serving with the Austrian Army, and reached Russell while its author was a prisoner of war near Monte Cassino in Italy. Its publication created a stir in Cambridge at the same time that Wittgenstein encountered the future members of the Vienna Circle, most of them pupils of Mach and already confirmed empiricists and anti-metaphysicians. Wittgenstein for his part had been influenced by Schopenhauer and retained a life-long interest in metaphysics, for all that he shared the empiricist conviction that metaphysical statements are incapable of proof. The *Tractatus* is the work of a scientifically trained philosopher who has done his best to suppress his mystical yearnings, but who does not hesitate to affirm that "the contemplation of the world *sub specie aeternitatis* is its contemplation as a limited whole", and that "the feeling of the world as a limited whole is the mystical feeling".[3] Between this way of looking at things and the authentic positivism of the Vienna Circle there was a radical discontinuity which all concerned, in the interest of forming a common front, decided to ignore.

Ludwig Josef Johann Wittgenstein was born in Vienna on 26 April 1889 and baptized in the Catholic faith of his mother, whereas his grandfather was a convert from the Jewish faith to Protestantism. His father was an engineer and a leading figure in the iron and steel industry. Both he and his wife were musical and Johannes Brahms, the composer, was a friend of the family. After having been educated at home until the age of fourteen, and then at a school at Linz in Upper Austria, Ludwig Wittgenstein proceeded to the Technical High School in Berlin where he remained until the spring of 1908. He then went to England, registered as a research student of engineering at Manchester, and in 1911 went to Jena in Germany to discuss his plans with the eminent mathematician Gottlob Frege, who advised him to study at Cambridge under Russell. Wittgenstein followed the advice and stayed at Cambridge for all three terms of the year 1912 and the first two terms of 1913, whereafter he spent some time in Norway. At Cambridge he became intimate with Russell and also saw a good deal of Moore and Whitehead. Besides philosophy he did some experimental work in psychology concerning rhythm in music. On the outbreak of war in 1914 he volunteered for service in the Austrian Army, spending most of the war years on the Eastern front until in 1918 he was ordered south, just in time to be captured by the Italians consequent upon the collapse of the Austro-Hungarian Army in October–November 1918. When taken prisoner he had in his rucksack the manuscript of his *Logisch-philosophische Abhandlung*, better known as the *Tractatus Logico-Philosophicus*. While still in captivity he managed to transmit the manuscript to Russell, who eventually arranged for its translation after it had been published in German. After 1919 Wittgenstein, who in 1912 had inherited a large fortune from his father, but given all of it away on his return from the war, took up the vocation of schoolmaster and from 1920 to 1926 taught in various remote villages in Lower Austria. Having resigned the last of these posts for personal reasons he briefly went to work as a gardener's assistant with the monks at Hütteldorf near Vienna, and then turned to architecture and sculpture. Meanwhile his fame had begun to spread among the members of the future Vienna Circle, among whom Moritz Schlick and Friedrich Waismann established personal contact with him. He was also visited by a young Cambridge philosopher, Frank Ramsey, and in 1929 he was finally persuaded by his English friends to return to Cambridge, where in the following year he was made a Fellow of Trinity College. In 1938 he acquired British nationality and in 1939, on the retirement of G.E. Moore, he was elected to a professorial chair, but preferred to do war-work as an orderly in a London hospital and later in a medical laboratory in Newcastle. In 1947, at the age of fifty-eight, he resigned his chair at Cambridge and thereafter for a while lived in solitude in a cottage on the west coast of Ireland. He paid a brief visit to the United States and in 1949 returned to Cambridge, where he died of cancer on 29 April 1951, three days after his sixty-second birthday. From all accounts he detested academic life in general and Cambridge in particular. Nonetheless his influence on the small group of pupils whom he taught in the 1930s was profound, and the posthumous appearance of his *Philosophical Investigations* is generally regarded as a landmark in the history of linguistic philosophy. The work was probably begun in 1936 and finished in 1949. It represents a complete break with the doctrines set out in the *Tractatus*, so that strictly speaking there are two Wittgensteins: the youthful genius who believed he had solved all problems in philosophy, and the elderly recluse who had come to doubt whether there were any problems worth solving.[4]

It is of some relevance that Wittgenstein never did any systematic reading in the classics of philosophy. In his youth he was impressed by Schopenhauer. Later he came to value St Augustine, Kierkegaard, Tolstoy and Dostoyevsky. His thought moved on the borderland between philosophy and religion. This is already clear from the *Tractatus*, although in a technical sense he was then dealing with logical problems raised by Frege and Russell. In the 1930s there occurred a radical change in his thinking, so that it has been possible to say of the author of the *Philosophical Investigations* that he has no ancestors in philosophy. At any rate he had abandoned the doctrine which first made him famous and enabled the members of the Vienna Circle to treat him as an ally: the picture-theory of language, that is to say, the notion that the form of language corresponds to the form of reality. Meaningful statements, on this assumption, are statements which are in accordance with the structure of the real world. As Wittgenstein put it in the preface to the *Tractatus*: "What can be said at all can be said clearly; and whereof one cannot speak thereof one must be silent." Logic reveals the meaning of factual discourse, and so discloses the structure of reality which factual discourse reflects. This doctrine assumes that reality consists essentially of simple things and that its basic structure is mirrored in an *a priori* connection between a pair of factual propositions. But in the *Philosophische Bemerkungen* ("Philosophical Remarks") of 1930, which remained unpublished at the time, this standpoint is qualified. Wittgenstein now thinks that there are many specific features of reality which are reflected in the logical grammar of the words we use to classify what we experience. This was a step towards his final position of which it has been said that it treats the structure of reality as a projection of human thought expressed in language. The shift towards nominalism and conventionalism runs right through the *Philosophical Investigations* of 1953 and accounts for the fact that what was now called linguistic philosophy increasingly took the place of the older logical positivism. The ontology of the *Tractatus* offered an objective account of the general nature of the world; the later theory not only rejected the view that reality consists of simple entities: it denied that there is any valid argument from the present structure of language to the structure of reality. The choice of language is not forced on us by the nature of things; the ultimate explanation of a necessary truth is merely that we find it convenient to develop language in accordance with it.[5]

This conclusion was a long way removed from the basic beliefs of the Vienna Circle which had originally taken shape in the 1920s as an attempt to work out a coherent doctrine of empirical science. What had brought the Circle together was a common distaste for metaphysics, including the Kantian variety which maintained that there are entities lying beyond the reach of possible experience – 'things in themselves'. What the logical positivists opposed to all metaphysics, that of Kant included, was the 'principle of verifiability', i.e. the notion that the meaning of a proposition lies in its factual verification. All entities not accessible to observation and verification were dismissed as meaningless, from which it followed that metaphysics was literally nonsense. As for morality and religion, any statements associated with them were simply expressions of emotion for which no proof could be offered, and which were hence neither true nor false. So far as the English-speaking world in the 1930s is concerned, the extreme expression of this standpoint is to be found in Ayer's *Language, Truth and Logic*, but he was merely giving a popularized account of what he had learned in Vienna from Schlick and Carnap and their associates. They for their part found support for the principle of verifiability in Wittgenstein's *Tractatus*, even though its author affirmed that they had misunderstood his position. Whatever its origin, the verifiability principle – first explicitly stated by Waismann in his "Logische Analyse des Wahrscheinlichkeitsbegriffs" (*Erkenntnis*, 1930) – became the central tenet of logical positivism, at any rate until 1934, when Popper, in his *Logik der Forschung* replaced it by the criterion of falsifiability: a theoretical statement forms part of empirical science if in principle it can be disproved. Popper was something of an outsider so far as the Circle was concerned, and although an empiricist he never regarded himself as a logical positivist in the strict sense. But these were internal differences within a group of thinkers who were in agreement on essentials. In their antagonism to what they termed 'metaphysics' they formed a common front.[6]

Objections were promptly raised against verifiability as an ultimate test of truth, one of the counter-arguments being that the principle of verifiability, since it was neither an empirical generalization nor a tautology, had no proper logical status. It was also observed that the ultimate verifiers of a proposition cannot themselves be propositions. There was a further difficulty: Schlick had argued that philosophy, while as a mental activity it may help us to understand what we are saying, does not itself say anything, from which it followed that there could be no such thing as a 'scientific philosophy'. To this it was objected that Schlick himself was putting forward philosophical theses – for example, the principle of verifiability. Wittgenstein, in the *Tractatus*, tried to get around this difficulty by suggesting that the propositions of the *Tractatus*, in so far as they were philosophical, were indeed nonsensical, but nonetheless illuminating, in that anyone who understood them could thereafter throw away the ladder and dispense with philosophy altogether. But Wittgenstein was essentially an irrationalist who held that "even if *all possible* scientific questions be answered, the problems of life have still not been touched at all".[7] The genuine positivists of the Vienna Circle were quite satisfied with science as a substitute for philosophy. Schlick followed Mach in holding that questions such as 'What is the meaning of life?' are unanswerable. Wittgenstein agreed to the extent of arguing that they are unanswerable *by science*, but he clearly hankered for something beyond science, even though he had committed himself to the thesis that this something was not philosophy. As Russell noted in his Introduction to the English translation of the *Tractatus*, "The totalities concerning which Mr Wittgenstein holds that it is impossible to speak logically are nevertheless thought by him to exist, and are the subject matter of his mysticism." This was the real issue between Wittgenstein and the radical positivists such as Carnap, Schlick and Neurath, and their British exponent, A. J. Ayer. The gulf was never bridged, and the popular notion of Wittgenstein as a representative of logical positivism continued to rest on a misunderstanding.

In addition to being dissatisfied with Wittgenstein's mysticism, the leading positivists were at odds among themselves over verification and what Neurath called "protocol sentences". The latter differed from "basic" or "atomic" sentences (metaphysical, according to Neurath), in that they were subject to correction. In *The Logical Syntax of Language* (1934) Carnap tried to deal with this problem as well as a number of others. On protocol sentences he steered midway between Neurath and Popper, all three being concerned to construct a proper language of science. For the rest he dismissed all statements about transcendental entities as senseless and shouldered the full burden of maintaining that ethical and metaphysical statements tell us nothing about the world. "The logic of science takes the place of the inextricable tangle of problems which is known as philosophy."[8] As to verification he had by 1935 abandoned "verifiable" for "testable", whereas Popper, as we have seen, proposed the alternative of "falsifiable". These differences were comparatively minor by comparison with the basic tenet of logical positivism, as expounded with great success by Ayer in 1936: the assertion that philosophy cannot disclose metaphysical verities. In view of what has already been said about the interaction between Cambridge and Vienna, it is not surprising that Ayer should have been able to name Locke, Berkeley and Hume as predecessors of Russell, and to treat the latter's theory of description as the British counterpart of Continental logical positivism. Nonetheless British empiricism and Viennese positivism, for all their family resemblances, pursued different aims. Of Ayer's *The Foundations of Empirical Knowledge* (1940) it has been observed that it is concerned with the traditional problem of British empiricism – "our knowledge of the external world" – and in his later writings he stayed even more closely within the British tradition. Meanwhile Carnap gradually moved away from logical positivism towards a form of conventionalism: mathematical necessity attaches to a mathematical proposition in virtue of its being the necessary consequence of the adoption of certain rules or axioms. The later Wittgenstein for his part arrived at the conclusion that the mathematician does not *discover* mathematical relations, but rather *invents* them, decimal notation being a good example.[9]

Let us now try to describe the precise link between empiricism of the British variety and logical positivism in the sense given to the term by the members of the Vienna Circle. It has already been pointed out that Wittgenstein started his philosophical career in Cambridge before 1914 under the auspices of Russell, who for his part had been influenced by Frege. Russell's original problem after 1900 was to find a philosophical foundation for mathematics, and the account of mathematical knowledge he then gave was one having to do with a realm of abstract entities, accessible to the intellect, but not to the senses. He was a rationalist, since he acknowledged the existence of a realm of abstract or logical propositions – universals in traditional language – independent of matter on the one hand and state of mind on the other. Wittgenstein thereafter convinced Russell that mathematical propositions are really tautologies – that is to say, purely conceptual truths, not stating any information about a self-subsisting realm of universals. This was a conclusion Russell was unwilling to accept, but he did in the end concur. The nature of truth and meaning thereupon became a problem for both thinkers, and eventually Wittgenstein put forward the *Tractatus*, where he raised the question what it is for a statement to be meaningful. The answer he gave was that for a proposition to have a meaning it must picture a fact, and that the world is a collocation of facts. This in turn led to the verification principle, i.e., the doctrine that for a form of words to have meaning it must be correlated with some type of experience which can be either verified or falsified. Mathematical knowledge was purely conceptual; metaphysical statements were not verifiable and hence nonsensical. This was the doctrine briefly summarized by Ayer in 1936, and for a few years it looked as though positivism had been integrated within the tradition of British empiricism. But then something unexpected happened: Wittgenstein returned to Cambridge and began to revise his own theory, while at the same time it turned out that the verification principle could not be formulated in a satisfactory manner. Logical positivism had underwritten the privileged status of science and mathematics. Now Wittgenstein began to suspect that the language of science, so far from being the basic structure of knowledge, was just one language among many others. There could be other meanings and other languages. The outcome of this radical revision of his earlier standpoint came to be known as linguistic philosophy, an attempt to investigate the actual use of words in their social context. This was empiricism with a vengeance, but it was no longer compatible with logical positivism. And so once more the British empiricists – Ryle and Austin being the leading figures of the post-1945 school – found themselves moving away from the positivism of the Continentals. It is true that they could appeal to the Wittgenstein of the *Philosophical Investigations*, but as a result of their work British post-war philosophy – now for the most part associated with Oxford rather than Cambridge – acquired a somewhat insular character.[10]

In a certain fundamental sense, therefore, logical positivism faded out or was eclipsed, in that it was no longer held that mathematics and physics were privileged forms of thought. The shift towards linguistics entailed a recognition that there could be a great variety of ways in which words might be significantly employed. While Russell emphatically dissented, as did Popper, the Oxford school came around to the conclusion that the meaningful use of language was itself the principal topic of an up-to-date philosophy. The problem now was to identify the fundamental subjects of everyday discourse, so as to make it possible to talk about other matters. Linguistic philosophy, whatever the personal interests and commitments of its practitioners, did not say anything about the world. Logical positivism, and its offshoot, scientism, had concerned themselves with the realm of physics and, at a remove, with the practice of technology. Linguistic philosophy busied itself with the everyday world and the commonsensible use of words. Neither had any pretension to that unification of critical thinking and practical action which had once figured among the aims of philosophy – German idealism above all.

It remains to be said that the members of the Vienna Circle, in accordance with their general disparagement of non-scientific state-ments, were tolerant in political matters, politics – like ethics and aesthetics – being a question of metaphysics and/or private feeling. Neurath and Carnap were socialists, and so until 1934 was Karl Popper. Schlick inherited Mach's progressivism together with his chair. Wittgenstein, as we have seen, volunteered for service in the Austrian Army in 1914, and after 1938 became a British subject solely because Hitler's occupation of Austria left him no choice. Others adhered to conventional liberalism. None were Marxists in philosophy – not even those among them who in 1919 had briefly toyed with Communism under the impact of the Russian Revolution. For Marxism descended from Hegel and was consequently suspect as a 'metaphysical' system, quite apart from the fact that the later Engels had in fact constructed a materialist ontology which in due course became the official creed of the Communist movement, after Lenin and his suc-cessors had imposed it on Russia. It is of some interest that to the neo-Marxists of the Frankfurt school, whom we shall encounter in the next section, logical positivism was abhorrent as a departure from the great tradition of German idealism. Nor, for obvious reasons, did positivism make an appeal to religious traditionalists, Wittgenstein's private mystical cravings notwithstanding. Like Freudian psychoanalysis, whose fate it shared when Austria was incorporated in the German *Reich*, logical positivism was the creation of an intellectual circle which had inherited the cautious empiricism of Ernst Mach. Intel-lectually, its closest allies were the Polish logicians around A.Tarski whose *Introduction to Logic and to the Methodology of the Deductive Sciences* (1936) appeared in an English translation in 1941. The Polish school of the inter-war period was an impressive phenomenon and one of the major casualties of the Hitler–Stalin age. Writers like Twardowski and Tarski deserve to be better known outside their native country, but we cannot go into the subject here and must content ourselves with referring the reader to the bibliographical note appended to this chapter.[11]

B MARXISM

The 1920s and 1930s witnessed a considerable upsurge in Marxist theorizing, largely though not wholly stimulated by the Russian Revolution and the emergence of an international Communist movement. In taking note of this phenomenon it is important to avoid the common misconception of identifying the prominence of Marxist literature with the spread of what passed for philosophy in the USSR, both before and after the official codification of what came to be known as Marxism–Leninism. An analogy may help to clarify the situation: the French Revolution left deep traces in German thought, whereas in France itself its accomplishments were almost wholly practical. No French thinker of the first order emerged from the tumult of 1789–1814, while across the Rhine German philosophy was entirely reconstructed under the impact of the tremendous happenings in France. With a few qualifications the same applies to the development of Marxism after 1917. Although Lenin had briefly dabbled in philosophy, and Bukharin in 1922 produced a dull textbook on historical materialism, Soviet Marxism was not taken very seriously by West European Communists with philosophical inclinations in the 1920s; and when during the Stalinist era this situation began to change, it did so because by then nearly all independent thinkers had broken with the Communist International. The two major exceptions to this rule, as noted before, were the Italian Communist theoretician Antonio Gramsci and the Hungarian philosopher-critic Georg Lukács, who somehow managed to adapt himself to Leninist orthodoxy, while preserving a private fund of heretical notions on which he cautiously drew after Stalin had left the scene. French Marxism was a post-1945 phenomenon and therefore lies outside our immediate theme. For practical purposes the only significant development of Marxist theorizing during the 1920s and 1930s occurred in Central Europe, and its authors were heretics whose writings remained highly suspect from the Soviet–Marxist standpoint. The Communist habit of identifying Marxism with Leninism has obscured this circumstance, just as it has successfully blurred the fact that the only significant contribution Lenin made to Marxist theorizing was his work on imperialism: written in Switzerland during the war and legally published before the first Russian Revolution of February 1917.[12]

A discussion of the subject is not rendered easier by the circumstance that the standard interpretations, both in the USSR and in the West, are wholly mistaken in attributing what is known as 'dialectical materialism' to Marx, whereas its source is to be found in the works of the later Engels, from which the doctrine found its way into the writings of G.V.Plekhanov (1856–1918) and his philosophical pupil Lenin. As part of this general misconception it is sometimes suggested that Marx never emancipated himself from Hegel's system, whereas Engels was more sympathetic to empiricism; in actual fact the situation was exactly the other way around. Again, it is frequently suggested that Lenin after 1914 made a decisive break with the philosophical interpretation of Marxism associated with Karl Kautsky (1854–1938). Nothing could be further from the truth. The doctrine set out by Engels in his writings of the 1880s – an eclectic composite of Marx's naturalism, Hegel's logic and contemporary positivism – became the treasured possession of the Third International: a circumstance briefly alluded to by Lukács in his heretical essay collection *Geschichte und Klassenbewusstsein* ("History and Class Consciousness") (1923) and expounded at some length by the German Communist theoretician Karl Korsch in the same year.[13] For Lenin as for Engels, the dialectic represented "the science of the general laws of motion and development of nature, human society and thought".[14] This particular manner of 'standing Hegel on his feet' retained the ontological character of his metaphysics, the sole difference being that the Absolute was now termed 'matter', instead of being called 'spirit'. This is really all that needs to be said of Soviet philosophy, and not surprisingly it made little headway among Western Socialists. On those occasions when Engels abandoned Hegel's ontology in favour of the positivist notion that philosophy must confine itself to logic, the Soviet philosophers characteristically refused to follow him. They were determined to work out an all-embracing system applicable to nature and history alike, and in the end they had their way.

In saying this one has to take account of a circumstance quite unrelated to Marxism, namely the fact that Russia shares with Spain the distinction of never having produced anything worth being called philosophy. In this respect there is not a great deal to choose between Lenin's *Materialism and Empirio-Criticism* (1909) and the thinkers listed in Louis J.Shein's *Readings in Russian Philosophical Thought*.[15] Solovyov, Lopatin, Lossky, Berdyaev, S.L.Frank and the rest were theologians or idealist metaphysicians whose problematic had been set for them by the disintegration of religious faith and the inroads of scientism or, as it was then called, materialism. Some of them were indebted to Schelling, which is why their writings make an immediate appeal to anyone brought up on the tradition of German Romantic philosophy. Their Marxist opponents, from Plekhanov onward, were in a similar position, the chief difference being that they were in search of a 'materialist' philosophy, whereas Marx and Engels, during their formative years in the 1840s, had aimed at the critical supersession of philosophy as such.[16] Engels' later backslidings in the 1870s and 1880s supplied a foundation for the Russian Marxists, whereas their idealist opponents continued the time-honoured search for an ontology that would underpin revealed religion. Most of them relied heavily on mystical intuition, while the practical direction of their thinking was primarily ethical, a trait they shared with the classics of Russian literature. In this respect at least they had more in common with their Russian Communist critics than with Western thinkers (whether Marxists or not) who had moved beyond the naive anthropocentrism of theology. In place of the dialectical interrelation of being and consciousness which Marx (following Hegel) had taken for granted, Soviet Marxism reproduced the pre-Hegelian, and indeed pre-Kantian, notion that knowledge is the passive reflection of an objective and absolute Being in a subjective Consciousness. In 1923 Lukács and Korsch rebelled against this retrogression. In later years Lukács affected to share Lenin's standpoint, thereby sterilizing his own thought and reducing most of his critical output to a level which immunized Western readers to the doctrines he tried to put across.

Given the philosophical nullity of Soviet Marxism, the absence before 1945 of any serious Marxist literature in France, and the fact that Gramsci's prison notebooks only became available in the 1950s, the task of continuing the tradition of classical Marxism fell to a handful of thinkers in Central Europe. Apart from Korsch and Lukács, who have already been mentioned, they were for the most part connected with the Frankfurt *Institut für Sozialforschung* whose major publications began to appear from 1932 onward. After 1933 these writers were obliged to emigrate and the *Zeitschrift für Sozialforschung* had to be published in Paris. The principal members of the group – Max Horkheimer, Theodor Adorno, Herbert Marcuse, Leo Lowenthal, Friedrich Pollock, Karl Wittfogel and Erich Fromm – eventually found refuge in the United States, as did Korsch. Franz Borkenau, the author of an important study on seventeenth-century philosophy,[17] spent most of the Hitler years in Britain. Walter Benjamin, already known to a few insiders in the 1920s as an eminent critic of literature, settled in Paris and in 1940 committed suicide in the wake of the French military defeat and the general turmoil that followed, while trying unsuccessfully to cross the Spanish frontier. Horkheimer and Adorno returned to Frankfurt in 1949, and thereafter achieved a prominence denied to them during the closing years of the Weimar Republic, as did Benjamin whose posthumous fame in West Germany contrasted strangely with his almost complete isolation in the 1920s and 1930s. The Institute, which had survived in New York and California during the war years, was reconstituted by Horkheimer and Adorno after 1949 as an integral part of Frankfurt University, but changed its character, its founders having abandoned the Communist position they held (with some qualifications) in 1933, although they continued to regard themselves as Marxists. Of the other adherents of the original circle, Korsch, Marcuse, Wittfogel, Lowenthal and Fromm remained in the United States; Borkenau returned to Germany, where he spent most of his time until his sudden death in 1957. Others settled down in Britain. From the 1950s onward the intellectual tradition originally associated with the Institute was continued, with suitable modifications, by those of its former adherents who had returned to Frankfurt, where in the 1960s their inheritance was passed on to a new generation of scholars.[18]

Like the Vienna Circle the Frankfurt School was riven by internal dissensions which became more pronounced after 1945, when some of its members reverted to liberalism in politics, while others retained a socialist standpoint. There had never been complete unanimity in political questions, or for that matter in regard to the evaluation of psychoanalysis. Whether it was possible to 'combine' Marx and Freud remained a matter for debate. Again, some of the original contributors to the *Zeitschrift* were a good deal closer to Max Weber than to Marx in their understanding of sociology. There was, however, a solid central core of Hegelian and Marxian thinking, principally represented by Horkheimer and Adorno, which was quite specifically directed against empiricism in general and logical positivism in particular. Horkheimer's important essay *Der neueste Angriff auf die Metaphysik* (1937)[19] deals critically with Russell, Wittgenstein, Schlick, Carnap, Neurath and Reichenbach, as purveyors of a positivist 'logic of science' which had tried, but failed, to usurp the place of traditional philosophy. He makes the nice point that rationalist thinking in the seventeenth century undermined the prevalent belief in witchcraft, whereas the logical positivists, when faced with such a mass of amply corroborated 'protocol sentences' about witches, would not have dared to question their probability. "On the other hand, they treat Aristotle, Kant and Hegel as confusionists, their philosophy as scientifically nil, merely because it does not fit their logic and because its relation to the 'basic notions' and 'elementary perceptions' of empiricism is dubious."[20]

So far as philosophy was concerned, the Frankfurt School was handicapped not merely by external circumstances, but by the fact that the writings of the young Marx – notably the celebrated *Paris Manuscripts* of 1844 – became publicly available only in 1932. A two-volume edition of his early writings, edited and published by S. Landshut and J. P. Mayer in that year under the title *Der Historische Materialismus*, had hardly seen the light when the triumph of National Socialism put an end to the public discussion of Marx's thought in the land of his birth. The even more important *Grundrisse der Kritik der Politischen Ökonomie*, composed by Marx in 1857–8 before he got down to the writing of *Capital*, did not become generally available until 1953, when they were reprinted in East Berlin from an earlier Moscow edition published in 1939–41. For these and other reasons there was no systematic discussion of Marxism in the *Zeitschrift für Sozialforschung*, whose editors in the 1930s developed what they styled "the critical theory". Where the *Zeitschrift* scored was in the analysis of cultural and sociological topics neglected by the members of the Vienna Circle and the logical positivists in general. Being indebted to Hegel and Kant (in Horkheimer's case also to Schopenhauer), the leading figures of the Frankfurt School had no use for British empiricism, or for the doctrines of Wittgenstein and Popper. The resulting cleavage became glaringly obvious when Karl Popper, who had spent the war years in New Zealand, in 1945 published *The Open Society and its Enemies*: a two-volume diatribe against Plato, Aristotle, Hegel and Marx of which it may charitably be observed that no Hegel scholar has ever been able to take it seriously.[21] Popper, a one-time socialist, had by then worked around to the strange conclusion that Marx was in some sense the intellectual descendant of Plato. That this is not in fact the case has in recent years been tacitly accepted even by empiricist philosophers who are critical of both Hegel and Marx.[22]

Marxist economics experienced a revival in the 1930s and 1940s under the impact of the world-wide economic depression. Two notable literary products of this revived interest in the author of *Capital* were Joan Robinson's *An Essay on Marxian Economics*[23] and Oskar Lange's and Fred M. Taylor's joint study *On the Economic Theory of Socialism*.[24] Marxist sociology, on the other hand, became frozen for reasons not entirely obvious at the time.[25] At first it merely looked as though the Stalinist regime had simply made any serious discussion of Marx impossible, as indeed was the case. Only later, after 1945, did it become clear that the new society which had arisen from the ashes of the Second World War was in important respects no longer analysable in terms of market relations and class conflicts resulting therefrom. The collapse of the unregulated market economy in the 1930s, the growth of state intervention, and the Stalinist 'revolution from above' which radically altered the economic infrastructure of Russian society, had created a situation to which classical Marxism was not wholly relevant. The problems resulting therefrom will be briefly discussed when we come to the post-1945 era. Here we merely register the fact that neither the Social Democratic nor the Communist variant of Marxist theory in the 1930s gave rise to a satisfactory analysis of the phenomenon of Fascism. The standard Communist description of Fascism as a movement born from the misery and confusion of what was called 'the petty bourgeoisie' was wide of the mark. In particular it failed to explain why the Third Reich, unlike the Weimar Republic, had been able to do away with mass unemployment. Social Democratic theorizing after 1933 was practically non-existent. The explanation favoured by the Frankfurt School – that liberalism had produced its own opposite by a kind of dialectical process within the culture of a collapsing bourgeois society – ignored the circumstance that Fascism had triumphed in a country the bulk of whose middle class had never accepted the tenets of the Enlightenment. In the end it was not really possible to argue that liberalism had given birth to totalitarianism by a sort of logical necessity, although this thesis was to have an unexpected revival in the 1960s.[26]

Against the general background sketched in this chapter it may be useful to pick out an issue central to the interpretation of Marxist theory as a systematic body of thought relevant to the understanding of man and society. In 1938 Karl Korsch – a veteran of the German Communist movement from which he was expelled in 1926 for 'ultra-leftist' deviations, but also a trained philosopher and at one time a lecturer at Jena University – had the following to say about the relevance of historical materialism:

> Just as positivism could not move with freedom in the new field of social science, but remained tied to the specific concepts and methods of natural science, so Marx's historical materialism has not entirely freed itself from the spell of Hegel's philosophical method which in its day overshadowed all contemporary thought. This was not a materialistic science of society which had developed on its own basis. Rather it was a materialistic theory which had just emerged from idealistic philosophy; a theory, therefore, which still showed in its contents, its methods, and its terminology the birth-marks of the old Hegelian philosophy from whose womb it sprang. All these imperfections were unavoidable under the circumstances out of which Marx's materialistic social research arose.[27]

Three years later, in his influential study *Reason and Revolution*, sub-titled 'Hegel and the Rise of Social Theory', Herbert Marcuse took a rather different view: the Hegelian dialectic, and particularly Hegel's treatment of logic, "marked the first step in the direction of unifying theory and practice".[28] For Hegel, "History . . . is the long road of mankind to conceptual and practical domination of nature and society, which comes to pass when man has been brought to reason and to a possession of the world as reason."[29] Hegel was thus seen as the precursor of Marx, even though in characteristic German professorial fashion he had contented himself with elaborating a 'system of science'. It is true that for Marcuse, too, "the transition from Hegel to Marx is, in all respects, a transition to an essentially different order of truth, not to be interpreted in terms of philosophy. . . . Even Marx's early writings are not philosophical."[30] The reason is that "in Hegel's system all categories terminate in the existing order, while in Marx's they refer to the negation of this order. . . . Marx's theory is a 'critique' in the sense that all concepts are an indictment of the totality of the existing order."[31] But Marcuse nowhere suggests that the Hegelian heritage was an unfortunate encumbrance which prevented Marx from evolving a genuinely scientific theory of society. To have done so would have been to meet the positivists at least halfway, and for Marcuse, as for the Frankfurt School in general, positivism was a wretched abortion, whereas the Hegelian dialectic, for all its faults, transcended the narrow empirical understanding of reality, that is to say, the specific accomplishment of what Hegel termed the 'understanding', as distinct from 'reason'. Reason may be hampered by metaphysical idealism, but it is nonetheless related, however obscurely, to the totality of the world, whereas science merely duplicates the environment in which it finds itself. "For Marx, as for Hegel, the dialectic takes note of the fact that the negation inherent in reality is 'the moving and creating principle'."[32] The 'overcoming' of Hegel's standpoint leaves intact the heritage of Critical Reason, which is something very different from the procedure of the natural and social sciences. Like the Vienna Circle, the Frankfurt School had its touchstone for the evaluation of philosophy: in its case the preservation of what had once been known as the heritage of German Idealism.

Marcuse's subsequent critique of Soviet Marxism, although published in the 1950s, belongs thematically to the range of topics we have already briefly considered. This must be the justification for giving some space to it here, instead of reserving it to later treatment. After the 1930s there occurred no significant change in the official interpretation of philosophy laid down during the Stalinist era. Nor for that matter did the pre-Stalinist representatives of Soviet Marxism – principally Abram Deborin and Nikolai Bukharin – diverge from the line already laid down by Lenin in his *Materialism and Empirio-Criticism*. In consequence what Marcuse in 1958 had to say about the Stalinist version of Marxism applies substantially to Leninism as a whole, a circumstance already obvious to the Frankfurt School in the 1930s:[33]

Perhaps nothing is more revealing in the development of Soviet Marxism than its treatment of dialectic. Dialectical logic is the cornerstone of Marxian theory. . . . But while not a single of the basic dialectical concepts has been revised or rejected in Soviet Marxism, the function of dialectic itself has undergone a significant change: it has been transformed from a mode of critical thought into a universal 'world outlook' and universal method with rigidly fixed rules and regulations, and this transformation destroys the dialectic more thoroughly than any revision. The change corresponds to that of Marxism itself from theory to ideology. . . . As Marxian theory ceases to be the organon of revolutionary consciousness and practice and enters the superstructure of an established system of domination, the movement of dialectical thought is codified into a philosophical system. . . .

Marcuse is obliged to note that "the first step in this direction was made by Engels in his Dialectics of Nature (which he did not publish), and his notes have provided the skeleton for the Soviet Marxist codification". Since Engels' and Lenin's revolutionary disposition is not subject to doubt, a purely sociological interpretation of Soviet Marxism is clearly inadequate. The fact is that Engels in his later years took some tentative steps towards that 'dialectical materialism' (so described by the 'father of Russian Marxism', G.V.Plekhanov) which in due course became the 'world outlook' of the party founded by Lenin and then transformed by Stalin. Lenin for his part (writing in 1908 in ignorance of Engels' unpublished work) thought it important to shift the emphasis from dialectic to materialism for reasons having to do with the pre-1914 intellectual situation in Tsarist Russia – a backward country on the eve of a 'bourgeois' revolution, where 'materialism' signified above all a radical break with religion, as it had done in eighteenth-century France. When in due course Soviet Marxism took shape, it did so under the dual inspiration of Engels' rather amateurish excursion into Hegelian philosophy and Lenin's quite unrelated effort to bring materialism up to date. Not surprisingly, Western Marxists such as Lukács, Korsch, the Frankfurt group, Gramsci and the post-1945 French philosophers did not quite know what to make of this strange confection. In the end Lukács adapted himself to it (at least in public), while the others went their separate ways. Marcuse adhered to his own brand of neo-Hegelianism; Korsch adopted a quasi-positivist standpoint; French thinkers such as Sartre and Merleau-Ponty abandoned Lenin and went back to Marx, while trying to bring him up to date. For our purpose it is relevant that during the critical 1930s the Communist movement was committed to a philosophy which had cut its connection with the development of thought in Western Europe. In the circumstances Soviet Marxism became the intellectual counterpart of Stalin's 'Socialism in one country': the official philosophy of what by European standards was a backward society struggling with problems the West had left behind.

In saying this due allowance has been made for Gramsci, thanks to whom the Italian Communist movement acquired an identity of its own and ultimately proved able to play an important part in the political and intellectual life of its country, after the Fascist dictatorship had been dislodged. Having helped to found the Communist Party in 1921, and then played a leading role in it until his incarceration in 1926, Gramsci after his death in 1937 became something like an apostolic figure, and in the 1960s his authority could be invoked by the party leaders whenever they felt like returning from Leninism to Marxism. This became an important issue once it had become clear that in a civilized country such as Italy the Communist party could hope to win power only if it accepted democracy – as all European Marxists had done until 1917. Gramsci's own adaptation of Leninism in the 1920s had been qualified by considerations which stemmed from his Syndicalist past. All told, he became vitally important to the party when it set out to invent an "Italian road to socialism".[34]

For our purpose we may note that Gramsci – unlike Lenin and Bukharin, who both specialized in economics – had undergone an academic training in philosophy at Turin between 1911 and 1915, at a time when Croce's influence was at its peak. As late as 1917, when he was deeply involved in anti-war activities as a left-wing Socialist, he still maintained that Croce was the greatest thinker then living in Europe. This is less paradoxical than it sounds. Croce after all was in the Hegelian tradition, and Italian Marxism, ever since its inception in the 1890s, had been heavily impregnated with Hegelian concepts, thanks to Antonia Labriola (1843–1904), then professor of philosophy in Rome, who had matured intellectually among the neo-Hegelians in Naples. It has been observed with truth that Gramsci's relationship to Croce resembled that of Marx to Hegel. He was acutely aware that Croce had established an intellectual dictatorship over Italian liberalism, and that the liberals in turn owed their political power to what he described as their 'hegemony' over Italy's cultural life. This led to the interesting notion that the working class must, in the fullness of time, establish its own cultural 'hegemony', a process necessarily mediated by the intellectuals. *Egemonia* is a key concept in Gramsci's writings, carefully distinguished from political *dittatura*. This did not make Gramsci less of a Leninist in politics, but he wore his Leninism with a difference. Though on occasion he paid tribute to Lenin's understanding of the fact that the new society had to be reintegrated in a superior cultural order if it was to survive, his own approach differed radically from the Bolshevik notion that a political *coup d'état* might precede the forcible indoctrination of the masses. For Gramsci, in this respect closer to Marx than to Lenin, the cultural 'superstructure' was a reality, not something to be worked out by purely political means. The victory of socialism was an 'ethico-political' matter. It is easy to imagine what he would have thought of the reality of Stalinism had he lived to witness its unfolding.[35]

Egemonia represents a social order held in equilibrium by a moral and intellectual consensus diffused through all strata of the population and informing their daily lives. While the change-over from an old order of society to a new one demands a temporary political *dittatura*, the establishment of a new consensus is a long and wearisome affair, since it entails a cultural reorientation. This latter cannot be dictated from above, but must evolve from the gradual dissemination of new values. In this process the intellectuals have a key role to play, since it is they who generate the new culture and then make it available to the whole of society. It is not a question of 'moulding' the masses by bringing an enlightened 'vanguard' into action and then investing it with dictatorial powers. The new consciousness must spring from the working class itself and then be transmitted to other social categories, until an integrated culture has come into being. Gramsci does not altogether avoid the ambiguity of bringing *egemonia* into harmony with *dittatura*, but in the last analysis he comes down on the side of freedom:

> It seems necessary that the hard work of research into new truths and into better, more coherent and clearer formulations of the truths themselves should be left to the free initiative of individual scholars, even if the very principles which seem most essential are continually put in question.[36]

Croce's pupil was not prepared to cast the heritage of liberalism overboard: indeed Croce himself (as well as Freud) was to be absorbed into the new synthesis, much as Marx had absorbed Hegel. One can see why Gramsci appealed to Italian intellectuals after 1945. One can also see why he continues to appeal to American, British and French Marxists, whereas he has had no visible effect on the ruling elites of the Soviet bloc.

C FROM IDEALISM TO EXISTENTIALISM

In turning to the third member of our triad, the Existentialist movement in European philosophy and theology between the wars, we run the risk of being accused of undue partiality for one particular area of the Continent. But in the first place it is simply a fact that Existentialism arose in Central Europe before it was taken up by French philosophers after 1940: Sartre, Merleau-Ponty and Gabriel Marcel being the best known. Secondly, it is possible to do justice, however briefly, to the lingering Idealist tradition before embarking upon our quest. As it happens, the leading figures of what for brevity's sake one may call neo-Hegelianism during the period under review – Benedetto Croce, R.G.Collingwood and G.R.G.Mure – represent two countries seldom mentioned in connection with Hegel: Italy and Great Britain. Had the last surviving Russian Marxists not been silenced or exterminated by the Stalinist regime in the 1930s it might be possible as well to say something about the fate of Hegelianism in the Soviet Union. The problem does not arise and the topic may be set aside. But it is impossible to ignore Croce, just as it would have been unreasonable to give a brief account of Marxism in the 1930s without at least mentioning Gramsci. Benedetto Croce (1866–1952) was the central figure in Italian philosophy between 1900 and 1950, just as in his political capacity he was the leading intellectual representative of the rather conservative and cautious Italian liberalism of the period. This dual role was anchored in the fact that around 1900 Croce had abandoned a brief and superficial flirtation with Marxism in favour of the comforting doctrine that Reality is Spirit.[37] He made his mark, at home and abroad, as a critic, an aesthetician and a historian before turning to philosophy proper, and it is not altogether easy to spot the precise significance for his work of Vico on the one hand and Hegel on the other.[38] But there is no question that he was heavily indebted to Hegel: more so than the German founder of *Geisteswissenschaft*, Wilhelm Dilthey (1833–1911), who is occasionally mentioned in the same context.[39] For some reason Croce was never comfortable with the 'neo-Hegelian' label his admirers as well as his opponents applied to his work, and in 1907 he actually published a brief study under the title *What is Living and What is Dead in the Philosophy of Hegel.*[40] Possibly he felt that in rejecting both God and Transcendence he had rescued historicism from the somewhat obscure position in which Hegel had left it; but since he also rejected Nature in favour of Spirit, he had opted for Idealism, much to the regret of those among his Marxist pupils – Gramsci being the foremost – who admired his work. They had reason to do so, for Croce had gradually worked around to the position that philosophy is "the methodology of history". Being himself a practising historian this conclusion came naturally to him, just as it seemed natural to the logical positivists that philosophy should be, or try to become, the methodology of science. History for Croce is the movement of the human mind, and this movement comes to self-awareness in philosophy. Croce dispensed with the Hegelian system, and his conception of history, although not cyclical, was indebted to Vico. But with this qualification he may safely be counted among the heirs of German Idealism.

In his seminal work, the *Estetica* of 1902, and in his later writings, Croce developed a relativist theory of history in general, and art history in particular, that was in tune with the neo-Hegelianism to which he had become a convert in the 1890s. His acceptance of contemporary German psychology reinforced his belief that reality consists of subjective mental images. All our knowledge is either intuitive or logical. Intuitive knowledge deals with the particular, logical thought with the general. The intellect is concerned with universals, the intuition with what is individual. Intuition is active not only in aesthetics, but also in historical investigation, which is not a science but an art. Written history is the narrative of particular incidents and their imaginative reconstruction: the treatment of subjective mental images as reality. All history is written from the standpoint of the historian who projects his intuitive understanding back into the past. Historiography does not yield scientific laws, or for that matter judgements valid for all time. Its value lies in the fact that it establishes some kind of continuity between ourselves and our ancestors whose lives the historian reconstructs with the aid of authenticated documents, but always from the standpoint of the present age. Written history, since it changes from generation to generation, embodies among others the aesthetic preferences of the writer. *A fortiori* the history of art presents the subjective intuitional understanding of the art historian when confronted with images which are themselves mental. Croce does not deny the function of logical reasoning, but maintains that in creating and then appreciating a work of art the mind operates at the intuitive level. To what level of mind does philosophy itself belong? Since it can be no more than a description of the general principles exhibited in the movement of mind it ultimately describes the method of historical reconstruction by which the philosopher is guided. There is a dialectic whereby the mind conceptualizes what it intuits, and then returns to intuition for fresh inspiration. Intellectual advance occurs as a by-product of this constant zig-zag. To understand is to see historically, and conversely it is by way of historical reconstruction that genuine intellectual progress occurs.

R. G. Collingwood (1891–1943) took up where Croce had left off: with an analysis of art, religion, science, history and philosophy, published in 1924 under the title *Speculum Mentis or The Map of Knowledge*. From there the road runs to the *Essay on Philosophical Method* (*1933*), the *Essay on Metaphysics* (1940) and the manuscript notes edited after his death under the titles *The Idea of Nature* and *The Idea of History*.[41] The connecting link was Hegel, or to be precise, the notion that history rather than physics introduces the mind to the real nature of things. The actual analysis of Hegel's philosophy was undertaken by a different thinker, G. R. G. Mure.[42] Collingwood took Hegel for granted and then tried to move beyond him, albeit not in a direction a Marxist would have chosen. As the Editor of *The Idea of History* remarked in his preface, Collingwood's "doctrine of absolute presuppositions, with its religious and theological background, has affinities with Kierkegaard and even Karl Barth". Indeed we are not so very far removed here from the main theme of this chapter. *Speculum Mentis* opens with the lapidary statement "All thought exists for the sake of action", and the *Essay on Metaphysics* takes issue with Kant's critique of the so-called 'ontological' proof of God's existence.[43] For Collingwood, the statement "God exists" is not a proposition (it cannot be proved either true or false), but a presupposition. It is something Christians believe. Hence the logical positivists are wasting their time when they treat it as a proposition that cannot be verified.[44] This kind of argument does have affinities with the 'dialectical theology' of Barth and Bultmann, and with Existentialist philosophy as well. Collingwood would not have described himself in these terms, but the historian is entitled to do it on his behalf.

At the same time it has to be recognized that Collingwood's defence of metaphysics against positivism presupposes a great many things besides the theological presupposition that God exists, without which indeed there would never have been any theology. As Collingwood sees it, "all thinking involves absolute presuppositions", and this is true of scientific thought as well as of any other.[45] Hence the title of this chapter in his book is "Positivist Metaphysics". For although positivists stand committed to the principle that metaphysics is impossible, they themselves operate with absolute presuppositions of which they are unconscious, such as Mill's belief that all events happen according to laws. Now Collingwood holds that such presuppositions are in fact inevitable in every branch of knowledge, and that metaphysics is "the science of absolute presuppositions". He congratulates Aristotle on having made this discovery, but at the same time blames him for "having initiated the barren search for a science of pure being."[46] No such science is possible. "There is not even a pseudo-science of pure being."[47] Berkeley, Hume, Kant and Hegel are cited in support, and Collingwood expressly underwrites Hegel's statement that pure being is the same as nothing. Thus there can be no ontology, or science of pure being, but there can and must be a systematic investigation into ultimate presuppositions, such as the belief that events have causes. This investigation is the true business of metaphysics. Aristotle brought to light the ultimate presuppositions of Greek science, Kant those of Newtonian physics, and so on. Presuppositions change from time to time, and philosophy thus becomes a historical enterprise, disentangling the presuppositions of a particular time and place. The notions of true and false do not apply to them, but they may be more or less adequate, and additionally they reflect historical and social circumstances. Thus Collingwood is in the end committed to a historicism as radical as that of Croce, and of course this side of his thought is uncongenial to theologians or ontologists in search of 'pure being'. The same applies to the Hegelian argument developed in *Speculum Mentis*: religion mistakes imagining for thinking and asserts the reality of what is only symbol. Christianity solves the religious problem of reconciling God to man and thus prepares the way for its own supersession by philosophy. This sceptical strain was later replaced by the doctrine that reason and faith are indispensable to each other: each is an independent source of knowledge. In his late work

Collingwood combines historicism (absolute presuppositions of faith are always historically conditioned) with a peculiar kind of dogmatism: our attitude to our own absolute presuppositions is to be one of "unquestioning acceptance". Since suppositions are not propositions, Ayer's argument in *Language, Truth and Logic* does not apply to them and the positivist critique of metaphysics is mistaken.[48] But if suppositions are subject to historic change one does not quite see why ten pages further on the reader is told that they must be accepted without question if civilization is to survive, or that a genuine metaphysician is one who realizes that absolute presuppositions "neither stand in need of justification nor can in fact be justified".[49] The sceptic and the dogmatist in Collingwood were never wholly reconciled.

After this brief dip into the Idealist tradition we are in a better position to appreciate what was novel about the two European schools of thought respectively known as Phenomenology and Existentialism. In an earlier part of this study (see Chapter 5) reference was made to the founder of Phenomenology, Edmund Husserl (1859–1938) and to his seminal work, the *Logical Investigations* of 1900, as well as to some of his later writings. The point that now needs making is that Husserl, quite without intending it, became one of the fathers of the Existentialist movement represented by Karl Jaspers, Max Scheler, Martin Heidegger and the French thinkers already mentioned at the start of this section. At first sight this must seem distinctly odd, for Husserl's training had been in mathematics before in the 1890s he turned to logic; and when he launched out upon his philosophical career he did so in a spirit of unflinching commitment to rationalism.[50] Paradoxically, however, it was this very commitment which in the end transformed Phenomenology into something not far removed from an ontology, that is to say, a 'science of Being', thus in turn helping to give rise to the Existentialist movement. Husserl had started as a pupil of the philosopher Franz Brentano who turned his attention from mathematics to logic, having previously induced him to occupy himself with the work of the mathematician Bernard Bolzano. From there he might have travelled along a road similar to that taken by Russell, who had likewise at one stage been influenced by Brentano.[51] Instead Husserl chose a direction which led from a critique of Kant to a rationalism more extreme than that of Descartes. As he saw it, Kant had contented himself with a knowledge that was purely formal, whereas the true aim of philosophy could only be fulfilled if there was a completely rational science of all reality. Husserl accepted Kant's 'Copernican revolution' which had *inter alia* refuted the scepticism of Hume. But whereas Kant had in the end postulated an unaccountable 'X', the 'thing-in-itself', Husserl was determined to have done with what he termed "dualism". The entire essential content of reality was to be found in the phenomena themselves, that is to say, in consciousness. Husserl seems not to have made a thorough study of Hegel, whose critique of Kant anticipated his own. In consequence he never developed a subject–object dialectic. Instead he devoted his life's work to the task of demonstrating that reality could be grasped by locating the 'essence' of phenomena.[52]

This approach had far-reaching consequences. It led Husserl to develop a technique whereby existence is "screened out" so as to make it possible for the mind to grasp the pure essence of what is given in consciousness. All that merely happens to exist is simply left out of consideration, so as to achieve a purified awareness of the phenomenon present to the mind. The aim is to close the gap between subject and object. Phenomenology does not necessarily seek new knowledge, but rather a more profound awareness of the knowledge one already has. From there it was only a step to what Sartre and other French thinkers were later to describe as *"prise de conscience"*. Thus by an extraordinary turn-about Husserl's search for a scientific method of investigation more radical than that of Descartes landed his French followers in a different kind of Cartesianism – one that was both phenomenological and existential. Sartre's *Being and Nothingness* (1943) was in part a rejoinder to Heidegger's *Being and Time* (1927), first published under Husserl's auspices, at a time when the younger man had not yet emancipated himself from his teacher to the extent of giving full vent to his Romantic longings.[53]

The link between Phenomenology and Existentialism is supplied by the concept of 'being'. Since according to Husserl it is possible to know what being is independently of existence, a science of being is both possible and necessary. Husserl aimed at a strictly rational method which would turn philosophy into something as scientific as mathematics. Philosophy, on this interpretation, is the science that investigates the being which all the particular sciences take for granted. To a thinker whose first work had borne the title *Philosophy of Arithmetic* it seemed evident that true knowledge of reality is not to be found in a contingent world of things existing independently of consciousness, but in consciousness itself. As Husserl put it in the article he contributed to the *Encyclopaedia Britannica*:

Phenomenology denotes a new, descriptive, philosophical method which, since the concluding years of the last century, has established (1) an a priori psychological discipline, able to provide the only secure basis on which a strong empirical psychology can be built, and (2) a universal philosophy which can supply an organum for the methodical revision of all the sciences.

Towards the close of the article he proclaims:

Thus the antique conception of philosophy as the universal science, philosophy in the Platonic, philosophy in the Cartesian sense, that shall embrace all knowledge, is once more justly restored. . . . Phenomenology is not less than man's whole occupation with himself in the service of the universal reason. . . . Metaphysical, teleological, ethical problems, and problems of the history of philosophy, the problem of judgment, all significant problems in general, and the transcendental bonds uniting them, lie within phenomenology's capability.

These were large claims indeed, and to his pupils they appeared to have been validated, in part at least, by Husserl's successful battle against any merely psychological explanation of logical concepts. The positivists shrugged him off, but the Kantians did not. They were, after all, concerned with moral problems, and they had it on the authority of Wittgenstein's *Tractatus* that "when all possible scientific questions have been answered, the problems of life remain completely untouched". This did not necessarily incline them to accept Husserl's method, but it did facilitate the rise of what came to be known as Existentialism.

As a mode of thought, Existentialism properly so described goes back to Soren Kierkegaard (1813–55) who actually invented the term after breaking away from Hegel's system.[54] Kierkegaard's rejection of speculative metaphysics has, however, been more consequential for modern Protestant theologians than for philosophers such as Heidegger and Jaspers who took over some of his ideas without following him all the way. There are thus two different ways of looking at the phenomenon called Existentialism. One can treat it as a forerunner of post-1918 German Protestant theology, or alternatively as one strain within a system of thought that has its roots in German metaphysics, and indeed ultimately in Kant. Then there is the additional difficulty that whereas the core of Kierkegaard's thinking was Christian, Nietzsche – whom Karl Jaspers and others have regarded as another ancestor of Existentialism – was an avowed atheist. About the only thing they had in common was their opposition to systematic philosophy. Further, one has to face the improbable circumstance that there is a Marxist version of Existentialism, represented by Sartre (1905–) and by British thinkers who have come under his influence.[55] When it is added that the Jewish-born French Catholic mystic Simone Weil (1909–43) and the well-known French Catholic philosopher Gabriel Marcel (1889–) likewise had or have affinities with Existentialism, it begins to look as though the term is impossible to define. Nonetheless there is something common to them all, namely the insistence that the human situation is the proper subject of philosophy. The customary definition of the central concept, the statement that *existence precedes essence*, does not get one very far, since it is really relevant only to

Sartre's work of 1943 which preceded his conversion to Marxism. One may therefore just as well ignore it. On the other hand, one cannot ignore the fact that this way of thinking goes back to Kierkegaard's original revolt against Hegel.[56]

When Hegel and other philosophers (Kierkegaard argued) urged people to be 'objective', what they meant was that the individual should forget his own *Existenz* and concentrate on disembodied entities called 'essences'. Now we have seen that this was precisely what Husserl attempted to do, and we have also seen that Heidegger was at one time Husserl's disciple. One can get out of the difficulty by arguing that Heidegger broke with Husserl, and that Husserl for his part had no great faith in the value of the younger man's work, even before the advent of Hitler in 1933 caused an irreparable breach between them. But when one then turns to the other important German Existentialist thinker, Karl Jaspers (1883–), one finds that his philosophy is rooted in Kant and that in his *Reason and Anti-Reason in our Time* (1950, English translation 1952) he reacted against Sartre to the extent of preferring to have his own thinking described as a "philosophy of reason".[57] This had not always been his attitude. In his early *Psychologie der Weltanschauungen* ('Psychology of World-Views', 1919) he had bracketed Nietzsche and Kierkegaard, while twelve years later, in *Die geistige Situation der Zeit*, he defined Existentialism as a philosophy which does not cognize objects (Husserl's aim), but rather "elucidates and makes actual the being of the thinker". The Cartesian ideal of scientific philosophy was specifically rejected, as were (for other reasons) Darwin, Freud and Marx. Jaspers is in fact a rather old-fashioned thinker in the tradition of German Idealism. This may be the reason why his influence has not spread far beyond the German-speaking world.

Although committed to a variant of Existentialism, Jaspers rarely refers to Heidegger (1889–) whose background was one of training as a Jesuit seminarian, and whose early work (1915) dealt with the scholastic metaphysics of Duns Scotus. After passing through a phenomenological phase Heidegger published *Being and Time* (1927) which established him as a major influence in German academic life between the wars. Of this treatise it has been said with much truth that it can be read "as an attack upon the ontological assumptions which lie behind British empiricism, to which ... neo-Kantianism was closely allied".[58] Heidegger is concerned with "the problem of being" rather than "the problem of knowledge", even though in 1929 he made an impressive effort to come to grips with the latter (*Kant und das Problem der Metaphysik*). Ultimately he rejects both Kant and the empiricists on the ground that they demand the impossible, namely proof of the existence of an external world, as though an isolated subject were capable of asking for an answer to such questions. In reality, according to Heidegger, the characteristic feature of human existence is that it always finds itself as a "being-in-the-world". Man cannot step back and assume the attitude of a disinterested spectator. He does indeed stand in a peculiar relationship to the world, inasmuch as he is the only being who raises questions about Being as such. But these questions relate to *his* world, and more especially to the fact of his mortality. Man does not simply perceive: he 'cares' about the world as a bundle of things which relate to him in a practical fashion, helping or hindering him, and all the time involving him in relations with other men. On these grounds it has been suggested that Heidegger's way of thought has something in common with American pragmatism, notably as represented by John Dewey. It is certainly the case that Heidegger places a great deal of emphasis upon the fact that men must die, and the extraordinary lengths to which they go to conceal this truth from themselves. This line of thought descends from Kierkegaard and leads on to Sartre's quest for 'authentic' existence, that is to say, for a form of experience in which man confronts the truth about himself and the world. Heidegger also has a kind word for Marx, on the gounds that he had grasped the 'alienation' of modern man. "Because Marx, in experiencing alienation, descends into an important dimension of history, the Marxist view of history is superior to all others." This surprising observation occurs in a *Letter on Humanism* addressed to a French correspondent in 1947, and was evidently provoked by the post-war vogue of Sartre's philosophy, of which Heidegger was critical on other grounds. It marked a notable change from his earlier writings and lectures on Nietzsche between 1936 and 1946, but then Heidegger had always possessed an uncanny sense for what was topical.[59]

One reason why Heidegger in 1947 and later felt it necessary to differentiate himself from Sartre had to do with the latter's exposition of Existentialism in his own *Being and Nothingness* (1943). Sartre then laid all the stress on being-in-the-world to the exclusion of metaphysics. But Heidegger was not content to be ranked with Kierkegaard's and Nietzsche's followers. "My philosophical tendencies," he wrote in a letter to Jean Wahl, "cannot be classified as existentialist; the question which principally concerns me is not that of man's *Existenz*; it is Being in its totality and as such." This is indeed the case, notwithstanding his admiration for Nietzsche who had denounced the quest for Being as senseless. Then why is so much of Heidegger's *Being and Time* devoted to human existence? Because, he argues, man has – in a sense to which Plato drew attention – "a vague average understanding of Being".[60] Consequently, by studying human existence, the philosopher is led to Being, and likewise to Nothing, which latter Heidegger treats as the dialectical counterpart of Being. He maintains that this procedure is not traditional metaphysics or ontology, an affirmation which reads strangely, but which recurs in his later writings, where the poet acquires an authority as great as that of the philosopher. "Poetry is the establishment of Being by means of the word", and Parmenides rather than Plato is the model philosopher. Being can be glimpsed in poetry, while Nothing is experienced in Dread. These concepts are peculiar to Heidegger and constitute his originality as a thinker. They have no counterpart in Sartre, to whose philosophy we shall turn in Part Three of this study. For the moment let us conclude our survey of the inter-war period with a brief glance at German theology.

Liberal Protestantism in Germany was one of the casualties of the 1914–18 war.[61] This statement applies not only to 'official' theologians such as Adolf Harnack, but also to outsiders like Albert Schweitzer whose *Quest of the Historical Jesus* (1910) had already demolished the amiable notion of Jesus as a religious reformer.[62] Schweitzer's missionary activities in Africa, his "reverence for life" ethic, and his interest in Indian thought[63] subsequently gained him a large following in the English-speaking world, but in Germany the kind of theology he stood for increasingly lost ground after 1918 to the neo-orthodox challenge represented by Karl Barth and others. Schweitzer held to his position and as late as 1934 declared that Barth's courageous resistance to the 'Germanic Christianity' sponsored by the Hitler government showed his entire theological approach to have been mistaken: religion could not be divorced from ethics, and Barth's decision to defend it against the State demonstrated the impossibility of his earlier attempt to turn his back on the world.[64] In due course, Barth's own pupil, Dietrich Bonhoeffer (1906–45), was to reach similar conclusions when compelled by his conscience to take part in the anti-Hitler resistance movement.[65] But in the troubled years after 1918, when *Kulturprotestantismus* had disclosed its bankruptcy and the official Churches seemed to have nothing to say, Barth (1886–1968) won an important following among the more erudite with what became known as the 'Theology of Crisis'.[66] This was essentially an attempt to reaffirm the central tenets of Reformation faith in language adapted to the modern world, although unlike his erstwhile ally and subsequent critic Rudolf Bultmann (1884–), Barth resisted the temptation to employ the vocabulary of Existentialism.[67]

What Barth and Bultmann had in common – at any rate until Bultmann's subsequent attempt to 'de-mythologise' Christianity, which made its real impact only after the Second World War and was then popularized in the 1960s – was the conviction that the 'spirit of the age' had to be resisted. In its extreme form this belief was held only by Barth and his closest followers who had been stirred from their spiritual lethargy by Barth's fundamentalist *Commentary on Romans* (*Der*

Römerbrief) of 1918. A Swiss by birth, Barth was appointed successively to various German universities, and in 1934 he became one of the founders of the so-called Confessing Church whose celebrated Barmen Declaration of 1934 rejected the 'blood and soil' cult and the attempt to set up a 'German Christian' Church purified of all traces of Judaism. Bultmann, while as a German citizen inevitably less active in his opposition to the Hitler dictatorship than the Swiss Barth (who was forced out of Germany in 1935), likewise played an important part in the Confessing Church. The profound theological differences between the two men became a matter for public controversy after 1945, when Bultmann in a fashion reverted to liberalism, but in the 1920s and 1930s they formed a common front. The central issue, so far as they were concerned, was the absoluteness of the claim made by revealed religion. The human mind – for Barth at any rate – had access to God only by way of revelation. "He would not hear of 'Revelation *and* Reason, God's Grace *and* Man's activity'." [68] Rather it was a matter of "Either – Or". Kierkegaard had been right: the Protestant Church had been corrupted by worldliness, and as for Roman Catholicism, with its belief in natural theology and its reliance on Thomist metaphysics grounded in Aristotle, it was the enemy of true faith and always had been. Barth accepted much of what Kierkegaard and Dostoyevsky had had to say about historic Christianity. What was needed was a return to the prophetic teaching of the Bible and the early Reformers. In 1922 he published a second, drastically revised, edition of *Der Römerbrief*, thereby inaugurating what came to be called 'dialectical theology' or 'theology of crisis'. In 1932 the first volume of his immense *Kirchliche Dogmatik* saw the light, and a year later he plunged into the political activity which was to result in his expulsion from Germany and in a series of increasingly resolute calls on his part for resistance – armed resistance if necessary – to Hitler and all he stood for. [69]

The paradox of an other-worldliness leading to such a determined political stand was resolved by Barth in language derived from the Prophets and the early Reformers. He had always held that the real spiritual disaster of modern Protestantism in general, and German Protestantism in particular, was the pantheist confusion of God and man. In his eyes, the Hitlerite attempt to root out the Biblical faith and replace it by something called 'German Christendom' was only the final consequence of Romanticism in its peculiarly German setting. The rot had set in with Hegel and Schleiermacher, with the identification of God's Spirit and religious self-consciousness. No wonder Ludwig Feuerbach had drawn the conclusion that 'God' was but a projection of the human spirit, thereby inaugurating the Marxist faith! Barth – a Social Democrat by political conviction – was tolerant of Marxism as an offspring of German Idealism. National Socialism was another matter.

Unlike Communism it did not content itself with being atheist: it was a counter-religion, an appeal to the submerged pre-Christian pantheism of the German people, and as such a mortal threat to the Church, whereas Communism was not really to be taken seriously. This attitude exposed Barth to the charge of partiality, but it was grounded in theological convictions he had formed before the European civil war got under way. He reaffirmed his theologico-political stand at Amsterdam in 1948, when to the annoyance of many conservatives he refused to join the anti-Communist crusade. So far as he was concerned the main enemy was not in Moscow but in Rome – a position modified somewhat when the Second Vatican Council gave promise that the Roman Catholic Church might not be entirely beyond hope of gradual reformation.

Given his Biblical fundamentalism, Barth could not fail to be roused to opposition when his erstwhile ally Rudolf Bultmann in the 1940s developed the notion that the New Testament *kerygma*, or gospel message, was embedded in the mythological setting of ancient Jewish cosmology and Gnostic redemption hopes. Bultmann firmly maintained that for modern man the three-storied universe of heaven, earth and hell had become incredible. Moreover, there was nothing specifically Christian about it, so that it might just as well be jettisoned. The New Testament message had been expressed in the language of ancient mythology. The purpose of myth is to present man's understanding of himself in the world, and Christian myth is no exception – a conclusion for which Bultmann was indebted to Heidegger. All theological statements are to be understood as statements about human life, whence the relevance of Existentialism. Thus by a circuitous route Bultmann after 1945 rejoined the liberal tradition which in 1918 he had set out to destroy. From the Barthian standpoint he had relapsed into the ancient mistake of trying to make philosophy do the work of theology. To his followers in Germany, Britain and America he had opened the way to an interpretation of faith which made sense to modern man. In particular, his claim that the Existentialist analysis of man's being stood in a special relation to faith evoked an echo among students of philosophy and theology alike. In the face of this new heresy, Barth's fundamentalism had by the time of his death acquired a somewhat old-fashioned look, although there were those who maintained that Bultmann's rival approach must issue in subjectivism. The two men, allies in the struggle against the Third Reich and its neo-paganism, had become irreconcilable antagonists. By the 1960s it was possible for J.M.Robinson (*A New Quest for the Historical Jesus*, pp. 11 ff.) to say that "Germany is just as nearly 'Bultmannian' today as it was 'Barthian' a generation ago – and Bultmann's works and ideas have become Germany's dominant theological export throughout the world".

NOTES

1 John Passmore, *A Hundred Years of Philosophy* (London: Penguin Books, 1968; New York: Basic Books, 1966), pp. 367 ff. For Wittgenstein see Norman Malcolm, *Ludwig Wittgenstein* (London: Oxford University Press, 1958; New York: Oxford University Press, 1967), with a biographical sketch by Georg Henrik von Wright; also David Pears, *Ludwig Wittgenstein* (New York: The Viking Press, 1970); Justus Harnack, *Wittgenstein and Modern Philosophy*, tr. from the Danish original by Maurice Cranston (New York: Doubleday, 1965); G.E.M.Anscombe, *An Introduction to Wittgenstein's Tractatus* (London: Hutchinson, 1959 and 1967; New York: Humanities Press, 1970). The *Tractatus* was published in 1922 by Routledge & Kegan Paul in London, in a German–English parallel text with an introduction by Russell. In the previous year the German text had been published in the last issue of Ostwald's *Annalen der Naturphilosophie*. The fifth English impression, published by Routledge & Kegan Paul in 1951, contains a few corrections. Further light is shed on Wittgenstein's personality and his later development by Paul Engelmann, *Letters from Ludwig Wittgenstein: With a Memoir* (Oxford: Blackwell, 1967), and by C.A.Van Peursen, *Ludwig Wittgenstein: An Introduction to his Philosophy*, tr. from the Dutch by Rex Ambler (London: Faber & Faber, 1969). The study of the *Tractatus* is facilitated by consulting the *Notebooks 1914–16*, edited by G.H.von Wright and G.E.M. Anscombe (Oxford: Basil Blackwell; New York: Harper & Row, 1961); the preliminary studies for the *Philosophical Investigations* generally known as *The Blue and Brown Books* (Oxford: Blackwell, 1958; New York: Barnes & Noble, 28th ed., 1969); and the *Philosophical Investigations* themselves, tr. from the German by G.E.M.Anscombe and published in a German–English parallel text by Basil Blackwell (Oxford: 1953); see also Ludwig Wittgenstein, *Schriften*, published in two volumes by Suhrkamp (Frankfurt am Main) in 1960 and 1964. Vol. I contains the *Tractatus*, the *Tagebücher 1914–16* and the *Philosophische Untersuchungen*; vol. II is titled *Philosophische Bemerkungen: aus dem Nachlass herausgegeben von Rush Rhees*. For Wittgenstein's posthumously published studies in mathematics see his *Remarks on the Foundations of Mathematics*, tr. by G.E.M. Anscombe (Oxford: Blackwell, 1956). A compilation from notes taken by some of his students between 1938 and 1946 appeared in 1966 under the title *L. Wittgenstein: Lectures and Conversations on Aesthetics, Psychology and Religious Beliefs* (Oxford: Basil Blackwell; Berkeley, Calif.: University of California Press, 1967).

2 For details see Passmore, *op. cit.*, pp. 368 ff.; Ayer's essay was reprinted in a revised edition in 1946 (London: Gollancz); see also Ayer, *The Foundations of Empirical Knowledge* (London: Macmillan, 1940, 1947; New York: St Martin's Press, 1961) as well as the collection of essays titled *Logical Positivism* and edited by Ayer (London: Macmillan, 1959; Glencoe: The Free Press, 1959), with contributions by Russell, Schlick, Carnap and others. Ayer's *Philosophical Essays* (London: Macmillan; New York: St Martin's Press, 1954, 1965) appeared at a time when logical

positivism had run out of steam and the author had revised some of his earlier opinions. Popper's *Logic of Scientific Discovery* was translated into English in 1959 (London: Hutchinson; New York: Basic Books) and republished in a revised paperback edition in 1965 (New York: Harper & Row). Carnap's intellectual autobiography is available in P.A.Schilpp ed., *The Philosophy of Rudolf Carnap* (London: Cambridge University Press, 1964; Evanston and Chicago: Northwestern University, 1963). Reichenbach's later views are concisely summed up in his *The Rise of Scientific Philosophy* (Berkeley, Calif.: University of California Press, 1959).

3 For the citation from the *Tractatus* see p. 187 of the 1951 edition, para. 6.45. Strictly speaking it would have been more appropriate to translate the second part of the statement as follows: "The *sense* of the world as a finite whole is the mystical sense."

4 For the above see von Wright's biographical sketch in Norman Malcolm, *op. cit.*, and Justus Harnack, *op. cit.*, Introduction. There are some slight discrepancies; e.g., Harnack dates Wittgenstein's earliest stay in Cambridge from 1911 to 1913, whereas von Wright gives 1912–13 as the correct date.

5 For an elaboration of this point see in particular David Pears, *Ludwig Wittgenstein*, pp. 95 ff.

6 For Popper's exposition of his standpoint see *The Logic of Scientific Discovery*, pp. 78 ff. For a recent critique see Imre Lakatos, "Falsification and the Methodology of Scientific Research Programmes", in Lakatos and Musgrave ed., *Criticism and the Growth of Knowledge* (Cambridge and New York: Cambridge University Press, 1970).

7 *Tractatus*, para. 6.52, p. 187.

8 Passmore, *op. cit.*, p. 379.

9 *Ibid.*, p. 434.

10 See Gilbert Ryle, *The Concept of Mind* (London: Hutchinson; New York: Barnes & Noble, 1949); J.L.Austin, *How to do Things with Words* (Oxford: Clarendon Press; Cambridge, Mass.: Harvard University Press, 1962), and the same author's *Sense and Sensibilia* (Oxford: Clarendon Press, 1962; New York: Oxford University Press, 1964); P.F.Strawson, *The Bounds of Reason* (London: Methuen; New York: Barnes & Noble, 1966); Stuart Hampshire, *Thought and Action* (London: Chatto & Windus, 1959; New York: The Viking Press, 1960). For a critical dissection of the school see Ernest Gellner, *Words and Things* (London: Gollancz, 1959; Boston: Beacon Press, 1960). For a critique of scientism see Michael Polanyi, *Personal Knowledge* (London: Routledge & Kegan Paul; Chicago: University of Chicago Press, 1958).

11 For the fate of Polish philosophy between and after the two European wars of this century see Z.A.Jordan, *Philosophy and Ideology* (Dordrecht: D. Reidel, 1963; New York: Humanities Press, 1963). See also Henryk Skolimowski, *Polish Analytical Philosophy* (London: Routledge & Kegan Paul; New York: Humanities Press, 1967); Tadeusz Kotarbinski, *Gnosiology* (New York and London: Pergamon Press, 1968), and the same author's *Praxiology* (New York and London: Pergamon Press, 1967), the former dating back to 1929, the latter originally published in Polish

under a different title in 1955, during the post-Stalin 'thaw'. Polish
Marxism after 1945 is generally associated with the names of Adam
Schaff and Leszek Kolakowski, the latter of whom was obliged to emi-
grate in 1968. See Schaff, *A Philosophy of Man* (London: Lawrence and
Wishart, 1962) and the same author's *Einführung die Semantik* (Frankfurt:
Europäische Verlagsanstalt, 1969); for Kolakowski see *The Alienation of
Reason* (Garden City, N.Y.: Doubleday, 1968) and *Der Mensch ohne Alterna-
tive* (Munich: Piper, 1960).

12 V.I.Lenin, *Imperialism, the Highest Stage of Capitalism* in Lenin, *Selected
Works* (Moscow: Progress Publishers, 1967), vol. I, pp. 673 ff.; for Lenin's
Philosophical Notebooks – for the most part a conspectus of Hegel's *Logic*,
jotted down in 1914–15 and published from 1929–30 onward – see Lenin,
Collected Works, vol. 38 (Moscow: Foreign Languages Publishing House,
1961). N.Bukharin's rather wooden exposition of historical materialism
for beginners appeared in German under the title *Theorie des Historischen
Materialismus* (Hamburg: Verlag der Kommunistischen Internationale,
1922) and was subjected to a polite but deadly critical dissection by
Lukács in the *Archiv für die Geschichte des Sozialismus und der Arbeiterbewegung*
(Frankfurt, 1925). For Gramsci see John M. Cammett, *Antonio Gramsci and
the origins of Italian Communism* (Stanford, Calif.: Stanford University
Press, 1967). For the history of Russian Marxist philosophy before and
after the Revolution, see Gustav A.Wetter, *Dialectical Materialism* (London: Routledge & Kegan Paul; New York: Praeger Publishers, 1958);
first published in German by Herder Verlag (Vienna 1952) as *Der
Dialektische Materialismus*. For the general development of dialectical
materialism, from its original source in Engels to its codification in Soviet
thought, see Z.A.Jordan, *The Evolution of Dialectical Materialism* (London:
Macmillan; New York: St Martin's Press, 1967). See also Abram Deborin
and Nikolai Bukharin, *Kontroversen über dialektischen und mechanistischen
Materialismus* (Frankfurt: Suhrkamp, 1969).

13 K.Korsch, *Marxismus und Philosophie: zweite vermehrte Auflage* (Leipzig:
Hirschfeld, 1930); see also the same author's critical dissection of Kautsky,
Die Materialistische Geschichtsauffassung (Leipzig: Hirschfeld, 1929); cf.
Karl Korsch, *Marxism and Philosophy* (London: New Left Books, 1970).
For Lukács' heretical treatise of 1923 see *History and Class Consciousness*
(London: Merlin Press, 1971), and vol. 2 of the collected works published
in West Germany during the 1960s: *Georg Lukács Werke*, Frühschriften II
(1968). For the literature of Stalinism see Wetter, *passim*. There is no
need to refer to Stalin's 'philosophical' writings, not to mention those of
Mao Tse-tung, which possess the singular merit of having reduced Marxism to an intellectual level appropriate to the comprehension of Asian
peasants only recently emancipated from belief in ancient fertility cults.

14 *Anti-Dühring* (Moscow: Foreign Languages Publishing House, 1954), p.
195. This popular tract, originally published in book form in 1878, does
not carry the full authority of Marx who only contributed a chapter on
economics.

15 *Op. cit.* (The Hague: Mouton, 1968).

16 Korsch, *Marxism and Philosophy*, p. 45.

17 Borkenau, *Der Übergang vom feudalen zum bürgerlichen Weltbild* (Paris: Felix Alcan, 1934).

18 Korsch's most important publication during the years of emigration was his *Karl Marx* (London: Chapman & Hall, 1938; New York: Russell & Russell, 1963). Borkenau published a brief study of Pareto in 1936 (London: Chapman & Hall), a history of the Communist International in 1938 (London: Faber & Faber; New York: Norton, 1939), and thereafter a number of political writings centering upon the analysis and critique of totalitarianism. In the field of political science two important publications not strictly adhering to the doctrines of the original circle (since their author was a Social Democrat) are Franz Neumann's *Behemoth: The Structure and Practice of National Socialism* (London: Oxford University Press, 1946; New York: Oxford University Press, 1942, 1944) and the same author's essay collection *The Democratic and the Authoritarian State* (Glencoe: Free Press, 1957). Benjamin's critical essays, as well as his letters, were collected and published in the 1960s by Suhrkamp (Frankfurt) as were numerous writings by Adorno, culminating in his *Negative Dialektik* of 1966. For the evolution of Horkheimer's theoretical and political standpoint compare his contributions to the *Zeitschrift für Sozialforschung* in the 1930s (reprinted in two volumes under the title *Kritische Theorie* by the S. Fischer Verlag, Frankfurt, in 1968) with his later writings collected under the title *Zur Kritik der Instrumentellen Vernunft*, ed. A. Schmidt (Frankfurt: S. Fischer Verlag, 1967) and with his and Adorno's *Dialektik der Aufklärung* (Amsterdam: Querido, 1947; Frankfurt: S. Fischer, 1969). Marcuse's principal work, *Reason and Revolution*, a critical dissection of Hegel's philosophy, appeared in 1941 (New York: Oxford University Press) and was republished with a supplementary chapter in 1955 (London: Routledge & Kegan Paul). His later writings belong to the post-1945 period. An early work, *Hegels Ontologie und die Grundlegung einer Theorie der Geschichtlichkeit* (Frankfurt: Klostermann, 1932), reflects the influence of Heidegger.

19 See *Kritische Theorie*, vol. II, pp. 82 ff.

20 *Ibid.*, p. 124.

21 *Op. cit.*, 4th revised edition (London: Routledge & Kegan Paul, 1962).

22 Eugene Kamenka, *The Ethical Foundations of Marxism* (London: Routledge & Kegan Paul; New York; Praeger Publishers, 1962); see also the same author's *Marxism and Ethics* (London: Macmillan; New York: St Martin's Press, 1969).

23 First published in 1942; the latest available edition appeared in 1966 (London: Macmillan; New York: St Martin's Press).

24 First published by the University of Minnesota in 1938; McGraw-Hill paperback edition, 1964.

25 T.B.Bottomore, *Sociology* (London: Allen & Unwin; Englewood Cliffs, N.J.: Prentice Hall, 1962), *passim*; W.G.Runciman, *Social Science and Political Theory* (Cambridge: University Press; New York: Cambridge University Press, 1963), *passim*; Stanislaw Ossowski, *Class Structure in the Social Consciousness*, tr. from the Polish (London: Routledge & Kegan Paul; New York: Free Press, Macmillan, 1963), pp. 69 ff.

26 Principally associated with the later writings of Herbert Marcuse. The subject cannot be pursued here.

27 Karl Korsch, *Karl Marx*, p. 231; see also Korsch, *Marxism and Philosophy*, pp. 29 ff.; for a more systematic appraisal of Hegel's influence on Marx see Jordan, *The Evolution of Dialectical Materialism*, pp. 65 ff.

28 Marcuse, *op. cit.*, p. 102.

29 *Ibid.*, p. 168.

30 *Ibid.*, p. 258.

31 *Idem.*

32 *Ibid.*, p. 282.

33 For this and the following see Herbert Marcuse, *Soviet Marxism* (New York: Columbia University Press; London: Routledge & Kegan Paul, 1958), pp. 136 ff.

34 For Gramsci, apart from Cammett's biography, see in particular the French essay collection titled *A. Gramsci: Oeuvres choisies* (Paris: Editions Sociales, 1959); also Antonio Gramsci, *Lettres de la prison* (Paris: Editions Sociales, 1953). The *Studi Gramsciani* produced by the Gramsci Institute (Rome: Editori Riuniti, 1958) are intended for specialists, and the same applies to the *Collected Works* published by Einaudi.

35 For Gramsci's philosophy see in particular Gwyn A. Williams, "The Concept of 'Egemonia' in the Thought of Antonio Gramsci", *Journal of the History of Ideas* (New York), vol. XXI, No. 4, Oct.–Dec. 1960.

36 Gramsci, *Il materialismo storico e la filosofia di Benedetto Croce* (Einaudi, 1955), p. 18.

37 Passmore, *op. cit.*, p. 300. For a representative selection from the philosopher's work see the volume titled *Benedetto Croce, Filosofia-Poesia-Storia* (Milano–Napoli: Riccardo Ricciardi Editore, n.d.); Eng. tr. introduced by Cecil Sprigge, *Philosophy–Poetry–History: An Anthology of Essays by Benedetto Croce* (London–New York–Toronto: Oxford University Press, 1966). For a brief statement by Croce of his own position see "My Philosophy", translated as part of a collection of essays by E.F. Carritt (London: Allen & Unwin, 1949).

38 See Enrico del Mas, "Vico and Italian Thought" in *Giambattatista Vico: An International Symposium* (Baltimore: Johns Hopkins Press, 1969), pp. 147 ff., and Hayden F. White's essay in the same volume, pp. 379 ff.

39 See Carlo Antoni, *From History to Sociology* (London: Merlin Press, 1962; Detroit, Mich.: Wayne State University Press, 1959); tr. from the Italian *Dallo storicismo alla sociologia*, with a Foreword by Croce, written in 1940.

40 Later revised and incorporated in *Saggio sullo Hegel* (1913).

41 Published respectively in 1945 and 1946 (Oxford: Clarendon Press). The earlier works mentioned also appeared under the imprint of the Clarendon Press.

42 G.R.G. Mure, *An Introduction to Hegel* (Oxford: Clarendon Press; New York: Oxford University Press, 1940) and *A Study of Hegel's Logic* (Oxford: Clarendon Press, 1950; New York: Oxford University Press, 1950); see also the same author's *Retreat from Truth* (Oxford: Basil Blackwell; New York: Fernhill House, 1958).

43 Collingwood, *op. cit.*, pp. 189–90.

44 *Ibid.*, pp. 185-6.
45 *Ibid.*, pp. 146-7.
46 *Ibid.*, p. 61.
47 *Ibid.*, p. 15.
48 *Ibid.*, p. 163.
49 *Ibid.*, p. 233.
50 For a brief and lucid introduction to the topic see Joseph Quentin Lauer, *Phenomenology: Its Genesis and Prospects* (New York: Harper & Row, 1965); Husserl's mature standpoint is most clearly expressed in his *Cartesian Meditations*, tr. Dorion Cairns (The Hague: Martinus Nijhoff, 1960): originally published in French under the title *Méditations cartésiennes* (Paris: Colin, 1931) and re-edited in 1957 (Paris: Vrin). Not until 1950 did the Husserl Archives in Louvain bring out the German text, *Cartesianische Meditationen*, ed. S. Strasser (The Hague: Martinus Nijhoff), which is more complete than the French version. See also Husserl's important essay, "Philosophie als Strenge Wissenschaft", *Logos* I (1910-11). For this as well as the concluding stage of his thought see *Phenomenology and the Crisis of Philosophy* (New York and London: Harper & Row, 1965), an edition by Quentin Lauer of "Philosophy as Rigorous Science" (1911) and "Philosophy and the Crisis of European Man" (1935). The first two sections of Husserl's last great work made their appearance in the Belgrade review *Philosophia* in 1936, and the entire text was published in 1954 under its original German title, *Die Krisis der europäischen Wissenschaften und die transzendentale Phänomenologie* (The Hague: Martinus Nijhoff) as vol. VI of the *Husserliana* edited at Louvain. What Lauer translated was only the text of a lecture delivered in Vienna on 7 and 10 May 1935, and reproduced as an annex to the 1954 volume, pp. 314 ff.
51 See Bertrand Russell, *My Philosophical Development* (London: Allen & Unwin; New York: Simon and Schuster, 1959), p. 134.
52 Lauer, *Phenomenology*, pp. 20 ff., 46 ff.
53 Jean-Paul Sartre, *L'Être et le Néant* (Paris: Gallimard, 1943; Eng. trans. London: Methuen, 1957); Martin Heidegger, *Sein und Zeit*; first published in Husserl's *Jahrbuch für Phänomenologie und phänomenologische Forschung* in the spring of 1927; for a later edition see *Sein und Zeit* (Tübingen: Niemeyer, 1953).
54 *A Kierkegaard Anthology*, ed. Robert Bretall (London: Geoffrey Cumberledge, Oxford University Press, 1947; Princeton, N.J.: Princeton University Press, 1946); James Collins, *The Mind of Kierkegaard* (London: Secker & Warburg, 1954; Chicago: Henry Regnery Co., 1965); H.J.Blackham, *Six Existentialist Thinkers* (London: Routledge & Kegan Paul, 1952; New York: Humanities Press, 1952); John Passmore, *A Hundred Years of Philosophy* (London: Penguin Books, 1968; New York: Basic Books, 3rd ed., 1966) pp. 466 ff.; Theodor W.Adorno, *Kierkegaard* (Frankfurt a. M.: Suhrkamp, 1962).
55 M.Warnock, *Existentialist Ethics* (London: Macmillan; New York: St Martin's Press, 1967); E.W.F.Tomlin, *Simone Weil* (Cambridge: Bowes & Bowes; New York: Hillary House, 1954); Iris Murdoch, *Sartre: Romantic Rationalist* (Cambridge: Bowes & Bowes; New Haven, Conn.: Yale

University Press, 1953); Jean-Paul Sartre, *Existentialism and Humanism* (London: Methuen, 1948), tr. by Philip Mairet from the French original, *L'Existentialisme est un humanisme* (Paris: Les Editions Nagel, 1946).

56 See Alasdair MacIntyre, *Marxism and Christianity* (London: Gerald Duckworth, 1969; New York: Schocken Books, 1968); *Secularization and Moral Change* (London and New York: Oxford University Press, 1967).

57 Passmore, *op. cit.*, p. 475; for a full-scale discussion of Jaspers's work by a number of prominent writers see P.A.Schilpp ed., *The Philosophy of Karl Jaspers* (London: Cambridge University Press; New York: Tudor Publishing Co., 1957); Jaspers's major works, notably his *Philosophie* (3 vols 1932) and *Von der Wahrheit* (1947) have not been translated into English. His earlier essay *Die geistige Situation der Zeit* (1931) appeared in 1933 in an English translation under the title *Man in the Modern Age*. His *Der philosophische Glaube* (1948) was translated in 1949 as *The Perennial Scope of Philosophy*. For his views on Nietzsche and Kierkegaard see his *Nietzsche* (1936, English translation 1965).

58 Passmore, *op. cit.*, p. 477.

59 Heidegger's two-volume *Nietzsche* of 1961 had gradually been elaborated between 1936 and 1946 and was couched in language wholly congruent with the Nietzsche of *The Will to Power*, not to mention Heidegger's own Rectoral address at Freiburg in 1933, when he briefly but emphatically committed himself to the Third Reich. The "Letter on Humanism" was reprinted in Heidegger's *Platons Lehre von der Wahrheit* (Bern: Francke, 1947), pp. 53 ff. For a critical analysis of Heidegger's work see Karl Löwith, *Heidegger: Denker in dürftiger Zeit* (Göttingen: Vandenhoeck & Ruprecht, 1960).

60 Passmore, *op. cit.*, p. 484.

61 Andrew Landale Drummond, *German Protestantism Since Luther* (London: Epworth Press; Naperville, Ill.: Allenson, 1951), p. 151.

62 Originally published in German under the title *Von Reimarus zu Wrede* in 1906. For an assessment of Schweitzer's life and work see George Seaver, *Albert Schweitzer: The Man and His Mind* (London: Albert & Charles Black; New York: Harper & Row, 1947).

63 See his *Die Weltanschauung der indischen Denker* (Munich: C.H.Beck, 1935); tr. in 1936 as *Indian Thought and its Development*.

64 See his article "Religion in Modern Civilization", *The Christian Century* (New York), 21 and 28 November 1934.

65 Dietrich Bonhoeffer, *Widerstand und Ergebung*, ed. Eberhard Bethge (Munich: Chr. Kaiser Verlag, 1951).

66 For a brief exposition of Barth's standpoint see his *God in Action* (Edinburgh: T. & T.Clark, 1936). The multi-volume *Kirchliche Dogmatik* launched in 1932 constitutes his principal claim to eminence as a theologian. See also *Parrhesia: Karl Barth zum achtzigsten Geburtstag* (Zurich: EVZ-Verlag, 1966). Barth's *Die protestantische Theologie im 19. Jahrhundert* (Zurich: EVZ-Verlag, 1947) is perhaps the best introduction to his thought, as well as being a fascinating account of the subject.

67 For Bultmann see in particular the three-volume essay collection titled *Glauben und Verstehen* (Tübingen: J.C.B.Mohr, 1964–5); the two volume

essay collection *Kerygma und Mythos* (Hamburg: Evangelischer Verlag, 1951–2), and the 1955 Gifford Lectures published under the title *The Presence of Eternity* (New York: Harper & Row, 1957) with the sub-title *History and Eschatology*, under which title the lectures were published in Britain by the Edinburgh University Press. See also James M.Robinson and John B.Cobb Jr. eds., *The Later Heidegger and Theology* (New York: Harper & Row, 1963). For the earlier German discussion between Emil Brunner and Karl Barth see John Baillie ed., *Natural Theology* (London: Geoffrey Bles, 1946; Ann Arbor: University of Michigan Press, 1962). For the post-war debate between Barth and Bultmann see Karl Barth, *Rudolf Bultmann: Ein Versuch, ihn zu verstehen* (Zurich: Evangelischer Verlag, 1952).

68 Drummond, *op. cit.*, p. 155.
69 Karl Barth, *Eine Schweizer Stimme 1938–1945* (Zurich: Evangelischer Verlag, 1945).

PART THREE

CHAPTER 12

THE SECOND WORLD WAR 1939–45

A BLITZKRIEG IN POLAND AND FRANCE

The outbreak of war in September 1939 confirmed the prescience of Marshal Foch who in 1919 had observed of the Versailles settlement: "This is not peace. It is an armistice for twenty years."[1] More generally it confirmed the pessimistic view taken throughout the inter-war period, and more particularly after Hitler's coming to power in 1933, by the French authorities in regard to Germany's capacities and intentions. In this respect there was a substantial difference not merely between French and British public opinion, but also between the national leaders in both countries. For whereas the French political elite – notably the military establishment and the professional diplomats – from the start had few illusions about Hitler's intentions, their opposite numbers in Britain tended to believe that the German threat could be 'contained' by a suitable mixture of concessions and veiled threats. The British, with few exceptions, thought the Versailles settlement could and should be peacefully revised, whereas the French were convinced that its revision, once undertaken, would end by making Germany the paramount power in Europe. From 1934 onwards these considerations induced a succession of fundamentally conservative French governments to seek a rapprochement with the Soviet Union, in so far as such a policy was compatible with France's obligations to Poland. The prevailing British attitude in the mid-thirties was accurately portrayed by the eminent liberal historian H.A.L.Fisher, whose widely acclaimed *History of Europe*, published in 1936, had this to say about the Third Reich:

> The Hitler revolution is a sufficient guarantee that Russian Communism will not spread westward. The solid German *bourgeois* hold the central fortress of Europe.[2]

At bottom this was the view taken by all those who, in the common parlance of the time, favoured what was known as the policy of 'appeasement'. Stripped of its moralistic trappings this line of thought amounted to giving Germany a 'free hand' in Eastern Europe, while standing on the watch so as to guard the Low Countries and France. Those who pursued this course mistook Hitler for a conservative like themselves, a misunderstanding that underlay the Munich agreement and much besides. When in March 1939 it became impossible to disregard the fact that Germany aimed at European hegemony, it was still possible to believe that British and French guarantees to Poland and Rumania, plus vague negotiations with the Soviet Union, would give Hitler pause. The folly of this course was denounced in the spring and early summer of 1939 by Winston Churchill and the aged Lloyd George, but to no avail. Following the 'rape of Prague" on 15 March 1939, when German troops marched in and the truncated remnant of Czechoslovakia was turned into a German protectorate, the British government turned a somersault and (after a preliminary statement on 31 March) on 6 April signed an agreement with Poland guaranteeing that country's territorial integrity: an agreement Britain had no power to enforce. Chamberlain and his colleagues – principally Lord Halifax, Sir Samuel Hoare and Sir John Simon – went further. Following Mussolini's invasion of Albania on 7 April, they concluded treaties of mutual assistance with Rumania and Greece on 13 April, and with Turkey a month later. On 26 April the government, for the first time in British history, announced the introduction of conscription in peace time. Thus in a matter of weeks Britain had been committed to the defence of Poland, Rumania, Greece and Turkey against both Germany and Italy, with only two divisions available for dispatch to the Continent should the guarantee be invoked, and with a compulsory service system which could only produce a few further divisions at the end of twelve months. This was indeed "the very midsummer of madness" the phrase Chamberlain had employed to damn and bury the collective security system of the League in the summer of 1936, when there was a question of applying sanctions against Italy over the assault on Abyssinia. For in the absence of a military alliance with Russia all these undertakings were worthless, a circumstance to which both Lloyd George and Churchill, as well as the Labour leaders Arthur Greenwood and Hugh Dalton, drew attention in the Commons debate of 3 April on the proposed guarantee to Poland.[3] On the same day Hitler instructed his generals to prepare to invade Poland on 1 September, and on 28 April he publicly denounced both the Anglo-German naval treaty of 18 June 1935, and his own 1934 non-aggression pact with Poland. He went on to demand the return of Danzig to the *Reich*, as well as a route and railway line through the Polish corridor. In itself these requests were more reasonable than the forcible *Anschluss* with Austria or the so-called 'return' of the Sudetenland, for which no justification existed either in history or in the principle of self-determination. The trouble was that by 1939 no one in Europe believed any longer that Hitler would content himself with the revision of the Versailles settlement. It was becoming plain that he was bent on military hegemony, and it was precisely this growing awareness which (as noted in an earlier chapter) induced Stalin and Molotov to conclude a pact with him on 23 August, in preference to an alliance with the Western democracies.

The possibility of such a realignment had become apparent since 3 May, when an official communiqué in Moscow announced that Maxim Litvinov (a Jew and as such unacceptable to Hitler, as well as being a believer in 'collective security') had been relieved from the office of Foreign Commissar and replaced by Vyacheslav Molotov, Stalin's closest collaborator. Molotov promptly embarked upon a policy of coming to an arrangement with Germany at the expense of Poland. The French (but not the British) realized this at once. On 7 May the French Ambassador in Berlin notified Paris that his secret informants had told him a new partition of Poland would be the basis of a Russo-German alliance.[4] Yet the Soviet government kept its options open until the last, and the decision to conclude a pact with Germany was taken only on 19 August, after months of fruitless discussions with the Western Powers had shown beyond doubt that they were either unable or unwilling to coerce Poland into an alliance with Russia. Three years later, in the course of a memorable conversation between Churchill and Stalin in the Kremlin, the Soviet dictator presented his version of what had occurred at the time. On this subject it is simplest to let Churchill speak:

At the Kremlin in August, 1942, Stalin, in the early hours of the morning, gave me one aspect of the Soviet position. "We formed the impression", said Stalin, "that the British and French Governments were not resolved to go to war if Poland were attacked, but that they hoped the diplomatic line-up of Britain, France and Russia would deter Hitler. We were sure it would not." "How many divisions", Stalin had asked, "will France send against Germany on mobilisation?" The answer was: "About a hundred." He then asked: "How many will England send?" The answer was : "Two and two more later." "Ah, two and two more later", Stalin had repeated. "Do you know", he asked, "how many divisions we shall have to put on the Russian front if we go to war with Germany," There was a pause. "More than three hundred." I was not told with whom this conversation took place or its date. It must be recognised that this was solid ground. . . . It was judged necessary by Stalin and Molotov for bargaining purposes to conceal their true intentions till the last possible moment. Remarkable skill in duplicity was shown by Molotov and his subordinates in all their contacts with both sides. . . .[5]

This description of what took place in 1939 would have gained in plausibility had Stalin added that the Soviet–German non-aggression pact signed by Molotov and Ribbentrop on 23 August, and thereafter solemnly toasted by Stalin ("I know how much the German nation loves its Führer, I should therefore like to drink to his health") included not only a demarcation line for the partition of Poland, but also a recognition on Germany's part that Finland, Latvia and Estonia (but not Lithuania) fell within the Soviet sphere of interest. This was more than the Western Powers could have granted, even had the Polish government been less determined not to tolerate Russian troops on its soil in the guise of allies. Finland and the Baltic States, not to mention Poland, had been created in 1919–20 as a *cordon sanitaire* to keep the Bolshevik infection out of Europe. The Soviet proposals endlessly debated in London and Paris between April and August 1939 amounted to this: the Russians wanted all these States to be guaranteed against Germany, whether their governments desired such a guarantee or not. This involved the passage of Soviet troops through their territory in case of war, and the near-certainty that these troops would never leave. The British and French were caught in the logic of their diplomacy. Having sold Czechoslovakia to Germany and then decided to save Poland, they were unwilling to sell the Baltic States to Russia; but the Russians were determined to have control of the Baltic, and subsequently fought a war with Finland in the winter of 1939–40 to achieve this aim. Hitler for his part saw no incompatibility between his tactical bargain with Stalin and the German–Italian military alliance (grandiosely described as the "Pact of Steel") of 22 May 1939, whereby Italy became Germany's partner (albeit Mussolini inserted a secret clause to the effect that no major war was to be undertaken by Italy before 1943). Hitler was confident that the decadent democracies would back down. When neither they nor the Poles obliged, he launched his assault against Poland on 1 September, thereby provoking the Anglo-French declaration of war delivered on 3 September. This did not greatly disconcert him, although it annoyed him. He was convinced that the Western Powers, having saved their honour, would return to the conference table once Poland had been crushed. Given their previous record it was not an unreasonable assumption.

Other currents had for months been steadily flowing in the same direction. The Spanish civil war, which had been going on since July 1936, virtually terminated in January 1939, when the Republican front in Catalonia collapsed and Barcelona fell to the Nationalists. Half a million refugees poured across the French frontier during the weeks that followed, half of them civilians, the others survivors of the beaten Republican forces. Thereafter, the surrender of Madrid in March was a foregone conclusion, although heavy fighting continued to the end, as did the massacre of prisoners by Franco's forces. In early January the Italian Foreign Minister, Ciano, noting that the only danger was a last-minute French intervention, had instructed his Ambassador in

London to state that such an event would bring 'regular' Italian divisions to Spain.[6] With the British Cabinet still pursuing its appeasement policy (on 12 January Halifax suggested to Ciano, on the occasion of a visit to Rome in Chamberlain's company, that he hoped Franco would "settle the Spanish question"), there was little danger of the French government doing more than allowing some arms to reach Catalonia, and when this occurred a few days later, Republican resistance had already collapsed. Léon Blum's criticism of the Daladier government for not doing more could have applied to his own government of 1936–7, which had substantially adhered to the British formula of 'non-intervention' – a fiction so far as Italy and Germany were concerned. The dramatic collapse of the Spanish Republic between January and March 1939 showed the Western democracies at their worst: the British government welcoming Franco's victory, the French wringing their hands and herding the refugees into makeshift camps, where thousands (including the poet Antonio Machado) died of injuries and neglect. The official recognition of Franco by Britain and France occurred on 27 February, with Anthony Eden supporting the Chamberlain government in the ensuing Commons debate, on the grounds that to delay recognition might prolong the war.[7] Churchill absented himself. He did not favour Franco's cause, but could not bring himself to make a public stand on behalf of a Spanish Republican regime which by then was effectively run by the Communists. By 31 March it was all over and Franco was able to acknowledge a telegram of congratulation from the new Pope, Pius XII: "Lifting up our hearts we give sincere thanks with your excellency for Spain's Catholic victory." The former Papal Secretary of State, Pacelli, had become Pope four weeks earlier, on 3 March, and at the suggestion of the German Cardinals in Rome had addressed the first of the customary notifications to Hitler, with whom he hoped to establish good terms. Here were the Papal divisions whose supposed non-existence provoked Stalin's ignorant scorn in 1945. Pacelli's predecessor, Pius XI, had towards the end of his life become disenchanted with Hitler, notwithstanding the Concordat of July 1933 which guaranteed the status of Catholic schools – the only thing that mattered to the German hierarchy, which had thereupon entered into a wholehearted alliance with the Third Reich. Pius XII was determined to relax the tension between State and Church which had made itself felt in 1937 as a consequence of the National Socialist war of attrition against the confessional schools. He could point to the fact that the German and Austrian bishops had faithfully applauded Hitler's every move in foreign policy – culminating in the abject surrender of the Austrian hierarchy after the *Anschluss* of March 1938. On that occasion Cardinal Innitzer, archbishop of Vienna, had visited Hitler, whereupon the Catholic episcopate of Austria issued a widely publicized statement (largely drafted by Hitler's underlings) asking the faithful to approve the union with Germany.[8] Now the victorious conclusion of the Spanish civil war sealed the alliance between Fascism and Catholicism, which had been the basis of Mussolini's rule for many years and which Hitler had been able to take for granted ever since the Catholic Centre Party, on 24 March 1933, voted in the Reichstag for the Enabling Act conferring dictatorial powers upon the Reich Cabinet – in other words, upon Hitler and his chosen colleagues.[9]

These undercurrents were not extraneous to the British government's 'appeasement' policy, which throughout had rested upon the assumption that Hitler could be won over to a respectable kind of conservative anti-Communism. "Germany is the bulwark of the West against Bolshevism", Hitler had declared in an interview with the foreign press in November 1935.[10] The bulwark looked odd in September 1939, when the German forces, in alliance with Bolshevik Russia, assaulted Catholic Poland. Hence the violent revulsion of the British Tories, from Chamberlain and Halifax downward, against the policy they had obstinately pursued for years. The French, having fewer illusions to lose, were less shocked, but no less determined to come to Poland's assistance: all except the Communists who, after 23 August 1939, obediently forgot their anti-Fascist declamations and denounced the Anglo-French declaration of war as an imperialist crime. They were to turn an even bigger somersault on 22 June 1941 when Hitler invaded their spiritual fatherland. For the time being their energies were devoted to the task of representing the Molotov–Ribbentrop pact as an attempt to preserve peace in the face of Anglo-French warmongering, and the carve-up of Poland as a triumph for socialism. Their task would have been eased had they been allowed to carry on the struggle against Fascism, while excusing Stalin's tactical manoeuvre as a reluctant concession to *Realpolitik*. But no such permission was granted by Moscow to its followers: they had to swallow whole the Soviet–German agreement and make themselves and others believe in its 'progressive' character. Anything short of such sophistry was viewed as betrayal by Stalin and his associates; those Communists, in Czechoslovakia and elsewhere, who in 1939 dared to question the official line were duly liquidated by the Soviet secret police and its helpers in the bloody post-war purges in conquered Eastern Europe after 1948.

The Polish campaign of 1939 proved a political turning-point, in that it induced the British and French governments to declare war on Germany. In so doing they fulfilled their recent obligations, but it would be a mistake to infer that this outcome had been visible from the start of Hitler's assumption of power in 1933. The Polish government in those days was guided by fear of Germany's resurgence leading to a European four-power directorate composed of Germany, Britain,

France and Italy. This would have displaced Poland as France's principal ally. The other possibility was a Russo-German war fought on Polish territory. It was therefore largely on Polish initiative that in January 1934 a ten-year non-aggression pact had been negotiated between Germany and Poland.[11] At the time of the Munich 'agreement' of 30 September 1938, the Polish government promptly demanded and obtained the handing over of the Czech frontier district of Teschen.[12] Pilsudski's successors in Warsaw, animated by the vain and foolish Foreign Minister, Colonel Beck, were not without hope of being able to tear a large chunk of territory out of Russia, assuming that Hitler was prepared to treat them as allies in his anti-Bolshevik crusade. These hopes were dashed when he tore up the German–Polish treaty of 1934, giving as his reason the recent Anglo-Polish guarantee. Thereafter the Poles had to rely once more on the Western Powers coming to their aid, an expectation which was due to be disappointed. While the German *Blitzkrieg* of September 1939 destroyed the Polish forces in less than three weeks, and the Russians came in on 17 September to claim their share of the loot, Britain and France did precisely nothing. The French gave as excuse that they needed more time for their mobilization, the British that their air force was not ready. Both had expected the Polish campaign to go on for at least six months, and so had the Polish military leaders upon whose advice they relied. Churchill, drawing what comfort he could from a very awkward situation, stuck to his post at the Admiralty, to which he had gone on the outbreak of war, and for the rest found consolation in the thought that Russia and Germany now faced each other directly over the corpse of Poland. In a paper written for the War Cabinet on 25 September he struck what he himself in his memoirs described as a cool note:

Although the Russians were guilty of the grossest bad faith in the recent negotiations, their demand made by Marshal Voroshilov that Russian armies should occupy Vilna and Lemberg if they were to be allies of Poland, was a perfectly valid military request. It was rejected by Poland on grounds which, though natural, can now be seen to have been insufficient. In the result Russia has occupied the same line and positions as the enemy of Poland, which possibly she might have occupied as a very doubtful and suspected friend. The difference in fact is not so great as it might seem. The Russians have mobilised very large forces and have shown themselves able to advance fast and far from their pre-war positions. They are now limitrophe with Germany, and it is quite impossible for Germany to denude the eastern front. A large German army must be left to watch it. . . . An eastern front is therefore potentially in existence.[13]

This assessment was accurate so far as it went, but as time went on it became evident that the Germans were able to concentrate increasingly large forces in the West. On the outbreak of war they had only forty-two divisions along the entire front from Aix-la-Chapelle to the Swiss border facing seventy French divisions which remained virtually motionless, the French General Staff having decided to adopt a defensive posture and await the expected German move through Belgium. By 10 May, when the storm burst over Holland, Belgium and France alike, the Germans had assembled a total of 155 divisions, ten of them armoured, and 126 were available for the onslaught in the West. Opposite Russia, according to General Halder, the German Chief of Staff, there was "no more than a light covering force, scarcely fit for collecting customs duties".[14] Moreover, in the interval the Russians had obtained a new frontier with Finland as a result of the 'winter war' fought between December 1939 and March 1940; while the Germans had overrun Denmark and Norway, in the process beating off a feeble and badly conducted Anglo-French countermove. This gave Hitler control of the Norwegian coastline and unhindered access to the Swedish iron ore on which a large part of the German war effort depended.[15] In consequence of these comparatively minor disasters, the Chamberlain government resigned on 10 May, and Churchill, the day following, formed a new administration, including the Labour and Liberal Parties alongside the Conservatives, on whose behalf Chamberlain and Halifax continued to sit in the Inner Cabinet, while Eden went to the War Office. Churchill himself became Minister of Defence as well as Prime Minister. His immediate task was to deal with the catastrophe that had befallen the Allies in France and Belgium.

The Polish campaign of 1939 had already made plain the decisive role of armour in the new kind of mobile warfare, especially when combined with dive-bombing. The new strategy had been worked out in the 1930s by the Generals of the *Reichswehr*, and on the French side by Colonel de Gaulle, although he did not give due weight to the crucial role of the dive-bomber. In London a few tank enthusiasts, spurred on by Captain B.H.Liddell Hart, had done what they could to introduce these ideas, but in May 1940 Britain, the birthplace of the tank, had only just completed the formation of her first armoured division (328 tanks), which was still in England when the storm burst. There were ten British divisions in France, but none of them were armoured in the modern sense, although they had some tanks. The French had ninety-four divisions, six of them mechanized, but of their total deployment of 2,300 tanks (most of them light) about half were held in dispersed battalions for cooperation with the infantry. The ten Dutch divisions laid down their arms when their government capitulated on 15 May, and the twenty Belgian divisions followed suit on 27 May, when King Leopold ordered them to cease fire. The German assault was spearheaded by ten *Panzer* divisions comprising nearly 3,000 armoured vehicles, of which at least a third were heavy tanks. The Germans also had control of the air, their fighter aircraft being superior to the French in numbers and quality, while on the British side about half the total fighter strength, including the most modern aircraft, were kept in England as a strategic reserve. Neither the British nor the French had equipped themselves with dive-bombers, which in May–June 1940 played an important role in demoralizing the French infantry. Moreover, their strategic dispositions were awkward. Belgium being neutral, it was not judged possible to enter Belgian territory until requested to do so by the government in Brussels. The construction by the British armies of an anti-tank ditch along their sector of the Franco-Belgian frontier was the only measure open to them, while the French failed to construct strong defences along the Meuse river, in the gap between the northern end of the heavily fortified Maginot Line and the beginning of the British front. Marshal Pétain and the other French military leaders had laid it down before the war that the Ardennes sector could not be rapidly traversed and that in consequence there was no danger of a German break-through at this dangerous spot, from which a short road led to Paris. In fact the German Army Command had planned a massive armoured onrush through the Ardennes, so as to sever the Allied armies as they moved forward into Belgium after 10 May. To cap everything the French High Command possessed no strategic reserve, a circumstance disclosed to Churchill by their Commander-in-Chief, General Gamelin, on 16 May, when a meeting of British and French political and military leaders took place in Paris to consider the situation created by the German armoured break-through at Sedan and along the Meuse. The French Prime Minister, M. Paul Reynaud, had already given up the battle for lost, although he was determined to continue the war from North Africa: a decision subsequently overruled by his colleagues under pressure from Pétain and Weygand, Gamelin's successor. Now the French military leaders informed their British colleagues that all their plans had collapsed. The Maginot Line, with its massive underground forts, had been turned by a flanking movement; the Anglo-French armies in Belgium had been severed from the rest and faced destruction; and the remainder of the French army was shattered and demoralized. It was the reckoning after years of cowardly and imbecilic political leadership – years when an ultimatum would have been sufficient to make the Germans withdraw from the Rhineland, or even to overthrow Hitler with the help of the German Army leaders who distrusted his judgement. Now he had triumphed all along the line, and there was no longer the smallest chance of rousing an effective opposition against him in Germany. The question was rather whether Britain might not be obliged to follow the French example and sue for peace terms.[16]

In his history of the war, Churchill devotes some of his most effective rhetoric to this momentous turn of events:

Within three weeks the long-famed French Army was to collapse in rout and ruin, and our only British army to be hurled into the sea with all its equipment lost. Within six weeks we were to find ourselves alone, almost disarmed, with triumphant Germany and Italy at our throats, with the whole of Europe open to Hitler's power, and Japan glowering at the other side of the globe.[17]

He goes on to draw up an account of the losses suffered then and subsequently by the British Empire throughout the six years of war that ended in September 1945:

The British total dead, and missing, presumed dead, of the armed forces amounted to 303,240, to which should be added over 109,000 from the Dominions, India, and the Colonies, a total of over 412,240. This figure does not include 60,500 civilians killed in the air raids on the United Kingdom, nor the losses of our Merchant Navy and fishermen, which amounted to about 30,000. Against this figure the United States mourn the deaths in the Army and Air Force, the Navy, Marines and Coastguard, of 322,188.[18]

British losses were in fact substantially less than during the First World War, due to the avoidance of battles on the scale of the Somme or Flanders in 1916–17. The French, who lost a million and a half killed in 1914–18, got off far more lightly in 1940, although they paid for defeat with the occupation of their country and the drafting of hundreds of thousands of prisoners to do forced labour in Germany under inhuman conditions. More important from the standpoint of the French political and military elites, France's prestige was gone. That some of it was subsequently recovered was due to the resistance movement which formed itself spontaneously after the conclusion of the Franco-German armistice late in June: a movement of which Brigadier (as he then was) Charles de Gaulle became the external symbol, since as Reynaud's Under-Secretary for War he was the only Frenchman holding both political and military rank around whom the 'Free French' movement could rally, once he had reached London on 18 June and set up headquarters on British soil.[19]

During the brief campaign in May preceding the hurried embarcation of the British expeditionary force at Dunkirk, he had distinguished himself at the head of one of the French armoured divisions. Now he was suddenly called upon to shoulder political responsibilities, the Pétain government formed after Reynaud's resignation on 16 June having decided to surrender. There was some historic justice in Pétain at the age of eighty-four being thrust into the role of chief capitulator, for during the inter-war period he had borne the heaviest responsibility for the fatal decision then taken to rely on the fortified Maginot Line constructed in the 1930s. While political nonentities like Albert Sarraut and Édouard Daladier presided over phantom administrations, Pétain employed his prestige as the 'victor of Verdun' (in 1916) for the purpose of preventing the modernization of the French Army. He was not even consistent in stressing fortification. In 1934, as Minister for War in the short-lived Doumergue government, he told the Army committee of the Senate that it was unnecessary to extend the Maginot Line from the Luxembourg frontier to the Channel, since with a few destructions the Ardennes could be made impassable, while to defend the northern frontier "one must go into Belgium", which turned out to be impossible for political reasons. In May–June 1940 the French paid for this kind of wisdom. Since they lost 120,000 men in dead alone, it is wrong to say that they did not fight; what is undeniable is that their generals were as incompetent as their politicians. In the circumstances one could not expect high morale on the part of the ordinary soldier. The nation had for years been fed on myths, the chief of them being the supposed impregnability of its defences. When the *Luftwaffe* and the *Panzer* corps made their appearance on the Meuse, the result was a general panic culminating in the exodus of millions of civilians. Moreover, what to the British was the 'miracle of Dunkirk' – the successful extrication of their army between 28 May and 4 June – to the French looked like 'desertion': an argument of which Laval, Flandin and the other seedy politicians around Pétain made full use in the years that followed. The British, it was suggested, were ready to fight to the last Frenchman. This propaganda line had originally been suggested by Goebbels during the 'phoney war' winter of 1939–40. It was now taken up by his French opposite numbers. In the circumstances the resistance movement could at the outset only be the cause of a small minority. Years of German occupation had to pass before it was joined by masses of Frenchmen, civilian and military, who had gradually lost their faith in the aged victor of Verdun.

Those leaders who had given a good account of themselves during the brief but bitter campaign – de Gaulle at Abbeville, de Lattre de Tassigny at Rethel – were marked out as future chiefs of the resistance, but of them all only de Gaulle possessed political as well as military talent. Churchill had taken note of him during the general collapse in June, when alone among Reynaud's military advisers he preserved an air of unruffled calm.[20] Some hopes were briefly built on Admiral Darlan, who on 12 June solemnly promised Churchill that the French Fleet would never come under German control. The Admiral's subsequent behaviour was decidedly equivocal. At one moment, on 17 June, he appeared ready to order the Fleet to make for Britain or North Africa. The next day he changed his mind, having meantime become Pétain's

Minister of Marine. His assassination in Algiers, in December 1942, removed Pétain's principal subordinate and the chief of all those who believed that the wisest course lay in letting the Germans exhaust their energies in Russia.

Churchill and de Gaulle having emerged in 1945 from the great trial as leaders of their respective nations, it is tempting to suppose that they must have been right in all their pre-war forecasts. The temptation has to be resisted. When de Gaulle in 1934 published his celebrated tract on modern warfare, *Vers l'armée de métier*,[21] he correctly foresaw the central significance of mechanization ("the professional army will move entirely on caterpillar wheels"), but he missed the point about close coordination between armoured forces and air power. Churchill for his part erred in overrating the strength of the German Air Force and in believing that it was designed to bomb Germany's opponents into surrender. The *Luftwaffe* was not as strong as he made out in his warning speeches from 1933 onwards (like many others he was taken in by Hitler's boasts), and it was not designed for bombing cities but for supporting the ground forces.[22] It had originally been conceived as a tactical weapon, not as a strategic force in total war against enemy populations. This was lucky for Britain, for when matters were put to the test in 1940, Göring was unable to make good his promise to Hitler to bomb London into defeat and chaos. It was the British, not the Germans, who thereafter systematically employed the giant bomber as a strategic weapon against enemy cities, although there was no lack of ruthlessness on the German side, merely lack of power. Churchill's misjudgements in this sphere were to have unfortunate consequences, culminating in the disastrous and wholly unnecessary destruction of Dresden in February 1945, when the war was already as good as won. But these errors pale in comparison with Hitler's belief that the British would make peace once France had been knocked out; or that the Russian Army would not fight; or that America would stay out of the war. In the long run it was Hitler's dictatorial power that made the German catastrophe inevitable. His advisers dared not contradict him, and the hold he had gained over the mass of the people made it certain that the war would be fought out to the bitter end. In military terms he was well prepared: from March 1933 to March 1939 the Third Reich spent about half as much again on armaments as Britain and France put together.[23] But the strategy of the *Blitzkrieg* could only work if the war was not protracted. In the end, Russia's successful resistance and America's belated entry in 1941 combined to produce a set of circumstances which made Germany's defeat in 1945 far more overwhelming than the narrowly fought decision in 1918.

B BRITAIN AT BAY

The scene over which Churchill had come to preside in the summer of 1940 was of a kind to evoke fitting historical parallels from a Prime Minister who had written a biography of his distant ancestor John Churchill, better known as Marlborough.[24] Britain stood alone and the entire European Continent lay open to the enemy. The War Cabinet, as formally constituted on 11 May, consisted of Churchill, Chamberlain, Halifax, C.R.Attlee and Arthur Greenwood, the last two representing the Labour Party. These five men were (as Churchill put it in his memoirs years later) "the only ones who had the right to have their heads cut off on Tower Hill if we did not win".[25] The Shakespearean language of this passage fails to convey an adequate sense of the fact that, viewed from Berlin, the British War Cabinet did not look very formidable. Chamberlain and Halifax after all had entered the struggle only with the greatest reluctance, and the Labour leaders had to reckon with pacifist sentiments in their party: not to mention Communist propaganda designed to represent any war as 'imperialist' unless it happened to threaten the safety of the Soviet Empire. For the rest, the aged Lloyd George was widely believed to hold defeatist views which might well have catapulted him into a role not unlike that of Pétain, had the Germans been able to break Britain's resistance. In his memoirs Churchill conveys the impression that the government was wholly united in its pursuit of resistance to Hitler and indifferent to his peace offers. This does not quite tally with the documentary evidence since made available. The records show Chamberlain and Halifax in late May 1940 urging their colleagues to seek peace terms from Hitler via Mussolini, before the latter had taken the plunge on 10 June and stabbed France in the back. They were outvoted by Churchill and his two Labour colleagues.[26] Thus the decision to fight on was taken by an extremely narrow margin. However, Chamberlain was stricken with cancer in August and died on 9 November, while Halifax was got rid of in December by being sent as Ambassador to Washington, where he could not do much harm, President Roosevelt and his principal associates being strongly committed to the British cause. His departure made it possible to shift Eden back to his old place at the Foreign Office, from which he had resigned in February 1938, in protest against Chamberlain's habit of directing foreign policy over the head, or behind the back, of the Foreign Secretary. The War Cabinet was strengthened when in August–September 1940 it was joined by Lord Beaverbrook (then in charge of aircraft production) and Ernest Bevin, greatest of British trade union leaders. Only from that time onwards could the country be said to have a political leadership adequate to its task and wholly determined to fight the war to a finish.[27]

These important events were preceded by the rather unreal project of a formal Anglo-French Union. A solemn declaration to this effect was hurriedly drafted on 14–15 June by some eminent British and French personalities, including Sir Robert Vansittart, General de Gaulle and M. Jean Monnet; endorsed the following day by the War Cabinet; and telephoned through to Bordeaux, where the French Council of Ministers was in session. The majority of its members promptly rejected it, abandoned Reynaud and rallied to Pétain. A Declaration of Union having been proposed and flatly rejected, Churchill felt free to give orders for all French naval vessels to be taken over or – as in the case of the French squadron at Oran on 3 July – attacked and sunk or damaged by the British Fleet on hand in the Western Mediterranean. De Gaulle, who made a stirring broadcast appeal from London on 18 June, thus had to launch his movement under the double handicap of being on British soil and obliged to support a deadly stroke against his country's navy. He never faltered, just as he had previously supported Churchill's refusal to send what remained of the British fighter squardons to France, when Monnet made an impassioned plea to this effect on 16 June.[28] Churchill on that occasion found himself confirmed in his earlier impression of de Gaulle, "Here is the Constable of France." He never managed to convey this certitude to Roosevelt, who from a mixture of ignorance and petty spite persisted throughout the war years in treating de Gaulle as a megalomaniac and an obstacle to Anglo-American strategy. It is true that, unlike the various Pétainists whom the Americans tried to recruit between 1940 and 1943, de Gaulle was not disposed to take orders from either Churchill or Roosevelt. This made him a difficult partner, but it also preserved the morale of his followers, and eventually it induced the internal resistance movement in France to accept him as their political leader.[29]

Others also during these troubled months behaved in accordance with their habits. Molotov, on being formally notified by the German Ambassador in Moscow on 10 May of the onslaught on France and the Low Countries, told Schulenburg that he quite understood: "Germany had to protect herself against Anglo-French attack". On 18 June, when France had virtually surrendered, Schulenburg reported to Hitler: "Molotov summoned me this evening to his office and expressed the warmest congratulations of the Soviet Government on the splendid success of the German Armed Forces."[30] Nor was this merely the small change of conventional diplomacy. As soon as the Germans had installed themselves in Paris they were approached by the leaders of the French Communist Party (then underground for obvious reasons) with a proposal for having the Communist daily *l'Humanité* legally published: the obvious implication being that it would contain nothing objectionable from the German standpoint. The offer was declined, whereupon the

French CP issued a tract which cast the responsibility for France's defeat on the handful of leaders who had remained true to the Jacobin tradition of patriotism; former Communist deputies offered to testify against Blum, Daladier, Reynaud and Mandel at the trial then in preparation, and subsequently changed their minds only because in the interval the Germans had invaded Russia; and de Gaulle until June 1941 was monotonously described in Communist literature as an agent of British imperialism in general and the City of London in particular. Thereafter – the USSR having been attacked by Hitler – he suddenly became a patriot with whom the Communists could cooperate. After the war, fraudulent 'documents' were produced by the French Communist Party to make it appear that its leaders had from the start called for resistance to the Germans. They could not well admit that Stalin's compact with Hitler had made it obligatory for all Communists to support the German cause, or at least not to hinder it.[31]

The Soviet government had not been slow to profit from the military triumphs scored by Germany in the West. On 14 June, the day Paris fell, Moscow sent an ultimatum to Lithuania, accusing its government and those of the two other Baltic Republics of having entered into a military conspiracy against the USSR. On the following day the Russian Army invaded the country and President Smetona fled to East Prussia. Latvia and Estonia got the same treatment. The President of Latvia was arrested and deported, his country occupied by Soviet troops, while Vyshinsky (the chief manager of the Moscow 'trials' in 1936–8, when the Bolshevik Old Guard was destroyed and discredited) supervised the installation of a 'friendly' regime. On 19 June Zhdanov, a member of the Politbureau and one of Stalin's closest colleagues, arrived in Tallinn to execute the same sort of operation. On 3–6 August all pretence was swept away by a decree annexing the Baltic States to the Soviet Union. Meanwhile a Russian ultimatum had been delivered to Rumania on 26 June demanding the cession of Bessarabia and the northern part of the province of Bukovina. The Bucharest government bowed to force on the following day, and the territories in question passed into Russian hands. All these measures were taken in conformity with the Soviet–German pact of August 1939, although the Germans resented the speed with which the Kremlin had imposed its wishes. It was not in Germany's interest to see Soviet forces installed on the shore of the Baltic and at the mouth of the Danube, not far from the Rumanian oil fields on which the German Army was largely dependent. Like the partition of Poland in the preceding year, the Russian advance to the Baltic and the Danube brought nearer the day when Hitler would decide to turn on Stalin, who for his part may have regarded the entire operation as a precautionary move. Within the Baltic States large-scale measures of deportation liquidated the political elite which for two decades had preserved the independence of these small countries. The secret police followed on the heels of the Soviet Army and was soon busy purging and deporting all unreliable elements. It was a foretaste of the much greater expansionary movement which occurred in 1945–8.

The summer of 1940 thus witnessed the end of a great many illusions, including those of the 1939–40 'phoney war' period. The British Cabinet papers released for public inspection in 1970 and 1971 contain some very odd material indeed. There is the American Ambassador, Mr Joseph Kennedy, remarking that "the proper way to attack both Count Ciano [the Italian Foreign Minister] and Signor Mussolini was to send six American chorus girls to Rome". There is Chamberlain telling his Cabinet colleagues that after Prague he had come to the conclusion "that Herr Hitler's attitude made it impossible to continue to negotiate on the old basis with the Nazi regime", and adding in the very next breath that "this did not mean negotiations with the German people were impossible". By "the German people" he presumably meant big business and the Army leaders, but it was too late for this sort of thing. Yet Chamberlain and Halifax went on hoping down to May 1940 that some more 'reasonable' German leadership would emerge, or alternatively that Mussolini could be induced to play the part of mediator: if necessary at the cost of letting him have Gibraltar and Malta. (This was also Reynaud's view late in May 1940, when things already looked black for the Allies, but before France had surrendered.) There is Churchill giving it as his opinion in September 1939 that "the Balkans were gradually veering towards the Allies" (as though it made the faintest difference which way they were veering) and that Turkey might be brought into the war: the very last thing the Turks intended. Fortunately none of this nonsense mattered. What did make a difference, once Churchill had become Prime Minister and rid himself of the appeasers, was the impact of his personality. On this topic we have the evidence of a senior civil servant, Sir Oliver Franks, who in 1957 told Churchill's medical adviser, Lord Moran:

> I remember early in the war attending a meeting on the roof of the Ministry of Supply when Winston addressed us. I came away more happy about things. He dispelled our misgivings and set at rest our fears. . . . He gave us faith. There was in him a demonic element, as in Calvin and Luther. He was a spiritual force.[32]

Winston Spencer Churchill (1874–1965) had not always stood so high in the estimation of his colleagues, or of the politically conscious governing elite generally. Down to 1940, when he suddenly assumed towering shape, his political career had been dogged by frequent blunders and by a reputation for being 'unsound' on major issues. His involvement in the unsuccessful attempt to seize Constantinople during the First World War temporarily cost him his Cabinet seat in 1915 and prejudiced the Admiralty against him. His espousal of armed intervention against the Soviet regime in 1919-20 aroused the political Left, while his verbal onslaught on the trade unions, during and after the general strike of May 1926, marked him out as an enemy of organized labour. To the Liberal followers of Lloyd George and J.M. Keynes in the later 1920s he was the man who in 1925 had yielded to orthodox financial opinion and pegged sterling at its pre-war gold value, thereby imposing an unnecessary burden upon the British economy.[33] Veteran Tories remembered that he had broken with their party over free trade in 1904 and only returned to the fold in 1924, when the Liberals had run out of steam. Radical intellectuals were repelled by his praise of Mussolini and his openly expressed conviction that as between Russian Bolshevism and Italian Fascism, the latter was much to be preferred. Moderate Conservatives thought him misguided in opposing Baldwin's cautious advance towards Indian independence between 1931 and 1935. He was a 'liberal imperialist' of pre-1914 vintage who had somehow survived into the modern age; a Whig historian who expressed obsolete sentiments in the language of Macaulay; a brilliant amateur who was the despair of his advisers; above all a man who appeared to be bored unless there was a major war going on. All these judgements were true, and all were irrelevant in 1940. In that dreadful year Churchill saved his country, and no one else could have done it. Moreover, the records show that, having at long last become Prime Minister, he generally moved with caution, listened to professional advice, and in particular knew how to work both with the Chiefs of Staff and with the Foreign Office.[34]

The first essential was to get ready for the inevitable air and sea battle around the British Isles. This was partly a technical problem having to do with the output of fighter aircraft and the effectiveness of the newly installed radar screen which gave early warning of the approach of enemy aircraft.[35] But it also involved high-level policy decisions affecting Britain's relations with the United States. On 4 June Churchill told the House of Commons there would be no surrender, and he concluded his speech by affirming that if the British Isles were to be subjugated "then our Empire beyond the seas, armed and guarded by the British Fleet, would carry on the struggle, until . . . the New World, with all its power and might, steps forth to the rescue and the liberation of the Old". Lord Lothian, then British Ambassador in Washington, felt that this statement might give encouragement to those who expected Britain to go under, whereupon the Fleet would somehow cross the Atlantic to North America. Churchill thereupon instructed him to discourage any notion on Roosevelt's part "that they will pick up the *débris* of the British Empire by their present policy. On the contrary, they run the terrible risk that their sea-power will be completely over-matched." If Britain broke under the strain of a German invasion, "a pro-German government might obtain far easier terms from Germany by surrendering the Fleet, thus making Germany and Japan masters of the New World".[36] The veiled threat implicit in this message played its part in inducing the US administration at the end of August to trade fifty over-age American destroyers in exchange for a number of naval bases in the West Indies. So as to make the transaction look less like a naked surrender of British-controlled territory in exchange for fifty aged ships, Churchill informed Parliament on 20 August that it was all a matter of coordinating the air and naval defences of Britain, Canada and the United States. This face-saving formula was embodied in the declaration whereby a week later the British government 'leased' to the United States, for a period of ninety-nine years, a number of naval and air bases in Newfoundland, Bermuda, the Bahamas, Jamaica, Antigua, St Lucia, Trinidad and British Guiana.[37] In exchange, Roosevelt – who had to think about his re-election to an unprecedented third presidential term in November – made available the ships, and on 5 September Churchill was able to inform the House of Commons of "the memorable transactions" whereby the Admiralty obtained the fifty American destroyers. "Only very ignorant persons," he went on, "would suggest that the transfer of American destroyers to the British flag constitutes the slightest violation of international law, or affects in the smallest degree the non-belligerency of the United States." Since in the very next sentence he observed that Hitler would probably resent the transaction, one may suppose that the emphasis upon US neutrality was for the benefit of Congress and the American voter. Roosevelt's triumphant re-election in November was in fact conditioned by his ability to persuade the electorate that he had no intention of taking America into the war. For his part, Churchill repeated an earlier assurance about not scuttling or surrendering the British Fleet. "I regarded all these as parallel transactions, and as acts of goodwill performed on their merits and not as bargains. The President found it more acceptable to present them to Congress as a connected whole. We neither of us contradicted each other, and both countries were satisfied."[38] It would have been truer to say that Churchill acted in accordance with his life-long conviction the the English-speaking peoples had a common destiny, whereas Roosevelt thought in terms of the 'American century'. In any event the United States had indirectly associated themselves with the British war effort. For the moment this was sufficient.

But in order to bring America into the war it was essential that the United Kingdom should beat off the German air attack in the summer and autumn of 1940. Here the British had an unexpected stroke of luck.

Contrary to the myths spread at the time by the Germans and various neutrals, there did not exist any serious plan for the invasion of Britain; the German Navy was inadequate to the task of protecting an invasion force if it ever set out; and Göring's *Luftwaffe* had to overcome not only the resistance of the Royal Air Force, but the pre-war invention of radar, to which the Germans had paid little attention.[39] The device had been worked out in 1935 by Robert Watson Watt who took his invention to Sir Henry Tizard, a senior civil servant and an influential middleman between the scientists and the military services. It consisted of an instrument whereby distant objects could be detected in the air. By 1939 radar stations covered most of the area over which enemy bombers were likely to make their appearance, thus giving the British fighter squadrons adequate warning of their approach. When the battle of Britain was fought in earnest, in the summer of 1940, radar was still in its infancy, but the radio signals emanating from its stations gave warning of air raids approaching the British coast, while an Observer Corps numbering upwards of 50,000 men and women was busy, with the help of field-glasses and portable telephones, sending information about raiders flying overland to the experts in the bomb-proof underground Operations Room from where the aerial defence was being directed. This included anti-aircraft batteries as well as the fighter squadrons, whose exploits Churchill immortalized on 20 August in his praise of 'the few" on whom everything depended. When years later he came to write his six-volume history of the war, he noted that the German air assault on Britain was "a tale of divided counsels, conflicting purposes, and never fully accomplished plans".[40] At the time this could not be known, but with the wisdom of hindsight we are now able to perceive that the German Air Force was inadequate for the purpose, while the Naval command had serious doubts about "Operation Sea Lion", the code term by which the enterprise was known when Hitler committed himself to it in late July. The United Kingdom was beyond the reach of the kind of *Blitzkrieg* to which France had succumbed in less than six weeks. Even so, Göring's bombers did a lot of damage in south-east England, though owing to Hitler's obsession with the bombardment of London they failed to concentrate on the British fighter bases, whose destruction would have crippled the Royal Air Force. Spectacular raids on the British capital meant more to Hitler than the crucially important task of wearing the RAF down. In the end, the Germans ran out of time. They had planned for an invasion not later than the last week in September, but their great air assault on 15 September was beaten off with heavy losses (though not as heavy as was claimed at the time). The fact is that Göring had available too few bombers and fighters to destroy the British installations on the ground, while at the same time shooting the RAF out of the sky. All told, the

Germans, from July until the end of October, lost 1,733 aircraft while the RAF lost 915 fighters. The two opposing fighter forces were about equally matched in numbers and technical performance, while morale was higher on the British side, as was the level of strategic direction. By the end of September, just when the British fighter command had been worn down by heavy losses, the weather became so unfavourable that Hitler's directive of 1 August for the *Luftwaffe* to "destroy the enemy air force as soon as possible" was replaced by fresh orders which in fact amounted to an abandonment of 'Sea Lion'. The Germans then switched to pure terror tactics designed to break British morale, while the British retaliated with what were called 'area attacks' on German cities. This duel persisted long after the invasion had been formally called off by Hitler on 12 October, when it was postponed until the following spring, by which time he was busy with plans for attacking his Russian partner.[41] Göring still clung to the belief that bombing would break morale, and the late autumn and winter months witnessed heavy night attacks on London, Birmingham, Coventry, Plymouth and other cities. But it had become a slogging match. After 15 September, when the decision for a few days hung in the balance, a combination of worsening weather and growing German bomber losses shifted the strategic balance in Britain's favour, and what had originally been conceived by Hitler as another *Blitzkrieg* became a war of attrition centred upon the night bombing of cities and industrial concentrations.

These were also the months when the United States drew closer to the point of formal involvement in the war. At a press conference in November 1940, Roosevelt – having been re-elected to a third presidential term – announced that half of America's armament output was being made available to Britain, and negotiations began soon thereafter for supplying the RAF with four-engined 'Flying Fortress' bombers. In the following month plans were announced for stepping up the supply of cargo ships to Britain, and on 18 December Roosevelt announced his intention of placing before Congress a 'Lend–Lease' arrangement whereby the US government would guarantee to manufacturers payment for war materials ordered by Britain. In his message to Congress of 6 January 1941 Roosevelt called upon the country to regard itself as "an arsenal" for "those nations which are now in actual war against aggressor nations". He was repeating Wilson's performance a quarter of a century earlier, but with greater tactical ability and with a determination born from the knowledge that if the British bastion fell, the United States would have to face a triumphant Germany allied to an increasingly warlike Japan in the Far East. Since Japanese militarism, albeit lacking a populist mass basis of the Fascist kind, bore some resemblance to the Third Reich (and even more to the Second Reich of William II in 1914), it was possible to represent the Anglo-American alliance as a direct continuation of the earlier effort to "make the world safe for democracy". Nor was this claim as unfounded as one might suppose from the self-critical afterthoughts of 'revisionist' or 'isolationist' American historians. Fascism was a real and present threat to everything Britain and America stood for, as well as being the belated reaction of the European counter-revolution to the democratic tradition inaugurated in 1789 and 1793. In this sense Churchill merely expressed the obvious when in a broadcast on 9 February 1941 he translated the secret Anglo-American staff conferences then in progress into the famous phrase: "Give us the tools and we shall finish the job." It was of course beyond Britain's power to do anything of the kind, but there was no need to trumpet this fact abroad. For the rest, the German assault on Russia in June 1941, and the Japanese surprise attack on America's Pacific bastions less than six months later, terminated the most critical phase of the war: that in which everything depended on the defence of the British Isles.

In retrospect it is clear that both sides fought an air battle for which they were not properly prepared. RAF fighter command had excellent aircraft, but not enough pilots. The *Luftwaffe* had been primarily designed for tactical cooperation with ground forces, although Göring was a believer in 'absolute air war' – the doctrine that the enemy could be defeated by bombing alone. Similar beliefs were held by influential political and military figures on the British side where it was pessimistically assumed before 1940 that in a war with Germany enormous civilian casualties would result from air raids. Baldwin had committed himself to the notion that "the bomber will always get through", even though it was during his premiership that the radar screen began to be developed. At the time of Munich, in September 1938, it was thought in London that a German bombing attack lasting sixty days would result in 600,000 dead and twice that number of wounded. In actual fact, civilian casualties from air attacks on Britain during the six years of war came to a total of 300,000, of whom 60,000 were killed. German civilian losses by 1945 were ten times this figure – a consequence of the bombing offensive developed by the combined British and American air forces. Even so, the range of destruction was held within limits which permitted German industrial production to continue, whereas in 1945 a single nuclear bomb was sufficient to obliterate an entire Japanese city. The Anglo-German air battle of 1940 was politically decisive, because of the rebuff given to Hitler, who thereupon turned away from 'Sea Lion' in favour of an orthodox land campaign against Russia; but in terms of modern technology the Battle of Britain belongs to the age that ended in August 1945: an age in which the European nation state was still capable of waging war with all the weapons at its command in the knowledge that the civilian population would survive.

C HITLER'S EUROPE

By the summer of 1940 the internal structure of the National Socialist regime had become fully totalitarian, with the Party in undisputed control over the administration of the new German Empire, and its military core, the SS, elevated to a position of supremacy over the regular armed forces as well as the more plebeian SA, whose leaders had been purged in June 1934. Since February 1938 Hitler had personally assumed the immediate power of command over all the armed forces and created a High Command, the *Oberkommando der Wehrmacht* (OKW), to carry out the routine duties hitherto performed by the War Ministry. It was partly in reaction against this move that some senior commanders began to make contact, at the time of the Munich crisis, with a conservative civilian opposition represented by Schacht, Gördeler and a group of officials in the Foreign Ministry. In the course of the next eighteen months this alliance dwindled away, the Army High Command (OKH) having been diluted by new appointments which replaced some of the more traditionalist military leaders. Neither the Chief of Staff, Halder, nor the Commander-in-Chief of the Army, Brauchitsch, felt able to oppose Hitler's orders, once victory in the West had vindicated his judgement. Their misgivings were to revive with the Russian campaign, but in the interval the politicization of the Army continued with the setting up of a 'National Socialist Guidance Staff' inside the High Command to coordinate political training. As a step towards the creation of a new 'People's Officer Corps', various educational qualifications hitherto required for an officer's career were abolished, and "unconditional readiness for action for the Führer, the People and the Fatherland" substituted for earlier and more traditional criteria of selection.[42]

In all these respects the regime remained true to its populist and plebeian character, the importance of which was constantly misjudged abroad: less so at home, where the Army leaders and their conservative allies in the bureaucracy were confronted with the facts of life. The decree of 1 August 1934, whereby Hitler on Hindenburg's death combined the offices of President and Chancellor, entailed an oath of loyalty to his person on the part of the armed forces and their leaders. At first it suited him to leave the actual military command in the hands of the former *Reichswehr* generals. When from 1938 onwards he began to encroach on their preserve, he was able to build on the political loyalty of younger officers, most of whom had by then been converted to National Socialism. At the same time the gradual expansion of the SS empire – originally confined to the concentration camps – and the enrolment of volunteers in the so-called *Waffen*-SS units enabled him to create a counterweight to the regular armed forces. This was all the more important since the systematic extermination of Jews and other 'sub-humans' became the special province of the SS, while the *Waffen*-SS was transformed into a military elite in possession of the latest arms. At the top an uneasy balance prevailed between Party leaders such as Hermann Göring, Commander-in-Chief of the Air Force with the historically unique rank of *Reichsmarschall*; Joseph Goebbels, Reich Propaganda Minister; Heinrich Himmler, head of the SS and eventually Commander of the Home Army and Supervisor of the Prisoner of War Administration; and Martin Bormann, Head of the Party Chancellory and successor to the mentally unbalanced Rudolf Hess, who had flown off in a private plane to Scotland in May 1941, in the hope of contacting eminent British personalities who would make peace with Germany and let Hitler have a free hand in the East. The former architect and subsequent Armaments Minister, Albert Speer, contrary to legend carried no political weight, and neither did the chief ideologist of the Party, Alfred Rosenberg, even though in 1942 Hitler appointed him "sole delegate of the Reich Government in matters of policy relating to all peoples of the former Soviet territories".[43]

Given the character of the regime, the total suppression of all political parties and the mass execution or imprisonment of former Socialist and Communist functionaries, the only effective opposition during the war was to be found among those conservatives who in 1933–4 had entered into an alliance with Hitler, only to be disillusioned by the increasingly terrorist and irrational traits of his personality. On the military side there was a small nucleus of conspirators led by the former Army Chief of Staff, Ludwig Beck, Admiral Wilhelm Canaris (head of the *Abwehr* military intelligence) and some of his closest collaborators, and a somewhat larger group of generals, including a few Army commanders who toyed with the notion of a *Putsch* whenever the military situation looked desperate, but could not bring themselves to take action against Hitler until their doubts were resolved by the luckless Count Stauffenberg in July 1944. Stauffenberg, who finally planted an ineffective bomb under Hitler's seat, was the link between the military conspirators and a civilian opposition which consisted of two distinct and overlapping circles: on the one hand conservatives such as Schacht, who had been President of the Reichsbank until 1939; Gördeler, National Price Commissioner under Brüning and Mayor of Leipzig until 1936; and a group of Foreign Service officers with British and American connections; on the other hand the so-called 'Kreisau Circle', which included a few prominent Social Democrats, as well as Bismarckian aristocrats like Helmuth von Moltke and Lutheran Church leaders like Eugen Gerstenmaier. By the end of 1943 both groups had become more or less committed to a programme drafted by Gördeler which called for peace and Christian democracy, with a few concessions to the Socialists in the economic sphere. It was in some ways a realistic forecast of the future German Federal Republic, but as such it naturally made no appeal to the Communists. Neither did it make much of an appeal to the Western Allies (in so far as they were aware of it), since it presupposed a compromise peace and something like the frontiers of 1914, whereas the American and British governments had since January 1943 committed themselves to a policy of unconditional surrender.[44]

Hitler's war aims assumed definite shape after the signing of the Tripartite Pact between Germany, Italy and Japan on 27 September 1940, whereby Japan recognized "the leadership of Germany and Italy in the establishment of a new order in Europe", while Germany and Italy made an identical declaration in regard to Japan's position in Asia. A "free exchange of trade" should (according to Ribbentrop) take place "along generous lines" between the "Euro-African hemisphere" under the leadership of Germany and the East Asian sphere "led" by Japan.[45] European countries whose colonies lay within the Japanese "living-space" (e.g. Holland) would be compensated by a share in the exploitation of the European *Grossraum*. Rosenberg and other German theorists, who propagated these ideas, were at pains to stress that the Tripartite Pact was not directed against Russia, but "exclusively against American warmongers". In fact the Soviet government came very close to joining this peculiar association when in November 1940 Molotov paid a visit to Berlin. At this stage Hitler was still uncertain where to turn next. As he put it to Molotov on 13 November, the first order of the day was to concentrate upon the "bankrupt estate" of the British Empire.[46] He explained that he did not want to annex France, as the Russians appeared to think but rather to create a coalition of interested Powers which would consist of Germany, Russia, Japan, Italy, France and Spain, extending from North Africa to East Asia and embracing all those who wanted to be satisfied at the expense of the British Empire.[47] Germany had "defined her spheres of influence with Russia", and after the establishment of a New Order in Western Europe would seek *Lebensraum* in Central Africa. As an earnest of this orientation, Hitler and Ribbentrop were prepared to insert into the first 'Secret Protocol' to the draft agreement which was to bring the Soviet Union into the partnership a declaration to the effect that Germany's principal aims, apart from territorial revisions in Europe, would centre on Africa.[48] Molotov for his part indicated that the USSR could only join if there was a clearer understanding concerning its share in the New Order. In particular, there were issues to be clarified regarding Russia's Balkan and Black Sea interests, notably concerning Bulgaria, Rumania and Turkey. He expressed agreement with Hitler's observations about Britain and America. Russia's adherence to the Tripartite Pact appeared to him entirely acceptable in principle. Hitler replied that the British Empire would be apportioned as a gigantic world-wide estate in bankruptcy of forty million square kilometres. In this vast sphere there would be for Russia access to the ice-free ocean. Molotov while expressing complete agreement in principle, returned to his earlier point about delimiting spheres of interest before any agreement could be concluded. On this note the participants separated, and Molotov returned to Moscow in order to report to Stalin. A few weeks later Hitler changed his mind about Russia: the Soviet counter-proposals of 26 November were too far-reaching for his taste. Stalin wanted not only Finland and Bulgaria, but military and naval bases within range of the Bosphorus and the Dardanelles, as well as a general recognition that the area south of Batum and Baku, in the general direction of the Persian Gulf, should be recognized as a Soviet sphere. No answer was returned to these proposals. Instead, Hitler on 18 December issued his Directive No. 21, code-named 'Operation Barbarossa', for an early invasion of the Soviet Union.[49]

This decision represented a return to the doctrine originally laid down in *Mein Kampf*, save that in those days Hitler had thought in terms of an alliance with the British Empire. With the wisdom of hindsight it is plain that Britain's unexpected resistance in 1940 had the effect of diverting him eastward. Thus what the Chamberlainites had hoped for – war between Russia and Germany – was actually brought about by Churchill. The attack on Russia in June 1941 gave birth to a concept of *Raumordnung* which was Continental and easily understood by Germans habituated by decades of Pan-German agitation to think in terms of colonial expansion in the Slav world. It also had the advantage of reviving the anti-Bolshevist theme. This was the spirit in which the German press and radio hailed the summoning of Axis and satellite representatives to Berlin to renew the Anti-Comintern Pact in the 'State Act' of 25 November 1941, only a year after the Hitler–Molotov talks.[50] This "first European congress", as Ribbentrop's spokesman called it, was to mark the identification of the 'New Order' with the European 'crusade' in the East, and in commemoration of the occasion the German radio stations broadcast a new 'Song of Europe', while the Post Office issued a special rubber stamp inscribed "European United Front Against Bolshevism" and showing a map of Europe decorated with a swastika and a sword. National Socialist ideology was sufficiently elastic to permit a sudden switch from dreams of a German Empire in Central Africa to projects for the colonization of Russian territory by millions of German and other peasants who would erect a *Bauernwall* against Bolshevism. Three million Dutchmen, it was declared after the establishment of the *Nederlandsche Oost-Compagnie* in June 1942, could take up a new life in the conquered territories. German peasants would likewise benefit, thereby fulfilling one of the most cherished dreams of

Hitler's followers: Germany must break through the narrow boundaries of the Bismarckian era to become a *Grossraum*, that is to say, a supra-national empire limited in space only by the *Herrenvolk's* ability to rule the lesser breeds. It was only after the defeat at Stalingrad early in 1943 that these heady visions were replaced by the more traditional theme of European defence against Bolshevism. [51]

It has been suggested that Hitler's ambiguity on the subject of the New Order was most clearly expressed by Goebbels in a Sportpalast speech of 11 February 1941, when he declared that Germany was fighting for *Lebensraum* (living space), "and what that is we can discuss after the war".[52] It is certainly the case that between the annexation of France, the dismemberment of the British Empire, and the destruction of Russia, Hitler – like the Pan-Germans before him – was quite prepared to make an arbitrary choice at any moment. If the British Empire refused to fall and looked like getting American support, he was ready to turn eastward. He was likewise generous in portioning out conquered territories even before they had actually been secured. At a conference held at his headquarters on 16 July 1941, a few weeks after the assault on Russia, he discussed the future organization of the Eastern Territories. The entire Baltic region was to become an integral part of Germany, while Leningrad must be razed to the ground and then handed over to Finland. In the south, the Crimea, with the largest possible hinterland, must be cleared of its inhabitants. Then, having been resettled with Germans, it must become *Reich* territory, as must the Volga German area and the "area around Baku".[53] As has rightly been remarked, Hitler's Europe was essentially an SS empire. The 'Germanic' ideal, as interpreted by the SS and its ideological inspirers, was central to Hitler's concept of the future 'New Order'. It was a source of considerable disappointment to him that the Quisling regime installed in Norway encountered so much popular resistance, and that Denmark, although occupied and helpless, likewise proved rebellious in spirit. For that matter the Dutch did not evince a great deal of enthusiasm for the New Order. Nonetheless the SS leaders persisted with the recruitment of 'Germanic' volunteers to the *Waffen*-SS. These units swore an oath of allegiance to Hitler as the 'Germanic Führer', whereas the non-Germanic formations of the *Waffen*-SS recruited their men on the principle of exploiting the anti-Bolshevik theme.[54]

The 'final solution' of the 'Jewish problem' was an aspect of this eastward turn. By December 1941 the bureaucracy of the German Foreign Ministry was ready with a detailed scheme for making the satellites conform to Hitler's wishes on the subject. A memorandum drawn up by an official appropriately named Luther, Under-Secretary of State in charge of the 'Deutschland' Department, outlined the steps to be taken. They included the deportation "to the east" of all Jews residing in the

Reich, as well as those in Serbia, Croatia and Slovakia; all German Jews in the occupied territories who had lost their citizenship, all those handed over to the Germans by the Hungarian government (which proved very refractory until the Germans actually occupied the country in March 1944), and sundry measures relating to Rumania and other satellites. Of these, Bulgaria and Finland were uncooperative until the end, while the Rumanians made no difficulty. At the notorious 'Wannsee Conference' on 20 January 1942 these aspects of the 'final solution' were given a thorough airing by Heydrich and other SS leaders.[55]

The SS had from 1933 onwards been placed in charge of the concentration camps, Dachau being among the more notorious. In the spring of 1936 their numbers were increased from 1,800 to 3,500 and they were renamed SS-*Totenkopfverbände* (Death's Head Units). The *Waffen*-SS, which eventually grew into a small army, was a military outcrop of this terrorist organization which from the start had been imbued with Nietzschean notions about the need to purify Germany from racially inferior elements. The whole complex was headed by Himmler, and ultimately by Hitler in person. It was outside the law – even of such law as still remained in Germany after 1933. The systematic tormenting of prisoners was part of a training course which culminated in the murder of some eleven million defenceless human beings – about half of them Jews, the others Poles or Russians. In 1938–9 the concentration camp population began to swell with the annexation of Austria and Bohemia, and simultaneously the SS leadership embarked on the task of preparing for the 'final solution'. As more and more East European territories fell under German occupation, Himmler was made responsible by Hitler for expelling and eventually liquidating millions of 'racially inferior' Jews and Slavs and colonizing the newly gained territories with German peasants. After the conquest of Poland the great death camp at Auschwitz (in Polish Oswiecim) was opened twenty miles east of Katowice. In addition to being a detention camp, and ultimately a murder camp, Auschwitz was a factory working for I.G.Farben. The gas-chambers were a later addition. Even before they had been instituted, the 'final solution' was applied by SS detachments to Jews in conquered Russian territories after Hitler had embarked upon his war against the Soviet Union. The mass execution of Jewish civilians was part of an extermination drive which also resulted in the death by starvation of millions of Russian war prisoners. In addition, the notorious *Kommissarbefehl* of 8 June·(a fortnight before the actual invasion of Russia) placed all active Communist Party officials on the death list. The German Army commanders tolerated all this, a circumstance which did not prevent them from claiming after the event that they had been opposed to these measures. To relieve their consciences the SS were made wholly responsible for the murder campaign. It was after all what they were for.[56]

In one of its aspects, extermination by gassing was an extension of Hitler's and Himmler's policy of euthanasia applied to the inmates of German hospitals and asylums without distinction of race or creed. The aim was to get rid of people who were obviously 'unfit' by Nietzschean or Social Darwinist standards. On 1 September 1939 Hitler issued a secret order to kill all those suffering from incurable diseases. He had postponed earlier action on this sector of the racial front because of worry about possible Church reaction. The start of the war seemed a propitious moment for getting on with his eugenic programme.[57] In the first euthanasia installation opened in December 1939 the victims were shot. As the programme expanded, gassing in rooms disguised as showerbaths was introduced. The next of kin were notified that the patients had died of disease and that their bodies had been cremated. Until August 1941, when the programme was stopped, some 70,000 patients had been gassed, including a good many who suffered from nothing worse than a nervous breakdown. Meanwhile, although the whole matter was classified as top secret, word of it gradually leaked out and on 11 August 1940 Cardinal Bertram, on behalf of the Catholic episcopate, lodged a protest with the head of the *Reich* Chancellery, Lammers; a few months later Cardinal Faulhaber protested to the Minister of Justice. These and other protests were ignored, and the killings continued, whereupon Bishop Galen of Münster, in a sermon delivered on 3 August 1941, made the whole matter public and branded these deeds as criminal. Shortly thereafter the euthanasia programme was halted by a *Führerbefehl*, even though Bormann and other Party officials considered that the bishop ought to be hanged. The victims had been Germans, which of course made all the difference. The Jews were less fortunate, in that neither the Catholic hierarchy nor the Protestants ever made a public stand on their behalf.

On Hitler's behalf it may be said that he had made no secret of his intentions. In a speech delivered on 30 January 1939 and broadcast all over the world he declared: "If international Jewish finance should succeed, inside Europe or elsewhere, in plunging the nations once more into a world war, the result will not be the Bolshevization of the world and with it the victory of Judaism, but the extermination of the Jewish race in Europe."[58] A decree of 1 September 1941 provided that all Jews over the age of six must appear in public marked with a yellow star. On 15 October mass deportations of German Jews to the east began, and meanwhile the special *Einsatzgruppen* of the SS in occupied Russia had already begun their mass executions of Jewish civilians, women and children included. By December the first death camp was opened near Lodz. Sobibor, Treblinka and Auschwitz went into full operation in the course of 1942. In August 1942 Colonel Kurt Gerstein, who had joined the SS in order to discover what was happening, tried to tell his story to the Papal Nuncio in Berlin, Orsenigo, who refused to receive him. He then informed Bishop Preysing of Berlin and others, and requested that his report be forwarded to the Holy See.[59] Both the Vatican and the German episcopate were in fact kept fully informed through reports emanating from Catholic officers serving in Poland and Russia and passed on to the hierarchy by Catholic officials in the Ministry of the Interior and other sections of the German administration. No action ever resulted, the German Catholic hierarchy being fully committed to Hitler's 'struggle against Bolshevism'. The desire of the Holy See not to weaken the German war effort was presumably responsible for the fact that Pius XII, although urged repeatedly by Britain and the United States, never issued a public denunciation of German atrocities against the Jews.[60]

The mass murder of the European Jews was part of a larger programme. From September 1939 onwards the SS had begun to carry out the Führer's order to solve the Polish problem by murdering the country's intelligentsia. The clergy were among the victims. In October and November of that year 214 Polish priests were executed, among them the entire chapter of the bishopric of Pelplin, and by the end of 1939 some 1,000 members of the Polish secular and regular clergy had been imprisoned, many of them in hastily constructed concentration camps.[61] On this occasion the Vatican radio and the official *Osservatore Romano* told the story to the world, but without any effect on the German bishops, who continued to a man to support the war effort. On 26 June 1941, four days after Hitler's invasion of Russia, a joint pastoral letter issued by the Fulda Bishops' Conference repeated the standard exhortation to the faithful to fulfil their duty to the fatherland. Thereafter the struggle against Bolshevism, and the duty of all good Christians to support it, became the theme of countless pastoral letters and sermons addressed to the faithful. This is all the more remarkable in that by 1941 the German episcopate was aware of what the SS was doing to the Polish clergy. A report circulating among the diocesan chanceries on conditions in Poland showed that as of 1 October 1941, in the archdiocese of Posen alone, seventy-four priests had been shot or had died in concentration camps and 451 were held in prisons or camps. Of the 441 churches of the archdiocese only thirty were still open for the Poles. It was Hitler's declared intention to exterminate the Polish intelligentsia, including the clergy, and to turn the remainder of the populace into helots working for their German overlords. In the light of these facts it is noteworthy that the German episcopate contented itself with occasional private protests against the treatment of the Polish Church.[62]

The precise status of what was officially described as the 'General

Government' of Poland – that is, territories not annexed to the Reich, but administered by German officials – was never made wholly clear, but it seems to have been Hitler's intention to create a Polish puppet state, with all the strings controlling its movement held in German hands. The original plan appears to have been to set up a native government similar to that of Bohemia-Moravia, but this aim was defeated by the failure to find any Polish leader who would lend himself to the purpose. After the Western Powers had rejected Hitler's first peace overtures, his decree of 12 October 1939, "concerning the administration of the Occupied Polish Territories" became the foundation of further administrative measures. These were sometimes contradictory; thus the forced migration of Poles and Jews from the incorporated territories into the General Government suggested an intention to preserve the latter's Polish character, but this trend was accompanied by measures pointing to Germanization, such as the destruction of Polish monuments and the establishment of schools in excess of the needs of the *Volksdeutsche* – the German-speaking minority. After the war it turned out that by a secret decree of 7 October 1939, Himmler and the SS had been placed in charge of the Germanization policy, including the elimination of 'harmful influences'. On the whole one may say that the General Government was regarded as a German colony, and was to be recognized as such by the 'inferior' peoples, who included the Poles as well as the Jews. The immediate aim was the liquidation of the Polish intelligentsia. All Polish institutions of higher learning were abolished; only primary and vocational education was envisaged for the Poles, and this under German supervision and in the German language. The subject population was physically starved as the war continued, and after the great Warsaw insurrection of August 1944 (which the Soviet government permitted to be crushed, while its victorious army stood idly by), no further restraints were placed on the SS in dealing with the Polish underground resistance movement and the population generally.

A distinction must nonetheless be drawn between the extermination of the Jews and the savage treatment of the Slav populations in occupied Eastern Europe. It was an essential aspect of the 'New Order' that Poland and Russia should be deprived of their politically conscious minorities, so that after the war they could be turned into German colonies. However, in the short run the extermination programme was limited to the Jews. They were machine-gunned, gassed or starved in every town and city entered by the invaders, as well as in Rumania, where the atrocities committed by the local authorities, after Rumania had joined Germany in the onslaught on Russia, rivalled those of the SS themselves. In 1942 and 1943, when the death camps had come into operation, transports of victims were sent eastward from France, Belgium and Holland, in addition to those from Central Europe. By the time the machinery had been perfected it had become possible at Auschwitz to kill 2,000 people in a single operation lasting only a quarter of an hour, and to repeat the performance three or four times a day. On occasion this mechanical efficiency led to errors being committed, as when a transport of Germans evacuated from Hamburg were seized, stripped and gassed by the Gestapo before it was discovered that they were not Jews at all.[63] Altogether in the Auschwitz death factory alone, according to the post-war testimony of the German camp commandant, some two and a half million people, most of them Jews, were gassed, while another half million died of starvation and disease. The last great consignment was 400,000 Jews from Hungary in the summer of 1944. In the autumn, when Germany's defeat had become probable, Himmler gave orders for the massacres to stop, although local SS squads persisted until the end.

The death of nearly four million Russian prisoners of war has not received the same publicity, largely because it was underplayed by the Soviet authorities. The presentation of the Russian case during the Nuremberg Trials in February 1946 went on for sixteen days and filled 530 pages of the British transcript, yet only one-tenth of it was devoted to charges concerning the treatment of Soviet soldiers. The disproportion is the more remarkable in that the Germans themselves admitted that at least 3,700,000 Russian prisoners died at their hands. This was almost exactly the number of Red Army soldiers who surrendered to the Germans in the summer and autumn of 1941, when the Russian armies virtually disintegrated. By the end of the war the Germans had taken more than five and a half million Russian prisoners of whom nearly four million died of starvation, while 800,000 changed sides and put on German uniforms to fight alongside the other satellite armies against the USSR. Since this enormous number of prisoners and deserters was never officially admitted by the Stalinist regime, the fate of the prisoners was obscured at Nuremberg by the casual manner in which the Soviet prosecution put their case. They could not well be expected to state in public that in 1941 their armies at the front had fallen apart. For the rest, the Soviet government not having signed the Geneva Convention on the treatment of war prisoners, the International Red Cross had no access either to the millions of Russian prisoners or to Germans taken prisoner by the Russians when the tide had begun to turn.[64]

The total of Russian and German casualties between June 1941 and the end of the war in May 1945 is difficult to compute, but in general it is accepted by historians that Russian losses were far higher than German. There is no official Soviet estimate of war dead. On 22 June 1944, in a speech commemorating the third anniversary of the war, Stalin declared that 5,300,000 Red Army men were dead, missing or prisoners – a manifest understatement.[65] In May 1945 the Soviet High Command claimed that they held over three million German prisoners, but this offers no clue, since the great bulk had surrendered during the last days of the war. It has been estimated that in all some four million Germans died throughout the war on active service, not counting a million or so who were taken prisoner and failed to return from Russia. The great majority of those killed in fighting, some nine-tenths, died on the Eastern front. Russian military losses, including prisoners taken by the Germans and then left to starve, cannot have been less than 15 million, to which one must add the millions of civilian dead from famine in Leningrad and the Ukraine, and some 750,000 Russian Jews slaughtered on the spot by the SS *Einsatzgruppen*. On all counts the Soviet Union probably lost some twenty million citizens, the Germans between six and seven million, including more than five million in the East alone, if one estimates at one million the number of civilians who in 1945–6 succumbed during the mass migration of more than ten million Germans from Polish and Central European territories overrun by the Soviet Army. Germany also lost some 600,000 civilians from air bombardment. Diminished births were of course an additional source of population decrease, and on these grounds it has sometimes been suggested that Soviet war losses, direct and indirect, may have run to as high as thirty or forty million, but this kind of estimate is speculative. The population of the Soviet Union in January 1959 was officially given as close to 209 million, against some 170 million in 1939, the increase being partly accounted for by the incorporation in the USSR of the three Baltic States, besides formerly Polish or Rumanian territories of White Russia, the Ukraine and Bessarabia. Assuming a real population in all these lands of 190 million in 1939, the enlarged Soviet Union in 1959 might, according to some estimates, have had something like 250 million inhabitants, instead of 209 million, assuming an unchanged birth-rate and no war. This would give a total loss from all causes, including diminished births, of forty million – probably five times the corresponding German figure for the period. In the nature of the case, all such estimates are problematic.[66]

Statistical imprecision likewise blocks the path of the historian in relation to the wars fought in the Balkans after the Italian assault on Greece in October 1940 and the German invasion of Yugoslavia six months later. The Greek imbroglio led to a three-cornered struggle between the Italian and eventually German occupants, the regular Greek forces, whose resistance collapsed in 1941 despite British efforts to aid them, and the various guerrilla movements who were fighting both each other and the occupying forces. The same tragedy on a larger scale was enacted in Yugoslavia, where after the rapid ending of organized resistance in April 1941 a prolonged partisan struggle took

Art and literature in the twentieth century

18 Robert Wiene's *The Cabinet of Dr Caligari* (1919), one of the classic pieces of German Expressionism.

19 (top) The famous scene on the steps at Odessa in Sergei Eisenstein's *The Battleship Potemkin* (1925), an example of his innovative editing techniques; (below) Jean Cocteau's surrealist *Sang d'un Poète* (1931).

20 (above) *Les Enfants du Paradis* (1943–5). Made during the occupation of France, it was quickly hailed as a masterpiece, though its romantic fatalism went out of fashion after the war; (below left) scene from the Berliner Ensemble production of Brecht's *Mother Courage* (1949).

21 (below right) Bergmann's *The Seventh Seal* (1957), one of the first films to bring him international notice.

22 (above left) The
Catalonian architect
Antoni Gaudí's Casa
Milà, Barcelona
(1905–10)
23 (below left) Peter
Behrens' AEG turbine
factory, Berlin (1908–9);
Behrens was
commissioned by the
AEG (German electric
company) to design not
only their buildings, but
their electrical products,
packaging, stationery
and advertisements.
24 (right) The
stalactite shapes of the
interior of Max
Reinhardt's Grosses
Schauspielhaus, Berlin
(1919).

25 The Bauhaus, the highly influential school of architecture and design founded by
Walter Gropius in 1919. The headquarters at Dessau (above) was designed by
Gropius (1925–6).

26 The pilgrimage church of Notre Dame du Haut at Ronchamp (1950–5) by the Swiss architect Le Corbusier.

27 Picasso's *Les Demoiselles d'Avignon* (1907), a controversial and highly influential work that marks the beginning of cubism.

28 Two masters of cubism: (above) Georges Braque, *Maisons à l'Estaque* (1908); (right) Marcel Duchamp, *Nude Descending a Staircase* no. 2 (1912).

NU DESCENDANT UN ESCALIER

29 Expressionism and Futurism: (above far left) Ernst Kirchner's *Five Women in the Street* (1913); (above left) Umberto Boccioni's *Unique Forms of Continuity in Space* (1913).
30 (below left) The Russian Vassily Kandinsky, one of the pioneers of abstract art, abandoned representation of objects altogether: his *Composition 8, no. 260* (1923).
31 (above) The brilliant colours and ornamental patterns characteristic of the work of Henri Matisse are illustrated in his *Decorative Figure on an Ornamental Background* (c. 1927).

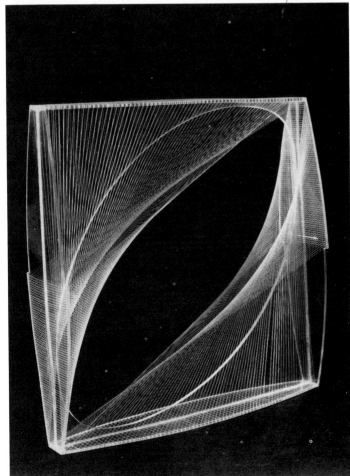

32 Constantin
Brancusi's work
eliminated descriptive
detail and decorative
design in favour of
simplicity and the
synthesis of pure form;
(above) *Fish* (1930);
(left) Naum Gabo's
Linear Construction
(1942–3). Gabo, with
his brother Antoine
Pevsner, was one of
the founders of
Constructivism, which
explored the
possibilities of form
independent of
volume.

33 D. H. Lawrence
(1885–1930)
34 Marcel Proust
(1871–1922)
35 Sigmund Freud
(1856–1939)

36 James Joyce (1882–1941)   37 Albert Einstein (1879–1955)

38 Sir Alexander Fleming (1881–1955) in his laboratory at St Mary's Hospital, Paddington.

39 Georg Lukačs (1885–1971)

40 Benedetto Croce (1866–1952)

41 Jean-Paul Sartre addresses the crowd during a demonstration against the Algerian war, 2 November 1961.

42 Bertrand Russell (1872–1970)

enormous toll of the population. While Yugoslavia was overrun in a week by the Germans, Greek resistance smashed in three weeks and the British expeditionary force destroyed or flung back to North Africa, partisan warfare went on until 1945. The various resistance movements – some Communist-led, some not – were soon at each other's throats, and in Yugoslavia the situation was further complicated by the murderous hatred opposing the Serb majority to the Croat minority – a conflict further exacerbated by religious differences. In the end, the resistance movement was taken over by the Communists whose leader, Josip Broz Tito, was a Croat and thus better able to bridge the national gulf than the more conventional Serb nationalist Mihailović who led the royalist forces. Mihailović's Cetnici were essentially Serb and as such loyal to the Orthodox Church, while the Croat Fascists, locally known as Ustaša, enjoyed Roman Catholic backing as well as German and Italian military support. By the time this complex struggle had come to an end in 1945, perhaps a million and a half people had been killed – largely in massacres directed by the Germans and the Ustaša Croats against the Serbs. It was the Communist Party's ability to transcend the national-religious division which in the end permitted it to triumph under the leadership of Tito whose movement attracted Serb and Slovene support, while the Cetnici never rose above their national and religious parochialism. When it was all over, the country had been devastated and one-tenth of its population wiped out, but at least the national split had been overcome.

The subjugation of the conquered Slavs and the extermination of the Jews were specific features of the SS empire which gradually came into being during the war. In other respects the 'New Order' was in tune with the older Pan-German programme Hitler had inherited from his German and Austrian predecessors, including theorists like Karl Haushofer who had built up the pseudo-science of geopolitics. Viewed from the geopolitical angle, the Greater German *Reich* was a connecting link between the Baltic and the Mediterranean, and was so conceived by the Axis propagandists who attempted to popularize this conception. The existence of Italy as a nominally equal partner in the enterprise, and the need to make provision for a French satellite state, as well as a Spanish zone in Africa, led to the conception of 'Euro-Africa' as a single *Grossraum*, with Italy, France and Spain dividing North Africa between them, in proportion to their respective contributions to the war effort. This part of the programme was from the first complicated by the equivocal attitude of Pétain's government at Vichy; by Italy's failure to make military headway in North Africa against numerically small British forces; and by Franco's refusal to let the Germans march through Spain. By the end of 1942, when the joint German–Italian forces commanded by Rommel had been defeated at Alamein, while French

North Africa had come in on the Allied side, the whole enterprise had begun to wear a fantastic look; but in the summer of 1942 it seemed possible that the Germans might overrun the Caucasus and occupy Persia, while Mussolini had serious hopes of entering Cairo in triumph. As late as the spring of 1943 the Axis partners wasted a quarter of a million men in an attempt to conserve their hold on Tunisia in the face of vastly stronger American and British forces. 'Euro-Africa' was not surrendered without a major battle. Conversely, the British war effort was seriously hampered for three years by the need to assemble large forces for the defence of Egypt.[67]

The differing characters of the Italian, French and Spanish regime-made it impossible to coordinate their activities in what from the Gers man standpoint looked like a rational manner. Italy, in theory a co-equal partner of the Axis, was in fact Germany's chief satellite, and after Mussolini's fall in July 1943 became a military liability, since it had to be defended against an Anglo-American invasion helped by French and Italian troops who at this stage had changed sides and joined the Allies. The Pétain government at Vichy rested upon the loyalty of its North African proconsuls and of the French Navy commanded by Admiral Darlan. The latter in November 1942 ordered most of its ships to be scuttled at Toulon so as not to be captured by the Germans, who by then had occupied Southern France and terminated the pretence of an autonomous French government under their remote control. Spain was another disappointment in that Franco clung to his precarious neutrality. In the event of a German victory there would have been Italian and Spanish claims upon the French Empire in North Africa, and this circumstance played a part in causing the local French military and naval commanders to throw in their lot with the Allies, once it was clear that the United States was determined to crush the Axis and restore North Africa to France. The gradual emergence of Roosevelt's America as a Power overshadowing Great Britain was likewise a factor in determining the Italian King and the High Command to depose Mussolini on 25 July 1943. What they chiefly looked for was security against Communism, and this could be taken for granted once the United States had emerged as a military giant balancing the Soviet Union in the East. Hitler's Europe therefore began to crumble in 1943, starting from the military defeat at Stalingrad in January of that year, when the Soviet armies destroyed the greater part of the German forces assembled for the conquest of South Russia and the Caucasus. From then onwards the Germans were defending what their propagandists termed 'Fortress Europe', and what was in reality the old *Mitteleuropa* of Pan-Germanism, plus outlying areas in the east and south, as well as Norway, which had been occupied at an early stage in the war.

276

Germany was by then faced with the need for carrying on a war of attrition against greatly superior forces, and once the Western Allies had successfully invaded France in June 1944 it became plain to the German military leaders that the war could not be won in Hitler's sense of the term. This is just why the conspiracy which had been brewing for years took shape in July 1944: the conservative opposition could now at long last count on the support of Army leaders who in the event of Hitler's death would lend their aid to the establishment of a 'respectable' regime. Whether the scheme would have worked, even if the conspirators had been less amateurish and more successful in bringing off the attempt on Hitler's life on 20 July, must remain an open question. The mass of the soldiers and junior officers were loyal to the Führer rather than to the elderly generals who held command of his armies, and it is by no means certain that they would have rallied to a conservative regime. In any event the attempt came to nothing, the conspirators were massacred by the Gestapo and SS, and the war continued until the Russians had stormed Berlin and Hitler had committed suicide on 30 April. Two days earlier Mussolini and his mistress Claretta Petacci were caught and shot by a band of Italian partisans near Lake Como. The 'New Order' perished as it had begun, in blood and terror. Typically, Hitler towards the end instructed his regional commissioners to destroy all waterworks and industrial plants, so as to create a 'desert' in the Allied path. When Speer protested, Hitler retorted: "If the war is lost, the German nation will perish, so there is no need to consider what the people require for their continued existence." It was in this Wagnerian spirit that the Führer rang the curtain down on the Third Reich. The formal surrender of the German armed forces followed as a matter of course a week later.

D THE GRAND ALLIANCE

Germany's assault on the USSR in June 1941, and Japan's entry into the war six months later, transformed what had hitherto been a European struggle into a world conflict. These events also made it necessary for America, Britain and Russia to coordinate their respective strategies. When Hitler attacked Russia on 22 June 1941, Churchill promptly announced his acceptance of the Soviet Union as an ally, and Roosevelt supported Churchill's position although the United States was not yet officially involved. With the Japanese air assault on the American fleet at Pearl Harbour in Hawaii on 7 December 1941, and the temporary loss of Western air and naval supremacy in the Pacific, it became necessary to decide whether the European or the Asian theatre should have precedence. The decision to concentrate on the defeat of Germany, leaving Japan until later, was born from the realization that the Soviet forces were tying down some 200 German and satellite divisions whose freeing for other purposes would make it impossible for the Western Powers to defeat the Axis and recover control of the Mediterranean, France and Western Europe generally. Relations between the Allies were dominated by this crucial circumstance until the Anglo-American landing in France on 6 June 1944, and even beyond that date, since it was evident that Germany could not be defeated if Russia either succumbed or made a separate peace. Fortunately for the Western Powers, the tide gradually turned in Russia's favour all along the Eastern front, while at the same time the 'total' character of Hitler's assault on the USSR ruled out the danger of a separate peace. It therefore became possible to clear North Africa of the Axis forces and to knock Italy out of the war in 1943, while all the time building up for the decisive assault on occupied France. Russia bore the heaviest burden in military losses, while the Western Allies were obliged for two years to concentrate on shipbuilding and the anti-submarine war. At the same time an Anglo-American air offensive against Germany developed whose purpose it was to destroy Germany's industries and weaken the morale of her civilian population by razing her cities to the ground. This latter aim was not officially avowed, so as to spare religious and humanitarian sensibilities, but it was central to the Anglo-American war effort.[68]

British Air Staff doctrine at the time is summed up in the Official History written by Sir Charles Webster and Dr Noble Frankland, *The Strategic Air Offensive Against Germany*:

The strategic air offensive is a means of direct attack on the enemy state with the object of depriving it of the means or will to continue the war. It may, in itself, be the instrument of victory or it may be the means by which victory can be won by other forces. It differs from all previous kinds of armed attack in that it alone can be brought to bear immediately, directly and destructively against the heartland of the enemy. Its sphere of activity is, therefore, not only above, but also beyond that of armies or navies.[69]

The doctrine of strategic air attack went back to the 1920s, but was not put into practice until the 1940s. It must not be confused with the parallel emergence of the theory and practice of close cooperation between air forces and armoured land formations. Strategic bombing was meant to level cities and industries and to wreck the morale of the civilian population. The same applies to the rocket attacks on London which Hitler developed in the closing months of the war.[70] The air superiority which the Russians gradually developed along the eastern front still formed part of conventional warfare, and the same applies to the impressive air cover by about 11,000 first-line machines which enabled the Anglo-American forces to storm ashore in June 1944 on the coast of Normandy, after an armada of 4,000 ships, plus several thousand smaller craft, had crossed the Channel: almost exactly four years to the day when the remnants of the British expeditionary force had been flung into the sea at Dunkirk by the triumphant Germans. The sustained bomber offensive against the German heartland from 1943 onward was something else again. The targets now chosen were industrial centres, especially the Ruhr, and great coastal cities such as Hamburg and Bremen. The Casablanca directive issued by the Combined Chiefs of Staff to the British and American Bomber Commands on 4 February 1943 gave them as their task "the progressive destruction and dislocation of the German military, industrial and economic system, and the undermining of the morale of the German people to a point where their capacity for armed resistance is fatally weakened".[71] This was a notable departure from previous forms of warfare: a departure already heralded by the Germans in 1939–40 and therefore morally justified in the eyes of the British and American governments. Nonetheless, care was taken not to spell out all the consequences in so many words. When in February 1945 the policy of levelling enemy cities to the ground culminated in the totally senseless destruction of Dresden and the incineration of more than 100,000 civilians, a reaction set in among those responsible. After the war had ended a US Strategic Bombing Survey estimated that the bombing offensive, which cost the lives of 160,000 American and British airmen, had not prevented German war production from attaining its peak in August 1944, by which time the Allies were already in Paris. In 1943 no qualms were felt, and the need to relieve the pressure on Russia by bombing German industrial concentrations enjoyed both official and popular support.

Relations among the Allies were then at their closest and most cordial: so much so that at the Teheran conference between Churchill, Roosevelt and Stalin, from 28 November to 1 December 1943, no exception was taken on grounds of principle when Stalin asked for East Prussia, notably the city of Königsberg, to be incorporated in the USSR.[72] Such difficulties as arose had to do with the frontier between Russia and Poland, a problem eventually solved by letting the Russians have the Molotov–Ribbentrop line of 1939, while Poland was compensated by being given large stretches of German territory. These and the related arrangements for giving Poland a government 'friendly to the Soviet Union' were worked out in greater detail at the subsequent Yalta conference in February 1945, by which time the decline in British military power by comparison with American coincided with a decline in Roosevelt's health and his powers of judgement. The Yalta settlement marked the high point of Soviet–American cooperation, whereas the Potsdam meeting in July 1945 – by which time Roosevelt had been succeeded by Truman – witnessed the beginning of an increasingly acrimonious argument over the division of Germany and the character of the satellite regimes implanted by the Russians in Eastern Europe.[73]

But Potsdam was noteworthy also for another reason. It was on this occasion that the decision was taken to drop the first two atomic bombs upon Japanese cities – and this at a moment when for all practical purposes Japan was already defeated and suing for terms. In the sixth and final volume of his reminiscences, Churchill has presented his grounds for concurring in the desire of the American political and military leaders to employ the new weapon against Japan:

On 17 July world-shaking news had arrived. In the afternoon Stimson called at my abode and laid before me a sheet of paper on which was written, "Babies satisfactorily born". By his manner I saw something extraordinary had happened. "It means," he said, "that the experiment in the Mexican desert has come off. The atomic bomb is a reality." . . . Next morning a plane arrived with a full description of this tremendous event in the human story. . . . The bomb, or its equivalent, had been detonated at the top of a pylon 100 feet high. . . . The blast had been terrific. An enormous column of flame and smoke shot up to the fringe of the atmosphere of our poor earth. Devastation inside a one-mile circle was absolute. Here then was a speedy end to the Second World War, and perhaps to much else besides. . . .

Up to this moment we had shaped our ideas towards an assault upon the homeland of Japan by terrific air bombing and by the invasion of very large armies. . . . Now all this nightmare picture had vanished. . . . Moreover, we should not need the Russians. The end of the Japanese war no longer depended upon the pouring in of their armies for the final and perhaps protracted slaughter. We had no need to ask favours of them. A few days later I minuted to Mr Eden: "It is quite clear that the United States do not at the present time desire Russian participation in the war against Japan."[74]

There were some who felt doubts about the propriety of using this weapon against civilians, but the leading scientists appear to have had few qualms, and President Truman's advisers saw in the atomic bomb a quick and easy way of finishing the war against Japan. The Soviet government had undertaken to declare war upon Japan within three months of the German capitulation, and in fact did so on 8 August. It can hardly be thought a coincidence that the first atomic bomb was dropped on Hiroshima on 6 August, followed three days later by another one upon Nagasaki. The Hiroshima bomb is estimated to have killed 80,000 people – a quarter of the town's inhabitants. That on Nagasaki was no less devastating. Coupled with the Russian declaration of war these blows had the effect of precipitating the Japanese surrender, which had become a certainty even before the bombs fell. Why then were they used? Stalin's demand at Potsdam to share in the occupation of Japan was embarrassing to the United States, and the Americans clearly preferred to obtain Japan's surrender on their own terms. Another reason was disclosed by Truman's Chief of Staff, Admiral

Leahy: the scientists and administrators in charge of the project, into which two billion dollars had been poured, were eager to demonstrate the bomb's effectiveness. One of the officers concerned in the operation, the code name for which was 'Manhattan District Project', put the point clearly when he said: "The bomb simply had to be a success – so much money had been expended on it ... The relief to everyone concerned when the bomb was finished and dropped was enormous." [75] The feeling of relief evidently did not extend to the Japanese population, nor to those Europeans and Americans who even in August 1945 foresaw what the development of these new powers of destruction would mean to their own security. From the standpoint of the Western Allies, possession of nuclear weapons served to balance Russia's preponderance on land, which after the German defeat had become a major source of worry. In this sense the decision to bomb Japan may be said to have initiated what in later years became colloquially known as the 'cold war'. However, the alliance with Russia was kept up for another two years, and when it disintegrated in 1947, it did so because the Soviet Union – contrary to assurances given at Yalta and naïvely accepted by Roosevelt – was determined to monopolize control of Eastern Europe. This decision inevitably entailed the imposition of rival forms of government upon the two halves of Europe, with a split running through the middle of Germany. The sequence of events was to show that Stalinism and liberal democracy were incompatible. The belief that coalition governments friendly to the USSR, but not under complete Communist control, could be established in Eastern Europe, never had any foundation in reality, and by February 1948, with the Communist takeover in Prague, lost whatever plausibility it had once possessed.

Even before this decisive turning-point it had become clear that the Allies were unable to agree about the future of Germany. At the Yalta conference in February 1945 the Russians brought forward proposals for the political dismemberment of Germany, plus reparations payments in kind to an extent which would have reduced German heavy industry by about eighty per cent. [76] The removal of dismantled industries was to be completed within two years, while reparations payment was to be made by the delivery of goods over a period of ten years. The total amount demanded in these two forms was to be set at twenty billion dollars, of which the Soviet Union would obtain half, plus German labour to reconstruct the devastated regions. Stalin and Molotov explained that two or three million German workers should be employed for a period of ten years doing forced labour in the Soviet Union. Churchill and Eden protested that reparations on this scale could never be collected and would reduce Germany to starvation. The Americans, who did not in fact intend to take reparations for themselves, finally proposed at Potsdam that each of the three Powers should take reparation in kind from their respective zones of occupation, and that the Russians, who had already removed large quantities of machinery from their zone, should be given additional deliveries from the Western territories. These arrangements necessarily lapsed with the partition of Germany in 1948–9 and the establishment of rival governing authorities in Eastern and Western Germany.

A project dear to the heart of Roosevelt and his advisers, the establishment of a future world organization, was also settled at these conferences. After some inconclusive discussions at Teheran, agreement in principle was reached at Yalta, where the Russians secured the veto power on which their minds were set from the start. A general conference for the establishment of the United Nations opened at San Francisco on 25 April 1945, a fortnight after Roosevelt's death. It resulted in agreement on the main points of the Charter, including the veto power of the five permanent members of the Security Council – the USA, USSR, Britain, France and China. The inclusion of France was largely due to British insistence. China was included because of the American commitment to the government of Chiang Kai-shek, soon to be displaced by the victorious Communist armies led by Mao Tse-tung. The resulting paradoxical situation whereby China's seat on the Security Council was held after 1949 by a government whose actual authority was limited to the island of Formosa had not been foreseen at Yalta, when Roosevelt and his advisers did their best to bring China into the inner ring of those who would control the future world organization.

The spring and summer of 1945 witnessed important personal and political changes affecting the alliance. Roosevelt's death on 12 April led to a hardening of American attitudes towards Russia on subjects such as the composition of the Polish government, the holding of elections in Eastern Europe and the future control of Germany. On 26 July, with the announcement of the British general election results, Churchill ceased to be Prime Minister and was succeeded by Attlee, who fought a determined rearguard action during the closing stages of the Potsdam conference, but – unlike Churchill in the preceding May – showed no disposition to question Soviet control over the occupation zone in Central Germany allotted to the Russians at Yalta. In France, de Gaulle secured his hold and, notwithstanding his exclusion from the Potsdam decisions, succeeded in bringing his country back into the councils of the Allies. The government over which he presided included Communist ministers, and the same was true of the coalition government formed in Italy after the extrusion of Mussolini and the Germans. Contrary to a legend widespread then and later, there never was any chance of the Communist Party seizing control in these two Western countries, in the face of widespread popular opposition and the certainty that the bulk of the armed forces would hold out against them. The only country in which the Communists captured the lead of the anti-German resistance movement during the war, and led the armed struggle against the German and Italian occupants and their local allies, was Yugoslavia, and it was in consequence of this fact that the Allies had to put up with the formation of a Communist regime led by Tito and his associates. A similar attempt by the Communists in Greece to seize control of the resistance movement came near to success, but was blocked in December 1944 by British armed intervention on behalf of the remaining conservative elements. Military presence on the spot did not always determine the political outcome. In Berlin and Vienna, where the Soviet Army shared control with the Western Powers, the workers for the most part stuck to their traditional Social Democratic allegiance. This circumstance became decisive when in 1948 the Russians tried to blockade Berlin, and supplies had to be flown in from the West by air. But for the fact that the bulk of the Berlin workers – like those in Western Germany – preferred Social Democracy to Communism, the prolonged Berlin blockade of 1948–9 would not have resulted in a climb-down on the part of the Russians. The same applies to Austria, where the ending of the military occupation in 1955 was materially helped by the gradual realization that the Communist Party had behind it only a small minority of the working class. Matters took a different turn in Poland and Czechoslovakia, where the post-war fusion of Stalinism and pan-Slavism was greatly aided by the atrocities committed by the Germans against the Slav populations under their control. East Germany, an island in a Slav sea, came to represent an anomaly, in that it was successfully incorporated in the Soviet Empire. The latter also came to embrace Hungary and Rumania, where the replacement of Fascism by Stalinism occurred as a natural consequence of the victorious Soviet advance in 1944–5.

Overall the Grand Alliance came apart in 1947–8 because the Big Three had fallen out over the interpretation of the Yalta and Potsdam agreements. It was not the intention of the Western Allies to let Russia have complete control of Eastern Europe, but they might have put up with it if Stalin and his associates had not given every sign of wanting control of Germany as well. At Potsdam, the British (first Churchill and Eden, then Attlee and Bevin) did what they could to secure free elections in Poland, in exchange for letting Poland have German territory up to the western Neisse, thereby displacing some ten million Germans in addition to three million who were expelled from Czechoslovakia. There was never any chance of the Russians permitting such elections, since they could not conceivably have resulted in Communist victories. When the process of clamping down one-party control was extended to Eastern Germany as well it became evident that 'democracy' meant different things to the Russians and their war-time allies. The Second World War in consequence resulted in the effective partition of Europe. In part this was due to the fact that the Soviet government thought in old-fashioned military terms: it meant to create a security zone by controlling the governments of all the states on Russia's western boundary as far as its armies could reach. But in the final analysis it was the totalitarian one-party state of Stalinism that made compromise impossible. Even in Czechoslovakia, where the Communist Party was followed by something like one-third of the electorate, and where the government of President Benes was wholly committed to cooperation with the USSR, Stalin and Molotov were not content with anything short of complete control. On the other hand, the USA from 1947 onwards stepped into Britain's shoes in Greece and Turkey, and later in the Middle East as well. The creation in 1949 of the North Atlantic Treaty Organization grouping all the Western European countries under American leadership was the response to Moscow's determination to have complete control in the East. The two great alliances facing each other across a wall of mutual suspicion in the centre of Europe had become publicly identified with the opposing creeds of communism and democracy, even though both made provision for military dictatorships as well. Thus was the ground laid for what in common parlance came to be known as the cold war.

Even without the strains arising from the nature of the Stalinist regime, Russia's share in the common victory was bound to bring up awkward questions at any peace conference. Military triumph after years of desperate fighting along the whole eastern front, with the bulk of Germany's forces matched against hers, had revived Russian patriotism and pan-Slavism, thinly overlaid by Communist sentiments. For all practical purposes the Soviet Union was a Great Power like any other, and certain to behave like one. A victorious Russia could hardly be expected to put up with the results of military defeat in 1905 and 1918. The Japanese as well as the Germans were in for a reckoning. At the very least there was bound to be a demand for the cancellation of the Treaty of Portsmouth, which shut Russia out of Manchuria and Korea, and that of Brest Litovsk, which deprived her of the Baltic States and important territories subsequently handed over to Poland.[77] This was the logic of imperialism, and the USSR was no less an imperialist Power for having adopted a state-controlled economy. Moreover, imperialism, pan-Slavism and Communism all marched together, since every territorial annexation could be justified as an expansion of 'Socialism'. The fact that Stalin had dissolved the Comintern in 1943 made no difference to the behaviour of Moscow-controlled Communist parties in areas where the Red Army had taken over from the Germans. It is true that Stalin treated the Yugoslav Communists with contempt, both before and after their seizure of power, but they benefited from the expansion of Russia's military might all the same. For the rest it was foolish to suppose that, having defeated Germany, Russia would renounce the annexations of 1939-40. As for the notion of bestowing a 'coalition government' upon Poland, once the Soviet Army had occupied the country, it ignored all the murderous realities of East European politics. The Soviet Empire, dressed up in Communist colours, was bound to spread as far and as fast as its armies. By 1948 the internal logic of the system had produced both a Communist take-over in Prague and a mortal quarrel with the Yugoslavs: fellow-Communists who had risen to power on a wave of patriotic feeling and were not disposed to take orders from Moscow. The essentially Russian quality of the Stalinist regime was better understood in Belgrade than in Washington.

Important parts of the 1945 peace settlement were never ratified, but (like the post-Napoleonic arrangements in 1815) they entered into the structure of legal and political relations. The fundamental fact was that in 1945 there had been established a fairly equal balance of power between the United States and the Soviet Union. Every significant territorial gain made by Russia in 1945 was secured during the closing months of the war.[78] Thereafter deadlock set in, and eventually this deadlock was baptized 'cold war', for no better reason than that someone had thought of the phrase to describe a relationship which in some ways resembled the Anglo-Russian rivalry after the close of the Napoleonic era. The Potsdam conference – the nearest thing to a peace settlement that the Powers were able to achieve – took place at a time when nothing on earth could stop the Russians from imposing their control over Poland, Hungary, Rumania and Bulgaria, and indirectly over Finland as well, although that country retained its democratic institutions, as did Austria. In 1945 Russia could have annexed Finland, disputed the West's share in the control of Austria, demanded a say in the political settlement of Italy and Greece, asked for a share in Italy's African colonies and clamoured for a revision of the existing arrangements concerning the Turkish Straits. In fact all these questions were raised by Stalin and Molotov in 1943-5, but only as bargaining points to be abandoned when Russia's basic requirement – complete control of Eastern Europe – had been met. Within this sphere the Russians could do as they liked. A smaller Poland and a larger East Germany might have suited the long-range purposes of Soviet diplomacy just as well as the arrangements that were actually made. Only uncertainty as to permanent Soviet control of East Germany can account for the determination to annex East Prussia and to push Poland's western frontier as far as the the Oder–Neisse line.[79]

Nor were Anglo-American relations as harmonious as they looked on the surface. The Atlantic Charter proclaimed by Roosevelt and Churchill in August 1941 – before America had come into the war, but at a time when her help was essential to Britain's survival – was fundamentally incompatible with the preservation of the British Empire.[80] For Roosevelt and his advisers the right of self-determination entailed the emancipation of Britain's colonies and above all of India. This was perceived by Churchill, who fought a resolute rearguard action in this area and on one occasion went so far as to proclaim in public that he had not become Prime Minister in order to preside over the liquidation of the British Empire. De Gaulle might have employed similar language, especially after the Anglo-American descent on North Africa, the Casablanca conference which followed it and Roosevelt's semi-public hints to the Sultan of Morocco that French control of his country would be called in question after the war.[81] Roosevelt's naïve 'anti-imperialism', which was shared by his advisers and the State Department, was an expression of the fact that the United States had become ready to play a world role. It never occurred to him that in urging the British and French to give up their colonies and protectorates he was promoting American imperial interests. Or to be exact, it did not occur to him that American interests could be imperialist. The reason was quite simply that, like all American liberals, he identified imperialism with European colonialism. That there might be such a thing as liberal imperialism – the creation of a global empire held together by economic ties – was plainer to Churchill than to Roosevelt, who imagined himself to be playing a liberating role in relation to British India and French North Africa. The Americans did what the British had done before them: they rose to world eminence in the name of liberalism. Roosevelt's Secretary of State, Cordell Hull, was a Wilsonian for whom free trade equalled peace, while protectionism spelled war.[82]

These convictions were no less sincerely held for being in large measure self-serving. American and British interests were bound to clash in the economic sphere, even though Washington and London worked together for the construction of a post-war world run on liberal lines – if only because Britain had become dependent on American support. The Americans were wholly committed to free trade and the Open Door, not only in China, but throughout the sterling area. The British were torn between their imperial interests and the need to conciliate American opinion. The conflict was fought out behind closed doors. So far as the general public was concerned, America and Britain stood for identical principles. The realization that Britain had become financially dependent on the United States entered the public mind only after the war had terminated in September 1945 and Britain had begun to request a free grant-in-aid to take the place of the Lend–Lease system. What the Attlee government, which by then had succeeded Churchill in office, actually got was a loan of £1,100 million repayable in fifty annual instalments with interest at two per cent. No part of the loan could be used to reduce Britain's debts to other countries, and by 1947 sterling was to be rendered freely convertible in other currencies: an experiment that lasted for exactly five weeks before it had perforce to be terminated to stop the drain on Britain's remaining gold and dollar reserves. The heroic age was over. The era of imperial self-liquidation had begun.

NOTES

1 Winston S.Churchill, *The Second World War*, vol. I (London: Cassell, 1948; Racine, Wis.: Golden Press, Western Publishing Co., 1960), p. 7.
2 L.C.B.Seaman, *Post-Victorian Britain 1902–51* (London: Methuen, 1967; New York: Barnes & Noble, 1966), p. 252.
3 Seaman, *op. cit.*, p. 308.
4 Churchill, *op. cit.*, p. 289.
5 *Ibid.*, p. 305.
6 Hugh Thomas, *The Spanish Civil War* (London: Eyre and Spottiswoode; New York: Harper & Row, 1963), p. 571.
7 *Ibid.*, p. 584.
8 Guenther Lewy, *The Catholic Church and Nazi Germany* (London: Weidenfeld & Nicolson, 1964; New York: McGraw-Hill, 1965), p. 212.
9 *Ibid.*, p. 35.
10 *Ibid.*, p. 205.
11 Seaman, *op. cit.*, p. 259.
12 Churchill, *op. cit.*, p. 252.
13 *Ibid.*, p. 351.
14 Churchill, *op. cit.*, vol. II, p. 27.
15 *Ibid.*, vol. I, p. 420.
16 Churchill, *op. cit.*, vol. II, pp. 36 ff. and *passim*; see also B.H.Liddell Hart, *History of the Second World War* (London: Cassell, 1970), pp. 65 ff.; Sir Edward Spears, *The Fall of France* (London: Heinemann, 1954), *passim*.
17 *Op. cit.*, p. 4.
18 *Ibid.*, p. 5.
19 Paul Reynaud, *Au coeur de la mêlée* (Paris: Flammarion, 1951); tr. and abridged, *In the Thick of the Fight 1930–1945* (London: Cassell; New York: Simon & Schuster, 1955); Robert Aron, *The Vichy Regime 1940–44* (London: Putnam, 1958; Boston: Beacon Press, 1969); tr. and abridged from the French original, *Histoire de Vichy 1940–44* (1955); Guy Chapman, *Why France Collapsed* (London: Cassell; New York: Holt, Rinehart & Winston, 1969).
20 Churchill, *op. cit.*, vol II, p. 162.
21 *The Army of the Future* (London: Hutchinson, 1940; Philadelphia: Lippincott, 1941). For the author's political philosophy see *Le Fil de l'épée* (Paris: Berger–Levrault, 1932).
22 Seaman, *op. cit.*, p. 260.

23 T.W.Mason, "Some Origins of the Second World War", *Past and Present*, No. 29, December 1964, p. 80.

24 Winston Churchill, *Marlborough: His Life and Times* (London: Harrap, 1933–4; New York: Scribners, 1933–8).

25 Churchill, *The Second World War*, vol. II, p. 12.

26 Mark Arnold-Forster, in The *Guardian* of 1 January 1971, on the Cabinet papers published that day under the thirty-years rule.

27 Churchill, *op. cit.*, vol. II, p. 287.

28 *Ibid.*, p. 189.

29 Charles de Gaulle, *Mémoires de Guerre*, 3 vols. (Paris: Librairie Plon, 1954–9; London: Weidenfeld & Nicolson, 1960; New York: Simon & Schuster, 1959–60), *passim*.

30 Churchill, *op. cit.*, vol. II, pp. 118–19.

31 See "Les Communistes et la Résistance", in *Contrat Social*, vol. VIII, No. 4 (Paris: July–August 1964); for fuller documentation see A. Rossi, *Les Communistes français pendant la drôle de guerre* (Paris: Les Iles d'Or, 1951).

32 Lord Moran, *Winston Churchill: The Struggle for Survival 1940–65* (London: Constable; Boston: Houghton Mifflin, 1966), p. 773. See also John Wheeler-Bennett ed., *Action This Day: Working with Churchill* (London: Macmillan, 1968; New York: St Martin's Press, 1969); Alan Bullock, *The Life and Times of Ernest Bevin*, vol. II: *Minister of Labour 1940–45* (London: Heinemann, 1967).

33 J.M.Keynes, "The Economic Consequences of Mr Churchill (1925)". *See Essays in Persuasion* (London: Macmillan, 1933; New York: Norton, 1963), pp. 244 ff.

34 Llewellyn Woodward, *British Foreign Policy in the Second World War* (London: HM Stationery Office, 1970). For details of Churchill's career after 1914 see A.J.P.Taylor, *English History 1914–1945* (New York and Oxford: Oxford University Press, 1965), *passim*. For Churchill's own account of various topics that at one time or another engaged his passing attention, see his essay collection *Great Contemporaries* (London: Thornton Butterworth, 1937; New York: Macmillan, 1942). For a critical view of Churchill's contribution to grand strategy see Arthur Bryant, *The Turn of the Tide 1939–1943: A Study based on the Diaries and Autobiographical Notes of Field Marshal the Viscount Alanbrooke* (London: Collins, 1957).

35 Churchill, *The Second World War*, vol. II, pp. 294, 338, 346. Liddell Hart, *History of the Second World War*, pp. 94 ff.

36 Churchill, *The Second World War*, vol. II, p. 355.

37 *Ibid.*, p. 366.

38 *Ibid.*, p. 368.

39 Seaman, *op. cit.*, p. 337. For details see Liddell Hart, *op. cit.*, pp. 87 ff.; Churchill, *The Second World War*, vol. II, pp. 266 ff. Churchill's attention had been drawn to the matter before the war by his scientific adviser, Frederick Lindemann (later Lord Cherwell), but it was Tizard's Committee for the Scientific Survey of Air Defence that played the key role between 1935 and 1940. For the conflict between Tizard and Lindemann see C.P.Snow, *Science and Government* (London: Oxford University Press, 1961).

40 Churchill, *The Second World War*, vol. II, p. 301.

41 *Ibid.*, p . 297.

42 Clifton J.Child, "The Political Structure of Hitler's Europe", in Arnold Toynbee and Veronica N.Toynbee eds., *Hitler's Europe: Survey of International Affairs 1939-1946* (London–New York–Toronto: Oxford University Press, 1954), pp. 11 ff.; Alan S.Milward, *The German Economy at War* (London: Athlone Press, 1965); Albert Speer, *Inside the Third Reich* (New York: Macmillan, 1970). For the political background see Karl Dietrich Bracher, *Die Deutsche Diktatur* (Cologne: Kiepenheuer & Witsch, 1969; Eng. tr. London: Weidenfeld & Nicolson; New York: Praeger, 1971); Hans-Adolf Jacobsen, *Nationalsozialistische Aussenpolitik, 1933-1938* (Frankfurt: Metzner, 1969). For the German Army's role since 1918 see John W.Wheeler-Bennett, *The Nemesis of Power: The German Army in Politics 1918-1945* (London: Macmillan; New York: St Martin's Press, 1953); Francis L.Carsten, *Reichswehr und Politik 1918-1933* (Cologne: Kiepenheuer & Witsch, 1964), Eng. trans. *The Reichswehr and Politics* (London: Oxford University Press, 1966). For the ultimately unsuccessful conservative resistance movement see Christopher Sykes, *Tormented Loyalty* (New York: Harper & Row, 1969); Roger Manvell and Heinrich Fraenkel, *The Canaris Conspiracy* (London: Heinemann; New York: McKay, 1969); Gerhard Ritter, *Carl Gördeler und die deutsche Widerstandsbewegung* (Stuttgart: Deutsche Verlags-Anstalt, 1954); Peter Hoffmann, *Widerstand, Staatsstreich, Attentat* (Munich: Piper, 1970). For the Social-Democratic opposition see Erich Matthias, *Sozialdemokratie und Nation* (Stuttgart: Deutsche Verlags-Anstalt, 1952).

43 Clifton J.Child, "The Ukraine under German Occupation", in *Hitler's Europe*, p. 644.

44 The aims of the conservative opposition are analysed at length in Ritter's biography of Gördeler. Speer's memoirs (see above) represent an apologetic account of what the situation looked like from the standpoint of one of Hitler's closest collaborators who towards the end had lost his faith in the Führer. In the summer of 1939 some of the leading conspirators, including Gördeler and Adam von Trott zu Solz, descended on London to try their luck with the Chamberlain–Halifax government. By then their plans, which provided for a military *coup d'état* and the restoration of the Monarchy, were no longer taken seriously by the British government. Subsequently von Trott made it clear that he and his friends did not think in terms of surrendering either Austria or Czechoslovakia. See Wheeler-Bennett in the *New York Review of Books*, 11 September 1969. For an apologia of the conspirators see Hans Rothfels, *The German Opposition to Hitler* (London: Oswald Wolff, 1961; Chicago: Henry Regnery Co., 1962).

45 Child, "The Political Structure of Hitler's Europe", in *Hitler's Europe*, p. 48.

46 See *Nazi–Soviet Relations, 1939-1941: Documents from the Archives of the German Foreign Office*, ed. R.J.Sontag and J.S.Beddie, Department of State Publication 3023 (Washington: USGPO, 1948), *passim*.

47 *Ibid.*, p. 243.

48 Conversation with Molotov of 12 November 1940, *ibid.*, pp. 221 and 257.

49 Churchill, *The Second World War*, vol. II, pp. 512–24.

50 Child, "The Political Structure of Hitler's Europe", in *Hitler's Europe*, p. 50.

51 *Ibid.*, pp. 51–3.

52 *Ibid.*, pp. 56–7.

53 *Ibid.*, pp. 60–1.

54 *Ibid.*, pp. 75 ff.

55 *Ibid.*, pp. 72–3. On this subject see in particular Raul Hilberg, *The Destruction of the European Jews* (London: W.H.Allen; Chicago: Quadrangle Books, 1961), *passim*, and Gerald Reitlinger, *The Final Solution* (London: Vallentine, Mitchell & Co., 1953; Cranbury, N.J.: A.S. Barnes, rev. ed., 1961), *passim*. For the peculiar role of the US State Department in sabotaging all attempts to facilitate Jewish emigration to America after 1933 see Arthur D.Morse, *While Six Million Died* (London: Secker & Warburg; New York: Random House, 1968), *passim*. For the ideological background see Norman Cohn, *Warrant for Genocide: The Myth of the Jewish World-Conspiracy and the Protocols of the Elders of Zion* (London: Eyre & Spottiswoode, 1967; New York: Harper & Row, 1966, 1967). For the attitude of the Catholic Church see Saul Friedländer, *Pius XII and the Third Reich* (London: Chatto & Windus; New York: Knopf, 1966); Guenther Lewy, *The Catholic Church and Nazi Germany* (London: Weidenfeld & Nicolson, 1964; New York: McGraw-Hill, 1965).

56 Gerald Reitlinger, *The House Built on Sand: The Conflicts of German Policy in Russia 1939–1945* (London: Weidenfeld & Nicolson; New York: The Viking Press, 1960), pp. 66 ff. and *passim*. For details see Hilberg, *passim*, and Reitlinger, *The Final Solution*. Hannah Arendt's *Eichmann in Jerusalem* (London: Faber & Faber, 1964; New York: The Viking Press, 1963) is replete with factual errors and more concerned to establish the responsibility of the Jewish Councils in the ghettoes in making possible the 'final solution' than to give an exact account of what actually happened during those years.

57 Guenther Lewy, *op. cit.*, pp. 263 ff.

58 James Parkes, "The German Treatment of the Jews", in *Hitler's Europe*, p. 153.

59 Pierre Joffroy, *A Spy for God: The Ordeal of Kurt Gerstein* (London: Collins; New York: Harcourt Brace Jovanovich, 1971).

60 Friedländer, *op. cit.*, pp. 59 ff., 76 ff., 103 ff.

61 Lewy, *op. cit.*, p. 227.

62 *Ibid.*, p. 233.

63 Parkes, *op. cit.*, p. 160.

64 Reitlinger, *The House Built on Sand*, pp. 98 ff.; see *Trial of the Major German War Criminals* (London: HMSO, 1946–51), vol. X, p. 132.

65 Reitlinger, *op. cit.*, p. 448.

66 *Ibid.*, pp. 446–9. The Soviet population census of January 1959 gave a figure of 208,826,000. In contrast the two Germanys in 1956 had a combined population of a little over sixty-eight million: rather less than the population of Weimar Germany when Hitler came to power in 1933.

67 For details see Churchill, *The Second World War*, vols. III and IV; Liddell Hart, *op. cit.*, pp. 241 ff., 397 ff.; Bryant, *op. cit.*, pp. 487 ff.

68 From the Western standpoint the most important primary sources bearing upon the Anglo-American alliance, relations with the Soviet Union, and with the various European resistance movements, are Winston Churchill's *The Second World War* (notably the later volumes) and Charles de Gaulle's *Mémoires de Guerre*. The actual course of military operations is briefly but succinctly set out in B.H.Liddell Hart's *History of the Second World War*. The state of Europe under the German occupation is described in A. and V.M.Toynbee eds., *Hitler's Europe*, to which reference has already been made. The studies collected in this impressive volume are particularly valuable for their detailed analysis of the German administration, the system of forced labour and other aspects of the war economy. Vichy France and the Free French movement are also dealt with at some length. A brief account of the military and diplomatic moves shaping Allied strategy is to be found in the two concluding chapters of the *New Cambridge Modern History*, vol. XII (second edition) published by the Cambridge University Press in 1968. The background of American, British and Russian policies is critically analysed in Gabriel Kolko, *The Politics of War: Allied Diplomacy and the World Crisis of 1943-45* (London: Weidenfeld & Nicolson; New York: Random House, 1969). Special weight is given in this heavily documented survey to American economic policy and the extent of Anglo-American rivalry underlying America's and Britain's joint resistance to Soviet expansion. A more conventional treatment of the topic is to be found in Herbert Feis, *Churchill–Roosevelt–Stalin: The War They Waged and the Peace They Sought* (London: Oxford University Press; Princeton, N.J.: Princeton University Press, 1957). See also Adam B. Ulam, *Expansion and Coexistence: The History of Soviet Foreign Policy 1917–67* (London: Secker & Warburg; New York: Praeger, 1968); F.H.Hinsley, *Power and the Pursuit of Peace* (Cambridge and New York: Cambridge University Press, 1967, 1968), pp. 335 ff.; L.C.B.Seaman, *Post-Victorian Britain 1902–1951* (London: Methuen; New York: Barnes & Noble, 1966), pp. 363 ff.

69 Liddell Hart, *op. cit.*, p. 590, citing the four-volume history of the strategic bombing offensive, *The Strategic Air Offensive against Germany 1939–1945* (London: HMSO, 1961).

70 Churchill, *The Second World War*, vol. VI, pp. 34 ff.

71 *Op. cit.*, vol. V, p. 458.

72 *Ibid.*, p. 357.

73 *Op. cit.*, vol. VI, pp. 520 ff.; Feis, *op. cit.*, pp. 283 ff., 441 ff.; Kolko, *op. cit.*, pp. 389 ff.; Ulam, *op. cit.*, pp. 378 ff.

74 Churchill, *The Second World War*, vol. VI, pp. 551–3.

75 B.H.Liddell Hart, "The Second World War", in *New Cambridge Modern History*, vol. XII (rev. ed.), pp. 792–3.

76 Llewellyn Woodward, "Diplomatic History of the Second World War", in *New Cambridge Modern History*, vol. XII, pp. 798 ff.; Feis, *op. cit.*, pp. 534 ff.; Kolko, *op. cit.*, pp. 350 ff.

77 Seaman, *op. cit.*, p. 366.

78 Hinsley, *op. cit.*, p. 352.
79 *Ibid.*
80 Seaman, *op. cit.*, p. 367.
81 Robert Murphy, *Diplomat Among Warriors* (London: Collins; New York: Doubleday, 1964), pp. 152-3, 172-3.
82 Kolko, *op. cit.*, p. 244.

CHAPTER 13

COLD WAR AND COEXISTENCE

The cold war began in 1945 with Poland providing the immediate cause of conflict, just as it had done in 1939.[1] The Western Powers had nominally gone to war for the sake of Poland, and it was not easy for them to renounce all interest in that country, even though the Poles had been compensated with German lands for the cession of territory to the Soviet Union. Russian insistence on turning the Polish Government of National Unity into an instrument of the Communist Lublin–Warsaw regime posed a problem for which conventional diplomacy had no solution. The same applied to the situation in Czechoslovakia, where President Benes, after a trip to Moscow, felt obliged to include several Communists in his government and to entrust the premiership to the fellow-travelling Zdenek Fierlinger. Spheres of influence on the classic pattern made no provision for the complications arising from a state of affairs where one political party differed from the rest in that it aimed at total control. It had been assumed in Moscow that the Americans and the British would recognize these realities. When they began to insist on genuine elections and authentic coalition governments being formed in Eastern Europe, Stalin and Molotov could only conclude that they were going back on their previous undertakings. The two sides did not speak the same political language. The Russians thought in terms of complete control; the Western leaders aimed at a compromise which would give the Communists a share in the government – a ludicrous misconception which ignored the nature of the Stalinist regime. The quarrel over Poland set the stage for prolonged bickering over the percentage of Soviet influence in other East European countries. Only in 1948, when the Communists had taken over in Prague, while in France and Italy they had been expelled from the coalition governments set up in 1944–5, did this meaningless dispute come to an end.

The ensuing state of affairs was not simply a prolongation of the tug between Communism and anti-Communism which had been going on all over Europe since 1917. It reflected the fact that America and Russia had simultaneously arrived at the status of Great Powers, and that they had done so on the ruins of Central Europe. Both sides were conscious of their position; they were also afraid of each other; and they represented incompatible systems. Liberalism and Communism were universal ideas; they were mutually exclusive; and both were profoundly corrupted by the imperial ambitions of the two Powers who faced each other across the no-man's-land dividing Eastern Germany from what in 1949 became the German Federal Republic. For some time Western Socialists generally, and British Labourites in particular, cherished the illusion that this split could be overcome if the European nations identified themselves with the ideas and values of democratic socialism. The British Labour government's experience with Soviet diplomacy after 1945 soon dispelled these fancies. Stalin and his associates had no use for Social Democrats. They actually preferred Conservatives who did not talk about socialism and consequently posed no serious threat. The Stalinization of Eastern Europe had for its counterpart the exclusion of the Communists from all positions of influence in the West, and the formation of governments based on Christian Democrats and Social Democrats, or a coalition of both. There was no middle ground between Stalinism and anti-Stalinism; there was only the fragile hope that the two systems might be able to exist in relative peace, beneath the menace of the nuclear bomb. In this sense, 'cold war' and 'coexistence' were two sides of the same coin. What these terms signified was that America and Russia would attempt by all means short of war to extend and fortify their respective zones of influence. The dividing line ran through the centre of Germany, ultimately through the centre of Berlin. It was never crossed, and in due course the two nuclear super-powers learned to put up with each other.[2]

Contrary to legend this tacit understanding did not have to await the passing of Stalin in March 1953 and the advent of Khrushchev two years later. Stalin on the whole pursued a fairly cautious policy of expansion, took few risks while Russia did not as yet have nuclear arms, and thereafter adopted the long view, which in his case amounted to a conviction that Western capitalism would before long find itself struggling once more with the problems of the 1930s. Meantime the Soviet Union would recover from the war, consolidate its hold on Eastern Europe, keep Germany divided and continue the pre-war policy of trying to catch up industrially with the more advanced countries. It is questionable whether Stalin grasped at once the full implications of the nuclear explosion in New Mexico, which by an agreeable irony occurred on 16 July, the day on which the Potsdam conference assembled. His apparent nonchalance when acquainted with the fact by Truman may have been due to innate conservatism as much as to foreknowledge gained by way of secret intelligence and the certainty that within a few years the USSR would have its own nuclear weapons.

Meanwhile he possessed overwhelming superiority in conventional arms within the European heartland, so that the American nuclear arsenal at most reinforced his cautious adherence to a policy of consolidating the gains made in 1944–5. He also benefited for a few years from American eagerness to demobilize and from the curious notion that it was possible to dispense with spheres of influence and the balance of power. It took Washington a couple of years to grasp that the alternative to balance was imbalance, and that if there were no recognized spheres of influence the conflict of interests would be fought out (not necessarily by arms) within the same sphere. American public opinion was somewhat shocked when Churchill, in a speech delivered at Fulton (Missouri) in the presence of President Truman on 5 March 1946, invoked the menace of Soviet expansion. By that time Churchill was no longer in office, but the Attlee government had quietly begun to invest millions of pounds in atomic research without informing Parliament of the fact. The British were ahead of the Americans in recognizing that peace had become dependent on a balance of terror. Their weakness was imperial nostalgia and a failure to realize that after 1945 there were only two giants left on the world scene. A year after Churchill's Fulton speech the moment of truth arrived for the planners in Whitehall: they had to inform the Americans that the burden of keeping troops in Greece and helping the Turks to modernize their army had become too much for a Britain impoverished by six years of war. The response came on 12 March 1947 in the form of a Presidential address to a joint session of Congress: America would step in to block Soviet expansion, whether direct as in the case of Turkey, or indirect through the Communist movement in Greece. The cold war was on in earnest.[3]

How far was it a matter of totalitarianism versus democracy? In Greece, civil war had been going on since 1944, with the Communists plainly trying to seize power by violence. In Turkey there were hardly any Communists, and the Soviet demand for Turkish territory (accompanied by the massing of troops on the frontier) was in the best, or worst, Tsarist tradition. When the United States blocked Russian expansion in this area, one imperial Power checkmated another, much as Britain had supported Turkey against Russia in the nineteenth century. Palmerston and Disraeli would have understood every move in the game, as would their Russian opponents. The same consideration does not apply to Truman's rhetoric in March 1947 when he tried to alert American public opinion to the danger by dwelling upon the insuperable gulf dividing Communist tyranny from Christian democracy. What was the relevance of democracy to America's allies in Turkey or in China? When Truman invoked the traditional catalogue of liberal principles – free elections, freedom of speech and the rest – he must have known that Chiang Kai-shek took no more account of these freedoms than did Stalin. The cold war involved a massive outpouring of hypocritical nonsense on both sides of the divide. The Russian excuse was that they were promoting socialism, the American that they were defending democracy. Both, according to their lights, were as sincere as it is possible for embattled rivals to be.

The Truman Doctrine was soon succeeded by the Marshall Plan – an attempt to put the European economy back on its feet. The initial proposal in June 1947 for a massive injection of American economic aid was addressed impartially to all European governments, Communist and non-Communist alike, and there may have been some embarrassment in Washington when Moscow responded by sending Molotov to Paris on 27 June. His opening statement at the conference was reasonably conciliatory in tone, and when a few days later he reversed himself, he did so on instructions from Stalin, who in the interval had changed his mind about the whole matter. Thereafter the satellites, including Czechoslovakia, were ordered to withdraw their acceptance of invitations to attend meetings on the subject, the argument being that the Marshall Plan infringed on the sovereignty of those taking part in it. What was officially known as the European Recovery Programme thus came to benefit only the western half of the Continent, while the eastern countries were integrated into a Moscow-controlled bloc of their own. This was the logic of Stalinism. It was plainly contrary to the interests of countries such as Poland and Czechoslovakia, not to mention the French and Italian Communist parties who in consequence lost their influence on the governments of their respective countries. As the Russians saw it, massive transfers of American aid could only result in the liquidation of the 'socialist' empire Moscow had built up since 1939. The Yugoslavs disproved this thesis when in 1948 they broke loose from the Kremlin, accepted Western economic aid and still retained their planned economy. There was no inherent reason why the USSR and its dependencies could not have done the same, and but for Stalin's pathological distrust of the West they might in fact have opted for 'competitive coexistence' then and there, instead of waiting for Khrushchev and his successors to initiate something of the kind, very cautiously and on a tentative scale, years later. Instead in January 1949 they set up their own Council of Mutual Economic Assistance (Comecon), which in the circumstances could only become an instrument for pumping surplus value out of the satellites into the Russian centre of the Soviet Empire. It was imperialism with a difference, but the difference would not have seemed important to Lenin.

In retrospect it is plain that the interests of the major Powers were in conflict, as were their ideologies. That was what the cold war was about and what made it inevitable. Churchill and de Gaulle recognized this from 1943 onwards. Roosevelt failed to recognize it, and the discovery was left to his successor. By 1950 the deadlock over Berlin had been superimposed upon the tacit acceptance that Germany was not to be re-united, which in the circumstances meant that Eastern Germany would be governed by the Communists, the Federal Republic by their opponents. Paradoxically, it proved easiest to preserve peace where spheres of interest were clearly demarcated, as they were in Central Europe. Elsewhere – notably in the Middle East and in what until 1954 was known as French Indo-China – local wars, political confusion and uncertainty over territorial boundaries repeatedly threatened to involve the Big Four, who by the 1960s had become the Big Two (or Three, if mainland China was included). The Russians showed from an early date that they were determined to play the imperial game according to time-honoured rules. As early as 1945–6 Molotov raised the question of a Soviet mandate over Tripolitania. What would Lenin have thought of that? For that matter, what would he have made of the bargain whereby, in return for a promise to enter the war against Japan, Stalin at Yalta obtained American recognition of Soviet control over Outer Mongolia and a promise regarding the rights once possessed by Tsarist Russia in Manchuria?[4] When in February 1950, under a treaty signed in Moscow by Stalin and Mao in person, the Manchurian Railway and the Soviet-held base of Port Arthur reverted back to China, the Soviet Government ceded to the new regime in Peking what in 1945 it had extracted from the Americans and their Chinese allies, the Kuomintang. These rights and possessions had belonged to Tsarist Russia until they were lost to Japan in 1905, twelve years before the Revolution. The Soviet Union had no title to them except the 'historic' one based on Tsarist annexation. Yet it took months of hard bargaining to make Stalin part with them, and Peking was obliged to recognize Moscow's suzerainty over Outer Mongolia. Relations between the two countries were now on a footing of equality, but this was due to Mao Tse-tung's victory in the Chinese civil war – a victory the Russians had neither foreseen nor tried to bring about.

All this was in the classic tradition of *Realpolitik*, as was Moscow's recognition in 1945 that American possession of the atomic bomb ruled out further Soviet territorial conquests for the time being. What was new and unprecedented was the development of technology to a point where the hypothetical use of nuclear arms became self-defeating. When after 1950 the United States and the Soviet Union confronted each other in the guise of nuclear super-powers, a major war became improbable, and for the same reason it became relatively easy to push minor conflicts to the point of armed escalation without risking the ultimate reprisal. The Korean war of 1950 sprang from mutual miscalculation, and was then kept going by the Chinese who did not share the view that nuclear arms had made conventional warfare too risky.

The lengthy struggle between the French and the nationalists in Indo-China began as a popular resistance movement and ended with a military victory over a demoralized French army. The Anglo-French Suez expedition in 1956 was called off under joint pressure from Washington and Moscow. In all these cases the participants operated on the tacit assumption that nuclear arms would not be employed, and the same applied to the protracted warfare in Algeria from 1954 to 1962, which terminated with another nationalist triumph and the eviction of the French settler population. The only occasion on which nuclear war looked like a genuine possibility was afforded by the Cuban crisis of 1962, when the Russians first installed rockets on the island and then withdrew them under pressure of what amounted to an American ultimatum. Thereafter the arms race was stepped up to the point where the Soviet Union began to feel that it had achieved parity with the United States. Britain and France were left behind, and so was Japan which had been compulsorily disarmed in 1945. China, on the other hand, made every effort to join the ranks of the nuclear super-powers and at the same time renounced its alliance with the USSR, a circumstance which from 1960 onwards altered the whole aspect of world affairs.

So far as Europe was concerned, the advent of 'peaceful coexistence' in the 1960s did not alter the fundamental alignment dating back to the signing of the North Atlantic Treaty in Washington on 4 April 1949 and the subsequent decision of the Western Allies to permit the gradual rearmament of West Germany. NATO, as it came to be called for short, was born from the spectacular Berlin blockade of 1948–9, when an Anglo-American air lift provided the population of West Berlin with the essentials of living for almost a year. The blockade in turn was the sequel to the earlier breakdown of Four Power control over an undivided Germany and the institution of a Stalinist regime in East Berlin which naturally attempted to annex the western half of the former German capital. The trial of strength ended in a stalemate and in May 1949 the Soviet blockade was lifted. Both sides now proceeded to set up their own German states: the Federal Republic, with Bonn as its capital, in the West, the 'German Democratic Republic' in the East: with a fairly open frontier running through the middle of Berlin until August 1961, when the East German authorities set up the Berlin Wall to stop the drain of manpower. They had lost some three million citizens to the West, and any further departure of skilled workers would have undermined their economy. From then on, every move to make 'peaceful coexistence' sound more plausible was inevitably tied up with the notion of a Berlin settlement. In practice coexistence turned out to be synonymous with cold war. There was no meeting of minds and no way of unifying the two Germanies. As they drew further apart it became evident that Hitler's war had made an end of Germany as a nation.[5]

The post-1945 international scene was thus marked by an inevitable polarization between the two giant Powers which had emerged from the struggle. But it also reflected the inherent impossibility of reducing liberal democracy and Stalinism to a common denominator. In the words of an historian already cited: "On the morrow of Russia's greatest victory and her emergence as one of the world's two super-powers, the regime seemed to be panic-stricken not by a foreign invader, but by what a few writers, scholars, musicians, etc., might do to the Soviet people's internal cohesion and sense of purpose."[6] The United States for its part was swept by an almost equally unreasoning and dis-proportionate fear of Communism, as of some strange foreign bacillus which might poison the healthy life of the American people. These paranoiac sentiments interacted to the point where all sense of reality was lost. The European countries, having only recently emerged from the bloodbath of 1939–45, were in no position to assume the role of moderators. The Continent had been split down the middle, and the duel between the United States and the Soviet Union reflected itself in the politics of their respective allies and satellites. Only in the 1960s, with the consolidation of the Gaullist regime in France, the partial de-Stalinization of the USSR, and the consequent worsening of relations between Moscow and Peking, did it become possible for Europeans of differing political views to transcend the crisis atmosphere of the pre-ceding decade. This did not mean that cold war had given way to coexistence: merely that their identity had at last been perceived. At the same time the integration of Western Germany within an economic community plainly designed to evolve into a West European confedera-tion of states and nations took some of the sting out of the Berlin situa-tion. As the Federal Republic of Konrad Adenauer and his successors in Bonn took shape, it became evident that the bulk of West German opinion, given the choice between the status quo and national reunion on Communist terms, preferred the status quo. At first limited to the ruling Christian Democrats and their Liberal allies, this orientation eventually came to dominate the Social Democrats as well. At the same time, de Gaulle's pragmatic view of the cold war as an ordinary power struggle, his withdrawal from Algeria, and his recognition in 1964 of Communist China, put an end to the public rhetoric predominant in the 1950s. It gradually became apparent that the 1945 settlement was not going to be seriously challenged.[7]

Even before this realization had sunk in, a kind of atmospheric change had begun to make itself felt on both sides. Stalin's death on 5 March 1953 was undoubtedly a major turning-point in that it removed the more bizarre features of a political system which sprang less from its inner nature than from the pathological character of the aged tyrant who presided over a series of bloody purges of his 'comrades'. In February 1956 matters reached a stage where N.S.Khrushchev stood out among his successors, to the point of feeling able to confront the Twentieth Congress of the Soviet Communist Party with a dramatic account of the late dictator's crazier actions: a speech which was not published in the USSR, but gained widespread notoriety abroad and even shook the faith of hard-core Stalinists in Poland and other satellite states. This move towards liberalization was soon checked by the Hungarian bloodbath of November 1956 and the entry of Soviet troops into that country following the attempt of Imre Nagy and other reform-minded Communist leaders to democratize the system and remove its terrorist aspect. After a pause de-Stalinization was resumed in the USSR and brought to a climax at the Twenty-Second Congress of the Soviet Party in October 1961, when the 'secret speech' of 1956 was succeeded by an open condemnation of Stalin and the simultaneous adoption by the CPSU of a new programme promising a more rapid advance towards full equality.[8] Meanwhile the American atmosphere had begun to unfreeze slightly with the election to the Presidency of John Kennedy in November 1960. From that time onwards the two super-powers began to grope for something like a stable *modus vivendi*, helped by the gradual recovery of Europe and the emergence of con-ciliatory tendencies in the Catholic Church consequent upon the election to the Papacy of John xxiii in 1958.[9]

Neither the *aggiornamento* of the Church nor the cautious de-Stalin-ization of the CPSU went beyond the boundaries of what was considered prudent by their respective hierarchies, but doubts were sown and some of the faithful on both sides of the ideological frontier acquired the potentially dangerous habit of thinking for themselves. Revisionist Communists such as the French philosophy professor Roger Garaudy (who was expelled from his Party in 1970) found their counterparts in unorthodox theologians such as Teilhard de Chardin who revived the heresy of 'modernism'. By 1963 Paul vi, formerly Cardinal Montini, had succeeded John xxiii, while on the Soviet side Khrushchev was overthrown in October 1964 by a 'collective leadership' which plainly sought to rehabilitate Stalin and revive some features of his unique regime. In the United States, too, the short-lived liberal era associated with John Kennedy came to an end with his assassination in November 1963, a few months after the signing of a Soviet–American agreement prohibiting nuclear tests in the atmosphere, under water and in outer space. 'Competitive coexistence' did not die with Kennedy and Khrushchev, but it assumed the familiar form of an arms race which neither side could reasonably hope to 'win'. The Cuban confrontation of October 1962, when Moscow backed down in the face of overwhelming American nuclear power, taught the collective leadership in the Kremlin the importance of attaining parity. As the United States from 1965 onwards sank ever deeper into the bloody morass of the Vietnamese war, Brezhnev and his colleagues in Moscow put their own gloss on 'coexistence' in August 1968, when they sent their tanks rolling into Czechoslovakia, to terminate the reform experiment begun by the new Communist leadership headed by Alexander Dubcek. This time there was no bloodbath as there had been in Hungary in 1956: the Czechoslovak armed forces offered no resistance, and the workers did not go on strike. All the same, it was becoming plain that the notion of reforming Stalinism from above, or from within, was implausible. What was accomplished along these lines in Poland, Rumania and Hungary during the 1960s did not touch upon the essential feature of the regime: the omnipotence of the Party, a self-propelling force equipped with its own version of infallibility.

Was then the entire reform era of 1956–63 nothing but a mirage in the desert of the cold war? No, for it habituated all concerned to a quasi-rational form of behaviour which had been lacking at the peak of the Stalin era. The CPSU and its satellite parties learned to do without bloody purges, while the American Establishment learned to put up with socialist regimes in the Western hemisphere, and with Gaullist forms of neutralism in Western Europe. Indeed, de Gaulle became the symbol of the new era, notably after he had withdrawn France from NATO in 1966–7, recognized Poland's post-war frontiers and urged the Bonn government to do the same. By contrast, the British governments of the period, whether Conservative or Labour, were too closely tied to the USA to risk major departures from post-war orthodoxy. Their dependence on America also lessened their chance of entering the European Economic Community, from which indeed they were formally barred by de Gaulle in 1963 and 1967. Their diplomats were not behind the French in recognizing that cold war and coexistence were two sides of the same coin. But the French, once de Gaulle was in the saddle, became adept at playing the game of mediating between the super-powers, whereas the British clung to their dwindling status as America's favoured ally. The 'special relationship' established during the Second World War between the American and British military staffs and their scientific advisers survived Britain's loss of empire and continued to give Whitehall privileged access to American nuclear research; but it also became an embarrassment to Washington and a barrier to Britain's integration into an increasingly self-confident Western Europe: centred upon a France ruled by de Gaulle's successors and a Federal Germany now governed by the Social Democrats, who in 1970 began to complement Adenauer's *Westpolitik* (reconciliation with France) by an *Ostpolitik* which could only signify reconciliation with Poland and Czechoslovakia. The trend was encouraged by Washington and Moscow alike – a notable departure from the immediate post-war situation, when the Germans dreamed not merely of reunion but of recovering the lost territories. By 1970 these fantasies had been quietly abandoned. This did not in any way signify the end of the cold war: merely a growing recognition that the 1945 frontiers were destined to last.

As the nuclear stalemate gave place to something like veiled cooperation between Washington and Moscow, it became fashionable among Western observers to attribute this state of affairs to an underlying convergence between the two opposing systems. Western capitalism and Eastern socialism, it was argued, had both given birth to a new kind of society organized along 'managerial' lines. Private property was losing ground in the West, central planning in the East. In the end, the cold war might lose its ideological character altogether and turn into a pragmatic debate as to the respective merits of the two systems, with the 'mixed economies' of Britain and Scandinavia, plus the decentralized socialism of Yugoslavia, pointing towards a possible compromise. These notions appealed to Western sociologists who had never taken Marxism seriously or asked themselves why the Russians should continue to pay lip service to Lenin's doctrines while disregarding them in practice. If the East–West conflict became less acute, then presumably the North–South split between industrially developed countries and the remainder would be perceived as the major issue of the age. For understandable reasons, the Soviet regime was reluctant to permit the propagation of such doctrines, which found favour principally among socially and intellectually privileged members of the so-called 'new class' – notably scientists with an insecure hold upon sociological concepts. On the extreme Left, Maoist and Trotskyist writers, albeit actuated by different motives, in some cases came to similar conclusions: the Soviet regime was not socialist in the Marxian sense at all, but rather state-capitalist. The more consistent Trotskyists affirmed that Mao's China, for all its egalitarianism, was state-capitalist as well. The State having replaced the private owners of capital, the mass of exploited peasants and workers now confronted a new enemy – the bureaucracy organized in the Communist Party.

The notion of there being such a thing as 'state capitalism' is attended by serious logical difficulties, for reasons explained by a leading Austrian Marxist more than three decades ago.[10] Capitalism, by definition, is a market economy wherein prices result from competition among private owners of means of production. It is this circumstance which in the final analysis determines what and how much is produced, how much profit is accumulated and where the accumulation occurs. If the State takes over the means of production, the consequent destruc-

tion of the market mechanism renders capitalist accumulation inoperative. This is not to say that wages and prices disappear from the scene,
but they are no longer controlled by the automatism of the market.
Instead, wage-fixing and price-fixing is done by a central planning
commission, which also decides what is to be produced and in what
quantities. As for the accumulation of an economic surplus for investment purposes, this may be greatly facilitated by state ownership, but
it is not for this reason to be described as an accumulation of capital:
at any rate not by Marxists, who ought to know that for Marx the
term 'capital' was not synonymous with means of production. Capitalism in the Marxist meaning of the term relates only to means of production which produce a profit, the private appropriation of which
supplies the competitive dynamic of the system. A completely state-
owned economy, in which accumulation takes place under the control
of a central planning body, is not a capitalist economy. Surplus production (over and above the needs of the immediate producers) is not
specifically capitalist: it occurs under any conceivable system, except
possibly the most primitive kind of tribal economy. It is therefore quite
meaningless to infer the 'state-capitalist' character of the Russian or
the Chinese system from the fact that the State accumulates a surplus:
it did so under the Manchus and in Pharaonic Egypt. What is peculiar
to capitalism – competition among private owners in a market, with
profit as the source of ever-growing economic expansion – is just what
is lacking in a totalitarian state economy. Nor does it help much to be
told that the bourgeoisie has been replaced by a new exploiting class,
the bureaucracy, which does the job of accumulation. The fact that a
state-controlled economy accumulates a surplus does not make it a
capitalist economy, for what is being accumulated is not capital.
Moreover, the bureaucracy is at the mercy of its political masters who
may at any moment change course and decide to expand production
along different lines. If it be argued that these decisions are in fact being
taken by a 'new class' which controls both the Communist Party and
the State, there still remains the problem of finding a suitable label for
the regime. 'State capitalism' will not do, for the simple reason that
the State has taken the place of the capitalists. Under a system of this
kind, the political sphere no longer reflects the movement of the economic 'infrastructure'. On the contrary, the economy is shaped by the
State. If the latter is democratically controlled, the society may be
described as socialist. If it is totalitarian and despotic it may be called
Stalinist for want of a better term. In either case, the distinction between
'economic base' and 'political superstructure' ceases to be operative.
So does the identification of the surplus product with 'surplus value' –
a phenomenon which occurs only under capitalism. As for the system
being 'managerial', the task of expanding production always falls to

the managers, and even under ideal socialist conditions – with the producers in full democratic control – there would have to be a surplus to make expansion possible. In fact of course the producers are nowhere in control, and where attempts were made to institute social democracy – in Hungary in 1956, in Czechoslovakia in 1968 – the Kremlin promptly intervened. It did not do so to uphold 'state capitalism', but because the totalitarian control of society by a single political centre was in danger. Stalinists cannot share power. The creation of a totalitarian structure obeying political impulses alone is their supreme aim, and where it has been attained, the system becomes self-perpetuating.

All this is not to say that the notion of a societal 'convergence' underlying the process of 'competitive coexistence' between the two rival blocs on the world scene is wholly without merit. In so far as Western capitalism has to some extent been bureaucratized since 1945, it is arguable that the bureaucrats on both sides of the political frontier find it easier to adopt a common language. This, however, does not apply to their political masters. Fascist Germany had many notable traits in common with Stalinist Russia, yet the outcome was not convergence but war. Political and military conflict between rival forms of totalitarianism is just as likely to occur as 'confrontation' between West and East. Stalinists, Maoists and Fascists may or may not go to war against each other – the decision depends on political factors not deducible from the character of their respective societies. One must guard against the temptation to employ liberal or Marxian categories to the dynamic of totalitarian systems in which the State – that is to say, the political authority – decides what the 'economic base' is to look like and how the bureaucracy is to behave. If those in control come to recognize that 'cold war' and 'competitive coexistence' are (a) identical and (b) preferable to nuclear war, the balance of power dating back to the 1945 settlement will endure, as did the post-Napoleonic arrangement of 1815. If the international system breaks down, it will not be due to the automatism of rival economic systems, but to incompatible political ambitions on the part of the nuclear super-powers. The stakes have grown too high for commercial rivalry to play the role it did in 1914, and still to some extent in 1939. Nor is the East–West antagonism reducible to a conflict between capitalist and socialist systems. In short, the Leninist perspective of the 1920s has ceased to apply. Were it otherwise, there ought to be a Leninist explanation for the growing enmity between Russia and China. The fact that there is none demonstrates that the age of economic rivalry giving rise to political conflict has been left behind.

NOTES

1 Adam B.Ulam, *Expansion and Coexistence: The History of Soviet Foreign Policy 1917–1967* (London: Secker & Warburg; New York: Praeger, 1968), pp. 378 ff.

2 André Fontaine, *History of the Cold War*, vol. II, tr. from the French by Renaud Bruce (London: Secker & Warburg, 1970; New York: Pantheon, 1969). The first volume of this *History* starts from 1917 and thus adopts a perspective more suitable to a general discussion of Communism than to the term 'cold war', popularized, if not invented, by Mr Walter Lippmann. See also *The Impact of the Russian Revolution 1917–1967*, issued under the auspices of the Royal Institute of International Affairs (London–New York–Toronto: Oxford University Press, 1967); Isaac Deutscher, *The Unfinished Revolution: Russia 1917–1967* (London–New York–Toronto: Oxford University Press, 1967); E.H.Carr, *1917: Before and After* (London: Macmillan, 1969); Walter Laqueur, *Europe Since Hitler* (London: Weidenfeld & Nicolson, 1970); Zbigniev K.Brzezinski, *The Soviet Bloc: Unity and Conflict* (New York and London: Praeger, 1961); Philip E.Mosely, *The Kremlin and World Politics* (New York: Vintage Books, 1960); Robert Conquest, *Power and Policy in the USSR* (London: Macmillan; New York: St Martin's Press, 1961); Alec Nove, *The Soviet Economy* (London: Allen & Unwin, 1961; New York: Praeger, 2nd ed., 1969); Leonard Schapiro ed., *The USSR and the Future* (London: Pall Mall; New York: Praeger, 1963); John Keep and Liliana Brisby eds., *Contemporary History in the Soviet Mirror* (London: Allen & Unwin; New York: Praeger, 1964); Alexander Dallin ed., *Diversity in International Communism* (London and New York: Columbia University Press, 1963); Richard Lowenthal, *World Communism: The Disintegration of a Secular Faith* (London and New York: Oxford University Press, 1966); Milovan Djilas, *Conversations with Stalin* (London: Rupert Hart-Davies; New York: Harcourt, Brace, 1962).

3 Ulam, *op. cit.*, pp. 430–2.

4 *Ibid.*, p. 371.

5 *Ibid.*, pp. 440 ff., 456 ff., 496 ff.

6 *Ibid.*, p. 402.

7 D.W.Brogan, *Worlds in Conflict* (London: Hamish Hamilton; New York: Harper & Row, 1967); George W.Ball, *The Discipline of Power* (London: The Bodley Head; Boston: Atlantic Monthly Press, Little, Brown, 1968); Ronald Steel, *Pax Americana* (London: Hamish Hamilton; New York: The Viking Press, 1967); Stanley Hoffmann, *Gulliver's Troubles, Or the Setting of American Foreign Policy* (New York: McGraw-Hill, 1968); Claude Julien, *L'Empire américain* (Paris: Grasset, 1968); Louis Armand and Michel Drancourt, *Le Pari européen* (Paris: Fayard, 1968), Eng. trans. *The European Challenge* (London: Weidenfeld & Nicolson, 1969); Raymond Aron, *Paix et Guerre entre les nations* (Paris: Calmann-Lévy, 1962), Eng. trans. *Peace and War* (London: Weidenfeld & Nicolson, 1967; New York: Doubleday, 1966); *Le Grand Débat* (Paris: Calmann-Lévy, 1963); Paul-Marie de la Gorce, *De Gaulle entre deux mondes* (Paris: Fayard, 1964).

8 L.Schapiro ed., *op. cit.*, Introduction and *passim*.

9 W.Laqueur, *op. cit.*, p. 229.
10 Rudolf Hilferding, "State Capitalism or Totalitarian State Economy", first published in the *Socialist Courier*, a Menshevik journal issued in Paris in 1940; reprinted in I.Howe ed., *Essential Works of Socialism* (New York: Bantam Books, 1971), pp. 511–17.

CHAPTER 14

THE NEW EUROPE

A   ECONOMIC RECOVERY[1]

In 1945, when the dust of battle cleared, Europe's former eminence in world affairs was found to be among the casualties of the Second World War. In the place of the familiar 'concert of Europe' there had emerged a global confrontation between the Soviet Union and the United States, with a deeply shaken British Empire (soon to be transformed into a Commonwealth of nominally equal states and nations) uncertainly poised on the edge of the European Continent. The separation of Britain from Continental Europe had been accentuated by the outcome of the war, which appeared to have left the British Empire intact as one of the Big Three responsible for the ordering of the post-war world. So far as public opinion was concerned, this position was confirmed by the Churchillian doctrine that Britain operated within three circles – the imperial, the Anglo-American and the European – and that this tri-angularity gave her a unique position in the world.[2] On a celebrated occasion in June 1944, Churchill, in the presence of Eden and Bevin, had told de Gaulle: "Here is something you should know: whenever we have to choose between Europe and the open sea, we shall always choose the open sea. Whenever I have to choose between you and Roosevelt, I shall always choose Roosevelt".[3] Since Roosevelt had by 1944 made it clear that he proposed to exclude France from the direction of the post-war settlement, this impassioned declaration amounted to saying that Churchill preferred a secondary status within the Anglo-American alliance to the role of Europe's defender. The subsequent behaviour of various British post-war governments, whether headed by Attlee, Eden or Macmillan, did nothing to alter this picture. As late as December 1962, Harold Macmillan coupled an application for entry into the European Economic Community (EEC) with a public demon-stration of Anglo-American nuclear partnership at the ill-fated Nassau conference with President Kennedy. De Gaulle responded on 14 Janu-ary 1963 by vetoing Britain's entry into the EEC.

But for such a dramatic confrontation between Britain and France to become possible in 1963, it was first necessary for all the West European countries to emerge from the ruins of 1945. Broadly speaking, this recovery had been accomplished by 1960 under the protective umbrella of American nuclear power and economic assistance. From then onwards, Britain, France, West Germany and Italy, with the smaller countries in their wake, consolidated their respective positions to a degree where it became safe to quarrel in public over the economic organization of Western Europe. For this to happen, the German Federal Republic had to become solidly committed to West European integration. It did so under the leadership of the aged Konrad Adenauer and his Christian Democrats between 1949 and 1963. Taking office at the age of seventy-three, Adenauer (1876–1967) committed his country to a firm political alliance with France, and would have led it into a supra-national European Defence Community as well, if the French government of the day had not torpedoed it in 1954.[4] On the French side, the prolonged rule of Charles de Gaulle, from 1958 to 1969, created the preconditions for a stable foreign policy. Between 1947 and 1958 no less than twenty-one French Cabinets had flitted across the scene of the Fourth Republic established in 1945–6. The Gaullist Fifth Republic, with ministerial changes held in check by the authority of a President who (after the constitutional amendment of 1962) had to be elected by popular vote, made it possible to institute long-range planning.[5] Contrary to some alarmist forecasts, de Gaulle did not go back on the essentials of French post-war policy, as laid down by the then Foreign Minister, Robert Schuman, on 9 May 1950, when he surprised a press conference with the announcement that France proposed "to place all Franco-German coal and steel production under a common High Authority, in an organization open to the participation of the other countries of Europe". This was the moment when Franco-German cooperation became the cornerstone of all future West European arrangements. It was also the moment when the British government missed the boat and renounced the European role it might have secured.[6]

Schuman was determined that the revolutionary nature of his proposals should be universally recognized. "Five years almost to the day after the Germans' unconditional surrender," he told his press conference, "France is carrying out the first decisive step in the construction of Europe, in partnership with Germany." The moment chosen for this breakthrough was uniquely favourable. Adenauer and Alcide de Gasperi (1881–1954), both Catholic democrats who had never compromised with Fascism, were in charge of West German and Italian affairs, while another Christian Democrat held the key post of Foreign Minister in France. For Robert Schuman, who had been born in Luxemburg in 1886, taken his doctorate in Strasbourg in 1910, served in the German Army during the 1914–18 war, and become a French citizen only in

1919 when Alsace-Lorraine reverted to France, this was the supreme moment of his career. Franco-German reconciliation under his aegis became and remained the keystone of the European arch. De Gasperi, another conservative democrat with strong Catholic backing, completed the triumvirate. The link between the Vatican and political reaction, embodied in the person of Pius XII, had been ruptured by the Allied victory in 1945, the disappearance of the Italian Monarchy and the electoral triumph of Christian Democracy. Where the old alliance persisted, as in Franco's Spain and Salazar's Portugal, there could be no question of including these regimes in the new Europe, although they might enter the wider NATO coalition organized under American leadership. The European community was democratic or it was nothing. It could count on Socialist support and Communist hostility, especially in Italy, France and Belgium. The German Social Democrats proved slow and reluctant converts, their leader Kurt Schumacher (1895–1952) preferring to chase the rainbow of German unification. When this aim proved unattainable, German Socialism added its considerable weight to the forces making for West European unification.

European federalism was in its origins a Continental movement in which the British did not take an active part because they were still under the illusion that the United Kingdom was the centre of a world empire. This did not prevent Churchill from accepting the post of President of Honour when a 'Congress of Europe' was held at The Hague from 8 to 10 May 1948, with 713 delegates from sixteen countries present. They could afford to feel hopeful, for on 17 March 1948 the governments of Britain, France, Belgium, Holland and Luxemburg had signed the Brussels Treaty providing for the creation of a Consultative Council of Foreign Ministers. The 'European Movement' International Committee set up on 25 October 1948 was once again headed by Churchill, flanked by M. Léon Blum for France, M. Paul-Henri Spaak for Belgium and Signor Alcide de Gasperi representing Italy. The subsequent agreement to establish a Committee of Ministers and a Consultative Assembly, together forming the Council of Europe, almost coincided with the signing of the North Atlantic Treaty on 4 April 1949. The British took part, not least because the Americans (in the words of a State Department declaration issued in July 1948) "strongly favoured" the "progressively closer integration of the free nations of Western Europe". But the British continued to regard themselves as a link between Europe and the United States, an attitude made clear by British delegates of all parties in the subsequent meetings of the European Assembly at Strasbourg. Since the Assembly, unlike the Council of Ministers, was a parliamentary body consisting of members of the various national legislatures acting in their individual capacities, these expressions of feeling may be regarded as having been spontaneous and unrehearsed. London's attitude to European federalism began to change only in the 1960s when the Commonwealth had begun to dissolve, while the United Kingdom was falling behind its continental neighbours in the economic race.

The movement ran parallel with the economic restoration of Western Europe as such. The USSR having refused to take part in the post-war American endeavours to put the European economy back on its feet, the key organization turned into a West European one. By April 1948, sixteen associated governments had established the Organization for European Economic Cooperation (OEEC) to which Western Germany was admitted in October 1949. The United States and Canada became observer members of the organization in 1950, and subsequently cooperation was developed impartially with Communist Yugoslavia and Fascist Spain.[7] By 1960 the original framework had been extended to embrace the United States, Canada and Japan as full members of an Organization for Economic Cooperation and Development (OECD), but it was the earlier OEEC whose establishment coincided with the signing in March 1948 of the Brussels treaty linking Britain, France, Belgium, the Netherlands and Luxemburg. Ostensibly directed against a hypothetical German military danger, this agreement preceded by a year the signing in April 1949 of the North Atlantic treaty by the United States, Canada and ten European countries, thereby shielding Western Europe against Russia and institutionalizing the American presence in Europe. In form an alliance among equals, NATO was in fact so heavily dependent on American air power, and especially nuclear power, as to constitute an American protectorate over Western Europe. Although a few ideologists affected to regard it as the forerunner of an Atlantic Community, it remained a purely military association within which the United States inevitably predominated. With the waning of the Russian menace in the later 1960s, the tacit recognition by all concerned of the 1945 frontiers and France's ostentatious departure from NATO in 1966–7, it became possible to differentiate between European and Atlantic planning. The original Brussels treaty of 1948 had already been expanded in 1954 to include the ex-enemies Germany and Italy and renamed Western European Union (WEU). This was more than a bureaucratic reshuffle: it pointed to a not so distant future when the West Europeans would become less dependent on American leadership. In 1948, and for some years thereafter, this dependence was overwhelming. The Marshall Plan – so called because its original outline had been suggested by the US Secretary of State, General George Marshall, in a speech made at Harvard University on 5 June 1947 – eventually took the form of a European Recovery Programme under which more than eleven billion dollars of aid were made available by 1951 to the principal West European countries. Of this total Britain received twenty-four per cent, France twenty per cent, West Germany eleven per cent and Italy ten per cent. With this help the West European economies by 1951 recovered their pre-war levels and were able to relax some of their controls over foreign trade and payments. Once this process had been set in motion, it also became possible to think in terms of West European economic integration, whereas in the immediate post-war period the various governments concerned were simply concerned to survive and to rebuild their shattered economies.

The increasing role played within NATO by Western Europe, and within Western Europe by France, was bound up with the idiosyncratic personality of Charles de Gaulle (1890–1970) who managed for a decade to place his stamp upon European affairs.[8] By origin and upbringing a conservative aristocrat with authoritarian leanings, de Gaulle in 1940 broke with his class, as well as with the Vichy regime, and transformed himself into a national leader who in 1944–6 presided over a quasi-revolutionary reorganisation of society. Recalled to power in 1958 in the midst of the turmoil into which the Algerian war of 1954–62 had plunged his country, he gave it a new constitution, ten years of stability and an orientation that led away from the idea of an Atlantic Union centred upon the United States. He also presided over an industrial transformation facilitated by the lessening importance of coal and the growing significance of oil, natural gas, electricity and nuclear energy. The development of nuclear power became a national priority as part of a deliberate attempt to develop a modern technology through an unprecedented concentration on *industries de pointe* (aerospace, cars, electronics, chemicals).[9] The political thunderbolts which accompanied this silent transformation – foremost among them the Evian agreement of 1962 which gave independence to Algeria, the two vetos of 1963 and 1967 on British entry into the Common Market of the Six, the recognition of Germany's 1945 frontiers, the departure from NATO and the General's public condemnation of American policy in Vietnam and towards China – held the public spellbound and even exerted a certain influence on the comportment of the Soviet government; but in essentials de Gaulle did not depart from the European priorities laid down by his Socialist and Christian Democratic predecessors in office during the stormy years of the Fourth Republic. Franco-German reconciliation remained the keystone of the structure, and the European Economic Community formed in 1955–7 by the governments of West Germany, France, Italy and the three Benelux countries was obstinately defended against Anglo-American encroachments. Indeed, the General's principal reason for excluding the British was widely believed to be his conviction that Britain would act the part of America's Trojan horse.

De Gaulle inherited two commitments made by his predecessors – the decision that France should become a nuclear power, and the Rome

Treaty of 25 March 1957, inaugurating the European Economic Community popularly known as the Common Market. He added a third element: resistance to American economic domination. This had become a genuine problem with the growing technological gap between the two halves of the Western world. American capital was not merely being invested in post-war Europe's key industries – it was threatening to turn them into American satellites.[10] The reaction to this challenge took two interrelated forms: Europeanism and the growth of state control. If the USA not merely predominated within the capitalist world, as Britain had done between 1815 and 1914, but actually became the centre of all basic decision-making in the economic sphere, the European countries and Japan were bound to sink into the role of clients of an American empire sprawling the globe. This state of affairs might be concealed behind the decorous façade of something called 'Atlantic Union', but it would be a genuine empire nonetheless. In point of fact this did not occur, although in the 1950s there were those who thought it would – especially if the British Empire (or Commonwealth) was liquidated under American pressure. The United States obtained a very large share of world trade and production in the key industries, but the only parts of the world which were really taken over by American capital were Canada and some of the less important Latin American countries. Elsewhere, a balance established itself, not least because Germany and Japan got on their feet much more rapidly than anyone had thought possible in 1950; also because Washington's increasing involvement in the global competition with Moscow encouraged an unproductive outlay upon arms which proved a burden upon the American economy rather than a stimulant. The upshot was that continental Western Europe and Japan managed to hold their own, while British influence declined as Commonwealth markets were increasingly taken over by Britain's American, European and Japanese competitors. American capital investment in Canada, Western Europe and Japan rose from 7·2 billion dollars in 1949 to 60 billion in 1967, but only Canada was genuinely satellized. During the 1950s and 1960s the key industries of Western Europe and Japan, so far from being held back by American competition, developed more rapidly than those of the United States – in part at least because of the massive inflow of American capital and technology. The figures speak for themselves. In 1947 Western Europe's share of international trade had fallen to less than thirty-four per cent of the global total, whereas by 1965 it had risen to over forty, against eighteen for the USA and Canada combined, while Japan's share rose from less than one per cent to 4·5 of the world aggregate, including the Soviet-controlled Eastern bloc. In 1967 the USA produced 118·1 million tons of crude iron, against 90 million for the Six of the EEC, 24·2 million for Britain and 62·1 million for Japan. In car production the

TABLE 2 GROSS DOMESTIC PRODUCT 1948–63*

Compound Annual Rates of Growth (%)[2]

Austria	5·8
Belgium	3·2
Denmark	3·6
France	4·6
Germany	7·6
Italy	6·0
Netherlands	4·7
Norway	3·5
Sweden	3·4
Switzerland	5·1
United Kingdom	2·5

* Source: M. Postan, *An Economic History of Western Europe 1945–1964* (London: Methuen, 1967), p. 12.

TABLE 3 EUROPEAN EXPORTS*

Values: £1,000 million
Index (1958 = 100)

1948	16·24	40
1953	26·67	70
1956	35·93	92
1959	42·14	111
1962	54·22	138

* Countries included: Austria, Belgium, Denmark, France, Germany, Italy, Netherlands, Norway, Sweden, Switzerland, United Kingdom, Source: Postan, *op. cit.*, p. 90.

relevant figures in that year were 7·4 million for the USA, 5·7 million for the EEC, 1·5 million for Britain and 3·1 million (including trucks) for Japan.[11] It was the same story in most other branches of production, and overall the combined output of all the Western European countries, including Britain, had by 1965 reached seventy per cent of the US total. Even though some key industries – notably cars and computers – had been largely taken over by American capital, it would have been absurd to speak of Western Europe being 'colonized' by the USA. The growth of the public sector in Britain, France and Italy was a sufficient guarantee against this happening. As for Western Germany and Japan, their relative freedom from the burden of unproductive arms expenditure, joined to the other factors which had enabled them to industrialize rapidly in the past, ensured their economic independence and even enabled them to invade the American domestic market for durable consumer goods.[12]

Why then did American capital influx nonetheless act as a spur to

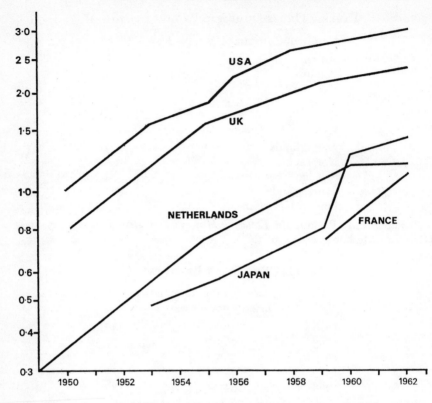

Europeanization? Principally because it was concentrated in certain key sectors in which the technological gap between the USA and the various European nation-states threatened to become permanent. In 1965 the European Economic Commission in Brussels estimated that eighty per cent of Common Market computer production, twenty-four per cent of the motor industry, fifteen per cent of synthetic rubber output and ten per cent of petro-chemicals were being managed by American subsidiaries.[13] This circumstance gave rise to the alarmist forecast that American industry in Europe would by 1980 overshadow its native competitors. European big business responded with a series of mergers, while the governments of the Six increasingly tightened the institutional framework laid down in the Treaty of Rome. There were in fact two possible reactions to the American challenge – Gaullism and Europeanism – and both came into play during the later 1960s, on occasion in such a manner as to counteract each other. Ultimately, the reason why both the more committed 'Europeans' among the Six and important sectors of British public opinion had by 1970 become converted to supra-nationalism lay in the disparity between the American industrial giants and their European competitors. If cooperation in scientific research could give rise to the highly successful European Centre for Nuclear Research (CERN) at Geneva, there was no apparent reason why the process should not be extended to the aerospace industries, telecommunications, electronics, chemicals and other key industries. Whether this kind of fusion necessitated a corresponding degree of political supra-nationalism – ultimately leading perhaps to a popularly elected European Parliament with genuine powers of control – continued to be debated, as did the merits of British participation in the EEC. But the trend towards Europeanization was unmistakable, extending as it did from business mergers to the increased mobility of labour. The point which needs stressing is that the original drive after 1945 came from politicians and intellectuals who were far ahead of the businessmen in their respective countries. Two disastrous wars had broken the deeply rooted nationalism of the masses in the leading European countries and given a unique opportunity to a political elite which at a decisive moment was able to turn Europeanism into a popular creed. That it did so in response to the Soviet–American antagonism is indisputable. That European federalism was never anything but an ideological veil cast over the reality of capitalist interpenetration is a fantasy entertained by people who have transformed Marxism into the most tedious kind of economic determinism. What lay at the back of the European movement in the 1950s was not cartelization but the common experience of the Resistance movement, plus democratic convictions and the will to make an end of senseless inter-state rivalries. This kind of political idealism – ably exploited by Social Democratic and Christian Democratic politicians who for a brief period held power in their respective countries – was strong enough to override the fears of the business community, which had to be dragged into the Common Market very much against its protectionist inclinations. This is how history really operates, which is why even the most perceptive economists rarely prove good prophets where the actual march of events is concerned.

European supra-nationalism in its more ambitious form having proved inapplicable to Britain and Scandinavia, the Franco-German alliance already referred to became the core of the EEC, whose members committed themselves to do away with internal customs duties and establish a single external tariff within twelve to fifteen years; to let capital and labour cross national frontiers; and to equate their respective social policies. While all this was going on, Britain proposed a free-trade area embracing the Six as a unit and the eleven remaining members of the OEEC. Within this area, internal barriers to industrial, but not to agricultural trade would be eliminated; there would be no common external tariff, and each associate would maintain existing preferences, such as the imperial preferences granted by Britain to Australia, New

Zealand and other overseas territories. Nothing came of this scheme, and Britain was thrown back upon the EFTA association with Scandinavia, Austria, Switzerland and Portugal, until Europeanism gained the upper hand after 1970.[14]

TABLE 4 RATE OF GROWTH OF OUTPUT AND RELATIONSHIP
BETWEEN INVESTMENT AND OUTPUT IN 1949–62*

	1 Annual rate of growth in real Gross *Domestic* Product (% per annum)	2 Gross *domestic* fixed capital formation[a] (% of Gross Domestic Product)	3 Incremental capital-output ratios
Austria	5·8	23·3	3·9
Belgium	3·0	16·9	5·6
Denmark	3·8	17·5	5·5
France	4·8	20·6	4·6
Italy	6·0	22·0	3·7
Netherlands	5·0	25·0	5·2
Norway	3·5	32·6	9·5
Sweden	3·5	21·4	6·3
Switzerland	5·0	23·6	4·5
United Kingdom	2·5	16·1	6·7
Germany	6·8	24·3	3·3

[a] At constant prices, the period covered for most countries is 1949–59 inclusive.

* The table is based on the figures in UNO, *Economic Survey of Europe 1961*, part 2, Geneva, 1964, Ch. II, Table 6, supplemented by figures for 1960–2 derived mainly from OECD annual surveys of individual countries, and adjusted for the United Kingdom on the basis of the figures in the paper by R.C.O.Matthews, "Some Aspects of Post-War Growth in the British Economy in Relation to Historical Experience", *Manchester Statistical Society*, 1964. Table originally appeared in Postan, *op. cit.*, p. 115.

The question why Britain did not in this period achieve a growth rate comparable with that of its main Continental competitors has been endlessly debated.[15] Perhaps the only statement that would commend itself to all the participants in this discussion is the retrospective recognition that Britain entered the 1960s with an overvalued currency. But it would seem that the slowdown had started already in 1955, when the post-war boom was over. The subsequent failure to sustain growth at a steady rate of three or four per cent annually cost the country thousands of millions of pounds, reduced its share of world trade, left British goods unable to compete in foreign markets, and in the end precipitated a devaluation of the pound in November 1967, following an earlier and even more drastic one in 1949. The explanation favoured by some economists – that an excessive concern for the defence of the sterling area led to an obsession with the balance of payments, at the expense of industrial growth – raised the question whether the interests of the City of London were not in some ways incompatible with rapid industrial development. Successive governments tried and failed to maintain a balance between these conflicting claims. The problem was not peculiar to Britain, but the Continentals – West Germany above all – were more successful in solving it. Paradoxically, the Germans were favoured by the absence of heavy defence requirements, which left their industries free to concentrate on the production of export goods. Overall, West Germany combined rapid growth with a much smaller rise in prices than that experienced by Britain. Between 1950 and 1960, consumer prices at home rose by fifty per cent in Britain, compared to only twenty per cent in West Germany. During the same period British industrial output grew by about forty per cent, while German output more than doubled.[16] It was substantially the same story during the 1960s, when moreover German real wages began to outpace those paid to British workers, whose gains were largely fictitious, being wiped out by rising prices. France, Italy and the Benelux countries were also substantially more successful in raising their growth rates. The basic feature of the post-war period in fact was the relatively slow expansion of the British economy compared to that of its rivals. This circumstance was at first overlaid by the catastrophic military defeats inflicted on Germany, Italy and Japan, and the devastation suffered by France and the Low Countries as a result of the German occupation. But once the immediate consequences of the war had worn off, these countries in the 1950s and 1960s began to outpace the United Kingdom. Taking the decade 1953–4 to 1963–4, Britain's rate of growth is estimated to have been 2·7 per cent a year, as against 4·9 per cent in France, 5·6 in Italy, 6 per cent in Germany, and no less than 9·6 per cent in Japan.[17] Setting aside the abnormal Japanese performance, which reflected that country's belated industrialization, the difference between British and Continental growth rates had become very marked by the 1970s, causing some leading economists to wonder whether built-in structural obstacles might not have to be regarded as permanent.

One favoured popular explanation – namely that Britain had, as a result of the war, lost its inherited wealth – was simply due to ignorance. "As late as 1950, when receipts from overseas investments were known to be greater than before the war, ministerial statements claimed that all overseas investments had been lost."[18] Subsequently, a heavy outflow of capital to the sterling area and other regions yielded a mounting income, which served to mask the relative failure of exports to expand with sufficient rapidity to make up for the growth of imports whenever the country approached a condition of near-full employment. The crucial failure lay in inadequate capital formation, lack of competitive ability and a consequent shrinkage of Britain's relative share in a rapidly expanding world market. Even so, national income increased from 1950 to 1966 by forty-nine per cent in total and by thirty-four per cent per person employed – more rapidly than during any comparable period in the past.[19]

What matters in a competitive world, however, is not so much absolute progress as growth in relation to actual and potential rivals. In relative terms Britain was near the bottom of the growth stakes over the whole period since 1950.[20] The USA, whose performance was even worse, started from a much higher absolute level of income and was less dependent on foreign trade. It is of course arguable that real progress in welfare terms is not measurable, and that if people choose to take their increased wealth in the form of greater leisure rather than more goods, this does not represent a check to economic advance:

> Healthy city environments, comfortable travel conditions and other public amenities are part of welfare; and an addition to physical output incurred at the expense of a greater cost in noise, smell, dirt or destruction of beauty is not a growth of welfare but a diminution of it. . . . There would, nevertheless, have had to be an extremely large systematic bias against Continental countries and in favour of Britain in changes in leisure, or in other unmeasured amenities, or in the statistical comparability of the figures, to bridge the gap shown in growth rates for the period as a whole.[21]

On balance it seems that a greater emphasis on welfare or leisure cannot account for Britain's relatively poor economic performance during this period, and that the Continental countries – with Sweden and Switzerland in the lead, followed at a distance by the Six of the EEC – were at least equally successful in making increased provision for social and cultural purposes, from old-age pensions to socialized medicine and paid holidays. In none of them did any significant distribution of wealth take place, but living standards rose faster on the Continent. Several of them, notably France, were also more successful in adapting to the new age of state planning and conscious control of the economy.[22] If central planning is the basic feature of the new capitalism, it must be thought a minor paradox that the homeland of Keynesian economics proved relatively resistant to the theory and practice of governmental direction of the economy, and that it did so under Labour and Tory governments alike.

Another unchanging feature throughout the 1950s and 1960s was the readiness of successive British governments to shoulder the burden of the sterling area. In essence this was a combination of nations, for the most part belonging to the Commonwealth, in whose monetary transactions the pound sterling served as the medium of payment and as a security for the local currency. This mechanism provided them with a means for settling their mutual accounts without the restrictions imposed elsewhere by the shortage of dollars. But from the British point of view the sterling balances held in London were not an unmixed benefit. They represented a large volume of foreign indebtedness – between £3,000 million and £4,000 million in the 1960s – and an obligation to defend the pound sterling as a medium of payment for a volume of commercial transactions greatly in excess of Britain's own foreign trade and her gold reserves. Whenever the British balance of payments showed a deficit, there was a tendency for sterling holders to convert into dollars or other currencies, thus threatening the central reserves. The British bank rate had to be kept high in order to retain foreign funds in London, and the resulting annual cost of servicing the sterling balances grew into a heavy burden. In so far as these debt charges had to be remitted abroad, they aggravated the payments unbalance which the high interest rates were meant to alleviate. By 1971 the whole system – ultimately an inheritance from the imperial past – had become so burdensome that Britain's projected entry into the European Economic Community of the Six came to be linked with schemes for terminating the sterling area as such. It was one symptom among several which to foreign observers suggested that after 1945 the United Kingdom had assumed military and financial obligations disproportionate to its strength.

B SOCIAL TRENDS

It has already been made plain in the course of our survey that the 'Europe' of this chapter is not the geographer's Europe, which is usually defined as the area north of the Bosphorus and west of the Ural mountains, thus including the Soviet satellites of Eastern Europe, as well as a large portion of the USSR itself. The designation 'Western Europe' is not wholly satisfactory either, for some parts of Eastern Europe are farther west than Greece, Finland or Yugoslavia. For practical purposes, the term 'Western Europe' is commonly used interchangeably with 'Europe', so as to specify the group of countries not included in the Soviet Empire; but if cultural criteria are applied, Turkey forms part of the Middle East, whereas East Germany, Poland, Hungary, Rumania and Czechoslovakia unquestionably belong to Europe. In terms of the political nomenclature invented in 1948–9 it was plainly absurd to include Spain within a region bearing the proud title 'The Free World'. There is no satisfactory solution of the problem, and there will be none until the Russian and American armies, whose vanguards met on the river Elbe in 1945, have returned to their respective homelands. Once this has occurred, the relevance of Poland's centrally planned economy to the 'European' status of that country will appear in its true light: that is to say, it will be generally accepted as wholly irrelevant. The plain fact is that the division of Europe into two blocs respectively controlled from Washington and Moscow has imposed a terminology for which there is no historical justification. This judgement differs from the opinion expressed by two historians who in 1966 concluded an account of *Independent Eastern Europe* with the words:

> With 1945, in any case, an entirely new era begins. In that year the flame of independence, where it had still flickered on throughout the war, was blown out in all 'Eastern Europe' except in the four peripheral states of Finland, Austria, Greece and Turkey. Three years later it sprang up again in Yugoslavia, but this did not alter the truth that the 'independent Eastern Europe' of our pages no longer existed.[23]

The standard American viewpoint was formulated in 1961 by an influential group of scholars for whom 'Europe' had come to signify the group of countries bound together in the OECD, which did not include Finland (and until recently had not included Spain), but did include Turkey.[24] Yugoslavia was left out, on the grounds that its centrally planned economy implied a wholly eastward orientation. This criterion is quite arbitrary, to say nothing of the fact that in recent years Yugoslavia has become heavily dependent on Western Germany and Austria as outlets for its surplus labour. The sensible procedure consists in ignoring politico-military structures such as NATO and the Warsaw Pact. This is not to say that the historic division between Eastern and Western Europe has lost its significance: it has, if anything, been accentuated by the consequences of the Second World War. On the other hand, the difficulty Moscow has been having in imposing its rule upon Eastern and Central Europe points to the importance of not making too much of political frontiers. Culturally, Europe represents a unity quite distinct from the Eurasian land mass of the USSR on the one hand, the United States on the other. It is arguable that in 1914 Russia formed part of Europe, and it is probable that some of its dissident intellectuals today would like to resort to this state of affairs; but for our purpose the USSR, as presently constituted, is a Eurasian empire midway between Europe and Asia. As for the East European countries of the Soviet bloc, their political fate is linked to that of the USSR, and so is the management of their state-controlled economies. The latter feature does not render them less European, but it imposes a need to treat them separately whenever one generalizes about socio-political trends. To the invisible nexus linking Western Europe and North America there corresponds the forcible integration of the East European economies with that of the Soviet Union. Where this process was momentarily threatened, as in Czechoslovakia in 1968, the connection was restored by military force. For political purposes, therefore, Europe remains divided. In what follows, the Soviet bloc is for the most part ignored and attention is mainly focused upon Western Europe plus its appendages. Students concerned to analyse the Soviet model have ample material at their disposal.[25]

At first glance it might seem that concepts such as 'industrial society', 'technological change' or 'the managerial revolution' supply a means of theorizing on a Continental scale, without troubling about political or ideological frontiers. Thus even though one may agree that 'Europe' was absent at Yalta and Potsdam, and has been non-existent as a political entity ever since, it is arguable that this does not really matter because the fundamental convergence of the two great power blocs, in the age of space rivalry and the computer, will bring about a common civilization. There is indeed a level of scientific generality at which politics ceases to be important, but then the same is true of table tennis. In 1944, Ernest Bevin – since 1940 Churchill's colleague as Minister of Labour in the war-time coalition government – declared: "I think it is true to say that science has not merely a place in industry, but does in fact dominate it now."[26] More was to be heard of this technological enthusiasm in the years that followed, culminating in the general explosion of feeling in 1969, when a team of American space explorers made the first successful landing on the surface of the moon. Soviet–American rivalry in this sphere underscored the effective absence of Europe from any serious international power competition since 1945. In this perspective, the political frontier separating Eastern from Western Europe was in fact negligible, a circumstance which in the 1970s gave additional impetus to the movement for Western European integration: better half a loaf than nothing at all. Yet 'convergence' in this domain is more likely to perpetuate the space race between the USA and the USSR than to promote the unification of Europe. As for the trend towards managerialism – in concrete terms: the replacement of the owner-manager by the salaried manager *tout court* – it has for decades been going forward all over the world, without for that reason making much of an impact upon the political divisions separating the two halves of the European Continent.[27] For that matter, the divorce of ownership from control was noted by Marx in the third volume of *Capital*: a century before there was any talk about technocratic managerialism overcoming the East–West split. The fact is that all these sociological insights have very little bearing upon our perception of the actual historical process. Stalinism and Fascism had much in common, and Stalin murdered more Communists than did all the Fascist regimes combined. This did not prevent the 1941–5 war between Germany and Russia from being the bloodiest in history. 'Convergence' between East and West will have to become a reality at the level of political decision-making before there is any let-up in the cold war. The mere emergence of a managerial stratum within the increasingly industrialized societies of Western and Eastern Europe is not by itself going to promote significant political changes, and the same applies to the new technology.

It is nonetheless a fact that since 1945 the world has witnessed a rate of technological progress more rapid and widespread than anything that occurred before this date. If one is determined to disregard political frontiers, one may note that the modern aircraft industry was for the most part a post-war development. The same applies to electronics – the production not only of radio and television equipment, but of various electronic devices for measurements, signals and telecommunication, as well as computers and transfer devices which form the basis of the modern automation and cybernetic techniques. The coming of the transistor in the 1950s opened a new era. Modern plastics, synthetic resins and man-made fibres were for the most part post-war commodities: products of the new hydrocarbon chemistry and the petrochemical industry based on it.[28] The civilian use of atomic power, although still in its infancy by the 1970s, promised to inaugurate the greatest revolution of all. Among numberless other inventions, the use of satellites to scan clouds over the world and to assist in the study of weather conditions foreshadowed a time when it may become possible to control the weather, thereby increasing rainfall in arid regions.[29] A great deal of the new technology originated in the 1939–45 war and was put to peaceful uses thereafter. Most of the radio and radar development of the 1950s and 1960s stemmed from the war years, and the same applies to electronics and computer techniques. The new petrochemical industry owed its development to the technology of high-octane fuels required for the last generation of reciprocating aircraft engines, as well as to the German and American search for synthetic rubbers and petrols. As for the military and 'space' stimulus behind the theory and practice of rocketry, it requires no special emphasis.[30]

On the principle that scientific, technical and economic developments are bound to interact, it is plausible to conclude that the technological speed-up since 1945 must in the end reflect itself in the political sphere. Hitherto it has done so primarily by encouraging an arms race and a space race from which Europe is effectively excluded. The political fragmentation of the Continent has obviously been responsible, and on these grounds it has been possible for historians to suggest that the two wars of 1914–18 and 1939–45 did for Europe what the Peloponnesian War did for Greece. In this perspective, the debate over the respective merits of capitalism and socialism is obviously irrelevant, at any rate if it is conducted along the lines of the East–West dialogue. What is not irrelevant is the notion that if central planning of the sort practised in France since 1946 were extended to the whole of Western Europe, or at least to the EEC, the foundation could be laid for a Federal Government in charge of the West European economy. Such proposals have in fact been advanced from time to time by French spokesmen concerned to make Western Europe less dependent on the United States. The link between technological change, economic growthmanship and long-term political planning is evident when one considers that the inter-penetration of European and American capital and technology has taken place precisely in the newer industries just mentioned. The fact that France should have taken the lead in this field is attributable to a complex of political and intellectual attitudes, some of which antedate the 1940s. National planning was invested with a special mystique by the Gaullist regime in 1946, and once more after 1958, but the ideas behind it were of socialist origin. The same set of attitudes underlay much of European federalism, with the obvious proviso that the supra-national aspect of Europeanism was unacceptable to Frenchmen who had made a fetish of national planning in order to overcome France's industrial backwardness. Once the principle of conscious control had been accepted by nationalists and federalists alike, it was possible to conduct a rational debate on the subject of investing the concept of Western European planning with an operational meaning. The question then was to what extent the national state would have to be transcended, in the interest of giving Western Europe a technological armature adequate to the new age. For obvious reasons, a corresponding dis-cussion could not be conducted in Eastern Europe – at any rate not in public. The trend away from nationalism there took the form of sub-ordination to the USSR in the name of international socialism. One may regard this as a perversion of an intrinsically sound idea. Be that as it may, the respective merits of a federalized Europe and an *Europe des patries* were debated in the West: principally within France and, at the governmental level, between the French and their West European part-ners in the EEC. To what extent national planning on the French post-war model was compatible with European planning had by the 1970s become a key problem in international relations.[31]

French central planning went through several stages. Its immediate post-war sponsors included de Gaulle and Jean Monnet, who in January 1946 cooperated in the establishment of a planning commissariat (*Com-missariat Général au Plan*) for the purpose of drawing up a Plan of Modernization. During the hectic years of the Fourth Republic, between 1946 and 1958, planning was largely carried on by the bureaucracy behind the back of Parliament, but with its general consent. A typical device of this period was the *loi-programme* – a legislative arrangement introduced by M. Mendès France, when he was briefly Prime Minister in 1954, to allow the planners to draw on public funds independently of the annual budget. In this as in other respects, Mendèsism turned out to be a precursor of Gaullism: a circumstance not observed by the literary intelligentsia of the *Quartier Latin*, but noted with interest by sociologists. With the advent of the Fifth Republic in 1958, national economic planning became the established doctrine of the regime. "France now had a government which prided itself on an indifference to short-term considerations and on its exclusive concern with the 'permanent' interests of the nation. The Plan was its chosen medium for expressing this fact in the field of economic and social affairs."[32] None of this would have been possible if in 1944–7 a large sector of French industry and banking had not been nationalized in the first flush of post-war enthusiasm, but the planning technique also required an interventionist spirit on the part of the higher echelons in the bureaucracy – ultimately a Saint-Simonian inheritance to which there was the Fabian equivalent in Britain. As noted before, the French were more successful in this sphere than the British, who even under nominally socialist governments in 1945–51 and 1964–70 were held back by an inherited reluctance to invest the central political authorities with genuine power to plan the shape of the national economy. France – and the same applies to Italy – had to overcome economic backwardness, and this circumstance acted as a spur to central planning, which by its nature is most effective where it is a question of concentrating the modernization process in selected key industries. In West Germany, where state control had acquired a bad reputation during the Third Reich, planning was nonetheless effectively pursued by tacit connivance between the political authorities, the trade unions and the leading banks.[33] In Austria the socialist component was stronger, and the same applies to Holland, Belgium and the Scandinavian countries. Overall, the mixed economy came to rest upon a balance of public and private planning even in the absence of a large public sector. To this M. Mendès France in 1962 added the startling, but very sensible, idea of supplementing the elected legislature with a second chamber openly devoted to the representation of economic interest groups.[34]

The Italians for their part benefited from that aspect of the Fascist legacy which dated back to Mussolini's socialist past: his insistence that economic liberalism was inadequate to the task of industrializing the country.[35] The consequent proliferation of nationalized and semi-public enterprises was of great help when the post-war democratic regime set about the task of modernization in earnest. The essential point about socialism had always been its refusal to accept the decisions of the market-place as a necessary guide to action. In any underdeveloped country – and Italy in the 1920s was merely poised on the brink of 'take-off' – the political authority must see to it that long-term economic interests are made to prevail, even if the sum total of individual short-term producer decisions points in another direction. Italian Socialism having missed the boat after 1919, the political Right gained mass support for its programme with the help of nationalist slogans, and then imposed a dictatorship which did away with Parliament and individual liberties. After 1945 the reverse took place: Fascism having been discredited, the democratic Centre-Left promoted economic modernization by discreetly using the tools of the discarded political regime it had come to replace. There was no return to the sort of economic liberalism which between 1870 and 1913 had given Italy the lowest growth rate in Western Europe, thereby promoting mass emigration to North and South America and ultimately discrediting liberal democracy as such. The change can be read off from the following table compiled in the 1960s by professional economists with no political axe to grind:

TABLE 5 RATE OF GROWTH OF OUTPUT PER HEAD OF POPULATION*

	(a) 1870–1913	(b) 1948–1962	
Belgium	1·8	2·2	
Denmark	2·1	2·8	
France	1·4	3·4	
Germany	1·8	6·8	(Federal Republic)
Italy	0·7	5·6	
Norway	1·4	2·9	
Sweden	2·3	2·6	
United Kingdom	1·3	2·4	

* Source: Postan, *op. cit.*, p. 18.

What makes the Italian performance after the Second World War so remarkable is that Italy was the most extreme example of public enterprise and intervention in Western Europe, followed at a short distance by Austria, where the Socialists had won political control after 1945. The State's activities were more extensive even, though less coherent, than in France. Economic left-overs of Fascism, such as the *Istituto per la Ricostruzione Industriale* (IRI), were placed in the service of economic growth, the prime aim being to build up quasi-monopolistic giants in modern industry, whether privately owned or (as in the case of electricity) ultimately nationalized, to serve as pace-makers for the rest. The classic case (apart from IRI, which was based on bankrupt companies taken over by the State in the 1930s) was the *Ente Nazionale Idrocarburi* (ENI) founded in 1953 to take charge of oil and natural gas. Although belonging to the public sector, it was run on capitalist lines, thus giving rise to a hybrid typical of the new age of mixed public and corporate planning. Together, IRI and ENI were responsible in the early 1960s for over one-fifth of all capital investment in industry and transport.[36] The great achievement of ENI was the development of Italy's recently discovered reserves of natural gas. It is questionable whether this could have been done without a lavish outpouring of public money. Public sector intervention to speed the rate of growth thus became an aspect of the new planned and controlled capitalism. It was not socialism – the workers had no say in the matter – but it was not traditional liberalism either.

Industrialization, notably in France and Italy, but also in the other West European countries, was bound to affect the class structure, inasmuch as it diminished the number of people employed in agriculture. If reliable statistics were available for the Soviet bloc, it would be possible to compare the relative impact of capitalist and state-socialist forms of modernization upon the composition of the population. In principle, urbanization gives rise to social problems quite irrespective of whether the means of industrial production are state-owned or belong to private firms. The chief advantage of state ownership and central planning lies in the increased power the system conveys upon the authorities responsible for making economic growth rhyme with social priorities such as housing. Inversely, the responsible politicians and administrators in a system of the Stalinist type cannot take shelter behind impersonal economic changes imposed by the market. Any decisions affecting the wage level or the general well-being of the population are immediately traceable to the political authorities – in the case of Eastern Europe to the leadership of the Communist Party. Hence the dramatic events in Poland in December 1970, when a price rise decreed by the central authorities ten days before Christmas detonated a series of bloody riots, which might have turned into a general strike and a popular uprising if the political leadership had not hastily retreated: in the process discarding the veteran General Secretary of the Party and replacing him by a relative newcomer with a reputation for being a 'technocrat' more interested in economic performance than in political doctrine. The advantage of possessing a democratic mechanism for the solution of social conflicts was made manifest in May 1968, when a general strike in France involving ten million workers and the entire student population was settled at the expense of only half a dozen lives, whereas the Polish insurrection of December 1970 reputedly resulted in the killing of hundreds of people by the security forces (no believable figures were ever published). The contrast was the more glaring in that Poland was officially declared to be a 'socialist' country, albeit the majority of the population was still engaged in private farming, an earlier attempt at collectivization on the Russian model having been abandoned in 1956, when the more rigid Stalinists made way for a new leadership headed by Wladislaw Gomulka. By 1970 the one-time rebel against Soviet orthodoxy had in his turn become the chief obstacle to administrative reforms propagated by the younger and less hidebound leaders of the Party apparatus. The question to what extent this cycle was due to the institutional shortcomings of the system continued

to be the principal issue at stake between Lenin's followers and Socialists who remembered Rosa Luxemburg's warning that socialism without
democracy was bound to turn into a monstrosity. Meanwhile the industrialization of Poland went on, though apparently at a less rapid pace
than that of Italy, where similar strains on occasion likewise expressed
themselves in street riots, but in principle were manageable through the
familiar mechanism of liberal (or social) democracy. The polar opposite
to the Polish regime was supplied by Spain, where military dictatorship
went hand-in-hand with the growing political influence of a Roman
Catholic secret society organized on hierarchical lines and prominent in
the country's political and administrative elite: the Opus Dei. The fact
that Poland, Spain and Italy, albeit governed on very different lines, all
belonged to a group of Catholic countries which had begun to industrialize in earnest at a relatively late date, supplied the historian with
fascinating topics not reducible to partisan slogans. The least that could
be said – taking the performance of these three countries since 1920 as a
whole – was that Communism and Fascism both seemed to flourish
against a background of relative economic stagnation which had somehow to be broken by political means. In Italy this stage had been passed
by 1945, when Fascism collapsed. In Spain and Poland, democracy
appeared to those in control to be incompatible with social order as late
as the 1970s. The same applied to Greece, a country governed in 1970
along familiar authoritarian lines by a group of provincial militarists
bereft of anything in the nature of a coherent ideology.[37]

If one abstracts once more from differences in the political system,
Eastern and Western Europe alike faced the same basic problem in the
1950s and 1960s: the peasantry had to be safeguarded at an acceptable
economic level, while industrialization was being speeded up. The towns
required a food surplus which could only be obtained if farming became
more productive, at the same time that industry needed workers who
could only come from the land. Agriculture, that is to say, was expected
to feed the growing population, to contribute to exports and to provide
manpower for industry. The problem was not insoluble, given a sharp
rise in agricultural productivity such that diminishing numbers of
peasant-farmers turned out a growing surplus of food. Those European
countries where electoral democracy put pressure on the authorities to
safeguard the peasantry's social standing adopted policies designed to
secure for farmers and their labourers incomes comparable with those of
the urban population. In France this aim, which was anyhow in tune
with Gaullist social philosophy, found expression in the 'Loi d'orientation' of 1960 designed to establish economic and social parity between
farming and other sectors of the economy. In West Germany the
Agricultural Law of 1955 was drawn up with similar aims in view, and
the same applies to the Austrian legislation of 1960.[38] These legislative

enterprises had the incidental effect of reinforcing the electoral clientele of Conservative movements, while the flight from the land, which occurred nonetheless, enlarged the mass basis of Socialist and Communist parties. British farming being for the most part in the hands of large and medium-sized commercial producers, the problem of protecting the peasantry did not arise in the United Kingdom. Not so on the Continent, where for the first time in history the entire peasant economy as such faced the prospect of complete erosion.[39] If the small family farm was no longer viable as the most productive form of agricultural enterprise, the choice lay between cooperation and large-scale commercialized farming of the British type. This was by far the most explosive socio-political issue of the period beginning in the 1950s, when the proportion of non-viable farming units – that is, units too small to provide their occupants with adequate sustenance – was estimated to vary from forty per cent in France to sixty-four per cent in Italy.[40] Under these conditions, the movement of population away from agriculture posed a social problem which the West European governments and the EEC tried to solve by massive subsidies at the expense of the urban consumer. The chief legislative instrument to this end was price support, coupled with measures designed to create viable farming units in place of the ancient small-scale peasant agriculture inherited from the past. By 1970 most West European countries were more or less committed to such legislation. The object was to shield the family farm

TABLE 6 NUMBER OF TRACTORS IN AGRICULTURE*

	1950	1962
Belgium	8,059	57,420
Denmark	17,182	141,000
France	142,000	900,000
Germany	139,493	960,000
Italy	56,941	300,000
Netherlands	17,488	75,000
Norway	11,000	51,000
Sweden	63,750	180,000
Switzerland	13,096	55,000
United Kingdom	325,000	443,000

*Source: OECD *Agriculture and Economic Growth* (Paris: 1965), Appendix, table 7. Table originally appeared in Postan, *op. cit.*, p. 175.

during a transitional period until the attainment of a new equilibrium, when farming would at last become sufficiently productive to secure for all land workers incomes comparable with those in industrial employments. The most optimistic forecasts did not expect such a state of affairs to occur before the 1980s, and then only on the assumption that the proportion of the peasantry within the total population would in the meantime have declined by a half or two-thirds. Whether this process would leave the family farm intact, at least for the remainder of those staying on the land and equipped with modern implements, was a matter for debate. Doubt on this score accounted for the fact that even in Scandinavia agrarian conservatism continued to hinder the formation of Socialist governments based on stable majorities. In West Germany, France and Italy, where the problem was more acute because of the vast proportion of non-viable farming units, political conservatism drew what sustenance it possessed from the belief that left-wing governments would prove unsympathetic to the preservation of the peasantry. This circumstance in turn induced the French and Italian Communist parties to pose, more or less successfully, as defenders of the family farm against the inroads of capitalism and mechanization.

Because of the close connection between economic change and altera-tions in the social structure, the maintenance of a satisfactory urban–rural balance became a political issue in all the countries under review, including those that did not possess the institutions of political de-mocracy, and where in consequence the authorities could proceed by decree. Industrialization had priority in Eastern and Western Europe alike, with the difference that the West European governments (outside Spain and Portugal) had to pay closer attention to what the populations under their control actually wanted. In a semi-planned economy of the French type, crowned by political institutions of a democratic kind, the resultant tug between the planners and the defenders of traditional peasant farming normally resulted in a compromise. In Eastern Europe the post–1948 Communist regimes proved very effective in overriding both peasant attitudes and consumer interests, at the expense of a gigantic political convulsion in Hungary and two minor ones in Poland. Yugoslavia found an uneasy solution by accepting economic aid from the West and allowing its unemployed to seek work abroad. Czecho-slovakia – already fully industrialized in 1948 and thus in no need of Stalinist surgery – watched its industries falling below the pre-war level in comparative efficiency, the reason being quite simply that the country had been integrated into a political bloc dominated by the Soviet Union with its backward economy. East Germany escaped a similar fate through concentrated capital investment in modern industry and became the most efficient producer of the Soviet-controlled bloc.

In the West, Britain had by 1970 fallen behind the Federal German Republic, a country of roughly comparable size and population. This may have been due in part to the higher quality of technical training in Germany, a feature of that country's progress since the early years of the century.[41] The trouble is that while there is plainly a connection between technical education and technological progress, the available evidence does not permit a clear-cut reply to the question why the pace of technological advance should have differed markedly as between one West European country and another over a given period:

On almost every count popular education in the United Kingdom progressed farther and faster since 1945, or indeed since 1920, than elsewhere in Europe. As a result, British educational levels, judged by purely material standards, had by the early sixties risen as high, or even higher, than in almost any other country. On some counts the Belgian record was almost equally good, whereas that of Germany and Sweden – the paragons of economic and educational virtues – stood rather low.[42]

These circumstances suggest that while in broad historical perspective there is some correlation between education and economic growth, specific performances over relatively short periods cannot be attributed to a single factor such as the provision of higher education. Other things being equal, managerial ability and traditional attitudes on the part of organized labour evidently play a decisive role in raising or lowering the level of competitive efficiency. 'Other things' evidently include governmental willingness and ability to operate the monetary mechanism available since the 1930s as a consequence of the so-called 'Keynesian revolution'. On the other hand, the British experience since 1945 demonstrates that a national commitment to the avoidance of heavy unemployment is not by itself sufficent to overcome built-in handicaps inherited from the past, while the sensational progress of Japan shows what can be done by a country which concentrates its resources on technological innovation, and does so unhampered by the need to keep declining industries going.

It must be emphasized that Keynesian monetary management, or even commitment to full employment, has nothing whatever to do with socialism. The latter term acquires significance only at the level of political decision-making having to do with priorities set by a national plan which aims at something more than the maximum rate of growth. Planning is socialist to the extent that it runs counter to market decisions based on profit expectations. For this reason 'capitalist planning' is a meaningless term, unless it is simply taken to signify the coordination of all the major decisions made by monopolistic firms in their respective branches of production. Some such coordination may impose itself even where the central political authorities have no aim beyond the steady enlargement of the aggregate volume of output. Socialism comes into play only at the stage where the planners consciously set themselves aims other than those which the market would produce if left to itself.[43] The Stalinist extreme of a totally state-owned economy, run by planners not subject to any sort of democratic control, may be treated as a perversion of what is undoubtedly central to socialism: namely the belief that the market cannot be left to decide what sort of shape society should take.

This is because market prices do not measure social costs, quite apart from the fact that under the conditions of monopolistic capitalism 'consumer choice' is largely illusory. The only consistent defence of a market economy rests upon the supposition that market prices reflect the priorities of individual consumers. But even if this were the case, the sum total of all individual decisions may result in the virtual destruction of social benefits and amenities which in principle ought to be available to all citizens. Because the market cannot measure social values, the public authorities are obliged to step in, to the end of imposing a minimum of rationality, not to mention social goals such as equality, over which public opinion divides at election time, if the political process permits free discussion. Where it does not do so, bureaucrats and technocrats are free to plan, but only Stalinists or Fascists are likely to welcome the result.

C TECHNOCRACY AND DEMOCRACY[44]

An attempt must now be made to extract the general significance, if any, of the economic and socio-political changes described in the two preceding sections. Fortunately it is possible to do this without becoming involved in the not very fascinating debate over the respective merits of Marx's and Max Weber's approach, a debate which has now been going on for over half a century. Marx's theory of social change, often condemned as mono-causal and determinist, is in fact neither.[45] But those who, for some reason or other, dislike it can turn to Weber and his disciples (Raymond Aron among them) for an alternative approach which likewise has the merit of focussing attention upon the problem of relating technological and social changes to each other.[46] For the purpose of this section it makes no great difference whether one starts from Marx or Weber, or from the eclectic compromise between them proposed by Karl Mannheim.[47] This is because both Marx and Weber proceed from the assumption that there exists a complex interconnection between material and immaterial factors in social change. In Marx's theory, the 'productive forces' are the determining factor, but only in the last resort, and moreover they include the input of science and technology. This makes it unnecessary to transpose the argument to the philosophical plane. If the development of the productive forces is increasingly dependent upon the growth of science, the distinction between material and non-material factors loses much of the importance it possessed in the nineteenth century. The situation here is analogous to the interrelation between 'base' and 'superstructure' to employ the familiar Marxian terms. Central planning – whether of the capitalist or the socialist variety – is incompatible with the maintenance of a rigid conceptual barrier between 'forces of production' and 'relations of production', since planning consists in remodelling the economic sub-structure in the light of what the planners conceive as rational social goals. These goals *may be* the 'ideological reflex' of the existing class structure, but they may also run counter to it, in which case we have the phenomenon commonly known as a revolution (whether peaceful or not is quite immaterial). The aims set by the planners reflect norms which in the final analysis are subject to political choice. As for the supposed difference between a sociology that is philosophically 'loaded' and one that is 'value-free', it has already been noted that Weber's employment of the term 'rationalization' is as crucial to his scheme as the concept of 'alienation' is to Marx.[48]

If we now work back from these general considerations to the specific problems briefly discussed in the preceding section, we come up against the question whether there corresponds to the phenomenon of economic planning the emergence of a new class structure and the rise of a new social stratum. Let it be repeated that even if the answer is in the affirmative, nothing in particular follows so far as international relations are concerned. There is no reason why centrally planned societies cannot engage in military hostilities against one another, as well as against third parties. On the evidence of Stalino–Fascist collusion and conflict in the 1930s and 1940s, almost anything in this domain is possible. This does not, however, absolve us from the duty of inquiring whether a phenomenon to which the label 'technocracy' can be pinned is in fact about to emerge in East and West alike. If something of the sort is happening we shall be obliged to conclude that the distinction between capitalist and socialist society, although still valid, has lost some of its significance. We shall also have to raise the question to what extent political democracy is compatible with social technocracy. And lastly we shall have to take a critical look at the neo-positivist outlook commonly associated with the affirmation that modern society has outgrown the rival ideologies of the nineteenth century.

Now the difficulty is that in order to decide whether 'technocratic' tendencies are present in contemporary society, we must already have some sort of notion of what is meant by 'technocracy', and this prelimin-ary employment of the term will, in part at least, be guided by a critical diagnosis of the technocratic ideology, as it manifests itself *inter alia* in contemporary writing. That is to say, we make the assumption that something in the nature of industrial society corresponds to a particular kind of intellectual self-awareness on the part of theorists whom we subsume under a label which they themselves have not chosen. This kind of circle is unavoidable, and the only way to validate the procedure consists in demonstrating that we have in fact stumbled upon a new phenomenon. The critical analysis of the situation takes its necessary starting-point from a particular kind of consciousness, but it does not limit itself to the theoretical explanations offered by the ideologists of the system. To take an analogous case, the peculiar rationality of the capitalist market economy could only be grasped after Ricardo, and following him Marx and others, had isolated what was unique about the new mode of production from what it had in common with the production of goods in general. Similarly, the specific nature of technocracy – if there is such a thing – must be something distinct from the general advance of technology: that is to say, from man's methods and tools for manipulating physical forces and material things.[49] It must also be distinct from bureaucracy, which is as old as the State.[50] And lastly it cannot simply be synonymous with what Weber described as rationality. Either the term 'technocracy' signifies a new historical phenomenon, or it signifies nothing at all.

The kind of sudden technological advance which has made large-scale economic organization possible in this century has often been described. A brief résumé is to be found in the work of an American sociologist who, towards the end of his career, was also among the critics of what for convenience we may call the new technocratic ethos:

Most of the thirty-odd billion dollar corporations of today began in the nineteenth century. Their growth was made possible not only by machine technology but by the now primitive office instruments of typewriters, calculators, telephones and rapid printing, and, of course, the transportation grid. Now the technique of electronic communication and control of information is becoming such that further centralization is entirely possible. Closed-circuit television and the electronic calculator put control of an enormous array of production units – no matter how decentralized such technical units may be – under the control of the man in the front office. The intricately specialized apparatus of the corporation will inevitably be more easily held together and controlled.[51]

The social counterpart of this process has attracted the attention of writers who have emphasized the growing divorce of ownership from control. Among a flock of economists, more or less distinguished in their profession, who have popularized this concept, we may choose J.K. Galbraith:

With the rise of the modern corporation, the emergence of the organization required by modern technology and planning, and the divorce of the owner of the capital from control of the enterprise, the entrepreneur no longer exists as an individual person in the mature industrial enterprise. Everyday discourse, except in the economics textbooks, recognizes this change. It replaces the entrepreneur, as the directing force of the enterprise, with management. This is a collective and imperfectly defined entity. ... It includes, however, only a small proportion of those who, as participants, contribute information to group decisions. This latter group is very large. ...

It embraces all who bring specialized knowledge, talent or experience to group-making decisions. This, not the management, is the guiding intelligence – the brain – of the enterprise. . . . I propose to call this organization the Technostructure.[52]

The Marxist counterpoint to this technological self-interpretation was provided almost simultaneously by a German philosopher domiciled in the United States, Professor Herbert Marcuse:

In the social reality, despite all change, the domination of man by man is still the historical continuum that links pre-technological and technological Reason. However, the society which projects and undertakes the technological transformation of nature alters the base of domination by gradually replacing personal dependence (of the slave on the master, the serf on the lord of the manor, the lord on the donor of the fief, etc.) with dependence on the "objective order of things" (on economic laws, the market, etc.). To be sure, the "objective order of things" is itself the result of domination, but it is nevertheless true that domination now generates a higher rationality – that of a society which sustains its hierarchic structure while exploiting ever more efficiently the natural and mental resources, and distributing the benefits of this exploitation on an ever-larger scale. The limits of this rationality, and its sinister force, appear in the progressive enslavement of man by a productive apparatus which perpetuates the struggle for existence and extends it to a total international struggle which ruins the lives of those who build and use this apparatus.[53]

It has been observed by a German author that Marcuse's vision of applied rationality as a specific historical phenomenon owes something to Husserl and Heidegger.[54] Where he differs from them is in treating the "political content of technical progress" as the key to the understanding of advanced industrial society. "The incessant dynamic of technical progress has become permeated with political content, and the Logos of technics has been made into the Logos of continued servitude. The liberating force of technology – the instrumentalization of things – turns into a fetter of liberation, the instrumentalization of man."[55] The implication that this state of affairs is peculiar to capitalism is disputed by a French sociologist convinced that 'technocracy' is a phenomenon which respects no political frontiers:

No technocrat – even if he be a socialist – likes the disorder of revolutions. Whether it develops under a capitalist or a socialist regime, technocracy presents itself as an assurance against this disorder. By means of progressive reforms, made in good time and with due knowledge of the matter, thanks to the control of economic and social life by appropriate governmental techniques – ranging from credit control and fiscal measures to investment decisions and planification – technocracy claims to be able to avoid revolutionary situations, to prevent economic crises and to regulate social and political conflicts by negotiating procedures among organized interest groups, by the amelioration of living standards and the organization of work, by distributing social benefits, lastly through the diffusion of mass culture and the de-politicization of social problems. Supple planification and the concerted economy are the present French variants of this technocratic reformism. . . .[56]

The same author has no doubt that a technocratic ideology already exists and that it is not limited to France, where it obtained public encouragement in the 1960s and found support among influential writers and organs of opinion. "This ideology has its roots in Saint-Simonism, in positivism, in the sociology of Thorstein Veblen, in the ideas of Rathenau and Howard Scott."[57] Its principal notions may be summarized as follows: human societies exist for the purpose of developing and for no other; nature having been tamed by science, the task remains, with the help of the 'human sciences', to develop the techniques necessary to master human relations; industrial civilization levels the barriers between classes, races and traditional cultures; the only remaining social stratification is a meritocratic one based on productivity and competence; the ancient political cleavages between the parties, between liberalism and conservatism, capitalism and socialism, are outdated and linked to dead ideologies; the system of boundless wealth-production marks the end of ideology and the de-politicization of society; the age of automation leaves only one opposition: that between the planners and the planned. "Like those academics who dream of a university without students, the technocrat dreams of a state without citizens."[58]

In so far as such tendencies are characteristic of advanced industrial society as such, they apply equally to planned capitalism and to the more bureaucratic forms of socialism. Now this 'convergence' is itself one of the goals of the politically conscious technocrats in East and West alike. We are thus confronted with a circle: the establishment of a new mode of existence – centralized, administered, de-politicized – gives rise to forms of thought which are themselves the effective instruments for bringing about the new way of life. In principle this is nothing new. It corresponds to the process whereby natural-law systems became the ideological justification of those political upheavals which in the seventeenth, eighteenth and nineteenth centuries brought bourgeois society into being.[59] The re-structuring of the prevalent world-view was both cause and consequence of the emergence of a new kind of society. The difference lies in the fact that whereas the market economy, and the society based upon it, developed slowly and spontaneously over a period of several centuries, the new social order is being consciously planned by the political authorities and their managerial allies. Hence the increasing difficulty of discriminating systematically between 'material base' and 'ideological superstructure' in the Marxian manner. In retrospect, Marx's critique of liberalism as the 'ideology' of bourgeois society turns out to have been possible because around the middle of the nineteenth century the legitimacy of the social order had become questionable: the capitalist mode of production, as it affected the wage-earner, was in plain contradiction to the democratic tenets inherited from the heroic age of liberalism. The critique of political economy pierced the ideological veil spun by the classical economists, who had extolled the institution of free wage labour as the guarantee of personal liberty. In this context, 'ideology' signifies 'false consciousness': that is to say a consciousness which quite genuinely and naively mistakes the shadow (legal equality) for the substance (authentic personal freedom). It does not signify that the prevailing consciousness is 'false' in the sense of being an imposture; rather it suggests that its carriers do not perceive their own role as the (unconscious) agents of a particular kind of social consensus. This situation is radically altered if the ideologists do in fact see themselves as the propagandists of a new order, as was the case under Fascism. The extent to which the technocratic ethos is an ideology in the Marxian sense depends upon the degree to which its promoters are able to reflect critically upon their own motivations.

These motivations are plainly not identical with those of the apologists of classical liberalism. On the contrary, it is the explicit aim of the planners to promote a social equilibrium no longer subject to the periodic economic crises which were part of the price paid by modern society for the institution of a market economy. Ever since the start of the present century, governmental regulation of the economic process has gone hand-in-hand with the decay of the ancient entrepreneurial function.[60] The dramatic speed-up of this process during and after the two world wars of this century was brought about by political upheavals such as the Russian Revolution and the rise of Fascism, but it also corresponded to the slow erosion of the social ethos characteristic of the nineteenth century: an ethos which itself reflected the establishment of a predominantly middle-class order of society. What matters for our purpose is the consequent re-politicization of the process of economic decision-making. If the self-regulating economy of liberal capitalism had to be sacrificed, because the price of periodic mass unemployment and political turmoil was too great, the fiction of governmental indifference to what was going on in the social sphere could not long survive. But this signified that the previous sharp distinction between state and society was no longer tenable. It has taken both liberals and socialists some time to realize what this entails, and it is not certain that all of them have yet grasped the consequences. The point is quite simply this: if the institutional framework of economic life is once more made subject to political decisions – as was universally the case before the triumph of liberalism – then the political realm ceases to be a mere 'superstructure', and its motions can no longer be treated as delayed reflections of an autonomous economic order. As a further consequence of this altered state of affairs it follows that a critique of society can no longer take the form of an analysis of the economic system and its theoretical reflex in the predominant academic orthodoxy. This is among the reasons why the 'Keynesian revolution' has made so little impact upon the public mind, save in so far as it legitimized the goal of full employment under the conditions of a regulated market economy. Once the autonomy of a supposedly self-regulating system is sacrificed to the overriding concerns of the State, the political realm recovers the central role it had temporarily lost at the peak of the liberal era. Marx's "critique of political economy" was both a theory of bourgeois society and a challenge to its ideology. The new society is no longer bourgeois, and its critique is no longer functionally dependent upon an analysis of economic theory. In its place there arises a critical assessment of the part played by science and technology in legitimizing the new mode of existence.[61]

We are now in a better position to assess the significance of Marcuse's later writings, and this quite irrespective of the circumstance that much of his doom-laden prose is irrelevant to the actual functioning of capitalism in the United States and elsewhere.[62] The point he wants to bring out is that a critical theory of social life must nowadays centre on the analysis of the 'superstructure', for the simple reason that the steadily growing input of science has eroded the contradiction between 'forces of production' and 'relations of production'. It is the latter, not the former, which increasingly tend to determine the operation of the system. In consequence, the centre of gravity, from the standpoint of radical theorizing, shifts to the socio-cultural sphere:

The distinguishing feature of advanced industrial society is its effective suffocation of those needs which demand liberation – liberation also from that which is tolerable and rewarding and comfortable – while it sustains and absolves the destructive power and repressive function of the affluent society. Here, the social controls exact the overwhelming need for the production and consumption of waste; the need for stupefying work where it is no longer a real necessity; the need for modes of relaxation which soothe and prolong this stupefication; the need for maintaining such deceptive liberties as free competition at administered prices, a free press which censors itself, free choice between brands and gadgets.[63]

It is nothing to the purpose to object that, in the United States at least, full employment and the welfare state still have to be fought for, and that the historic instrument for the attainment of these aims is the labour movement. The radical critic could accept this without yielding on the point that matters to him: the automatic self-regulation of a social system which, just because it fulfils most primary material needs, legitimizes itself in terms of technical efficiency alone. In actual fact the institutions of political democracy (which Marcuse does not take into account) alter the horizon of possibility not only for marginal social groups and outcasts, but for the mass of wage-earners too. Radical criticism of the status quo spreads from the universities (where it is the privilege of a minority not subjected to immediate economic pressure) to the body of society at large, and it does so because in fact everyone suffers from the operation of a system which literally poisons the atmosphere. It might be objected, however, that this is merely a social lag due to the fact that a technocratic elite with an adequate sense of its responsibilities has not yet formed, or is not yet in charge of the political realm. Once this obstacle has been overcome – as is largely the case in Western Europe – the system might make itself invulnerable by altering the terms of political discourse in such a way as to render democracy in the classical sense inoperative. What counts in such circumstances is no longer the will of a politically mature citizenry, but the programmed reaction of a mass of consumers to the manipulations of those in control. This was the alarming perspective suggested in literature by Huxley and Orwell, in response to the Wellsian optimism of the pre-1914 era. The homogeneous social structure presupposed by all these writers leaves ample room for manipulation and thus confirms the cultural pessimism of the surviving libertarians, whether classical liberals or utopian anarchists. In the actual reality of present-day industrial society, in East and West alike, no such homogeneity exists as yet – fortunately no doubt.[64]

The point is connected with the survival of class conflict, both in its traditional form under the conditions of 'free' unregulated capitalism, and in the guise of spontaneous rebellions against the operation of a bureaucratized system run by the planners in the absence of democratic controls. At one extreme, in the pre-industrial hinterland of the modern world, class conflict involves the peasantry and an unemployed urban mob which has not yet transformed itself into an authentic working class. Here the political model of the French Revolution, or alternatively the Russian Revolution, retains its relevance, for the simple reason that neither modern capitalism nor a bureaucratic form of socialism has yet come into existence. For the same reason, the resulting political tensions can still be discussed in time-honoured language – Jacobin, Blanquist, Bakuninist, Leninist or a mixture of all these traditions. At the other end of the scale, industrial society (whether capitalist or nominally socialist) has taken shape and given rise to an unprecedented rate of technological progress, with all the social consequences flowing from it: urbanization, de-politicization, the spread of a popular culture promoted by the mass media, and the growth of new social tensions due to the antagonism between the planners and the planned. Where the system leaves no room for democratic expressions of popular feelings, violent explosions will occur from time to time and will be repressed by the bureaucracy of the one-party state in the name of socialism. Where democracy has survived, mass movements such as the French general strike of May–June 1968 may nonetheless interfere with the functioning of the mechanism, to the point where the authority of the government is called in question. At this stage the success or failure of the movement – 'the revolution' in traditional parlance – depends upon the availability of an alternative political elite which makes an effective appeal to popular confidence. An elite of this kind is unlikely to call into question the basic purpose of centralized economic planning: it may even elevate it to the distinction of a principle, while condemning the actual holders of power as servants of monopolistic private interests. In the perspective of an Ultra-Left which represents marginal groups of the population or sections of the unemployed intelligentsia, an opposition party of this sort appears reformist and/or technocratic, even if it still employs traditional socialist or communist language. The replacement of a conservative governing elite by a radical one does not necessarily constitute a social revolution – that much is anyhow plain from past experience. For the particular case under discussion, the question that needs an answer is whether or not a profound structural transformation of the classical revolutionary type is still conceivable, once the institution of a reasonably well functioning planning mechanism has removed the spectre of disastrous economic crises. If revolution on the classic pattern is a response to a situation where 'base' and 'superstructure' are seriously out of step, it is arguable that a crisis of this type need not arise under conditions where the planners can reshape the 'base': either to suit their own convenience or to take the steam out of inchoate mass movements precipitated by a temporary malfunctioning of the system. If this is in fact the typically novel feature of the present situation, then something like political convergence between East and West begins to look like a distant possibility. The belief that such a convergence is in the nature of things, and is only blocked by irrational attitudes inherited from the past, forms part and parcel of the technocratic mode of thought.

From the technocratic standpoint, political upheavals of the type associated with the magic dates 1789 and 1917 belong to the past. They occurred because there was as yet no such thing as a scientific organization of production and an equally scientific regulation of the social process taken as a whole. As for democracy, it reduces itself in the technocratic perspective to a choice between competing political elites having the same basic ends in view. This manner of thinking goes back to the older positivism associated with Comte; in Central Europe it is associated with the names of Max Weber and Joseph Schumpeter. Its popularization since the 1950s is clearly linked to the structural reorientation of Western European society described in an earlier section. So far as Marxism is concerned it appears from this standpoint as a system

339

of thought centred upon a unique and irrecoverable experience: the bourgeois revolution which prepared the ground for the mature industrial society of the modern age. Revolutions of this type are still possible, but only in backward countries which have not yet crossed the watershed that separates them from modernity. As for the anarchist notion that a revolutionary movement can be based upon racial or social minorities temporarily or permanently excluded from the general march of progress, it can be dismissed as an aberration due to a failure to perceive that such groups are not social classes in the Marxian sense. Their rebellions cannot undermine the social order, for the simple reason that the economic system is not dependent upon them: any more than the Western world depends upon those among its former colonies which lead a precarious existence trying to sell a few unimportant raw materials in the world market. The growing disparity between the industrially advanced societies and the third world appears from this standpoint as a misfortune which does not seriously endanger the stability of the system – unless it becomes a factor in promoting military conflicts.[65]

Now clearly it is possible to describe this way of looking at the world as ideological, without for this reason characterizing it as an illusion. It is perfectly possible for a new social order to give birth to a more or less coherent view of the world which distorts significant aspects of reality and is yet not classifiable as a mere fantasy. The new ideology, like the older liberalism it has replaced, omits those features of the real world which disturb the perennial craving for harmony and coherence, but it does not follow that it can be shown up as an intellectual confection produced for the benefit of a hypothetical 'new class' or 'power elite'. Even the idolization of science, which is the centrepiece of the new *Weltanschauung*, cannot simply be treated as a manifestation of the obvious circumstance that scientists (including social scientists) have a vested interest in the creation of a world dominated by an elite of scientifically trained managers. It corresponds to an actual state of affairs – the emergence of a type of society in which the production of material goods depends to an increasing extent on scientific technology. The circularity of a system which renders society dependent on applied science, and then appeals to scientific criteria for the purpose of judging whether or not the social whole is rational, is indeed obvious. But the circle cannot be broken by dismissing scientific endeavour as a subordinate form of rationality, radically severed from critical reason in the traditional philosophic sense of the term. If a corrective is to be applied to the neo-positivist ideology which is one aspect of technocratic thinking, the critique must take for its starting-point those elements of scientific reasoning which by their own nature press beyond the artificially foreshortened world-view of the technocrat.

The simplest way of doing this is to confront the positivist under-standing of science with the general concept of rationality which has come down to us from the Enlightenment. Historically, the new self-interpretation of man in the eighteenth century comprised both an emancipation from theology and the vision of a social order in which (to cite Marx's formulation) "the free development of each is the condition for the free development of all". This goal was common to liberals and socialists alike, though they differed over the means of attaining it. The separate development of scientific rationality and critical reasoning about society has given rise to the philosophical problem of re-stating the assumptions common to both branches of the Enlightenment; it does not signify that scientific and critical reason are radically discord-ant. [66] Still less does it follow from the critical analysis of modern empiri-cism that the aims traditionally enshrined in socialist theorizing can be restated with the help of a transcendental metaphysics whose theological provenance was patent to its radical nineteenth-century opponents. A 'critical theory' which holds fast to the heritage of German idealism in its Hegelian form is in some danger of looking wholly obsolete to people who have absorbed what Wittgenstein, Popper, Carnap and the more up-to-date psychologists and sociologists of the past half century have contributed to the sum of knowledge. At the same time, it has clearly become necessary to discriminate between the genuinely enlightening and emancipatory aspects of present-day natural and social science, and the misuse of scientific empiricism for the purpose of underwriting the status quo. There exists a variant of 'value-free' positivism which accounts for the fact that distinguished scientists were and are able in all innocence to wash their hands of the catastrophic social and political consequences of their own research into physical phenomena. But to overcome this split we are not obliged to revive traditional metaphysics. Positive science and the humanist understanding of society have a common root in the rational critique of a sub-human reality. In principle this is conceded by empiricists who have retained the liberal heritage, even though their social conservatism blinds them to the fact that classical liberalism has become inoperative. [67]

Scientists and technicians, by and large, take the existing social structure for granted. This is as true of the bureaucratized form of socialism established under the aegis of the East European police state as it is of liberal democracy in the West. The older 'critical theory' of the 1930s, with its roots in Marxism, had not yet lost its confidence in the emancipatory role of the labour movement, and in consequence de-nounced the positivism of the Vienna Circle as 'bourgeois'. With the emergence of technocracy as the dominant ideology of the new, post-liberal (but not post-capitalist) social order, the really important line of division no longer separates conservatives from socialists, but democrats from technocrats. This is the background to the reformulation of the 'critical theory' by the original founders of the Frankfurt School and their post-1945 disciples, who in some cases have broken entirely new ground.[68] The reconstruction of neo-Marxism which Horkheimer, Adorno and Marcuse had attempted in the 1930s constituted a pol-emical counterpoint to the project of the Vienna neo-positivists. By the 1960s it had become obvious that the critical theory would have to become self-critical if it was to retain any relevance. Its reformulation by Habermas and his pupils started from the recognition that classical liberalism and classical Marxism alike had lost much of their relevance: the former because the notion of a society of free and autonomous citizens, who are also owners of private property, was historically outmoded; the latter because the European working class had failed to play the revolutionary role assigned to it in the Marxist prospectus. To that extent the heirs of the Frankfurt School, no less than the survivors of the Vienna Circle, had come to accept the standpoint of their Anglo-American contemporaries. Where they differed from them was in their retention of a critical attitude which transcended the horizon of empiri-cal sociology. The aim of a 'critical theory' is not exhausted by the correct description of social or linguistic structures. It is inherently subversive of the existing order, even though it can no longer specify a social class which is regarded as the predestined instrument of an approaching revolution. What makes the theory subversive is quite simply its insistence upon the emancipatory function of rationality, taken in the larger sense of the term. The divorce of scientism from humanism appears from this standpoint as a misconception which can be corrected by critical reflection. Whether this is in fact possible, given the managerial and technocratic structure of a social order largely administered by scientists, remains to be seen. At any rate it represents a more promising approach than the rejection of scientism in the name of metaphysical Reason. Scientists and technicians, too, are citizens, and the creation of a genuinely conflict-free society is as much in their inter-est as in that of everyone else.

This circumstance, however, does not eliminate the basic difference between positivist scientism and a 'critical theory' which in the last analysis is derived from what was once a doctrine of social revolution. "The truth of critical social theory is a *vérité à faire*; in the last analysis, it [the theory] can legitimize itself only through the success of emancipa-tion: from this there results the peculiar hypothetical-practical status of the theory."[69] Critical theory, in the neo-Marxian understanding of the term, does not attempt to replace ideological by scientific thinking – that is the business of positivism; its purpose is to promote social emancipation by transforming 'false consciousness' into something else. This 'something else' is an awareness of the contrast between the existing reality and the kind of life which men *might* lead if their social relations were not distorted by the heritage of the past *and* by the technocratic deformation of the present. The latter is not limited to capitalist society. It also comprises the bureaucratic degeneration of socialism: a degeneration in part at least promoted by the scientist ideology peculiar to Stalinism. This ideology is technocratic in the precise sense that it invests a privileged minority (privileged because it alone is supposed to be in possession of authentic insight into the inevitable march of history) with the task of creating a new social order, by force, from above. The reformist variant of this 'science of revolution' centres upon the proposition that socialism will necessarily emerge from capitalism by an evolution inherent in the automatism of the economic process. As noted before, this kind of determinism can also be placed in the service of yet another version of the technocratic creed: the authoritarian faith in the coming rule of an elite which has (a) done with 'ideology' and (b) made an end of 'history' in the traditional sense of the term. In point of fact, all these notions are to be encountered in contemporary literature, conservative and radical alike.[70]

In the new historical situation of the 1960s and 1970s this state of affairs could no longer be discussed in the terminology of the 1930s, when the founders of the Frankfurt School counterposed classical Marxism and the labour movement to what they conceived to be the ultimate (Fascist) stage of capitalism. The only effective opposition to the status quo now being represented by the student movement, the later development of the 'critical theory' assumed the guise of an attempt to understand the world, rather than a decision to transform it. At the same time, however, the continuing dialogue between the Vienna school (Popper, Topitsch) and the inheritors of the Frankfurt tradition (Habermas and his pupils) undercut the positivist self-assurance. It has been observed that from the positivist standpoint, which treats physics as the paradigm of the 'value-free' sciences, even a distinguished physicist such as Max Born was guilty of metaphysical Romanticism in giving utterance to sentiments such as these: "I belong to a generation which still distinguishes between understanding and reason. From this point of view, space flight is a triumph for the understanding but a tragic failure for reason."[71] The distinction between reason and understanding goes back to Kant and cannot therefore simply be debited to the neo-Hegelians, from whom the dialectical philosophers and sociologists of the Frankfurt school may be said to be descended. In the perspective of a consistent positivist like Topitsch, anyone who maintains with Kant that there is such a thing as 'practical reason', i.e. a normative dimension of the human intellect, must appear as a belated Romantic. If he takes his norms from the past he is likely to be a Christian traditionalist. If he affirms that there are supra-empirical norms pointing the way to a

343

desirable future (one that *ought* to be brought about) he will probably be a Marxist of some kind. In either case he will have broken with Max Weber's neo-Kantian assertion (in fact an adaptation of the Kantian heritage to positivism) that the sciences are value-free.[72]

Now clearly the critique of technocracy cannot content itself with mere desiderata if it is not to turn into Romanticism. There is no point in decreeing that society 'must' take another shape if one cannot point to actual contradictions within the system which act as a spur to renovation. The belief that the system can successfully deal with its own immanent contradictions accounts for the pessimism of the later Adorno and of Marcuse, just as it underlies the genial optimism of the French technocrats already cited (and their Soviet counterparts). At the same time, critical reflection cannot even reach the stage of self-interpretation unless it adheres to the (Kantian, Hegelian and Marxian) notion that theoretical reason itself provides a normative basis for the ordering of human sociability. If the new scientific culture carries its own theoretical justification, then the first critical step consists in demonstrating that technical progress is not synonymous with human emancipation. Habermas' distinction between *techne* and *praxis* is a step in this direction. So is his defence of the early Hegel, for whom 'spirit' was tied to the symbolic interaction between individuals which takes place in everyday language.[73] The technocratic vision of a 'post-industrial' society, as a self-regulating system in which information is the crucial input, can only be criticized from a meta-scientific standpoint which does not confuse reason with rationalization. Criticism in turn becomes practical if it encounters genuine human needs not satisfied by the prevailing system. The difficulty of preventing meta-science from turning into quasi-theological metaphysics is as patent as the problematical status of a critique which, for the time being, can only appeal to socially marginal groups and is in danger of substituting generational for social conflict, thereby relapsing into Romanticism. A totally integrated society run by technocrats according to 'value-free' principles is, however, just as difficult to conceive as a successful rebellion founded on nothing more substantial than a vague dissatisfaction with the boredom of suburban existence. For one thing, technocracy does not do away with the wage relationship, which will become increasingly intolerable as industrial society grows more productive and eliminates actual poverty. Moreover, the fundamental pre-condition of a genuinely functioning technocratic 'post-industrial' system – the abolition of war and the institution of an authentic world authority transcending the sovereign state – appears utopian from our present standpoint. Precisely for this reason it calls for *practical* efforts whose *theoretical* justification is meta-scientific: there simply is no way of demonstrating the desirability of a pacified universe without having recourse to norms and values lying beyond the horizon of science. Nor is it possible at this level to juxtapose neutral fact-picturing, in the positivist manner, to what is actually desired, for what is actually desired might be some Orwellian monstrosity of permanently conflicting world empires. The rational choice in these circumstances is not calculable in factual terms. It can only be grounded in a philosophical anthropology which makes sense of human history as a whole. The displacement of Europe from its central role in the political cosmos does not exclude the possibility that the elaboration of a new intellectual consensus will be Europe's legacy to the unified and pacified world of the future.

NOTES

1 For literature see *Europe's Needs and Resources: Trends and Prospects in Eighteen Countries* (New York: Twentieth Century Fund; London: Macmillan, 1961); Stanley Rothman, *European Society and Politics* (Indianapolis and New York: Bobbs-Merrill Co., 1970); Andrew Shonfield, *Modern Capitalism* (London–New York–Toronto: Oxford University Press, 1965); Peter Calvocoressi, *World Politics Since 1945* (London: Longmans, Green & Co.; New York: Praeger, 1968); F. Roy Willis, *France, Germany and the New Europe 1945–1967* (London: Oxford University Press, 1968; Stanford University Press, 1965, 1968); J. E. Meade ed., *Case Studies in European Economic Union* (London–New York–Toronto: Oxford University Press, 1962); Anthony Harrison, *The Framework of Economic Activity* (London: Macmillan; New York: St Martin's Press, 1967); Emile Benoit, *Europe at Sixes and Sevens* (New York and London: Columbia University Press, 1961); Hans A. Schmitt, *The Path to European Union* (Baton Rouge: Louisiana University Press, 1962); Michael Shanks and John Lambert, *Britain and the New Europe* (London: Chatto & Windus; New York: Praeger, 1962); J. F. Deniau, *The Common Market* (London: Barrie and Rockliff, with Pall Mall Press, 1960; New York: Fernhill House, 4th ed., 1967); tr. from the French original, *Le Marché Commun* (Paris: Presses Universitaires de France, 1959); E. Strauss, *European Reckoning* (London: Allen & Unwin, 1962).
2 Calvocoressi, *op. cit.*, p. 124.
3 Charles de Gaulle, *Mémoires de Guerre*, vol. II (Paris: Plon, 1956), p. 224. English trans. London: Weidenfeld & Nicolson; New York: Simon & Schuster, 1959.
4 Willis, *op. cit.*, pp. 178–84.
5 Charles de Gaulle, *Mémoires d'Espoir*, 2 vols. (Paris: Plon, 1970, 1971; English trans. *Memoirs of Hope* (London: Weidenfeld & Nicolson, 1971).
6 Willis, *op. cit.*, p. 80. For an involuntary confirmation see the Prologue to the first volume of Macmillan's memoirs, *Winds of Change 1914–1939* (London: Macmillan; New York: Harper & Row, 1966), especially the remark on p. 29: "To sum up, as my story unfolds, it will be found that Anglo-American cooperation was an essential thread running through the whole tangled skein." For the European imbroglio of the 1950s see

Anthony Eden, *Full Circle* (London: Cassell; Boston: Houghton Mifflin, 1960), pp. 146 ff.

7 Calvocoressi, *op. cit.*, p. 116.

8 Willis, *op. cit.*, pp. 273 ff. For the French political background see Philip Williams, *Crisis and Compromise: Politics in the Fourth Republic* (London: Longmans; Hamden, Conn.: Shoe String Press, 3rd ed., 1964), *passim*; also the same author's *The French Parliament* (London: Allen & Unwin; New York: Praeger, 1968).

9 Wolf Mendl, "After de Gaulle: Continuity and Change in French Foreign Policy", *The World Today* (London: Chatham House, January 1971).

10 Jean-Jacques Servan-Schreiber, *Le défi américain* (Paris: Denoël, 1967); Eng. trans. *The American Challenge* (Harmondsworth: Penguin Books, 1969); for a Marxist critique see Ernest Mandel, *Europe versus America* (London: NLB; New York: Monthly Review Press, 1970); first published as *Die EWG und die Konkurrenz Europa-Amerika* (Frankfurt: Europäische Verlagsanstalt, 1968); see also Michael Kidron, *Western Capitalism since the War* (London: Weidenfeld & Nicolson, 1968; Baltimore: Penguin, 1970).

11 Mandel, *op. cit.*, pp. 15–16.

12 For French post-war economic planning see Jean Fourastié and Jean-Paul Courthéoux, *La Planification économique en France* (Paris: Presses Universitaires de France, 1963); Pierre Bauchet, *La Planification française* (Paris: Editions du Seuil, 1962) Eng. trans. *Economic Planning: the French Experience* (London: Heinemann; New York: Praeger, 1964); *Le Plan Sauvy* (Paris: Calmann-Lévy, 1960); Pierre Naville, *Vers l'automatisme social* (Paris: Gallimard, 1963); François Perroux, *Industrie et création collective* (Paris: Presses Universitaires de France, 1964); Michel Crozier, *Le phénomène bureaucratique* (Paris: Editions du Seuil, 1963) Eng. trans. *The Bureaucratic Phenomenon* (London: Tavistock; Chicago: University of Chicago Press, 1964); Serge Mallet, *La Nouvelle classe ouvrière* (Paris: Editions du Seuil, 1963). For the political aspects of state planning in a democracy see *Pour une démocratie économique* (Paris: Editions du Seuil, 1964); Jacques Mandrin, *Socialisme ou social-médiocratie?* (Paris: Editions du Seuil, 1969); André Gorz, *Le Socialisme difficile* (Paris: Editions du Seuil, 1967).

13 Mandel, *op. cit.*, p. 21.

14 Calvocoressi, *op. cit.*, pp. 129–30; G. Lichtheim, *Europe and America* (London: Thames & Hudson, 1963), pp. 55 ff.

15 Michael Barratt Brown, *After Imperialism* (London: Heinemann; New York: Hillary House & Humanities Press, 1963), pp. 307 ff.; A. J. Youngson, *Britain's Economic Growth 1920–1966* (London: Allen & Unwin, New York: Kelley, 1968); U. W. Kitzinger, *The Challenge of the Common Market* (Oxford: Blackwell, 1961); Samuel Brittan, *Steering the Economy* (London: Penguin Books, 1971), *passim*; Michael Shanks, *The Innovators* (London: Penguin Books, 1967), pp. 102 ff.; Nicholas Kaldor, *Causes of the Slow Rate of Economic Growth in the United Kingdom* (Cambridge University Press, 1966); A. R. Conan, *The Problem of Sterling* (London: Macmillan; New York: St Martin's Press, 1966.)

16 Barratt Brown, *op. cit.*, p. 315.

17 Kaldor, *op. cit.*, p. 1.

18 Conan, *op. cit.*, p. 108.

19 *The Economist*, 29 June 1968; citing *Britain's Economic Prospects*, edited by Richard E. Caves for the Brookings Institution in Washington (London: Allen & Unwin; Washington: Brookings Institution, 1968).

20 Brittan, *op. cit.*, p. 420.

21 *Ibid.*, p. 421.

22 Shonfield, *op. cit.*, pp. 121 ff.

23 C. A. Macartney and A. W. Palmer, *Independent Eastern Europe* (London: Macmillan; New York: St Martin's Press, 1966), p. 450.

24 *Europe's Needs and Resources* (New York: Twentieth Century Fund, 1961).

25 Alec Nove, *An Economic History of the USSR* (London: Allen Lane, the Penguin Press, 1969), *passim*; Zbigniew Brzezinski, *The Soviet Bloc: Unity and Conflict* (New York and London: Praeger, rev. ed., 1961); "America and Europe", *Foreign Affairs*, October 1970; Walter Laqueur, *Europe Since Hitler* (London: Weidenfeld & Nicolson, 1970), pp. 180 ff.; Philip E. Mosely ed., *The Soviet Union 1922–1962* (New York and London: Praeger, 1963); Nicholas Bethell, *Gomulka, his Poland and his Communism* (London: Longmans; New York: Holt, Rinehart & Winston, 1969); Milovan Djilas, *The Unperfect Society*, tr. by Dorian Cooke (London: Methuen; New York: Harcourt, Brace & World, 1969).

26 Arthur Marwick, *Britain in the Century of Total War* (London: The Bodley Head; Boston: Atlantic Monthly Press, Little, Brown, 1968), p. 286.

27 M. M. Postan, *An Economic History of Western Europe 1945–1964* (London: Methuen, 1967), pp. 230 ff.

28 *Ibid.*, p. 143.

29 J. D. Bernal, *Science in History* (London: C. A. Watts & Pelican Books 1969; New York: Hawthorn Books, 1965), vol. IV, p. 1303.

30 Postan, *op. cit.*, pp. 145–6.

31 *Ibid.*, pp. 30 ff.; Shonfield, *op. cit.*, pp. 130 ff.

32 Shonfield, *op. cit.*, pp. 132–3.

33 *Ibid.*, pp. 239 ff.

34 Pierre Mendès France, *La République moderne* (Paris: Gallimard, 1962), Eng. trans. *A Modern French Republic* (London: Weidenfeld & Nicolson, 1963); Francois Bloch-Lainé, *Pour une réforme de l'entreprise* (Paris: Editions du Seuil, 1963); Club Jean Moulin, *Pour une politique étrangère de l'Europe* (Paris: Editions du Seuil, 1966).

35 Shonfield, *op. cit.*, p. 178.

36 Shonfield, *op. cit.*, p. 184.

37 For the Polish events of December 1970 see Stefan Markowski, "Mr Gomulka's Economic Legacy: the Roots of Dissent", *The World Today* (London: Chatham House), February 1971.

38 Postan, *op. cit.*, p. 180.

39 *Ibid.*, p. 184.

40 *Ibid.*, p. 185.

41 *Ibid.*, p. 157.

42 *Ibid.*, pp. 160–1.

43 Shonfield, *op. cit.*, pp. 226–7.

44 The title of this section has been taken from Raymond Boisdé, *Technocratie et Démocratie* (Paris: Plon, 1964); see also the essay collection titled *Liberté et organisation dans le monde actuel* (Paris: Desclée de Brouwer, 1969); for the general background see Raymond Aron, *Dix-huit leçons sur la société industrielle* (Paris: Gallimard, 1962), Eng. trans. *18 Lectures on Industrial Society* (London: Weidenfeld & Nicolson, 1967); and the same author's *La lutte de classes* (Paris: Gallimard, 1964); for a specialized study of French working-class existence and changes in the social consciousness see Andrée Andrieux and Jean Lignon, *L'Ouvrier d'aujourd'hui* (Paris: Rivière, 1960).

45 T. B. Bottomore, *Sociology* (London: Allen & Unwin; Englewood Cliffs, N.J.: Prentice-Hall, 1962), pp. 280–1.

46 W. G. Runciman, "Karl Marx and Max Weber" in *Social Science and Political Theory* (Cambridge and New York: Cambridge University Press, 1963); see also the same author's *Sociology in its Place and Other Essays* (Cambridge and New York: Cambridge University Press, 1970).

47 For a specimen of the eclectic school see Donald Macrae, *Ideology and Society* (London: Heinemann, 1961; New York: Free Press, Macmillan, 1962), pp. 63 ff.

48 Runciman (citing Karl Löwith), *Social Science and Political Theory*, pp. 54–5 (see Part One, Ch. 4).

49 See the article "Technology" in vol. XV of the *International Encyclopedia of the Social Sciences* (New York: Crowell Collier & Macmillan, 2nd ed. 1968).

50 Jean William Lapierre, "Révolution et technocratie", in *Liberté et organisation dans le monde actuel* (see above); see also, among the literature cited by Lapierre, Jean Fourastié, *La Civilisation de 1975* (Paris: Presses Universitaires de France, 1964) and Alain Touraine, *Sociologie de l'Action* (Paris: Editions du Seuil, 1965).

51 C. Wright Mills, *The Power Elite* (London and New York: Oxford University Press, 1957), p. 123.

52 John Kenneth Galbraith, *The New Industrial State* (London: Hamish Hamilton, 1967; Boston: Houghton-Mifflin, 1969), p. 71. See also Daniel Bell, *Work and Its Discontents* (Boston: Beacon Press, 1956).

53 Herbert Marcuse, *One-Dimensional Man* (London and Boston: Beacon Press, 1964), p. 144.

54 Jürgen Habermas, *Technik und Wissenschaft als 'Ideologie'* (Frankfurt: Suhrkamp, 1968), p. 53.

55 Marcuse, *op. cit.*, p. 159.

56 Lapierre, *loc. cit.*, p. 52.

57 *Ibid.*, p. 45.

58 *Ibid.*, p. 46.

59 Habermas, *op. cit.*, p. 73.

60 Joseph Schumpeter, *Capitalism, Socialism and Democracy* (London: Allen & Unwin; New York: Harper & Row, 1950), pp. 131 ff.

61 Habermas, *op. cit.*, pp. 75–6.

62 See Peter Sedgwick, "Natural Science and Human Theory", in *The Socialist Register* (London: Merlin Press, 1966), pp. 163 ff.; Alasdair MacIntyre, "Herbert Marcuse", in *Survey* (London: Information Bulletin Ltd, January 1967), pp. 38 ff.

63 Marcuse, *op. cit.*, p. 7.

64 For a more optimistic assessment of the contemporary situation, in the spirit of neo-liberalism, see Ernest Gellner, *Thought and Change* (London: Weidenfeld & Nicolson, 1964; Chicago: University of Chicago Press, 1965); Ralf Dahrendorf, *Society and Democracy in Germany* (London: Weidenfeld & Nicolson, 1968; New York: Doubleday, 1967): first published under the title *Gesellschaft und Demokratie in Deutschland* (Munich: Piper, 1965); and the same author's *Gesellschaft und Freiheit* (Munich: Piper, 1961).

65 Habermas, *op. cit.*, p. 87.

66 Sedgwick, *loc. cit.*, pp. 176 ff.

67 Albrecht Wellmer, *Kritische Gesellschaftstheorie und Positivismus* (Frankfurt: Suhrkamp, 1969), pp. 19–20.

68 See Habermas, *Erkenntnis und Interesse* (Frankfurt: Suhrkamp, 1968), *passim*.

69 Wellmer, *op. cit.*, p. 75.

70 For the conservative version see among others Arnold Gehlen, *Anthropologische Forschung* (Hamburg: Rowohlt, 1961); Hans-Georg Gadamer, *Wahrheit und Methode* (Tübingen: J. C. B. Mohr, 1960); Karl Löwith, *Gesammelte Abhandlungen* (Stuttgart: Kohlhammer, 1960).

71 Cited by Paul Lorenzen, "Enlightenment and Reason", *Continuum* (Chicago, spring–summer 1970), p. 5.

72 Ernst Topitsch, *Vom Ursprung und Ende der Metaphysik* (Vienna: Springer, 1958); *Sozialphilosophie zwischen Ideologie und Wissenschaft* (Neuwied: Luchterhand, 1961).

73 Habermas, "Arbeit und Interaktion", in *Technik und Wissenschaft als 'Ideologie'*, pp. 9 ff. See also Trent Schroyer, "Marx and Habermas", in *Continuum*, pp. 52 ff.

CHAPTER 15

THE POST-EUROPEAN AGE

A SHRINKING HORIZONS

The age which terminated in 1945 can be called 'European' in the sense that the pre-eminence of Europe as the centre of global politics was not seriously in question. By the end of the Second World War, Europe had been effectively divided along a line which gradually became the frontier between the Western world and the Soviet Union plus its satellites. The resultant attempt to constitute a West European federation has been briefly described in the preceding chapter. One reason for its relative failure to make progress lay in the ambivalent attitude of British public opinion. "Even Mr Churchill, who at Zürich in September 1946 had called for the building of 'a kind of United States of Europe', was unwilling in the last resort to participate in any kind of federation on the continent if it jeopardized relations with America."[1] Inversely, the Eurocentrism of France blocked Britain's halting movement towards the Continent, at any rate until the death in November 1970 of France's and Europe's last great political figure, Charles de Gaulle.[2] The faceless mediocrities who succeeded Churchill and de Gaulle in the governments of their respective countries symbolized by their lack of intellectual and moral stature the condition of the body politic. The quarrel over Atlantic as against European institutions was enacted against the background of an increasingly parochial public mood, itself the faithful reflex of the nation state's decline in an age of continental empires. Rivals in space flight, in nuclear weaponry, and in the ability to organize the remainder of the world according to their competing principles, the USA and the USSR could not be accommodated within the mental framework inherited from Europe's past. If de Gaulle's *Europe des patries* was an anachronism, federation promised at best to remove Western Europe from the area of conflict between the super-powers. The other familiar Gaullist concept, that of a Europe united from the Atlantic to the Urals, presupposed Russia's readiness to play a European rather than a global role: hardly to be expected from the rulers of a country bordering on China and engaged in a

350

permanent competitive race with America. By the standards of the age which opened in 1815 and closed in 1945, the new era could only be described as post-European.

It is arguable that the 'dwarfing of Europe' was already foreshadowed at the beginning of the century by the first attempts to create a modern China around 1912 and by Japan's military victory over Russia a few years earlier. These events gave warning that the future of Asia was not to be decided by the European Powers – nor for that matter by the United States. It was, however, the two wars of 1914–18 and 1939–45 that determined the issue. By 1950 European hegemony was gone, the former colonies were becoming independent, the Soviet Union had turned into a Eurasian giant, and China began to modernize in earnest under the aegis of Communism: in its origins a European creed, but by now so profoundly transmuted as to have become unrecognizable to Western Marxists. Parallel to these developments came the sudden recognition that the world was in the midst of a 'population explosion' which had raised the number of the globe's inhabitants from roughly 1,000 million in 1850 to double that figure in 1930, some 3,000 million in 1962 and a probable 4,000 million in 1977, barely fifteen years later.[3] The problem of procuring an adequate food supply for these new multitudes aggravated the already existing contrast between the industrialized countries and the remainder. New fertilizers and pesticides promised an increase in food production, while at the same time threatening the balance of nature. Meanwhile discoveries in biology and genetics threw open quite novel and revolutionary perspectives – not only in helping to limit population growth, but in determining the physical characteristics of future generations. Even the creation of human beings by artificial means could no longer be excluded.[4]

While the backward pre-industrial countries of Asia, Africa and Latin America were thrown into revolutionary turmoil by the population explosion and the urgent need to increase their food supply, the advanced countries of Europe had by 1970 begun to face a set of different but no less intractable problems centering upon the very modernization process which had lifted them out of their former poverty. The possibility that the world's oil reserves might be exhausted by the year 2000 was coming into view, thereby enhancing the significance of nuclear energy while placing a large question mark over the future of the motor industry. The development of computers and the growth of automation promised to do away with much tedious labour, but at the same time the world's great cities were being made uninhabitable by the reckless discharge of industrial waste and the ravages of the internal combustion machine. Commercial aviation across the oceans, another triumph of the post-1945 age, facilitated trade at the expense of growing noise and lessening amenities for city dwellers unlucky enough to find themselves in the vicinity of airports constantly swelling in size. At the politico-military level, the proliferation of nuclear weapons underscored both the universality of science and Europe's reduced status in an age of super-powers who alone could hope to survive a nuclear strike. The competitive exploration of space likewise enhanced the role of the USA and the USSR at the expense of their European clients. The launching of the first man-made satellite by the Russians in 1957 gave the signal for a race in which the Americans scored a temporary advance with the first landing on the moon in 1969. The consequent bipolarity of world politics lent additional stimulus to movements as distinct from each other as European federalism, Japan's sensationally successful drive to become a major industrial power and China's attempt to give political leadership to the 'third world' of undeveloped countries. Against this background the residual quarrels among the Western European nations assumed a distinctly parochial aspect. At the same time Scandinavia, followed at a distance by Britain, pioneered in the practical application of social democracy.

The dwarfing of Europe was rendered notable in international affairs by the diminished role of the leading European nation states in the United Nations Organization: itself the offspring of America's second attempt, after the earlier failure of the League, to establish a political framework for the emerging world society of sovereign and competing states. Although by courtesy holders of permanent seats on the Security Council, Britain and France by the 1970s no longer ranked as major powers. Economically all the West European countries were meanwhile being outclassed by Japan whose gross national product seemed likely by 1975 to equal that of Britain and West Germany combined. An extrapolation of present trends suggested that Japan's foreign investments might rise from 2,000 million dollars in 1968 to ten times that figure in 1975 and a possible range of 100,000 million dollars in the 1980s.[5] No such development was in prospect for any Western European country, or even for all of them taken together. Their energies seemed more likely to flow into publicly controlled efforts to render life more tolerable for the inhabitants of highly industrialized countries by reducing hours of work and expanding social benefits of all kinds. The alternation of Social Democratic and Christian Democratic governments (the latter paying more attention to the rural population) went far to produce an intellectual climate very different from that of the 1930s and 1940s. "The encyclicals of Pope John XXIII were almost Saint-Simonian in their commitment to material, social and moral progress, and a traditionalist might seek in vain for the mention of sin in *Pacem in Terris*."[6] Marxist traditionalists had similar troubles when scanning the political platforms of nominally Socialist parties from which all mention of class conflict had disappeared. Political differences were more sharply accentuated where socio-cultural issues came to the fore: another sign that economic pressures had become less acute, save for immigrants and racial minorities for whom the political system provided no recognized outlet.

What matters for our topic is that the decline of the nation state as the ultimate seat of sovereign power went *pari passu* with the decay of liberal democracy in its classical nineteenth-century form. The material precondition of a functioning liberal-democratic system is a clear-cut distinction between society (itself based upon the market economy) and the State. A system of this type enables the middle class – though not the working class – to acquire the requisite knowledge and experience for the management of public affairs. It does so because the individual citizen (who for practical purposes is á property owner) can normally educate himself up to a level where he possesses an adequate grasp of what is at stake in governmental matters. Under circumstances of this kind, public opinion constitutes a real force, even though it is confined to the opinion of the educated middle class. A mass electorate counterposed to a governmental structure in full or partial control of the economy is an altogether different affair, which is why democratic socialists have had a difficult time since 1945, except in small and easily governed countries of the Scandinavian type. With the best will the rulers of a major industrial country are constantly obliged to take decisions over a wide range of subjects which are not really amenable to public control because the individual citizen is no longer able to assess the merits of the case. To take an extreme instance, the proper balance between nuclear and conventional forces simply cannot be judged by the electorate, although the voters can (and should) decide whether their country ought to possess nuclear arms at all. To the extent that the exercise of judgement is still possible, it devolves for the most part upon organized bodies advised by professional experts: political parties, corporations, trade unions and the like. This is a far cry from the classical theory of democracy, which to be sure never applied to the whole population. If democratic socialism is to take the place of liberalism, the conclusion seems to follow that the system is going to be workable only in countries which have effectively contracted out of the power struggle between the nuclear giants.

Uneasiness over the fate of Europe in the new age probably accounts for the proliferation of philosophies of history, whose authors in some cases took for their theme the advent of a new Hellenistic era: the European nation state having presumably followed the ancient city state into oblivion. The fashion had been set by Spengler in 1918 and was continued thereafter by Arnold Toynbee and the deservedly less well known Pitirim Sorokin; by theologians such as Nicholas Berdyaev and Reinhold Niebuhr; by liberal philosophers like Karl Jaspers; and

by Catholic historians such as Christopher Dawson; not to mention the
evolutionary theology of Teilhard de Chardin which provided some of
the impetus behind the Vatican's rather half-hearted attempt to rejuvenate itself. Revisionist Marxists like Roger Garaudy joined the
debate without contributing notably to the lessening of philosophical
differences.[7] So far as the development of systematic thinking about man-
made history was concerned, the entire trend of thought went back to
Vico, the tercentenary of whose birth in 1668 furnished the occasion
for a massive anthology.[8] The urge to place themselves within a historical
time sequence was understandably most pronounced among German
writers, but the public success of Toynbee's multi-volume *Study of
History* testified to the Europeanization of Britain. In a more confident
age his elaborate attempt to account for the rise and fall of civilizations
in quasi-theological terms would have been unlikely to evoke so widespread a response. Soviet authors were not represented in the general
chorus, being officially committed to the eighteenth-century French
doctrine of unilinear and unlimited progress: a residue of classical
bourgeois optimism presumably intended to compensate its benefi-
ciaries for the material privations imposed by the need to keep up with
America in the space race. The Russians may be thought to have been
dimly conscious of the advantage of being situated at the centre of one
of the great multi-national units in which power was concentrated
after 1945. Such units may be described as civilizations, which is why
the Soviet–American antagonism (or, for that matter, the Sino–Soviet
one) cannot be adequately discussed in a terminology left over from
the age of competing European nation states. There is a Russian civilization, just as there is an American, a Chinese and a European one.
For a brief moment around 1945 it looked as though the British Commonwealth might evolve into a distinctive unit of the same supra-
national or multi-national kind.[9] The opportunity – if it ever existed –
was missed, and by the 1970s Britain found itself uneasily perched on
the edge of the European Continent, uncertain whether or not to
work for European federalism: a movement whose aim could only be
to extinguish or transcend the nation state as the supreme embodiment
of political loyalty.

Spengler's *Decline of the West* and Toynbee's *Study of History* both
treated the concept of civilization, rather than that of the nation, as the
unit of historical thought. The same may be said of Dawson's attempt
to expound a philosophy of history from a Roman Catholic standpoint.[10] Spengler was first in the field and – as befitted a German scholar
writing in the conservative and Romantic tradition – he operated on
the principle that the history of human society must be conceived on
the analogy of an organism: each culture has an individual style or
personality which can be seized intuitively and whose ramifications

354

extend to all the arts and sciences, not excluding mathematics. From there it was only a step to demands for a 'German physics' purged of Jewish traits, and the step was duly taken by Spengler's and Hitler's followers, who included the eminent political theorist Carl Schmitt and other academic dignitaries.[11] Spengler, like Nietzsche before him, had no use for the concept of truth. "There are no eternal truths. Each philosophy is an expression of its own age, and only of its own age, and there are no two ages which possess the same philosophical intentions."[12] From this it follows that the values specific to each cultural organism are unique and incommunicable, since they owe nothing to a human reason which transcends the experience of a people and its history. But if each culture is a world to itself, hermetically sealed against all others, it becomes incomprehensible how Spengler manages to grasp the life-cycle of an organism different from that to which he himself belongs. On this subject it may be best to let a Catholic historian speak:

In reality, since our civilization is the work of several peoples, it embraces several parallel life-cycles. The most representative of these is no doubt that of the French, which stands midway between the early ripening of the Italians and the late maturity of the Germans. Indeed in many respects France has a similar importance for our culture to that which Hellas possessed for the culture of antiquity. Nevertheless this is but an average standard, and it can only be applied with exactitude to the French portion of the Western European culture-area.[13]

Toynbee, while influenced by Spengler and likewise much given to metaphorical borrowing from biology, avoided his precursor's self-destructive relativism. His twenty-one (or twenty-three) civilizations are autonomous entities, but he does not treat them as organisms in the full biological sense: that is to say, as completely self-enclosed micro-cosms, each with its own philosophy, religion, art and science. On Spengler's assumptions the historian cannot get outside his own culture and see history as a whole. Toynbee recognized the danger of this procedure and tried to solve the problem by injecting a moral absolutism derived from his own religious convictions: civilizations rise and fall, more or less in the Spenglerian manner, but they are not in all respects philosophically equivalent. The rise of the Higher Religions introduces a principle enabling us to judge where each particular civilization stood and stands. In the place of Spengler's succession of closed cycles there is a progressive unfolding: from the innumerable primitive societies, via the primitive and secondary civilizations, to the Higher Religions (which are apparently twelve in number, ranging from Christianity and Islam to the worship of Isis and Osiris), and then forward again to the eight Tertiary Civilizations and the Secondary Higher Religions which have developed out of them. The entire construction is extremely involved and far more elaborate than Spengler's relatively simple scheme. It also entails a value-judgement, namely the belief that civilization fulfils its mandate by giving rise to the Higher Religions.[14] In the end the latter become the only intelligible field of study. In our context it is of interest that Toynbee treats Western civilization as the only existing representative of the species which is not currently in process of material disintegration, while expressing considerable scepticism as to its capacity for unifying and pacifying the globe. Western civilization is of course not co-extensive with Europe – not even for Toynbee. On the other hand he does tend to suggest that since the two wars of this century the condition of Europe has become similar to that of the ancient world in the Hellenistic age. Ultimately his message amounts to the statement that the modern age represents a dead end: the only remaining purpose of Western civilization is to bring forth a new syncretistic religion. It is perhaps superfluous to remark that Toynbee treats the terms 'society' and 'civilization' as interchangeable. Sociology in fact never enters his horizon, nor does he seem to have given any thought to the possibility that the industrial revolution of the past two centuries may have represented the sharpest break history has witnessed since the rise of settled agricultural communities made city life possible. In all these respects Toynbee's philosophy of history represents the kind of learned curiosity appropriate to a declining class and culture: in his case that of the elite which once governed the now defunct British Empire.[15]

What needs stressing is that a discussion of this type cannot limit itself to historiography. When we inquire into the current standing of political doctrines such as conservatism, liberalism or socialism, we are obliged to take account of social science and ultimately of political philosophy. This principle also applies to the genesis of the two great European wars in this century and the consequent decline of the European nation state from the eminence it enjoyed in 1914. A distinguished social scientist has proposed the following schematic picture of the situation as it evolved since the close of the Napoleonic era:

1815: Archetypes: England and France.

1815–1914: Three-level system: six 'Great Powers' of which two (Russia and Austria-Hungary) were not nation states; a moderate number of other 'recognized states', of which the USA was one; a world of non-states, partly left alone, partly devoured or 'protected' by stronger powers.

1919: A legally constituted world of nation states formally organized in a League of Nations, a system recognizing seven Great Powers (USA, USSR, UK, Germany, France, Italy, Japan, which were never all within the League at the same time), and (as of 1935) 54 others of varying rank.

1945: A world still based on nation states formally organized in the United Nations Organization: but an effective two-power situation, with the USA and the USSR dominant, each with major and minor satellites; an excluded China comprising at least one-fifth of mankind; and a cloud of camp followers, the total growing from about 80 in 1945 to about 120 in 1965[16]

To this one may add that by the 1970s it had become possible to project a situation around 1985 when China would have joined the ranks of the nuclear super-powers, while lagging far behind Japan economically. The global scene would then presumably feature four major industrial and scientific concentrations (USA, USSR, Japan, and a more or less united Western Europe); three great military blocs (USA, USSR, China); and a sharp division between the economically advanced countries and the rest, with population curves rising ominously in India, Latin America and Africa. The last-named area would also in all probability have a peculiar set of political problems, in that its evolution seemed likely to be patterned on that of Latin America in the nineteenth century: with military dictatorships predominating, a relatively slow rate of economic growth and a not very successful attempt to establish modern political institutions – including the nation state – in an environment still deeply marked by tribal residues. Assuming this global set-up, political and military conflicts would be likely to be (a) racial and (b) continental rather than national. Given the fact that European history since the sixteenth century has been co-terminous with the emergence of rival nation states, one would have to conclude that the 'European' age of world politics is already pretty much over and by the year 2000 will be no more than a dim memory. To the survivors of an age in which Britain, Germany, France and the rest held the remainder of the world spellbound, while they confronted each other in a ceaseless search for European hegemony, this conclusion must seem rather depressing, but there is no getting around it. One may, of course, envisage a federalized Western Europe as an actual or potential Great Power, but after what the Europeans have been through in this century it takes a deal of wishful thinking to imagine that they will want to rival the USA, the USSR and China in the capacity to deliver overwhelming nuclear strikes upon a hypothetical enemy. It appears more likely that Western Europe will in the 1980s begin to look and sound increasingly like an enlarged version of the Swiss Confederacy.

In making this kind of forecast one necessarily extrapolates from the current situation. This is an exercise in political science rather than in the writing of history, but then the two have a way of overlapping.[17] It is no longer possible to conceive history in the manner of those classical authors who preceded Vico, Hegel and Marx, and who for all their sophistication had not really departed very far from the Tacitean model: a knowledge of history was held to be essential to statesmen because human nature was always the same, and so was the nature of politics.

We have all learned that the real movement of history comports total and irreversible changes. It is now likewise generally accepted that historiography cannot proceed from abstract considerations about the nature of man. "Various old problems about 'man and society' vanish if one recognizes that man does not exist except as a social animal. Outside society he is not a man."[18] Inside society, on the other hand, he is involved in contradictions and conflicts which propel the system forward. The structuralist notion that man does not act in society, rather it is society which acts through men, represents a useful corrective to liberal individualism. But taken literally it reduces consciousness to a kind of descriptive analysis from which the critical element has been eliminated. This is to suppose the existence of a conflict-free society which, fortunately or unfortunately, does not exist. Historiography is not an exact science, and where it is closest to scientific accuracy it deals with the past, not the future. It is possible to specify trends, not to state historical laws on the model of the natural sciences – the characteristic fault of nineteenth-century positivism. The neopositivist version of structuralism confounds history with nature, forgetting that man is not merely the continuation of nature, but also its contrary. Socialization represents a break with the kind of self-regulating system that has become the model of structuralist theorizing ever since Norbert Wiener, of the Massachusetts Institute of Technology, in 1948 invented a new science which he called cybernetics: *kybernetes* meaning pilot or helmsman. If anything is certain about the socio-cultural organism it is that it does not work on cybernetic principles.

B CULTURAL DILEMMAS

With the concluding remarks of the preceding section we have crossed the narrow boundary separating the philosophy of history from the history of philosophy. Attention has been drawn to the revival of Vico's mode of thought by Spengler and Toynbee in the aftermath of the two great European wars of this century, and the suggestion has been hazarded that the prominence of cyclical thinking about history in Germany and England after 1918 had something to do with loss of confidence in Europe's future. But this merely helps to explain why the topic became fashionable at a certain moment. It does not account for the Vichian revival associated with the names of Croce and Sorel before the First World War. Nor does it explain why Croce, opening a congress of philosophers in Rome on 25 October 1920, in his capacity as Minister of Public Instruction, thought it right to tell his hearers that the labour movement had encountered Vico and Hegel by way of Marx.[19] He may of course simply have given vent to a pet notion of his, namely that Vico had on some important points anticipated Hegel. A decade later Trotsky quoted Vico on the opening page of his *History of the Russian Revolution*, but he did not do so because Vico was important to Russian Marxists: he never had been, even though the more learned among them knew that Marx had mentioned Vico in *Capital* in 1867 (and five years earlier in a letter to Lassalle). The Marxian doctrine that "men make their own history" *may* be an echo of Vico, whose *New Science* had appeared in a revised French translation in 1844; and then again it may not. The only Marxist theorist to have made systematic use of Vico is Antonio Gramsci, to whom reference has already been made in another context, and in his case the motivation is quite clear: he had somehow to break the spell of Croce if Marxism was to be made palatable to Italian intellectuals, and he did it by elaborating on the notion that socialism is the heir to the whole of Western culture, including of course the Hegelian idealism of Croce. This was a notable departure from Leninist orthodoxy, but then Gramsci had a mind of his own and was quite willing to assimilate the bourgeois heritage. In this he followed the example of Marx rather than that of the Russian Marxists. Moreover, to an Italian theorist brought up on Hegel and Croce it was obvious that Vico had not simply anticipated the Enlightenment, but on some points transcended it: notably in suggesting that Descartes' physicalism could never become a method suitable to the study of history. The anti-Cartesian bent is marked in Croce and Sorel. It is also to be found in Collingwood whose conception of history is plainly influenced by Vico's doctrine that men can only understand what they themselves have made: *verum et factum convertuntur*.[20] We have already encountered Collingwood in an earlier chapter among the heirs of speculative idealism. We can now see him as a contemporary of Croce who made it his business to equip the working historian with a methodology suited to his task.

The Vichian revival, then, needs to be considered in its dual aspect: as an expression of 'post-European' pessimism about the state of the world; and as an attempt to make the study of history truly historical – that is to say, independent of the criteria laid down by the Cartesians and their logical-positivist heirs. As to the first, there is no particular mystery concerning the sudden popularity of an author who as early as 1725 had suggested that every classical age is followed by a decline into barbarism, which in turn prepares the ground for a new upsurge. It is perhaps as well to bear in mind that Vico's cyclical movement is not a closed circle, but a spiral which always creates something new and unprecedented. Thus the Christian barbarism of the Middle Ages differs from the pagan barbarism of the Homeric age by virtue of everything that makes the medieval age an expression of the Christian mind. On this assumption Christian conservatives and Marxist radicals alike could and did find support in Vico. The strictly philosophical import of his doctrine lay elsewhere: in its anti-Cartesianism. Descartes had taken for his starting-point the validity of mathematical knowledge and the application of the mathematical model to the natural sciences. History, politics and the study of languages and literatures were assigned a peripheral place. Ever since the early nineteenth century – to be exact since the appearance in 1822 of a German translation of the *Scienza nuova* – the German historical school had done what it could to restore the balance, and by the early twentieth century Dilthey had worked out a conceptual framework for the study of history which owed a good deal to Hegel: another anti-Cartesian who in due course came under fire from the epigones of the Vienna Circle. The Cartesian problematic has to do with the relation between ideas and things, and ultimately with the question whether there really is such a thing as the material world. From Vico's standpoint this question is irrelevant:

Descartes, looking at the fire, asked himself whether in addition to his own idea of the fire there was also a real fire. For Vico, looking at such a thing as the Italian language of his own day, no parallel question could arise. The distinction between the idea of such an historical reality and the reality itself would be meaningless. The Italian language is exactly what the people who use it think it is. For the historian, the human point of view is final. What God thinks about the Italian language is a question which he need not ask, and which he knows he could not answer. Search for the thing in itself is for him as pointless as it is futile.[21]

This evacuation of theology, however, was only half the story. Vico's conception of historiography as a philosophically justifiable form of knowledge also signified that the historian could dispense with theories of cognition derived from the Cartesian problematic. In substance this had been Hegel's standpoint, which is why Marx (unlike Engels and Lenin) took no interest in Kant. Neither the Cartesian nor the Kantian has anything to say to the historian or the sociologist. Precisely for this reason the Vienna Circle and the Frankfurt School never found a common language. On the other side of the Alps, as noted before, the heritage of Vico and Hegel was preserved by Croce, who from 1900 to 1950 exercised something like an intellectual dictatorship in Italy. By way of Croce's *Estetica* (1902) and his later writings Vico in turn came to the attention of James Joyce who seems to have become progressively more inclined towards a cyclical view of man's history. It is a critical commonplace that the structure of *Finnegans Wake* (and to some extent that of *Ulysses*) is Vichian.[22] Does this matter in an evaluation of the intellectual climate of Western Europe between and after the two great wars? The answer depends on the status allotted to literature in a society increasingly marked by a cleavage between the 'two cultures': that of the natural sciences and that of the humanities. From the standpoint of the scientific culture, as represented in philosophy by logical positivism and among the general public by writers such as C.P.Snow, the fact that an important novelist should have taken Vico as a guide may seem to be no more than a literary curiosity. It acquires genuine significance only if there is ground for holding that the Vichian revival after 1900 was part of the general crisis of European society to which attention has been directed in the opening chapters of this study.

The 'two cultures' debate exploded around 1960, at a time of relative political tranquillity and in a milieu which by Continental European standards was stable and conservative. But it also occurred at a time when Europe in general, and Britain in particular, had become very conscious of their diminished role, and it was no accident that unflattering comparisons with the state of affairs in the USA and the USSR played a large part in the argument set out by the advocates of greater reliance on technical and scientific training.[23] The chief protagonists, C.P.Snow and F.R.Leavis, were eminently qualified to represent 'scientism' and 'literarism' (to employ the somewhat misleading terminology coined by Aldous Huxley for use against Leavis). As the debate ran its course it became increasingly evident that neither history nor the social sciences could be accommodated within the terms of a discussion pitting the study of literature (including the classics) against the claims of natural science. Notwithstanding a few casual references to social change, what Snow chose to describe as "the scientific revolution" turned out on inspection to be nothing more sensational than the expansion of scientific training to promote a more rapid rate of technological change. His critics for their part were reduced to a rearguard action on behalf of their conception of the university as a counterweight to specialization and the computer. For all their insistence that "there is only *one* culture", their prescriptions did sound like a defensive reaction on behalf of the traditional culture – that based on the humanities – against the inroads of science. The point is connected with the rise of technocracy to which reference was made in the preceding chapter. The technocratic ideology in its current form assumes that all major social problems can be solved by the intelligent application of advanced technology, which is why Snow, in his controversial Rede lecture of 1959, moved very rapidly from the teaching of applied science to the widening gap between the industrialized countries and the remainder. The poor countries, he reminded his hearers, comprised a vast sector of the world's population and they were determined not to stay poor. "The West has got to help in this transformation. The trouble is, the West with its divided culture finds it hard to grasp just how big, and above all just how fast, the transformation must be."[24] This appeared to place the responsibility where it did *not* belong – on the "divided culture" – instead of on the shoulders of statesmen and electorates. Moreover, the rather cursory glance at China ("not yet over the industrial hump, but probably getting there") omitted the important factor of self-help, which has played the major part in China's economic development since 1949, when the Communists took over and began to apply Snow's favourite remedy: technical education. On Vichian principles it is at least arguable that the Chinese situation looks relatively hopeful because there has been a *ricorso* which trampled the traditional culture into the mud. But this particular problem is irrelevant to Europe, where scientism has been only too successful in raising the gross national product without doing much in the way of creating a sense of well-being.

Since for our purpose the central area between 'literarism' and 'scientism' is occupied by sociology, we may as well cite the celebrated passage from the *Scienza nuova* which for the first time spelled out the *verum-factum* principle:

But in the thick night of darkness enveloping the earliest antiquity, so remote from ourselves, there shines the eternal and never failing light of a truth beyond all question: that the world of civil society has certainly been made by men, and that its principles are therefore to be found within the modifications of our own human mind. Whoever reflects on this cannot but marvel that the philosophers should have bent all their energies to the study of the world of nature, which, since God made it, He alone knows; and that they should have neglected the study of the world of nations, or civil world, which, since men had made it, men could come to know.[25]

This premature statement of the basic principle underlying the study of society may be contrasted with the *cri de coeur* uttered, some two and a half centuries later, by an American propagandist for the anti-scientific 'counter-culture' of the young, or rather the middle-class young who could afford to take material security for granted:

We have C. P. Snow to thank for the notion of the 'two cultures'. But Snow, the scientific propagandist, scarcely grasps the terrible pathos that divides these two cultures; nor for that matter do most of our social scientists and scientistic humanists. While the art and literature of our time tell us with ever more desperation that the disease from which our age is dying is that of alienation, the sciences, in their relentless pursuit of objectivity, raise alienation to its apotheosis as our *only* means of achieving a valid relationship to reality. Objective consciousness *is* alienated life promoted to its most honorific status as the scientific method. Under its auspices we subordinate nature to our command only by estranging ourselves from more and more of what we experience, until the reality about which objectivity tells us so much finally becomes a universe of congealed alienation.[26]

The philosophy underlying this by now familiar complaint was that of Marcuse, the protagonist of a *Weltanschauung* synthesizing the young Marx and the mature Freud. Specifically it was the Marcuse of *One-Dimensional Man* (1964) whom we have already encountered in the preceding chapter. By an agreeable irony Snow's scientism had simultaneously come to be perceived as a technocratic delusion by the elder statesman of the Frankfurt School and by the veteran defender of traditional Cambridge humanism:

. . . Science is obviously of great importance to mankind; it's of great cultural importance. But to say that is to make a value-judgment – a human judgment of value. The criteria of judgments of value and importance are determined by a sense of human nature and human need, and can't be arrived at by science itself; they aren't and can't be, a product of scientific method, or anything like it. They are an expression of human responsibility.[27]

Leavis, unlike Marcuse, had no philosophical creed with which to buttress his position. Being unable to fall back on Hegel or Husserl, he appealed to commonsense. His German–American contemporary, having digested Husserl's critique of scientific rationalism in 1935–6, undertook a more sweeping revaluation of values:

The Cartesian division of the world has also been questioned on its own grounds. Husserl pointed out that the Cartesian *Ego* was, in the last analysis, not really an independent substance, but rather the 'residue' or limit of quantification; it seems that Galileo's ideal of the world as a "universal and absolutely pure" *res extensa* dominated *a priori* the Cartesian conception. In which case the Cartesian dualism would be deceptive, and Descartes' thinking ego-substance would be akin to the *res extensa*, anticipating the scientific subject of quantifiable observation and measurement. Descartes' dualism would already imply its negation; it would clear rather than block the road toward the establishment of a one-dimensional scientific universe in which nature is "objectively of the mind", that is, of the subject. . . . The science of nature develops under the *technological a priori* which projects nature as potential instrumentality, stuff of control and organization.[28]

What then was the 'two cultures' debate really about? Snow had originally counterposed the literary intellectuals to the scientists, and affirmed that they were separated by a gulf of mutual incomprehension. To his critics it looked rather as though science (including a domesticated social science purged of Marxist residues) was becoming the ideology of a new kind of society: one run on technocratic principles. In this context, the term 'positivism' plainly signified what it had done to Comte and his contemporaries: (1) the validation of cognitive thought by factual experience; (2) the pre-eminence of the physical sciences as models of exactness; (3) the conviction that social progress depended on this orientation.[29] The logical positivism of the Vienna School and its Anglo-American epigones, if not strictly speaking identical with the older Comtean version, was compatible with it. Marxism was not – at any rate not as interpreted by the Frankfurt School, or by the East European 'revisionists'. But then it was arguable that different interpretations were possible, and that in its 'official' form Marxism had become the ideology of a technocratic ruling stratum. This process of adaptation could be held to correspond to what had simultaneously happened in the West to philosophy under the impact of logical positivism and linguistics. Wittgenstein's affirmation that philosophy "leaves everything as it is" evidently ruled out any critical, meta-scientific function. "The self-styled poverty of philosophy" (Marcuse) corresponded to its actual inefficacy in a society organized on Snow's principles (or for that matter on those of his opposite numbers in the East).

With the foregoing remarks the area of debate has evidently shifted from sociology to philosophy. How does this circumstance accord with the suggestion that the middle ground between 'literarism' and 'scientism' is occupied by the study of society? The link, it would seem, lies in the commonly held belief that facts are neutral because objectively established, whereas values are personal and subjective:

Hence arises that common, if inconsistent, attitude which holds both by the notion that there are objective standards underlying and authenticating that list of the virtues of which the agent's group is the bearer, and at the same time by the incompatible notion that what values a man has depends upon his free choice and that nobody has the right to act as moral legislator for anyone else.[30]

The dilemma is familiar from the literature of Existentialism, including the writings of Sartre in his earlier, pre-Marxist, phase.[31] How is it to be resolved? Not (according to Mr Alasdair MacIntyre, from whose 1964 Riddell Memorial Lecture the above quotation was excerpted) by going back to traditional Christianity – "the kind of Sermon about Hell that is found for instance in Joyce's *Portrait of the Artist as a Young Man*".[32] But not in the theological liberalism of Paul Tillich, Dietrich Bonhoeffer and Dr John Robinson either, for:

Tillich's theism is merely a familiar form of atheism baptized with a new name. When Feuerbach explained that he did not believe in the God of orthodoxy because God could at best only be a name for man's ultimate concerns, he was not regarded by theologians as being a particularly subtle defender of the Christian religion. In fact the evacuation of the notion of God of its substantial content through re-definition seems the only possible outcome of the whole Tillichian (or Robinsonian) enterprise here.[33]

This latest attempt to reform theology "is yet another recognition that traditional Christian ethics is no longer applicable in an entirely changed social and institutional situation, but ... what is put in its place is not a new and relevant morality, but an entirely vacuous one."[34] "The Gospels were written against a background of the kind of morality which our society has lost."[35] The sociologist, then, is able to put the theologian in his place because sociology tells us that we live in the kind of society in which there is no longer a genuine moral consensus:

The impact of industrialism and of a liberal and individualist ethos destroys this conception of human relationships in terms of norms and functions. . . . Theologians like Bonhoeffer or Robinson want a single notion which will supply a motive at every point in the moral life and yet have some specific content. The requirement of generality and the requirement of content are, however, incompatible.[36]

If this is accepted it follows that the gulf between 'literarism' and 'scientism' cannot be bridged by appealing to religion. Is humanism in better shape? To Sartre, writing in 1946, freedom of choice was axiomatic. But freedom to choose what sort of goal? "What is at the very heart and centre of existentialism is the absolute character of the free commitment by which every man realises himself in realising a type of humanity . . . and its bearing upon the relativity of the cultural pattern which may result from such absolute commitment."[37] To the argument that there seem to be no objective grounds for choosing anything in particular (or nothing at all), Sartre replies that "man finds himself in an organised situation in which he is himself involved: his choice involves mankind in its entirety, and he cannot avoid choosing".[38] But what if he chooses Fascism, whereas Sartre under the German occupation chose the reverse? Then he becomes responsible for the consequences of his actions, but he cannot know in advance that it is the wrong choice. After all, if he has read Nietzsche rather than Sartre, he may see nothing wrong in the proposition that the strong should rule or exterminate the weak. Existentialism, like theology (from which in the last analysis it is derived), supplies no firm guide.

Those defenders of the traditional culture who are able to back their arguments by appealing to the *philosophia perennis* are evidently in a happier position than the Existentialist, for whom the purity of the solitary will is the only intelligible ground of moral choice. For proof let us cite Iris Murdoch:

It is totally misleading to speak, for instance, of 'two cultures', one literary-humane and the other scientific, as if these were of equal status. There is only one culture, of which science, so interesting and so dangerous, is now an important part. But the most essential and fundamental aspect of culture is the study of literature, since this is an education in how to picture and understand human situations. We are men and we are moral agents before we are scientists, and the place of science in human life must be discussed in *words*. This is why it is and always will be more important to know about Shakespeare than to know about any scientist: and if there is a 'Shakespeare of science' his name is Aristotle.[39]

This qualification leaves open the possibility that there may arise another 'Shakespeare of science' who will presumably be a philosopher. Miss Murdoch is firmly enlisted on Dr Leavis' side, but she is able to hold her ground only because in the last resort philosophy matters more to her than literature. And indeed, what reasons are there for holding that Aristotle obtained his insights by consulting the *literature* of his age? We are men and we are moral agents before we are literary critics.

Sartre having been cited, a brief inquiry into his mode of thought imposes itself. After what has been said in an earlier section (see Chapter 11) there is no need to revert to the German origins of the Existentialist school. What concerns us here is the French variant which suddenly went out of fashion two decades later.[40]

Being and Nothingness (to cite the English title) was first published in 1943, during the German occupation of France, by the author of *La Nausée* (1938) who was then already committed to Existentialism, but not as yet to Marxism. Its theme was the familiar one of Dread, Death and Despair in a universe which held no meaning whatever for the solitary individual. God was dead. Man was "a useless passion" ('*l'homme est une passion inutile*'), history made no sense, and consciousness was mostly self-deception put up to shelter human beings from true insight into their condition. By 1948, having in the meantime become politically active on the fringe of the Communist Party, Sartre had changed his ground. Freedom of choice was still conceived as absolute, but the liberty of each now depended upon the liberty of all. In creating his own values, man creates the values of his age, and he must behave on the sound Kantian principle that only acts which can in principle be universalized are truly moral. From this it follows that Fascism must be rejected, since its proponents cannot universalize their creed without destroying or enslaving the bulk of mankind. Does it also follow that the philosopher must join the Communist Party? Not necessarily, for the Communists are equipped with an obsolete determinist doctrine, and moreover (as the revelations about Stalin and the Hungarian revolt of 1956 have shown), Communist rule may conflict with personal freedom. By now we have reached the Sartre of the *Critique de la Raison dialectique* (1960) who has accepted Marxism, but rejected its Leninist–Stalinist deformation as an historically inevitable, but nonetheless tragic, departure from democracy. On the other hand, anarchism leads nowhere and some form of organization is necessary. What this form may be in a Western country remains to be seen, but the chief problem will be to prevent the bureaucracy from taking over. The events of May–June 1968, moreover, have shown that the French Communist Party is incapable of leading a revolution. This was Sartre's judgement in 1969–70. Meanwhile there is the autobiographical Sartre of *Les Mots* (1964) – very much a Parisian intellectual reflecting nostalgically upon a typically bourgeois childhood. What is one to make of it all?

The first and worst mistake to be avoided is to identify Sartre with either of the two cultures. Intentionally at least he belongs to neither, or rather he seeks to transcend them. This is a consequence of his belated acceptance of Marxism, which in his interpretation is both a scientific and a libertarian creed. Marxists are committed to changing the world, but Sartre is also committed to the preservation of the traditional culture. He is a revolutionary for whom it is supremely important to understand what Flaubert was about when he analysed his own emotions. Furthermore, he is concerned to make the most of Freud (minus the "mechanistic cramp" due to Freud's scientific upbringing). Even though he rejects the standard Freudian description of the unconscious, he believes in the importance of dreams. He also holds that the philosophy of *L'Être et le Néant* was vitiated by its Cartesian rationalism which in the end cannot account for processes in what Freudians call the unconsciousness and what Sartre now describes as the realm of "lived experience" which has not (yet) attained an adequate awareness of itself. In brief, the individual has not lost his importance for Sartre, even though he has come to believe that Existentialism is parasitic on Marxism – the only philosophy relevant to the present age.

In terms of his intellectual biography, then, Sartre has gone through two distinct phases interrupted (or linked) by the 1939–45 war. In *L'Être et le Néant* he borrowed extensively from Husserl and Heidegger, but translated them into his own Cartesian idiom. In the *Critique de la Raison dialectique* he relied on Hegel and Marx, but without surrendering his Existentialist concern for the *condition humaine*. The outcome was an existentialized Marxism which sought to incorporate psychology and sociology. Sartre's explicit aim in 1960 was a Marxist anthropology wherein the significance of history would disclose itself through an analysis of human nature. The link between the earlier and the later work lay in the attempt to "reconquer man inside Marxism" through the introduction of the (Husserlian) notion of intentionality. Orthodox Marxism, in Sartre's view, has become a scholastic system incapable of understanding the true nature of history, because it takes no account of men's concrete needs, desires and struggles since the dawn of society. All human relationships occur against a background of scarcity, and it is this which has turned men against one another, necessitating the establishment of class distinctions and the State. From this it would appear to follow that socialism presupposes the overcoming of scarcity, but in point of fact socialist revolutions have hitherto occurred in poor countries, and socialism has in consequence become the rival of capitalism rather than its successor. This circumstance poses a political problem for Sartre (and accounts for his qualified support of Maoism), but it does not seriously compromise his reading of history. Socialism remains a hope in advanced countries, and a necessity for backward ones which must somehow accomplish the primary task of producing a food surplus. What lies outside history does not concern Sartre as a theorist. In particular he rejects the notion of a dialectic inherent in nature.[41]

Sartre is of course much more than an ordinary philosopher of history. He is also the author of *La Nausée*, of *Les Chemins de la liberté* (a trilogy dealing with the Resistance movement), of plays such as *Les Mouches*, *Les Mains Sales* and *Huis Clos*, of important critical essays, and of polemical writings, some of them directed against former allies such as Albert Camus, whose *La Peste* (1947) remains to this day a notable example of an Existentialist novel with political undertones barely perceptible to the reader.[42] But whereas Camus can be classified as the French contemporary and counterpart of George Orwell, it is not possible to find an Anglo-American, or for that matter a German, Italian or Russian writer who can stand comparison with Sartre. There simply is no other author who between 1935 and 1970 has excelled simultaneously as a dramatist, a novelist, a literary critic of distinction, a political controversialist and a professional philosopher operating at the highest level of abstraction. For that Sartre is indeed a philosopher, not a *littérateur* writing about philosophy, there can be no doubt whatever. André Malraux may be his superior as a novelist, Maurice Merleau-Ponty as a scholarly exponent of phenomenology, Henri Lefebvre as a Marxologist and Raymond Aron as a political publicist; but Sartre is unique in having combined all these roles and having done so for over three decades.

It is true that he has had to pay a price. Whereas in his novels, notably in *La Nausée*, he conveys an overpowering sense of what it is like for a man to experience the sheer contingency of existence, as well as his freedom to create his own nature through an act of choice, he has been less successful in blending his intuitive sense of reality with a systematic philosophical doctrine. In the words of an author already cited, "We read Sartre's novels, then, as psychological studies; it is quite another matter to express this schizophrenic point of view as an ontology, as Sartre attempts to do in *Being and Nothingness*."[43] Nor was Sartre's subsequent attempt to replace an Existentialist ontology by a Marxist anthropology altogether successful. The *Critique de la Raison dialectique* contains some brilliant passages, but it adds nothing to Marxist theory. If in the earlier work he attempted to translate psychological theories into ontology, in the *Critique* he is busy hypostatizing the Marxian notions of history, necessity and *praxis* into supra-historical categories applicable to the *condition humaine* in every age and under every sky. The 'structuralist' reaction to Sartre's philosophy of freedom – represented by the cult of Lévi-Strauss and the vogue of Louis Althusser among the Parisian Marxists of the later 1960s – was the penalty of a grandiose attempt to erect a philosophical synthesis on questionable foundations. For a Cartesian to fuse Hegel, Husserl, Marx, Freud and Heidegger into a systematic union was certainly an astonishing *tour de force*, especially when one considers that the fusion operated simultaneously at the level of drama, the novel, psychology, ontology, Marxist historicism and the critical analysis of Flaubert; but it seems legitimate to suggest that Sartre has been more successful in acclimatizing German philosophy and psychology in France than in solving the problems posed by his intellectual ancestors.[44]

C CONCLUSION

We may terminate our survey by taking as a starting point two contrasting generalizations about the process which has shaped European history since the Renaissance: Marx's celebrated formulation of historical materialism, and the disillusioned judgement of two former Marxists almost a century later:

The mode of production of material life conditions the social, political and intellectual life process in general. It is not the consciousness of men that determines their being, but on the contrary their social being that determines their consciousness. At a certain stage of their development, the material productive forces of society come in conflict with the existing relations of production, or – what is but a legal expression for the same thing – with the property relations within which they have been at work hitherto. From forms of development of the productive forces these relations turn into their fetters. Then begins an epoch of social revolution. With the change of the economic foundation the entire immense superstructure is more or less rapidly transformed. (Marx, Preface to the *Critique of Political Economy*, 1859)[45]

Our second citation is taken from a rather esoteric work which was destined to provide the philosophic credo of an intellectual elite among German academics after the Second World War:

Enlightenment, in the most comprehensive sense of progressive thought, has from the start pursued the aim of liberating men from fear and installing them as masters. But the wholly enlightened globe radiates triumphant disaster.[46]

The change of tone, from mid-Victorian self-confidence to post-European resignation, is so marked as to constitute something like a cultural reorientation. Where Marx looked forward to a social revolution for which bourgeois society was unwittingly providing the material means, his erstwhile disciples, living in the shadow of the nuclear superpowers, were reduced to gloomy reflections on the "dialectic of Enlightenment": by now perceived as a self-contradictory process which threatened humanity with destruction unless brought under control:

What is at stake is not culture as a value, in the sense of the critics of civilization – Huxley, Jaspers, Ortega y Gasset and others; rather the Enlightenment must become self-reflective if mankind is not to be betrayed for good. It is not a question of conserving the past, but of implementing a one-time hope. . . . Under present circumstances, the products of welfare themselves are transformed into elements of disaster. . . .[47]

By now the argument has become familiar, and not only in Central Europe, where in 1945 the pile of debris reached heavenwards. By the later 1960s a leading representative of the French structuralist school felt able to announce that 'Man' was a recent invention and probably about to go out of fashion shortly[48] From the death of God in the philosophy of the Enlightenment to the disappearance of Man (and of the Cartesian *cogito*) only two centuries had elapsed: time enough for the experiment of putting Man in God's place to have exposed its inherent dangers.

Now plainly there is something unsatisfactory about a writer who proclaims in all seriousness that before the nineteenth century life, language and work did not exist. What Foucault presumably means is that the industrial revolution has made a radical break in human continuity. It is arguable that the critique of political economy is no longer the key to the understanding of society, for the good and sufficient reason that bourgeois society is being transformed into something else. But this criticism of traditional sociology does not of necessity entail the paradoxical statement that humanity was invented by the philosophers of the Enlightenment. Viewed from the other side of the Channel, the situation in the 1960s looked quite different:

It seems to me that we are living through a long revolution, which our best descriptions only in part interpret. It is a genuine revolution, transforming men and institutions; continually extended and deepened by the actions of millions, continually and variously opposed by explicit reaction and by the pressure of habitual forms and ideas. Yet it is a difficult revolution to define, and its uneven action is taking place over so long a period that it is almost impossible not to get lost in its exceptionally complicated process. The democratic revolution commands our political attention. Here the conflicts are most explicit, and the questions of power involved make it very uneven and confused. Yet in any general view it is impossible to mistake the rising determination, almost everywhere, that people should govern themselves, and make their own decisions, without concession of this right to any particular group, nationality or class. In sixty years of this century the politics of the world have already been changed beyond recognition in any earlier terms. . . .[49]

If this sounds unduly optimistic, given the perils of the nuclear age and the population explosion in the 'third world', at least it does not introduce metaphysical concepts such as 'the death of Man' into the consideration of present-day society. If, in the Parisian context, Christians, Marxists and Existentialists lined up against the modish message of the neo-positivists, the latter had only themselves to thank. When all is said and done it ought to be possible to discuss the diminishing relevance of classical liberalism and classical Marxism without dragging in the supposed disappearance of Man.

It was remarked in an earlier chapter that Freud, Lévi-Strauss and Chomsky share a common concern to lay bare the material foundation of mental phenomena such as dreams, speech and myth. All three look for a materialist explanation of the concordance between man's cerebral structure and his perception of reality. From here the road leads to the structuralist trend in sociology, but on the evidence we possess it seems premature, to say the least, to draw the sort of conclusion that has become fashionable among theorists who confuse the end of European history with the termination of history as such. There clearly is a connection between the contemporary prominence of material processes such as automation and the emergence of a view of life that recalls the mechanical materialism of the eighteenth century. Nonetheless it ought to be possible to revive Cartesian linguistics without relapsing into determinism.[50] The historian in particular will be on his guard when confronted with a mode of thought that pre-dates the rise of historical consciousness in Vico, Hegel and Marx. The prestige of the physical sciences, and the dissolution of traditional metaphysics, have jointly brought about a revival of positivism. Just because this is the case it has become necessary to subject the theory of science to critical reflexion. "The denial of reflexion *is* positivism."[51] In its currently fashionable form "the notion of structure is seen to overlap, or even to collapse into, the notion of system . . .",[52] whence the assertion that social institutions cannot be explained in historical terms: they must be seen as self-equilibrating systems on the cybernetic model. Structuralism, then, is a form of systems-analysis which deliberately abstracts from the system's historical origin. Being an abstraction it is necessarily incomplete. "There is no such thing as a purely synchronic sociological explanation any more than an explanation in terms of a unique and self-insulated historical sequence."[53]

But how did this situation ever arise? Why has it become possible for an influential school of thought to assert that the study of social wholes can be divorced from an examination of their history? The excesses of historicism – whether of the Hegelian or any other variety – cannot be held altogether accountable for so pronounced a swing in the other direction. There has been a change in the intellectual climate, due to the exhaustion of rationalism in its classical form, which underlay the theory and practice of political liberalism. The representative thinkers of the Enlightenment were not confronted, as we are, with the split between the physical sciences and the humanities – or, what amounts to the same, the distinction between theoretical and practical reason.[54] They supposed in all innocence that the understanding of society (and consequently its reform in accordance with the normative principles held by all 'reasonable' people) was in essentials no different from the understanding of nature. Two centuries and several revolutions later, 'science' had come to signify a 'value-free' investigation into facts: the reason being that in the meantime it had come to be accepted that scientific thought, left to itself, was unable to furnish standards for practical behaviour. The new scientism, unlike that of the Enlightenment, carried no normative implications. The counterpart of this objectivity was pure decisionism in the style of Max Weber. The structuralist treatment of sociology is one aspect of this retreat from philosophy to scientism. Its ultimate aim is a general theory of human behaviour which will account for the manner in which particular social systems operate. This project clearly lacks any practical or critical purpose. Like Wittgenstein's philosophy, it leaves everything as it is.

If this is not to be the end of the European story in the realm of thought, there will have to be a successful reassertion of the – Kantian, Hegelian and Marxian – principle that theoretical reason carries its own practical, normative implications. From the standpoint of the Vienna School and its adherents in the Anglo-American world, this of course is sheer romanticism, a return to metaphysics. For anyone who is dissatisfied by the positivist world-picture it is an affirmation of what ought really to be a commonplace: namely that it is the business of philosophy to bring reason into the world, including the world of the sciences. To renounce this claim is to surrender the whole field of human action to the automatism of technology and to the material interests which reproduce a given social structure. The emancipation of science from philosophy has celebrated its greatest triumph in the nuclear domain, and by this very fact has reminded us all of the limitations inherent in the logic of science. If practical reason is to come into its own, this trend will have to be reversed.

NOTES

1 Geoffrey Barraclough, *European Unity in Thought and Action* (Oxford: Basil Blackwell, 1963; New York: Fernhill House, 1969), p. 49.

2 André Malraux, *Les chênes qu'on abat* (Paris: Gallimard, 1971). For background see H. Stuart Hughes, *The Obstructed Path* (London and New York: Harper & Row, 1968).

3 *The New Cambridge Modern History*, vol. XII (2nd ed.) (Cambridge: University Press, 1968), p. 3.

4 For an introduction to modern biology see P. B. Medawar, *The Future of Man* (London: Methuen; New York: Barnes & Noble, 1960); for a critique of Teilhardian speculation see the same author's *The Art of The Soluble* (London: Methuen; New York: Barnes & Noble, 1967), pp. 71 ff.

See also Pierre Teilhard de Chardin, *The Phenomenon of Man*, with an introduction by Sir Julian Huxley (London: Collins; New York: Harper & Row, 1959); Hans Jonas, *The Phenomenon of Life* (London and New York: Harper & Row, 1966): Marjorie Grene, *The Knower and the Known* (London: Faber; New York: Basic Books, 1966).

5 Hiroshi Kitamura, "Japan's economic growth and its international implications", *The World Today* (London: Chatham House), May 1971.

6 Frank E. Manuel, *Shapes of Philosophical History* (London: Allen and Unwin; Stanford, Calif.: University of California Press, 1965), p. 141.

7 See Roger Garaudy, *Perspectives de l'homme: Existentialisme, Pensée Catholique, Marxisme* (Paris: Presses Universitaires de France, 1961); for a more rigidly Marxist–Leninist exposition of the doctrine see Louis Althusser, *Pour Marx* (Paris: Maspero, 1966); the continuity of Hegelian and Marxian thought is stressed by Jean Hyppolite, *Études sur Marx et Hegel* (Paris: Rivière, 1955); for the traditional Thomist view of the matter see Jacques Maritain, *La philosophie morale* (Paris: Gallimard, 1960), Eng. trans. *Moral Philosophy* (London: Bles; New York: Scribner's, 1964); for an illuminating critique of neo-Marxist scholasticism see Raymond Aron, *D'une Sainte Famille à l'autre* (Paris: Gallimard, 1969).

8 Giorgio Tagliacozzo and Hayden V. White eds., *Giambattista Vico: An International Symposium* (Baltimore: Johns Hopkins Press, 1969).

9 E. H. Carr, *Nationalism and After* (London: Macmillan; New York: St Martin's Press, 1945), p. 52.

10 Christopher Dawson, *The Dynamics of World History* (London and New York: Sheed & Ward, 1956).

11 Jürgen Habermas, *Philosophisch-politische Profile* (Frankfurt: Suhrkamp, 1971), p. 64. In 1936 Schmitt opened a scholarly gathering with a public tribute to the "grandiose struggle waged by Gauleiter Julius Streicher" against Jewish influence.

12 *Der Untergang des Abendlandes* (Munich: C. H. Beck, 1923), vol. I, p. 55.

13 Dawson, *op. cit.*, p. 385.

14 *Ibid.*, pp. 390 ff.

15 For a similar manifestation of the syncretistic mentality see R. Z. Zaehner, *Evolution in Religion: A Study in Sri Aurobindo and Pierre Teilhard de Chardin* (Oxford: Clarendon Press, 1971).

16 W. J. M. Mackenzie, *Politics and Social Science* (London and Baltimore: Penguin Books, 1967), p. 38.

17 Arthur Marwick, *The Nature of History* (London: Macmillan, 1970), pp. 97 ff.

18 Mackenzie, *op. cit.*, p. 89.

19 Eugene Kamenka, "Vico and Marxism", in Tagliacozzo and Hayden, eds., *Giambattista Vico*, p. 139.

20 R. G. Collingwood, *The Idea of History* (Oxford: Clarendon Press; New York: Oxford University Press, 1946), pp. 63–71; Croce's *La filosofia di Giambattista Vico* (1911) was translated by Collingwood.

21 Collingwood, *op. cit.*, p. 66.

22 A. Walton Litz, "Vico and Joyce", in *Giambattista Vico*, pp. 245 ff.

23 C. P. Snow, *The Two Cultures and A Second Look* (Cambridge: University

Press, 1965; New York: Mentor Books, New American Library, 1964);
F. R. Leavis, *Two Cultures? The Significance of C. P. Snow*, with an Essay on
Sir Charles Snow's Rede Lecture by Michael Yudkin (London: Chatto &
Windus, 1962; New York: Pantheon, 1963); see also F. R. Leavis, " 'Liter-
arism' versus 'Scientism' ", *The Times Literary Supplement*, 23 April 1970.
For the general background to the controversy see *A Selection from Scrutiny*,
compiled by F. R. Leavis, 2 vols. (Cambridge and New York: Cambridge
University Press, 1968).

24 Snow, *op. cit.*, p. 42.
25 Cited by H. Stuart Hughes, in *Giambattista Vico*, p. 321, from Max H.
Fisch's and Thomas G. Berlin's translation, *The New Science of Giambattista
Vico* (London and Garden City, N.Y.: Anchor Books, Doubleday, 1961),
pp. 52–3. This is an abridged version of the 1744 edition of the *Scienza
Nuova*. The introduction has been reprinted in the revised edition of
their unabridged 1948 translation (Ithaca, N.Y.: Cornell University
Press, 1968).
26 Theodore Roszak, *The Making of a Counter-Culture: Reflections on the Technocratic Society and Its Youthful Opposition* (London: Faber and Faber, 1970;
Garden City, N.Y.: Doubleday, 1969), pp. 232–3.
27 F. R. Leavis, 'Literarism' versus 'Scientism' *loc. cit.*
28 *One-Dimensional Man* (Boston: Beacon Press, 1964), p. 153.
29 *Ibid.*, p. 172.
30 Alasdair MacIntyre, *Secularization and Moral Change* (London and New
York: Oxford University Press, 1967), p. 45.
31 Jean-Paul Sartre, *Existentialism and Humanism* (London: Methuen, 1948);
tr. by Philip Mairet from the French original, *L'Existentialisme est un
humanisme* (Paris: Éditions Nagel, 1946). See also Iris Murdoch, *Sartre –
Romantic Rationalist* (Cambridge: Bowes & Bowes; New Haven, Conn.:
Yale University Press, 1953); E. W. F. Tomlin, *Simone Weil* (Cambridge:
Bowes & Bowes, 1954; New York: Hillary House & Humanities Press,
1951).
32 MacIntyre, *op. cit.*, p. 70.
33 *Ibid.*, p. 69.
34 *Ibid.*, p. 71.
35 *Ibid.*, p. 73.
36 *Ibid.*, p. 72.
37 Sartre, *op. cit.*, p. 47.
38 *Ibid.*, p. 48.
39 Iris Murdoch, *The Sovereignty of Good* (London: Routledge & Kegan
Paul, 1970; New York: Cambridge University Press, 1967), p. 34.
40 J.-P. Sartre, *L'Être et le Néant* (Paris: Gallimard, 1950), Eng. trans. *Being
and Nothingness* (London: Methuen, 1957); *Critique de la Raison dialectique*
(Paris: Gallimard, 1960); *Sartre par lui-même: Images et textes présentés par
Francis Jeanson* (Paris: Éditions du Seuil, 1955); H. J. Blackham, *Six
Existentialist Thinkers* (London: Routledge & Kegan Paul; New York:
Humanities Press, 1952), pp. 110 ff.; see also the interview with Sartre in
the November–December 1969 number of the London *New Left Review*.
41 Henri Lefebvre, "Critique de la Critique non-critique", *Nouvelle Revue*

Marxiste, July 1961; see also the same author's *Introduction à la modernité* (Paris: Éditions de Minuit, 1962). For a radical rejection of the Leninist heritage see Bruno Rizzi, *La Lezione dello Stalinismo* (Rome: Opere Nuove, 1962).

42 See Conor Cruise O'Brien, *Albert Camus* (New York: The Viking Press, 1970).

43 John Passmore, *A Hundred Years of Philosophy* (London: Penguin Books, 1968; New York: Basic Books, 1966), p. 494.

44 For a brief critique of Sartre's existentialized Marxism see Raymond Aron, *D'une Sainte Famille à l'autre* (Paris: Gallimard, 1969); for the structuralist version of Marxism see Louis Althusser, *Pour Marx* (Paris: Maspero, 1966); for an attempt to bring Marxism up to date see Louis Soubise, *Le Marxisme après Marx* (Paris: Éditions Montaigne, 1967); also Pierre Thévenaz, *De Husserl à Merleau-Ponty* (Neuchatel: Éditions de la Baconnière, 1966) and the symposium entitled *Qu'est-ce que le structuralisme?* (Paris: Éditions du Seuil, 1968).

45 See Marx and Engels, *Selected Works* (London: Lawrence and Wishart, 1968; Baltimore: Penguin, 1967), pp. 182–3.

46 Max Horkheimer and Theodor W. Adorno, *Dialektik der Aufklärung* (Amsterdam: Querido, 1947; reprinted with new preface by S. Fischer, Frankfurt-am-Main, 1969), p. 9.

47 *Ibid.*, p. 5.

48 Michel Foucault, *Les Mots et les Choses* (Paris: Gallimard, 1966; London: Tavistock, 1968), p. 319: "Avant la fin du XVIIIe siècle, *l'homme* n'existait pas. Non pas plus que la puissance de la vie, la fécondité du travail, ou l'épaisseur historique du langage. C'est une toute récente créature que la démiurgie du savoir a fabriquée de ses mains, il y a moins de deux cents ans." See also the same author's *L'Archéologie du savoir* (Paris: Gallimard, 1969).

49 Raymond Williams, *The Long Revolution* (London: Penguin Books, 1965; New York: Columbia University Press, 1961), p. 10. See also the same author's *Culture and Society 1780–1950* (London: Penguin Books, 1961; New York. Columbia University Press, 1958), p. 38.

50 Hans Jonas, "Cybernetics and Purpose: A Critique", in *The Phenomenon of Life* (London and New York: Harper & Row, 1966), pp. 108–34. Compare Chomsky's observation that "the speaker of a language knows a great deal that he has not learned", in *Cartesian Linguistics* (London and New York: Harper & Row, 1966), p. 73.

51 Jürgen Habermas, *Erkenntnis und Interesse* (Frankfurt: Suhrkamp, 1968), p. 9.

52 W. G. Runciman, *Sociology in its Place and Other Essays* (Cambridge and New York: Cambridge University Press, 1970), p. 46.

53 *Ibid.*, p. 48. See also p. 56 for the difference between Lévi-Strauss' conceptual model and that of Jean Piaget whose studies in child psychology have exercised a marked influence upon specialists in the field.

54 Paul Lorenzen, "Enlightenment and Reason", *Continuum*, vol. VIII, no. 1, p. 6.

BIBLIOGRAPHICAL NOTE

Although for practical purposes the bibliography is contained in the Notes, it may be useful to single out a number of works which stand out both for their general usefulness and for their accessibility to the student. The 1968 edition of the American *Encyclopedia of the Social Sciences* takes pride of place, closely followed by the concluding volume of *The New Cambridge Modern History*. Oswald Spengler's *Decline of the West* (1918–22) and Arnold Toynbee's twelve-volume *Study of History* (1934–61) are classics of a peculiar sort, in that they are essential to the understanding of what is signified by the term 'philosophy of history', without therefore being particularly useful to the working historian. Spengler's *Untergang des Abendlandes* (to give it its proper title) was re-issued in Munich in 1950. It is best read in conjunction with works such as Christopher Dawson's *Dynamics of World History* (1956) and Friedrich Heer's *Intellectual History of Europe* (1966). General introductions to the theme of modern European history are to be found in Solomon F. Bloom's *Europe and America* (1961), George L. Mosse's *The Culture of Western Europe* (1961), H. Stuart Hughes' *Contemporary Europe: A History* (1961); the same author's *Consciousness and Society: The Reorientation of European Social Thought 1890–1930* (1958); and his study of modern French history, *The Obstructed Path* (1968). Hugh Seton-Watson's *The Russian Empire 1801–1917* (1967) and Raymond Carr's *Spain: 1808–1939* (1966) belong to the same general category, as does Karl Dietrich Bracher's *Die deutsche Diktatur* (1969), Fritz Fischer's *Germany's Aims in the First World War* (1967) Leonard Schapiro's *The Communist Party of the Soviet Union* (1960), A.J.P. Taylor's *English History 1914–45* (1965) and L.C.B. Seaman's *Post-Victorian Britain 1902–1951* (1966).

The general topic of imperialism in the modern age is extensively analysed in George W.F. Hallgarten's *Imperialismus vor 1914* (1951); for the typology of nationalism see Alfred Cobban, *The Nation State and National Self-Determination* (1969); the principal Marxist contributions to this theme are Rosa Luxemburg, *Die Akkumulation des Kapitals* (1913), an English translation of which appeared in 1951; and V.I. Lenin, *Imperialism, the Highest Stage of Capitalism* (1916), reprinted in the three-volume

377

edition of Lenin's *Selected Works* (1967); Alexander Gerschenkron's *Economic Backwardness in Historical Perspective* (1962) brings together a number of essays essential to the understanding of Russia's peculiar problems before and after 1917; E.H.Carr's multi-volume *History of Soviet Russia* (1950–71) covers the period down to 1929, while Alec Nove's *An Economic History of the USSR* presents a concise survey of the fifty years following the 1917 upheaval. Ernst Nolte's *Der Faschismus in seiner Epoche* (1963; Eng. tr. *Three Faces of Fascism*, 1966) surveys a subject which is given briefer treatment in F.L.Carsten, *The Rise of Fascism* (1967); Hugh Thomas, *The Spanish Civil War* (1961), Gerald Brenan, *The Spanish Labyrinth* (1943–1967) and Franz Borkenau, *The Spanish Cockpit* (1937) treat one particular aspect of this topic; for the decline of Italian liberalism and the rise of Fascism see Denis Mack Smith, *Italy: A Modern History* (1959). The roots of Hitlerism are discussed by Fritz Stern, *The Politics of Cultural Despair* (1965), Walter Laqueur, *Young Germany* (1962) and P.G.J.Pulzer, *The Rise of Political Anti-Semitism in Germany and Austria* (1964).

European intellectual life on the eve of 1914 has been the subject of a comprehensive literature, from which one may cite Reinhard Bendix, *Max Weber. An Intellectual Portrait* (1960), Franz Borkenau, *Pareto* (1936), James H.Meisel, *The Myth of the Ruling Class* (1958) and Raymond Aron, *German Sociology* (1957); the best general history of science is J.D.Bernal's *Science in History* (1969); John Passmore's *A Hundred Years of Philosophy* (1968) is essential equipment for the student; the volumes devoted to G.E.Moore, Bertrand Russell and Alfred Whitehead in Schilpp. ed., *The Library of Living Philosophers* provide access to the world of British empiricism and its critics both before and after 1914.

New movements in the arts and literature, before and after the 1914–18 war, are discussed in the fourth volume of Arnold Hauser's *The Social History of Art* (1962); in the concluding volume of Wilfrid Mellers, *Man and his Music* (1969); in Paul West, *The Modern Novel* (1967); and in Richard Ellmann's study *James Joyce* (1966); see also Ernst Fischer, *The Necessity of Art* (1963) and G.S.Fraser, *The Modern Writer and his World* (1964). Herbert Read ed., *The Styles of European Art* (1965) and E.H. Gombrich, *The Story of Art* (1967) are indispensable background reading for anyone who wants to understand what happened to the arts in this century, starting from the modernist movement which formed itself on the eve of the First World War. For the German contribution see John Willett, *Expressionism* (1971).

The two world wars are discussed from the British standpoint in Arthur Marwick, *Britain in the Century of Total War* (1968). Winston Churchill's *The World Crisis 1911–1918* (1931) remains the most readable introduction to the topic, if not the most impartial; B.H.Liddell Hart, *A History of the World War 1914–18* (1934) is the standard work in this field; Franz Borkenau, *The Communist International* (1938) offers a brilliant sketch of a subject the documentary side of which is exhaustively treated in Jane Degras ed., *The Communist International 1919–1943* (1956); the Versailles Treaty found its classic critique in J.M.Keynes, *The Economic Consequences of the Peace* (1920); for the inter-war period see Elizabeth Wiskemann, *The Rome–Berlin Axis* (1949); C.A.Macartney and A.W.Palmer, *Independent Eastern Europe* (1966); L.B.Namier, *Europe in Decay* (1950) and the same author's *Diplomatic Prelude 1938–39* (1948); Elie Kedourie, *The Chatham House Version and Other Middle-Eastern Studies* (1970) presents a critique of British imperial policy in that part of the world.

The crisis of liberal democracy in Western Europe is documented in Charles Loch Mowat, *Britain Between the Wars 1918–1940* (1955); for the French scene see in particular Charles de Gaulle, *Le Fil de l'épée* (1932), *Vers l'armée de métier* (1934) and Paul-Marie de la Gorce, *De Gaulle entre deux mondes* (1964); George L.Mosse, *Nazi Culture: Intellectual, Cultural and Social Life in The Third Reich* (1966) and Peter Gay, *Weimar Culture: The Outsider as Insider* (1970) deal with different aspects of the German catastrophe. For the general intellectual background of the period see among others Robert Thomson, *The Pelican History of Psychology* (1968); J.A.C.Brown, *Freud and the post-Freudians* (1961); David Stafford-Clark, *What Freud Really Said* (1965); Charles Rycroft ed., *Psychoanalysis Observed* (1966); Edward Glover, *Freud or Jung* (1950); Bronislaw Malinowski, *Argonauts of the Western Pacific* (1922); Karl Korsch, *Marxismus und Philosophie* (1930) and *Karl Marx* (1938); Georg Lukács, *Geschichte und Klassenbewusstsein* (1923); Norman Malcolm, *Ludwig Wittgenstein* (1958); L.Wittgenstein, *Tractatus Logico-Philosophicus* (1922); Karl Popper, *Die Logik der Forschung* (1934); A.J.Ayer, *Language, Truth and Logic* (1946); G.R.G.Mure, *An Introduction to Hegel* (1940); Edmund Husserl, *Die Krisis der europäischen Wissenschaften und die transzendentale Phänomenologie* (1936); Martin Heidegger, *Sein und Zeit* (1927); Jean-Paul Sartre, *L'Être et le Néant* (1943); Karl Jaspers, *Von der Wahrheit* (1947); Karl Barth, *Die Protestantische Theologie im 19. Jahrhundert* (1947); Rudolf Bultmann, *Kerygma und Mythos* (1951–2).

The 1939–45 war is the subject of an immense literature. For practical purposes Winston Churchill's six-volume *The Second World War* (1948–54) remains the best general introduction, but the student in search of exact military information must turn to B.H.Liddell Hart's *History of the Second World War* (1970) for a precise account of what actually occurred on the major battlefields; Paul Reynaud, *Au coeur de la mêlée* (1951), presents a personal apologia; Robert Aron, *The Vichy Regime 1940–44* (1958), presents a scholarly discussion of the subject; Guenther Lewy, *The Catholic Church and Nazi Germany* (1965), casts some light on a painful topic; Charles de Gaulle, *Mémoires de Guerre* (1954–59), documents the rise of the only French soldier of the time who was also a statesman; among official accounts of the war issued by the British government, *The Strategic Air Offensive against Germany* (1961) runs to four volumes; F.H. Hinsley, *Power and the Pursuit of Peace* (1967), goes into the historic origins of the European power balance; John Wheeler-Bennett, *The Nemesis of Power: The German Army in Politics 1918–1945* is indispensable to the serious student, and so is the essay collection published by Chatham House under the title *Hitler's Europe* (1954); Raul Hilberg, *The Destruction of the European Jews* (1961) tells its story with an abundance of documentation; for briefer treatment see Gerald Reitlinger, *The Final Solution* (1953); Herbert Feis, *Churchill–Roosevelt–Stalin* (1957), gives a succinct account of the war-time grand alliance; Adam B.Ulam, *Expansion and Coexistence* (1968), explains the unfolding of the cold war and its historical background; Philip E.Mosely, *The Kremlin and World Politics* (1960), can be commended for its brevity and lucidity. Among a mass of literature devoted to the cold war, Alexander Dallin, *Diversity in International Communism* (1963), is remarkable for its scholarly tone.

The reconstruction of Europe after 1945 is the chief topic of the massive study published in 1961 by the Twentieth Century Fund under the title *Europe's Needs and Resources*; Andrew Shonfield, *Modern Capitalism* (1965), goes into the structural transformation of Western Europe since 1945; F.Roy Willis, *France, Germany and the New Europe 1945–1967* (1968), gives a well documented account of the movement leading to the rise of the European Economic Community; Peter Calvocoressi, *World Politics Since 1945* (1968), summarizes a great deal of factual material; for the French political background see Philip Williams, *Crisis and Compromise: Politics in the Fourth Republic* (1964); Pierre Bauchet, *La Planification française* (1962) supplies a useful introduction to a controversial topic, as does Serge Mallet, *La Nouvelle classe ouvrière* (1963); Michael Barratt-Brown, *After Imperialism* (1963), represents a scholarly Marxist study free from the usual Leninist simplifications; Samuel Brittan, *Steering the Economy* (1971), analyses Britain's economic troubles; M.M.Postan, *An Economic History of Western Europe 1945–1964* (1967), lives up to the promise of its title; Raymond Boisdé, *Technocratie et Démocratie* (1964), comes to grips with a controversial topic; see also Raymond Aron, *Dix-huit leçons sur la société industrielle* (1962); and W.G. Runciman, *Social Science and Political Theory* (1963) for a confrontation of Marx and Weber; for the neo-Marxist school in post-war Western Germany, see Jürgen Habermas, *Technik und Wissenschaft als 'Ideologie'* (1968) and the same author's *Erkenntnis und Interesse* (1968); for a Marxist critique of neo-positivism see Albrecht Wellmer, *Kritische Gesellschafts-theorie und Positivismus* (1969); for the positivist school see Ernst Topitsch, *Vom Ursprung und Ende der Metaphysik* (1958).

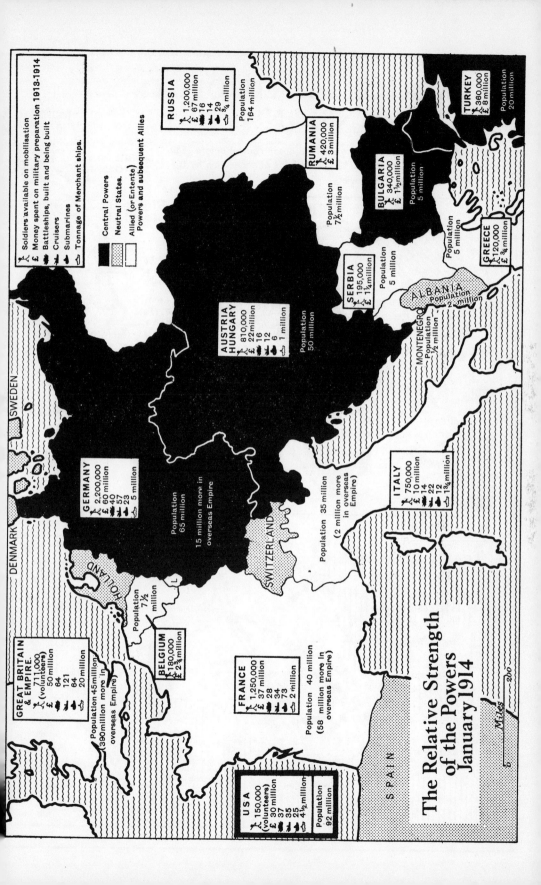

The Relative Strength of the Powers January 1914

Key:

🏃 Soldiers available on mobilisation
£ Money spent on military preparation 1913-1914
🚢 Battleships, built and being built
⛴ Cruisers
🛥 Submarines
⚓ Tonnage of Merchant ships.

■ Central Powers
▦ Neutral States.
□ Allied (or Entente) Powers and subsequent Allies

RUSSIA
🏃 1,200,000
£ 67 million
🚢 16
⛴ 14
🛥 29
⚓ ¾ million
Population 164 million

RUMANIA
🏃 420,000
£ 3 million
Population 7½ million

BULGARIA
🏃 340,000
£ 1½ million
Population 5 million

TURKEY
🏃 360,000
£ 8 million
Population 20 million

GREECE
🏃 120,000
£ ¾ million
Population 5 million

SERBIA
🏃 195,000
£ 1¼ million
Population 5 million

ALBANIA Population 2 million

MONTENEGRO Population ½ million

AUSTRIA HUNGARY
🏃 810,000
£ 22 million
🚢 12
⛴ 6
🛥 1 million
Population 50 million

GERMANY
🏃 2,200,000
£ 60 million
🚢 40
⛴ 23
⚓ 5 million
Population 65 million
15 million more in overseas Empire

SWEDEN
DENMARK
HOLLAND
Population 7½ million

BELGIUM
🏃 180,000
£ 2¾ million
Population 7½ million

GREAT BRITAIN & EMPIRE.
🏃 711,000 (volunteers)
£ 50 million
🚢 64
⛴ 121
🛥 84
⚓ 20 million
Population 45 million 390 million more in overseas Empire

SWITZERLAND

ITALY
🏃 750,000
£ 10 million
🚢 14
⛴ 22
🛥 12
⚓ 1¾ million
Population 35 million (2 million more in overseas Empire)

FRANCE
🏃 1,250,000
£ 37 million
🚢 28
⛴ 34
🛥 73
⚓ 2 million
Population 40 million (58 million more in overseas Empire)

SPAIN

USA
🏃 150,000 (volunteers)
£ 30 million
🚢 37
⛴ 35
🛥 25
⚓ 4½ million
Population 92 million

Miles
0   200

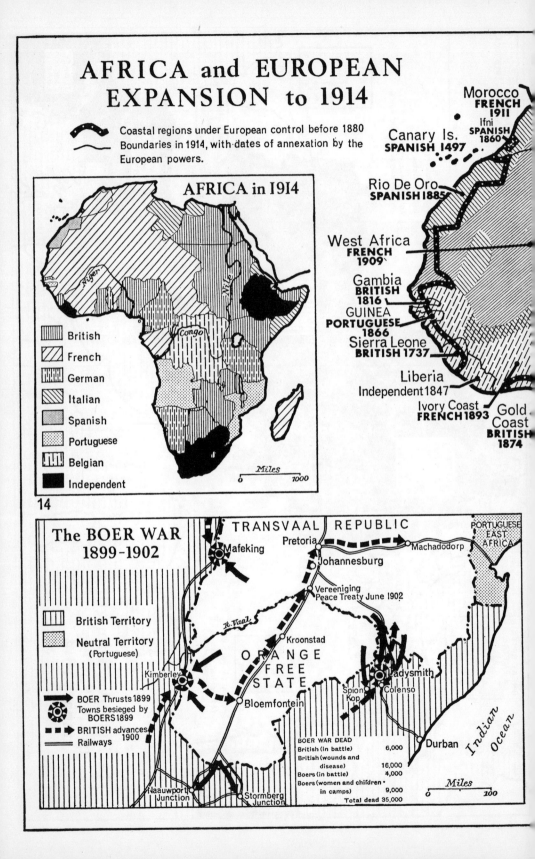

AFRICA and EUROPEAN EXPANSION to 1914

Coastal regions under European control before 1880
Boundaries in 1914, with dates of annexation by the European powers.

AFRICA in 1914

- British
- French
- German
- Italian
- Spanish
- Portuguese
- Belgian
- Independent

Miles
0   1000

Morocco
FRENCH 1911
Ifni
SPANISH 1860
Canary Is.
SPANISH 1497
Rio De Oro
SPANISH 1885
West Africa
FRENCH 1909
Gambia
BRITISH 1816
GUINEA
PORTUGUESE 1866
Sierra Leone
BRITISH 1737
Liberia
Independent 1847
Ivory Coast
FRENCH 1893
Gold Coast
BRITISH 1874

Niger
Congo
Nile

14

The BOER WAR 1899-1902

TRANSVAAL REPUBLIC

PORTUGUESE EAST AFRICA

- British Territory
- Neutral Territory (Portuguese)
- BOER Thrusts 1899
- Towns besieged by BOERS 1899
- BRITISH advances 1900
- Railways

Mafeking
Pretoria
Machadodorp
Johannesburg
Vereeniging
Peace Treaty June 1902
R. Vaal
Kroonstad
ORANGE FREE STATE
Kimberley
Bloemfontein
Spion Kop
Ladysmith
Colenso
Durban
Naauwport Junction
Stormberg Junction

Indian Ocean

BOER WAR DEAD	
British (in battle)	6,000
British (wounds and disease)	16,000
Boers (in battle)	4,000
Boers (women and children in camps)	9,000
Total dead	35,000

Miles
0   100

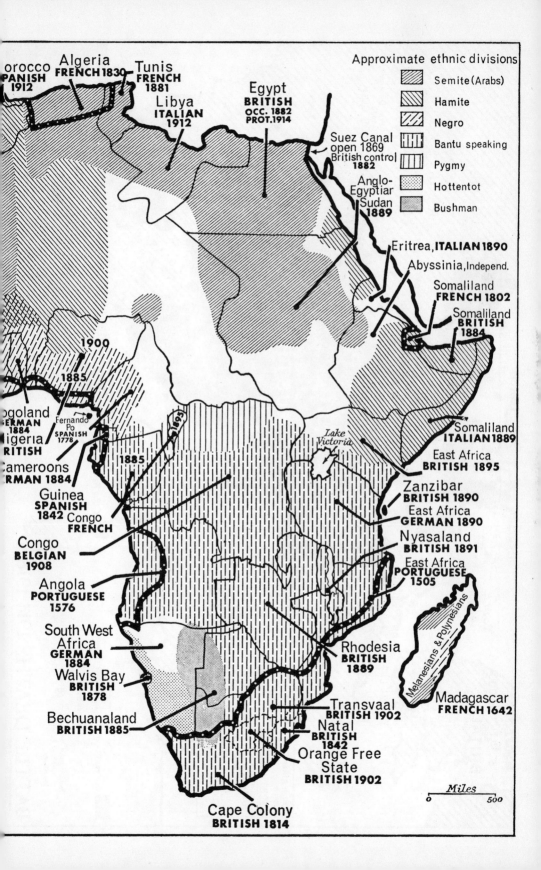

Morocco
SPANISH 1912

Algeria
FRENCH 1830

Tunis
FRENCH 1881

Libya
ITALIAN 1912

Egypt
BRITISH
OCC. 1882
PROT. 1914

Suez Canal
open 1869
British control
1882

Anglo-
Egyptian
Sudan
1889

Approximate ethnic divisions

Semite (Arabs)
Hamite
Negro
Bantu speaking
Pygmy
Hottentot
Bushman

Eritrea, ITALIAN 1890

Abyssinia, Independ.

Somaliland
FRENCH 1802

Somaliland
BRITISH
1884

1900

1885

Togoland
GERMAN
1884

Nigeria
BRITISH

Cameroons
GERMAN 1884

Fernando Po
SPANISH
1778

1885

1893

Lake
Victoria

Somaliland
ITALIAN 1889

East Africa
BRITISH 1895

Guinea
SPANISH
1842
Congo
FRENCH

Congo
BELGIAN
1908

Angola
PORTUGUESE
1576

South West
Africa
GERMAN
1884

Walvis Bay
BRITISH
1878

Bechuanaland
BRITISH 1885

Zanzibar
BRITISH 1890
East Africa
GERMAN 1890

Nyasaland
BRITISH 1891

East Africa
PORTUGUESE
1505

Rhodesia
BRITISH
1889

Melanesians & Polynesians

Transvaal
BRITISH 1902

Natal
BRITISH
1842

Orange Free
State
BRITISH 1902

Madagascar
FRENCH 1642

Miles
0   500

Cape Colony
BRITISH 1814

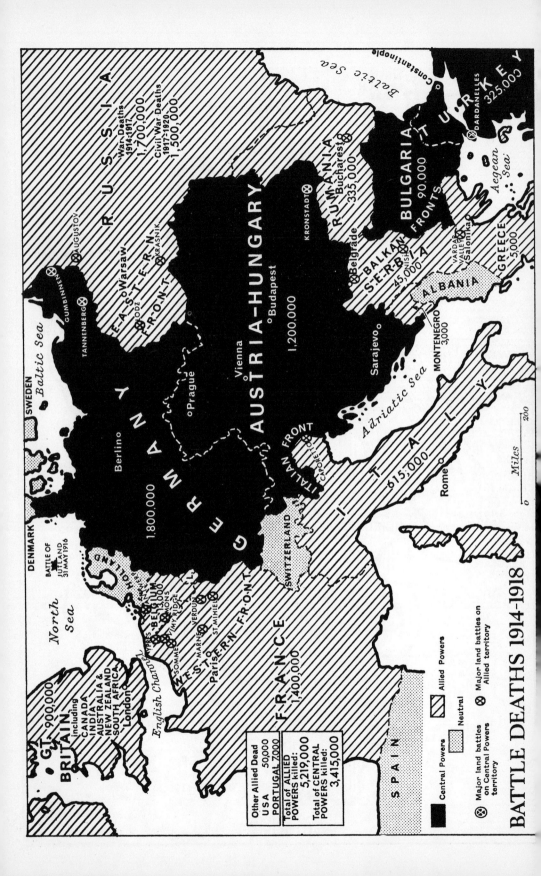

BATTLE DEATHS 1914–1918

War Deaths
1914–1917
1,700,000
Civil War Deaths
1917–1920
1,500,000

TURKEY
325,000
DARDANELLES
Aegean Sea

R U S S I A

Baltic Sea
Constantinople

BULGARIA
90,000
FRONTS

RUMANIA
335,000
Bucharest ⊗

KRONSTADT ⊗

E-A-S-T-E-R-N
F-R-O-N-T

Warsaw
Lodz
KRASNIK

AUGUSTOV ⊗
⊗ GUMBINNEN
TANNENBERG ⊗

GREECE
5,000
VARDAR
VALLEY
Salonika ⊗

BALKAN
S-E-R-B-I-A
45,000
NISH ⊗
Belgrade ⊗

ALBANIA

MONTENEGRO
3,000

Sarajevo ○

AUSTRIA-HUNGARY
1,200,000
Budapest ○
Vienna ○

Adriatic Sea

North
Sea

Baltic Sea

SWEDEN
DENMARK
BATTLE OF
JUTLAND
31 MAY 1916

Berlin ○

G E R M A N Y
1,800,000

Prague ○

I T A L Y

CAPORETTO ○
ITALIAN FRONT
615,000

HOLLAND
BELGIUM
YPRES
VIMY RIDGE ⊗
MONS ⊗
SOMME ⊗
VERDUN ⊗ ST MIHIEL
MARNE ⊗
WESTERN-FRONT

SWITZERLAND

GT.
BRITAIN
900,000
including
CANADA
INDIA
AUSTRALIA &
NEW ZEALAND
SOUTH AFRICA
London ○

English Channel

F R A N C E
1,400,000

Rome ○

S P A I N

200
Miles
0

Other Allied Dead
USA   50,000
PORTUGAL 7,000
Total of ALLIED
POWERS killed:
5,219,000
Total of CENTRAL
POWERS killed:
3,415,000

Central Powers
Allied Powers
Neutral
⊗ Major land battles
on Central Powers
territory
⊗ Major land battles on
Allied territory

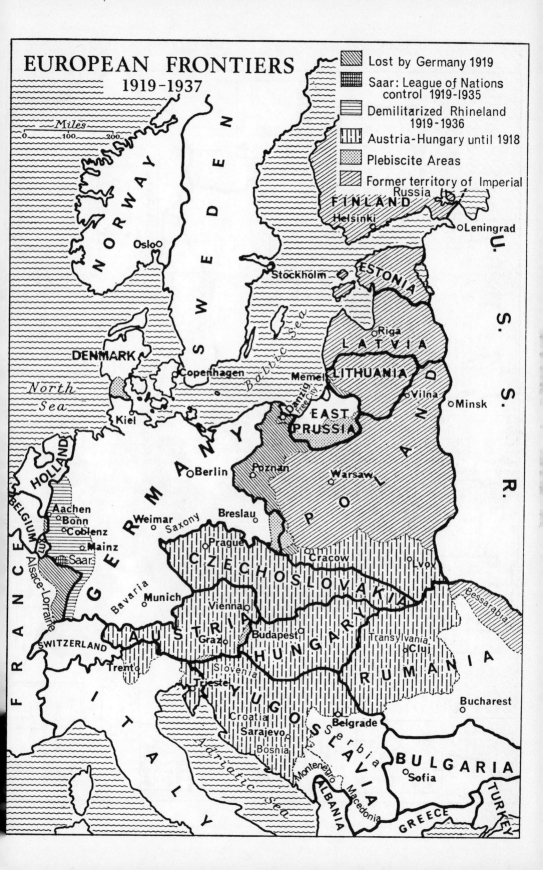

EUROPEAN FRONTIERS
1919–1937

Miles
0   100   200

Lost by Germany 1919
Saar: League of Nations control 1919–1935
Demilitarized Rhineland 1919–1936
Austria-Hungary until 1918
Plebiscite Areas
Former territory of Imperial Russia

NORWAY

SWEDEN

Oslo

Stockholm

FINLAND

Helsinki

Leningrad

ESTONIA

Riga

LATVIA

LITHUANIA

Vilna

Minsk

DENMARK

Copenhagen

Baltic Sea

North Sea

Kiel

Memel

Danzig Free City

EAST PRUSSIA

POLAND

HOLLAND

BELGIUM

Aachen

Bonn

Coblenz

Mainz

Saar

GERMANY

Berlin

Poznan

Warsaw

Weimar

Saxony

Breslau

Cracow

Lvov

Alsace-Lorraine

FRANCE

SWITZERLAND

Bavaria

Munich

Prague

CZECHOSLOVAKIA

Vienna

AUSTRIA

Graz

Budapest

HUNGARY

Transylvania

Cluj

Bessarabia

RUMANIA

Bucharest

Trento

ITALY

Slovenia

Trieste

YUGOSLAVIA

Croatia

Sarajevo

Bosnia

Slovenia

Adriatic Sea

Montenegro

Macedonia

ALBANIA

Serbia

Belgrade

BULGARIA

Sofia

GREECE

TURKEY

U. S. S. R.

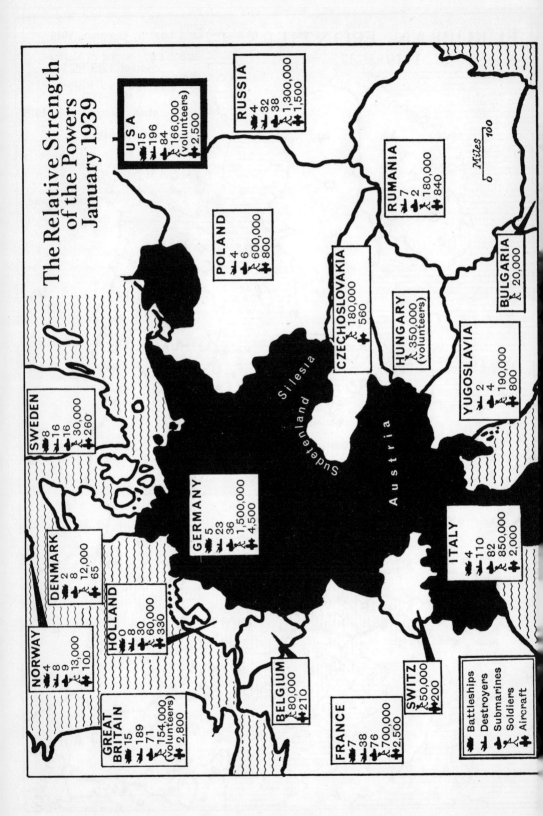

The Relative Strength
of the Powers
January 1939

USA
🚢 15
⚓ 196
84
👤 166,000
(volunteers)
✈ 2,500

RUSSIA
🚢 4
⚓ 32
38
👤 1,300,000
✈ 1,500

RUMANIA
⚓ 7
2
👤 180,000
✈ 840

POLAND
🚢 4
6
👤 600,000
✈ 800

CZECHOSLOVAKIA
👤 180,000
✈ 560

HUNGARY
👤 350,000
(volunteers)

BULGARIA
👤 20,000

YUGOSLAVIA
🚢 2
⚓ 4
👤 190,000
✈ 800

SWEDEN
🚢 8
⚓ 16
16
👤 30,000
✈ 260

GERMANY
🚢 5
⚓ 23
36
👤 1,500,000
✈ 4,500

DENMARK
🚢 2
⚓ 8
👤 12,000
✈ 65

HOLLAND
🚢 0
⚓ 8
30
👤 60,000
✈ 330

ITALY
🚢 4
⚓ 110
82
👤 850,000
✈ 2,000

NORWAY
🚢 4
⚓ 8
9
👤 13,000
✈ 100

GREAT BRITAIN
🚢 15
⚓ 189
71
👤 154,000
(volunteers)
✈ 2,800

BELGIUM
👤 80,000
✈ 210

FRANCE
🚢 7
⚓ 38
👤 700,000
✈ 2,500

SWITZ
👤 50,000
✈ 200

Silesia

Sudetenland

Austria

Miles
0 ___ 100

🚢 Battleships
⚓ Destroyers
Submarines
👤 Soldiers
✈ Aircraft

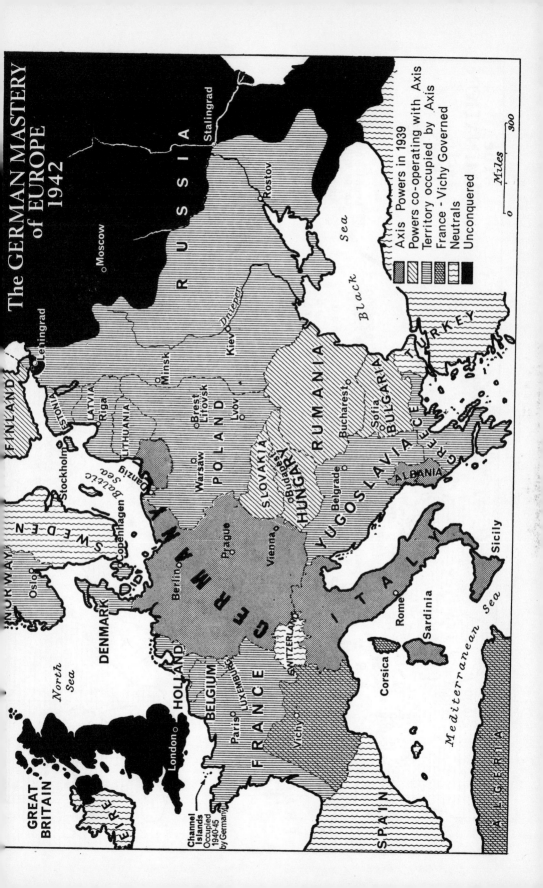

The German MASTERY
of EUROPE
1942

Axis Powers in 1939
Powers co-operating with Axis
Territory occupied by Axis
France - Vichy Governed
Neutrals
Unconquered

Miles
0   300

R U S S I A
Stalingrad
Moscow
Leningrad
Rostov
Kiev
Minsk
Dnieper
Brest
Litovsk
Lvov
ESTONIA
LATVIA
Riga
LITHUANIA
Black Sea
TURKEY
POLAND
Warsaw
Danzig
Baltic Sea
Stockholm
SWEDEN
Oslo
NORWAY
FINLAND
GREAT BRITAIN
London
EIRE
North Sea
DENMARK
Copenhagen
HOLLAND
BELGIUM
Channel Islands
Occupied 1940-45
by Germany
Paris
LUXEMBURG
FRANCE
Vichy
SWITZERLAND
Prague
Berlin
G E R M A N Y
Vienna
SLOVAKIA
HUNGARY
Budapest
RUMANIA
Bucharest
Belgrade
YUGOSLAVIA
Sofia
BULGARIA
ALBANIA
GREECE
I T A L Y
Rome
Sardinia
Corsica
Sicily
Mediterranean Sea
SPAIN
ALGERIA

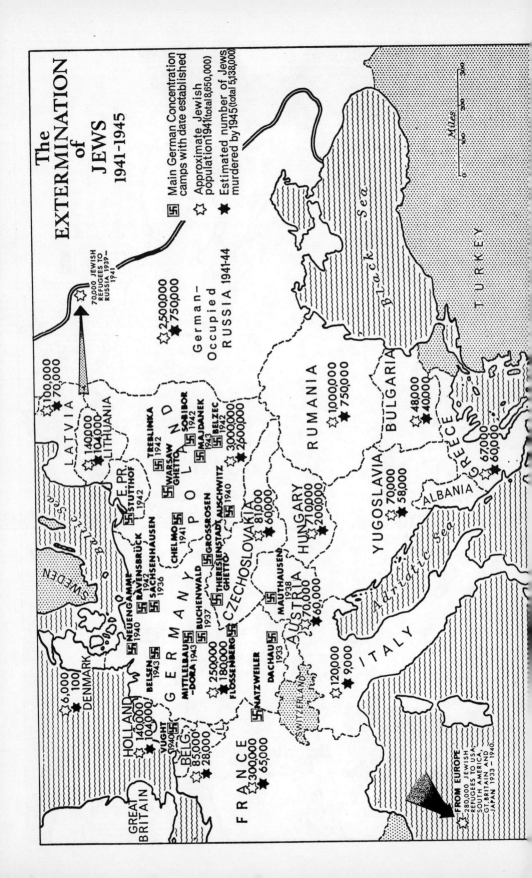

The
EXTERMINATION
of
JEWS
1941–1945

🔲 Main German Concentration camps with date established

☆ Approximate Jewish population 1941 (total 8,650,000)

★ Estimated number of Jews murdered by 1945 (total 5,138,000)

70,000 JEWISH REFUGEES TO RUSSIA 1939–1941

☆ 2,500,000
★ 750,000
German–Occupied
RUSSIA 1941-44

GREAT BRITAIN

SWEDEN

DENMARK
☆ 6,000
★ 100

HOLLAND
☆ 140,000
★ 104,000

BELG.
☆ 85,000
★ 28,000

VUGHT 1940 🔲

FRANCE
☆ 300,000
★ 65,000

NATZWEILER 🔲

SWITZERLAND

NEUENGAMME 🔲 1940
RAVENSBRÜCK 1942
SACHSENHAUSEN 1936
BELSEN 1943
BUCHENWALD 🔲 1937
MITTELBAU–DORA 1943
☆ 250,000
★ 180,000
FLOSSENBERG 🔲
DACHAU 🔲 1933

GERMANY

E.PR.
STUTTHOF 1942 🔲
LATVIA
☆ 100,000
★ 70,000
☆ 140,000
★ 104,000
LITHUANIA

CHELMO 1941 🔲
WARSAW GHETTO 🔲
TREBLINKA 1942
SOBIBOR 1942
MAJDANEK
BELZEC 1942
☆ 3,000,000
★ 2,600,000
P O L A N D

GROSSROSEN 🔲
AUSCHWITZ 🔲 1940
THERESIENSTADT GHETTO 🔲
CZECHOSLOVAKIA
☆ 81,000
★ 60,000

MAUTHAUSEN 🔲
AUSTRIA 1938
☆ 70,000
★ 60,000

☆ 120,000
★ 9,000

ITALY

HUNGARY
☆ 710,000
★ 200,000

RUMANIA
☆ 1,000,000
★ 750,000

YUGOSLAVIA
☆ 70,000
★ 58,000

ALBANIA

BULGARIA
☆ 48,000
★ 40,000

GREECE
☆ 67,000
★ 60,000

Black Sea

Adriatic Sea

TURKEY

Miles
0   100   200   300

FROM EUROPE
☆ 280,000 JEWISH REFUGEES TO USA, SOUTH AMERICA, GT.BRITAIN AND JAPAN 1933–1940.

INDEX

Abraham, Karl, 75
Absolute Idealism, 71; *see also* Idealism
abstract art, 84, 184
Abwehr (German military intelligence), 265
Abyssinian war (1935), 131, 244
Action française, 37–8, 47, 49, 198
Adenauer, Konrad, 299, 301, 308
Adler, Alfred, 75, 174, 177
Adorno, Theodor, 213, 214, 342, 344, 369–70
Adventures of Ideas (Whitehead), 70
aestheticism, 47, 84
Africa, 3, 6, 101, 102, 104, 119, 120, 133–4, 144, 154, 266, 351, 357
African Negro Art, 84
Agricultural Law (West Germany, 1955), 327–8
agriculture, 24; pre-1914 peasantry, 18–19, 20–21; invention of tractor, 64; Soviet collectivization of, 140, 142–3, 190, 326; use of nitrogen fertilizer in, 165–6; effect of post-1945 industrialization on, 327–9
aircraft, aircraft industry, 28, 38, 39, 43, 64, 99–100, 107, 155–6, 167–8, 250, 251, 311, 315, 322, 351; *see also* space flight
Alamein, Battle of (1942), 275
À la recherche du temps perdu (Proust), 83–4, 90
Alain, *see* Chartier, Emile-Auguste
Albania, Mussolini's invasion of, 244
Alexander, Samuel, 70
Algerian war (1954–62), 298, 299, 311; Evian agreement terminates, 311
Alsace-Lorraine, 36; cession to Germany (1870), 19, 25; in First World War, 103, 105; restored to France in Versailles treaty, 108, 110, 118, 308

Althusser, Louis, 368
anarchism, anarcho-syndicalism, 5, 26, 141, 366
Andreyev, Leonid, 189
Anglo-French Union, Declaration of (1940), 256
Anglo-German Naval Agreement (1935), 134, 244
Anglo-Japanese alliance (1902), 12
Animal Farm (Orwell), 199
L'année sociologique, 52
d'Annunzio, Gabriele, 38, 39, 131
Anschluss, see Austria
anthropology, 75–6, 177–80
Anti-Comintern Pact, 267
anti-Semitism, pre-1914, 34–5, 36, 37, 39; Nazi, 126, 128, 130, 152, 265, 268–71, 272–3, 274, 275; inter-war growth of, 129–30; *see also* Zionism
Apollinaire, Guillaume, 84
appeasement, 243–4, 247; *see also* Munich agreement
architecture, 64, 82, 84–5, 86, 88, 184
Argonauts of the Western Pacific (Malinowski), 177
Aristotle, 215, 223, 365, 366
Armenia, 139
arms race, *see* nuclear weapons; rearmament
Arnold, Matthew, 23
Aron, Raymond, 331, 368
Art Nouveau, 85
Asia, 6, 101, 120, 144, 154, 351, 357
Asquith, H.H., 40, 102
astronomy, 66, 67
Atlantic Charter (1941), 286
atom bomb, *see* nuclear weapons
atomic energy, *see* nuclear energy
Attlee, C.R., 255, 282, 283, 287, 307

INDEX

Pétain, Marshal Henri Philippe, 109, 141, 251, 252–3, 254, 255, 256, 275, 276, 311
petro-chemicals, *see* chemical industry
Petrushka (Stravinsky), 88
Pevsner, Antoine, 191
phenomenology, 71–2, 73, 78, 224–6
Philippines, 7
Philosophical Investigations (Wittgenstein), 205, 206, 209
Philosophical Remarks (Wittgenstein), 206
philosophy, *see* individual writers and movements
Philosophy of Arithmetic (Husserl), 225
The Philosophy of Bertrand Russell (ed. Schilpp), 69
physics, 64–7, 91, 167; *see also* nuclear weapons; science and technology
Picasso, Pablo, 64, 84, 85, 86, 87, 184, 185
Pilnyak, Boris, 190
Pilsudski, Marshal Józef, 121, 249
Pirandello, Luigi, 186, 200
Pius XI, 247
Pius XII (Pacelli), 161, 247, 271, 309
Planck, Max, 65, 66, 68, 79, 168
plastics industry, 28, 322
Plato, Platonism, 70, 215, 228, 229
Plekhanov, G.V., 212, 218
Poincaré, Henri, 67
Poincaré, Raymond, 123
Poland, 118, 319; independence of (1919), 25, 110, 111, 112; First World War and, 103, 105; inter-war alliance with France, 120, 135, 243; revisionist claims against, 122–3, 132; Hitler's attitude towards, 129; anti-Semitism in, 129–30; Allied guarantees to, 136, 244, 249; defeat of Red Army in (1920), 140; Hitler's preparations for invasion of, 244; Nazi–Soviet Pact declared over, 246, 248; *Blitzkrieg* in, 248, 249, 250; and Soviet occupation of territory in, 249; extermination of Jew in, 269, 271; post-1945 frontiers of, 279, 282, 283, 285, 301; and Soviet control of, 283, 285, 293, 296, 301; social effects of industrialization in, 326–7, 329
Polish Corridor, 110, 118
Pollock, Friedrich, 213
Popolari (Italian Catholic Party), 131
Popper, Karl, 78, 203, 207, 208, 210, 215, 341, 343

Popular Front (France: 1936–7), 141, 153
population growth, 16–17, 24, 29, 165, 274, 351, 357
Portsmouth, Treaty of, 284
Portugal, 134, 309, 329
positivism, 28, 45, 47, 50–61, 150, 223, 339, 340–1, 343, 363, 371; *see also* logical positivism
post-Impressionism, 64, 92
Potsdam Conference, 279–80, 282, 283, 285, 294, 321
pragmatism (American school of), 67, 68, 69, 228
Preysing, Bishop (of Berlin), 271
Principia Mathematica (Russell and White-head), 69, 70, 203
Principles of Mathematics (Russell), 69, 203
Principles of Scientific Management (Taylor), 172
Process and Reality (Whitehead), 70
protectionism, 8, 10, 20, 21–2, 23, 29, 30, 147, 286
Protestantism, Protestants, 202; link between capitalism and, 52, 58–60; Existentialism and, 226; German 'Theology of Crisis' movement, 229–31; and Bultmannism, 229, 231
protocol sentences, *see* logical positivism
Protocols of the Elders of Zion, 130
Proust, Marcel, 83–4, 89, 90, 183–4, 185, 186–7, 198
psychology, psychoanalysis, 64, 66, 67, 72–8, 89, 91, 148, 171–8, 210; *see also* individual writers and movements
Pudovkin, Vsevolod I., 189
Puntila (Brecht), 193
Purism, 84, 85

quantum theory, Planck's, 66, 79, 168

racialism, racism, 29, 34, 36; National Socialism and, 124–5, 157; *see also* anti-Semitism
radar, use in Second World War of, 259, 261; post-1945, 322
Radcliffe-Brown, A.R., 178
radioactivity, discovery of, 64, 65, 168; *see also* nuclear weapons, research
Ramsey, Frank, 205
Rathenau, Walter, 21, 104
Ravel, Maurice, 87, 89